# A HISTORY

OF THE

# PEOPLE OF THE UNITED STATES,

## FROM THE REVOLUTION TO THE CIVIL WAR.

BY

### JOHN BACH McMASTER,

UNIVERSITY OF PENNSYLVANIA.

*IN EIGHT VOLUMES.*

VOLUME I.

1784-1790.

NEW YORK AND LONDON

D. APPLETON AND COMPANY

1914

# CONTENTS OF VOLUME I.

## CHAPTER I.

# CONTENTS.

## CHAPTER III.

# CONTENTS.

## CHAPTER IV.

# CONTENTS.

## CHAPTER V.

## CHAPTER VI.

# HISTORY

OF THE

# PEOPLE OF THE UNITED STATES.

## CHAPTER I.

### THE STATE OF AMERICA IN 1784.

*Indep → Civil War*
*1850*

THE subject of my narrative is the history of the people of the United States of America from the close of the war for independence down to the opening of the war between the States. In the course of this narrative much, indeed, must be written of wars, conspiracies, and rebellions; of presidents, of congresses, of embassies, of treaties, of the ambition of political leaders in the senate-house, and of the rise of great parties in the nation. Yet the history of the people shall be the chief theme. At every stage of the splendid progress which separates the America of Washington and Adams from the America in which we live, it shall be my purpose to describe the dress, the occupations, the amusements, the literary canons of the times; to note the changes of manners and morals; to trace the growth of that humane spirit which abolished punishment for debt, which reformed the discipline of prisons and of jails, and which has, in our own time, destroyed slavery and lessened the miseries of dumb brutes. Nor shall it be less my aim to recount the manifold improvements which, in a thousand ways, have multiplied the conveniences of life and ministered to the happiness of our race; to describe the rise and progress of that long series of mechanical inventions and discoveries which is now the admiration of the world, and our just pride and boast; to tell how, under the benign influence of liberty and peace, there sprang up, in the course of a single century, a prosperity unparalleled in the annals of human affairs; how, from a state of great poverty and feebleness, our country grew rapidly to one of opulence and power; how her agriculture and her manufactures flourished together; how, by a wise system of free education and a free press, knowledge was disseminated, and the arts and sciences advanced; how the ingenuity of her people became fruitful of wonders far more astonishing than any of which the alchemists had ever dreamed.

Such a mingling of social with political history is necessary to a correct understanding of the peculiar circumstances under which our nation was formed and grew up. Other people in other times have become weary of their rulers, have thrown off the yoke, have come out of the house of bondage and set up that form of government which has always been thought the freest and most perfect. But our ancestors were indeed a highly favored people. They were descended from the most persevering, the most energetic, the most thrifty of races. They enjoyed the highest form of civilization; their climate was salubrious; their soil rich; their country boundless; they were hampered by no traditions; they were surrounded by no nations of whom they stood in fear. Almost alone, in a new land, they were free to work out their own form of government in accordance with their own will. The consequence has been such a moral and social advancement as the world has never seen before. The Americans who, toward the close of 1783, celebrated with bonfires, with cannon, and with bell-ringing, the acknowledgment of independence and the return of peace, lived in a very different country from that with which their descendants are familiar. Indeed, could we, under the potent influence of some magician's drugs, be carried back through one hundred years, we should find ourselves in a country utterly new to us. Rip Van Winkle, who fell asleep when his townsmen were throwing up their hats and drinking their bumpers to good King George, and awoke when a generation that knew him not was shouting the names of men and parties unknown to him, did not find himself in a land more strange. The area of the republic would shrink to less than half its present extent. The number of the States would diminish to thirteen, nor

would many of them be contained in their present limits or
exhibit their present appearance. Vast stretches of upland,
which are now an endless succession of wheat-fields and cornfields and orchards, would appear overgrown with dense forests abandoned to savage beasts and yet more savage men.
The hamlets of a few fishermen would mark the sites of
wealthy havens now bristling with innumerable masts, and
the great cities themselves would dwindle to dimensions scarce
exceeding those of some rude settlement far to the west of
the Colorado river. Of the inventions and discoveries which
abridge distance, which annihilate time, which extend commerce, which aid agriculture, which save labor, which trans-
mit speech, which turn the darkness of the night into the
brilliancy of the day, which alleviate pain, which destroy disease, which lighten even the infirmities of age, not one existed. Fulton was still a portrait-painter, Fitch and Rumsey
had not yet begun to study the steam-engine, Whitney had
not yet gone up to college. Howe and Morse, M'Cormick
and Fairbanks, Goodyear and Colt, Dr. Morton and Dr. Bell,
were yet to be born.

By the treaty which secured the independence of the
colonies, the boundaries of the region given up by the mother
country were clearly defined. The territory ceded stretched
from the Atlantic Ocean westward to the banks of the Mississippi, and from a line running along the great lakes on the
north it spread southward to the thirty-first parallel and the
southern border of Georgia. This vast tract was parcelled
out among the thirteen original States. Of the thirteen, seven
had well-defined boundaries; of the remaining six, some laid
claim to lands since given to other States, while a few would
content themselves with no limits short of the waters of the
Mississippi river.

But, though the Fourth of July orators then boasted that
their country extended over fifteen hundred miles in length,
and spread westward across plains of marvellous fertility into
regions yet unexplored by man, they had but to look about
them to see that the States were indeed but little better than
a great wilderness. A narrow line of towns and hamlets extended, with many breaks, along the coast from the province

of Maine to Georgia. Maine was still owned by Massachusetts, and did not contain one hundred thousand souls. Port-
land existed, then Falmouth, and along the shore were a few
fishers' cots, built of rough-hewn logs, and thatched with sea-
weed. But an almost unbroken solitude lay between Port-
land and the St. Lawrence. In New Hampshire a few hardy
adventurers had marked out the sites of villages in the White
Mountains. In New York, Albany was settled, and Schenectady ; but the rich valleys through which the Mohawk and the
Genesee flow down to join the Hudson and the lake, were the
hunting-grounds of the Oneidas, the Mohawks, the Cayugas.
In Pennsylvania, dense forests and impassable morasses covered that region where rich deposits of iron and of coal have
since produced the Birmingham of America. In Virginia,
a straggling village or two was to be found about the head-
waters of the Potomac and the James. Beyond the Blue
Ridge, Daniel Boone was fighting the Cherokees in the canebrakes of Kentucky. Some villages of log huts surrounded
by stockades were rising on the fertile plains of western
Tennessee. A handful of pioneers had settled at Natchez.
Pittsburgh was a military post. St. Louis was begun, but the
very name of the village was unknown to nine tenths of the
Americans. So late as 1795, Cincinnati consisted of ninety-
five log cabins and five hundred souls. In truth, that splendid section of our country drained by the Ohio and the Tennessee was one vast solitude. Buffaloes wandered in herds
over the rich plains now the granaries of Europe. Forests
of oak and sycamore grew thick on the site of many great
and opulent cities whose population now exceeds that of Virginia during the revolution, and whose names are spoken
in the remotest corner of the civilized world. No white
man had yet beheld the source of the Mississippi river.
Of the country beyond the Mississippi little more was
known than of the heart of Africa. Now and then some
weather - beaten trapper came from it to the frontiers of
the States with stories of great plains as level as the floor,
where the grass grew higher than the waist, where the
flowers were more beautiful than in the best kept garden,
where trees were never seen, and where the Indians still

looked upon the white man as a god. But this country lay far to the west of the frontier, and the frontier was wilder then than Wyoming is now. There the white man lived in an unending war with the red man.

The opinion which many careful and just-minded persons of our time have formed touching the Indians of whom the settlers in the border-land then stood in constant dread, is a singular mixture of truth and romance. Time and absence have softened all that is vile and repulsive in his character, and left in full relief all that is good and alluring. We are in no danger of being tomahawked. We are not terrified by his war-whoop. An Indian in his paint and feathers is now a much rarer show than a Bengal tiger or a white bear from the Polar sea. Of the fifty millions of human beings scattered over the land, not five millions have ever in their lives looked upon an Indian. We are therefore much more disposed to pity than to hate. But, one hundred years ago, there were to be found, from Cape Ann to Georgia, few men who had not many times in their lives seen numbers of Indians, while thousands could be found scattered through every State, whose cattle had been driven off, and whose homes had been laid in ashes by the braves of the Six Nations, who had fought with them from behind trees and rocks, and carried the scars of wounds received in hand-to-hand encounters. In every city were to be seen women who had fled at the dead of night from their burning cabins; who had, perhaps, witnessed the destruction of Schenectady; or were by a merciful Providence spared in the massacre of the Minisink; whose husbands had gone down in the universal slaughter of Wyoming; or whose children had, on that terrible day when Brant came into Orange county, stood in the door of the school-house when the master was dragged out, when their playmates were scalped, when their aprons were marked with the black mark which, like the blood upon the door-posts, a second time staid the hand of the Angel of Death. The opinion which such men and women held of the noble red man was, we may be sure, very different from those current among the present generation, and formed on no better authority than the novels of Cooper, and the lives of such warriors as Red Jacket and Brant.

Of the true character of the Indian it is difficult to give any notion to those who are acquainted with it only as it appears exalted or debased in the pages of fiction. In him were united in a most singular manner all the vices and all the arts which form the weapons, offensive and defensive, of the weak, with many of those high qualities which are always found associated with courage and strength. He was, essentially, a child of Nature, and his character was precisely such as circumstances made it. His life was one long struggle for food. His daily food depended not on the fertility of the soil or the abundance of the crops, but on the skill with which he used his bow; on the courage with which he fought, single-handed, the largest and fiercest of beasts; on the quickness with which he tracked, and the cunning with which he outwitted the most timid and keen-scented of creatures. His knowledge of the habits of animals surpassed that of Audubon. The shrewd devices with which he snared them would have elicited the applause of Ulysses; the clearness of his vision excelled that of the oldest sailor; the sharpness of his hearing was not equalled by that of the deer. Men of a less-gifted race were astounded at the rapidity with which he followed the most obscure trail over the most difficult ground; at the perfection with which he imitated the bark of the wolf, the hoot of the owl, the whistle of the whippoorwill; at the cat-like tread with which, over beds of autumn-leaves and heaps of dried twigs, he walked to the very side of the grazing deer. Nor was his success in the hunt without its effect. Many of the qualities of the creatures he hunted were, as he believed, imbibed with their blood. Courage, such as enables a man to go through a campaign or a battle with credit, such as makes him first in the breach and last in the retreat, and sends him, with a measured step and cool head, to the cannon's mouth, the brave possessed in the highest degree. Nor did he lack a more exalted fortitude. While he underwent the most excruciating torture the ingenuity of his enemies could devise, while his ears were being lopped off, while his nose was being slit, while slices of flesh were being cut from his body and the bleeding wounds smeared with hot ashes, while his feet were roasting, while his limbs were being torn with hot splinters, while the flames leaped high about him, he shouted his death-song with a steady voice till his tormentors plucked out his tongue or brained him with a tomahawk.

Yet this man whose courage was unquestionable, was given to the dark and crooked ways which are the resort of the cowardly and the weak. Much as he loved war, the fair and open fight had no charms for him. To his mind it was madness to take the scalp of an enemy at the risk of his own, when he might waylay him in an ambuscade, or shoot him with a gun or an arrow from behind a tree. He was never so happy as when, at the dead of night, he roused his sleeping enemies with an unearthly yell, and massacred them by the light of their burning homes. Cool and brave men who have heard that whoop, have left us a striking testimony of its nature; how that no number of repetitions could strip it of its terrors; how that, to the very last, at the sound of it the blood curdled, the heart ceased to beat, and a strange paralysis seized upon the body. The contrast between the savage on the war-path and the savage in his wigwam was indeed striking. When the hatchet was dug up, when the war-paint was put on, when the peace-pipe was broken, the idle, shiftless savage was all activity. Patient of hunger, patient of cold, he would march all day through the snow with the thermometer far below zero; and at night, rolled in buffalo robes, go hungry to sleep. But when the chase was over, when the war was done, and the peace-pipe smoked out, he abandoned himself to debauchery and idleness. To sleep all day in a wigwam of painted skins, filthy and blackened with smoke, adorned with scalps, and hung with tomahawks and arrows, to dance in the shine of the new moon to music made from the skin of snakes, to tell stories of witches and evil spirits, to gamble, to sing, to jest, to boast of his achievements in war, and to sit with a solemn gravity at the councils of his chief, constituted his most serious employment. His squaw was his slave. With no more affection than a coyote feels for its mate, he brought her to his wigwam that she might gratify the basest of his passions and administer to his wants. It was Starlight or Cooing Dove that brought the wood for his fire and the water for his drink, that ploughed the field and

sowed the maize. The bead-work which adorned his mocca-
sins, the porcupine quills which set off his cloak, were arranged by her hands. When he travelled she trudged along
with the pappoose on her back beside the led-horse that carried the wigwam and the few pots and jars of sun-baked clay.

The mental attainments of the Indian were quite of a piece
with his character. His imagination was singularly strong,
his reason singularly weak. He was as superstitious as a Hot-
tentot negro and as unreasonable as a child. When a long
succession of fasts and gorgings, when bad food and fire-
water had done their worst, he awoke screaming from his
dreams to assert that a wolf had sat upon his breast, that he
had been in the clutches of Pauguk. Every twig that fell
upon him in the forest was an omen. The simplest occur-
rences of life were full of significance. If he were sick some
enemy had brought it on him. If misfortune overtook him
it was the work of a medicine man or a witch whose anger
he had excited. Then it was that, in his hour of need, he
betook himself to the magic of his medicine bag and the skill
of the medicine man, and, during incantations and strange
mutterings and exorcisms, was beaten and bruised from head
to foot and finally made to believe that a toad or a bright
stone had been taken out of him, and was the cause of his
ills. Gay colors pleased him beyond expression. Over a red
blanket or a patchwork quilt the sedate and dignified savage
would go into raptures of delight. To possess it he would
gladly part with a bundle of skins which exceeded it many
times in value, or with a hundred bushels of Indian corn.

Thus hemmed in on the east by the waters of the ocean,
and on the west by a crafty and ever vigilant foe, were scattered the inhabitants of the thirteen States. Unfortunately
the precise number of the population cannot now be ascertained
with any high degree of certainty. But from such information as we have, it is safe to say that, in 1784, the number
could not have been far from three millions and a quarter. It
has been estimated that at the opening of the war there were
in the country, both white and black, 2,750,000 souls.* Five

* This estimate is given by De Bow, as made from reliable sources. Vol. iii.
p. 404.

years later these, in spite of the ravages of war, had increased, it is thought, to 2,945,000.*  The first periodical counting of the people was made in 1790, and, from the returns then sent in, it appears that the population was 3,929,214 human beings †—less than are now to be found in the single State of New York, but a little over three times the number crowded within the city of New York, and not many more than a third of the number of the men who every four years cast their votes for a president.‡  We may, therefore, with confidence declare that when peace was announced the population of the country did not vary far from three and a quarter millions.

Nor were these by any means equally distributed.  More were in the southern than in the northern States.  Virginia alone contained a fifth, Pennsylvania a ninth, while the five states of Maryland, Virginia, the two Carolinas, and Georgia, counted as citizens almost one half of all the English-speaking people in America.#  The reason is obvious.  The southern colonies had long before the revolution become renowned as the seat of a lucrative agriculture.  Nowhere else could such tobacco be raised as was annually grown on the banks of the Rappahannock, the Potomac, and the James.  The best rice in the English market came from the swamps of the Carolinas. Georgia was already famous for pitch, for indigo, for tar.  New England, on the other hand, produced scarce enough corn and rye for the needs of her citizens.  Beyond a few stately trees,

---

* An estimate of the white population of the States made in 1783, for purposes of assessment, gives the number as 2,389,300.  American Remembrancer, Part ii, 1783, p. 64.

† See United States Census for 1870.

‡ The popular vote in the presidential election in the fall of 1880 was, all told, 9,192,595.

# The population of the States in 1790, soon increased to fifteen by the admis sion of Kentucky and of Vermont, was—

| | | | |
|---|---|---|---|
| Connecticut | = 237,946. | New Jersey | = 184,139. |
| Delaware | = 59,094. | New York | = 340,120. |
| Georgia | = 82,548. | North Carolina | = 393,751. |
| Kentucky | = 73,677. | Rhode Island | = 68,825. |
| Maryland | = 319,728. | South Carolina | = 240,073. |
| { Massachusetts | = 378,787. | Vermont | = 85,425. |
| { Maine | = 96,540. | Virginia | = 747,610. |
| New Hampshire | = 141,885. | Pennsylvania | = 434,373. |

suitable for masts for his Majesty's ships of war, the eastern States grew nothing the mother country wished to buy.* There men built ships, sailed the ocean, caught fish, extracted oil from the blubber of whales, put up great warehouses, and kept great shops; but found the climate of a country where snow lay deep on the ground for five months out of twelve too rigorous for profitable farming. That gigantic system of manufactures which has since made every stream and every river of Massachusetts and Connecticut an endless succession of mills, and covered the land with factory towns, had not begun to exist. Every housewife spun her own flax and made her own linen. Boston and New York were, indeed, the great centres of commerce; but the packets that entered the Narrows, or drew up at the long dock heavy laden, went back to Liverpool freighted with skins which the traders of the new world had purchased from the Indians for bushels of periwinkle shells or strings of wampum. Thus, under the favoring circumstances of climate and soil, agriculture flourished, and wealth and population rapidly increased in all the States south of Virginia, but especially in the Old Dominion. Nor is it to be forgotten that probably one seventh of the population was in slavery.

Diverse as the inhabitants of the States thus were in occupations, they were not less diverse in opinions, in customs, and habits. Though lately united in a common league against a common foe, though now living, nominally, under a common government, many causes conspired to keep them anything but a united people. Differences of race, differences of nationality, of religious opinions, of manners, of tastes, even of

---

* New England pine-trees were famous, and were guarded with great care. Foresters were appointed by the Crown to range the woods, pick out such lofty pines as were suitable for masts for men-of-war, and mark them with a royal brand. Many years after the present century had come in, loggers in the forests of Maine continued to find, here and there, magnificent trees, which had been set apart for the use of King George's navy, and which still bore upon their trunks the marks of the royal axemen. James Allen, a noted poet of ante-revolutionary days, writing of the supplies England drew from America, says:

> " E'en the tall mast, that bears your flag on high,
> Grew in our soil, and ripened in our sky."

To cut any tree that was to be so used was a trespass. Bancroft, Hist. of U. S., vol. iii, p. 391.

speech, were still distinctly marked.   New England had been settled by the Puritans, and there the levelling spirit, the stern theology, the rigid and straitlaced morality were as unyielding as ever.   Virginia had been settled by the cavaliers, and was still the stronghold of aristocracy, of social refinement and episcopacy.   In New York the Dutch element prevailed and the language of Holland was very generally spoken. Maryland was the home of the English Catholics; Pennsylvania of the Germans and the Quakers.   Along the Delaware river were flourishing settlements of Swedes.   In the Carolinas might be found many villages where the inhabitants were all Highlanders, or all Huguenots.*

In truth, the traveller who at that day, prompted by curiosity to see the youngest republic, had the hardihood to endure the discomforts and dangers of a journey over the bad roads and through the almost desolate lands of the States, saw nothing more noticeable to put down in his journal than the marked difference of manners, of customs, of taste and refinement which prevailed in the country.   Such a traveller usually landed in Boston after a seven weeks' voyage in a packet, and found himself in a city which then ranked third in importance, but would now be thought mean and poor. Indeed, carried back to the close of the revolution Boston would present a strange contrast to its present appearance. But for a few time-worn landmarks yet remaining a Bostonian of to-day would seek in vain to recognise the provincial town of 1784 in the great city of 1882.   He would not be able to find his own office, his own house, the street in which he lives. Cows were pastured where the houses of a dense population now crowd each other for room.   Boys played ball in streets now noisy with the rush of traffic.   Faneuil Hall, the Old South, the Old State-House, and a few other relics of ancient times still exist; but so many houses of that time are gone, or to go, that, before another generation has passed away, Old Boston will be known in tradition only.   The city in 1784 stood on the three hills which gave to it the second name of Trimoun-

---

* The Highlanders came over in ship-loads after the suppression of the rebellions of 1715 and 1745.   Ramsay's History of South Carolina, vol. i, p. 11.   The Huguenots, Ramsay says, came over after the revocation of the edict of Nantes.

tain and contained, all told, fifteen thousand souls. There was then no bridge over Charles river, and, when the tides were up, the neck being entirely submerged, it often happened that the town was cut off from all connection with the mainland.* The importance of a bridge was quite manifest, and the matter was carefully discussed in the taverns and coffee-houses by all classes, till three opinions prevailed. Many of the better educated who had travelled far for that day, and whose knowledge of the applied sciences was, therefore, above question, held that it was quite impossible to build a bridge because of the great depth of the water in the channel of Charles river. Others of a bolder turn of mind asserted that the depth of the water could offer no insurmountable obstacle, but that the ice of the first winter would surely carry away the bridge however stout. But the merchants deprecated the idea, and proved from statistics drawn from the customs that such a structure would be highly injurious to navigation. It was not till 1786 that the river was spanned by a bridge.† In the mean time a rude ferry-boat plied between the North End and Charlestown.‡

The streets of the city were laid out with no regularity, and were given names which, either from their English associations or the coarseness of the times they recalled, were, by a more refined generation, gradually changed. George street has thus become Hancock street; King has been changed to

---

* The neck seems to have been quite a barrier to the daily travel between Boston and Roxbury. Thomas, who had often been over it, says: "There was no bridge then, and at very high tides the neck by which the peninsula on which the town is built is connected with the main-land, was sometimes overflowed." Reminiscences of the Last Sixty-five Years, S. E. Thomas, p. 14. "Within the recollection of persons now living, the water has been known to stand up to the knees of horses in the season of full tides at some places on the road on the neck." Drake, Landmarks of Boston, p. 419.

† The building of the bridge was looked upon as a great feat of engineering. Indeed, Cox, the mechanic who built it, made such a reputation by his work that he was called over to Ireland to build the bridge at Londonderry. He was loudly praised for using on the Irish structure American timber and workmen. For a description of the Charlestown bridge, see Boston Gazette, June 6, 1786. For the ceremonies of the opening of the bridge, see Boston Gazette, or the New York Gazette, June 6, 1786. An ode written for the occasion, June 17, 1786, is printed in American Museum, February, 1787.

‡ Thomas's Reminiscences of the Last Sixty-five Years, p. 14.

State ; Queen to Court ; Marlborough to Washington. What was once Black Horse lane is now Prince street; Cow lane is now High street ; Frog lane is now Orange street; Hog alley is Avery street; Longacre has become Tremont street; Love lane has been changed to Tileston; Pond to Bedford; Paddy's alley to North Centre ; Flounder lane is now merged in the south end of Broad street.*

The carriage-way along these narrow lanes and alleys was unpaved. The sidewalks or footways were unflagged. Each was, in the language of the time, pitched with large pebbles, and the footway was marked off from the carriage-way by a line of posts and a gutter, after the manner of many old English towns. The roads were such as would now excite the indignation of a country newspaper. The pebbles were ill-laid and ill-kept. Yet travellers admitted the road was as good as could then be found in many parts of London, and the horseman who galloped over it was fined to the amount of three shillings and fourpence. As to the houses which lined the streets on either side, they were, in the older portion of the city, mean and squalid. Built entirely of wood, with unpainted weatherboard sides and shingle roofs surmounted by ugly wooden railings, within which, every washing-day, shirts and petticoats flapped in the wind, they contrasted strongly with the better class of dwellings on the west side of town.† There the streets were neater. There the houses of brick with Corinthian pilasters up the front, and columns of the same order supporting the porch, and handsome entrances to which led up a long flight of sandstone steps, stood back in little gardens dense with English elms and shrubs. Honeysuckles twined round the porch and high damask roses grew under the windows.

The furniture in these dwellings was often imported from England. The side-boards were heavy with articles of porce-

---

* An interesting account of the Boston of the revolution may be read in Drake's Landmarks of Boston. So, also, in the Memoirs of Josiah Quincy; Life of Dr. John Warren ; Henry Wansey's Excursion in the United States of North America in the Summer of 1794 ; and in A Description of Boston : With a View of the Town of Boston, finely engraved. Columbian Magazine, December, 1787.

† Henry Wansey's Excursion to the United States of North America in the Summer of 1794, p. 39.

lain and china, many of them of the celebrated Wedgwood ware, whereon blue lovers walked by the side of blue waters and blue deer lay down to rest in the shade of blue trees. The crockery that adorned the table gave evidence of the good taste of the lady of the house, and not seldom was mingled with silver plate and cut-glass articles such as the épergne Josiah Quincy saw broken at a dinner in Governor Hancock's banqueting room.* In the corners of the rooms, or on the landing of the stairs, stood the high clocks of English make, many of which yet remain to attest the excellence of the manufacture. Some were surmounted by an allegorical representation of Time. Others had a moving disk to illustrate the phases of the moon and show when it was crescent, when in the second quarter, and when full. Still others at the final stroke of every hour chimed forth a tune which, when the Sabbath came round, was such a one as our grandfathers sang to their hymns in meeting. There were high candelabra to be drawn about the room on rollers, and huge fireplaces adorned with scripture tiles whose rudeness excited the disgust of Franklin, and brass andirons that shone like gold. On the walls were pictures by the brush of Copley or West, or engravings such as Trumbull copied in the library at Cambridge.†

The library was a strange assortment of good books and books so gone out of fashion that no second-hand dealer will buy them. Huge volumes, long since out of print, and now to be found, covered with dust, on the back shelves of public libraries, were then high in favor. Among the sober and sedate readers of Boston the puritanical taste was yet strong. The delightful novels of Richardson, of Fielding, of Smollett, and of Sterne found no place on their shelves.

---

* One of the best descriptions of the interiors of the Boston houses of that day is in the Life of Dr. John Warren. See, also, Life of Josiah Quincy.

† Colored engravings vilely executed were then the fashion. Among the most popular were " Joseph Interpreting," " Pharaoh's Cup Found," and " Apollo and the Muses on Mount Parnassus." Two others, often to be seen in the parlors of the well-to-do, were " African Slave Trade " and " African Hospitality." Each represented a scene on the African coast. In the one a band of negroes were being torn from their families and dragged to a ship. In the other, a band of negroes were struggling to save shipwrecked mariners. See Life of Warren.

Reading was a more serious business. "The Lives of the Martyrs ; or, The Dreadful Effects of Popery," stood side by side with Vattel's "Law of Nations" and Watts's "Improvement of the Mind." There might have been seen Young's "Night Thoughts," Anson's "Voyages," Lucas on "Happiness," Rollin's "Ancient History," "The Pilgrim's Progress," "The Letters of Junius," "The Spectator," but not the works of the hated author of "Taxation no Tyranny." If the owner had a taste for politics, and there were few who had not, no small space on the shelves was taken up with lampoons, with caricatures, with poems such as that in which Hopkinson celebrated the Battle of the Kegs, and pamphlets such as those in which Otis defended so ably the cause of the colonies, and Hamilton silenced the Westchester Farmer.

Uninviting as such a collection would now be thought, their contents were familiar not only to the master, but also to the lady of the house who, despite her many household cares, found much time for reading. The young woman of that day generally received her early education at home, or at the school taught by the minister of the parish and his wife, passed thence to some school kept in Boston, and came back to practice the more homely duties of a housewife. She learned embroidery and could draw and paint; knew less of novels and more of receipt-books than her descendants; knew little of French, nothing of German, and never went to a play in her life. Many a young damsel passed from girlhood to womanhood without ever having looked within the covers of Shakespeare or Sheridan, without ever having attended a dance, and could not tell whether the ace of spades was black or white, or if the king outranked the knave. Her musical acquirements were not such as her granddaughters would consider deserving of more than a smile. Her favorite instruments were the spinet and the harpsichord, instruments which, with the sombre and plaintive melodies once sung to their music, have long ago gone out of fashion.

The less austere, however, indulged in a round of festivities such as excited the horror of their more rigid neighbors. Their time was spent in dispensing hospitality to strangers, in paying and receiving calls, in attending quilting parties and

spinning-matches, and, once a fortnight, in going to the
public assemblies in Concert Hall where the minuet and
country dance still held the floor.  But the most fashionable
of entertainments were the dinners after the English fashion,
where the fun and jollity were prolonged till the candles had
long been lighted, and where, after the ladies had withdrawn,
discussions were held on politics, on religion, on the topics
of the day, over rare vintages of Madeira whose excellence
was acknowledged by all.

The mean appearance of the houses in Old Boston was,
to some extent, relieved by the rich display of painted and
sculptured signs which adorned the front of the taverns and
stores.  The numbering of shops and houses had not come
into fashion, and every business street was an endless succession of golden balls, of blue gloves, of crowns and sceptres,
dogs and rainbows, elephants and horseshoes.  They served
sometimes as advertisements of the business, sometimes merely
as designations of the shops which were indicated popularly
and in the newspapers by their signs.  The custom still lin-
gers among opticians, glove-makers, boot-makers, furriers, and
barbers.  But we are now accustomed to regard the sign as
bearing a direct relation to the character of the business it
advertises.  We should never seek for eye-glasses in a shop
over whose entrance hangs a gilt boot, nor inquire for gloves
in a shop before whose door stands an Indian in war-paint
and feathers.  One hundred years ago no such relation was
understood to exist, and it was not thought remarkable that
Philip Freeman should keep his famous book-store at the
" Blue Glove," on Union street.  From the notices given in
the newspapers of the time we may justly conclude that the
goods offered for sale in the shops, and designated often as
" men's stuffs " or " women's stuffs," did not differ greatly in
kind from those to be had in similar shops at present.  Many
of them, however, passed by names unknown to this generation.  This is especially true of the articles sold at the counters of the haberdashers.  There were to be found plushes,
lawns, and fine dyed jeans; galloons and silk-ferrets, crimson
velvets from Genoa, silks from China, linens from Ireland,
ich damasks and cambrics from England, Bellandine sewing

silk and Prussian flowered silk bonnets, then in the height of
fashion, swords, garterings, vest patterns, and figured silk
cloaks.  On the stalls on a market-day we would miss, again,
many of the fruits and vegetables now considered not as luxuries but as essentials.  The tomato was not only uncultivated,
but almost unknown.\*  Apples and pears were to be had in
abundance, but none of those exquisite varieties, the result of
long and assiduous nursing, grafting, and transplanting, which
are now to be had of every green-grocer.  The raspberries
and strawberries were such as grew wild on the hills, and
the best of them could bear comparison neither in flavor nor
in size with the poorest that are often to be seen at county
fairs.  Oranges and bananas were the luxury of the rich, and
were, with all the tropical fruits, rarely seen; for few packets could then make the voyage from the West Indies under
several weeks.  Since that day our dinner-tables have been
enriched by the cauliflower and the egg-plant.  No great companies existed as yet for the distribution of ice.  This article, since come to be regarded as much a necessity of life as
meat and bread, and which, in ten thousand ways, administers to our comfort and promotes our health, was almost, if
not quite, unused.  The coolest water the tavern could afford
came from the town pump.  Every thunder-storm curdled
the milk.  The butter was kept in the dampest and coolest
nook of the cellar, or hung in pails down the well.

With the exception of such vegetables and fruits as grew
among the rose-bushes and tulip-beds of their gardens, the
citizens of Boston depended for their daily food on the produce of the farms without the town.  We should indeed be
much mistaken if we pictured to ourselves the farms such as
Warren and Webster were reared upon, as the pleasant places
we know so well.  The lands were ill-fenced, the barns were
small and mean, nor could there be seen in the barn-yard, or
under the cow-shed, one of those implements of agriculture
with which American ingenuity has revolutionized a great
branch of human labor, has cheapened food, and brought

---

\* The seed of the tomato was brought over by emigrants from France.  For
many years after the present century came in the plant was used for ornament.
The fruit was thought to be poisonous, and called the love-apple.

millions of acres into a high state of cultivation. The first thrashing-machine was not invented till 1786; the cast-iron wheeled plough, the drill, the potato-digger, the reaper and binder, the hay-raker, the corn-cutter, are not fifty years old. The Massachusetts farmer who witnessed the revolution ploughed his land with the wooden bull-plough, sowed his grain broadcast, and, when it was ripe, cut it with a scythe, and thrashed it on his barn-floor with a flail. His house was without paint; his floors were without carpet. When darkness came on his light was derived from a few candles of home manufacture. The place of furnaces and stoves was supplied by huge cavernous fireplaces which took up one side of the room, and, sending half the smoke into the apartment, sent half the heat up the chimney. His food was of the simplest kind, was served in the coarsest of dishes, and eaten with the coarsest of implements. Beef and pork, salt fish, dried apples and vegetables, made up the daily fare from one year's end to another. Josiah Quincy has left us a pleasing picture of such a home.* There was then little, or indeed no communication with the South; and the bread, he tells us, was, therefore, of rye or Indian meal and not always well baked. The minister alone had white bread, for brown bread gave him the heart-burn and he could not preach upon it. Of this simple fare we may, perhaps, with justice, recognise some trace in the world-famous brown bread and baked beans which, on a Sunday morning, are now to be found on half the breakfast-tables of New England.

If the food of such a man was plain, so were his clothes. Indeed, his wardrobe would, by his descendants, be thought scanty in the extreme. For meeting on a Sabbath and state occasions during the week he had a suit of broadcloth or corduroy which lasted him a lifetime, and was at length bequeathed, little the worse for wear, with his cattle and his farm, to his son. The suit in which his neighbors commonly saw him, the suit in which he followed the plough, tended the cattle, and dozed in the chimney corner while Abigail or Comfort read to him from Edwards's sermons, was of homespun or linsey-woolsey. The entire sum annually laid out, in

* Life of Josiah Quincy.

those days, by a New England farmer on clothes for himself, his wife, and his eleven or thirteen children, was ridiculously small; nor is it too much to say that many a well-to-do father of to-day, with a less numerous family, expends each year on coats and frocks and finery a sum sufficient, one hundred years since, to have defrayed the public expenses of a flourishing village, school-master, constable, and highways included.*

It must not, however, be supposed that because the New England farmer of 1784 was not in possession of a well-stocked and highly-cultivated farm, that because he ate plain food and wore plain clothes, he was by any means an insignificant personage. His education, though not as profound as is within the reach of men of his class at present, was far from contemptible. His reading was not extended and was, in general, confined to such books as found their way into pedlers' packs. The newspaper he rarely saw unless it came wrapped about a bundle; but his inquisitiveness amply supplied its place. There is, undoubtedly, much exaggeration in the stories that have come down to us regarding this singular characteristic. Yet it is impossible to doubt in the presence of such a mass of evidence, that he was the most shrewd, the most talkative, the most inquisitive of mortals. The horseman who stopped at his door to inquire the road was astounded at the eagerness with which he sought for news. The jaded traveller at an inn, or, as the phrase went, a tavern, sat hungry at the board while the landlord plied him with question after question and gave him the latest bit of town scandal, or the last action of the committee men.†

---

* In a paper, called Cause of and Cure for Hard Times, published in 1787, an honest old farmer is made to say: "At this time my farm gave me and my whole family a good living on the produce of it, and left me, one year with another, one hundred and fifty silver dollars, for I never spent more than ten dollars a year, which was for salt, nails, and the like. Nothing to wear, eat, or drink, was purchased, as my farm provided all." American Museum, January, 1787. Connecticut Courant, August 18, 1788. Had his case been an uncommon one, the force and value of the paper would have been lost.

† It is almost impossible to take up a diary, written at that time by a foreigner, without finding some story or some comment on Yankee inquisitiveness. Anburey, who was a lieutenant in Burgoyne's army, narrates an amusing anecdote of the inquisitiveness of New England inn-keepers, told him by an officer of Virginia line. Anburey's Travels through the Interior Parts of America. Smyth, in

In politics he was a stanch patriot; in religion he was a Congregationalist. Neither his views on politics, nor his opinions on matters touching original sin, were the result of long and patient reflection. He was zealous in the cause of the States not because he considered taxation without representation as unjust, or the stamp act as tyrannical, but because the men he looked up to were patriots, and because he believed the King had serious intentions of making the Church of England the established church of America. He was a Congregationalist because his father and his grandfather had held such a belief before him. Yet he seemed not to know that his religious belief and his religious practices were very different from those of his ancestors, and that the changes then begun were to go silently on into our own time. Compared with his grandfather and his grandson, his opinions are as far removed from those of the one as from those of the other. To his grandson they seem to belong to a straitlaced, bigoted and narrow-minded man; to his grandfather they would have seemed such as became a man on the high road to episcopacy. He held it an abomination to read a novel, to see a play, to go to a dance, to make a jest, to sing a comic song, to eat a dinner cooked on a Sunday, or to give a present on Christmas-day.* Yet he would, at times, so far forget his austerity as

---

his Tour through the United States of America, in 1784, has some remarks on this characteristic, vol. ii, p. 346. Riedesel calls them "inquisitive and credulous." Riedesel Memoirs.

* The strictness of the New England Sabbath was the subject of considerable mirth and satire elsewhere. In an old poem it said that God had thought one day in seven sufficient for rest, but in New England men had improved on this, and set apart a day and a half:

> "And let it be enacted further still,
> That all our people strict observe our will;
> Five days and half shall men and women, too,
> Attend their bus'ness and their mirth pursue.
> But after that, no man without a fine
> Shall walk the streets or at a tavern dine.
> One day and half 'tis requisite to rest
> From toilsome labor and a tempting feast.
> Henceforth let none, on peril of their lives,
> Attempt a journey, or embrace their wives;
> No barber, foreign or domestic bred,
> Shall e'er presume to dress a lady's head;

to play a game of draughts with his wife, or spend an hour
at fox and geese with his children.   His conscience did
not smite him when he drank palm-tea at a quilting, or listened to the achievements of his better half at the spinning match.   He drank ale and cider at the apple-paring bees,
and laughed as loudly as any one when, at the corn-husk-
ing, the lucky finder of the red ear kissed his favorite daughter.   But the moment the fiddles were produced he went
home to his pipe and sermons, or to a long talk with the
school-master.

In few things is the great advance made in this country
during the past one hundred years more strikingly apparent
than in the change which has taken place in the social and
intellectual condition of the school-master.   The education of
the young has now become a lucrative profession by itself,
and numbers among its followers many of the choicest minds
of the age.   The school-master is specially prepared for his
work, and is in receipt of a sum sufficient to maintain him in
comfort, to enable him to procure books, and, if he be so
inclined, to travel.   Booksellers and publishers make a liberal
discount in his behalf.   The government allows him to import the text-books and apparatus used in his work duty free.
He is everywhere regarded as an eminently useful member of
society.   But the lot of the school-master who taught in the
district school-house three generations since fell in a very different time and among a very different people.*   School was
then held in the little red school-houses for two months in the
winter by a man, and for two months in the summer by a
woman.   The boys went in the winter, the girls in the sum-

---

No shop shall spare (half the preceding day)
A yard of riband or an ounce of tea."
    The Connecticut Sabbath.   See American Museum for February, 1787.
    A few of the laws of the Vermont Blue Book, which were copied from the
laws of Massachusetts, are given in Acts and Laws of Vermont, 1779; Slade's
State Papers, pp. 313, 315; Hall's History of Eastern Vermont, vol. ii, p. 579.
Whoever was guilty of any rude, profane, or unlawful conduct on the Lord's-day,
in words or action, by clamorous discourses, shouting, hallooing, screaming, running, riding, dancing, jumping, was to be fined forty shillings, and whipped upon
the naked back, not to exceed ten stripes.

    * In many parts of New England it must be owned the condition of the school-
master has improved but little since 1784.

mer. The master was generally a divinity student who had graduated at one of the academies, who had scarcely passed out of his teens, and who sought by the scanty profits derived from a winter's teaching to defray the expenses of his study at Harvard or at Yale. His pay was small, yet he was never called upon to lay out any portion of it for his keep. If the district were populous and wealthy a little sum was annually set apart for his board, and he was placed with the farmer who would, for that amount, board and lodge him the longest time. But this was a far too expensive method for many of the districts and the master was, therefore, expected to live with the parents of his pupils, regulating the length of his stay by the number of the boys in the family attending his school. Thus it happened that in the course of his teaching he became an inmate of all the houses of the district, and was not seldom forced to walk five miles, in the worst of weather over the worst of roads, to his school. Yet, mendicant though he was, it would be a great mistake to suppose that he was not always a welcome guest. He slept in the best room, sat in the warmest nook by the fire, and had the best food set before him at the table. In the long winter evenings he helped the boys with their lessons, held yarn for the daughters, or escorted them to spinning matches and quiltings. In return for his miserable pittance and his board the young student taught what would now be considered as the rudiments of an education. His daily labors were confined to teaching his scholars to read with a moderate degree of fluency, to write legibly, to spell with some regard for the rules of orthography, and to know as much of arithmetic as would enable them to calculate the interest on a debt, to keep the family accounts, and to make change in a shop.

Nor was making change a simple matter. We who are accustomed to but one unit of value and purchase with dollars and cents can form but a faint conception of the difficulties which beset our ancestors in their money payments. The Constitution had not yet been framed. There was, therefore, no supreme authority, and no national currency based upon a universally recognized unit. In every State there were at least two units of value; the State pound and the

Spanish milled dollar, which had been adopted by Congress in the early years of the revolution. But the values of these standards were by no means common ones. The pound in Georgia contained fifteen hundred and forty-seven silver grains; in Virginia it fell to twelve hundred and eighty-nine grains, which was also recognised as the pound in Massachusetts, Rhode Island, Connecticut, and New Hampshire. In New Jersey, Delaware, Pennsylvania, and Maryland, it fell to ten hundred and thirty-one and a quarter grains, while in New York and North Carolina it reached the minimum of nine hundred and sixty-six. The pound being divided into shillings, and the shillings into pence, made the value of the penny far from equal in the different States. These local or State pounds had no existence off the books of the merchants, nor out of the mouths of the people. They were used in keeping accounts and expressing debts; but when the debts were to be settled the pounds were translated into johannes, doubloons, moidores, dollars, or some other coin, and in such coin paid. Chief of the silver pieces was the Spanish milled dollar, then in general circulation, and divided into a half, a quarter, an eighth, and a sixteenth, each represented by a silver coin, and each containing more or less shillings or pence according to the section of the country into which it was taken. Thus, in New England and Virginia, six shillings, or seventy-two pence, were accounted a dollar. In New Jersey, Pennsylvania, Delaware, and Maryland, seven shillings and sixpence made a dollar; in New York and North Carolina, eight shillings, or ninety-six pence; in South Carolina and Georgia, four shillings and eight pence. The school-boy, therefore, was expected to convert, with some readiness, the local pounds and shillings of his State into dollars and joes, and to know the rules for turning York money into Pennsylvania money, and be able to tell how many shillings and pence a pistole contained in the various sections of the country.

As to geography, such books and maps as could then be procured were not of a kind likely to convey much knowledge to a lad of an inquiring mind. Monteith, and Olney, and Guyot had not yet appeared. That splendid series of school-books which now stands unrivalled had but just found a beginning in the spelling-book of Noah Webster.*

With the district school the education of half the lads in the country ended. A few, however, more fortunate, passed thence to a seminary kept by some minister, or to one of the famous academies which were regarded as the feeders of Harvard and of Yale. But those were still days of Puritan austerity, and the boy who quitted his home for school left behind him, too often, peace and happiness. Little Paul at the Blimbers, Smike at Dotheboys Hall, did not have a much harder fate. Indeed, the pedagogue who, in our day, should subject his pupils to the rigid discipline, to the hard fare, to the sermons, the prayers, and the flogging which then fell to the lot of the school-boy, would be held up by the press to universal execration, and might count himself fortunate if he escaped without a prosecution by a society for the prevention of cruelty to children. Masters knew no way of imparting knowledge but by the rod. To sit eight hours a day on the hardest of benches poring over Cheever's Accidence to puzzle over long words in Dilworth's speller; to commit to memory pages of words in Webster's American Institute; to read long chapters in the Bible; to learn by heart Dr. Watts's hymns for children; to be drilled in the Assembly Catechism; to go to bed at sundown, to get up at sunrise, and to live on brown bread and pork, porridge and beans, made up, with morning and evening prayer, the every-day life of the lads at most of the academies and schools of New England. When Sunday, or, as the boys would say, the Sabbath, came round, they found it anything but a day of rest. There were long prayers in the morning by the master, there were commentaries on some scripture text to be got by rote before meeting, to which, dressed in their best, they marched off with ink-pot and paper to take down the heads of the sermon, and give what account of it they could at evening prayers. Between morning and afternoon meeting they were indulged with a cold dinner.

The system of instruction was crude in the extreme. The

---

* Webster published his American Spelling-Book or First Part of a Grammatical Institute of the English Language, in 1784.

appliances of the modern teacher were wholly wanting. The maps and charts, the globes and models that enable the eye to make clear to the mind what might otherwise be confused, found no place in the school-room. To explain away the difficulties of the task, to elucidate the obscurities of pedants, to make smooth the rough path of knowledge, formed no part of the duty of the master. His business was to stand, rod in hand, while his pupils pondered hopelessly over lessons which ten words would have sufficed to make clear. Thus, Trumbull, the artist, spent three weeks in the vain endeavor to solve an example in long division. Josiah Quincy went over his Accidence " twenty times." *

From the academy the lad passed to Harvard or to Yale. Were it not for the old buildings which still remain, surrounded by the splendid memorials of later days, it would be impossible to recognize in the great university of our time any trace of the humble college which boasted of Adams, and whose students turned out in full force to welcome Lafayette. The faculty then would be outnumbered by the instructors in a single department now. Subjects of which Dr. Willard knew nothing are at present taught by the most distinguished men of the time, and illustrated by museums filled with collections far exceeding in value all the property the college then possessed. So little was understood of palæontology that the bones of a mastodon dug up at Claverack, on the Hudson, seventy-two years before, were still believed to be those of a giant. So little was known of geology that the drift and erratic bowlders of the Glacial Age were cited in the sermons of the time as evidence of the flood so conclusive as to silence all doubters. Of political economy nothing was heard. The same year which witnessed the publication of the Declaration of Independence had, indeed, also witnessed the publication of the Wealth of Nations. But it may well be questioned whether, in 1784, there could be found from Boston to Savannah one hundred copies of the book.

The four years of residence at college were spent in the

---

* For an account of school-life, see Life of Josiah Quincy, pp. 24, 25; Personal Memoirs of J. T. Buckingham, vol. i, pp. 17–19; Life of J. K. Paulding; Memoirs of Roger B. Taney.

acquisition of Latin and Greek, a smattering of mathematics, enough of logic to distinguish barbara from celarent, enough of rhetoric to know climax from metonymy, and as much of metaphysics as would enable one to talk learnedly about a subject he did not understand. The students lodged in the dormitories and ate at the commons. The food then partaken of with thankfulness would now be looked upon as prison fare. At breakfast, which was served at sunrise in summer and at daybreak in winter, there were doled out to each student a small can of unsettled coffee, a size of biscuit, and a size of butter weighing generally about an ounce. Dinner was the staple meal, and at this each student was regaled with a pound of meat. Two days in the week, Monday and Thursday, the meat was boiled, and, in college language, these were known as boiling days. On the five remaining days the meat was roasted, and to them the nickname of roasting days was fastened. With the flesh went always two potatoes. When boiling days came round, pudding and cabbage, wild peas and dandelions were added. The only delicacy to which no stint was applied was the cider, a beverage then fast supplanting the small beer of the colonial days. This was brought to the mess in pewter cans which were passed from mouth to mouth, and, when emptied, were again replenished. For supper there was a bowl of milk and a size of bread. The hungry Oliver who wished for more was forced to order, or, as the phrase went, "size it," from the kitchen.*

Rude as was the school system of New England, it was incomparably better than could be found in any other section of the country. In New York and Pennsylvania a schoolhouse was never seen outside of a village or a town. In other places, children attending school walked for miles through regions infested with wolves and bears.† In the

---

* A description of college life at Harvard at this time is given in the Harvard Book, vol. ii. See, also, Hall's Coll. Words and Customs, ed. 1856, pp. 115–117; New England Mag., iii, p. 239; Willard's Memories of Youth and Manhood, vol. ii, pp. 192, 193.

† "I was compelled to walk three miles through a deep and tangled forest, infested with wolves, wildcats, snakes, and other animals." Autobiography of Chas. Caldwell, p. 64. See, also, for scarcity of schools in Virginia, Life of Archibald Alexander, pp. 11, 12.

southern States education was almost wholly neglected, but nowhere to such an extent as in South Carolina. In that colony, prior to 1730, no such thing as a grammar-school existed. Between 1731 and 1776 there were five. During the revolution there were none.* Indeed, if the number of newspapers printed in any community may be taken as a gauge of the education of the people, the condition of the southern States as compared with the eastern and middle was most deplorable. In 1775, there were, in the entire country, thirty-seven papers in circulation. Fourteen of them were in New England, four were in New York, and nine in Pennsylvania. In Virginia and North Carolina there were two each, in Georgia one, in South Carolina three.† The same is true to-day. In 1870, the population of Georgia was, in round numbers, twelve hundred thousand souls, and the circulation of the newspapers less than fourteen and a half millions of copies. The population of Massachusetts was, at the same time, fifteen hundred thousand, but the newspaper circulation was far in excess of one hundred and seven and a half millions of copies.‡

Not less important than the school-master, in the opinion of his townsmen, was the doctor. With the exception of the minister and the judge, he was the most important personage in the district. His professional education would now be thought insufficient to admit him to practice; for there were then but two medical schools in the country, nor were they, by reason of the expense and dangers of travelling, by any means well attended. In general, the medical education of a doctor was such as he could pick up while serving an apprenticeship to some noted practitioner in Boston or New York, during which he combined the duties of a student with many of the menial offices of a servant. He ground the powders, mixed the pills, rode with the doctor on his rounds, held the basin when the patient was bled, helped to adjust plasters, to sew wounds, and ran with vials of medicine from one end of the town to the other. In the moments snatched from duties

---

* Ramsay's History of South Carolina.
† Hudson's History of Journalism in the U. S.
‡ Ninth United States Census.

such as these he swept out the office, cleaned the bottles and jars, wired skeletons, tended the night-bell, and, when a feast was given, stood in the hall to announce the guests.*

It was a white day with such a young man when he enjoyed the rare good fortune of dissecting a half-putrid arm, or examining a human heart and lungs. So great, indeed, was the difficulty of procuring anatomical subjects,† that even at the medical school which had just been started at Harvard College, a single body was made to do duty for a whole year's course of lectures.‡ It was only by filching from grave-yards or begging the dead bodies of criminals from the Governor that subjects could be obtained.#

Under such circumstances, the doctor's knowledge was derived from personal experience rather than from books, and the amount so obtained bore a direct relation to the sharpness of his powers of observation and the strength of his memory. If he were gifted with a keen observation, a logical mind, and a retentive memory, such a system of education was of the utmost value. For in medicine, as in mechanics, as in engineering, as in every science, in short, where experience and practical skill are of the highest importance, a practical education is most essential. The surgeon who has studied anatomy from a book without ever having dissected a human body, the physician who learns the names and symptoms of diseases from a work on pathology, and the remedies from the materia medica, without ever having seen the maladies in active operation and the remedies actually applied, is in a fair way

---

* Life of Dr. John Warren, p. 314.

† On the difficulty of procuring subjects for dissection, see Life of Dr. John Warren, pp. 228–231. Sometimes students were permitted to view the bodies of men and women who had died of an extraordinary disease. Life of Dr. John Warren, p. 226.

‡ Harvard Book, vol. i, pp. 240, 241. The school was started in 1783.

# A very innocent exposure of a limb from a window of a hospital in New York led, one Sunday in April, 1788, to a most serious riot, in which John Jay, Baron Steuben, and a number of prominent citizens, were hurt. The affray has come down to us under the name of The Doctors' Mob. The common practice was to rob the graves of negroes and strangers, but on this occasion the bodies of "respectable persons had been removed." See New York Packet, April 25, 1788; Pennsylvania Gazette, April 23, 1788; Life of John Jay; Life of Baron Steuben.

to kill far more patients than he will ever cure. But the value of knowledge obtainable from books alone is on that account not the less useful, and by no means to be despised. The student who has read much in his profession is in possession of the results of many centuries of experience derived from the labors of many thousands of men. He is saved from innumerable blunders. He is enabled to begin his career with a knowledge of things which, if left to his own experience to find out, would cost him years of patient waiting and careful observation. The advantages of such a system of study were, however, but sparingly enjoyed by the medical students of the last century when but few physicians boasted a medical library of fifty volumes.*

His apprenticeship ended, the half-educated lad returned to his native town to assume the practice and to follow in the footsteps of his father. There as years went by he grew in popularity and wealth. His genial face, his engaging manners, his hearty laugh, the twinkle with which he inquired of the blacksmith when the next boy was expected, the sincerity with which he asked after the health of the carpenter's daughter, the interest he took in the family of the poorest laborer, the good-nature with which he stopped to chat with the farm-hands about the prospect of the corn-crop and the turnip-crop, made him the favorite of the county for miles around. When he rode out he knew the names and personal history of the occupants of every house he passed. The farmers' lads pulled off their hats, and the girls dropped courtesies to him. Sunshine and rain, daylight and darkness, were alike to him. He would ride ten miles on the darkest night, over the worst of roads, in a pelting storm, to administer a dose of calomel to an old woman, or to attend a child in a fit. He was present at every birth; he attended every burial; he sat with the minister at every death-bed, and put his name with the lawyer to every will.

But a few of the simplest drugs were then to be found

---

* Dr. Hubbard, first president of the New Haven County Medical Society, organized in 1784, was, perhaps, the most wealthy practitioner in the county. Yet, when he died, his books were valued at $82. See Papers of the New Haven Colony Historical Society, vol. ii, pp. 260–262.

stowed away on the shelves of the village store, among heaps
of shoes, Rohan hats, balls of twine, packages of seed, and
flitches of bacon. The physician was, therefore, compelled to
combine the duties both of the doctor and the apothecary.
He pounded his own drugs, made his own tinctures, prepared
his own infusions, and put up his own prescriptions. His
saddle-bag was the only drug-store within forty miles, and
there, beside his horn balances and his china mortar, were
medicines now gone quite out of fashion, or at most but rarely
used. Homœopathy, with its tasteless mixtures and diminutive doses, was unknown, and it is not too much to say that
more medicine was then taken every year by the well than is
now taken in the same space of time by the sick. Each
spring the blood must be purified, the bowels must be purged,
the kidneys must be excited, the bile must be moved, and
large doses of senna and manna, and loathsome concoctions of
rhubarb and molasses, were taken daily. In a thousand ways
the practice of medicine has changed since that day, and
changed for the better. Remedies now in the medicine-box
of every farmer were then utterly unknown. Water was denied the patient tormented with fever, and in its stead he was
given small quantities of clam-juice. Mercurial compounds
were taken till the lips turned blue and the gums fell away
from the teeth. The damsel who fainted was bled pro-
fusely. Cupping and leeching were freely prescribed. The
alkaloid quinia was unknown till 1820. The only cure
for malarial diseases was powdered cinchona bark ; but the
amount required to restore the patient was so great, and the
supply so small, that the remedy was all but useless. Vacci-
nation was not made known by Jenner till 1798. Inoculation
was still held by many to be attended by divine punishment.
Small-pox was almost as prevalent as pneumonia now is. The
discovery of anæsthesia by the inhalation of ether or chloro-
form was not given to the world by Morton till 1846. Not
one of the many remedies which assuage pain, which destroy
disease, which hold in check the most loathsome maladies and
the most violent epidemics, was in use. Every few years during the dog-days the yellow fever raged with more violence
in the northern cities than it has ever done in this generation

in the cities of the far South. Whole streets were depopulated. Every night the dead-cart shot its scores of corpses into the pits of the Potters' Field. Better surgery is now generously given to every laborer injured by the fall of a scaffold than could then have been purchased at any price.

High as the doctors stood in the good graces of their fellow-men, the ministers formed a yet more respected class of New England society. In no other section of the country had religion so firm a hold on the affections of the people. Nowhere else were men so truly devout, and the minister held in such high esteem. It had, indeed, from the days of the founders of the colony been the fashion among New Englanders to look to the pastor with a profound reverence, not unmingled with awe. He was not to them as other men were. He was the just man made perfect; the oracle of divine will; the sure guide to truth. The heedless one who absented himself from the preaching on a Sabbath was hunted up by the tithing-man, was admonished severely, and, if he still persisted in his evil ways, was fined, exposed in the stocks, or imprisoned in the cage. To sit patiently on the rough board seats while the preacher turned the hour-glass for the third time, and, with his voice husky from shouting, and the sweat pouring in streams down his face, went on for an hour more, was a delectable privilege. In such a community the authority of the reverend man was almost supreme. To speak disrespectfully concerning him, to jeer at his sermons, or to laugh at his odd ways, was sure to bring down on the offender a heavy fine. His advice was often sought on matters of state, nor did he hesitate to give, unasked, his opinion on what he considered the arbitrary acts of the high functionaries of the province. In the years immediately preceding the war the power of the minister in matters of government and politics, had been greatly impaired by the rise of that class of laymen in the foremost rank of which stood Otis and Hancock and Samuel Adams. Yet his spiritual influence was as great as ever. He was still a member of the most learned and respected class in a community by no means ignorant. He was a divine, and came of a family of divines. Not a few of the preachers who

witnessed the revolution could trace descent through an unbroken line of ministers, stretching back from son to father
for three generations, to some canting, psalm-singing Puritan
who bore arms with distinction on the great day at Naseby,
or had prayed at the head of Oliver's troops, and had, at the
restoration, when the old soldiers of the Protector were turning their swords into reaping-hooks and their pikes into prun-
ing-knives, come over to New England to seek that liberty of
worship not to be found at home. Such a man had usually
received a learned education at Harvard or at Yale, and
would, in these days, be thought a scholar of high attainments. Of the men who Sunday after Sunday preached to
the farmers and blacksmiths of the petty villages, one had
explored the treasures of Hebrew literature, another was an
authority on matters of Greek grammar, while a third added
to his classical acquirements a knowledge of metaphysics
and philosophy. His narrow-mindedness and sectarianism,
his proneness to see in the commonest events of daily life
manifestations of Divine wrath, his absurd pedantry, his
fondness for scraps of Latin, may well seem laughable. Yet,
bigoted as he was, the views he held and the doctrines he
preached would by his great-grandfather have been despised
as latitudinarian. Compared with Cotton or Hooker, a
New England minister of 1784 had indeed made vast strides
toward toleration. He was a very different man from the
fanatics who burned Catholics at the stake, who drove out the
Quakers, who sent Roger Williams to find an asylum among
the Indians of Rhode Island, and sat in judgment on the
witches of Salem and Andover. In the general advance of
society from ignorance toward knowledge, the whole line was
going forward. The tail was constantly coming up to where
the head had been. Errors beaten down by the front rank
were in turn trampled on by those that followed, and truths,
once dimly discernible only to the far-sighted men who
marched foremost in the van, were becoming plainly visible
to the most short-sighted bigots who dragged along far in the
rear. Yet the distance between the head and the tail was as
great as ever, and the New England preacher seems liberal
only by contrast with men of an earlier time. Long after

Jefferson had secured complete religious toleration among the Episcopalians of Virginia, the Massachusetts divines were still denouncing that sect, were still cautioning their flocks never to suffer the wicked heresy to take root in the commonwealth,* and heard, with uplifted hands, that a parcel of nonjuring Bishops at Aberdeen had ordained a Bishop for Connecticut.†

Such doctrine, however, was confined to the sermons which he preached on Sabbaths, and to the papers which he contributed to the press. In the election sermon which he delivered on the return of every election-day, he taught a very different lesson, exerted his eloquence to set forth the equality of all men and the beauties of a pure democracy, and taxed his learning to defend his politics with passages from scripture and quotations from the writers of Greece.

Hatred of Kings and Princes had, indeed, always been a marked characteristic of his sect, and in the pre-revolutionary days he was among the most eager in the patriot cause. It cannot be denied that this show of patriotism was, in most cases, the result of personal interest rather than of a deeply rooted conviction of the necessity of resisting the oppression of England. If there was one sect of Christians which he detested above another, that sect was the Episcopalian. He firmly believed that the stupid King, who cared as little for the Church of England as for the Church of Scotland, was fully determined to make Episcopacy the established religion of the colonies. He was sure that His Majesty had even matured a plan for the establishment of the Church, and that, before many months had gone by, laws as odious as the Conventicle Act and the Five-Mile Act would be in full operation; that hundreds of dissenting divines would be ejected from their churches, stripped of their livings, and sent to starve among the Indians on the frontier.‡ While, therefore, the rectors

---

* A warm discussion on the propriety of admitting bishops into Massachusetts was carried on in one of the Boston papers early in 1785. Boston Gazette, January 3, 10, 17, 1785.

† When the news came of the ordination, which took place November 14, 1784, the Gazette exclaimed : "Two Wonders of the World—a stamp act in Boston and a Bishop in Connecticut." Boston Gazette, May 30, 1785.

‡ Fear of the Church of England "contributed as much as any other cause," says John Adams, "to arouse the attention, not only of the inquiring mind, but

of Virginia and the Carolinas were ranging themselves on the
Tory side, the ministers of the eastern colonies were all active
on the side of the Whigs.

When at last the independence the minister so much
wished was achieved, he found himself, with all his neighbors,
in the depths of poverty. His stipend, which had once been
paid with punctuality to the last pistareen, was now delayed
till long after the day of payment, and often consisted of barrels of turnips, bushels of corn, sacks of beans, and flitches of
bacon.* Patches appeared on his homespun suit, and, in
extreme need, he betook himself in his moments of leisure
to teaching school. His home was turned into a seminary for
a half dozen boys, whom he undertook, for a miserable pittance, to board, lodge, and fit for college. Yet his dignity
and self-complacency were never for a moment laid aside.
He had grown up among his flock. He had succeeded his
father in the pastorship of the little white meeting-house, and
he never left his charge till he was carried out to be laid
away in the shade of the elm and chestnut trees in the bury-
ing-ground beside the church. His sermon was the one event
of the week. There were no concerts, no plays, no lectures,
none of the amusements which, in the great towns like Boston, drew away the thoughts of men from religion. On a
Sabbath the whole village turned out in force with note-book
and pencil to take down the text and so much of the discussion as they could, and, when the services were over,

---

of the common people, and urge them to close thinking on the constitutional authority of parliament over the colonies." Works of John Adams, vol. x, p. 185.
" The establishment of a Protestant episcopate in America is very zealously contended for, . . . and we desire you would strenuously oppose it," was the instruction given by the Massachusetts Assembly to its agent in London in 1768.
Thompson, Church and State in the United States, pp. 42, 43.

* The salary of a minister a century ago was, unless he preached in a great
town, but a pittance ; was never the same two years in succession, and was rarely
paid in money. Few preachers stood higher than Joseph Buckminster. Yet "his
settlement was upon the value of wheat and Indian corn, and varied extremely in
different years ; but never did the amount, I think, exceed six or seven hundred
dollars." Memoir of Joseph Buckminster, D. D., p. 69. In more favored places
the preacher was allowed " £130 with glebe lands and parsonage, and the dona-
tion from strangers ; " that is, the money laid upon the plate, which in those
early times was placed in some conspicuous part of the meeting-house. Memoir
of Buckminster, p. 39.

drew up along the aisle to let the great man and his family pass out first.

Nor were his discourses altogether undeserving such marks of distinction. The theology of New England was strongly tinged with philosophy, and every Sabbath there went forth from half the pulpits of the eastern States elaborate discussions of the most obscure points of the most obscure of all sciences. Not a few of the sermons which have come down to our time are vigorous and logical arguments in behalf of the freedom of the will, and the presence of God in conscience. In truth, of the writers who, up to the peace, and for many years after, put forth treatises, arguments, and expositions on metaphysical themes, scarcely one can be named who was not a native of New England, and a pastor of a New England church. Each minister, therefore, felt in duty bound to discuss his text in a philosophical way, and, however crude his attempt, the reasons he advanced, the analogies he drew, the hints and suggestions he threw out, furnished each week many new topics for an evening's talk. And such topics were needed, for of news the dearth was great. Almost every means of collecting and distributing it familiar to this generation was unknown to our great-grandfathers. There were, indeed, newspapers. Forty-three had come safely through the long revolutionary struggle to publish the joyful tidings of peace. But, with a few exceptions, all were printed in the large towns, and news which depended on them for circulation was in much danger of never going fifty miles from the editor's door.

An interchange of papers did go on among the printers; and some copies of the "Spy" and the "Columbian Centinel" found their way to subscribers at New York. But the papers were not received by the post-office, and it was only by rewarding the post-riders that a place was made for a dozen copies in the portmanteaus containing the letters. Even then, on reaching New York, they were almost a week old, and had they been carried on to Charleston would have entered that city twenty days after the date of publication. Had the time been less it would have mattered little, for the news to be derived from them was usually of small value, and

likely to convey only the most general information. Even
the Connecticut "Courant," the Boston "Gazette," and the
Pennsylvania "Packet," the three best, rarely had much news,
and were badly printed with old-fashioned type on coarse paper,
which, under the influence of time and dust, has grown brown
and brittle. Few came out oftener than thrice in a week, or
numbered more than four small pages. The amount of reading matter which the whole forty-three contained each week
would not be sufficient to fill ten pages of ten daily issues of
the New York "Herald." Nothing in the nature of an edi-
torial page existed. Its place was given up to long essays on
politics or morals by some unknown writer who subscribed
himself "Seneca" or "Tully." The printer and the editor
were generally one, and it was "to the printer" that correspondents addressed their notes. It was seldom that he felt
himself called on to do more than make appeals, sometimes
serious, sometimes humorous, to his delinquent subscribers,
begging them to pay their bills, if not in money, in quarters
of wheat, in pounds of cheese, or the flesh of hogs.* The rest
of the paper was filled up with advertisements for runaway
slaves or stray horses, with scraps taken from other papers,
with letters written from distant places to friends of the editor,
a summary of the news brought by the last packet from Lisbon
or London, a proclamation by Congress, a note to the editor
posting some enemy as a coward in the most abusive and
scurrilous language, a long notice setting forth that a new
assortment of calamancoes and durants, colored tammies, shal-
loons, and rattinels were offered for sale at the shop of a
leading merchant, and, now and then, a proposal for the
reprinting of an old book. The columns devoted to such
advertisements were commonly adorned with rude wood-
cuts. A stage-coach, or a pair of top-boots, a prancing
horse, or a ship under full sail, a house, a plough, or a man
running away with a bundle and a stick in his hand, meet

* "In order to accommodate subscribers, any kind of grain will be taken in
payment at market rates." New Jersey Gazette, July 16, 1783. This consideration on the part of the editor was not appreciated, and in a little while the
Gazette ceased to come out. "Those who cannot pay cash or country produce,
it is expected will have no objection to acknowledge their accounts by notes."
New Jersey Journal, January 10, 1787.

the eye on almost every page. Occasionally odes, ballads, and bits of poetry made their appearance in the poet's corner. Now and then a paper of enterprise and spirit undertook to enlighten its readers and to fill its columns by the publication in instalments of works of considerable length and high literary merit. Robertson's "History of America" was reprinted in the "Weekly Advertiser" of Boston,* and ran through more than one hundred and fifty numbers. A "History of the American Revolution" came out in the "Spy," "Cook's Voyages" were published in the Pennsylvania "Packet," † while other papers of lesser note found room among essays and lampoons, epigrams, anecdotes, coarse "bon-mots," and town resolutions to discourage extravagance, for short treatises on geography and morals. But everything which now gives to the daily paper its peculiar value, and passes under the general name of news, was wanting. The student of history who seeks in the Packets and Advertisers of that day for information on matters which it concerns him to know, will, in all likelihood, search long and find but little. He will read much about the sins of idleness, about the value of economy, about the wretchedness of the wicked woman whose feet take hold on hell. But he will meet with nothing, or next to nothing, on many of the most exciting topics and important events of the time. He will, for instance, look in vain for any extensive information on the abhorrence which the people felt for the Cincinnati, on the proceedings of the Middletown convention, on the action against the Mayor's Court for its decision in the case of Rutgers against Waddington ; he will see scarce a word about the formation of the State of Franklin, or the rupture of the Committee of the States whereby the country was left without a government for many weeks. The reason is plain. What took place in Boston or New Haven, what was going on among the flatboatmen on the Ohio, or among the settlers on the Holston ; what prospect there was of a war with the Shawanese and Twightwees, what prospect there was of the people of Vir-

---

* See also Continental Journal for 1784, 1785.

† Pennsylvania Packets for the closing months of the year 1784 and opening of 1785.

ginia granting the impost, were matters concerning which an
editor two hundred miles away had no direct means of knowing.    To tell the readers of the New York Packet what they
already knew, that they hated Tories, and were indignant at
the Commutation Act, would, to him, have seemed absurd.    To
keep them posted as to what was doing elsewhere he found
a most difficult task.    He had not in every city and town a
well-paid correspondent, whose duty it was to collect the
freshest bits of scandal, to interview the latest public character, and to send accounts of the course of popular opinion.
For all this he was indebted to a source now rarely, if ever,
used even in a backwoods village or a prairie town.    Any
gentleman who was so fortunate as to receive a letter from a
distant part of the country was expected to display his public
spirit by sending to the printer such portions of it as were
likely to be of interest to the community.    Scarce a week,
therefore, went by but the Gazettes contained many scraps of
valuable information under such headings as, " A Letter from
a Gentleman at the Falls of the Ohio to his Friend in New
England," " A Letter from a Gentleman resident in Virginia
to his Friend in this City."    Sometimes these communications
would fill a column, and were almost always well worth a careful perusal.

In truth, the marvellous mechanical inventions that have
compressed the whole world to the limits of a single town,
and have made the collection and distribution of news so easy
and so quick, have brought about a great change in the art of
writing letters.    Men who were, a century since, separated by
three hundred miles, were, to all intents and purposes, much
farther away, and saw much less of each other, than men who
in our time are parted by three thousand miles.    It was no
uncommon thing for one who went on business or on pleasure
from Charleston to Boston or New York, if he were a prudent
and a cautious man, to consult the almanac before setting out,
to make his will, to give a dinner or a supper to his friends at
the tavern, and there bid them a formal good-by.    Many in-
centives, therefore, to letter-writing then existed which the
railroad, the steamboat and the telegraph have quite destroyed.
Men who were of the same family, who had grown up in the

same village, who had known each other at school, or had fought side by side under Washington or Gates, were constantly exchanging epistles or notes. The number who, at present, have the disposition and the time for a like correspondence is very small indeed; nor do they write of the same class of subjects. No merchant in New York would now think of acquainting his friends in Chicago with the result of a late election, with the last action of the Legislature, with the price of commodities, with opinions held on matters of state or national importance, with what took place on 'change or on the street, with anything in short, which can be read in the newspapers under the head of general news. Yet all this our ancestors thought worthy to be communicated to distant friends. No city in 1784 had its public library, no tavern its reading-room where papers from every State in the Union could be seen, and where even a busy man could, with a little pains, make himself as familiar with what went on a thousand miles away as with what went on at his very door. For such information he was dependent on his correspondents, and on his correspondents alone. He therefore wrote, and received in return, letters in which, among much that is of no concern to us, assurances of friendship and esteem, thanks for small favors conferred, are mingled many items full of interest to the historian of the times. It is from this source alone that a just and accurate knowledge is to be obtained of many great events and many stirring times; of the troubles in New England, of Shay's rebellion in Massachusetts, of the indignation felt at the conduct of Rhode Island, of the fears and anxiety of the people during the long secret session of the Federal Convention. It is therefore much to be deplored that so few have been saved from *autos-da-fé* more sweeping than that performed by the curate, the barber, and the house-keeper on the little library at La Mancha. Nor should it be forgotten that such missives were much prized by the recipient; for the difficulties of transmitting letters were many, and the rate of postage high.

In the early colonial times no such thing as a post existed. Indeed, two hundred years have not gone by since the first royal patent was issued to Thomas Neals creating him Postmas-

ter-General of "Virginia and other parts of North America."
The population, however, was at that time so scattered that
nothing ever came of the royal patent, and the postmaster
appears to have found little to do.  Three years later matters
had so much improved that in the course of a twelvemonth
eight mails passed from the banks of the Potomac northward
as far as Philadelphia.  The end of the first decade of the
eighteenth century had come before a line of posts ran from
Philadelphia to the Piscataqua.  This enterprise met with such
success that, a few years later, the service was extended to
Williamsburg, then an important town in Virginia.  But the
post-rider was not to leave the city till enough letters had
been lodged to pay all expenses of the trip.  At last, in 1753,
the post-office passed to the hands of Franklin, and long
before he was put out of office, in 1774, had become a source
of revenue to the Crown.  It was his boast that this branch
of the public service, which, till he assumed its charge, had
never. paid one penny to the King, yielded in his day more
than three times the income of the Irish post-office.  When
Franklin retired, Goddard, a brother printer of Baltimore,
proposed a plan for a "Constitutional American Post-office."
But the war broke out, and the duty of transmitting letters
was again given to Franklin, with authority to establish a line
of posts from Falmouth, in New England, to Savannah, in
Georgia, with as many cross-posts as should, in his judgment,
be thought necessary.  In the mean time Massachusetts had,
at her own charge, set up fourteen offices within her boundaries, and New Hampshire one.  The mail routes thus established ran out from Cambridge, already renowned as the seat
of Harvard College, and went as far north as Georgetown,
in Maine, and as far south as Falmouth, then a flourishing
hamlet, whose busy population were deeply concerned in the
whale-fishery.  From Cambridge mails also went out to Hav-
erhill, to Providence, to Woodstock by way of Worcester,
and from Worcester by way of Springfield, to Great Barrington.  At Falmouth the bags were taken in charge by riders
who travelled at the expense of Congress.  The average day's
journey of the postman was from thirty to fifty miles in summer, and considerably less in winter.  Nor was it till Jeffer-

son had been some years Secretary of State that the possibility of sending letters one hundred miles a day was seriously considered.* Not long after the opening of the war two packets were chartered by Congress, one to ply between the ports of Georgia, and one between the ports of North Carolina and such harbor as should at any time be most convenient to the seat of government.

Such was the humble beginning of that branch of the public service, which, more than any other, has aided the growth of trade and the prosperity of the nation. The sums now annually expended on the carriage of letters and newspapers exceed one half the amount of the domestic debt at which our ancestors stood appalled at the close of the revolution.† The number of letters carried from place to place in a twelvemonth exceeds six hundred millions; the distance traversed by these letters, over one hundred millions of miles. More mails are now each day sent out and received in New York than in Washington's time went from the same city to all parts of the country in the course of half a year. More letters are delivered in that city every four-and-twenty hours than, when Franklin held office, were distributed in the thirteen States in a whole year.‡ When the British evacuated New York, letters were sent to Boston thrice in a week during the summer months, and twice in a week during the winter. Six days were passed on the road. But at New Year's time, when the snow lay deep, the post-riders between these great cities rarely saw the church-spires of Boston till toward the close of the ninth day. Many years elapsed before the bulk and weight of the mails attained such proportions as to exceed the capacity of a pair of saddle-bags. That from New York to

---

* Jefferson's letter to Colonel Pickering, March 28, 1792. See Life of Pickering, vol. iii. Jefferson's Works, vol. iii, p. 158. Ed. 1830.

† In 1879, the amount expended in mail service was $20,012,872; the number of post-offices, 40,855; and the length of mail routes, 316,711 miles.

‡ The daily average of mail matter distributed at New York for 1882 was 2,400,000 pieces. In Barber and Howe's Historical Collections of New Jersey it is stated that, so late as 1791, there were but six post-offices in New Jersey. These were at Newark, Elizabeth, Bridgeton (now Rahway), New Brunswick, Princeton, and Trenton. The gross receipts were for the year ending October 15, 1791, $530. Of this the six postmasters received $108.20, leaving for net revenue $421.80.

Philadelphia went out five times in a week, and was for many
years carried by boys on horseback.

It was, however, in the small country towns far removed
from the great post-roads that the slowness and irregularity
of the mails were greatest. In the mountains of New Hamp
shire, in the hill-country of Pennsylvania, in the rice-swamps
of Georgia and the Carolinas, letters were longer in going to
their destination than they now are in reaching Pekin. Letters sent out from Philadelphia spent five weeks in winter
going a distance now passed over in a single afternoon.* In
more favored places they were received and dispatched once
a week, and that was an occasion of no small importance. On
the day when the post-rider was due, a day which was known
not by its name, as set down in the weekly calendar, but as
"post day," half the village assembled to be present at the
distribution of the mail, which, in good weather and in bad
alike, took place at the inn. The package for the whole village was generally made up of a roll of newspapers a week
old, and a few bundles of drugs for the doctor. It was a great
day whereon, in addition to the usual post, a half dozen letters
were given out. Then, as the townsmen pressed around the
inn-door to make arrangement for borrowing the "newsprint,"
or to hear the contents of it read aloud by the minister or the
landlord, the postman was carried home by one of the throng
to share the next repast, at which, as the listeners preserved
an admiring silence, he dispensed the news and the gossip
collected along the way. In some regions remote from
the travelled highways, it often happened that the post-rider
was a man stricken in years, who, as his beast jogged slowly
along, whiled the hours away by knitting woollen mittens and
stockings.† At other places the letters lay for months in the

---

* "The letter which you did me the honor to write to me on the 20th of last
month only came to my hands by the post preceding the date of this." Washington to R. H. Lee, December 14, 1784; Washington to Sir J. Jay, January 25,
1785; to L. W. Otto, December 5, 1785. "The bad weather, and the great care
which the post-riders take of themselves, prevented your letters of the 3d and 9th
of last month from getting to my hands till the 10th of this." Washington to
Knox, February 20, 1784; to Knox, March 20, 1784; to General Lincoln, February 6, 1786.

† Memoirs of the Life of Eliza S. M. Quincy, p. 29.

office, there being no money wherewith to pay their transportation.

For the security of mails carried over long distances there was no protection whatever. It was well known and loudly complained of that letters and packages were opened and their contents read and examined by the riders. That most salutary law which extends a sure protection to letters, and even to telegraphic messages, had no existence. Nor was it till many years later, when the bulk and number of the mails had greatly increased, and the carriers found no time to read the notes they bore, that this flagrant evil ceased to exist. For a long time after the revolution business men, and men holding high places in the state, were accustomed to correspond in cipher. Such was the practice of Madison, of Jefferson, of Monroe, and of Aaron Burr, against whom it has often been foolishly cited as a sure indication of a crafty and a cunning disposition.* As stage-wagons and coaches became more and more common between the large towns, letters were often intrusted to a friend, or even to a stranger, to be left at the Red Dragon, or some other inn frequented by the person to whom they were addressed.†

These precautions might insure a safe but not a speedy delivery, for a journey of any length was beset with innumerable difficulties and delays. Towns and cities between which we pass in an hour were a day's journey apart. For all purposes of trade and commerce two hundred and fifty miles was a greater distance then than twenty-five hundred miles now. A voyage across the ocean to London or Liverpool, a trip across the prairies to the Pacific coast, is at present performed with more ease and comfort, and with quite

---

* A few instances will suffice. "My two last, neither of which were in cipher, were written, as will be all future ones in the same situation, in expectation of their being read by the postmasters." Madison to Jefferson, October 17, 1784. "Your favor without date was brought by Thursday's post. It enclosed a cipher, for which I thank you, and which I shall make use of as occasion may require it." Madison to Monroe, November, 1784. See, also, Madison to Jefferson, September 7, 1784; Washington to Lafayette, September 1, 1785; Hamilton to G. Morris, June 22, 1792.

† Frequent references to this custom may be found in the letters of Washington, Franklin, Ames, Madison, Burr, indeed, in any collection of letters written a century ago.

as much expedition as, a hundred years since, a journey from
Boston to New York was made. It was commonly by stages
that both travellers and goods passed from city to city. In-
sufferably slow as such a mode of conveyance would seem to
an American of this generation, it had, in 1784, but lately
come in, and was hailed as a mark of wonderful progress.
The first coach and four in New England began its trips in
1744. The first stage between New York and Philadelphia,
then the two most populous cities in the colonies, was not set
up till 1756, and made the run in three days.* The same year
that the stamp act was passed a second stage was started.
This was advertised as a luxurious conveyance, "being a covered Jersey wagon," and was promised to make the trip in
three days, the charge being two pence the mile.† The success which attended this venture moved others, and in the
year following it was announced that a conveyance, described
as the Flying Machine, "being a good wagon, with seats on
springs," would perform the whole journey in the surprisingly
short time of two days. This increase of speed was, however,
accompanied by an increase of fare, the charge being twenty
shillings for the through trip and three pence per mile for
way passengers.

When the revolution came most of these vehicles ceased
to ply between the distant cities; horseback travelling was resumed, and a journey of any length became a matter of grave
consideration. On the day of departure the friends of the
traveller gathered at the inn, took a solemn leave of him,
drank his health in bumpers of punch, and wished him God-
speed on his way. The Quaker preacher, Hicks, setting out in
1779 for yearly meeting, remarks: "We took a solemn leave
of our families, they feeling much anxiety at parting with us
on account of the many dangers we were exposed to, having
to pass, not only through the lines of the armies, but the deserted and almost uninhabited country that lay between them."‡

---

* Watson, Historical Tales of the Olden Times in N. Y. City and State.

† Some account of the stage-coaches in New Jersey may be had in Historical
Collections of New Jersey, by Barber and Howe, pp. 43, 44. Rude cuts of the
stage-coaches may be seen in almost any number of the N. Y. Packet for 1784,
or after.

‡ Journal of the Life and Religious Labors of Elias Hicks, p. 18.

With the return of peace the stages again took the road; but many years elapsed before traffic over the highways became at all considerable. While Washington was serving his first term, two stages and twelve horses sufficed to carry all the travellers and goods passing between New York and Boston, then the two great commercial centres of the country. The conveyances were old and shackling; the harness made mostly of rope; the beasts were ill-fed and worn to skeletons. On summer days the stages usually made forty miles; but in winter, when the snow was deep and the darkness came on early in the afternoon, rarely more than twenty-five. In the hot months the traveller was oppressed by the heat and half choked by the dust. When cold weather came he could scarce keep from freezing.* One pair of horses usually dragged the stage some eighteen miles, when fresh ones were put on, and, if no accident occurred, the traveller was put down at the inn about ten at night. Cramped and weary he ate a frugal supper and betook himself to bed, with a notice from the landlord that he would be called at three the next morning. Then, whether it rained or snowed, he was forced to rise and make ready, by the light of a horn-lantern or a farthing candle, for another ride of eighteen hours. After a series of mishaps and accidents such as would suffice for an emigrant train crossing the plains, the stage rolled into New York at the end of the sixth day.† The discomforts and

---

* See, on the discomforts of stage-coaches, a letter from Fisher Ames to Dwight, October 30, 1791.

† Many gentlemen who lived through this period, and saw railroads and steamboats introduced, have left us amusing accounts of the difficulties of travel. Breck relates how on one occasion he set sail on the regular ferry-boat at Elizabethport for New York. The distance between the two places is fifteen miles; but, after waiting all day for a breeze to spring up, he was forced to hire a fisherman to put him ashore in his canoe. Recollections of Samuel Breck, p. 102. In another place he describes how, by getting up at three or four o'clock in the morning and prolonging the journey until late at night, he used to make the trip from New York to Boston in six days. Id., p. 90; see, also, pp. 99, 100, 103, 271–273. Josiah Quincy says that during such journeys travellers were called at three in the morning, made ready by the light of a horn-lantern and a farthing candle, and went on their way over the worst of roads till ten at night. Often they were forced to get down and lift the coach out of a quagmire or a rut, and when New York was reached, after a week's travelling, they used to wonder at the ease as well as the speed with which the journey was made. Life of Josiah

trials of such a trip, combined with the accidents by no means uncommon, the great distance from help in the solitary places through which the road ran, and the terrors of ferry-boats on the rivers, made a journey of any distance an event to be remembered to the end of one's days. Such was the crude state of the science of engineering that no bridge of any considerable length had been undertaken in the States. No large river had yet been spanned. While going from Boston to Philadelphia, in 1789, Breck crossed the Connecticut at Springfield, the Housatonic at Stratford, the Hudson at New York, the Hackensack and Passaic between Paulus Hook (now Jersey City) and Newark, the Raritan at New Brunswick, the Delaware at Trenton, and the Neshamung at Bristol on what were then known as ferry-boats.[*] The crossing of any of these streams was attended by much discomfort and danger; but the wide stretch of water which flowed between Paulus Hook and the city of New York was especially the dread of travellers. There, from December till late in March, great blocks of ice filled the river from either bank far out to the channel. On windy days the waves were high, and when the tide ran counter to the wind, covered with white-caps. Horse-boats had not yet come in; the hardy traveller was, therefore, rowed across in boats such as would now be thought scarcely better than scows. In one of her most touching letters to her husband, Mrs. Burr describes to him the alarm occasioned by his making the dangerous crossing.[†] How she had anxiously waited for his return, hoping that the dangers

---

Quincy, by Edmund Quincy, pp. 47, 48. On one occasion Quincy spent a month in his own coach, going from Boston to Washington. Id., p. 72; see, also, pp. 37, 56. For some of the difficulties that beset travellers between New York and Philadelphia, and New York and Albany, see the Letters of Aaron Burr to his wife; also, some curious Directions to Mrs. Arnold on her way to West Point, in Arnold's Life of Benedict Arnold, p. 235.

[*] Breck, p. 103.

[†] See a letter from Mrs. Burr to her husband, dated March 22, 1784. Though the letters of Theodosia Burr exhibit an unnecessary amount of apprehension for the safety of a worthless man, the letter is worth quoting as illustrative of the terrors of the river. "Every breath of wind whistled terror; every noise at the door was mingled with hope of thy return, and fear of thy perseverance, when Brown arrived with the word *embarked*, the wind high, the water rough. . . . A tedious hour elapsed when our son was the joyful messenger of thy safe landing at Paulus Hook."

of the passage would deter him; how, when she heard that
he was really embarked, she gave herself up to an agony of
fear as she thought of him exposed in the little boat to the
rough waters and the boisterous winds, and what thankfulness
she felt when her son brought word of his safe arrival at
Paulus Hook.*

Even a trip from Brooklyn to New York, across a river
scarce half as wide as that separating the city from New Jersey, was attended with risks and delays that would now be
thought intolerable. Then, and indeed till the day thirty
years later, when the rude steamboats of Fulton made their
appearance on the ferry, the only means of transportation for
man and beast were clumsy row-boats, flat-bottomed square-
ended scows with sprit-sails, and two-masted boats called peri-
aguas.† In one of these, if the day were fine, if the tide
were slack, if the watermen were sober, and if the boat did
not put back several times to take in belated passengers who
were seen running down the hill, the crossing might be made
with some degree of speed and comfort, and a landing effected
at the foot of the steps at the pier which, much enlarged,
still forms part of the Brooklyn slip of the Fulton Ferry.
But when the wind blew with the tide, when a strong flood
or an angry ebb was on, the boatmen made little headway,
and counted themselves happy if, at the end of an hour's hard
pulling, the passengers were put ashore opposite Governor's
island, or on the marshes around Wallabout bay.

In summer these delays, which happened almost daily,
were merely annoying and did no more harm than to bring

---

* Mrs. Quincy, on her way to the Commencement of Princeton College in 1790,
met with the following adventure on the Elizabethtown ferry: "We had a stormy
passage across the bay, and I was excessively frightened. Having arrived at the
ferry-house, we were shown into a room where a venerable old man was waiting
to go over to the city. The moment I entered he took off his great-coat, and
said to his wife: 'My dear, I do not go to New York to-day; the looks of that
young lady are enough to deter me.' This was the celebrated General Gates."
Memoirs of Eliza S. M. Quincy, p. 55. For the dangers of the ferry, see New
York Packet, June 17, 1788.

† Much information concerning the Brooklyn ferries is given in Stiles's His-
tory of the City of Brooklyn, vol. iii, pp. 504–540. Another reliable source is
An Historical Sketch of Fulton Ferry and its Associate Ferries, by a Director.
(H. E. Pierrepont.)

down some hearty curses on the boatmen and the tide. But when winter came, and the river began to fill with huge blocks of ice, crossing the ferry was hazardous enough to deter the most daring. Sometimes a row-boat would get in an ice-jam and be held there in the wind and cold for many hours. At others a periagua would go to pieces in the crush, and the passengers, forced to clamber on the ice, would drift up and down the harbor at the mercy of the tide. It is not improbable that the solicitude of Mrs. Burr for the safety of her husband was heightened by the recollection of such an occurrence which took place but a few months before.*

Nor were the scows, in the best of weather, less liable to accidents than the row-boats. It was on these that horses, wagons, and cattle were brought over from city to city, for the butchers of the Fly market drew their supplies of beef and mutton from the farms that lay on the hills toward Flatbush and what is now Williamsburg. Every week small herds of steers and flocks of sheep were driven to the ferry, shut up in pens, and brought over the river, a few at a time, on the scows. The calmest days, the smoothest water, and a slack tide, were, if possible, chosen for such trips. Yet even then whoever went upon a cattle-boat took his life in his hands.

If a sudden gust of wind struck the sails, or if one of the half dozen bullocks became restless, the scow was sure to upset.† No one, therefore, who was so fortunate as to own a fine horse or a handsome carriage would trust it on the boats if the wind and sea were high, or much ice in the river, but

---

* In January, 1784, a row-boat coming from Brooklyn was caught in the ice, crushed, and sunk within a few feet of the New York shore. Eight persons were on board. One was drowned, but the seven climbing upon the ice were swept into the East river, then back into the Hudson, and were finally carried down the bay to the Narrows, where some soldiers overtook them with a boat. New York Packet, January 22, 1784. Pennsylvania Packet, January 22, 1784.

† The newspapers of the times contain many accounts of such disasters. One Saturday, in 1784, as a ferry-boat with five horses on board was crossing the river, one of the horses became unmanageable, and so disturbed the rest that they all shifted to one side of the scow which immediately filled and went down. Independent Journal, 1784. Like accidents continued to be noticed till paddle-wheel boats came into use in 1814. See New York Journal and Post-Rider, December 17, 1795; New York Journal, April 3, 1798; American Citizen, May 27, 1801.

would wait two or three days for a gentle breeze and smooth water.

But it was not solely by coaches and ferry-boats that our ancestors travelled from place to place. Packet sloops plied between important points along the coast, and such of the inland cities as stood upon the banks of navigable rivers. The trip from New York to Philadelphia was thus often made by packet to South Amboy, thence by coach to Burlington, in New Jersey, where a packet was once more taken to the Quaker city. A similar line of vessels ran between New York and Providence, where coaches were in waiting to convey travellers to Boston. This mode of conveyance was thought to be far more comfortable than by stage-wagon, but it was, at the same time, far more uncertain. Nobody knew precisely when the sloops would set sail, nor, when once started, how soon they would reach their haven. The wind being favorable and the waters of the sound quite smooth, the run to Providence was often made in three days. But it was not seldom that nine days or two weeks were spent in the trip.* On the Hudson were many such sloops, bringing down grain, timber, and skins from Albany, to be exchanged for broadcloth, half-thicks, and tammies, at New York. They ceased to run, however, when the ice began to form in the river, trade was suspended, and the few travellers who went from one city to the other made the journey on horseback or in the coach. In summer, when the winds were light, two weeks were sometimes spent in sailing the one hundred and fifty miles. The difficulties, indeed, which beset the English traveller John Maude on his way to Albany, would now be rarely met with in a canoe voyage on the rivers of the Northwest.† Burr, on his way to Albany to attend court, changed from sloop to wagon, from wagon to canoe, and from canoe back to wagon ere his journey was ended.‡ Travellers by these packets often took boat as the vessel floated slowly down the river, rowed ashore and purchased eggs and milk at

---

* " I have myself," says Breck, " been that length of time (nine days) going from New York to Boston." Recollections of Samuel Breck, p. 90.

† Watson's Historical Tales of Olden Times in New York City and State.

‡ Letter of Burr to his wife, October 26, 1788.

the farm-houses near the bank, and overtook their vessel with ease.

The present century had long passed its first decade before any material improvement in locomotion became known. Our ancestors were not wholly unacquainted with the great motive-power which has within the life-time of a genera- tion revolutionized every branch of human industry, and en- abled great ships of iron to advance in the face of wind and waves, and long trains of cars to traverse the earth at a speed exceeding the pace of the fleetest horse. Before the close of 1787, Fitch at Philadelphia, and Rumsey at Shepherdstown, Virginia, had both moved vessels by steam. Before 1790, a steamboat company had been organized at Philadelphia, and a little craft built by Fitch had steamed up and down the Dela- ware to Burlington, to Bristol, to Bordentown, and Trenton. Before 1800, Samuel Morey had gone up the Connecticut river in a steamer of his own construction and design, and Elijah Ormsbee, a Rhode Island mechanic, had astonished the farmers along the banks of the Seekonk river with the sight of a boat driven by paddles.* Early in this century, Stevens placed upon the waters of the Hudson a boat moved by a Watt engine. The same year Oliver Evans ran a paddle- wheel vessel on the waters of the Delaware and the Schuyl- kill. Fulton, in 1807, made his trip to Albany in the famous Clermont, and used it as a passenger-boat till the end of the year. But he met with the same opposition which in our time we have seen expended on the telegraph and the sewing- machine, and which, some time far in the future, will be en- countered by inventions and discoveries of which we have not now the smallest conception. No man in his senses, it was asserted, would risk his life in such a fire-boat as the Clermont when the river was full of good packets. Before the year 1820 came, the first boat had steamed down the Mis- sissippi to New Orleans ; the first steamboat had appeared upon the lakes, and the Atlantic had been crossed by the steamship Savannah. But such amazing innovations as these found little favor with men accustomed from boyhood to the stage-coach and the sail-boat. In 1810, nine days were spent

---

* Westcott's Life of John Fitch.   Thurston's Growth of the Steam-Engine.

in going from Boston to Philadelphia. At the outbreak of
the second war with England, a light coach and three horses
went from Baltimore to Washington in a day and a half.
The mail-wagon, then thought to make the journey with surprising speed, left Pennsylvania avenue at five in the morning
and drew up at the post-office in Baltimore at eleven at night.*
Ocean travel was scarcely known. Nothing short of the most
pressing business, or an intense longing to see the wonders of
the Old World, could induce a gentleman of 1784 to leave his
comfortable home and his pleasant fields, shut himself up in
a packet, and breathe the foul air of the close and dingy cabin
for the month or seven weeks spent in crossing the Atlantic.
A passage in such a space of time would, moreover, have been
thought a short one, for it was no very uncommon occurrence
when a vessel was nine, ten, eleven weeks, or even three
months, on a voyage from Havre or L'Orient to New York.†
So formidable was this tedious sail, and the bad food and
loathsome water it entailed, that fewer men went over each
summer to London than now go every month to South America. In fact, an emigrant steamer brings out each passage
from Queenstown more human beings than, a hundred years
ago, crossed the ocean in both directions in the space of a
twelvemonth. So late as 1795, a gentleman who had been
abroad was pointed out in the streets even of the large cities
with the remark, " There goes a man who has been to
Europe." ‡

---

* S. E. Thomas's Reminiscences, vol. ii, p. 126.

† The letters of Jefferson, when Secretary of State, to William Short, *chargé* at
the French court, and William Carmichael, *chargé* at that of Madrid, are full of
evidence on this point. "I will state to you the dates of all your letters received by me, . . . and length of their passage. . . . You will perceive that they
average eleven weeks and a half; that the quickest are of nine weeks, and the
longest are of near eighteen weeks' coming. Our information through the English papers is of about five or six weeks. . . . " Jefferson to W. Short, July 26,
1790. Again he writes: ". . . I have received Nos. 45 and 50; the former in
three months and seven days, the latter in two months and seventeen days, by
the English packet, which had an uncommonly long passage." Jefferson to W.
Short, March 15, 1791. See also letters to Short, March 19, 1791, and to Carmichael, April 11, 1791.

‡ "At that time (1795), and for a number of years after, a man, not a seaman,
who had made a voyage to Europe, was pointed at in the streets as a curiosity,
with some such a remark as this : ' There goes a man who has been to London.' "

Much of the delay in land travelling was caused by the wretched condition of the highways. On the best lines of communication the ruts were deep, the descents precipitous. Travellers by coach were often compelled to alight and assist the driver to tug the vehicle out of the slough. Nor were such accidents limited to the desolate tracks of country. Near the great cities the state of the roads was so bad as to render all approach difficult and dangerous. Out of Philadelphia a quagmire of black mud covered a long stretch of road near the village of Rising Sun. There horses were often seen floundering in mud up to their bellies. On the York road long lines of wagons were every day to be met with, drawn up near Logan's hill, while the wagoners unhitched their teams, to assist each other in pulling through the mire. At some places stakes were set up to warn teams out of the quicksand pits; at others, the fences were pulled down, and a new road made through the fields.*

With such obstacles to communication between the different parts of the country, it is far from surprising that each city was broadly distinguished from every other by the habits and customs of its citizens. A Bostonian who found himself in New York, could spend an hour or two no more profitably than in strolling about the streets and noting the superiority of his own native city to the Dutch town at the mouth of the Hudson; and, indeed, his opinion was not an erroneous one, for the condition of the city after the war was very different from its condition before. Prior to the revolution the commerce of New York was surpassed by that of Boston alone. The number of the population rolled up to three-and-twenty thousand. In her streets were heard the languages of all the civilized nations of the world. But, after seven years of warfare, the city was almost ruined. On the day the last of the British soldiers sailed down the Narrows, her commerce was gone, her treasury was empty, her citizens starving in the wilds of New Jersey. The city, as the term was then understood, ended at Anthony street

---

S. E. Thomas, Reminiscences of the Last Sixty-five Years, p. 29. At Philadelphia, foreigners were stared at. American Daily Advertiser, August 19, 1791.

* Watson's Annals of Philadelphia and Pennsylvania in the Olden Time.

on the north; Harrison street was the last toward the Hudson river, as Rutgers was toward the East river. This region, which now consists for the most part of immense warehouses and counting-houses and public buildings, crowded by traders and their clerks during the day, and left almost in total solitude at night, was then the place not only of business, but of residence. Yet, even within these narrow limits, the houses were scattered and surrounded by large gardens, not a few of which ran down to the shores of the rivers, and were thick with hedges and trees. Innumerable creeks and kills flowed through broad meadows, or lost themselves in swamps and pools, where are now the sites of great mercantile houses; dwellings stand crowded together on land then covered with orchards and fields of buckwheat; farms spread out where is now the fashionable part of the city; men fished and snared fowl in ponds and in marshes long since given up to the wants of trade. So late as 1787, the seine was regularly drawn on the beach where Greenwich street now is; ducks were often shot in Beekman's swamp; wild pigeons were plentiful in Berkley's woods.

More than a third part of the old town lay in ashes; in the very week wherein Howe entered the city in triumph, a terrible fire destroyed five hundred houses on the west side of the city near the present Washington market. Again, three years later, a second fire consumed three hundred houses on the east side. But little building had been done, and, in 1784, the two sites were still covered with heaps of blackened plaster and fragments of burned brick. Between these sites lay the Common. Originally, this stretch of land had been rectangular, but the post-road ran through it, cutting off a large triangle. The present City Hall park occupies the piece of common known as the "Flat" or "Vlackte." What Faneuil Hall was to Boston, what Independence Hall was to Philadelphia, that was the Common to New York. There the Sons of Liberty, led by Seares and Scott and Lamb, met to denounce the stamp act; there they fought for their liberty-pole; there they ended the battle of Golden Hill.

North of the Common was the fresh-water pond, called, also, the Collect. In this sheet of sparkling water many a belated traveller and unwary fisherman had found an untimely grave; and around it many traditions and myths had gathered. The pond was reported, and the story was believed by the educated, to have no bottom; it was confidently affirmed by the ignorant to be the abode of strange sea-monsters. Every one knew it to be full of most excellent roach and sunfish. Below the Common, to the east, lay Beekman's swamp, a patch of low, flat land, overgrown with coarse grass and tangled briers, and, when the tides were unusually high, covered with water. There, fifty years before, Jacobus Roosevelt laid out his tanneries, and so began that branch of industry of which the Swamp is, to this day, the centre. Along the Bowery lane lay a succession of orchards and gardens; near Gramercy park was Crummashie hill; the Zant Berg hill lay above it, with the Minetta brook winding its way through a marshy valley to the river; Broadway disappeared in the meadows above Anthony street; to the west of Canal street the Lispenard meadows, a great resort of sportsmen, stretched away to the North river.

Three roads then ran out of town: the Kingsbridge road, a continuation of the Bowery lane, joined with the Southampton road, and went out by McGowan's pass to Kingsbridge, and along the river to Albany; the old Boston postroad started from the neighborhood of Madison square, and, winding its way to Harlem, crossed the river, and turned eastward toward Boston; the Middle road ran direct to Harlem.

Scattered here and there along these were the homes of many wealthy citizens. Not a few of them had been the scenes of revolutionary incidents. Thus, at Inclenbergh was the home of Robert Murray, father of the famous grammarian, and husband of the fair Quakeress who, when the American army was in full retreat, detained the British officers till the last man of Silliman's brigade was well on toward Harlem; higher up, on the Bloomingdale road, was Apthorpe mansion, where, on the same day, Washington waited for his scattered troops till the British came in sight, and barely escaped capture by a hasty flight; on the shore of the East river, hard by Turtle bay, was the Beekman mansion, beneath whose roof Nathan Hale, the martyr spy, was tried and sen-

tenced to execution; while high up, on the banks that over-
look the waters of the Harlem, stood the home of Colonel
Roger Morris, afterward the home of the famous Madame
Jumel.

In the city scarce a street was paved, and these few were
so illy done that Franklin observed that a New Yorker could
be told by his walk as he shuffled over the smooth pavements
of Philadelphia. Street-lamps, which came into fashion ten
years before, were few in number, and rarely lighted on wet
nights.* Nor was there indeed much need of them, for the
fashion of keeping late hours had not then come in. The
city was famous among all the colonial towns for routs and
riots, the luxury and display of its citizens, and for gayety and
festivity. But the rout was over, and the guests safe at home,
long before the watchman was heard crying in the streets,
"Nine o'clock and all's well."

Many of the old Dutch customs were still kept up. New
England could boast of no such day as New Year's day. Boston and Philadelphia saw no such scenes as on every Christmas and every Easter day were enacted in New York. For,
despite the boast that men speaking the tongue of every civilized people were to be found in the city, the Dutch element
was still strong, and the language and religion of Holland were
most prevalent. Half the signs on William street were in
Dutch. At the Hudson market, and along the slips of the
Hudson river, a knowledge of Dutch was absolutely indispensable. Until twenty years before, no sermon in the English
language had ever been preached in either of the three Dutch
churches, and, even after the revolution, prayers were still
made, and sermons still preached, at times, in the language
of the Stuyvesants and Van Dams. But a change in church
language had been attended by no change in church ceremonial. The dominie in his black silk gown still preached in
in the high pulpit. The hour-glass yet stood at his right hand,
and the huge sounding-board over his head. The first psalm
was still announced by movable numbers hung on three sides
of the pulpit; the clerk still sat in the deacon's pew, and when

---

* The papers of that and a later day contain many notices of gangs of ruffians
who frequented the streets at night, and waylaid and robbed passers-by.

the congregation were in their seats, when the preacher was in the pulpit, the psalm sung and the prayer made, prefaced the sermon with a chapter from the Bible at morning service, and by chanting the Apostles' Creed at evening service. To him were intrusted the notices to be read, which he fastened to the end of a long pole and passed up to the minister. When the last grain of sand had run out of the glass, his three raps brought the sermon to a close. Then the deacons rose in their pew, listened to a short address from the minister, and, with velvet bags and bells hung to long rods, went among the congregation collecting alms for the poor.*

Hard by the Dutch church stood a smaller and less pretentious chapel, on whose worshippers Episcopalians and Dissenters alike looked down with horror not unmingled with contempt. The building had been put up some sixteen years before. Yet the congregation was not numerous, and was made up chiefly of shopkeepers and negroes, for the Methodists were still a new sect. Indeed, the society at New York, though it dated no further back than 1766, could have boasted, with justice, of being the oldest Methodist society, and of worshipping in the oldest Methodist church in America.† The first of the sect to come to our shores was undoubtedly Whitfield, who preached and exhorted through the southern provinces in 1737. But the man who may well be called the father of American Methodism, the man who watched and tended it in its early years, who shaped its course, who found it weak and left it strong, was Francis Asbury. He was an Englishman of hard sense and strong religious feeling, and sprang from the great middle class, which has, in every generation, furnished numbers of men whose names are held in grateful remembrance. When he landed in America, in 1772,

---

* My description of the city of New York is made up of materials taken chiefly from M. L. Booth's History of the City of New York; Watson's Historical Tales of the Olden Times in New York City and State; Duer's New York as it was during the latter part of the Last Century; Valentine's History of the City of New York; Denton's Brief Description of New York; Dunlap's History of New Netherlands, and the history by the loyalist Jones.

† An Appendix to the Methodist Memorial, containing a Concise History of the Introduction of Methodism on the Continent of America, etc. Charles Atmore, Manchester, 1802.

there were scattered from New York to Georgia six preachers and a thousand members of the sect.* But such was the excitement of the time, the energy and force of the preacher, that, when Burgoyne surrendered, the membership had increased to seven thousand souls, and the ministers to forty.† This growth is the more remarkable as every English preacher except Asbury deserted his flock and went back to England when the war broke out.‡ When peace came, eighty-one men were spreading the Methodist worship through the States. Then, it seemed to Wesley, the time had come when the Methodist church in America should be separated from the Methodist church in England. Coke, therefore, was ordained, and a letter dispatched directing the American brethren to receive him and Asbury as joint superintendents of the flock. A few days later Coke was on the sea. A few weeks later he landed at New York, and went with all speed toward Baltimore. On Sunday, the fourteenth of November, 1784, the very day on which the first Protestant Episcopal Bishop for America was ordained at Aberdeen, he preached to a great crowd in a little meeting-house in the woods. When he was done, a rough-clad man came out of the crowd and kissed him. The man was Asbury, who, the next Christmas eve, at Baltimore, was raised to the dignity of Bishop.

It was long, however, before the Methodists made proselytes and built churches in the towns along the great river that flowed by New York. Chief among them was Albany.‖ The city, indeed, was next in importance to New York in the State, and sixth in rank in the country. The place had been laid out early in the seventeenth century, and, after an existence of over a hundred years, had grown to be a flourishing Dutch town of five hundred houses and thirty-eight hundred souls.ᐱ It could not, indeed, be said to have a rival on the river unless it was Poughkeepsie, then a village large enough

---

* Atmore's Appendix to the Methodist Memorial.
† Ibid.                                          ‡ Ibid.
‖ For an account of Albany, see Morse's American Geography, edition 1784, a most curious book ; Mrs. Grant's Diary of an American Lady; Watson's Historical Tales ; and the Scammel Letters, Historical Magazine, September, 1870.
ᐱ New York Gazette, August 17, 1786.

and prosperous enough to support a weekly journal. Troy
was not much more than a collection of the houses and barns
of a half-dozen Van Rensselaers. The site of Hudson was a
farm. Tarrytown was a pretty village. At Newburg a few
buildings clustered about an inn. Albany was, therefore, in
the estimation of the inhabitants, a great city. The prosperity of her merchants was the envy of far larger places.
Her steadily growing trade was the boast of her citizens. The
time, they said, was surely coming, nay, was almost at hand,
when she would rival Boston and Philadelphia in magnificence,
and become the emporium of northern trade. Did she not
stand at the very head of the navigable waters of the Hudson?
It was plain, therefore, that she need fear no northern rival.
Was she not surrounded by boundless forests of fir and pine?
Was she not on the only open route to Canada? Did she not
command the Indian trade of the North and North-west? Was
she not at the foot of that rich and splendid valley already
famous for its wheat-fields and corn-fields and rye? Did not
her commerce employ upward of ninety shallops? It was
simply a question of time then how soon her docks would be
crowded with sloops from the four quarters of the earth,
bringing the spices and rich fabrics of the South to be exchanged for the rare furs of the North; when her warehouses
would be filled with skins from Canada and Oswego; when
her yards would be stocked high with lumber from the mountains; when her streets would be blocked with long trains of
wagons laden with the products of the western farms; when,
after every harvest, her granaries would run over with wheat
and corn and rye from the fertile lands along the borders of
the Mohawk and the Genesee.

But with boasts of the citizens were mingled the invec-
tives and sarcasms of strangers. Travellers of every rank
complained bitterly of the inhospitality of the Albanians, and
the avarice and close-fistedness of the merchants. The fertility of American soil, the salubrity of an American climate,
had not, they said, modified one jot the cold, taciturn, stingy
Dutchman. They admitted that Albany was a place where a
man with a modest competence could, in time, acquire riches;
where a man with money could, in a short space of time,

amass a fortune. But nobody would ever go to Albany who could by any possibility stay away, nor, being there, would tarry one moment longer than necessary. There, Dutch names and families, Dutch habits and customs, survived for the longest time. Albanians continued to keep Kerstydt and Nieuw Jar, Paas, Pinxter, and San Claas, in the old Dutch fashion many years after they had been greatly modified at New York. It was remarked by an humble topographer that so late as 1784 they knew nothing of the plays and social amusements common in New York. The few who affected a life of ease and pleasure spent their time in walking and "sitting in mead-houses," went regularly to their favorite tavern at eleven o'clock, played cards, billiards, and chess, staid till dinner, and came home in the evening. The town water was so bad as to be undrinkable by a stranger, and was but sparingly indulged in by the inhabitants. Its place was therefore largely supplied by punch, schnapps, and Madeira. The principal streets ran parallel to the river, were wide, unpaved, and in many months of the year heavy with mud. Six or eight lanes crossing these almost at right angles completed the town. The shops, seventy in number, clustered along Pearl and Water streets. In them were offered for sale, among heaps of wampum and strings of glass beads, goods whose names are wholly unintelligible to the shopkeepers of this generation.* There were to be found tammies, half-thicks, persians and pelongs, blue sagatha and red bunts, ticklenburghs and black everlastings, and handkerchiefs known under the names of bandanoe, lungee, romals, culgee, puttical, and silk setetersoy.† The houses, scarce one of which can now be found in the city, were built after the Dutch Gothic style; three sides were of boards, or roughly squared

---

* Wampum, or white money, was originally made from the periwinkle; suckhannock, or black money, from the inside of the shell of the hard clam. The most valued money of the Indians—their gold, in fact—was a black glass bead about a third of an inch long, highly polished, and bored lengthways. Three pieces of black, and six of white money, made a penny, or a Dutch stuyver. Among the fur-traders at this time was the father of Gerrit Smith. See Life of Gerrit Smith, by O. B. Frothingham, p. 6. John Jacob Astor had but just landed at New York with his stock of violins.

† See the newspaper advertisements of the time.

timbers.  The fourth, always a gable end facing the street, was of yellow Holland brick, with a high pediment roof stepped off on each side like a flight of stairs, and surmounted by an iron horse as a weather-vane.  In the middle of the brick gable was the door, with a stoop flanked on each side by seats, where, in the long summer evenings, the whole family gathered.

But one other appendage to the house must be noticed, as it greatly excited the derision of travellers familiar with the neater streets of Boston and New York.  Tin gutters projected from the roofs far out over the foot-paths, and in rainy weather discharged torrents of water into the unpaved streets, drenching the horsemen and splashing the foot-traveller with mud from head to foot.*

Beyond the city, to the north and west, the country was an unbroken wilderness.  That beautiful region renowned for the majesty of its scenery, whose wilds are now the sites of watering-places famous from one end of the country to the other, whose mountains and forests are every summer the resort of artists and tourists, fishermen and hunters, was rarely explored by trappers.  The fertility of the valley of the Mohawk was indeed well known, but the power of the Six Nations was far from broken, and the jealousy with which the Indians beheld the slightest encroachment on their hunting ground made every attempt at opening up the country an undertaking full of danger.  As if the vengeance of the savage were not enough, there came up from the newly ploughed land a terrible malaria, known as the Genesee fever, which, unchecked by the rude medical knowledge of the time, swept off whole families of settlers.  It was not till 1789 that the tide of immigration began to set in strongly,

---

* A traveller who saw Albany in 1776 has left us a pleasing description of the place.  "I was not a little surprized to find Albany to be so durty a city the houses in the Dutch Taste, the Inside clean to a fault even their Cyder Barrels are kept scour'd as clean as their Dishes, their women are continually employ'd in scouring the floors, one drop of Ink In a house will breed a Riot, till it is erazed by Soap and sand, and Dishclouts, whilst their Streets are excessive durty, and the outside of the Houses resemble welchmans Breeches, void of all form and Comliness."  A letter to Miss Nabby Bishop, June 2, 1776.  In the Scammel Letters.  Historical Magazine, September, 1870.

and that thousands of ox-sleighs annually went out from Albany.

When Washington, in the summer of 1783, went through the central part of New York State with Clinton, Oswego was a military post on the extreme frontier, where a few enterprising traders carried on a flourishing commerce with the Cayugas, the Senecas, and the Tuscaroras, who brought thither skins of the buffalo, the bear, the otter, and the lynx, to exchange for strings of wampum, hundreds of periwinkle shells, and bits of colored glass. Deer browsed and black bears roamed at will over the plain where Rochester now stands. Foxes and wolves were plentiful on the site of Syracuse. At Saratoga, since renowned over the whole earth for its mineral-waters, a single spring, long known to the Indians for its medicinal properties, bubbled up through a barrel sunk in the ground.

It would indeed be tedious to enumerate the many towns now great and opulent which were then wretched hamlets, or whose streets had not yet been laid out. No manufacturing villages were to be found in all New England. Beavers built their dams unmolested along the banks of streams since crowded with mills and factories, each one of which finds work for more men and women than, to the end of the eighteenth century, made up the population of the largest country town of America. At Springfield a few houses were strung along the post-road ; Lawrence was a squalid hamlet ; Manchester was no better. When, in 1820, the fourth census was taken, the country around Lowell was a wilderness where sportsmen shot game. The splendid falls which now furnish power to innumerable looms were all unused, and the two hundred needy beings who comprised the whole population of the town found their sole support in the sturgeon and alewives taken from the waters of the Concord and the Merrimack.* Indeed, the condition of the manufactures at that time was most deplorable. With the exception of a few mills for the manufacture of paper, scarce so good in quality as that grocers are now accustomed to wrap around pounds of sugar and tea; a foundry or two, where iron was melted into rude pigs, or beaten into bars or nails ; a factory where cocked hats

---

* Miles's Lowell as it Was and as it Is, p. 10.

and felts were made, no manufactures could be said to exist. Cotton was never seen growing but in gardens among the rose-bushes and honeysuckle-vines. A little had indeed been sent to Liverpool five years before the fight at Lexington. Eight bags were again sent out in 1784, but when the ship sailed into that port the officers of the customs seized them, as it was well known that so much cotton could never have come from America.* The Constitution had been framed and adopted before the first Arkwright spinning-machine was set up in this country, before the first bounty was offered, or the first cotton-mill erected in Pawtucket. The place now held by cotton fabrics was filled by linen spun at every farmer's hearth, but nowhere so extensively as in New England. To spin well was then esteemed an accomplishment of which any damsel might well be proud. Nor were any means of encouragement left untried. To the poor, bounties were offered. The rich brought into fashion the "spinning bee," which continued in vogue in many country towns when the ladies of the great cities had long deserted the wheel for the harpsichord and the spinet. The bee was generally held in the town-hall; but if the village were not prosperous enough to own such a building, the house of some minister was chosen. Thither the women went with their spinning-wheels and flax, and, as they spun, were brought cake and wine and tea by the fine gentlemen of the town.

Though the inland towns were thus mean and squalid, those scattered along the sea-coast from Portsmouth to New London were thriving and populous. Their proximity to the water had made them great trading and fishing ports. Indeed, before the revolution, scarcely one could be found among them whose citizens had not some venture on the sea, either of a regular or irregular kind. The harsh restrictions laid by the mother country on the commerce of her colonies had led to smuggling, and smuggling had proved a sure road to wealth. In every town prominent characters could be pointed out who, when the States were under British rule, had constantly stowed away in their cellars and attics goods they would have

---

* Smithers' History of Liverpool, p. 129; De Bow's Industrial Resources of the United States, vol. i, pp. 119, 120.

been loath to have the officers of the customs see.  To these harbors came vessels built for speed and laden with contra-band ware gathered in the colonies of France and Spain.  Of this trade Boston was long the centre, and many a merchant of high repute did not disdain to engage in it.  Thus, on the very day when the farmers and ploughmen of Middlesex drove the British out of Lexington, John Hancock was to have stood trial for defrauding the customs.

The war changed all this.  Smuggling almost ceased, and the crews once engaged in it found occupation at the Grand Banks or on the whaling fleets that went out each year.  Spermaceti whales, now almost driven from the sea, were then most plentiful, came some seasons as far south as Cape Ann and Montauk Point, had been seen by old whalers in schools off the coast of Rhode Island and Connecticut, and were at times found stranded on the shores of Long Island sound.*

The oil obtained from these creatures commanded a ready sale and a high price.  The whale-fishery became, accordingly, in spite of its hardships and dangers, a favorite occupation of the fishermen of New England.  Falmouth and Barnstable, Martha's Vineyard and Cape Ann, were noted whaling ports; but foremost among them all was Nantucket.  The town stood on a little strip of sand scarce four miles wide and fifteen

---

* The fishermen of Cape Cod were the first to begin whale-fishing, and it was from them that the Nantucket fishers learned the use of the harpoon.  Sperma-ceti whales had from time to time been found dead on the Massachusetts and Rhode Island shore; but it was not till 1712 that the first living one was cap-tured by Christopher Hassey.  Hassey was a Nantucket fisherman, and had gone out in search of right whales, was caught in a storm, blown off shore and into a school of spermaceti whales.  One of them he killed and towed to land.  From that time forth great numbers were taken every year.  In 1726, as many as eighty-six were killed off the Nantucket coast.  In 1784, the favorite cruising-ground was the gulf of St. Lawrence, banks of Newfoundland, Davis's strait, straits of Belle Isle, and even so far away as Cape Desolation.  The crude oil then brought £24 per ton, and paid a duty of £18 per ton at the port of Liverpool.  It may be interesting to state that the first vessel that ever entered a British port bearing the stars and stripes was a Nantucket whaler laden with oil.  A good history of the New England whale-fishery has yet to be written, but some facts regarding it may be had from Hunt's Merchant's Magazine, vol. iii; North American Review, vol. xxxviii; and Obed Marcy's History of Nantucket.  See, also, Brown's Whaling Cruise, and History of the Whale-Fishery.

long, that rose from the ocean, and was, before the war, a
busy hive of seafaring men, where ships were built, where
cordage and rigging were made, and whence set sail each year
to the whaling grounds one hundred and fifty ships. When
the war closed, all this prosperity and greatness had ended.
The rope-walks were deserted. The docks and wharfs had
fallen into decay. A few old hulks were all that remained of
the once gallant little navy. The population had sadly decreased. Grass grew in the streets of the town. Of the
whalemen, a few were serving in the crews of privateers,
but the larger number, enticed by the liberal offers of England, had settled at Halifax to take part in the whaling ventures that went out from thence.*

To the south of New York no place of importance was to
be met with till Philadelphia was reached. The city was
then the greatest in the country. No other could boast of so
many streets, so many houses, so many people, so much renown.† There had been made the discoveries which carried the name of Franklin to the remotest spots of the civilized world. There had been put forth the Declaration of
Independence. There had long been held the deliberations
of Congress. No other city was so rich, so extravagant, so
fashionable. Seven years before, Lee had described the place
as an attractive scene of amusement and debauch.‡ Lovel #
had called it a place of crucifying expenses. And this reputation it still maintained. But the features that most impressed travellers from distant lands were the fineness of the
houses, the goodness of the pavement, the filthiness of the
carriage-ways,‖ the regular arrangement of the streets, and the

* See Obed Marcy's History of Nantucket Island; Letters from an American
Farmer, by Hector St. John Crèvecœur.

† In 1786, the number of houses in Philadelphia was 4,600; in New York,
3,500; in Boston, 2,100. The population of Philadelphia was 32,205; of New
York, 24,500; of Boston, 14,640. See New York Gazette, August 17, 1786.

‡ R. H. Lee to Washington. Sparks's Correspondence of the Revolution,
vol. i.

# James Lovel to Washington. Sparks's Correspondence of the Revolution,
vol. i.

‖ The streets of the city finally became so full of filth, dead cats and dead
dogs, that their condition was made the subject of a satire by Francis Hopkinson,
better known as the author of the Battle of the Kegs. In a piece which he

singular custom of numbering some and giving to others the names of forest-trees.*

One of these, Chestnut, long since given up to the demands of commerce, and lined with banks, with warehouses, and with shops, was the fashionable walk. There every fine day, when business was over, when the bank was closed, when the exchange was deserted, crowds of pleasure-seekers gathered to enjoy the air and display their rich clothes. If the dress that has displaced the garb of that period be less tasteful, it must be owned it is at least more convenient. A gentleman of the last century, if he were a man of fashion or of means, wore a three-cornered cocked hat heavily laced. His hair was done up in a cue, and its natural shade concealed by a profusion of powder. His coat was light-colored, with diminutive cape, marvellously long back, and silver buttons engraved with the letters of his name. His small clothes came scarce to his knees; his stockings were striped; his shoes pointed, and adorned with huge buckles; his vest had flap-pockets; his cuffs were loaded with lead. If he were so happy as to have seen some service during the war, he affected a military bearing, and had much to say of campaigns. When he bowed to the damsels that passed him, he took half the sidewalk as he flourished his cane and scraped his foot. Nor does the dress of the lady, as she gravely returned his salutation and courtesied almost to the earth, seem less strange to us. Those were the days of gorgeous brocades and taffetas, luxuriantly displayed over cumbrous hoops, which, flattened before and behind, stood out for two feet on each side; of tower-built hats, adorned with tall feathers; of calash and muskmelon-bonnets; of high wooden heels, fancifully cut; of gowns without fronts; of fine satin petticoats; and of implanted teeth. This singular custom had but lately been brought in by one La Mayeur, and had rapidly become fashionable. La Mayeur called himself a doctor, advertised his business ex-

---

called Dialogues of the Dead, a conversation is made to take place between the carcasses of a cat and dog lying in one of the streets. The dialogue is without wit, but is said to have aroused the street commissioners to a sense of duty. It was afterward republished in the American Museum for March, 1787.

* Smyth, in his Tour through the United States of America in 1784, comments on these singular appellations of the streets.

tensively, was largely patronized by the ladies, and, at the end of a few months, went off, it was believed, with a small fortune. One of his advertisements is yet extant. In it he announces to the people of Philadelphia that his business is to transplant teeth; that he has, within the six months just passed, successfully transplanted one hundred and twenty-three, and assures those having front teeth for sale that he will give two guineas for every sound one brought him.

The dreariness of winter evenings was broken by dancing assemblies and plays. The assemblies were of fortnightly occurrence, and very select.* The price of a season ticket was three pounds fifteen shillings. But it was thought highly improper that divertisements of this kind should be attended by young men under twenty, or by young women under eighteen. They were, therefore, rigorously excluded. Nor did such damsels as found admittance reap any benefit from beauty, from wit, or from the possession of any of those charms now so highly prized. The plainest and the fairest were treated alike. For partners were chosen by lot, and were partners for the evening.† They danced, walked, and flirted with no one else, and, when the dancing was over, partook together of rusks and tea. The next evening the gentleman came to sup with the parents of the young woman who had fallen to his lot at the assembly, an event which was made the occasion for a great display of plate, of china, and of ceremony.‡ Many of the table manners then in vogue have fallen into disuse and been utterly forgotten, but one has been preserved to us by

---

* In many of the old advertisements it is announced that these assemblies will open with a Passe-Pie and end with the Sarabund à l'Espagnole. See New York Packet, January 5, 1784.

† On the Ohio such matters were differently managed. One who was no mean observer has left us an amusing account of the routs and balls of Louisville: "The Manager who distributed the numbers, call'd Gent No. 1. He takes his stand.—Lady No. 1. she rises from her seat, the Manager leader to the floor & introduces the Gent[n] No. 1— & so on 'till the floor is ful. . . . At the refreshments, the Gent[n] will, by instinct, without Chesterfieldian monition, see that his better half (for the time being) has a quantum sufficit, of all the nice delicacies, & that without his cramming his *jaws* full untill he has reconducted her to the ball-room —then he is at liberty to absent himself a while." Autobiography of Major Samuel S. Forman. See Historical Magazine for December, 1869.

‡ Scharf's Chronicles of Baltimore, p. 229.

an anecdote that is worth citing. It would, it seems, have been thought as rude for the guest to refuse to partake of a dish a fourth or fifth time, if asked so to do, as it would have been thought negligent in the hostess to omit to press him. There seemed, therefore, to be no limit to the number of times the lady of the house was constrained to ask, and the number of times the visitor was constrained to accept. But, happily, there was in use a kind of freemasonry signals by which he conveyed, by the position of his plate, by the arrangement of his knife and fork, by the way in which he disposed of his spoon, his wish not to be invited to be helped again to slices of chicken and saucers of jam. This custom sorely puzzled the uninitiated, and gave rise to many amusing incidents, one of which happened to the Prince de Broglie. The prince, who travelled in our country in 1782, relates, in one of his letters, that he was invited to dine with the lady of Robert Morris; that he went; that he was repeatedly asked to have his cup refilled; that he consented; and that, when he had swallowed the twelfth cup of tea, his neighbor whispered in his ear and told him when he had had enough of the water diet he should place his spoon across his cup, else the hostess would go on urging him to drink tea till the crack of doom.*

From Philadelphia ran out the road to what was then the far West. Its course after leaving the city lay through the counties of Chester and Lancaster, then sparsely settled, now thick with towns and cities and penetrated with innumerable railways, and went over the Blue Ridge mountains to Shippensburg and the little town of Bedford. Thence it wound through the beautiful hills of western Pennsylvania, and crossed the Alleghany mountains to the head-waters of the Ohio. It was known to travellers as the northern route, and was declared to be execrable. In reality it was merely a passable road, broad and level in the lowlands, narrow and dangerous in the passes of the mountains, and beset with steep declivities. Yet it was the chief highway between the Mississippi valley and the East, and was constantly travelled in the summer months by thousands of emigrants to the western country, and by long trains

* Pennsylvania Magazine of History and Biography, 1878, vol. ii, No. 2, pp. 166, 167.

of wagons bringing the produce of the little farms on the banks of the Ohio to the markets of Philadelphia and Balti-more. In any other section of the country a road so fre-quented would have been considered as eminently pleasant and safe. But some years later the traveller who was forced to make the journey from Philadelphia to Pittsburg in his car-riage and four, beheld with dread the cloud of dust which marked the slow approach of a train of wagons. For nothing excited the anger of the sturdy teamsters more than the sight of a carriage. To them it was the unmistakable mark of aris-tocracy, and they were indeed in a particularly good humor when they suffered the despised vehicle to draw up by the road-side without breaking the shaft, or taking off the wheels, or tumbling it over into the ditch.* His troubles over, the traveller found himself at a small hamlet then known as Pittsburg. The place bore no likeness to the great and wealthy city now standing on the same spot and bearing the same name, whose streets are bordered with stately dwellings and stores, whose population numbers more than one hundred and fifty thousand, and whose air is thick with the smoke and soot of a hundred foundries, machine-shops, and factories.† Yet, small as was the town, many historical associations gath-ered about it. At that very point, where the Alleghany sweep-ing from the north, and the Monongahela from the south, mingle their waters to form the Ohio, had stood, years before,

---

* Such mishaps were, in 1784, quite unknown, for no carriages then found their way to so remote a spot as Pittsburg. But in a few years they became of com-mon occurrence, and continued to be when Madison was President.

† A good description of Pittsburg at that time was published in the Pitts-burg Gazette of July 29, 1786, the first number of the first newspaper ever printed west of the Alleghanies. H. H. Brackenridge, whose famous novel, Modern Chivalry, is still to be found on the shelves of circulating libraries, wrote it. See, also, Diary of Arthur Lee, 1784, and An Early Record of Pittsburg, in Historical Magazine, vol. ii. "The Towne," says one who saw it in 1789, "The Towne at that time was the muddiest place that I ever was in; and by reason of using so much Coal, being a great manufacturing place & kept in so much smoke & dust, as to effect the skin of the inhabitants." Autobiography of Major Sam-uel Forman, Historical Magazine, December, 1869. In 1795, the place is de-scribed as "a thriving Town containing at present about two hundred Houses, fifty of wch are brick and framed, & the remainder Log." Journal of Thomas Chapman, Historical Magazine, June, 1869. See, also, Craig's History of Pitts burg.

Fort Duquesne, one of the long chain of posts the French erected from the St. Lawrence to the Mississippi. Not far away was "Braddock's Fields," a little patch of land whereon the English general had sustained his memorable defeat, and whence the young Virginia captain had led the remnant of his troops. Just back of the town, and hard by the banks of the Monongahela, rose "Grant's Hill," on whose summit a detachment of Highlanders were surprised and massacred by the French and Indians. So late as 1784, the top was strewn with their whitened bones, and with arrow-heads and tomahawks used in the battle. Near by, on the same hill, was a mound thrown up by that prehistoric race whose tumuli are found on the crests of half the hills from the Mohawk to the Rio Grande.

On the destruction of Fort Duquesne, the place passed into the hands of the British, who built Fort Pitt. In 1764, at the end of the Indian war, Colonel Campbell laid out the town in four squares just without the walls of the fort, and named it Pittsburg, in honor of the great commoner. When Washington saw it in 1770, the town numbered twenty log huts along the Monongahela; but in the course of fourteen years many new settlers had come in, many new houses had been put up, till, in 1784, Pittsburg numbered one hundred dwellings and almost one thousand inhabitants. It was the centring point of emigrants to the West, and from it the travellers were carried in keel-boats, in Kentucky flat-boats, and Indian pirogues down the waters of the Ohio, past the beautiful island where long afterward Blennerhasset built his palace, to the filthy and squalid settlement at the falls of the Ohio, or on to the shores of the Mississippi, where La Clede, twenty years earlier, had laid the foundations of St. Louis. Two dangers constantly beset the voyager. The boat was at every moment likely to become entangled in the branches of the trees that skirted the river, or be fired into by the Indians who lurked in the woods. The cabin was therefore low, that it might safely glide under the limbs of the overhanging sycamores, and lined with blankets and with beds to guard the inmates from Indian bullets.* From St. Louis rude boats and

---

* For a description of one of these boats, and the trouble they had when

rafts floated down the river to Natchez and New Orleans. But of the many that went down the river scarce one ever came back, for the current was so rapid that it seemed hopeless to attempt a return. The boats were therefore hastily put together and sold at New Orleans as lumber.

Some settlements had been attempted in the region now portioned out between the States of Indiana and Illinois, but the most thickly settled portion of the valley lay along the banks of the Kentucky river, and the tributaries of the Licking. In all, upward of twelve thousand souls were there, most of them having come across the Blue Ridge mountains from the neighboring States of Georgia and Carolina. For in the three States of Georgia, North Carolina, and South Carolina were then living near one fifth of the population of the country. They could, therefore, well spare the restless colonists who yearly went out from them to dwell in the canebrakes and wilds of Kentucky. One cause of this emigration was, beyond a doubt, the extreme difficulty which the most helpless and dependent class of society, whose province it was to follow the plough, to tend the cattle, and to toil in the swamps, found in eking out even a miserable existence. Almost every acre of land close to the sea-ports was portioned out into plantations and held by the great landed proprietors. The labor was largely slave labor. The immense yield of the rice-fields and the indigo-fields, of pitch and rosin, had brought wealth, and with wealth had come in all the blessings and all the evils which flourish best in opulent societies. Nowhere else was good blood and noble descent held in such high esteem. Nowhere else was social rank so clearly defined. Toil was the only thing from which the rich planter abstained.

---

passing under trees, see Autobiography of Major Forman, Historical Magazine, December, 1869, pp. 325, 326.

All travellers down the Ohio comment on the great size of the trees. General Parsons measured a black-walnut near the Muskingum, and found the circumference, five feet from the ground, to be twenty-two feet. A sycamore near the same spot measured forty-four feet in circumference, five feet from the ground. See a pamphlet by Cutler, called An Explanation of the Map which delineates that part of the Federal Lands, etc., Salem, 1787, p. 10. This statement is copied by Morse in his Geography, edition 1789, p. 461. Connecticut Courant, September 1, 1788.

Horse-racing by day and deer-hunting by ni
gambling, made up, with the social festiviti
which he belonged, his sole occupation and p

The country lying to the south of the P
fore, to a New Englander or a Pennsylvania
strange as if it had been in the tropics.   T
shade of trees whose foliage bore no resembl
elms and chestnuts that grew along the stree
lage.  He rode for days through an endless succession of tobacco-
fields.  The rank vegetation of the Dismal Swamp; the rice-
fields covered with water; the sugar-cane growing higher
than he could reach; the great forests of pine yielding an
inexhaustible supply of pitch and tar; the indigo-plant, the
fruits, the very birds, filled him with astonishment; nor did
the people seem less strange to him than the country.  He
admired, indeed, their open hospitality, but their appreciation
of good blood excited only his derision.   Their pride, their
arrogance, their keen sense of what they were pleased to term
personal honor, inspired him with disgust.   He could not understand why men of sense and courage should be ever ready
to seek each other's lives in revenge for slights and insults
so trivial that they would, among his friends, scarcely have
elicited a hearty curse.   The appearance of the towns and
cities, the social customs and festivities of the people, were
unlike anything he had ever seen in Boston or Philadelphia.
The language seemed scarcely to be English.  Nor was he in
turn less an object of wonder to his host.  His walk, his
dress, the eagerness with which he plied his new friends
with questions, and the strange language in which he conveyed his feelings of surprise and pleasure, marked him out
at once as an object of interest.  The way he compacted his
vowel sounds and clipped his words; the long sound which
he gave to a; the broad sound with which he pronounced e;

---

* An account of the social life of Georgians and Carolinians before the revolution may be found in Ramsay's History of South Carolina, 1809.   See, also,
the American Museum for 1790.   It did not change much after the war.   In
1791, the grand jury for the district of Charleston, S. C., presented duelling "as a
grievance of a very serious and alarming nature."   Gazette of the United States,
July 6, 1791.

boldness with which he substituted that letter for *u*, and *u*
or *o*—excited many a good-natured laugh at his expense.
Odd phrases, delightful in vigor and made up of words long
gone out of use in the mother country, and to be found only
in the pages of Dryden, of Chapman, of Ben Jonson, were
constantly in his mouth.

Strange as this section of the country seemed to men from
the Eastern States, it never failed to impress visitors from the
continent with the many resemblances it bore to England.
Especially was this true of Virginia. There the traveller
journeying through the tide-water region may still meet,
along the banks of the Rappahannock and the James, with
the crumbling ruins and dilapidated remains of what, one
hundred years ago, were the spacious mansions of the rich
planters. Like the opulent families that once dwelt in them,
by far the larger number have long since fallen into decay,
while the few that still withstand the ravages of time bear
but feeble testimony to the ancient grandeur of their former
owners. Yet it is not impossible to form from them even
now some conception of what they were a century ago. The
house was usually of wood, one story and a half or two stories
high, for it dated back to a time when the country did not
yet furnish permanent building materials, except at vast expense, nor provided skilled architects to make use of them.
But the spacious gardens, laid out in the prim style, with the
terraces, the arbors, the box-borders, and the geometrically
shaped parterres so fashionable a century since; the cupola;
the broad veranda, supported on massive columns; the high
chimney of sun-baked bricks; the ample dimensions of the
structure, and the broad entrance, gave to it an aspect of state-
liness by no means diminished by the lack of architectural
adornments, and the windows full of diminutive panes of ill-
pressed glass. It was, however, in the internal arrangements
that the good taste and wealth of the owner were most
apparent. The spacious rooms were decorated with carved
oaken wainscoting, reaching above the mantel-piece in an
unbroken expanse of flowers, and grinning faces and armorial
devices in the corners. There were Chelsea figures, and
Japanese cabinets, and Kidderminster carpets ; sideboards

full of plate; and huge tiled fireplaces, whose brass andirons
shone like gold; nor were the stairways and landings wanting
in grandeur.

In such abodes the heads of the great families, whose estates stretched far inland from the banks of the Rappahannock, lived splendidly and hospitably. Numerous slaves and
white servants attended them in every capacity that use or os-
tentation could suggest. On their tables were to be found
the luxuries of the Old World and the New, and chief among
these stood Madeira wine and rum. That the men of that
generation drank more deeply than the men of this, is not to
be doubted. Then, and for many years after, whenever a
public character was to be entertained, or a day famous in
revolutionary history to be celebrated, a dinner was gotten
up and toasts drunk. The number of regular toasts was always equal to the number of States in the Union. But when
they were disposed of, "volunteers" were in order, and to
these there was no fixed limit. Sometimes as many as ten
would be offered and drunk to. Indeed, on more than one
occasion thirty toasts were responded to, and the bumpers by
which they were followed were strong Jamaica rum.

In the moments snatched from pleasures such as these, the
rich Virginian devoted himself to the care of his estate and
the performance of his public duties. He followed the
judges on their circuits; he voted bills and addresses in the
House of Deputies, and, if he were a military man, was present at the muster of the militia. No law had yet been
passed by Congress for the formation of a national militia.
Each State governed its own troops in its own way. Yet it
would be unjust to suppose that the military was not an efficient body of men. Among the officers were to be found
men with records of which any soldier might well be proud.
Not a few of the captains and majors who stood before the
ranks were veterans of a former war. Some had shared in the
victory of the Great Meadows; had defended to the last Fort
Necessity, and, when no longer tenable, marched out with all
the honors of war; had followed Washington and Braddock to
the fatal field of Monongahela, and, by their coolness and skill,
covered the disorderly retreat of the more disciplined soldiers

of England. Others, too young to have shared in such exploits, had hastened, when independence was declared, to join the army commanded by the illustrious Virginian, had stood by him in his retreat through the Jerseys, marched with him through the ice and snow of that glorious December morning when he charged the Hessian camp at Trenton, took part in the fight at Princeton, shared in the defeats at Brandywine and Germantown, and beat back the troops of Cornwallis when they sallied from the works at Yorktown.

The son of a great landed proprietor usually grew up to manhood on his father's plantation, rode every morning, attended by his servant, to the school kept in the neighboring parish by a clergyman of the English Church, passed thence to William and Mary's college, spent a winter at Richmond, and came back to the old hall an aspirant for a seat in the House of Deputies. His opinions respecting forms of government and forms of creed were not the result of long study or of deep meditation, but were inherited with his estate, which passed from father to son by the strictest laws of entail. Whether Catholicism or Protestantism embraced the purer creed or the more divine form of worship, whether nations were wiser, better governed, more prosperous, under hereditary monarchs, electoral princes, or presidents, were matters on which it would have puzzled him to give an opinion; he was devotedly attached to the ritual and polity of the Anglican Church because his father and grandfather had been so before him, and because he believed them to be a necessary badge of what he considered his patrician descent; he was a non-imposter, not because his reading had taught him that imposts were bad things, but because the men on whom he looked down with contempt were strongly in favor of the measure. The few deductions, indeed, which he derived from reading had much of a foreign character, for his books, like the lace for his hat and the frill for his shirt, his silver shoe-buckles and his sword, came from over the sea.

That he should import his books is far from strange, for, with few exceptions, all books came from beyond the Atlantic. Fully three fourths of every library were volumes written by English men of letters, and published by English printers.

No American writer had yet appeared whose compositions possessed more than an ephemeral interest, or were deemed worthy to be ranked with those of Goldsmith and Johnson, of Swift and Gibbon. It is true, indeed, that a few productions had come out during the revolutionary war, which had gained much notoriety for their authors, and had been widely read. It is true that Trumbull's "McFingal" went through as many editions when the population of the country was three millions, as did "Evangeline" when the numbers of the people had swollen to thirty millions. But the cause of the popularity of "McFingal" and the cause of the popularity of "Evangeline" are very different indeed. So long as the war lasted, phrases, expressions, whole pages of "McFingal," were on every tongue; but of the thousands who laughed over the first canto in 1775, not one in ten read the third canto in 1780, and not one in a hundred read the poem in 1784. Paine's "Crisis," it is true, had enjoyed an equal share of popularity, and was still reprinted and read. It is true, also, that Paine's little pamphlet, "Common Sense," had gained for him national reputation and national gratitude; but the circumstances which called it forth had passed away, and men were already beginning to forget the great services he had rendered to the cause of liberty.* Ramsay had not commenced his history; Gordon's was soon to come out. One author had indeed appeared, an author whose name has since become familiar to three genera-

---

* Toward the middle of the year 1784, a bill was brought in by some members of the Virginia house of deputies to reward the patriotism and public services of the now famous author of "Common Sense" by a grant of land known as the Secretary's land, on the eastern shore, equal to four thousand pounds sterling. The bill was known to have the approval of Washington, and was warmly supported by Madison; yet it was, on the third reading, thrown out. His friends again rallied, and proposed that the tract should be sold, and two thousand pounds of the money applied to the purchase of an estate for Mr. Paine. Even to this many of the deputies would not listen, and, after a sharp fight, the bill was again rejected by a single vote. See the letter of Washington to Madison, June 12, 1784, and that of Madison, in reply, July 2, 1784. The bill had passed two readings, when Arthur Lee made some statement which produced a sudden change in many votes. In New York he fared much better. The legislature, on the 19th of April, presented him with a farm in Westchester. Packet, May 29, 1784.

tions of school-boys, and whose works have, in our time, greatly changed our written language. Noah Webster, then a youth of four-and-twenty, had lately put forth his "American Institute," the first of a splendid series of spelling-books, and the forerunner of his dictionary, and had seen it introduced into many New England schools, and rapidly displacing the ancient Dilworth. But, with these few exceptions, and perhaps as many more in the domain of theology, no work had been produced which was, seventy-five years later, read by any but the curious.*

There is, in fact, no portion of our literary annals which presents a spectacle of so much dreariness as the one hundred and sixty years which followed the landing of the Pilgrims. In all that time scarcely any work of the imagination was produced which posterity has not willingly let die. It would be a hard task to the most assiduous compiler to glean from the literature of that period material enough to make what would now be thought a readable book. A few poems of the "Tenth Muse," an odd chapter from the "Magnalia Christi," a page or two from the essay on "The Freedom of the Will," some lyrics of Hopkinson, a satire by Trumbull, a pamphlet by Paine, would almost complete the book, and, when completed, it would not be a very large volume, nor one of a very high order of merit. It would not be worth fifty lines of "Evangeline," nor the half of "Thanatopsis." The men whose writings now form our national literature, the men we are accustomed to revere as intellectual patriarchs, all whose works have become classics, belong, without exception, to the generation which followed the revolution. Irving was not a year old when peace was declared. Cooper was born in the same year that Washington went into office. Halleck, one year later. Prescott, in the year Washington came out of office. The Constitution was five years old when Bryant was born. The first year of the present century witnessed the birth of Bancroft, and, before another decade had come and gone, Emerson

---

* In the list of text-books that came out in 1784, Morse's American Geography must not be omitted. It was full of errors, and received a scorching criticism in a pamphlet called Remarks on the American Universal Geography, by J. F., 1793.

was born, and Willis, and Longfellow, and Whittier, and Holmes, and Hawthorne, and Poe. Before the year 1825 was reached, "Thanatopsis" was published, Motley was born, the "Spy," the "Pioneer," and the "Pilot" were written, and Drake, after a short and splendid career, carried with honor to the grave. Scarcely a twelvemonth went by unmarked by the birth of a man long since renowned in the domain of letters—1783, 1789, 1790, 1791, 1794, 1795, 1796, 1800, 1803, 1806, 1807, 1808, 1809, 1811, 1814, such is the almost unbroken succession.

It may, at first sight, seem strange that, after so many years of intellectual weakness, of feeble tottering, and of blind gropings, there should suddenly have appeared so great a crowd of poets and novelists, historians and essayists, following hard upon the war for independence. But the fact is merely another illustration of a great truth with which the history of every people is replete with examples, the truth that periods of national commotion, disorder, and contention are invariably followed by periods of intellectual activity. Whatever can turn the minds of men from the channels in which they have long been running, and stir them to their inmost depths, has never yet failed to produce most salutary and lasting results.

The age of Pericles, of Augustus, of Leo and Elizabeth, of Louis Quatorze, and the splendors of the reign of Ferdinand, are but so many instances in point. The same is true of our own land. For the first time since white men began to inhabit America, the colonists were united in a common league against a common foe. For seven years the strife continued. When it ended, yet another seven years followed, during which the fury of war gave way to the rage of faction. There was never a moment of rest. No sooner was one storm over than another appeared on the horizon. Yet here again years of national commotion were followed by years of great mental activity the like of which our country had never witnessed before. Yet again were the evils of war succeeded by the fruits of genius.

Our ancestors were, therefore, in 1784, shut out from the only native authors whose writings are by this generation

thought worthy to be read.  They possessed no poets better
than Philip Freneau and Timothy Dwight.  No novelist, no
dramatist, no really great historian, had yet arisen.  Among
the living statesmen none had as yet produced anything more
enduring than a political pamphlet or a squib.  Hamilton and
Madison and Jay had not begun that noble series of essays
which finds no parallel in the English language save in the
" Letters of Junius."  A knowledge of German, of Italian, and
of Spanish was not considered a necessary part of the education of a gentleman.  Men of parts and refinement listened in
astonishment to the uncouth gutturals in which the officers of
the Hessian troops commanded their men to " carry arms "
and to " right wheel."  All, therefore, who did not understand
French, and they made up the majority of readers, were of
necessity compelled to peruse the works of English authors, or
read nothing, or what was worse than nothing.  They filled
their library-shelves, as a consequence, with volumes which are
at this day much more admired than studied.  The incom-
parable letters of Philip Francis to Woodfall were imitated by
numberless pamphleteers, who, over the signature of Cassius
or Brutus, reviled the Cincinnati, or set forth most urgent
reasons why no Tory refugee should ever again be allowed to
find a footing on American soil.  Damsels envious of distinction as correspondents made themselves familiar with the polished diction and pure English of the " Spectators " and the
" Tatlers."  Nor were they ignorant of many books which no
woman would now, without a blush, own to having read.  The
adventures of Peregrine Pickle and Roderic Random were
as well known to the women of that generation as were
those of Leatherstocking to the women of the succeeding.
It would, however, be a great mistake to suppose that they
read no novels of a less objectionable character than "Tom
Jones" and "Tristram Shandy." *  The lighter literature of

---

* The favorite novels of the young women of that age were Victoria, Lady Julia Mandeville, and Malvern Dale.  A critic who confessed to being a great novel-
reader has said of Lady Julia Mandeville: " The stile is beautiful, but the tale is
horrid."  Malvern Dale was, she thought, " something like Evelina, though not
so pretty."  Journal of a Young Lady of Virginia, pp. 12, 17, 25.  Edited by E.
V. Mason.  The Sylph also stood high.  Many others are advertised in the Pennsylvania Packet, January 28, 1785.

England had long been growing purer and purer. The reproach which from the time of Fielding and Smollett had lain on the novel was rapidly passing away. Even among grave and reflecting people the feeling against all works of fiction was far less strong that it had been when, a few years before, Sir Anthony Absolute pronounced the circulating library to be an evergreen-tree of diabolical knowledge. "Evelina" and "Camilla" had appeared, had been read with admiration, and had shown that a popular novel might be written without an amour or a debauch. From letters and journals still extant, it should seem that, with the exception of the few novels named, the staple reading was of a serious character. After years of patient toil, Gibbon had lately put forth the third volume of his majestic work; Robertson had published the first readable history of America.

The cost of such books was then much in excess of what it now is, yet the price, though high, was very considerably less than they could have been published for at home.* Paper was both scarce and expensive. Some few mills had recently been put up in Pennsylvania, but the machinery was rude, the workmen unskilled, the number of reams turned out each month by no means equal to the demand, and the quality of the paper not much better than that at present used for printing hand-bills and posters. Bristol-board seems not to have been made in the country, and so little of it was brought in from abroad that the lack of it was severely felt. A hundred uses to which it is now put were unknown. No tradesman notified his patrons, by a generous distribution of neatly printed and ornamented cards, of the arrival of a new stock of tammies and everlastings; the fine gentleman gave his name,

---

* In the advertisement of Ramsay's History of the Revolution in South Carolina, edition of 1786, it is stated: "The author has taken on himself the risk and expense of the whole edition, amounting to more than four thousand nine hundred dollars." An abridgment of the Lives of the Poets, in twenty-five numbers, paper covers, sold for thirty-seven shillings and sixpence, a sum that would not now be equalled by fifteen dollars; Claypole's History of Ireland brought half a guinea. Pennsylvania Packet, January 8, 1784. Moore's Travels sold at a dollar for each of the four volumes. Packet, March 27, 1784. It may be observed that the sale of Ramsay's History was prohibited in England. See a poem on the subject in the American Museum for February, 1787.

not his card, to the servant who courtesied before him at the
open door; the fine lady sent out no richly engraved invitations to her routs and her feasts; for such a purpose playing-
cards were made to do duty, for of these, as the taste for
whist, for ombre, and quadrille was universal, there was no
stint. The custom, indeed, lingered till the present century
had come in, and the descendants of many of the fashionable families of those days preserve, among the stately love-
letters of their grandmothers, queens of hearts and aces of
spades on the back of which are printed invitations to dancing assemblies and to balls.

Low as was the state of letters, that of the fine arts was
lower still; they were wholly neglected. There did not then
exist in the country a single piece of architecture which, when
tried even by the standard of that day, can be called respectable. Not a church, not a public building, not a hall has been
preserved to us that is not a deformity; here and there, in the
great towns, some merchant prince had put up a costly pile,
which was believed by his townsmen to rival in magnificence
the palace-like homes of the English aristocracy. Such an
one was the Walton house, at New York, whose spacious rooms
were long since turned into emigrants' lodgings and stores.
The home of Robert Morris, at Philadelphia, was another. It
was by far the most magnificent in the city; had called forth
the admiration of a distinguished foreigner accustomed to the
splendors of Paris and Versailles, and led him to comment on
the huge doors of solid mahogany, on the hinges of glittering
brass, and on the rich display of porcelain. But these were
the exception. The houses which made up the towns and
cities were of the low-brow, hip-roofed order, strung along the
streets in disorderly array; some had their gable-ends toward
the road, others stood back in small gardens full of sunflowers and hollyhocks. If of brick, they were commonly
smeared with stucco and defaced with pilasters; had great
wastes of wall between the stories, and windows which resembled nothing so much as a checker-board. Their beauty
consisted solely in spacious rooms, in costly furniture and
rich hangings; but among the hangings a landscape, a battle-
piece, or an interior, indeed, an oil-painting of any kind other

than a portrait by Smybert or a head by Copley, was never to be seen. A vague rumor of a gallery of pictures that once existed in New Jersey has come down to us. We are told how one Watson, a Scotchman, settled at Perth Amboy; how he loaned money, how he painted portraits, how he kept in a barn, which he dignified by the name of a gallery, a few pictures done in oil; how, at his death, they passed to his nephew, how the nephew took sides with the Tories, how he fled for his life, and how the militia so effectually scattered these works of art that not a trace of one of them can now be found. But with that exception, no extensive collection was made for more than twenty years. In truth, at the close of the revolution the country could boast neither of artists nor of paintings.* Of the men who, in after years, reached a questionable distinction as painters, some were busy with their tops and marbles, some were in long clothes, and some had not been born. Peale was at that time six years old, Allston was five, Sully was one. Of the three Americans who had already reached distinction in the fine arts, not one was in the country. West was in England daubing canvas with representations of Cupid, of Death on the Pale Horse, and with scenes drawn from the writings of Shakespeare, of Homer, and the Apostles. Gilbert Stuart, who first saw the light of day in the dingy garret of a Rhode Island snuff-mill, went abroad two years before the fight at Lexington, and did not return till Washington had been four years president. Copley, too, departed at the opening of the war, leaving behind him many excellent portraits of the beauties and fine gentlemen of colonial days. The place of

---

* In a paper, entitled Thoughts on American Genius, published in the American Museum, for March, 1787, some names and works are cited to "explode the European creed that we are infantine in our acquisitions and savage in our manners, because we are inhabitants of a new world, lately occupied by a race of savages." Among artists, the men of genius are West, Copley, and John Trumbull; Mr. Taylor, of Philadelphia, in landscape; Mr. Stuart, of Rhode Island, and Mr. Brown, of Boston, in portrait-painting. The best prose writer is Dr. Ramsay, of South Carolina. The finest poet is Barlow, whose Vision of Columbus is as far below the epics of Blackburn as the epics of Blackburn are beneath the epics of Homer. Some idea of the style of painting popular at that day may be had by reading the list of paintings that were drawn as prizes in Mrs. Pine's lottery at Philadelphia, in 1789. Pennsylvania Gazette, November 25, 1789.

these men was filled by foreigners. Smybert had long been busy in Boston. Pine, now chiefly remembered for his fine portrait of Washington, had just come over. He brought with him the first plaster cast of the "Venus de Medici" ever seen in the United States. But the women of Philadelphia were prudes; the statue was a nude one, and the cry of shame that went up was so strong that Pine was forced to show it to his friends in private. Nor did this unwholesome morality soon disappear. Twenty-two years later, when a new generation had grown up, the exhibition of the Philadelphia Academy of Fine Arts was held in the Rotunda. Among the pictures then shown were fifty casts of famous statues in the Louvre; but many of these were naked, were pronounced indecent, and the managers compelled to set apart one day in each week for women, and, on such days, to keep the naked figures carefully covered up. Nay, more: in our own time, when the "Greek Slave," one of the few works of art of which our country has reason to be proud, was shown at Cincinnati, the world was edified by the sight of a delegation of distinguished clergymen sent to view it, that Christian people might know if they could with safety behold it. Trumbull, himself an artist, spoke the truth when he assured a young friend that it would be better for him to learn to make shoes or to dig potatoes than to paint pictures in America. Thirty-six years later, a famous writer in the Edinburgh Review tauntingly asked, and his taunts were none the less galling because they were true: Who, in the four quarters of the globe, reads an American book, or goes to an American play, or looks at an American painting or statue? What does the world owe to American physicians or surgeons? What new substances have their chemists discovered? What new constellations have their astronomers discerned? Who drinks out of American glasses? Who eats from American plates? Who wears an American coat, or lies down to sleep in an American blanket?* The first quarter of the present cen-

---

* Edinburgh Review, 1820.

The feelings aroused by this performance were quite as bitter as any Mr. Dickens awakened by the American Notes, and everywhere editors and writers hastened to hurl foul scorn at the Review. Nor did the resentment soon die

tury passed away before a single painting or a single piece of statuary was produced which will, one hundred and fifty years from now, be examined by our descendants with pride.

There was, however, one art, an art which is half a fine art, not wholly neglected. It is true that in many parts of the community the theatre was still proscribed. In Massachusetts it was held in abhorrence, and the sharp laws of earlier times were in 1784 re-enacted. In New York and Philadelphia the stage was frowned upon, and plays and players pronounced immoral. But there remained many towns of lesser note where the actors were made welcome and rich. Such an one was Baltimore, for the city, small as it then was, had already achieved a high reputation for jollity.* Market street was the fashionable quarter, and ran out from the crowd of shops and taverns, far into the green fields and orchards of what was then the country, but is now covered with blocks of houses. The street was lined on either side by an endless succession of low, rambling houses, and was the particular pride of the citizens. They boasted that neither Philadelphia nor New York could show a street so long, so beautiful, and so gay. Nor was their pride altogether unfounded. The houses, brightly colored, some blue, some white and blue, others yellow, lighted up the deep shade of the locust-trees, while here and there loomed up the brick mansions of the rich merchants, with quaint entrances and great patches of wall between the windows. Along this highway, too, in the cool of the summer evening, sauntered a great throng of young men and damsels dressed in their best clothes, flirting, jesting, and enjoying the air. The spectacle, unimposing as it would seem to a generation accustomed to much finer ones, was still attractive to strangers, and led not a few of them to put down in their journals comments on the beauty of the women, on the gallantry of the men, and the rich display of brocades, of taffetas, and of hoops.

---

out, for, many years later, there appeared in the North American Review a vigorous reply, entitled, Who reads an American Book? North American Review, No. lv.

*See a lecture on Baltimore Long Ago, by J. P. Kennedy; also, Scharf's Chronicles of Baltimore for a good account of Baltimore at the revolution. Mr. Kennedy's lecture is quoted by Scharf, p. 231.

The favorite amusements of the Baltimoreans were balls, routs, and dancing assemblies. But in the intervals between assembly nights the theatre was the place of resort. The theatres to which the town then went to weep and applaud were wanting in the luxury, the richness and display of the rooms wherein we are accustomed to witness the impersonations of Salvini and of Booth. In the best of them the stage was narrow and contracted, the scenery wretched daubs, which produced little illusion in the dim light of a multitude of oil-lamps and candles. That portion of the house at present believed to contain the best seats was then known as the pit, was looked upon as the least desirable, and nightly filled with a rabble more noisy and obstreperous than is now to be found in the top gallery on the night of a benefit. In the boxes and stalls above the pit were the seats of the better class and the aristocracy of the town. The gallery was taken up by the lower classes. As the fashion of reserving seats had not yet come in, it was customary to send servants to occupy places as soon as the doors were thrown open, and hold them till their masters and mistresses arrived. It was, however, announced among the notices at the foot of the play-bills that the curtain would rise promptly at a quarter after six o'clock, and that all servants were then expected to leave. Other notices informed the audience that they were not to call upon the musicians to play their favorite airs, that if they did not bring exact change they could purchase no tickets, and that the managers would be greatly obliged, and the public much diverted, by the loan of any plays fit to be brought on the stage.* Among the plays considered as fit to be performed were one or two of Sheridan's, as many more of Shakespeare's, and some of O'Keefe's. But the taste of the public was not critical, and

---

* On some of the play-bills of 1784, and earlier, are notices as follows: "Any Gentlemen possessed of good Farces, and will lend or dispose of them to the Managers, will greatly oblige them." "Some Tunes having been called for by Persons in the Gallery which have given Offence to others, the Managers have resolved that no Music will be played but such as they shall order the Day before the Representation." "Children in Laps will not be admitted." Scharf's Chronicles of Baltimore. See, also, the play-bills printed in the Philadelphia papers of 1790–1796.

none called forth such rounds of applause as "Love in a Village" and "Miss in her Teens." The price of admission to the boxes was commonly one dollar, to the pit five shillings, to the gallery ninepence. This sum placed the luxury of a night at the theatre within the means of the poorest classes. Every night the playhouse was open, which rarely was more than thrice in a week, the gallery was crowded with apprentices, with shopkeepers, and with tradesmen. But on no occasion was the press so great, and the audience so jolly, as on an evening when it was expected that Harlequin would bound through hogsheads of fire and chests of drawers. Then the mob was wild with delight. They would call upon the fiddlers to play their favorite tunes, not always the most select, would sing snatches of lewd songs, would make coarse jokes, would shout to the people in the boxes, jeer one actor and applaud another, and, when Columbine was hard pressed, call upon Harlequin to come to her relief.

From such spectacles as these, however, a large part of the community kept aloof. Some pronounced them to be immoral, others denounced them as a piece of foolish and wicked extravagance. The country, they declared, was surely going to be ruined by the taste for expensive luxuries that was coming in. The times were full of signs. Coaches were becoming more and more common in the great towns. Shops were springing up filled with all manner of finery brought from beyond the sea. Damsels whose mothers had been content to wear homespun were quite unhappy unless they were tricked out in brocades, in taffetas, in Rohan hats. Young men now thought it becoming to scoff at sacred things, and frequented the playhouse much more than they did the church. A stop should be put to this, and as the theatre was the newest evil, it was quite fitting to begin the attack there. Some earnest moralists accordingly took up the matter. The discussion grew warmer and warmer, till in a little while the community was divided between the defenders and the detractors of the stage. All kinds of grounds were taken, and all manner of arguments advanced. Indeed, the whole range of history, ancient and modern, was ransacked for instances to prove that plays and shows had been made use of by tyrants as engines to destroy liberty; that they had been employed by virtuous rulers to promote liberty; that they were purely monarchical institutions; that they were eminently republican institutions; that they fostered vice; that they taught morality.

The dispute began at Philadelphia, and for several months the good points and the bad points of the theatre were sharply debated by several individuals under the names of Janus, Thespis, and Philo-Thespis.* Nothing came of the dispute, however, till in the following year it broke out in New York. Some champion of the good cause published, about the middle of September, 1785, an address to the citizens of New York. A new species of luxury and dissipation had, he said, lately come among them, and was making ground so rapidly as to give much cause for alarm. It was really true then that the measure of folly, of extravagance, and of pride was not yet full; and to fill it to overflowing the theatre must needs be set up in their midst. It was well, in such matters, to listen with attention to the warning voice of great moralists who knew whereof they spoke. Montesquieu had truly said that morality was the principle of republican government, and on this it would be an easy matter to prove that the playhouses were, in a political view, a pest. They would, beyond anything else, undermine the glorious fabric the sons of America had been rearing, and prepare the way for anarchy and monarchy. But the political was not the only view. Looking at the matter from a financial point, dramas were equally ruinous to the good of the community. There was a time for everything, and this was no time for gayety, for jollity, and for plays. Think for a moment on the situation. They were just emerging from the horrors of a protracted war. They were beginning as a new people. They were too poor to support an army, though the enemy was still on the frontier; or a navy, though they stood exposed to the depredations of the whole world. It was stark madness in such a situation to waste their money on a set of British players with their Harlequin trumpery. Yet a little while and these men would

---

* See The Freeman's Journal for February 11, 18, 25, and March 3, 10, 24, 1784.

squeeze a rich spoil in hard cash out of their dupes. Nay, more: they would perchance, if suffered to go on, soon teach their hearers to laugh at the exertions of those hardy spirits to whose efforts, under God, it was due that every American had a house to sit in without a British bayonet at his throat. Why did they seek to hide the true character of their performances under innocent names? The paltry titles of Moral Lecture, Serious Lecture, and the like, were at best but a trifling preface to the theatre. It was time the magistrates took up the matter; but if they did not, a party could easily be got together to lay the playhouse in the dust.*

Attacks like this were not suffered to pass unnoticed. They found so much approval, and seemed so important, that grave answers were put forth, in which all the merits of a good play were illustrated and defended by scraps of Latin from the early philosophers, and such bits of history as were familiar to men fresh from the high-schools and colleges. Plays, it was said, were by no means new and untried things. All well-regulated states had, in earlier times, thought it fitting, both in a political and moral sense, to have some kind of show for the amusement of the people. And what kind of show had been so much a favorite as well-acted dramas? Every man who knew anything of the history of Greece knew at what enormous expense the men of Athens kept up their theatre, what pains they were at to secure the finest actors, how often they made their favorite poets guardians of their liberties, or sent them forth to govern provinces and command armies. And was there ever a people so jealous of their liberties as the Athenians? Was there ever a people who knew so well that corruption and debauchery are the greatest foes of liberty, and that the freedom of the theatre is, next to the freedom of the senate, its best and safest foundation? Socrates, whose teachings seemed almost Christian, delighted to assist Euripides in his compositions. Solon, the wise legislator, whose laws had been the admiration of seventy generations of men, was, even in the decline of life, a frequenter of plays. Plutarch held the belief that plays were useful in polishing manners. Brutus, the virtuous, the moral Brutus,

---

* New York Packet, September 15, 1785.

thought his time well spent in journeying from Rome to Naples to see a play, and that, too, at a time when the imperial city was all tumult and confusion over Cæsar's death. Could anybody doubt that Mr. Addison had done great things as a moralist? Yet Mr. Addison wrote " Cato." Was there anything which breathed a more exalted piety than the " Night Thoughts "? Yet Doctor Young wrote " Busiris " and " The Revenge." *

To the arguments about the high regard the people of old held for the theatre, the reply was made that he who read Greek history in such wise read it ill. It was quite true that the stage had its birth at Athens. But even there both tragedy and comedy were soon abolished by public will. The Romans, also, were not adverse to plays. But so cautious were that people that they did not suffer a theatre when once put up to stand many days. How long was it before the theatre of Scaurus, which cost upward of a million sterling, came down? As for the opinions of Socrates and Solon, they were set off, and more than set off, by the opinions of Seneca and Tertullian, whose writings abounded in passages condemning such amusements. Who was it that wrote " Nihil est tam damnosum bonis moribus, quam in alioquo spectaculo desidere. Tunc enim per voluptatam facilius vitia surrepunt "? † Much was said about the advantages that would flow from a well-regulated theatre. What were they? Would the merchant choose to have his apprentice learn exactness and frugality of the stage? Was it a fact that men whose generosity had been strengthened by weeping over virtue in distress made the best paymasters? ‡ There were, on the other hand, a few evils which would perhaps flow from the boasted well-regulated theatre. It would promote discontent, it would create a taste for show. How contemptible and mean did the affairs of a family seem to the wife and daughter of a mechanic after the gaudy scenes of the stage! But, aside from all this, the theatre was improper because it tended to effeminate manners and corrupt that virtue which was the living principle of all good republican government. Let the intruders then be driven out!

---

* New York Packet, October 20, 1785.   † Ibid., January 23, 1786.
‡ Ibid., October 20, 1785.

And now the papers began to abound in addresses to the inhabitants of New York, in "Thoughts for the Rulers of the Free," * and the coffee-houses with petitions and memorials. One wit went so far as to assert, facetiously, that the name drama was derived from the custom of always having a dram-shop near the theatre.† Another besought all good men not to put their hands to the petition, then going the rounds, for the suppression of virtue and morality, as a counter one would shortly be offered them wherein the fallacy of every argument in favor of the theatre would be shown, and the impropriety of the drama clearly set forth.‡ A third remarked that, while he had no fault to find with the theatre, he had much to find with the plays. It was a shame that while the English language afforded so many energetic tragedies abounding in excellent morals, and so many comedies replete with the justest satire, they were made to listen to such trash as the "Genii of the Rock," "The Witches," "Harlequin in the Moon," and a thousand other pantomimic mummeries at which common-sense stood aghast. The paltry farces in two acts which preceded the dumb show were nothing. The hornpipe might perhaps have some meaning to one who had studied the laws of motion. Let the actors bring out good pieces, and the clap of approval would be heard from men who had emancipated half the world.#

In the midst of this discussion no small merriment was afforded by the news which came down the river from Albany. A party of strolling players had lately made their appearance in that staid city, had obtained permission of the Mayor to perform their parts, and, to the horror of the more sober inhabitants, drew large crowds. A petition was soon written, and presented with many signatures to the Mayor. His Honor was assured that, although the inhabitants were suspected of rusticity and a want of politeness, they had, it was hoped, enough common-sense to judge and declare that they stood in no need of plays and play-actors to instruct them in their duty and good manners. The pressing necessities of many families, after a long and distressing war, and the debts still due to the

<hr />

* New York Packet, January 23, 1786.    † Ibid., January 23, 1786.
‡ Ibid., January 16, 1786.    # Ibid., October 10, 1785.

public, called upon them to ask for an impartial reconsideration of the late resolution granting a license to the players. They would assurĕdly drain the people of much money, and instil into the minds of the giddy principles inconsistent with that virtue which is the true basis of republican liberty and happiness.*

The inhospitality, the rude manners, and the parsimony of the men at the head of the river, had long been a source of ill will to the men at the mouth of the river. The news, therefore, that the Albanians were really spending their money on theatrical shows excited much amusement. Many persons, it was said, had supposed the friends of the theatre to be confined to New York. But the delirium had spread far and wide. And, strange to relate, the honest, sober Dutchmen of Albany, who were once distinguished by industry and laudable parsimony, were now wasting their substance on shows.

Meanwhile a like discussion was going on in Philadelphia. The city had long been justly renowned for the extravagance of its people, and for the favor with which they looked on every kind of amusement. Yet there was in Philadelphia a respectable party, composed largely of Quakers, which held that the country had much more to fear from the theatre than from the weakness of Congress, the navigation act, and the quarrelsome disposition of the States put together. When, therefore, the bill for the suppression of vice and immorality was undergoing discussion in the Assembly, these men were much elated to hear that an attempt was being made to tack on to it a clause providing that whoever should put up a theatre, playhouse, stage or scaffold for tragedy, comedy, tragi-comedy, farce, prelude or interlude, should be heavily fined. It was proposed by a member named Whitehill, and boldly attacked by that General Wayne whose reckless, eccentric character had earned for him the title of Mad Anthony. He told the members that he for one hoped they would not think of introducing into the bill a clause for the suppression of the theatre; for a well-regulated theatre was everywhere acknowledged to improve morals, to polish manners, and to teach virtue. Should one be

---

* New York Packet, December 26, 1785.

set up in their midst, this would undoubtedly be the result.
For an illustration they had but to look to Paris. To this
Dr. Logan objected. The government under which it was
their happiness to live was a republican government. France
was an absolute monarchy, and no argument drawn from an
absolute monarchy could apply to a republic. Nobody liked
to see a well-acted tragedy better than he did. Yet he was
clearly of the opinion that theatres were suited to monarchies
and despotic governments. Look at the Genevese. They
abolished theatres; and immediately the King of France and
Sardinia, who had long sought to enslave them, attempted to
set up one in their midst. In this he failed; but he did succeed in building a playhouse within two or three miles of
their very gates. Look at Paris. Did they not have soldiers
with fixed bayonets in the theatres to keep down riot and
tumult? When the doctor had finished, General Wayne reminded the House that the whole city was desirous to have
Congress return, and told them that he was fully borne out in
saying that a theatre would be a great inducement for that
body to come back, as there were in it a number of young
fellows who did not intend to be debarred so innocent an
amusement. This was replied to by Mr. Smiley. The argument made by the gentleman from Chester was, he thought,
no argument at all. A theatre would bring back Congress
because some young fellows in that body were fond of plays!
Of all arguments this surely was the strongest against the
theatre. Had the gentleman said the drama would be an
inducement to the grave, the sober, and the wise, his reasoning would have had some weight. But the Legislature of
Pennsylvania did not intend to hold out inducements to the
dissolute, the thoughtless, and the giddy. Mr. Findley declared that he did not know what was meant by a well-regulated theatre. What should regulate it? Government? Then it
became indeed a dangerous tool. The stage, it was true, could
be made the source of most rational amusement. But it was
undeniable that it was frequently subservient to licentiousness
and immorality. Let any man read over a catalogue of plays.
Let him look into the plot of each narrowly. Ten to one he
would find the *dénoûment* in general to be the running away

with an only daughter, violating the chastity of a friend's wife, separating a married pair, or putting matrimony out of countenance, to say nothing of *doubles ententes*, which, as succedaneums for wit, were interspersed through the scenes. In England, to be sure, the dramatic taste was contradictory. Indelicacies were rigidly excluded from the new plays. Yet the indecent pieces written during the Augustan age of that nation, the age of Queen Anne, were played without any opposition, and a Farquhar, a Congreve, a Vanbrugh, held possession of the stage. "At present play-writers are at liberty, when they wish to throw their audiences into fits of laughter, to make a smutty joke, throw the ladies into confusion, and give the jessamies a chance of tittering to show their teeth." As a consequence not one of the many plays written during ten years past had done more than, by dint of puffing in the newspapers, eke out for the writer a miserable pittance from a third night's performance. Sensible of this, a Mr. O'Keefe, who had of late written several farces, "filled them with the most rank nonsense, which, from its very absurdity, forced even the stoic to grin." Mr. Findley then repeated, amid roars of laughter, several selections from the pieces of O'Keefe.* As to American plays, he was adverse to censorship. The manners and morals of his countrymen were too chaste to leave any reason to think that an improper comedy would be written by one of them for perhaps a century to come. Robert Morris replied to this, and when the question

---

* A couple of selections from the works of O'Keefe may perhaps serve to illustrate the " rank nonsense " to which Mr. Findley referred. The first is from the Castle of Andalusia :

"A master I have, and I am his man,
    Galloping dreary dun.
And he will get married as fast as he can,
    With my haily, gaily gambolarity,
    Giggling, niggling, galloping,
    Galloway dreary dun."

The chorus of another song is :

"Ditherum doodle, adgety,
    Nadgety, tragedy rum,
Goosterum foodle, fidgety,
    Nidgety, nagety mum,
        Goosterum foodle."

to postpone was called, the noes were twenty-nine, the ayes were thirty-four.*

In Boston the old Puritanic hatred of players and play-houses, though much weakened, was still strong. Indeed it was not till the close of Washington's first administration that a company of players dared to show themselves in the town. An attempt, it is true, was made in June, 1790, to break down the ancient prejudice against the stage, and a petition was sent in by one of the famous American Company of players for leave to open a theatre under proper regulations. But permission was flatly refused. The town was much disappointed, and a year later thirty-eight gentlemen signed a like petition to the select-men, begging them to take the sense of the people in town-meeting. This prayer was heard. A great meeting was held in Faneuil Hall, the morality of comedies and tragedies discussed in the usual way, and when the question, "Theatre or no Theatre," was put, the number in favor of the theatre was thought to be at least three to one.† Such an expression of town feeling soon had its result. The matter was carried to the General Court, and a bill brought in to regulate the expense and prevent the excess of theatrical shows. Gardiner was the champion of the showmen, and on the twenty-sixth of January, 1792, made a long and exhaustive speech.‡ Yet the best argument he could adduce was the profit such things would bring to tradesmen. The emolument, said he, that the masons, the carpenters, the white-smiths, the wood-carvers, and the painters must derive from building and repairing the playhouse will be very great. The milliners, too, would not be forgotten. They would furnish the silks, the laces, and the ducks, while the rope-walkers would be called on to supply rope to ring the bells and gibbet the villains and traitors. As to morality, he was as well acquainted

* Quite a full report of the debate in the Pennsylvania Assembly is given in New York Packets for December 5, 1785, and February 6 and 9, 1786. Also, in the Pennsylvania Packet, from which the New York report is copied. For other remarks on the theatre, see Carlisle Gazette, February 15, 1786; New York Packet, December 5 and 27, 1785; Ibid., April 6 and 10, 1786.

† See the Columbian Centinel, October 22, November 2, 12, 1791.

‡ See a pamphlet entitled A Speech in the Massachusetts House of Representatives, January 26, 1792.

with the scriptures as any man who heard him speak. Yet he
could recall nothing reflecting on actors. Nay, there were
many things in the Holy Book that partook of dramatic poetry
and action. Had not Saint Paul borrowed whole passages
from the Greek poets? The bill ultimately passed the House
and the Senate, and was signed by the Governor.*

Meanwhile a company of comedians, encouraged by the
townsfolk, began their season in an old stable that had been
hastily fitted up for the purpose in Broad Alley. To evade
the law against such performances, they called the theatre the
New Exhibition Room, and the plays Moral Lectures. On the
sixteenth of August the room was opened with tight-rope
dancing, tumbling, hornpipes, minuets, and a gallery of portraits.† No interference took place. The actors grew more
daring, and when September came, announced that on the
twenty-sixth of the month "Douglas and the Poor Soldier," a
moral lecture in five parts, would be presented. But Hancock
was Governor, and not a man to be deceived by a name or to
tolerate so bold an evasion of the law. One night in December,
therefore, while the company were playing the moral lecture
of "School for Scandal," and the play had gone as far as the
end of the second act, the sheriff suddenly rushed upon the
stage and carried off Sir Peter to the jail. The house in a fit
of fury denounced the Governor, damned liberty, and pulled
down and trampled under foot a painting of the Governor's
Arms that hung before the stage-box.‡ The next number of
the Centinel was full of cards. One expressed the thanks of
Harper, the arrested comedian, for the sympathy manifested by

---

* For the discussion over the theatre in Boston see the Independent Chronicle,
November 3, 18, and December 1, 8, 15, 1791. Also a pamphlet by W. Hali-
burton, called, Effects of the Stage on the Manners of a People and the Propriety of encouraging and establishing a Virtuous Theatre, Boston, 1792.

† Independent Chronicle, August 16, 1792.

‡ Some account of the disturbance is given in the Columbian Centinel, December 8, 1792. After the arrest of December 5th, threats were made of tar
and feathers and rotten eggs. See New York Journal, December 19, 1792,
and January 2, 1793. See, also, the slightly conflicting accounts given in Dunlap's History of the American Theatre, vol. i, pp. 244–252, and Thomas's Reminiscences of the last Sixty-five Years, vol. i, p. 28. Thomas says it was a portrait
of Hancock the mob pulled down. The newspapers say it was a painting of the
" Governor's Arms."

the audience on the evening of his arrest.  A second informed
the public that, at the request of the select-men, the performance
would be discontinued for a while.*  A third, it was pretended,
came from the tavern-keepers, and stated, amid a profusion of
thanks, that since the theatre had been stopped the tap-rooms
had been crowded, that the tapsters no longer slept over the
empty pots, and that the cry of "Coming, sirs, coming, sirs,"
was nightly heard on every side.†

The desire of the select-men to have the plays cease for a
while was the result of well-founded alarm.  On the Friday
after the arrest an angry discussion took place in the Apollo,
and threats of tearing down the theatre were made openly.
This so impressed a few sailors who were present, that they
collected a mob and went that night to Hancock's house and
asked for leave to pull the building to the ground.  The
Governor forbade it, scolded them mildly, and sent the crowd
home.‡  But the papers flatly accused him of having gathered
the mob himself.#

When the trial of Harper came on the arrest was declared
illegal, for, by a strange oversight, the complaint had not been
sworn to, and the warrant was, therefore, void by the fourteenth article of the Declaration of Rights.  Nothing more
was heard of the matter.‖  The plays were soon resumed,
and a year later the first theatre was put up.  A stock company built it.  The shares were one hundred and twenty
in number, and fifty pounds sterling apiece.  Yet when the
books were opened for subscription all were taken in a few
minutes.ᴬ

To know something of that great class of the community
whose republican principles and good morals could not, it was
feared, withstand the corrupting influence of the playhouse,
would indeed be most interesting.  Yet it is, unfortunately,
precisely the class concerning which our information is most

---

* Columbian Centinel, December 8, 1792.    † Ibid., December 15, 1792.

‡ Boston Gazette, December 24, 1792.

# Columbian Centinel, December 22, 1792.

‖ A town meeting was held on the matter of the theatre, December 21, 1792,
and instructions to the delegates in General Court adopted, December 27, 1792.
See Independent Chronicle, December 27, 1792.

ᴬ Gazette of the United States, April 24, 1793.

imperfect. There can, however, be no doubt that a wonderful amelioration has taken place since that day in the condition of the poor. Their houses were meaner, their food was coarser, their clothing was of commoner stuff, their wages were, despite the depreciation that has gone on in the value of money, lower by one half than at present. A man who performed what would now be called unskilled labor, who sawed wood, who dug ditches, who mended the roads, who mixed mortar, who carried boards to the carpenter and bricks to the mason, or helped to cut hay in the harvest-time, usually received as the fruit of his daily toil two shillings. Sometimes when the laborers were few he was paid more, and became the envy of his fellows if, at the end of a week, he took home to his family fifteen shillings, a sum now greatly exceeded by four dollars. Yet all authorities agree that in 1784 the hire of workmen was twice as great as in 1774.*

On such a pittance it was only by the strictest economy that a mechanic kept his children from starvation and himself from jail. In the low and dingy rooms which he called his home were wanting many articles of adornment and of use now to be found in the dwellings of the poorest of his class. Sand sprinkled on the floor did duty as a carpet. There was no glass on his table, there was no china in his cupboard, there were no prints on his wall. What a stove was he did not know, coal he had never seen, matches he had never heard of. Over a fire of fragments of boxes and barrels, which he lit with the sparks struck from a flint, or with live coals brought from a neighbor's hearth, his wife cooked up a rude meal and served it in pewter dishes. He rarely tasted fresh meat as often as once in a week, and paid for it a much higher price than his posterity. Everything, indeed, which ranked as a staple of life was very costly. Corn stood at three shillings the bushel, wheat at eight and sixpence, an assize of bread was fourpence, a pound of salt pork was tenpence. Many

---

* "On an average forty to fifty per cent. more can now be obtained for labour and country produce than their current price was in 1774." A Seventh Essay on Free Trade and Finance, January 10, 1785, Pelatiah Webster. Jay also complains of the "wages of mechanics and labourers, which are very extravagant." Jay to B. Vaughan, September 2, 1784.

other commodities now to be seen on the tables of the poor were either quite unknown, or far beyond the reach of his scanty means. Unenviable is the lot of that man who cannot, in the height of the season, when the wharfs and markets are heaped with baskets and crates of fruit, spare three cents for a pound of grapes or five cents for as many peaches, or, when Sunday comes round, indulge his family with watermelons or cantaloupes.* One hundred years ago the wretched fox-grape was the only kind that found its way to market, and was the luxury of the rich. Among the fruits and vegetables of which no one had then even heard are cantaloupes, many varieties of peaches and pears, tomatoes and rhubarb, sweet corn, the cauliflower, the egg-plant, head lettuce, and okra. On the window-benches of every tenement-house may be seen growing geraniums and verbenas, flowers not known a century ago. In truth, the best-kept gardens were then rank with hollyhocks and sunflowers, roses and snowballs, lilacs, pinks, tulips, and, above all, the Jerusalem cherry, a plant once much admired, but now scarcely seen.

If the food of an artisan would now be thought coarse, his clothes would be thought abominable. A pair of yellow buckskin or leathern breeches, a checked shirt, a red flannel jacket, a rusty felt hat cocked up at the corners, shoes of neat's-skin set off with huge buckles of brass, and a leathern apron, comprised his scanty wardrobe. The leather he smeared with grease to keep it soft and flexible. His sons followed in his footsteps, or were apprenticed to neighboring tradesmen. His daughter went out to service. She performed, indeed, all the duties at present exacted from women of her class; but with them were coupled many others rendered useless by the great improvement that has since taken place in the conveniences of life. She mended the clothes, she did up the ruffs, she ran on errands from one end of the town to the other, she milked the cows, made the butter, walked ten blocks for a pail of water, spun flax for the family linen, and, when the year was up, received ten pounds for her wages. Yet, small as was her pay, she had, before bestowing herself

---

* Cantaloupe-seed was first brought over from Tripoli by Colonel James Barron. To the French immigrants we owe the artichoke and okra.

in marriage on the footman or the gardener, laid away in her stocking enough guineas and joes to buy a few chairs, a table, and a bed.

But there is one other change which has, it must be admitted, done far more to increase the physical comforts of the poorest class than better food, higher wages, finer clothes. Men are no longer imprisoned for debt. No crime known to the law brought so many to the jails and prisons as the crime of debt, and the class most likely to get into debt was the most defenceless and dependent, the great body of servants, of artisans, and of laborers, those, in short, who depended on their daily wages for their daily bread. One hundred years ago the laborer who fell from a scaffold or lay sick of a fever was sure to be seized by the sheriff the moment he recovered, and be carried to jail for the bill of a few dollars which had been run up during his illness at the huckster's or the tavern.

It is pleasing to reflect that while our countrymen have been making such astonishing progress in all that administers to the comforts and conveniences of life, they have at the same time grown charitable and humane. There is indeed scarce a scrap of information bearing upon the subject extant which does not go to prove beyond question that the generation which witnessed the revolution was less merciful and tender-hearted than the generation which witnessed the civil war. Our ancestors, it is true, put up a just cry of horror at the brutal treatment of their captive countrymen in the prison ships and hulks. So great and bitter was their indignation, that money was to be stamped with representations of the atrocities of which they complained, that their descendants to the remotest generation might hold in remembrance the cruelty of the British and the suffering of the patriots. Yet even then the face of the land was dotted with prisons where deeds of cruelty were done, in comparison with which the foulest acts committed in the hulks sink to a contemptible insignificance. For more than fifty years after the peace there was in Connecticut an underground prison which surpassed in horrors the Black Hole of Calcutta. This den, known as the Newgate prison, was in an old worked-out copper-mine in the hills near

Granby.* The only entrance to it was by means of a ladder down a shaft which led to the caverns under ground. There, in little pens of wood, from thirty to one hundred culprits were immured, their feet made fast to iron bars, and their necks chained to beams in the roof. The darkness was intense; the caves reeked with filth; vermin abounded; water trickled from the roof and oozed from the sides of the caverns; huge masses of earth were perpetually falling off. In the dampness and the filth the clothing of the prisoners grew mouldy and rotted away, and their limbs became stiff with rheumatism. The Newgate prison was perhaps the worst in the country,† yet in every county were jails such as would now be thought unfit places of habitation for the vilest and most loathsome of beasts. At Northampton the cells were scarce four feet high, and filled with the noxious gases of the privy-vaults through which they were supposed to be ventilated. Light came in from two chinks in the wall. At the Worcester prison were a number of like cells, four feet high by eleven long, without a window or a chimney, or even a hole in the wall. Not a ray of light ever penetrated them. In other jails in Massachusetts the cells were so small that the prisoners were lodged in hammocks swung one over the other. In Philadelphia the keeps were eighteen feet by twenty feet, and so crowded that at night each prisoner had a space six feet by two to lie down in.

Into such pits and dungeons all classes of offenders of both sexes were indiscriminately thrust. It is therefore not at all surprising that they became seminaries of every conceivable form of vice, and centres of the most disgusting diseases. Prostitutes plied their calling openly in the presence of men and women of decent station, and guilty of no crime but an inability to pay their debts.‡ Men confined as wit-

---

* The mines were known as the Sinsbury, and the company that worked them, chartered in 1709, was the first incorporated mining company of any kind in the United States.

† An interesting account of the Newgate prison is to be found in a little tract entitled A History of the Newgate Prison, R. H. Phelps, 1844.

‡ "The grand jury on Monday last presented as a nuisance the general intercourse between the criminals of the different sexes in the jail, and likewise the indiscriminate mixture of debtors and criminals in the hall originally intended

nesses were compelled to mingle with the forger besmeared with the filth of the pillory, and the fornicator streaming with blood from the whipping-post, while here and there among the throng were culprits whose ears had just been cropped, or whose arms, fresh from the branding-iron, emitted the stench of scorched flesh. The entire system of punishment was such as cannot be contemplated without mingled feelings of pity and disgust. Offences to which a more merciful generation has attached no higher penalty than imprisonment and fine stood upon the statute-books as capital crimes. Modes of punishment long since driven from the prisons with execrations as worthy of an African kraal were looked upon by society with a profound indifference. The tread-mill was always going. The pillory and the stocks were never empty. The shears, the branding-iron, and the lash were never idle for a day. In Philadelphia the wheel-barrow men still went about the streets in gangs, or appeared with huge clogs and chains hung to their necks.* In Delaware, which to this hour treats her citizens with the degrading scenes of the whipping-post, twenty crimes were punished with a loss of life. Burglary and rape, sodomy and witchcraft, were among them. In Massachusetts ten crimes were declared by the General Court to be punishable with death. There the man who, in a fit of anger or in a fit of drunkenness, was heard cursing and swearing, or spreading evil reports of his neighbor, was first set in the stocks, and then carried off to the whipping-post and soundly flogged. If, however, he was so unfortunate as to be caught in the arms of a prostitute, he was suffered to escape with a fine. In Rhode Island, a perpetual mark of shame was for many offences

---

for debtors only." Philadelphia, September 22, 1787. This report declares that "the prison seems to them to be open as to a general intercourse between the criminals of the different sexes; and that there is not even the appearance of decency with respect to the scenes of debauchery that naturally arise from such a situation; insomuch that it appears to the jury, from undoubted information, that the gaol has become a desirable place for the more wicked and polluted of both sexes." Grand Jury of the County of Philadelphia to the Court of Oyer and Terminer. Pennsylvania Gazette, September 26, 1787.

* A great reform in the Penal Code of Pennsylvania was effected in 1790, when many crimes ceased to be capital, and the wheel-barrow punishment was abolished. See Journal of Prison Discipline, vol. i, p. 4.

judged to be a most fitting punishment. There a counterfeiter was punished with the loss of a piece of his ear, and distinguished from all other criminals by a large C deeply branded on his forehead. A wretch so hardened as to be recommitted was branded on the arm. Keepers knew no other mode of silencing the ravings of a madman than tying him up by the thumbs and flogging him till he was too exhausted to utter a groan.*

The misery of the unfortunate creatures cooped up in the cells, even of the most humanely kept prisons, surpasses in horror anything ever recorded in fiction. No attendance was provided for the sick. No clothes were distributed to the naked. Such a thing as a bed was rarely seen, and this soon became so foul with insects that the owner dispensed with it gladly. Many of the inmates of the prisons passed years without so much as washing themselves. Their hair grew long. Their bodies were covered with scabs and lice, and emitted a horrible stench. Their clothing rotted from their backs and exposed their bodies tormented with all manner of skin diseases and a yellow flesh cracking open with filth. The death-rate often stood as high as sixty in the thousand. As if such torments were not hard enough to bear, others were added by the half-maddened prisoners. No sooner did a new-comer enter the door of a cell than a rush was made for him by the inmates, who stripped him of his clothing and let him stand stark naked till it was redeemed by what in the peculiar jargon of the place was known as drink-money. It sometimes happened that the prisoners were in possession of a carefully preserved blanket. Then this ceremony, called garnishing,† was passed over for the yet more brutal one of blanketing. In spite of prayers and entreaties, the miserable stranger was bound, thrown into the blanket, and tossed till he was half dead and ready to give his tormentors every superfluous garment to sell for money. With the tolls thus exacted, liquor was bought, a fiendish revel was held, and, when bad rum and bad

---

* In Vermont the adulteress still wore the scarlet letter.

† For a definition of garnish, see a virulent pamphlet called Pigott's Political Dictionary, London, 1795.

tobacco had done their work, the few sober inmates of the cell witnessed such scenes as would be thought shocking in the dance-houses which cluster along the wharfs of our great sea-board towns.*

To a generation which has beheld great reforms in the statutes of criminal law and in the discipline of prisons and jails; to a generation which knows but two crimes worthy of death, that against the life of the individual, and that against the life of the State; which has expended fabulous sums in the erection of reformatories, asylums and penitentiaries, houses of correction, houses of refuge, and houses of detention, all over the land; which has furnished every State prison with a library, with a hospital, with workshops, and with schools, the brutal scenes on which our ancestors looked with indifference seem scarcely a reality. Yet it is well to recall them, for we cannot but turn from the contemplation of so much misery and so much suffering with a deep sense of thankfulness that our lot has fallen in a pitiful age, in an age when more compassion is felt for a galled horse or a dog run over at a street-crossing than our great-grandfathers felt for a woman beaten for cursing or a man imprisoned for debt.

---

* Some account of the state of the prisons may be found in Defence of the System of Solitary Confinement, G. W. Smith; also, North American Review, July, 1839.

# CHAPTER II.

## THE WEAKNESS OF THE CONFEDERATION.

WHEN the year 1784 opened, the revolution had been accomplished. The preliminary articles had been signed on the thirtieth of November, 1782, and the return of peace everywhere celebrated with bonfires, with rockets, with speeches, and with thanksgiving on the nineteenth of the following April, the eighth anniversary of the fight at Lexington. The definitive treaty had been signed at Paris on the third of September, 1783, and was soon to be ratified by the United States in Congress assembled. The last remnant of the British army in the east had sailed down the Narrows on the twenty-fifth of November, a day which, under the appellation of Evacuation Day, was long held in grateful remembrance by the inhabitants of New York, and was, till a few years since, annually celebrated with fireworks and with military display. Of the continental army scarce a remnant was then in the service of the States, and these few were under the command of General Knox. His great work of deliverance over, Washington had resigned his commission, had gone back to his estate on the banks of the Potomac, and was deeply engaged with plans for the improvement of his plantations. The retirement to private life of the American Fabius, as the newspapers delighted to call him, had been attended by many pleasing ceremonies, and had been made the occasion for new manifestations of affectionate regard by the people. The same day that witnessed the departure of Sir Guy Carleton from New York also witnessed the entry into that city of the army of the States. Nine days later Washington bid adieu to his officers. About noon on Thursday, the fourth of December, the chiefs

of the army assembled in the great room of Fraunces's Tavern,
then the resort of merchants and men of fashion, and there
Washington joined them.   Rarely as he gave way to his emo-
tions, he could not on that day get the mastery of them.   As
he beheld drawn up before him the men who, for eight long
years, had shared with him the perils and hardships of the
war, he was deeply moved.   He filled a glass from a decanter
that stood on the table, raised it with a trembling hand, and
said : " With a heart full of love and gratitude I now take
leave of you, and most devoutly wish your latter days may be
as prosperous and happy as your former ones have been glorious and honorable."   Then he drank to them, and, after a
pause, said : " I cannot come to each of you to take my leave,
but shall be obliged if you will each come and shake me by
the hand."   General Knox came forward first, and Washington embraced him.   The other officers approached one by one,
and silently took their leave.   A line of infantry had been
drawn up extending from the tavern to Whitehall ferry, where
a barge was in waiting to carry the commander across the
Hudson to Paulus Hook.   Washington, with his officers following, walked down the line of soldiers to the water.   The
streets, the balconies, the windows, were crowded with gazers.
All the churches in the city sent forth a joyous din.   Arrived
at the ferry, he entered the barge in silence, stood up, took off
his hat and waved farewell.   Then, as the boat moved slowly
out into the stream amid the shouts of the citizens, his companions in arms stood bareheaded on the shore till the form
of their illustrious commander was lost to view.

From Paulus Hook he journeyed by easy stages to Annapolis, where Congress was then in session.   The news of
his approach was spread throughout the country by the post-
riders, and the many villages and towns that lay along his
route vied with each other in doing him honor.   At every
step he was met by committees from the select-men, who, in
addresses full of allusions to Cincinnatus, thanked him for
the great things he had done for the country, and assured him
of the undying love and gratitude of his fellow-citizens.
Addresses of congratulation and thanks were voted by the
Legislatures of New Jersey, of Pennsylvania, and of Mary-

land.   The American Philosophical Society at Philadelphia turned from the consideration of learned papers on Improved Methods of Quilling a Harpsichord, and Observations on the Torporific Eel,* to do homage to the great chief, and their example was speedily followed by innumerable religious and mercantile organizations in the State.

It was not indeed till Friday, the nineteenth of the month, that he reached Annapolis.   Gates and Smallwood, who had served under him in the war, met him, with many of the chief characters of the place, a few miles from the city and escorted him to town.   As he entered the streets his arrival was made known to the citizens by the discharge of cannon. On Monday Congress gave him a dinner in the ballroom, where toasts were drunk to the United States, to the army, to the most Christian King, to the Peace Commissioners, and to the virtuous daughters of America.   When night came the Stadt-house was lit up, and a ball given by the General Assembly.†   The day following his arrival he dispatched a letter to Congress announcing his wish to resign his commission, and asking that he might be informed in what manner it would be most proper to tender his resignation, whether in writing, or at a public audience of Congress.   General Mifflin replied that it should be at a public audience of Congress, and appointed noon of the twenty-third of December, 1783, for the ceremony.   In the mean time a committee was appointed to make such preparations as the occasion seemed to require. On the committee were Jefferson, who sat for Virginia; Gerry, who represented Massachusetts; and McHenry, who cast his vote in the name of the State of Maryland.

Long before the hour of noon on the twenty-third the gallery and floor of the hall of Congress were filled with ladies, with high functionaries of the State, and with many officers of the army and navy.   The members of the House, twenty in number, were seated and covered as representatives of the sovereignty of the Union.   The gentlemen present were standing and uncovered.   At noon Washington was an-

---

* Transactions of the American Philosophical Society, vol. ii, edition of 1786, pp. 171, 183.

† Pennsylvania Packet, January 1, 1784.

nounced, and escorted by the Secretary of Congress to a seat which had been made ready for him in front of the President's chair. After a short silence General Mifflin informed him that the United States in Congress assembled were prepared to receive his communication. Washington then arose, and, with that dignified composure which never deserted him even when musket-balls and cannon-shots were whistling around him, delivered a short and solemn address, which of all his writings is most familiar to the men of this generation. Having returned his commission into the hands of the President, that official thanked him in the name of the people of the United States for the patriotism with which he had responded to the call of his country, and the ability with which he had defended her invaded rights. "You retire," said he, "from the theatre of action with the blessings of your fellow-citizens, but the glory of your virtues will not terminate with your military command; it will continue to animate the remotest ages."

The same evening Washington bid adieu to Annapolis, and, attended by the Governor of Maryland to the confines of the State, made all speed toward Mount Vernon, which he reached on Christmas eve.

But the outburst of love and gratitude which the resignation of the Commander-in-chief called forth soon subsided. The time for voting addresses and thanks soon went by. Letters and eulogies and odes on his Excellency soon ceased to fill the columns of the newspapers. Matters of a grave and serious nature began to occupy the thoughts of the people, and, as is always the case where the multitude undertake to discuss matters they do not understand, they fell into an ill humor. The revolution was at last accomplished. The evils it had removed being no longer felt, were speedily forgotten. The evils it had brought pressed heavily upon them. They could devise no remedy. They saw no way of escape. They soon began to grumble, became sullen, hard to please, dissatisfied with themselves and with everything done for them. The States, differing in habits, in customs, in occupations, had been during a few years united by a common danger. But the danger was gone; old animosities and jealousies broke forth again with all their strength, and the union seemed likely to be dissolved.

In this state of public discontent the House met at Philadelphia early in January, 1784. Some days were spent in examining credentials of new members, and in waiting for the delinquents to come in. It was not till the fourteenth of the month that the definitive treaty was taken under consideration and duly ratified. Nothing remained, therefore, but to carry out the stipulations with as much haste as possible. But there were some articles which the people had long before made up their minds never should be carried out. While the treaty was yet in course of preparation the royal commissioners had stoutly insisted on the introduction of articles providing for the return of the refugees and the payment of debts due to British subjects at the opening of the war. The commissioners on behalf of the United States, who well knew the tempers of their countrymen, had at first firmly stood out * against any such articles. But some concessions were afterward made by each party, and certain stipulations touching the debts and the refugees inserted. Adams, who wrote in the name of his fellow-commissioners, informed Secretary Livingston that he was well aware that some of the States had confiscated British debts; but that, in his opinion, no acts of government could dissolve obligations resulting from lawful contracts made by individuals of the two countries before the war. It was true that some British creditors were making common cause with the refugees and other enemies of independence. But it was equally true that sacrificing private justice to reasons of state and political convenience was always an odious measure, and the purity of the reputation of the United States in this respect was, in all the commercial cities of Europe, of infinitely more value than the money involved. As for the two articles respecting the Tories, they were indeed unsatisfactory. But had not England been particularly anxious to have the matter closed up at the precise time it was, to have framed them so nearly in accordance with the views

---

* "These articles (the fifth and sixth, respecting refugees) were among the first discussed and the last agreed to." Letter of the commissioners to Secretary Livingston, December 14, 1782.

of Congress as they were, would have been out of the question. When, too, it was considered that nothing could make them perfectly consistent both with American and British ideas of honor, he hoped that the middle line adopted would be approved.* The middle line to which Adams referred was that Congress should recommend the States to make no more seizures of the goods and property of men lately in arms against the Confederation, and to put no bar in the way of the recovery of such as had already been confiscated.

It was distinctly understood by each side that these were recommendations, and nothing more than recommendations. Yet no sooner were they made known than a shout of indignation and abuse went up from all parts of the country. The community in a moment was divided between three parties.† The smallest of the three was made up of the Tories, who still hoped for place and power, and still nursed the delusion that the past would be forgotten. Yet they daily contributed to keep the remembrance of it alive by a strong and avowed attachment to Great Britain.

Opposed to these was the large and influential body of violent Whigs, who insisted vehemently that every loyalist should instantly be driven from the States.

A less numerous and less violent body of Whigs constituted the third party. They were not prepared for extreme measures, and sought to soften the rigors of the laws against those who had been so misguided as to support the wrong side of the quarrel. They were opposed to banishment because of the clause in the treaty; because if the royalists were sent away they would settle at Nova Scotia and destroy the American fishery; because if suffered to remain they would enrich the country; and because they had no political influence what-

---

* These reasons are set forth in the course of some remarks on the preliminary treaty. See the letter from the commissioners to Secretary Livingston, December 14, 1782. We are assured that the original draft of the letter is in the handwriting of Mr. Adams. Works of John Adams, Boston, 1853, vol. viii, p. 18, note.

† The state of the political parties in 1784 is well explained in a letter of R. R. Livingston to John Jay, at that time abroad. The date is January 25, 1784. See Life of J. Jay.

ever.* At the same time these moderate Whigs protested they never for a moment thought of destroying all distinction between refugees and patriots, and giving the Tories a hold upon the reins of government.

The loyalists most wisely wrote little. The discussion was carried on by the two branches of the Whigs. Scores of sermons were preached,† and hundreds of pamphlets written, on the subject. The columns of the newspapers were for many months crowded with Letters to the Refugees; Last Advice to the Refugees; Considerations for the Refugees, that poured in upon the editors from all sides.‡ It was difficult, such was the language held by some of the writers, to understand the singular infatuation which led men of reputed sense and judgment to believe that the recommendation contained in the obnoxious fifth and sixth articles of the treaty would be complied with. It was simply preposterous to suppose for a moment that they would be listened to by the Legislature of a single State in the Union. If, on the one hand, the men in whose behalf the appeal had been made were to be considered citizens of the United States, then, independence having been secured, the people, through their legislators, had a perfect right to deal with them as they saw fit, and it was an open and gross insult for Great Britain to lay down rules for their treatment. If, on the other hand, the refugees were to be regarded as British subjects, then the insolence of the recommendation could be equalled only by its folly and absurdity. But the whole matter, from beginning to end, was quite of a piece with the usual stupidity of English ministers. Before the war they had refused to the people of the colonies the right of managing their own affairs. They had then proceeded to regulate matters for them, and had done the work

---

* See New York Gazette of March 11, 1784. The reasons given for the return of the refugees are there stated to be common arguments. Also, Boston Gazette, March 1, 1784.

† One deserving of mention is entitled The Reward of Toryism. A discourse delivered at the Tabernacle, in Salem, by Nathaniel Whittaker, D. D.

See The Case and Claim of an American Loyalist, 1783. The Claims of the American Loyalist Reviewed and Maintained, 1786.

‡ A good specimen of these letters is A Last Advice to the Tories and Refugees in New York. See New Jersey Gazette, April 16, 1783.

so ill that the colonies were soon free and independent States. Now, in the very paper in which this independence was acknowledged, England had the effrontery to prescribe how the United States should act toward American citizens. But this insolent folly should be treated with the contempt it so richly merited. Congress had been wise in confining itself to recommendations, for the people had already decided how to dispose of the Tories. What right had men, who for seven years had been destroying property, plundering, burning, killing, inciting Indian massacres, to expect kind and gentle treatment at the hands of a people they had so deeply injured? Was there ever a set of men so hard to please? For years past they had steadily opposed the government, had fought against it, had reviled it, had sought by every means in their power to overthrow it, and now they cried out in indignation because they were not permitted to live under it. If it were hateful to them in the past, what made it acceptable to them in the present? Why, after fighting for a monarchical government, did they on a sudden insist on becoming citizens under a republican government? Could any one doubt for a moment that some deeply meditated scheme lay at the bottom of all this? Was it that they might become good and loyal citizens of the republic, or was it that they might the more effectually destroy its liberties? They had wealth, and would gladly expend it in the acquisition of power. Many of them had, while their republican neighbors were starving in the continental armies, carried on a lucrative trade with England, or put away thousands of pounds by acting as sutlers and contractors to the troops of Clinton, of Cornwallis, and of Howe. Make them citizens, give them the right to vote, and in a few years the places of trust and influence would be held by Tories. Tory Governors and Tory Legislatures would rule in every State. The laws of which the refugees complained would be repealed, and others carefully framed to injure the patriots enacted. Decisions would be pronounced in the courts by Tory judges against Whig petitioners, and carried into execution by Tory sheriffs and Tory officers of the law. Nor would they stop there. They would confiscate property, found an aristocracy, levy taxes, and create a government whose tyranny would far exceed the tyranny of England. They would, in short, undo in a few years everything that had been done by an immense expenditure of treasure and of blood.

Sometimes the writer assumed the character of a grave and impartial witness, and cautioned the refugees not to trust too implicitly to the clemency of a much-abused and long-suffering people. They were assured that the wisest course was to consider all Americans, wherever found, as their very worst enemies. They were reminded of the phrase, so often in their mouths, the King can do no wrong, and urged not to hesitate a moment to throw themselves at his Majesty's feet. Whatever might be their treatment by Americans, they would at least have one consolation; that of knowing they would be rewarded by their King according to their deserts. And their deserts were great. They had done and suffered much in defence of his Majesty's rights. Surely a gracious sovereign would not forget them in their hour of trouble, as they had not forgotten him in his; he would provide for them most liberally. Even if the State Legislatures did act on the recommendation of Congress, pass acts of oblivion and make every loyalist a citizen of the United States, who would suspect them of the baseness of accepting such offers? They would not, of course, abjure the King they loved so well, and swear allegiance to the government they had with so much diligence sought to destroy. Some bad men among them had plundered houses, killed farmers, and done deeds for which, in the excited state of public feeling, they were now, as a class, to be held responsible. There was therefore but one thing to do, and that was to be gone instantly.*

Distasteful as such advice was, many followed it. Numbers sought a refuge in Florida, then a possession of Spain, and founded settlements which their descendants have since raised to prosperous and beautiful villages, renowned for groves of orange-trees and fields of cane. Others embarked on the British ships of war, and were carried to Canada† or

---

* New York Packet.

† For some account of their actions there, see a letter signed Philo Patriæ in the Boston Continental Journal, May 27, 1784.

the island of Bermuda; a few turned pirates, obtained a sloop, and scoured the waters of Chesapeake bay. * Many went to England, beset the ministry with petitions for relief, wearied the public with pathetic stories of the harsh ingratitude with which their sufferings had been requited,† and were accused, with much show of reason, by the Americans of urging the severe restrictions which England began to lay on American commerce. Many more, forgetful of the rigors of a northern climate, where for week after week the mercury never rose above ten degrees below zero, where water froze while being carried from the well to the house, and where the ground was white with snow for seven months in the year, set out for Nova Scotia.‡ On their arrival at St. John they were at first coldly received, then loudly ridiculed, and finally driven off in great numbers, to seek a home at Passamaquoddy. Of such treatment at the hands of those from whom they had expected nothing but kindness and help they complained with much bitterness. Their sufferings were, they said, among Englishmen and English subjects far greater than among the rebels. They had been lured thither to their destruction by falsehood and treachery. The King had graciously bestowed on them, as good and true subjects ruined in his behalf, what they were assured was rich and fertile land lying along the banks of gently flowing rivers; and they were told that when the fields had been cleared, when towns had been built, when law had been established, they were to send delegates to represent them in the halls of the Provin-

---

* New York Packet.

† One of these inveterate petitioners became so great a nuisance that he was popularly nick-named Crying Billy. He laid his damages at seventy thousand pounds sterling. Sir J. Johnston declared that he had lost three hundred thousand guineas. At this one of the English papers exclaimed: "Are there any gold and silver mines in England, Scotland, and Ireland? Surely they will be wanted to pay off these worthy American sufferers. All funds from taxation must be insufficient for such demands, which already draw nigh to twelve millions. Surely the American States must be, collectively, exceedingly rich and valuable if the few refugees who fled from that country left property behind them worth twelve or fourteen millions." Quoted in the New York Packet, October 10, 1785.

‡ For letters urging the refugees to come to St. John and Nova Scotia, see New York Gazette, March 29, 1783, and American Remembrancer, Part i, 1783, p. 307.

cial Assembly. Meanwhile agents and surveyors, appointed at great cost to the Crown, were to locate and lay out the farms of all such as chose to accept of the bounty of his Majesty; taxes were to be remitted for the space of seven years, and supplies of provisions doled out till such time as the earth should be made to yield her increase. Had these things been done? Far from it. The delays of the well-paid agents had brought them to the brink of ruin. Scarce an acre had been staked out by the surveyors; a few of the refugees had indeed, after much persevering, much worrying, and great expense, finally succeeded in having their claims located. They had then set out to take possession of their estates, only to find themselves in the wildest and most desolate of regions, to which not a road led, and in which no human industry could make so much as the grass to grow. The donations of the King had, in the mean time, been curtailed; and the supply of provisions would, in all likelihood, cease in May. *

The pitiable condition of these men was about this time depicted with much humor and sarcasm by a writer in the newspaper printed at St. John.† The industrious husbandman, fraught with expectations and glowing with the gratitude of his sovereign, went up the river, it was said, to settle on his lands with all convenient speed, and sat down on some cleared spot of earth, there to encamp till his lands were divined to him. But it generally happened that the spot so picked out was hard by the shelter of the cow-house or the barn of some republican, who speedily made it known to him by advertisement, or proclamation, or what not, that he must turn neither to the right hand nor to the left, but make straight away from the barn and the cow-house and abide in the wilderness till, at the pleasure of the would-be lords, he should be given a tract in the burned district. The paper was read with delight by the Tories of St. John, and the town was, a few days later, yet more diverted by hand-bills which appeared in every street and on the tables of every tavern. They purported to con-

---

* See a letter in the Packet of December 6, 1784, describing the suffering of the refugees at Shelburne, Nova Scotia. See, also, the Packet of May 20, 1784.

† This paper will be found copied in full in the New York Packet, March 8, 1784. It appeared at St. John in January.

tain a number of " Familiar Questions addressed to the Loyalists at St. John." " Were you," said the writer, who carefully concealed his name, " were you sent here to get land?
Did you get any? How are you refugees off for cash: are you
pretty flush? Is it true that the refugees up the river are
charged twenty-five dollars a ton for hay? Do you know how
the Hivites and the Jebusites looked on the children of Israel
when they came to take possession of the promised land?
Did you ever hear of a subaltern going with a file of men and
taking away the hay cut by refugees at Gagetown? Which
should you like better; a little snug water-lot where you might
cut grass and catch salmon, or a bit of burned tract with never
a road to it? Do you know that about four hundred of you
have signed to go to Passamaquoddy?" *

While the loyalists at St. John were being thus insulted
and reviled by those who ironically addressed them as brethren, their companions at New York were undergoing a like
treatment. The wits of the day affected to treat the sudden
and unceremonious departure of so many Tories as an epi-
demic. The name of independence fever † was fastened upon
it, and from one end of the country to the other the newspapers exulted in recording the numbers who in New York and
Philadelphia fell a prey to it each week. It was noted with
no small pleasure that a vessel carrying seven hundred of the
fever-stricken Tories had gone to pieces off the New England
coast, and scarce a soul been saved; that every week hundreds
of obnoxious faces were disappearing from the coffee-houses
and inns, and that the stages were doing a brisk business carrying loyalists up to town. The few that remained were
termed turn-coats, and it was facetiously said that in the great
towns the trade of tailoring was wellnigh ruined since so
many gentlemen of fashion had become so economical as to
turn their own coats. A writer in the Massachusetts Gazette
observed that the patriotic character of some who now made

---

* New York Packet, March 3, 1784. These Familiar Questions were afterward printed on hand-bills and scattered about New York.

† New Jersey Gazette, April 10, 1783. See, also, American Remembrancer,
Part ii, 1783, p. 712. " We hear from New York that the independence fever
rages there to such a degree among the Tories and refugees that it carries off
great numbers of them weekly." Boston, April 15, 1783.

a great figure in promoting conventions all over the country, and of others who, in Connecticut, were loud against commutation, brought to his mind the story of the Vicar of Bray with modern additions. The additions consisted of a few verses in which the vicar, after turning his coat for King George, is made to turn it again for Congress, and assert his willingness to die in its cause.*

The animosity which fired the more violent Whigs often led them to absurd extremes. A few men of the moderate branch of the party at New York took it into their heads on one occasion to attempt something for the benefit of their proscribed neighbors. To do anything outright for the betterment of the political condition of the unfortunates was impossible. But it seemed quite probable that if restored to their old places in society; if the houses of former friends were again opened to them; if their well-known faces were once more seen at routs and balls, and they were suffered to make and receive calls, the detestation felt toward them would gradually wear away, and in time the cruel laws inspired by that bitter hatred be repealed. To initiate this laudable plan, a dancing assembly was started in which many of the Tories were invited to take part. But the object of this piece of innocent amusement was quickly discovered and vigorously attacked. Could it be possible, the hotheads exclaimed, that men calling themselves Whigs could be so lost to every degree of sensibility, so inconsiderate as to engage in a measure cruel in its nature and pregnant with dangerous consequences? Did they mean to open old wounds afresh? What were they thinking of? Did they suppose all Whigs were pigeon-livered enough to look tamely on while a parcel of miscreants, of atrocious and obnoxious Tories, insulted their feelings and wantonly danced on the graves of their brave officers? This was going too far. Honor and justice forbade it, and the dancing must be stopped. †

---

* The poem was printed in the New York Packet for February 19, 1784.

† Pennsylvania Packet, January 5, 1784. " Time-serving Whigs and trimmers " were also accused of forming a political coalition with the Tories. Boston Gazette, February 2, 1784. The same paper declares that " the eyes of all America are fixed on the New York patriots, who it is expected will act with their usual decision,

But the comments of the press were not always in so mild and inoffensive a tone. They were in general full of savage threats, and written in the bombastic language in which stump orators were accustomed at every election to address audiences of ploughboys and drovers, and which is even now to be heard on the twenty-second of every February and the fourth of every July. The editor of a New England paper exhorted his readers never to make friends with those fiends the refugees. "As Hannibal," said the writer, "swore never to be at peace with the Romans, so let every Whig swear, by his abhorrence of slavery, by liberty and religion, by the shades of departed friends who have fallen in battle, by the ghosts of those of our brethren who have been destroyed on board of prison-ships and in loathsome dungeons, never to be at peace with those fiends, the refugees, whose thefts, murders, and treasons have filled the cup of woe. . . ." * At Worcester and at Stamford the Tories were forbidden to return.†

Absurd as such appeals now seem, they were, it must be remembered, but the timely fruit of the war, and their effect was very great. The intense animosity felt toward the unfortunate refugees became each day more and more bitter, and was not in the least allayed by the recollection of acts which had lately been done, and were constantly brought up as exhibiting a lack of good faith on the part of England. In direct violation, it was claimed, of the seventh article of the treaty, great numbers of negroes had been carried off by the departing troops. Sir Guy Carleton had been remonstrated with and called upon to take strong measures to prevent the recurrence of such deeds. He had given no heed to the remonstrances, and had attempted to justify himself by excuses worthy of the casuists. He knew, he said, that some negroes had been taken away; but they could not be considered as property. He had found them freemen; he could not reduce them to a state of slavery. On this plea their departure was

---

firmness, and vigor with respect to the spaniels, tools, and minions of Britain now remaining in their capital."

* Massachusetts Chronicle, May, 1783. See, also, Boston Gazette for October 25, 1784, and April 14, 1785.

† American Remembrancer, Part i, 1783, pp. 264, 265; and Part ii, 1783, p. 249.

held to be a voluntary act. But the Whigs were not to be blinded by sophistical excuses. It was denied that they were freemen; the Tories were accused of taking them off by violence, and payment for them was demanded of the English Government. The number taken, undoubtedly large, was magnified by popular report to several thousands. The alarm was great, for the article had been framed expressly for the benefit of the slave-holding States, and the most populous of the States were of this class. If this went on, it was said, there was no telling what the consequences might be. Every slave dissatisfied with his master had but to steal away from his cabin on some stormy night, make his way to the nearest seaport, and claim the protection of some departing Tory, who, glad to inflict so severe a loss upon the master, would willingly carry the servant to England. The multitude, inflamed by such reasoning, and, as was but natural, ready to put the worst construction on everything done by the Tories, loudly accused England of bad faith. The treaty was held to be violated, and a new plea thus furnished for the justification of many sharp acts against the refugees.[*] Harsh laws, passed while the war was still raging, were, in many of the States, re-enacted or suffered to remain unchanged on the statute-books.[†] But in New York the most severe acts were required to satisfy the angry multitude.[‡]

Of all the great cities, New York had undoubtedly suffered most at the hands of the enemy. No other had been so long under British control. Howe had been compelled to evacuate Boston; Clinton had been driven from Philadelphia. But from the day when Howe entered New York in 1776 to the day when Carleton sailed out of its harbor in 1783, the peaceful possession of the city by the British had never for a moment been disturbed. It became, therefore, during the war and after the peace, a place of refuge for the Tories.

---

[*] Virginia passed a resolution that England had, by carrying off the negroes, violated the treaty, January 22, 1784.

[†] See laws passed by Massachusetts, November, 1784.

[‡] By New York, July 12, 1782, March 17, 1783, and May 12, 1784. See, also, Secret Journals of Congress, vol. iv, pp. 267, 269–274. See, also, a pamphlet entitled A Collection of Laws Relative to American Loyalists in Massachusetts, and their Property, 1785.

There privateers were fitted out, and ships bearing arms and ammunition to the armies of the King sailed in and out of the spacious harbor with as much safety as if upon the waters of the Mersey or the Thames. The churches and jail were filled with prisoners of war. The prison-ships Jersey and Stromboli, whose names our ancestors could never mention without a shudder, lay at anchor off the Battery shore. The Whig citizens were driven from their homes, their property confiscated, their houses seized and occupied under military orders, and they, penniless and deprived of every means of subsistence, sent across the Hudson to starve, or live upon the charity of the Dutch farmers of New Jersey.* When, therefore, the day of retribution, so long delayed, came, when the banished, despoiled and persecuted Whigs were free to return and take vengeance on their persecutors for the ills they had borne for many years, they did so with the exultant malignity of men who, half maddened by the desire for revenge, are beside themselves with joy in their hour of triumph. At a time when the inhabitants of the New Jersey towns were hurrying to sign papers expressing their willingness to forgive and forget, and bidding the Tories to come and live among them;† at a time when the committee-men at New Haven were writing their report, and assuring their fellow-townsmen that no reason could be found why the loyalists should not be free to come back;‡ that it was contrary to good sense, to good policy, nay, to humanity, to deprive of the rights of a citizen any Tory who had not carried arms in the great struggle, the inhabitants of New York were crying out wildly for vengeance. Nothing but extreme measures would satisfy their thirst. The Legislature, indeed, was scarce assembled before a memorial drawn up by the Whig citizens was brought in. The signatures were many in number, and were

---

* The hardships and suffering of the Whig refugees in New Jersey are pleasantly told in the memoirs of Eliza S. M. Quincy, the wife of Josiah Quincy. Mrs. Quincy was at the time of her parents' flight from the city a girl of thirteen years.

† See New York Packet for March 8, 1784. Many signatures were obtained at New Brunswick, Piscataway, Amboy, and neighboring towns.

‡ See New York Packet for March 8, 1784, and American Remembrancer, Part iii, 1783, p. 324.

those, not of demagogues, but of persons of high rank, of stainless character, and good ability. The instrument humbly set forth that the petitioners had lately returned to their native city to take possession of what little remained to them from the ravages of war. They were, however, greatly alarmed and incensed to find numbers of the bitterest enemies of the liberty and independence of the United States so audacious, so impudent, as to expose themselves to their much injured and angry countrymen. If these men were longer allowed to go at large about the town, the peace of the citizens would be seriously endangered, the harmony essential to prosperity would constantly be destroyed, the blessings of peace would be turned into curses, and there was much reason to fear that riot and bloodshed would be of frequent occurrence. They firmly believed that these turn-coats, even while living in their midst, would remain enemies to independence. They believed this to be so because, in the first place, the renegades had, with inveteracy and uniformity, during the whole course of the dubious struggle for liberty, made the utmost efforts against the country; because, in the second place, they had, when the near prospect of peace opened to their view, manifested their disapprobation in terms of the deepest rancor and malignity; and because, in the third place, the bitter remembrance of innumerable murders, injuries, and cruelties done by them still rankled in the bosoms of the citizens. It was quite impossible to be at peace with creatures of this stamp. If the Tories stayed the Whigs must go, and it seemed but reasonable that the Whigs, who had suffered so much and so long for liberty, should, when liberty came, be permitted to enjoy all its blessings in quiet. They had therefore watched with much anxiety the slow progress of the Alienation Bill, and deeply regretted that it had not yet passed. Indeed, they earnestly hoped that the Legislature would at once use every possible means to pass the bill into a law.*

The statement made in the memorial of the angry feelings of the people was, as the Legislature well knew, mildly expressed. Tories, in fact Englishmen, were scarcely safe; for though they usually behaved with much sense and discretion,

---

* New York Packet, February, 1784.

they were at times, when goaded to desperation by the taunts
and jeers flung at them in the coffee-houses and on the streets,
provoked into making ill-timed replies.  It was well for them
if on such occasions summary vengeance were not instantly
wreaked.  Others, whose talk had not been public, were informed that if they did not moderate their language a watchman who had overheard what was said would send their names
to the newspaper.  Should the newspaper refuse to make
their names public after its fashion, he would make them
public after his fashion, and, as he went his rounds at night
cry out, "Past ten o'clock, and ———— is a vile hypocrite and
an enemy of freedom." *

That he would have done so, and that he would have been
loudly praised for doing so, there can be no doubt.  The delay of the Legislature had wearied and disgusted the people.
It was true, the Assembly had been by no means backward in
enacting vigorous laws against the Tories.  It was true that
the Governors of the twelve sister States had been urged to
exchange lists of the proscribed persons, that not one of them
might find a resting-place in the country.  It was true that
such persons had been disfranchised, † and that when election
day came round no one suspected of the slightest tinge of
toryism could cast his vote till he had first cleared himself of the charge of hostility to the government.  It was
true that the petitions of such refugees as were entitled by
the sixth article of the treaty to make application for liberty
to return from exile were invariably thrown out.  It was true
that a Trespass Act had been passed and an Alienation Bill
brought in; but all this fell far short of the demands of the
people.  Every day the clamor of the multitude grew louder
and more menacing.  One day, late in March, hand-bills were
scattered about the town, calling on the sons of liberty to
assemble at Vandewater's, a noted coffee-house in the fields.‡

The meeting was a large one.  All classes were represented,

---

* New York Packet, March 1, 1784.

† The bill passed the Legislature, but not the revisionary council.  It would,
the council said, so utterly depopulate whole districts that there would not be men
enough left in them to fill the necessary offices at election.

‡ The hand-bills were dated March 25, 1784.  The meeting was held a few
days later.  New York Packet, April 6, 1784.

and strong language was, for the first time, heard from the lips of many of the most eminent merchants of the city. A series of resolutions set forth the sense of those present. It was impossible that Whigs and Tories could ever mingle in harmony; that they could not consider the government as completely established while the faces of so many wealthy and influential royalists continued to be seen in the streets; that they would on no pretence whatever consent to live in society with any man who had served in the British army in any capacity, or had fled to the city while in British hands, or had come over from England during the war, and that they seriously recommended all such characters to remove from the city before the first of May. But when the first of May came the detested Tories were still as numerous as ever, and continued to show themselves with the old effrontery. Then the wrath of the Whigs flamed high. This, then, was the return made to them for a most foolish forbearance. They had begun by intimating to the Tories that it would be well to go out from the presence of the men they had so deeply injured; from intimations they had gone on to hints; from hints to plain requests; from requests to menaces and threats; but intimations, hints, requests, and threats were alike of no use. Now their patience was exhausted, and they would resort to harsher measures. Since the Legislature had given little heed to their petition on the Alien Bill, they would address that body in unmistakable language. Accordingly, the Whig freeholders of Westchester county assembled and drew up instructions to their representatives. They were seriously alarmed, so the instructions ran, that after so long a sitting the Legislature had seen fit to take no means to re-move from their midst the most obnoxious of those who, while the war was raging, had deserted friends and country and gone over to the enemy. Six reasons were then given why the Tories should no longer be suffered to live among them, and the representatives bidden to spare no pains to obtain an act of discrimination. It might possibly happen that the Legislature would think them a parcel of malcontents forming a very inconsiderable part of the community. They were, in that event, prepared to lay before the Legislature a most unanswerable argument. They would go and present themselves, to a man, before the Assembly, and they would pledge their honor to go and return in the most peaceable and orderly manner.*

These instructions were scarcely dispatched before the Whig Society took up the matter. The Whig Society was a company of pleasant gentlemen, who, had they dared to use so obnoxious a term, would have called themselves the aristocracy of the city. Among them were many of the soundest merchants, ablest lawyers, and most skilful physicians New York then boasted of. They were all stanch Whigs, and the few who had not been in the army had been, as they termed it, in exile, and often entertained the assembled company with laughable accounts of their sufferings and adventures. They met on stated evenings in the long room at the coffee-house, and discussed, over bowls of grog, punch, or sangaree, the impost, the theatre, the paper-money scheme, the bank, or whatever else might happen to be occupying the thoughts of the people. Often these meetings had much the appearance of the session of a debating club. The subject to be discussed was put in the form of a question, a negative and affirmative side chosen, and speakers, noted in the society for their skill in debate, pitted against each other. The floor was then open to any member, and not a few young men, who hoped some day for a seat in the Assembly or the Senate, gladly availed themselves of such opportunities to display their political sagacity and their oratory. On the present occasion the question to be debated was whether it would conduce to the public peace and safety to pass a law removing from the State certain characters of influence who had uniformly manifested an inveterate opposition to the liberties of the people. The question was so important that almost every member was in his seat, and the debate was warm and rancorous, for some members, while they disliked the Tories, disliked still more any measure looking to a forcible expulsion. But despite their arguments, when a show of hands was called on the merits of

---

* New York Packet, May 4, 1784. For the resolutions of the inhabitants of the small towns in the other parts of the State, see American Remembrancer, Part iii, 1783, pp. 58–61, 96, 97, 123, 267, 269.

the debate, almost every hand in the room went up in the
affirmative.   It was then determined to make public these
proceedings, and to appoint another evening for a yet further
discussion of the question.*

But the debate in the Whig Society had scarce been made
known when news came which greatly amused the Whigs.   A
petition had for some time past been going from town to town
through northern New Jersey.   The petition set forth that
the signers condemned the harsh treatment their more zealous
brethren had subjected the Tories to in New York, and invited all such injured ones to come, be made welcome, and
live in peace and friendship with the farmers of New Jersey.   Many names were obtained in different towns, but nowhere in such numbers as in Amboy, New Brunswick, and
Piscataway.   To these places the Tories had therefore gone
in crowds, and among those who went were Thomas Crowell
and Elias Barnes.   Crowell and Barnes had at first settled in
Amboy, but at length determined to try their fortunes at the
little village of Woodbridge, some five miles distant.   Thither
they went; but no sooner was their arrival known than a
town-meeting was held, and a committee appointed to bid them
welcome.   The committee waited on them, informed them of
the great joy entertained by the village at their arrival, and
assured them that they were just the sort of men that were
wanted.   The Tories were much pleased, thanked the committee, and said they were at first of a mind to settle at Port
Roseway, a place they believed of great plenty, but, having
been urgently invited to come to Jersey, and assured that all
such as were heavy-laden would find at Amboy a place of rest,
they had come, desiring to be made good citizens.   The committee in return thanked the Tories for their unexpected
goodness, when one, more forward than the rest, declared that
"for his part he was touched to the heart at such a meeting;
he was desperately afraid the Tories would all go to Scotia."
He then expressed his sorrow at being compelled to inform
his new friends that the people of Woodbridge had determined that no Tories should settle among them till they had
first been tarred and feathered.   Barnes and Crowell were

---

* New York Packet, May 25, 1784.

for a moment dumfounded. They stoutly protested, talked much of the sixth article of the treaty, of the recommendation of Congress, of the conduct of the good people of Piscataway, of New Brunswick, of Amboy, but all to no purpose. In a few minutes they were stripped naked, and tarred and feathered "as completely," said a witness, "as if it had been done in one of those seminaries of the art, Boston or Connecticut." *

In Philadelphia some bitter complaints were made that a great number of those miscreants who called themselves loyalists were daily seen flashing among the citizens, claiming protection under the treaty, and pretending to have business to transact. The only business they had, it was alleged, was to put Americans at variance with the King of France. Nothing could be done with them because of the articles in the treaty; but it would not be amiss, the moment a Tory came to town, to find out his business, set a guard over him, conduct him through the streets, and, when his work was done, show him out of the city.†

But, of the many legal proceedings of the time, none bore such strong marks of a fierce and implacable hatred as the Trespass Act. By the terms of this law, an action of trespass for the recovery of damages was given to all persons who had fled from their homes in consequence of invasion, against such persons as had subsequently entered and remained in possession. The only plea which the possessors could advance in justification was that they had been placed in possession by a military order. A military order was therefore declared, by the provisions of the act, to be no justification of the seizure, and the Tories thus deprived of all ground of defence.

No sooner did this law go into operation than every householder whose home had, for the shortest space of time, been in the possession of an enemy, hastened to seek indemnity in an action of trespass with enormous damages. The lawyers were beset with clients; the court calendars were crowded

---

* New York Packet, June 26, 1784. For the state of feeling at New Brunswick, see Pennsylvania Packet, March 20, 1784.

† Freeman's Journal, Philadelphia, August 5, 1784. See, also, American Remembrancer, Part ii, 1783, pp. 273, 278.

with actions for trespass. The work, however, of clearing the calendars went rapidly on, and many cases had already been disposed of when one was reached which had long been looked forward to with increasing interest, and whose unexpected decision caused no small consternation. There was nothing in the matter in action to distinguish the case from the hundreds that had gone before it. The plaintiff was a widow who, alone and defenceless, had left home and property and fled in terror for her life in the dark days when the soldiers of Howe ran riot in the streets of New York. The defendant was a rich Tory merchant, who, by a military order, had been placed in possession of the abandoned property, had from that time continued to hold it, and was fully determined not to yield it without a contest in the courts.* Each side had secured the services of eminent counsel, but a murmur of surprise not unmingled with indignation went through the coffee-houses and taverns when it was known that the detested Tory was to be defended by Alexander Hamilton.

Of all the men who, in the judgment of posterity, are ranked high among the founders of the republic and the framers and defenders of the Constitution, by far the most brilliant and versatile was Hamilton. His temper was gentle; his manner engaging; his spirit, high and resolute, was raised above the influence both of cupidity and of fear; his parts were quick; his industry unwearied; his attainments various. He was at once a skilful officer, a brilliant pamphleteer, an active political leader, an impressive debater, a wise statesman, an able financier, a political economist of rare sagacity. In his veins was mingled the blood of two distinctly opposite races. In his mind and character were combined the choicest traits of each. From his father, a cool, deliberate, calculating Scotchman, he inherited the shrewdness, the logical habits of thought, which constitute the peculiar glory of the Scottish mind. From his mother, a lady of French extraction, and the daughter of a Huguenot exile, he inherited the easy manners, the liveliness and vivacity, the keen sense of humor, the

---

* See a pamphlet called The Case of Elizabeth Rutgers *vs.* Joshua Waddington, determined in the Mayor's Court in the City of New York, August 7, 1784. H. B. Dawson.

desire and the ability to please, which so eminently distinguish the children of the Celtic race.  Born within fifteen degrees of the equator, the rare powers of his mind ripened in him at a time when, in the natives of a colder climate, they have scarcely begun to bloom.  Since the time of William of Orange the world had rarely seen an instance of so mature a mind in so young a lad.  At an age when even the most precocious of young men are still poring over Horace and Xenophon, he had, under the impulse of the moment, risen up in a grave and temperate meeting of his townsmen and delivered a speech which called forth loud comments of praise.  At seventeen he was already renowned through the colonies as a political writer, and saw with delight his anonymous pamphlet attributed to the mature hands of Clinton and of Jay.  Before he was eighteen he had become a frequent contributor to a Whig sheet published in New York by John Holt, sending now a paper of a grave and argumentative character, now a satire in the best vein of Swift.  At twenty-three, in an hour of gloom, when the national treasury was empty, it was proposed to send him with Lafayette to the French court to negotiate a new loan.  When the war opened he hastened to join the army, soon attained to the rank of captain of artillery, was made aide-de-camp to Washington, and took a brilliant part in the campaign which ended with the surrender of Cornwallis.  At the close of the war he had chosen the law as his profession, and was now, in his twenty-ninth year, acknowledged by his worst enemy to be second to none of the many able men who pleaded at the bar of New York.  He had recently been sent to Congress, and had there introduced many resolutions which show his views to have been far in advance of his age.  He soon became an authority on the affairs of the army, was on the committee to model the peace establishment, and distinguished himself by an earnest support of every measure for the relief of the troops.

But the case in which he was now retained was one far more likely to cover him with infamy than with glory.  Never since the day when John Adams had stood up in court to defend the British soldiers charged with the murder of citizens in the "Boston Massacre" had a stanch patriot attempted to find excuses for the doings of Tories. The service he had undertaken was held by his fellow-citizens to be of no honorable kind, and he was plainly told so. But the fee was large, the opportunity for a display of forensic ability was not to be thrown away with impunity, nor can it in justice be denied that an honest conviction that the Tories were ill-used had much weight in determining his action. The case was soon brought to trial, was sharply contested, and a verdict finally rendered in behalf of the defendant. While the verdict did much to increase the reputation of Hamilton as a learned and skilful advocate, it added nothing to his popularity. His conduct was severely criticised, and it was long before he regained his former high place in the opinion of his townsmen.

It was at this time that he put forth the first of his letters of Phocion. In them he proceeded to take a calm and dignified review of the opinions held by the people on matters of politics, pointed out the absurdity of many, and furnished a collection of excellent arguments for a more humane and honorable treatment of the refugees and Tories.

The letters were well received, widely read, and replied to with much asperity by Isaac Ledyard. It was then the fashion among pamphleteers and letter-writers to put forth their productions over a name borrowed from the classics. Ledyard chose that of Mentor. Ledyard was a man of parts, a fluent writer, an easy speaker, and one of a company of boon companions who met every day at the same hour at the same coffee-house to discuss politics, and, when deep in their cups, to harangue against Congress, against standing armies, and the refugees. The letters of Phocion had given high displeasure to this company of revellers, and Ledyard undertook to refute them. The reply of Mentor, which was far from an able performance, called forth a second letter from Phocion, which was in turn followed by another letter from Mentor. As letter after letter came forth, the superiority of Hamilton over his antagonist in candor, in weight of argument, and in brilliancy of style became quite apparent. Indeed, before the letters ceased to appear, the town had made up its mind that the victory was with Phocion.

There still remained, however, one other weapon, armed with which the friends of Ledyard believed they could prove a match, nay, more than a match for Hamilton. To this they now betook themselves. His pride, his courage, his high sense of personal honor were well known to them. They determined therefore to call him out. They would form themselves into a club, would bind themselves by a solemn oath to secrecy, and, one by one, challenge Phocion to duel after duel till he fell dead before the pistol of one of the company. Much as he hated his rival, the stout heart of Ledyard revolted from murder. He would have revenge, but it should be revenge of an honorable kind. He accordingly interfered, and the evil design of his friends was never carried into execution. That such a scheme should have been meditated, not by villains and cutthroats, but by men who passed in the world as refined and polished gentlemen, throws much light on the morality of the times, and the bitterness of the passions the war had aroused.*

In the Southern States the Trimmers and Vicars of Bray, so the Tories were nick-named, were yet more severely dealt with. All were compelled to flee for their lives. A few who were bold enough to return were put to death. But it must in justice be owned that a great number of cruel and bloody deeds can be cited in extenuation of such acts. While the redcoats of Tarleton were overrunning South Carolina, to murder Whig farmers in the dead of night, to burn Whig houses and barns, and run off the cattle of men who were serving under Marion or Sumter, was a favorite amusement of many bands of Tories who made their homes in the mountains, and sallied thence to plunder and kill. But when the day of retribution came, the odium of their deeds was such that they shrank from the presence of men they had so deeply wronged, left lands and beeves, and fled with the troops. Three years had gone by, and a few of the refugees, finding exile intolerable, began to think of coming back. They threw themselves, they said, upon the mercy of the people. If they might only be allowed to return, not a word should be said about estates that had been confiscated, or debts that were

---

* Morse's Life of Hamilton, vol. i, pp. 149, 150.

due.* They wished merely to become good and peaceful citizens. Many sent petitions to the Legislature; but the news soon became public, and the papers solemnly warned them not to set foot on the land they had reddened with blood. Some took the hint and stayed away. Others, trusting to the provisions of the treaty, came back, and, while the Assembly deliberated on their cases, set out for their former homes. A party of twelve went up in a body to take possession of their abandoned plantations on the banks of a little brook called Fishing creek, were promptly waited upon by old friends and neighbors, told they were obnoxious to those whose houses they had plundered and burned, and were given twenty days in which to quit the country. When the prescribed time expired not one of them had budged. The Whigs lost all patience, flew into a passion, and, after three days more of grace, attacked the Tories, put eight to death, and suffered four to flee with all speed to the coast.† There a better reception seemed to await them, for the Legislature had passed a bill granting leave to a number of refugees to remain in the State. But the people of Charleston took up the matter, vowed that no turn-coat should find an asylum in their city, held a meeting, formed a procession, marched up and down the streets, and raised a riot which lasted several days.‡

A strange infatuation appears, however, to have seized upon the refugees. While these events were still fresh in the public mind, a fellow named Love, who had distinguished himself for cruel and barbarous deeds, had the front to show himself in his native village of Ninety-Six. It is said of Love that while the troops of Balfour and Cunningham roamed the State he joined them, and became a principal actor in a most shocking piece of work. During the winter of 1781 a party of thirty-five Americans were surprised by Cunningham in a house hard by the banks of Bush river. A spirited defence was made, but reasonable terms being offered, the Americans marched out and threw down their arms. Nineteen were instantly shot. After the slaughter was over, Love traversed

---

the ground where lay the dead and dying, his former neighbors and old acquaintances, and, as he saw signs of life in any
of them, ran his sword through and dispatched them. Those
already dead he stabbed again. To others seemingly without
life, but whose bodies twitched involuntarily as his sword
passed through them, he gave new wounds.

From that day Love was a marked man. He fled with
the British, and nothing more was heard of him till, one day
in November, 1784, he appeared in the neighborhood of
Ninety-Six. A justice of the peace took him into custody
and sent him to jail. The State's attorney pressed the matter
before the Court of Sessions. Ædanus Burke, an eccentric
Irishman and a noted character in the State, presided, over-
ruled the prosecution, declared that conscience could alone
punish the prisoner, and dismissed the case. No demonstration was made in the court-room, but, as the hated Tory walked
insultingly out, he was laid hold of, placed on horseback, hurried to a clump of trees without the village, and hanged.*

The open contempt with which, in all parts of the country, the people treated the recommendation of Congress concerning the refugees and the payment of the debts, was no
more than any man of ordinary sagacity could have foretold.
Indeed, the state into which Congress had fallen was most
wretched. Rudely formed amid the agonies of a revolution,
the Confederation had never been revised and brought nearer
to perfection in a season of tranquillity. Each of the thirteen
States the Union bound together retained all the rights of
sovereignty, and asserted them punctiliously against the central government. Each reserved to itself the right to put up
mints, to strike money, to levy taxes, to raise armies, to say
what articles should come into its ports free and what should
be made to pay duty. Toward the Continental Government
they acted precisely as if they were dealing with a foreign
power. In truth, one of the truest patriots of New England
had not been ashamed to stand up in his place in the Massachusetts House of Deputies and speak of the Congress of the

* See a letter from Mr. Justice Burke to Governor Guerard, December 14,
1784. This was published in the papers of the time, and afterward in the American Museum for February, 1787, p. 126.

States as a foreign government.  Every act of that body was scrutinized with the utmost care.  The transfer of the most trivial authority beyond the borders of the State was made with protestations, with trembling, and with fear.  Under such circumstances, each delegate felt himself to have much the character, and to be clothed with very much of the power, of ambassadors.  He was not responsible to men, he was responsible to a State.  The opinions which he expressed, the measures which he advanced, were not those of a great party, nor even such as found favor among the men of his own district or of his own town.  They were such as he believed to be in accordance with the will of a majority of the members of that Legislature which had sent him to the post he filled.  To him the smallest interest of the little patch of earth he called his native State was of far more importance than the greatest interest of the Confederation of States.

From beginning to end the system of representation was bad.  By the Articles of Confederation each of the thirteen little republics was annually to send to Congress not more than seven and not less than two delegates.  No thought was taken of population.  The immense State of Virginia, whose domains stretched along the valley of the Ohio and the shores of the lakes, and who boasted that upon her lands were the homes of seven hundred thousand human beings, was to command no more votes and to have no more influence in the councils of the nation than the petty State of Rhode Island, where the lists of the census-takers did not add up to seventy thousand souls.  But this absolute equality of the States was more apparent than real.  Congress possessed no revenue.  The burden of supporting the delegates was cast on those who sent them, and, as the charge was not light, a motive was at once created for preferring a representation of two to a representation of seven, or, indeed, for sending none at all.

While the war was still raging and the enemy marching and counter-marching within the border of every State, a sense of fear kept up the number of delegates to at least two.  Indeed, some of the wealthier and more populous States often had as many as four congressmen on the floor of the House.  But the war was now over.  The stimulus derived from the

presence of a hostile army was withdrawn, and the representation and attendance fell off fast. Delaware and Georgia
ceased to be represented. From the ratification of the treaty
to the organization of the Government under the Constitution
six years elapsed, and during those six years Congress, though
entitled to ninety-one members, was rarely attended by twenty-five. The House was repeatedly forced to adjourn day
after day for want of a quorum. On more than one occasion
these adjournments covered a period of thirteen consecutive
days.* Resolutions were passed condemning this, and appeals
made in the strongest language.† The Legislatures were assured that, while they were represented in Congress by two
delegates only, such an unanimity for conducting important
public concerns as was necessary could rarely be had; that,
if each of the thirteen States should send but two congressmen, it would be possible for five out of the twenty-six to
negative any measure requiring the consent of nine States;
that eleven States were then on the floor of Congress; that
nine of these eleven had but two delegates each, and that it
was therefore in the power of three men to negative measures of the greatest weight, such as the ratification of a treaty
of commerce, the emission of bills of credit, the appropriation
of money to the discharge of the interest on the debt, or the
raising of a land force to fight the Indians on the frontier.
But the appeal went, like all other appeals, like that for an
impost, for an established revenue, for the right to manage
trade, unheeded. No occasion, however impressive or important, could call out a large attendance. Seven States,
represented by twenty delegates, witnessed the resignation of
Washington.‡ Twenty-three members, sitting for eleven
States, voted for the ratification of the treaty.#

On such questions as came up from day to day; should the
accounts of some quartermaster be audited, should a reward
be offered for the capture of a highwayman who had robbed
the mails, should some cannon be returned to New York,

---

* Journals of Congress for 1784. See, also, on the dilatoriness of Congress,
a letter from R. H. Lee to Samuel Adams, November 18, 1784. Life of Adams
by Wells.        † Ibid., April 19, 1784.        ‡ Ibid., December 22, 1783.
# Ibid., January 14, 1784.

should a committee be appointed to devise plans for cutting
up the western lands, who should be geographer for the
next year, what should be done with the man who had as-
saulted the French minister in Philadelphia, the assent of a
majority of the States was sufficient, and, on the largest ballot the House could cast, six votes could make the question
pass in the negative.    It is not surprising, therefore, that
Congress speedily degenerated into a debating club, and a
debating club of no very high order.    Neglected by its own
members, insulted and threatened by its mutinous troops, reviled by the press, and forced to wander from city to city in
search of an abiding place, its acts possessed no national importance whatever.    It voted monuments that never were put
up, rewarded meritorious services with sums of money that
never were paid, formed wise schemes for the relief of the
finances that never were carried out, and planned on paper a
great city that never was built.    In truth, to the scoffers and
malcontents of that day, nothing was more diverting than the
uncertain wanderings of Congress.    Driven from Philadelphia by the jibes and taunts of a band of drunken ploughmen,
it flees to Princeton, and there, under the guns of fifteen hundred regulars, passes its resolutions in Nassau Hall.    From
Princeton it adjourns to Annapolis, from Annapolis to Trenton, from Trenton to New York.    Meanwhile the press is
making merry.    In one squib Congress is likened to a pendulum vibrating between Annapolis and New York.    In another
an honest countryman is made to entreat the Lord to make it
like unto a wheel, and keep it rolling from Dan to Beersheba,
from Beersheba to Dan, and give it no rest on this side of
Jordan.

In the coffee-houses and taverns no toasts were drunk with
such uproarious applause as " A hoop to the barrel " and
" Cement to the Union "; toasts which not long before had
sprung up in the army and come rapidly into vogue.*

While the mockers and jesters were thus busy in the endeavor to bring down what little respect was still felt for
Congress, another and a very different class of men were

---

* In a letter to Washington, General Knox observes that no toasts were drunk
in the army but " A hoop to the barrel " and " Cement to the Union."

equally strenuous in the endeavor to bring over to that body the good-will and hearty support of the populace. The present state of public affairs was, they said,* most deplorable, and nobody regretted it more deeply than they did. It was idle, however, to seek for the cure in abuse, in ridicule, and in unjust complaints. The cause, it was evident, lay either with Congress, with the Legislatures of the States, or with the people. Congress had undoubtedly much to answer for, but it was at the same time to be remembered how really small its power for good or evil was. Congress possessed but the semblance of power. The States possessed the substance. Congress could merely entreat, persuade, suggest. The States could act. It was therefore idle folly to hold it personally responsible for the wretched state into which public matters were come. All the ills against which the grumblers were so loudly complaining began to exist while the framers of the Confederation still sat in Congress. The membership of that body had since been changed over and over again, and so completely changed that scarce one of the men who had signed their names to the articles was now to be found in the House. Yet the evils still continued unabated. Nor had any attempt been made to remove them. It was, to say the least, not a little singular that, while the constitutions of the various States had one by one undergone careful revisions, no steps had ever been taken to remedy the defects of the Articles of Confederation. No political sagacity was needed to detect them. They were many and glaring. Any one who would take the trouble to look about him could not help seeing that the Union was wholly unequal to the needs of the United States. It had been formed in the midst of hostilities, in an hour of extreme peril, to meet immediate exigencies. These dangers had now passed away. New and imminent dangers were soon to be encountered, and for these the Confederation was totally unprepared. If the Union were not to be dissolved, additional power must instantly be bestowed on Congress. The State governments were day by day growing more powerful. In the wicked hope of increasing their own

---

* Some of these views are well expressed in the New Jersey Gazette for July 16, 1783.

importance they were steadily undermining the power and influence of Congress. When the recommendations of that august body were in accordance with the aims and wishes of the Legislatures, they were adopted; but when some sacrifice for the good of the country was demanded, they were coldly disregarded or openly despised. Patriotism was now understood to mean devotion to the interests and welfare of one's native State.

Much blame also lay with the people. They seemed to forget that their situation in 1784 was very different from their situation in 1764. In 1764 the colonies, though acknowledging allegiance to a common King, were widely separated by diversities of tastes, of customs, of occupations, and by all manner of petty jealousies. But ten years of tyranny and oppression at last did for them what no amount of argument could ever have brought about—it united them. They forgot all differences, and joined in a common league against the common foe for the common good. Ten years more of suffering and warfare went by, and the purpose for which that league had been formed was fully accomplished. They were no longer British subjects. Neither were they separate and distinct colonies. They were parts of one great Confederation. It was high time that this fact was understood, and that all envy, hatred and malice were laid aside. Ten years ago the States were rivals; now the States were, or at least ought to be, partners. Ten years ago the States had no interest in common, unless it was that of self-preservation; now the States had no interests which were not in common. Yet there was great danger of the old jealousies, the old animosities, again breaking out with renewed vigor. They should, under the new order of things, forget old injuries, adjust petty disputes, and, joined in a firm union with Congress at their head, set forth on the great career that lay before them.

But the evils and the remedy were set forth by none with so much truth as by one who wrote over the signature of Yorick. He was not an American. He was an alien and a stranger. Yet he had been a close observer of every phase of political life, and, as he belonged to no particular faction and to no particular State, he was at the same time a dispas-

sionate observer, and saw many things which utterly escaped
the notice of his more factious neighbors.   He could not, he
said, but lament the small prospect he saw of a great, liberal,
energetic government in the republic.   It was astonishing, to
say the least, that a matter of so much magnitude, a matter
which so materially concerned the interest of America as that
of a great, solid, and efficient government, should have been
so long unthought of, or, if not unthought of, unattended to.
It was astonishing that in such stirring times no man had
stepped forward to lead his country to the source of national
happiness and prosperity.   "A selfish habitude of thinking
and reasoning," said he, "leads us into a fatal error the moment we begin to talk of the interests of America.   The fact
is, by the interests of America we mean only the interests of
that State to which property or accident has attached us.
Thus a citizen of Philadelphia, when he harangues on the
rights and liberties of America, is not aware the while that
he is merely advocating the rights and liberties of Pennsylvania.   And our fellow-citizen here labors to evince his interest and efforts in the well-being of America, when behold!
lead him to the westernmost banks of the Hudson, or beyond
the eastern boundary of our State, and his heart is as cold
and unconcerned as to the interests of Kouli Khan or the
Nabob of Arcot.   The same local policy pervades all America,
and the people, for want of a guide, are not sensible of their
error." *

Leaders, indeed, there were, whom the multitude followed
with much the same alacrity and thoughtlessness that a herd
of buffaloes follows the sturdiest of the bulls.   But among
these leaders there was not one who could rise above the interests of his own State.   The men who, in after years, came
to eminence as the framers of the Constitution, who became
renowned leaders of the Federalists, presidents, cabinet ministers, and constitutional statesmen, were then in private life,
abroad, or in the State Assemblies.   Washington was busy
with his negroes and tobacco; Adams was minister to Holland ; Jefferson still sat in Congress, but was soon to be sent
as minister to France; Madison sat in the Virginia House of

* New York Packet, August 30, 1784.

Deputies; Hamilton was wrangling with Livingston and Burr at the bar of New York; Jay was minister to Spain. Demagogues were constantly reminding the people that the United States were thirteen independent republics; that Congress was merely a committee of the States; that it was unsafe to enlarge its powers, and that such powers as it already possessed were but to enable it to dispatch business which it was inconvenient or inexpedient for the States to settle individually. If now and then a sturdy supporter of the impost and the revenue bill was bold enough to dispute these assertions, to advocate the increase of the powers of Congress, and to intimate that under the present system certain States were fast becoming too powerful for the good of their neighbors, he was plainly told that he was now talking nonsense, and it was hinted that it would not be amiss to disfranchise a man whose political principles were no better than the political principles of a Tory.

While such appeals were made to thinking men, the same arguments, expressed in the language of the market and the pot-house, were addressed to those on whose ears the most logical reasoning produced no impression but sound. The shopkeepers and tradesmen were told in squibs, in broadsides, and in hand-bills, that, if they persisted in their present opinions, they would surely find reason to repent when repentance was too late. One of these papers had a large circulation, and was called "A Shorter Catechism." It consisted of a series of thirty-two questions and answers, drawn up with no wit and little skill, in which the course pursued by men of honor toward their benefactors and creditors was strongly contrasted with that taken by the public toward those to whom were due great debts of gratitude and money. What, it was asked, was gratitude? A disposition to repay benefactors. What was public gratitude? Forgetfulness of benefits. What was patriotism? A hobby-horse. What was liberty? Licentiousness unbridled. What was independence? Dependence on nothing. Who had gained it for the States? The army. How should the soldiers be requited? Cheat them. Who had loaned the States money? France and Holland. How should they be repaid? "Laugh at 'em." Public credit was, according to the catechism, soldiers' notes at thirty per centum discount. Taxation was much ado about nothing. The excise was great cry and little wool. Commutation was the devil, and when it was asked who could lay him, it was sarcastically answered, the Middletown convention.*

That language of this sort was both wise and timely there can be no doubt, for the condition of the country was indeed critical. The people had just emerged from a long and exhausting war. After their struggles, their sufferings, their narrow escape, they were irritable and wavering. Everything about them was new. Old parties, old leaders, old forms of government had gone down in the storm of revolution, and no new ones had as yet arisen to take their places. Not a thing existed about which the people of every State could rally. They had yet to frame a foreign policy such as became the high rank they were soon to occupy in the family of nations, and a home policy such as would unite the conflicting interests of thirteen jealous republics. They were to pay off an enormous debt, to restore a depreciated currency and replace it by a national currency, to establish a public credit, and create a national commerce. Toward furthering all these things Congress could do nothing, or next to nothing, but advise, recommend, suggest. As a body it was absolutely destitute of that fundamental power when stripped of which no government, no society, no organization, known among men, can long hold together; that power which the African negro gives to his chief, which the Indian bestows upon his sachem, and which, even by thieves and pirates, is acknowledged to belong to the men who command them, the power of compelling obedience to decrees. Congress was graciously permitted by the States to make treaties, and was then forced to sit by in dumb submission and see article after article violated by the very States for whose benefit the treaty was framed. Congress was allowed, nay, compelled, to borrow money, and when an enormous debt had thus been contracted, was ungraciously refused the means of liquidating even the annually increasing interest. It could not levy a dollar, either by way of impost or assessment, on the property of a citizen.

---

* The catechism was printed in the New York Packet for February 5, 1784.

When the decrees of a Legislature were in direct conflict with the lawful and constitutional acts of Congress, and they often were so, they must be submitted to with the best grace possible, for no power to annul them existed.  When soldiers were needed to fill the depleted ranks of the Continental army, the most that Congress could do was to assign to each State its quota and wait patiently till such time as the States saw fit to enlist and equip them.  And now when money was imperatively wanted to pay the arrearage due the troops, and the interest on the sums generously advanced in the hour of need by France, Congress was once more brought to the degrading necessity of putting off with excuses and with promises the long-deferred day of payment, while the multitude discussed the dangers of establishing a revenue to be applied to no other purpose than the discharge of their debts.

This delay on the part of the States to comply with an eminently just and wise request is to be ascribed to the utter lack of anything approaching to a national spirit, to the prevalent dread of bestowing enlarged powers on Congress, and to the immensity of the sum required.  The cost of the war had been in round numbers one hundred and forty millions of dollars.*  Much of this had, however, been, one time and another, paid off, so that not more than forty-two millions of dollars of the domestic debt remained.  Yet this sum, far less in amount than is now annually yielded to the Government by the Internal Revenues, and about one sixty-seventh as much as was in our time expended by the Government on the war between the States,† seemed to our ancestors simply appalling.  The time, it was confidently affirmed by the grumblers, would never come when so large a debt would be extinguished.  Liberty had, indeed, been dearly purchased.  Nor can it be denied that there seemed to be much truth in the statement, for it was with difficulty that sufficient money could be wrung from the people to meet the current expenses of each year.  By the reduction made in the forces by the resolutions of the year previous, expenses were cut down to four hundred and fifty-eight thousand dollars; a sum less than is now laid out each year by the City of New York in water-

---

* Jefferson's estimate.            † The war debt in 1865 was $2,844,649,626.

pipes, paving-stones, and lamp-posts. An additional million was needed to meet the outstanding deficiencies of the year just closed, and three millions to pay the overdue interest on the public debt. The committee, therefore, who had the matter in charge, informed Congress that the sum needed for the year 1784 fell not far short of five and a half millions of dollars. This money it was proposed should be raised in three ways.

Many of the States, by the stipulations of their ancient charters, claimed jurisdiction over boundless tracts of lands, stretching from the shores of the Atlantic across the continent to the unknown regions which lay along the waters of the Mississippi. Scarce twenty thousand acres of the far western part of these immense domains had been surveyed and mapped. It may be doubted whether as many as ten thousand acres were under cultivation. Less was known of the country than of the heart of China. There the Indians hunted the buffalo and the deer, and the trappers, unmolested, laid snares for the beaver and the mink. The inhabitants of the eastern part, a gaunt, rawboned, poverty-stricken race, were as much objects of curiosity to the refined and polished natives of Boston and New York as an Esquimau or a Turk. They dwelt in the rudest kind of log-cabins, and knew no other money than whiskey and the skins of wild beasts. They yielded no revenue to the States claiming their allegiance, and were, in truth, but nominally under the authority of the Legislatures. No troops were stationed among them to enforce obedience to the laws of the land. No judges ever journeyed to them to correct abuses, to mete out justice, to vindicate the majesty of the law. But, left to themselves, the people administered a prompt and rude justice with the knife and the gun. Up to 1784 these lands had been little more than a source of contention and strife. But a use, it was thought, had at last been found for them. The States should relinquish all claim, and vest all rights to them in Congress.

The territory thus acquired, it was promised, should be cut up into States and sold, and the money applied to the payment of the public debt. The sale would of necessity be slow, and the sums yielded for many years to come small. But the reduction of the debt would go on steadily, and the interest must, in the mean time, be provided for. It was, therefore, further urged to bestow upon Congress a fixed and sure revenue to be used for the payment of the interest. This, it was acknowledged, was asking for a great deal of power. But it was alleged in defence, and supported by statistics drawn from the books of the Financier, that the system then in use of portioning out the expenses of government, and leaving each State to collect its share of the burden in its own way and in its own good time, had signally failed. Every year the States had been growing more and more dilatory in the payment of their quotas. Every year the interest on the debt had, in consequence, been steadily growing larger and larger, till now more than three millions of dollars remained unpaid. It was not surprising, then, that the ministers were constantly sending home the disheartening intelligence that the credit of the country had fallen so low that money could not be borrowed in the name of the United States on any exchange in Europe. What wonder was it that the French Government, justly incensed at the failure to pay so much as the interest on the sums so generously loaned, was becoming clamorous for payment of the principal? No American doubted for a moment that the debt would be paid, interest and principal, to the very last farthing. But this failure to meet the interest was only increasing the load so hard to be borne. The trouble lay not in the inability of the people to pay their taxes, but in the bad method of collecting them. A revenue system should at once be established.

Of the many ways through which a sure revenue might be made to flow into the treasury, none seemed to the supporters of Congress so desirable as an impost. This they vehemently urged; and that the duty thus to be imposed might fall on the rich, rather than on the poor, special rates were to be established for many articles in general use. Some difficulty was at first encountered in determining what these articles should be; but a careful examination of the records of importation was made, and seven classes of goods at last chosen.* These seven were liquors, sugars, teas, coffees, cocoa, molasses, and

---

* Journals of Congress, April 18, 1783.

pepper. The tax on each was to be determined by the amount imported, and the amounts yearly imported were so small that they would move a smile among the officials accustomed to the immense invoices which each week, nay, which each day, pass through the custom-houses of Boston and New York. In every great centre of commerce and of trade may now be found many small importers, brokers, and commission merchants, who each year import and sell more bags of coffee and boxes of tea, more hogsheads of molasses and casks of wine, than ninety-five years ago were, in the same space of time, imported by all the merchants in the thirteen States. No wine was then so great a favorite as Madeira. It held much the same place that is now accorded to champagne, was to be found on the table of every man of wealth, and was thought to be as indispensable at every dinner-party as the sweet-cakes and the bowls of tea. Yet of Madeira but one hundred thousand gallons were imported in the course of a twelvemonth. A tax, therefore, of twelve ninetieths of a dollar the gallon was to be imposed, and on all other wines half that amount. As Madeira was the beverage of the rich, so was Jamaica rum that of the poor. Scarce anything else was drunk by the fishermen of New England, or by the artisans and rustics who, on long winter evenings, assembled round the huge fireplaces in the taverns where the logs were blazing, to listen while one of their number expounded true Whig principles, and pronounced vengeance on the refugees and Tories. It was, moreover, applied to many uses since usurped by alcohol. Yet it was believed to be very doubtful whether more than two millions of gallons could be relied upon as coming into the country each year. The tax proposed was four ninetieths of a dollar the gallon. Of teas the preference for Bohea was very decided. More than twelve times as much of this brand was imported as of all the other brands put together. Yet it was found, after careful examination, that but a little over one pound of Bohea was consumed for every twelve persons in the country. Three hundred thousand pounds were therefore taken as the annual importation, and each taxed at six ninetieths of a dollar. Of the other brands, twenty-five thousand pounds were found to be as much as, in a twelvemonth, ever came over from

China, and the duty was fixed at twenty-four ninetieths of a dollar. This was the heaviest proposed to be laid. The lightest was one half of one ninetieth of a dollar, which was put on each pound of brown sugar. Loaf-sugar was to be taxed at two ninetieths the pound; all other sugars, as also molasses and coffee, at one ninetieth of a dollar per gallon or pound. Low as was the importation of tea, that of coffee was lower still by a third. Indeed, it was scarcely used outside of the great cities. Two hundred thousand pounds was considered as a very large yearly importation. Of molasses, two millions of gallons came into the country each year. A few hundreds of thousands of these were consumed as food. The remainder were hurried to the Massachusetts distilleries and there made into the far-famed New England rum, which, by the fishermen at the Grand Banks, was thought much finer than the best that came from Jamaica. All other goods brought into any port in the country were to be taxed at five per cent of their value.

This impost, it was rightly judged, would meet with bitter and violent opposition. No pains, therefore, were spared to bring over the States into whose ports the dutiable goods were likely to be brought. It was distinctly given out that the revenue yielded by the measure would be applied to the payment of the interest on the national debt, and to nothing else. The impost was to continue for twenty-five years, and not a day longer. The collectors of the revenue were to be appointed by each State for its own ports.

The interest on the public debt being thus disposed of, the attention of Congress was called to a measure providing for the current expenses of the Government. The system then in use was to determine the gross sum needed for a year, and portion it out among the States. This it was not proposed to alter in the least, but it was thought expedient that every State should establish a substantial and sufficient revenue for the payment of its quota. Precisely in what way the sum should be raised the framers of the plan did not so much as intimate. That, it was wisely said, was a matter for each member of the Confederation to settle in such way as it thought best. But, said the opponents of the measure, the expenses of Government are never the same for two years running;

the quotas will therefore vary, being some years more and some years less. The revenue, on the other hand, will prob-ably, for some years to come, remain about the same. The result will be that the amount assigned to a State, and the money provided by a State, will never balance. Sometimes the revenue will exceed the quota; sometimes the quota will exceed the revenue, and so the State will at all times be a sufferer. To remove this objection, which seemed to have much reason on its side, a clause was inserted stipulating that when the fund paid into the treasury by any State was greater than the amount required, the overplus should be returned; but that when a deficiency occurred, it should be immedi-ately made up. In this form the bill passed the House.*

These two resolutions, that recommending an impost, and that recommending the grant of what was popularly called the supplementary funds, made up the revenue system of 1783. They were no common resolutions, and sent to the States in no common way. They formed an appeal for life, and nothing that could give them weight with considerate men was omitted. With them went forth an address, a batch of papers showing the nature and origin of the debt and the meritorious character of the creditors, copies of the Newburg Addresses, of the action of the officers, of the contracts with the French King, and an answer, written with great power of argument and language, to the objections lodged by Rhode Island against the revenue system of two years before. Madi-son drew up the address. Hamilton wrote the answer. There were, the States were told, three classes of creditors. Chief among them was Louis, King of France. In an hour of dire necessity, when every resource seemed exhausted, when hope deferred had made every heart sick, Louis had stood forth the friend of the States, had loaned them of his army and his treasures, had added to his loans most bounteous donations, and had, in the very contracts he made, manifested his mag-nanimity. Next to the King came that noble army of heroes who had staked their fortunes and their lives, and poured out their blood like water for the good cause, and who now asked but so much of their just dues as would enable them to lay

* Journals of Congress, April 19, 1783.

down the sword and go back, with the means of getting daily bread, to private life. Finally, there were those who had cheerfully loaned their money to the State, or looked on with patience while their property was taken for the public use. The address closed with an urgent entreaty to the States to remember that they were about to take rank with the nations of the earth, and to set such an example as would save the cause of republican liberty from ignominy and shame.*

No stronger appeal was ever made to the good sense of any people. But it fell on dull ears. The plan for an impost and the supplementary funds had now been before the public for more than a year. The consent of nine States was necessary before it could become a law. Yet such was the animosity to any measure likely to increase the powers of Congress that but two States had, with many misgivings, yielded a reluctant assent.†

Indeed, nothing that Congress was able to do could silence the grumblers, who filled column after column of the newspapers with their complaints. This impost, said one of them, who, after the fashion of his time, wrote under the signature of Calca,‡ this impost brings up for consideration three important questions. Is it, in the first place, wise to fund the national debt? Is it, in the next place, wise, after having risked everything to establish thirteen free republics, to part with everything to establish one great sovereignty? Is it, in the last place, possible that such funded debt and such all-ruling sovereignty can be made compatible with liberty and with national happiness? To fund the debt is simply to perpetuate it by paying interest. We are told, it is true, that this funding, this impost, is to go on for twenty-five years, and no longer. But what reason is there for supposing that when the twenty-five years have come and gone the same arguments will not be urged for continuing it that are now used for establishing it? There is no reason whatever to suppose such a thing. The proposed revenue system may therefore be looked upon and reasoned upon as a perpetual revenue. Now,

---

* See the address in the Journals of Congress.

† These two States were Virginia and North Carolina.

‡ The paper was printed in the New York Packet of February 26, 1784.

what are the consequences of such a revenue? They are, said Calca, to be learned from the history of other countries, and with rare dexterity he chose the history of the most hateful of all countries to the men he addressed—the history of England. Debts were first funded, and perpetual revenues first granted to the supreme power in England after her great revolution. It is proposed to fund debts and grant revenues in America after her great revolution. May Heaven avert the omen! True, indeed, the English people, under the system, rapidly advanced to the utmost pinnacle of grandeur and power. But all this merely served to render the fall, when the fall came, more ignominious and more marked. The Government, armed with inexhaustible riches, became all-powerful. With power came abuse of power. The revenues were perverted and made the prolific parent of corruption. Corruption produced extravagance and wastefulness; then recklessness followed, and recklessness brought on a general war in Europe and the loss of her colonies. What security have we, what security can we have, that the same baneful effect will not attend funding in America? We are told that Congress is annual, that the King is perpetual. But even if Congress be annual, the power of Congress is perpetual, and the very fact that it can be enjoyed but for a few months will tend to make those who hold it all the more heedless and reckless in its use. There is, indeed, a good political maxim which should be engraved on the heart of every freeman, and that maxim is that difficulty in procuring money for public use is the best, the only security, for a proper and frugal use of it. How should the debt be paid? Paid as the Articles of Confederation provide. Because now and then a State, as Rhode Island, for example, does not pay, or is slow in paying, her quota, that is no argument that the system is a bad one. These failures have happened in war-times. But times are now changed, and there is no likelihood that such things will again come to pass. The public land in the West should, he thought, be sold. The cession made by New York three years ago has been accepted. That made by Virginia will in all probability speedily be accepted, and the sales of these immense tracts will be more than sufficient to extinguish the debt.

In much the same spirit was the complaint of A Rough
Hewer,* who, under that homely signature, expressed the feeling and opinion of a very considerable portion of the community.  At the beginning of the war, said he, the people
acted as implicitly up to the various recommendations of Congress as if they believed that honorable body could do no
wrong.  Now the people act as if they think Congress can do
no right.  It is not far to go for the reason.  In the war-times
Congress was cautious.  Then it seemed little disposed to take
risks, and much disposed to let things slip from its shoulders
to the shoulders of the Legislatures.  Now, on the other hand,
Congress acts as if it aimed at arrogating to itself what belongs
to the sovereignty of the people.  Congress a year ago recommended an impost.  The Legislature of Rhode Island has
stoutly refused to grant this impost, and the refusal has given
rise to two performances in which the Rhode Islanders are
held up in a wrong light.  It is admitted that the impost
will confer great power on Congress, but asserted that the frequent rotation of members will prevent an abuse of power.
This is a great mistake.  There is no safety in frequent
elections, and, if the States venture to act on the belief,
they will some day in the future find out that the boasted
security has but increased their encumbrances.  Rough Hewer
then proceeded to illustrate his meaning by a fable.  "Friend,"
said the fox, "I desire you by no means to disturb these honest blood-suckers that are now quartered upon me, and whose
bellies I fancy are pretty well filled; for if they should leave
me, a fresh swarm would take their places, and I should not
have a drop of blood left in my body."  It was truly painful
to see Congress grasping at a power which, if obtained, would
in all likelihood prove its ruin.

The recommendation touching the cession of western lands
met with a better fate.  Indeed, it is not a little curious and
interesting to observe that none gave so willing and unre-
served a consent as the States from which a violent opposi-

---

* New York Packet, February 26, 1784.  Rough Hewer was the signature
Robert Yates put to many papers he published during the war.  The sentiments of
this paper are so like those he afterward held that it is not improbable he was
the author.

tion had most reasonably been expected. No member of the Confederation possessed such extensive, such rich, such populous lands in the west as Virginia. Out of the territory then conceded to belong to her have been formed the States of Michigan and Wisconsin, and so much of Ohio, of Indiana, and of Illinois as lie between the turbid waters of the Ohio and the forty-first parallel of latitude. The great valley of the Ohio was then, it is true, but little better than a wilderness. It was infested by roving bands of Indians. It swarmed with wild beasts. Yet the fertility of the soil and the healthfulness of the climate had attracted great numbers of immigrants, who had already marked out the sites of many hamlets and settlements which have since become opulent and mighty cities. At the head of the river, under the guns of Fort Pitt, nestled the hundred cabins of Pittsburg. Farther down, on a flat that spread out at the foot of a low range of hills, were the squalid huts which marked the site of the village of Losantiville,* whose name St. Clair, six years later, changed to Cincinnati, in honor of the great society whose blue ribbon he wore. Still nearer the mouth of the river, and hard by the spot where its waters plunge down a ledge of limestone rock to make the falls of the Ohio, were the three streets and the cluster of cabins that bore the name of Louisville, renowned through all the lower valley as the only hamlet that could boast of a store.† The site of Vincennes had been marked out,

---

* The village of Losantiville was not laid out till 1788, but houses had been going up on the site since 1780. "On the first day of August, 1780," says Vickroy, "we crossed the Ohio river and built the two block-houses where Cincinnati now stands." Albach, Western Annals, p. 324. When the town was laid out in 1788, the name Losantiville was given it by Filson, a pedantic school-master. He compounded the word of *ville*, the town; *anti*, opposite; *os*, the mouth; *L*, the Licking; so that Losantiville, being interpreted, meant the town opposite the mouth of the Licking. See Perkins's Annals of the West, pp. 325, 326. Cincinnati Directory for 1819, p. 18; also, Cist's Cincinnati.

† Some facts regarding Louisville may be had from Casseday's History of Louisville. The place, it seems, was first settled in 1773, and called the Beargrass Settlement. But when, in the spring of 1780, three hundred flat-boats, bringing six hundred immigrants, came down the Ohio and settled at Beargrass, the place became so important that the Virginia Assembly, in May, 1780, "established the town of Louisville at the falls of Ohio." One authority (Western Annals, p. 419) asserts that in 1784 the town contained "sixty-three houses finished, thirty-seven partly finished, twenty-two raised but not covered, and more than one hun-

and of Limestone, better known to us as Maysville. A fort
had been built at the mouth of the Great Miami. Some rude
dwellings had gone up at Clarksville, called after the distinguished soldier who had founded the district of Kentucky,
had conquered Kaskaskia, and explored the river to the Mississippi, while along the banks of the Wabash and the Great
Miami were the block-houses of many hunters and trappers.
All this had been the work of a few years. In 1779 there
were, it was said, in the whole Kentucky district but one hundred and seventy-six white men.* In 1784 these numbers
had gone far up into the thousands, and each month hundreds
of immigrants came over the mountains from Carolina, or
down the Ohio from Pittsburg.† Wheatfields and cornfields
and orchards began to spring up in every direction, and already the wagons that brought out merchandise from Philadelphia went back laden with grain.

---

dred cabins. But another and a better authority, who saw it in 1787, says that
the town was laid out in three streets, parallel, but oblique to the river, and consisted of about one hundred buildings. See a letter in Pennsylvania Gazette,
March 29, 1787. The first store in the place was opened in the spring of 1783.
The goods came in wagons from Baltimore and Philadelphia, by way of Ligonier
and Cumberland to Redstone-Old-Fort and Pittsburg, and then went down the
river in flat-boats to Louisville. In 1784 another store was opened at Lexington.
Albach's Western Annals, p. 419.

* The rapidity with which hamlets and settlements in the Ohio valley grew to
be towns and cities has no parallel in the history of America, unless, indeed, it be
in California. The settlement of California was due to unusual and exceptional
causes. The settlement of Kentucky was in the natural course of immigration.
The population of California increased with marvellous rapidity for a time, stopped,
fell back, and has since grown but slowly. The population along the Ohio has
from the first gone on doubling and tripling every few years. Indeed, it appears
by the census of 1880 that more than one of the cities of that region has, within
the last ten years, increased the number of its inhabitants by more than seventy
per cent. Monette, in his Valley of the Mississippi, vol. ii, p. 143, asserts that
in 1783 the population of all the Kentucky settlements was upward of 12,000,
and that by the spring of 1784 it was 20,000. My authority for the statement
that in 1779 there were but 176 white men in Kentucky is a letter in the Pennsylvania Gazette of March 29, 1787, written by a gentleman at Fort Fenny.
His facts were undoubtedly gathered from good sources. The rage for western
emigration is noticed by John Jay in a letter to W. Bingham, May 31, 1785; also,
in one to Lafayette, January 19, 1785.

† In 1784 thirty thousand immigrants are said to have come from Virginia and
North Carolina. Western Annals, p. 419. This must be understood to mean
not thirty thousand, but a very great many.

The value of these lands was therefore, at that time, believed to be very great, and if any reliance was to be placed in human foresight, it was certain that this value would constantly increase.  When, however, the bill to cede them to Congress was brought into the Virginia House of Deputies, in the autumn of 1783, it passed with small opposition, and early in the following March the deed was delivered.  Some mutterings of dissatisfaction were indeed heard, but they came, in general, from beyond the mountains, and were little heeded.  A few malcontents, on the other hand, while they brought forward no valid objections to the cession, ridiculed the idea of there being anything to cede.  Where, they asked, did Virginia get her right and title to the lands she now proposed so generously to give away?  There was, they owned, some semblance of a title on paper which had been carefully preserved among the colonial records ; but it was well known to be a semblance to a title, and nothing more, and could not bear the test of a search half so careful as that usually given to the title to an estate.

The sneers and the sarcasm of these men would perhaps have been as little regarded as the mutterings that came up from the district of Kentucky and the regions that lay along the banks of the Miami and the Ohio, had they not been set forth with all the ingenuity, asperity, and wit at the command of the most consummate master of pamphleteering the age had produced.  We doubt whether any name in our revolutionary history, not excepting that of Benedict Arnold, is quite so odious as the name of Thomas Paine.  Arnold was a traitor.  Paine was an infidel.  Indeed, the terms in which he is commonly described, and the epithets which are commonly heaped upon him, should seem to imply that of all infidels Paine was the blackest, and that since the day when the "Age of Reason" came forth from the press the number of infidels has increased much more rapidly than it did before that book was written.  The truth is, he was one of the most remarkable men of his time.  It would be a difficult matter to find anywhere another such compound of baseness and nobleness, of goodness and badness, of greatness and littleness ; of so powerful a mind left unbalanced, and led astray by the worst of animal passions. At one time arguing and disputing in behalf of his adopted countrymen, cheering them in the dark hour of distress, and instilling the best and noblest of principles, he at another urges them to the acceptance of principles which, if once adopted, would have destroyed all that is most sacred in life, and sunk them in depths of misery. The contrast between the man and his work is indeed great. Of all the human kind he was the filthiest and the nastiest, and his disgusting habits grew upon him with his years. In his old age, when the frugal gifts of two States which remembered his good work had placed him beyond immediate want, he became a sight to behold. It was rare that he was sober; it was still rarer that he washed himself, and he suffered his nails to grow till, in the language of one who knew him well, they resembled the claws of birds. What gratitude was he did not know. For his word he had scarcely more regard than for his oath; and his oath he had repeatedly violated when he held offices of trust. To contempt and shame, even when heaped upon him in the most public way, he was utterly callous, and still continued to toil on unrewarded in the cause of those who had insulted him. Yet this man undertook and accomplished a work as important and as necessary to the success of the Revolution as any of the victories won by the skill of Washington or Gates. Paine was by birth an Englishman. He sprang from that great middle class whence have come so many Englishmen renowned in science, in literature, in art. His mother was the daughter of a well-to-do country attorney; his father was a Quaker and a stay-maker. But the disposition and the parts of Thomas were inherited from neither parent. Of all the boys in Thetford he was the most idle and shiftless. At thirteen he was taken from the free school and set to make stays in his father's shop; and from that time forth to the day when, fifty-nine years later, he lay down, hated and despised, to die in misery and filth, his life was stranger than a fiction. Indeed, it would furnish materials for innumerable fictions. From his father's shop he went to London. There he fell in with some companions who gave him such a glowing story of the fortunes to be made at sea that, at twenty-two, he became a foremastman on a privateer. But the hard fare, the still harder work, and the strict discipline on board the King of Prussia, were little to the taste of Paine, and he soon settled at Sandwich. There he made the acquaintance of a pretty girl, fell in love with her, and urged his suit so successfully that, under a promise of marriage, he borrowed ten pounds, and set himself up as a master stay-maker. This venture brought him nothing but debt, and as his mistress would loan him no more money, he broke with her, married the daughter of an exciseman, and went to Margate. His wife soon died of ill treatment; and from Margate he went to London, and from London wandered back once more to his father's shop, where he made stays till his father-in-law found him a place in the excise; but, after some years, the temptations of the excise were too great for Paine, and he was, in 1774, dismissed for a gross abuse of trust. He then, in conjunction with a widow, started a green-grocery shop at Lewes, and married her daughter; but the grocery shop, like the stay-making business, soon overwhelmed him in debt. Meanwhile his wife, weary of his abuse and his blows, left him. And now, separated from his wife, his place in the excise gone, his shop taken from him, Paine, in the depths of poverty, turned his steps once more to London; and there Franklin met him, a wretched, half-starved, Grub-street hack. He had by some means obtained a letter to the great philosopher, besought him piteously for aid, and was strongly recommended to go to America. The advice so well suited his roving disposition that he took it, and landed in Philadelphia in 1775, a few months before the affair at Lexington. Again he had recourse to his pen, and speedily became the editor of the Pennsylvania Magazine. The country was then in the wildest disorder. It seemed impossible that the government of England could longer be borne in peace and quiet. No act of separation had yet taken place. But the time had come for a bold and decisive blow, and Paine was, in the opinion of Dr. Rush, precisely the man to give it. He waited upon Paine, and urged him to prepare a strong pamphlet recommending separation from England. The bargain was soon struck. Paine agreed to write the pamphlet; Dr.

Rush agreed to find the publisher, which was at that time no easy matter. An obscure printer was, however, found who would take the risk of publication, and "Common Sense" was given to the public.* It is hard for us, after the lapse of a hundred and seven years, to form a just appreciation of the effect of this production. But it must have been immense; nor is it too much to say that "Common Sense" did for the revolution what the "Federalist" did for the Constitution. Innumerable copies were printed, and for years thereafter the fact had only to be known that a pamphlet or a newspaper letter was by the author of "Common Sense" to secure for it a wide circulation and a careful perusal. Paine had now found the one sphere in which he could be useful. His pen, in fact, soon became as necessary to the cause as the army. Perhaps the darkest days in all the war were those which immediately followed the defeat on Long Island and the retreat of Washington through New York. Then all seemed lost. Despondency was in every face; the army was hourly diminished by desertion; the Tories were exultant. But Paine again came to the help of the good cause in the "Crisis." The effect was immediate. The desertion ceased, the depleted ranks filled up, men became more hopeful than ever. The "Crisis" was everywhere read and admired, and whole pages of it committed to memory. One passage in particular was a great favorite, passed into the common language of the market and the street, and, continuing to our own day, is still heard from the lips of those who have never read the pamphlet, who know nothing of Paine except that he was an infidel, and are utterly ignorant that to him is to be ascribed the famous line: "These are the times that try men's souls." The next year he was made Secretary of the Committee on Foreign Affairs by Congress. This he held for two years, during which he continued, on every important occasion, to put forth numbers of the "Crisis" till they reached fifteen. In 1779 he became involved in the Silas Deane affair, and in an evil hour made so scandalous a breach of trust that he was ignominiously dismissed. Four years

---

* Common Sense appeared in January, 1776. American Remembrancer, 1776, Part i, pp. 238–241.

later, when Congress sat in Nassau Hall, Washington, who could not forget the good services Paine had done in days gone by, suggested that the illustrious author of "Common Sense" be rewarded with the office of Historiographer of the United States. A motion to the purpose was made in Congress, but was received with such an outburst of indignation that the unlucky mover made all haste to withdraw it. The remembrance of the Silas Deane letter was yet fresh. A year later Washington once more sought to obtain some reward for him from the Legislature of Virginia. He wrote a strong letter to Madison, and Madison warmly supported the motion in the House of Deputies; but it was twice thrown out, for Paine had again stood in his own light. He had published a pamphlet called "Public Good," in which he denied the claim of Virginia to the lands beyond the mountains. The sting of the pamphlet, which was not written in the author's best style, nor with his usual force of argument, soon wore off; but the recollection of it long rankled in the minds of a set of narrow men who, having kept him out of a fine estate and several thousand pounds of money, lost no opportunity to blacken his memory and his name.*

At the same time that the representatives of Virginia were instructed to prepare the deed of cession they were bidden to vote for the impost. The news of the passage of this act was received with much indignation and surprise. For nowhere did goods from over the sea find a more ready sale than in the markets of Virginia. From time immemorial the lords of the Virginia manor-houses had been accustomed to look to the Old World for the stuffs for their coats, their house-furniture, and their wines. Nor had the taste for such luxuries, thus handed down for many generations, been at all lessened by the poverty occasioned by the calamities of war. It was still as strong as ever, and must be gratified, whatever the cost. Could the money be had in no other way, more acres must be laid out in tobacco. Some of the plant which in colonial days would have been burned

---

* The sources of information touching the life and character of Paine are: Life of Thomas Paine, by Cheetham, vol. i, 1817; Letter of Washington, June 12, 1784; Letter of Madison, July 2, 1784.

in the presence of the inspector as too bad for the market might now, under a free government, be smuggled in with the finest leaves and command a high price.   If, indeed, the worst came to the worst, a wench might be hired out to service, or sent to the nearest mart and sold.   Virginia therefore stood first on the list of importing States.   Ships from Spain, from Madeira, and the Indies were constantly going in and out of her ports.   Her importations amounted to hundreds of thousands of dollars yearly.   It was under such circumstances not unnatural that factious and discontented persons should mutter, that they were quite at a loss to know on what principle of good government Virginia should at one and the same moment give away her rich possessions in the northwest, and consent to an impious tax which would press on no men so heavily as on her own citizens.

Yet the example set by Virginia was speedily followed by a near neighbor.   North Carolina was also the owner of great estates lying beyond the western foot hills of the Blue Ridge Mountains, and which, green with woods and waving grass, sloped gently down to the waters of the Mississippi and the Tennessee.   A handful of adventurers in the autumn of 1758 had crossed the mountains, had gone down into the wilderness, had made clearings, had driven out the Indians, had founded a settlement, and had sent back such glowing accounts of the richness of the soil that numbers of immigrants followed them.   At length, after the lapse of twenty-six years, a population of upward of ten thousand souls was gathered in the region lying between the Holston, the Cumberland, and the hills.*   But the country was still sparsely settled, and those splendid pastures, verdant even beyond the verdure of Kansas, which now feed some of the finest cattle in all our land, were then a virgin soil, over which each year the Chickasaws and Cherokees, hideous in paint and feathers, chased great herds of buffaloes and deer.   The colony was indeed little more than a source of expense to the parent State.   Yet it was deemed of much importance, and was permitted each year to send deputies to the Legislature of North Carolina.

In the spring of 1784 the Assembly was in session at Hills-

---

* Albach's Western Annals, p. 507.

borough, a small town hard by the banks of one of the branches of the Neuse river. Much business had been before it, but time had been found to take into consideration the three requests of Congress. Early in April the supplementary funds and the impost had been discussed and acceded to. The impost had been unreservedly granted; a special tax had also been laid, and, to the surprise of many, authority given to Congress to collect it. It was not, however, till June that a bill providing for the session of the western land was laid on the table of the House. This bill made over to the national Government the twenty-nine millons of acres of rich grass-land and woodland out of which, twelve years later, a new State was made and named from the great river whose huge bend prompted the Indians to bestow upon it the appellation of the Tennessee. Two years were given to Congress wherein to accept the grant. Meanwhile the authority of North Carolina was to be supreme. A few days after the bill became a law the House rose, and the deputies from the ceded counties immediately set out for home.

The way was long. The road was so bad, and, as it approached the Bald Mountains, so tortuous and steep, that the summer was wellnigh spent ere they reached the Holston, bringing with them the first intelligence of the cession act. There was then no newspaper, nay, no printing-press, west of the mountains.* The news was therefore carried from settlement to settlement by word of mouth, and as it spread, the fears and indignation of the people increased. It was evident, they said, in what estimation they were held by their friends of the tide-water region. Their calls for money had been met with charges of extravagance. Their calls for greater protection had at first been coldly disregarded, and had now been answered by taking away what little protection had before been grudgingly given.

Could any region in the whole country be pointed out which needed protection, and a strong protection, more? The settlements swarmed with men who, in the east, had avowed by

---

* The first newspaper printed in the State was the Knoxville Gazette. The first copy bears date November 5, 1791. See also T. W. Hume's Semi-Centennial Address; Ramsey's History of Tennessee, p. 557.

their actions an utter disregard of law and order. Refugees who had been proscribed and hunted from their homes as outcasts of society; thieves and cutthroats who had broken jail or escaped from the clutches of the law; men who had murdered their rivals in duels, or run them through the body in the dark, were constantly seeking an asylum on the Holston. Yet no supreme court had been established. Violations of law were unpunished except by the summary processes of the regulators whom the people had, in self-defence, been compelled to appoint. The Cherokees again were restless and aggressive. They might at any moment dig up the hatchet, put on the war-paint, dance the war-dance, and sweep through the settlements, burning, killing, and scalping. This was not only possible, but highly probable. Yet how were the people to defend themselves? There were indeed a few companies of militia. But they were without organization, and, what was worse, without a commander, for no brigadier-general had been appointed who could, at a moment's notice, call the forces into service. There was fortunately one sovereign remedy left, a remedy which under any other circumstances they should be loath to apply, and that was, for the people to waste no more time in petitioning a body of men glad to get rid of them, but take matters into their own hands. For if they failed to protect themselves, who was it that would protect them? Not Congress, surely, for Congress had not yet, and very likely never would accept them. Not the home Legislature, for if that body had rendered little assistance in the past it was sheer folly to expect it to do anything in the two years to come, during which their fate would be undecided. These two years would inevitably be times of anarchy and destruction unless the settlers availed themselves of the remedy, and that speedily.

This advice was most acceptable, and representatives were soon assembled in each of the counties. They were gravely, soberly, and with patience, to consider the state into which public affairs were come, and recommend some general course of action. Many plans were discussed, but the unanimous sense of the meeting was that a general election should take place, that deputies should be chosen in the four counties, and that they should meet at an early day at Jonesboro with full power to adopt such measures as the times required. Not a moment was lost in acting on this recommendation, and on the twenty-third of August the delegates were assembled in a log cabin. When the credentials were examined it was found that representatives were come from the three counties of Washington, Greene, and Sullivan. None came from Davidson. Again the evils complained of were discussed and the sufferings of the people gone over. Many remedies were brought forward, debated, and the sense of the delegates taken. In the course of these discussions a number of suggestions were brought out which agreed so thoroughly with the sentiments of all present that they were finally reduced to the form of a resolution.* This set forth as the sense of the assembly that the three counties represented should be formed into a new State; that so far as possible the laws of North Carolina should be laws of the State; that it was the undivided opinion of the assembly that it would be lawful to hold a convention, that it would be lawful for that convention to prescribe such regulations as circumstances required, and to petition Congress to accept the cession and admit the new State to the Union. No sooner had this been passed than a member was dispatched to the door of the hut to make it known to the crowd of trappers and backwoodsmen who impatiently awaited without.† The shouts which followed the reading of the resolution announced to the delegates that they had acted well.

But the shouts of joy sent up by a crowd of unthinking men in a moment of excitement was no sure indication that the resolution would be welcomed with equal pleasure by the multitude. The thousands yet to hear of and discuss it might receive it with bitter condemnation, might think the remedy worse than the disease, and seek refuge beyond the mountains or in other States, where law and order were supreme. An address to the people was therefore made ready, and copies multiplied as rapidly as could be done in a country where a printing-press would have been as great a wonder as in Africa

---

* A copy of the resolution as taken from the manuscript of Rev. S. Houston is given in Ramsey's Annals of Tennessee, p. 287.

† Ramsey's Tennessee, p. 288.

or Japan. The language and the arguments of this paper were not such as would have come from the pen of Hamilton, of Jefferson, or of Jay; but of a kind that became men who, more accustomed to fighting Indians and tracking bears than to making laws, sat down and, without the smallest knowledge of the road by which communities advance from ignorance and poverty to knowledge and to wealth, marked out such a course and cast about them for reasons to justify it. To remove the doubts of the scrupulous, to encourage the timid, and to induce all to enter into a firm association, such was the language of the address, a few things were to be maturely thought over. If the action recommended seemed hasty and ill-judged, it was to be remembered that the people had been driven to an extreme. Nay, more, the Legislature of North Carolina had, by ceding the counties to Congress, opened the way for, and invited, the action. There were undoubtedly many reasons why a separate government was not desirable. But there were also many reasons why a separate government was desirable. Once established, immigrants would, with a little persuasion and a little encouragement, come in and fill up the frontier. Agriculture and manufactures would flourish. Yet a little while, and the vast plains where the buffalo roamed would be interminable cornfields and wheatfields, and the lowing of cattle would be heard on the hills which then echoed the howl of the wolf and the yelp of the fox. Mills and factories would obstruct the waters of every stream, schools would spring up, knowledge would be diffused, literature would flourish. The seat of government once among them, gold and silver would no longer be drawn away. Where the capital was, there would money also be; and as none would go out, the stock would constantly be increasing. Much would be left by travellers prompted by curiosity to see the new State. Many ingenious schemes could be devised to draw in more.*

The address as thus presented looked well on paper and sounded well to the ear. But neither those who framed it nor those who heard it had the smallest conception of the means by which so many long-wished-for ends were to be

---

* Ramsey's Tennessee, pp. 288, 289.

attained.  Their hearts were bent upon creating a new State,
and, in their eagerness to point out the blessings that would
flow down to them from the new order of things, they
saw none save such as had through years of darkness and of
gloom been the subjects of their day-dreams and their prayers.
They longed to see the wilderness they had cleared thick with
cities and villages such as they had left beyond the mountains, and to have their cabins of rough-hewn logs give way to
stately edifices of brick and wood.  They looked forward to
the time when they should once more hear the coins chinking
in their pockets, and estimate their wealth not in skins of
wild beasts, but in heads of cattle and bushels of grain.  And
from all this they firmly believed they were separated by barriers which could be broken down by a few resolutions of their
delegates and a few votes of congressmen.

As soon as the convention had broken up, vigorous measures were set on foot for another election.  Five representatives were to be chosen from each county.  The fifteen were
to form a convention, draw up a constitution, and give a name
to the new State.  The sixteenth of September was set down
as the day for the meeting, and Jonesboro was selected as the
place.  But September and October came and went, and
November was far spent ere the delegates met, and they met
only to separate in angry confusion.  The unanimity of sentiment which had hitherto marked all their deliberations was no
longer with them.  Had it been the duty of the fifteen to lay
down a plan for the conduct of a summer campaign against the
Chickasaws, had they come together to deliberate on the best
way of defending the settlement against the inroads of the
Cherokees, they would in all probability have proceeded with
expedition and with perfect harmony to the business in hand,
and have accomplished results honorable to themselves and
pleasing to their constituents.  But they found themselves in
a position the like of which they had never stood in before,
and such as, till a few months previous, they never had in
their wildest dreams expected to occupy.  Each had all his
life long been used to see law and law-makers treated with
open contempt.  Now, in an hour of peril, the scoffers had
sent him to make laws, and precisely how a man should act

when a law-maker he did not know. He had, however, for ten years past, heard much of the duties of a delegate, and held the doctrine that a representative is bound by the will of his constituents in its crudest form. The minute, therefore, each one took his seat in the convention, he felt himself in honor bound to be the noisy advocate of the opinions of men whose votes had placed him there. And throughout the three counties no two constituent bodies could be found holding the same opinions. Scarce had one backwoodsman laid before the members the wild theories of government he had so often discussed with his boon companions as they sat around the tavern-door, than half a dozen others were instantly on their feet clamoring to be heard. Each advanced what he believed to be the most convincing arguments in behalf of his own scheme, and overwhelmed that of his neighbor with sarcasm and derision. The replies which followed these attacks were full of abuse, and abuse of that peculiar kind which flourishes best among men who, in a new country, labor in the van of settlement and progress. In a short time the convention, amid the utmost disorder, broke up.

But while the constitutional convention was wrangling at Jonesboro, the Legislature met at Newbern. And now that the damage was done, all haste was made to repair it. The measures resorted to were, however, much better adapted to preventing than to curing the disorder. The bill of cession was quickly repealed. The requests so long refused were granted. A bill was brought in, and hastily passed, to establish a supreme court at Jonesboro, to provide for the appointment of an attorney-general and an assistant judge, and to form the militia of Washington district into a brigade. These concessions were followed up by a dexterous distribution of the new honors.

Of the men sought to be won over by title and place, the foremost in parts, in courage, and in energy was John Sevier. Sevier was perhaps the only one in the settlements who could trace back an honorable descent through several generations of ancestors. He was a native American; but his family were of French extraction, were Huguenots, had long lived in France, and had there written the name Xavier. On the revocation of the Edict of Nantes, his grand-father fled with the family to London, and in time became a prosperous merchant. But ledgers and invoices had so little attraction for the son Valentine that he soon went over the sea to seek his fortunes in the colonies, and settled among the mountains which border the rich and beautiful valley where flow the waters of the river the Indians have named the Shen-andoah. There John Sevier was born; but while he was still a lad his parents went across the mountains and took up their abode on the banks of the Holston. Thenceforth his years were passed amid Indians and backwoodsmen, men whose talk was of trails and traps, of encounters with the savages and fights with bears, and whose ambition was to be renowned as the finest shot and the best hunter in the four counties. The fruits of this training became visible when in after years the boy was famous as a popular leader and Governor of the State of Franklin. He early acquired, and to the last re-tained, a reputation for intrepidity and decision. His bold-ness, indeed, often bordered upon rashness. What fear was he did not seem to know. He served with distinction in the war for independence, and bore an honorable part on that memorable day when the undisciplined frontiersmen charged again and again up the steep sides of King's Mountain. When peace came he went back to his home, and became one of the most noisy of the little knot of aspiring men who set them-selves to correct what they were pleased to consider the wrongs of the settlers. A fluent speaker, and of much better education than his companions, Sevier was always heard with respectful attention. When, therefore, the time came for ac-tion, when the ignorant multitude were casting about for a man of parts and decision, they turned to him.* He had been among the first to advocate the formation of a new State, had a seat in the convention which recommended this measure, and in the convention which in November broke up in confu-sion. Not long after he received a letter from Governor Martin acquainting him with the action of the mother State;

---

* The facts related of Sevier have been collected chiefly from Lippincott's Cabinet History of the States, Haywood's History of Tennessee, Ramsey's History of Tennessee, and from the newspapers and letters of the time.

how that courts had been organized, an attorney-general appointed, the militia formed into a brigade, and he made commander. He was not a little flattered. It seemed in truth much better to be a brigadier-general in the service of a great State than the leader of a noisy mob, which might, in a fit of jealous anger, hurl him from power and drive him beyond the Ohio. Sevier thought over the matter, and, when the fourteenth of December arrived and the new convention were about to meet, mounted the steps of the wretched building and read Martin's letter to the crowd. "You see," said he, "our grievances are redressed and we have nothing more to complain of. My advice is to cease all efforts to separate from North Carolina and remain firm and faithful to her laws." * But for once his advice was neglected. The members took their seats, opened the convention, and Sevier, as he could not stem the current wisely went with it and suffered himself to be made president of the meeting.

Meanwhile the example of Tennessee was being closely imitated by the Kentuckians. Early in the summer roving bands of Indians appeared along the southern border of the district, burning houses, destroying crops, and driving the settlers before them. Every day the news that came in from the back country grew more and more alarming, till there seemed much reason to believe that a general Indian rising was close at hand. In this extremity Benjamin Logan, a colonel in the militia and a man of some renown through the district, summoned the citizens to meet at Danville to deliberate on a plan for defence.

The condition of the district which Logan's convention was soon to discuss was well calculated to awaken fear. Yet, bad as it was, it was much better than that of the country across the Tennessee. The Kentuckians had not, like the Tennesseeans, been cast off by the parent State. Virginia still claimed their allegiance, still contributed to their support, and still looked upon the Kentucky district as the richest of her unrelinquished possessions in the West. While the petitions, the remonstrances, the complaints of Sevier and his friends had been coldly received in North Carolina, the murmurs of

---

* Ramsey's Tennessee; Haywood's Tennessee.

the men who assembled at Logan's call had been heard with attention at Richmond. Courts had been established, judges had been appointed, an attorney-general commissioned, lawyers had come among them, a session had already been held, and a court-house of roughly hewn logs besmeared with mud was fast rising in the town of Danville. But there were in Kentucky offenders who stood in no fear of judges and sheriffs, and against whom the law afforded no protection whatever. Savages could not be sued, nor imprisoned, nor fined, nor hanged. In every county were, indeed, militia companies, and thousands of men who, at a moment's notice, were ready to desert their traps and their cornfields, take down their muskets, mount their horses, and go upon a campaign against the Indians. But the Cherokees were vigilant, wary, prompt to act, and at the settlers' very doors. The only authority that could call the militia to arms was careless, slow to move, and over the mountains hundreds of miles away.

The moment, therefore, the convention was assembled at Danville and a plan for an expedition into the Indian country discussed, the question of the lawfulness of such an undertaking was raised. The lawyers were consulted and gave it as their opinion that a campaign could not legally be carried on against the Indian tribes. The power, it was said, of impressment had ceased with the war. Nor was there any power known to the law then present among them capable of calling out the militia however great the danger. No sooner had this opinion been announced than the cry was raised that the time had come to form a government independent of Virginia. But this the assembly had no power to do. It contented itself with sending out a recommendation that a new convention should be formed, that each company of the militia in the district should, on a certain day, elect one delegate, and that the delegates so chosen should meet at Danville on the twenty-seventh of December to consider the expediency of an appeal to Virginia for leave to form a new State. With this the gathering broke up.*

But long before the settlers of Kentucky and Tennessee were thus hastening to sign petitions, to form conventions, to

---

* Marshall's History of Kentucky, p. 190.    Collins's History of Kentucky.

draw up constitutions, and part out new States, Congress had
been engaged in a precisely similar work. The condition
of the northwestern territory had long been under the consideration of the House. Several committees had been appointed, and several schemes listened to, for laying out new
States, but it was not till the middle of April that a resolution
was finally reached. One plan was to divide the ceded and
purchased lands into seventeen States. Eight of these were
to lie between the banks of the Mississippi and a north and
south line through the falls of the Ohio. Eight more were
to be marked out between this line and a second one parallel
to it, and passing through the western bank of the mouth of
the Great Kanawha. What remained was to form the seventeenth State. But few supporters were found for the measure, and a committee, over which Jefferson presided, was
ordered to place before Congress a new scheme of division.
Chase and Howe assisted him, and the three devised a plan
whereby the prairie-lands were to be parted out among ten
new States. The divisions then marked down have utterly
disappeared, and the names given to them become so forgotten that nine tenths of the population which has, in our
time, covered the whole region with wealthy cities and prosperous villages, and turned it from a waste to a garden, have
never in their lives heard the words pronounced. Some
were borrowed from the Latin and some from the Greek;
while others were Latinized forms of the names the Indians
had given to the rivers. The States were to be, as far as possible, two degrees of latitude in width, and arranged in three
tiers. The Mississippi and a meridian through the falls of the
Ohio included the western tier. The meridian through the
falls of the Ohio and a second through the mouth of the Great
Kanawha, were the boundaries of the middle tier. Between
this and the Pennsylvania West Line lay the third tier. That
vast tract stretching from the forty-fifth parallel of latitude
to the Lake of the Woods, and dense with forests of pine, of
hickory, and of oak, they called Sylvania. It was the northern State of the western tier. To the long tongue of land
separating the water of Michigan from the waters of Erie
and Huron they gave the name Cherronesus. A narrow strip,

not more than two degrees of latitude in width, and stretching from Lake Michigan to the Mississippi, was called Michigania. As marked down on their rude maps, Michigania lay under Sylvania, in the very heart of what is now Wisconsin. South of this to the forty-first parallel of latitude was Assenisipia, a name derived from Assenisipi, the Indian title of the river now called the Rock. Eastward, along the shore of Lake Erie, the country was named Metropotamia. It took the name Mother of Rivers from the belief that within its boundary were the fountains of many rivers, the Muskingum, the two Miamis of Ohio, the Wabash, the Illinois, the Sandusky, and the Miami of the Lake. That part of Illinois between the thirty-ninth and forty-first parallels was called, from the river which waters it, Illinoia. On to the east was Saratoga, and beyond this lay Washington, a broad and level track shut in by the Ohio river, the waters of the lake, and the boundaries of Pennsylvania. Under Illinoia and Saratoga, and stretching along the Ohio, was the ninth State. Within its confines the waters of the Wabash, the Sawane, the Tanissee, the Illinois, and the Ohio were mingled with the waters of the Mississippi and Missouri. The committee therefore judged that a fitting name would be Polypotamia. Pelisipia was the tenth State. It lay to the east of Polypotamia, and was named from Pelisipi, a term the Cherokees often applied to the river Ohio.*

At the same time that the boundaries of the new States were defined, a code of laws was drawn up which should

---

* So little was generally known of this absurd plan of Jefferson that when, in 1856, an old French map was discovered in the New York State Library at Albany, containing the statement that ten new States were being formed in the Northwest, and giving their names badly spelled, a writer in the Albany Argus and Atlas of December 24, 1856, asked where the Frenchman got his idea of such a thing. A correspondent replied that he had found a like statement in Guthrie's Geography, published in Dublin in 1789. The mystery was solved by the New York Tribune, which printed the ordinance in full on December 30, 1856. The title of the map was: États Unis de l'Amérique Septentrionale avec Les Iles Royale, de Terre Neuve de St. Jean, L'Acadie, etc., 1785. The report of the committee and the ordinance may also be seen in Journals of Congress, March 1 and April 19, 1784; New York Packet, April 23, 1784; Randall's Life of Jefferson; in Jefferson's Collected Works; and in the Tribune Almanac for 1857. Guthrie's Geography, it may be well to say, became in its day quite a noted text-book, and found its way even to the rude settlements on the Ohio. See Drake's Pioneer Life in Kentucky.

serve as a constitution for each State, till twenty thousand free inhabitants acquired the right of self-government. The code was in no wise a remarkable performance, yet there were among its articles two which cannot be passed by in silence. One provided for the abolition of slavery after the year 1800. The other announced that no one holding an hereditary title should ever become a citizen of the new States. Each was struck out by the House. Yet each is deserving of notice. The one because it was the first attempt at a national condemnation of slavery, the other because it was a public expression of the dread with which our ancestors beheld the growth of the Society of the Cincinnati.

The Order of the Cincinnati was formed in April, 1783, at the suggestion of General Knox. Members were exclusively officers of the army and navy. They had, it was said, been united for eight years in defence of a common cause. They had shared the same dangers, the same privations, the same sufferings. Many strong friendships had, under these circumstances, grown up; and now that the hour of disbandment was near, it seemed but fitting that a great society should be formed to perpetuate in peace the friendships formed in war, to enable them to deliberate in secret on the welfare of the Union they had fought to maintain, and to hand down to their remotest descendant some more tangible honor than the recollection of their poverty and their wounds. The verdict of posterity has long since acquitted the founders of the Cincinnati of any evil designs against the life of the State. But it would indeed have been a hard task to have brought to this mind the men who, in 1783, heard, with mingled feelings of alarm and disgust, that a military order had been established, that its honors had been made hereditary, that Frenchmen had been admitted to its ranks, that a petition had been laid at the foot of the throne, had been graciously received, and that the eagle and the blue ribbon of the Cincinnati were daily to be seen in the proudest of courts, where no subject had ever before been permitted to wear the decorations of a foreign State.* Scarcely a larger share of public attention is now en-

---

* Major L'Enfant, in one of his letters, speaks of " La faveur que sa Majesté très Chrétienne a bien voulu nous accorder, en nous permettant de porter la

joyed by the society than is bestowed on the many social and literary clubs which from time to time hold receptions and give dinners to guests from over the sea. Then the sharpest laws were thought necessary to protect the new liberties of the State from its baneful influence. An election to membership is now an event of no more importance than the bestowal of the honorary degrees which, on the return of every June, are so liberally granted by innumerable colleges. Then the officer who subscribed to its laws laid down in many States his rights of citizenship. Ten thousand societies have since that day been organized by ill-disposed men, for ten thousand purposes inimical to the good of the State, or to the good of large classes in the State. Socialistic societies, communistic societies, societies of freethinkers, Fenian brotherhoods, and trades-unions without number, have sprung up, grown apace, and sunk utterly into oblivion, without exciting more comment than a few caustic lines in the morning papers. Nay, more : we beheld at the close of the rebellion another body of troops, numbering more than a million and a half of veterans, organizing grand armies, holding meetings, wearing badges, establishing posts and lodges all over the country, and exerting no small influence at elections. Yet no cry went up that the liberty of the State was in danger. No harsh laws were enacted. But the country ninety-nine years ago was in no temper to bear patiently with such societies. Nothing was more galling than that, having destroyed long-established orders of nobility, new orders should be set up by the very men who had aided so materially in pulling down the old.

The few who were eligible to membership were much inclined to treat the clamors of the people as the result of a wide-spread discontent, and as no fault of the society. " The public of New England," wrote General Greene, " seem to want something to quarrel with the officers about. Remove one thing, and they will soon find another. It is in the temper of the people, not in the matter complained of." * But the complaints against the officers were of no vulgar kind. A year

marque de notre union dans son royaume, où nul autre ordre étrangère est toleré." Proceedings New York Society of the Cincinnati, 1786, p. 16.

* Letter from Greene to Washington.

had now gone by since the members had hastened to sign the constitution of the order. Yet the fears of the multitude were as great as ever,* and were shared in by the most acute philosophers, the most sagacious statesmen, and the shrewdest diplomatists a country by no means wanting in such men had produced. Franklin, who then represented the people at the French court, wrote home ridiculing the order in his own peculiar way.† The united wisdom of the nation had, he said, in the Articles of Confederation, manifested a strong dislike to established ranks of nobility. He wondered, there-fore, that a number of gentlemen should, in the face of this, think proper to set themselves and their posterity apart from their fellow-citizens, and form an order of hereditary knight-hood. Such matters were much better managed in China. In China honors ascended. In America honors descended. In the Celestial Empire, if a man of the people, because of his learning, because of his wisdom in council, or his valor in bat-tle, be graciously raised by the Emperor to the rank of Man-darin, he shares his new distinction with his parents. From the moment of his elevation his father and his mother are entitled to wear the same decorations he wears, to receive the same tokens of honor that he receives, and to be treated with the same ceremony he is treated with. Franklin then went on, in that singular vein of pleasantry which his friends often mistook for humor, to demonstrate by arithmetic that as the descent became more and more remote, the glory grew less and less. A man's share in his family was, he said, but a half part; in the second generation but a fourth part; and when the ninth generation was reached but the five hundred and eleventh part. When, therefore, the badges and the titles of the Cincinnati had come down to the eldest son of the ninth generation, his share would be but the thousand and twenty-second part of that of the first recipient. The bad Latin of the motto reminded him of one of his inexhaustible fund of

---

* "The Cincinnati appears, however groundlessly, to be an object of jealousy. The idea is that it has been created by a foreign influence, in order to change our form of government." Knox to Washington, Boston, February 21, 1784.

† Letter from Franklin to Mrs. Bache. Franklin's Works. The letter is dated January 26, 1784.

stories which he then went on to narrate. But ill as the school-master had done his work, the artist had done worse, for the device was no less puzzling than the motto. The bird might be a turkey or a bald-headed eagle. Of the two the turkey was, in his estimation, the more honorable bird. The eagle was notoriously a bird of bad repute, was a coward and a thief, delighting to plunder smaller birds of the food they had collected by diligence and pains, but fled screaming from the presence of the little king-bird. The turkey, on the contrary, hated redcoats, and would attack them courageously.

The tone of Samuel Adams was less flippant, but not less severe. His views were those of a statesman, and however groundless they may now seem, were expressed after the manner of a statesman. He was, he said, as sensible as any man ought to be of the great things done by the late army; he was as desirous as any man ought to be that the merit of these things should be gratefully acknowledged and rewarded by the country. Indeed, the people would have richly rewarded their defenders, in spite of their prejudice against the gratuity of five years' pay, had not the officers adopted a plan so disgusting to their feelings. It was truly wonderful that men should imagine that a people, who had freely spent blood and treasure in support of equal rights, should, the moment the struggle was over, be reconciled to the odious hereditary distinction of families. The country must indeed be humiliated and debased when men would patiently bear to see their fellows strutting among them with their assumed badges, and proudly boasting, "These are the distinctions of our blood." It was scarcely reasonable to suppose that all the officers held such an idea of haughty pre-eminence. But the human mind fell an easy prey to the thought of being raised above the common crowd; and whatever the fathers might do in their day, it was not improbable that their sons, when they perceived that the multitude had grown dizzy with long gazing, would go much farther, and take to themselves much more than the pageantry of nobility. He could not but look upon the order as a stride toward an hereditary military nobility as rapid as ever was made in so short a time, and could not but lament, as a grievous misfortune to the States,

that so illustrious a man as Washington sanctioned it.* But
what was it that induced these Cincinnati gentlemen, who
had undertaken to deliberate on matters which might essentially " concern the happiness and future dignity of the American empire," to admit European military subjects into their
society ?  Was there then no danger that a foreign influence
might prevail in America ?  Were they ignorant that foreigners wished to have weight in our councils ?  What good
could possibly come of the union of the two nations, so different in their politics, to deliberate on matters concerning the
safety, honor, and welfare of one ?  They had indeed once
been united in the pursuit of the same object; they had indeed of late been fighting side by side; but was it well to be
so sure the two nations would not one day have different
views, and very national and interested ones, too ?  Admitting that the Cincinnati had a right to form an order, and
deliberate on national subjects, had they a right to call in
foreign aid ?  This step was as impolitic as preposterous ;
nay, as dangerous as it would be for the United States to
admit a delegation of Frenchmen into Congress.

On the same side with Samuel was his cousin, John Adams.
He understood, he said, that in a communication sent from
Amsterdam he was reputed to be very violent against the
Order of the Cincinnati, and to have denounced it as a French
blessing.† That he thoroughly disapproved of the society
was true.  That he was violent against it was not true.  He
was not, he thought, a violent man.  And while he could not
look on in indifference at the introduction into America of an
order of chivalry, he had disapproved of the measure with as
much tranquillity, as much self-recollection, as much phlegm,
as if he had been a native full-blooded Dutchman.  He disapproved of it because he believed it to be contrary to the Confederation, and against the constitutions of the several States.
The society had been founded without the consent of the
Government.  What, he should like to know, would be said

---

* Samuel Adams to Elbridge Gerry, April 23, 1784.  See also Adams to
Gerry, April 19, 1784, and September 15, 1785.  Samuel Adams to John Adams,
December 16, 1784.

† Adams to Lafayette, March 24, 1784.  Works of John Adams.

in any country of Europe if a party of private gentlemen set up a new order of nobility without consulting the sovereign? If these things went on the Government would become weak indeed.*

But while the statesmen were busy complaining, the people betook themselves to action. Lampoons, pamphlets, and broadsides were published, denouncing the society in the strongest language. Candidates for legislative honors found themselves in possession of a theme for unending invective. The Independent Chronicle, a sturdy Whig journal printed at Boston, set forth in a lengthy paper what was undoubtedly the feeling of its readers in the matter. The institution of the Cincinnati, said the writer, is concerted to establish a complete personal distinction between the military dignities and the people who will henceforth be dubbed plebeians. It has been publicly asserted, and it has not been disproved, that the Order of the Cincinnati is full of danger to the rights of man; that it tends to the rapid introduction of nobility into America, and that kind of nobility which for centuries plagued and domineered over Europe. If this be so, if the Order threatens to introduce even the mildest form of nobility, then it becomes the duty of legislators, of governors, of magistrates, above all, of electors, to prevent, by every judicious means in their power, such an institution from gaining any strength in the Commonwealth.† The hint was soon taken. One of the order, who, at the spring election at Boston was running for senator, found his chances of election so much impaired by his blue ribbon that he came down to the polls on the eve of the voting, and, in the most solemn manner, declared his determination to withdraw from the society.‡ The site of the great New England college and the presence

---

* The opinions of Adams were shared by almost all noted Americans abroad. "Most of the Americans here," writes Lafayette, "are virulent against our association. Wadsworth must be excepted, and Dr. Franklin says but little, but Jay, Adams, and all the others, warmly blame the army." Lafayette to Washington, Paris, March 9, 1784. Writing from the same city, Jay says: "The institution of the Order of Cincinnatus does not, in the opinion of the wisest men whom I have heard speak on the subject, either do credit to those who formed and patronize, or to those who suffered it." Jay to G. Morris, February 10, 1784.

† Independent Chronicle, 1784.

‡ Samuel Adams to Gerry, April 19, 1784.

of so many grave and learned doctors had raised Cambridge to a high place among New England towns. It was universally allowed to be the centre of polite learning, and the inhabitants were believed to have acquired, by some mysterious process, much of the gravity of the place and to be more calm and deliberate in their actions than their neighbors. Not a little stir, therefore, was made when it was known that the men of Cambridge had deliberately instructed their representative in General Court to use his endeavors to have the Society of the Cincinnati suppressed. But the legislators of Massachusetts were not prepared for so extreme a measure, and contented themselves with declaring the society to be " dangerous to the peace, liberty, and safety of the Union." * Rhode Island disfranchised such of her citizens as were members of the Order,† and the opposition then spread to South Carolina. Of the thirteen States, South Carolina was perhaps the one in which titles, honors, wealth, illustrious lineage, all things which in other lands make up nobility, were most highly prized. Yet the chief men of the State were, with scarce an exception, violent against the Cincinnati, and among the chief men the most bitter in opposition was Ædanus Burke. ‡ Burke was an Irishman. He had been educated at St. Omer for a priest. But his spirit was restless, and a life of wandering and excitement was more to his taste than a life of vigils and of prayers. He soon set forth on his travels, and went first to the West Indies, wandered from island to island, and, disgusted with the heat of the climate, the laziness of the people, and the swarm of loathsome creep-

---

* The action of the General Court is given in full in the American Remembrancer for 1783, Part iii, p. 364.

† " We hear that the State of Rhode Island is determined to disfranchise any and every person who is a member of the Order of the Cincinnati, and render them incapable of holding any post of honor and trust in the Government." Freeman's Journal, Philadelphia, April 28, 1784. For the feeling toward the Cincinnati in Philadelphia, see Pennsylvania Packet, June 12, 1784. General Knox, in his letter to Washington, February 21, 1784, mentions the appointment of a committee by the Massachusetts Legislature to investigate the Cincinnati, but expresses a doubt as to whether the committee would ever bring in any report.

‡ Much of my information regarding Burke has been derived from J. B. O'Neall's Bench and Bar of South Carolina, vol. i, pp. 35-53.

ing things, went on to Charleston. At Charleston he chose
to labor in that profession in which so many of his countrymen
have, in all parts of the world, risen to distinction. A fluent
speaker, a ready debater, a man never at a loss for a quick rep-
artee, he possessed what were then the requisites of a good lawyer. Practice soon came to him, and with practice came renown. It was not long before his jovial face, his good sayings,
his bulls, his brogue, and his "'fore God, sir," were as well
known in the State as in the court-room. His eccentricity, his
fits of absent-mindedness, his wit, furnished scores of amusing
anecdotes which have since his day, like the jests of Hiero-
cles, become the common property of newsmen and story-
tellers, and been related, with little change, of half the judges
and lawyers of the West. When the war opened Burke deserted his clients and joined the southern army as a volunteer
major, and served till, in 1778, he was elected judge. But
his judicial functions were brought to a speedy close when
the English troops overran the State. He then went back to
the army, served till the peace, when he took his seat on the
bench of the Supreme Court of South Carolina. But the
gravity, the deliberation, the even-handed justice which marked
all his rulings as a judge, seem to have deserted him when he
turned his thoughts to subjects not judicial. The moment he
put on his black gown and bands he was the impartial judge.
The moment he took up his pen to write he was the irascible
Irishman. As an Irishman he felt an intense hatred of aristocratic pretensions in general. As a stanch Whig he felt a
peculiar hatred of aristocratic pretensions in America in particular. When, therefore, the news came to him of the
founding of the Society of the Cincinnati, of its purpose,
and of the mummeries with which the members were initiated
at New York, his indignation went out of all bounds. He
determined to attack it. There was, at that time, but one
way in which the attack could be made, and that way was in
a pamphlet. Burke therefore put forth a pamphlet which he
called "Considerations on the Order of the Cincinnati," and,
as it would have been a most serious breach of custom to write
under his own name, he chose to do so under that of Cassius. His motto was, "Sound ye the Trumpet in Zion." The

pamphlet was a success from the first, was reprinted in every
State, was widely read, and attributed to many hands. A few
copies even crossed the Atlantic, and found their way to
Paris, where one of them fell in the way of Mirabeau.

The Count, who had but lately escaped from one of his
many imprisonments, was much taken both with the matter
and style of the book, and, though his time was greatly occupied with schemes for the completion of the Louvre, for the
formation of a national picture-gallery, with Cagliostro and
the diamond necklace, with the Bank of St. Charles, with long
dissertations on stock-jobbing and the opening of the Scheldt,
he turned from these diverting pursuits and put the pamphlet
of Cassius into French. But before his work was ended he
went over the channel, taking with him a bundle of half-finished manuscript and a letter from Dr. Franklin.* The book
came out in London,† and had some sale. It was indeed
twice translated into English, and afterward into German.‡
But in Paris it was coldly received. There the Cincinnati
were high in favor. They were patronized by the King;
they were petted by the Court. The decoration appeared
in the royal presence side by side with the collars of the
Golden Fleece. Men of all ranks hastened to lay claim to
the coveted eagle. One had stood upon the deck of the
Bon Homme Richard on that memorable day when Paul

---

* See a letter from Franklin to Benjamin Vaughan, September 7, 1784. It is
stated in Mémoires de Mirabeau, t. iv, p. 145, that "l'autre motif (for going to
England) était le besoin de compléter les documens dont il composait ses Consi-
dérations sur l'ordre de Cincinnatus."

† The book came out at London late in September, 1784, under the title, Con-
sidérations sur l'ordre de Cincinnatus ou imitation d'un pamphlet anglo-américain, par le comte de Mirabeau. Londres, J. Johnson, 1784, un vol. On the title-
page was the epigram, "La gloire des guerriers ne saurait être complète que
lorsqu'ils savent rempli les devoirs des citoyens."

‡ To the charge of plagiarism Mirabeau makes this defence: "J'ai donné mon
livre sur les Cincinnati pour l'imitation d'un pamphlet anglo-américain. C'est
dans ma préface que se trouve l'indication de la feuille de cet Ædanus Burke qui,
dit-on, réclame mon ouvrage. Et si ceux qui la citent aujourd'hui, l'avaient seu-
lement lue, ils auraient compris qu'ils réuissiraient difficilement à faire passer un
gros volume, deux fois traduit en anglais (à Londres et en Amérique), et qu'on
va publier en allemand, pour la traduction de 16 pages in-8°, ou 24 pages in-12°;
car le très-estimable pamphlet d'Ædanus Burke a été impremé sous ces deux
formats." Mémoires de Mirabeau, t. iv, p. 160, note, ed. 1834.

Jones, with his ship fast to the rigging of the Serapis, fought the English hand to hand. Another had been proclaimed at the head of the army for gallant services at the siege of Savannah. A third had languished in an English prison for the cause of the States. The eldest son of De Kalb spoke of the claims of his father. Chevalier de Lameth pointed to the wounds he received as he stormed the trenches at Yorktown.* Nor did this enthusiasm for the Cincinnati soon die out. On the twelfth of July, five years later, when the French Revolution may be said to have got really under way, Camille Desmoulins rushed from the Café de Foy, climbed upon a table, and proposed a cockade. "What," said he to the multitude that swayed about him, "What shall it be? Shall it be green, the color of hope? or shall it be blue, the color of the Cincinnati?" And the crowd shouted back, "Let it be green, green, the color of hope." †

At home the strictures of Burke called forth several replies, but they were judged such poor performances that they went off slowly, and many years afterward, when the present century was well advanced, when Jefferson was in the White House, when the Cincinnati were quite forgotten, copies were picked up in the bookstalls by the curious for a few coppers apiece.‡

Angry as the people were with the officers, they were in a still worse humor with the men. When the war was over, a clamor was raised that the army should instantly be disbanded.

---

* See a very interesting article on the Cincinnati in the Pennsylvania Magazine of History and Biography.

† The scene has been described by Mignet, one of the earliest historians of the French Revolution, and whose book, we are told, was revised by Lafayette. " Il (Camille Desmoulins) propose de prendre des cocades pour se reconnaître et pour se défendre: 'Voulez-vous,' dit-il, 'le vert, couleur de l'espérance, ou le rouge, couleur de l'ordre libre de Cincinnatus?' 'Le vert, le vert,' répond la multitude. S'orateur descend de la table, attache une feuille d'arbre à son chapeau, tout le monde l'imite; les marronniers du Palais sont presque depouillés de leur feuilles, et cette troupe se rendre en tumulte chez le sculpteur Curtius." Histoire de la Révolution Française depuis 1789 jusqu'en 1814, par F. A. Mignet, t. i, pp. 66, 67. Also, Camille Desmoulins, Œuvres, ed. 1879, t. ii, pp. 49, 50, 92.

‡ One of the most elaborate of the answers is Observations on a Late Pamphlet entitled, Considerations upon the Society or Order of the Cincinnati, etc. By an Obscure Individual, 1783. See, also, Considerations on the Order of the Cincinnati, Boston Gazette, May 26, 1788.

But a large arrearage of pay was due, and the troops seemed little inclined to lay down their arms till it had been paid to the last shilling. In this strait Congress passed several acts for the relief of the army. These the people received with great indignation, and on several occasions the wrath of the populace flamed so high that the objectionable acts were condemned at town-meetings.

Such had been the fate of the army bill for the commutation of half-pay for life to five years' full-pay at once. Late in the fall of 1783 a suggestion was made by Washington to give a life pension of half-pay to every officer and soldier who had served through the war. The idea seemed a good one, was highly approved, and a bill embodying it soon brought in and passed. This, a few months later, was repealed, and a new ordinance voted which commuted the life-pay into five years' full-pay in one sum. As to the wisdom of this course there can now be but one opinion. It was greatly to the advantage both of the Government and the army. It was no more than reasonable to suppose that the majority of the men who were to receive the money would live more than ten years. A great saving would therefore be effected by commuting the life pension to half-pay for ten, or, what was precisely the same thing, full-pay for five years. The pensioners would, moreover, be greatly assisted by the payment at one time of so large a sum. They were poor; their needs were many and pressing. Some time must necessarily elapse before they could establish themselves in any business or in any profession that would yield them a competence. The wages that would be doled out to them annually would be, at best, but a pittance. But if this pittance were increased tenfold, and paid down in one lump, the value of it would, by immediate payment, be increased tenfold more.

Considerations like these, however, had no weight with the multitude. When they contrasted the number of dollars it was proposed to give to each soldier, from the general down to the private, with the number of dollars yielded by their potato-patches and their wheatfields, they cried out that they were about to be loaded with unbearable taxes that an aris-

tocracy of money might be created.  All over the country the
Commutation Act met with small favor.  The war was over.
Peace had come.  Men forgot the services of the army, and
thought only of their own poverty and the great sum to be
wrung from them as a reward for their deliverers.  It was
all they could do, they declared, to pay the taxes now laid
upon them.  This new levy would take the houses from over
their heads and the clothes from off their backs before it was
paid.  The plain duty of Government was to cut down, not
to increase, expenditures.  This feeling was particularly strong
in New England.  In Massachusetts the voice of Samuel
Adams was against commutation, and the voice of Adams was
heard with respect.

Indeed, no man had for so long a time performed so great
a part in eastern politics.  He had come early into public
life, and was famous as a stanch patriot when men who afterwards sat in high places were busy with their school-books
or their toys.  Old men, whose memories went back to the
early part of the century, could remember no time for forty
years before the war when Adams had not been foremost in a
wise and temperate resistance to the encroachments of the
Crown.  In part this is to be ascribed to the natural bent of
his mind; but much is also due to his training.  The elder
Adams was a well-to-do Boston brewer who had always taken
a lively interest in colonial politics; had been a member of
that renowned club whose name, slightly corrupted, has enriched our language with the word caucus,* and had kept
open house for his political friends.†  The lad, therefore, grew
up surrounded by tax-collectors and select-men, judges and
pamphleteers, and it cannot be doubted that the discussions
he often overheard strongly affected his future career.  From
the day he entered Harvard he was constantly declaiming on

---

* It is stated on the authority of the celebrated Dr. Gordon, the historian,
that, in 1724, Samuel Adams, the elder, "and about twenty others, one or two
from the north end of the town, where all ship business was carried on, used to
meet, make a caucus, and lay their plans for introducing certain persons to public places of trust and power."  From this calkers' club of ship-building mechanics comes, by a slight corruption, the word caucus.  See some remarks in Wells's
Life of Samuel Adams, vol. i, p. 3.

† Life of Adams, vol. i, p. 3.

the theme of liberty. On the day he quitted Harvard he pronounced an able oration on the right of resistance, and from thenceforth to the close of his life was devoted to the interests of the colonies.\* No single man did so much to promote the success of the Revolution. While others were busy inciting the people, he was engaged in providing them with leaders. His eye was upon every young man of parts and promise. It was his delight to make their acquaintance, and, while he counselled and helped them in their worldly affairs, warned them of the dangers that threatened the country, and enlisted them heartily in the good cause.† He was the steady friend of Church, the poet, and of Joseph Warren, the martyr of Bunker Hill. He started Hancock upon his political career; he discovered the eloquence of Josiah Quincy; he gave John Adams that case which brought him for the first time into public notice.

In politics Samuel Adams was of the school of Otis and Thatcher. But his clear head and even temper enabled him to maintain that just balance without which his party would have rushed headlong to its destruction. When the fiery eloquence of more excitable men had persuaded the multitude that England should be defied, that the acts of Hutchinson should be withstood, that the Stamp Act should be resisted, Adams was chosen as the man to say how it should be done. He was as forward as any in resistance, but resistance of a strictly legal kind. He would countenance no violence till every means the ingenuity of lawyers could devise had been exhausted, and he would then have just so much as was necessary, and no more. When the people were calling for summary vengeance on the soldiers arrested in the Boston massacre, he insisted that they should be placed on trial. When the mob were for destroying the tea, he urged that it should be sent back to England. Some of the opinions he held, and some of the opposition he made, have, in later days, been shown to be erroneous and ill-timed. He disapproved of the return of the Tories. He pronounced the Cincinnati a dangerous body. It was only under great pressure that he was induced to cast his vote in favor of the Constitution. But it

---

\* Life of Adams, vol. i.    † Correspondence of J. Adams, vol. x, p. 364.

was well known that his opinion, whatever it might be, was
the result of careful deliberation, and that he stood out against
no measure except from a sincere conviction that it was not
likely to promote the public good.   At no time was this more
conspicuously illustrated than at the present.   He denounced
the commutation bill in unmeasured terms, yet it was about
to put several thousands of dollars into the pocket of his much-
loved son.*

In Connecticut a more vigorous resistance was offered.   A
State convention was called to meet at Middletown, and delegates from many towns came up.   Much invective was indulged in, and great complaints made.   But nothing was done.
The gathering broke up, and was for a long time made the subject of sport in bad poems and worse lampoons.†   Nor were
arguments of a better kind wanting.   Many noted characters
came to the support of Congress; but one of the most earnest
in their ranks was a young man then all unknown to fame,
but who, by the sheer force of his natural abilities, raised himself in after years to great eminence and made his name a
household word wherever the English language is spoken.
Noah Webster was then in his twenty-fifth year.   He believed
in commutation, strongly disapproved the conduct of the town-
meetings, and, in a series of essays, ‡ stoutly maintained the
justice and wisdom of the course pursued by Congress, pointed
out the short-sightedness of the pot-house politicians who were
clamoring so loudly against its acts, and adjured all men as
they loved liberty to stand firm on the side of Government.
These papers were far from contemptibly written, were widely
read, and elicited for the young author the hearty praises of
Governor Trumbull.

Thankless and ungrateful as may seem the ill-humor the
country was in with the army, no small part of it is to be ascribed to a number of acts for which the rank and file could
blame no one but themselves.   Not long after the cessation of

---

* Wells's Life of Samuel Adams, vol. iii, p. 178.

† The convention met on the sixteenth of December, 1783.   A good specimen
of the ridicule it aroused is a satirical poem on its proceedings in the Pennsylvania Packet, January 8, 1784.

‡ They came out in the Connecticut Courant under the name Honestus.

hostilities, and while the Peace Commissioners were still wrangling over the articles of the treaty, a cantonment of the troops was formed at Newburg not far from the spot where a few years before the boom had been thrown across the river to impede the progress of British vessels. The discipline of the camp was lax; the wants and sufferings of the troops many and great. They were ill-shod. Their clothes could with difficulty be kept from dropping off their backs. Often the misery of cold was augmented by the pangs of hunger, for the roads were in such a condition that, though the highest cash price was offered for corn and wheat, the farmers could not drag their produce to camp.* The thoughts of the soldiers, diverted from war, were speedily turned to their wretched condition. Complaints, at first heard but as muttered grumblings, were soon spoken boldly out at the mess-table and the camp-fire. The war, they said, was over. The very next packet from London might, not improbably, bring the treaty. The British troops would be withdrawn. American troops would no longer be needed. Congress would disband them, and what, in that event, would become of their hard-earned pay so long overdue? The policy of Congress was clearly to postpone all action on the matter till after the peace, and then turn them adrift to starve or live as best they could on the charity of the country. Good friends had repeatedly made known their condition to Congress. Nay, they had themselves presented to that body a memorial drawn up in the most respectful and becoming language. Yet no action had been taken, and, what was more, no disposition had been shown to take any action. While in this frame of mind the discontent of the army was yet more fomented by a few restless and aspiring spirits, till, one morning in April, 1783, the camp was white with copies of an address which appeared without signature. The pure English and the style were such as would at any other time, and under any other circumstances, have excited admiration and applause. But the spirit

---

* Pickering, in one of his letters written at this time, states that the roads were so bad that the farmers "could not bring their produce to market, though offered cash on delivery." Life of Timothy Pickering by Octavius Pickering, vol. i, p. 392. Pickering was the quartermaster.

was plainly one of mutiny and rebellion. The troops were, however, thoroughly out of humor, and the writer with great dexterity made use of just such arguments as had for many weeks past been going the rounds of the camp. He began the first address with some account of himself.* He was a soldier. He too had left his home to bear arms in defence of the rights of his injured country. He had endured much. He had felt the cold hand of poverty without a murmur, and beheld the insolence of wealth without a sigh. It had been his hope that, as the dark clouds of adversity scattered and the sunshine of peace and better fortune broke forth, the severity of Government would relax, and that justice, nay, more than justice, that gratitude would blaze out on the little band of men whose hands had upheld and steadied the Union in all the dark stages of its passage from impending servitude to acknowledged independence and to peace. After a pursuit of eight years their object was at last reached. They had placed the country in the chair of independency. Peace had now returned to bless whom? A country ready and willing to redress their wrongs, to cherish and fittingly reward their services? Had peace come to bless a land courting them to return to private life, and there enjoy the independency their courage had purchased? Was this the case? Or rather had peace come to a land trampling on their rights and turning a deaf ear to their cries of distress? More than once had they made known their wants to Congress. How had they been answered? If this were their treatment while their services were still indispensable to the security of the State, what might they not expect when no longer of use, when their

---

* The anonymous letter is given in full in the Journals of Congress for the year 1783. Who wrote the Newburg Addresses was long as much in dispute as who wrote the Letters of Junius. Gordon, whose History of the American Revolution came out a few months later, says (Letter XVII) that they were known to be the work of Major John Armstrong. But Johnson, the author of a Life of General Greene, many years later attributed them to the last man who would have written them, Gouverneur Morris. This was too much for Armstrong, and, in a review of the book that came out in the United States Magazine for January, 1823, he labored hard to prove a claim to the authorship of the addresses. He was successful. But he gained small credit There is now no doubt that Armstrong wrote them, that Gates set him on, and that Barbar, the assistant adjutant-general, copied and distributed them through the army.

swords should be taken from their sides, and no marks of military distinction left them but their poverty and their scars? Was it just that the army should be the only sufferer by the revolution? Was there one among the troops who would consent to the deep degradation of dragging out a life of poverty, or of wading through the vile mire of dependency? If so, let him go, and go knowing that he carried with him the jests of Whigs and Tories. Let him go, starve, and be forgotten. But it was high time that those who were of a different mind came to some determination as to what they would bear and suffer. Above all, let them change the milk-and-water style of their late memorial, act the man, and assume a bolder tone.

This document was read by the troops with strong manifestations of approval, and the next day named for the discussion of their grievances and the determination of a plan of action for their relief. Washington the next day heard with deep mortification of the action of his troops. With all speed he issued an address to the army, assembled his officers, assured them of his unalterable confidence in their loyalty, and avowed his disbelief that one of their number was the author of the letter. He then retired and left them to deliberate unrestrained by his presence. Gates was placed in the chair. Some ill-natured remarks were made, but an address was finally voted assuring the commander-in-chief of the undying love of his troops, of their disapproval of the sentiments of the letter, and their readiness to wait longer.

The storm had now spent itself. But the effect made on the people was deep and lasting. Nor was this at all diminished by an event which almost at the same time took place at Philadelphia. Indeed, the news of the disorders at Newburg had scarce been carried to the newspapers of Virginia when it was followed by intelligence of a yet more startling kind. Some raw recruits of the Pennsylvania line were in camp at Lancaster. Their pay was long overdue. They had become unruly, and shown signs of a spirit of mutiny that had with difficulty been kept down by the officers. Suddenly, on the nineteenth of June, 1783, word was sent to Congress that eighty of the troops were on their march to the city, that they were determined to have a settlement of their accounts, and were making threats against the bank. Late on the twentieth the mutineers entered Philadelphia, and on the twenty-first, joined by some veterans, drew up in line before the State House, where Congress was sitting. Good order was kept till the can had gone freely round, when a few windows were broken, and a volley of taunts, jibes, and obscene jests poured forth. Congress in alarm dispatched General St. Clair to expostulate, but with no effect. A message was then sent for the second time to the Council of the State, which sat under the same roof, demanding protection. The President answered that he could do nothing for the relief of Congress. It was true, he said, that he had a small body of militia at his command. But he could not venture to call them out, for he was by no means sure that they would act against their brothers in arms. Some outrage must first be committed; some property must be destroyed.* It was moved that Congress adjourn instantly. This, a member asserted, would be an exhibition of terror disgraceful to Congress as a body and to the members individually, and the motion was voted down. That night Congress rose and three days later fled to Princeton, where quarters were found in the college.†

The flight was viewed in many lights. A few men of sense, while they held that no danger was to have been apprehended, bitterly lamented the great lack of a proper federal spirit on the part of Pennsylvania. What, said they, will be thought abroad of a government which no State will, in an hour of need, undertake to defend? Others could see in it only matter for jest. But the multitude were mean enough in spirit to attribute it to motives worthy of their own bad hearts. Some shrewd ones, it was asserted, who hated Pennsylvania, had seized the opportunity to get Congress out of that State. They had magnified the danger. They had worked upon the cowardice of their fellows, and were now

---

* " He (Dickinson) thought that without some outrages on persons or property the militia could not be relied on." Madison Account in Elliot's Debates, vol. i, p. 92.

† An account of the whole affair is given by Madison in Elliot's Debates, vol. i, pp. 92–94; and by Hamilton in a letter to Reed. Hamilton's Works, vol. i, pp. 374–393.

congratulating each other on the success of the scheme.
This talk was firmly believed in Philadelphia and New York.*
No names were mentioned, but it was insinuated that Hamilton was one of the plotters. † Hamilton was a new member,
had been very active during the session, and was chairman of
the committee that sought aid of the Council. So flatly was
this charge made that, though a cautious man and not much
given to rushing into print, he thought quite seriously of vindicating himself and held a long correspondence with Madison on the subject.

While the indignation excited by these acts of the troops
was still fresh, a motion was made in Congress to create a land establishment of a few hundred men. The posts along the western frontier, it was argued, are, in defiance of the stipulations of the treaty, still in the hands of the British. Royal
agents are at work inciting the border tribes to constant acts
of depredation. The western settlements are too weak to defend themselves. To talk of the abolition of the army is,
therefore, to talk like a madman or a Tory. The opponents
of the measure, waiving all question of the need of troops,
vehemently denied the right of Congress to levy them. No
one, it was said, pretended to deny that the delegates of the
States in Congress assembled had the right to raise troops in
time of war. But it was far from clear that this authority
could be construed into a right to make requisitions on the
States for a land-force in times of peace. To say that the
number was small, only eight hundred and ninety-six men,
and the time limited to three years, was no defence. If the
law could be interpreted to justify a requisition for a small
number of men for a short time, what was there in it to forbid
a requisition for a great number of men for an unlimited
time? This was simply taking away the power of the States
to deliberate on the matter and leaving them but the duty of
obeying. More than this, it should be remembered that Congress was already clothed with power to make foreign and

---

* "The prevailing idea is (in Philadelphia) that the actors in the removal of
Congress were influenced by the desire of getting them out of the city, and the
generality of the remainder by timidity, some say passion." Hamilton to Madison, July 6, 1783.

† See a letter from Hamilton to Madison, June 29, 1783.

domestic loans and to issue bills of credit. Add to this the right to enlist troops in time of peace and that body would instantly be armed with such coercive means as might well be alarming to the country. The history of Greece, the history of Rome, and the history of England were then ransacked for examples of the ills of a standing army, and the conclusion reached that nothing but sophistry or Toryism could reconcile an army in time of peace with republican principles. Armed bodies of men were, it was claimed, and always had been dangerous to the liberty of a free people. They had often been made destructive weapons for the establishment of despotism. If a republic were to be set up in the very heart of Europe and surrounded on every hand by States hostile to the principles of liberty, maintaining great armies, and ready on a day's notice to send them over the border, then indeed a peace establishment would be absolutely necessary. But the United States was not in the heart of Europe. Three thousand miles of water, which it took a month to cross, separated her from the nearest warlike kingdom, and to talk of the need of a land-force in peaceful times, in such a country, was absurd. As to the Indians, every one knew they were no match for white men and could easily be held in check by small garrisons in the frontier forts assisted by the settlers.

Such was the persistency with which these objections were urged that Congress was soon as divided in opinion as the people. Motion after motion was brought forward to create a land-force, and as often lost. But at length a resolution was reached on a motion introduced by Elbridge Gerry. After a long preamble in which he rehearsed what may be regarded as the popular arguments against standing armies, he moved that a recommendation, not a requisition, be sent to the States to raise troops to do garrison duty in the frontier posts soon to be given up by England. In this form the motion was put and carried.* A week later the few troops in the service of Congress were disbanded. Eighty men were, however, retained. Twenty-five were sent to guard the military stores at Fort Pitt, and fifty-five to do a like duty at West Point. The day following an ordinance passed recom-

---

* Journals of Congress, May 26, 1784.

mending the four States of Connecticut, New York, New
Jersey, and Pennsylvania to raise seven hundred troops to
garrison the frontier for one year.*

The army having no longer any existence, the office of
Secretary of War, long held by General Lincoln, was left
vacant.   With Lincoln retired into private life one whose
name is, even at this distance of time, never mentioned without awakening sentiments of gratitude and respect.   While
the army matters were still under dispute Congress listened
with deep regret to the resignation of Robert Morris who,
for three years, had held the post of Financier.

Morris was an Englishman, but had come over to the colonies while a mere stripling, had grown up with the country,
as the phrase went, and had come to think himself in all
respects an American.   He was not long in Philadelphia when
he was put out to work and began to run errands and sweep
out a counting-house.   But he was no ordinary lad, and before he was thirty was a partner in the great mercantile house
of the Willings.   There he acquired immense wealth, and
that intimate knowledge of the intricacies of commerce and
of trade which stood him in such good need when, a few
years later, he found himself in Congress surrounded by judges
and lawyers, small traders, and petty farmers.   His riches, his
genial manners, and the princely hospitality he delighted to
display made his house a favorite resort in the city.   It was
accounted one of the most magnificent in the country, and
excited the admiration of men accustomed to the luxury and
splendor of kings.   When the war opened he was sent a
delegate to the Continental Congress, sat in that body for
three years, put his name to the Declaration of Independence,
signed the Articles of Confederation, and, though he was seldom on his feet to speak, exercised a powerful influence.   He
was a member of the secret committee charged with procuring
military supplies from abroad.   But it was as one of the commercial committee and of the committee of finance that he
particularly distinguished himself.   The great things which
he then did were long remembered, and, three years after, in
a day of trial, when the treasury was empty, when the credit

---

* Journals of Congress, June 3, 1784.

of the Government was gone, when the continental bills had ceased to circulate, Congress turned to him as the only man who could correct the disorders of the public money and establish a sound and healthy credit. The place of Superintendent of Finances was offered him. He took it, and almost immediately the effect of his business habits and vigorous mind was felt. Many reforms were instituted, many sources of expenditure were cut off. The requisitions on the States were more firmly enforced. Their quotas were more promptly paid, and, when the credit of the Government was not sufficient, he gladly pledged his own.

In this work he was assisted by a young man who, though he bore the same name, was not of the same blood. Gouverneur Morris was a native of New York, and came of that family whose name is still given to a vast district of the city beyond the Harlem river. Of all the young men who had then reached fame he was the most promising. He had been bred to the law and early became eminent at the bar. Before he was twenty-four he took his seat in the Colonial Assembly. Before he was twenty-six he was sent a delegate to the Continental Congress. There he soon approved himself a politician, a financier, an agreeable speaker, a fine scholar, a wit, a man devoted to business, yet noted for his social accomplishments. No one played a better hand at ombre or quadrille, told a better story, or made a more agreeable companion at a dinner-party or an assembly. But in Congress he was an indefatigable worker. An eloquent speaker, a close reasoner, a shrewd observer, he at all times commanded the ear of the House; but it was as a committeeman that he made himself especially felt. His name was down upon the journals as a member of three very important committees—that for the conduct of foreign negotiations, that for the organization of the army, and that on national finances. It was while busily engaged on the finances that his unusual abilities attracted the attention of Robert Morris. The knowledge which he displayed on the most puzzling money matters, and the acuteness with which he reasoned on the most intricate questions of commerce and trade would have done credit to the oldest merchant in the States, but was remarkable for one

whose life had been spent in drawing up briefs and trying
causes. When, therefore, the office of Superintendent of the
Finances was made in 1781, Gouverneur Morris became assistant to his illustrious namesake. Precisely what services
he rendered can now never be known. But one of his many
labors deserves extended mention. He was the founder of
our system of national coinage.

There is probably no man now living whose memory goes
back to a time when the American people were without a national coinage. There is therefore no man now living who
can form a perfectly just conception of the evils of the time
when there was no national treasury, no banks, and when the
old stockings of the people were full of coins bearing the
stamps of many foreign mints, called by all manner of names,
and expressing different values in different places. Yet there
are many men who can distinctly recall a time which nearly
resembles this; a time when the coinage, though national in
name, was not national in use ; when there was still one money
for account and another for exchange ; when tradesmen still
expressed the price of their wares in terms unknown to the
Federal system ; and when there were still in circulation coins
whose names are so utterly forgotten as to sound strange to
the ears of a generation accustomed to speak of cents, of
dimes, and of quarters. Fifty years ago the silver pieces
which passed from hand to hand under the name of small
change were largely made up of foreign coins. They had
been in circulation long before the war for independence,
had seen much service, and were none the better for the wear
and tear they had sustained. The two commonest were the
eighth and sixteenth of the Spanish milled dollar, and these,
taking the country through, passed under seven names. In
New York and North Carolina, where eight shillings made
a dollar, the eighth was a shilling, and went by that name.
From New Jersey to Maryland the same coin was nearly
equalled by eleven pence, and was there called the eleven-
penny-bit or the levy ; but became, for a like reason, ninepence in New England. In the same way the sixteenth of
a dollar was called sixpence in New York, five-penny-bit, or
the fip, in Pennsylvania, and fourpence in New England. In

Louisiana, the people called it the picayune. Sixpence, in Massachusetts, meant eight and a third cents; a shilling meant sixteen and two thirds cents; two and threepence was thirty-seven and a half cents; three shillings was fifty cents; four and six was seventy-five cents; nine shillings was a dollar and a half. A merchant, therefore, in place of asking twenty-five cents for a yard of his taffeta or a pound of his cheese, would have demanded one and six, a price which the purchaser of the taffeta or the cheese would, if he were so disposed, have paid by putting down the silver coin familiar to us as the quarter of a dollar. Some shilling pieces and sixpence pieces were to be found in circulation down even to the civil war, and were, with the fips, the levies, and the pistareens, the last relics of a time happily passed away. In 1830 only the small change was of foreign coinage. In 1784 the entire coin of the land, except coppers, was the product of foreign mints. English guineas, crowns, shillings and pence were still paid over the counters of shops and taverns, and with them were mingled many French and Spanish and some German coins. Indeed, the close connection the colonies had held with the traders of the Spanish Indies, and the nearness of the Spanish possessions at the mouth of the Mississippi and along the Gulf of Mexico, had made Americans familiar with all denominations of Spanish coins. They had long circulated freely among all classes of buyers and sellers. One of them, the Spanish milled dollar, had become as much a unit of value as the pound. Others were of great value, were carefully stowed away in secret drawers, or rolled in old stockings and hidden in the darkest hole in the attic, or buried under the boards of the floor, whence they emerged only as quarter-day came round, or the taxes fell due. Such an one was the Johannes, always called the joe, a gold coin which in June, 1784, was received and paid at the newly established Bank of New York at sixteen dollars.* Next to the joe in value was the doubloon, then

---

* New York Packet of June 7, 1784. The value of the English guinea is there given as $4$\frac{9}{8}$; of the French guinea as $4\frac{5}{9}$; of the carolin as $4\frac{7}{9}$; of the chequin as $1\frac{9}{8}$. In the Carolinas three other pieces of coin circulated that were seldom seen in the north—the German piece, worth £1 3s. 4d.; the half-German piece, valued at 11s. 8d.; and the ducat, worth 9s. 4d. There also were quarter-joes and eighth-joes. See Pennsylvania Packet, November 28, 1785.

considered to be worth fifteen dollars. The half-joe went at eight dollars, the double Spanish pistole at seven dollars and forty-eight ninety sixths, and the pistole at half that value. The moidore was a six-dollar piece. These, with the English guinea and half-guinea, the French guinea, the carolin, the five and the two and a half moidore, the double johannes, the chequin, the quarter and eighth johannes, and the French pistole, made up the list of gold coins. The small change was of silver; and among the silver coins were the Spanish milled dollar, the half, quarter, eighth, and sixteenth of a dollar, the English crown, the French crown, the English shilling, the sixpence, and the pistareen. The copper coins were pennies and French sous. Each of these coins, again, expressed five different values, for it could be translated into sterling money and the four local currencies of the States.*

These values, of course, applied to no pieces which were not true and of full weight, for counterfeiters and clippers had long been busy, and had at last brought the coin to such a state that it passed by weight and not by tale. One of the favorite tricks of the counterfeiters was to turn French sous into Spanish moidores. The sou was a small copper piece, worth about a cent, so closely resembling the gold moidore that when it was gilded over it readily passed with the careless for the Spanish piece worth thirty-six shillings. Another trick was to wash coppers with silver and pass them off in a handful of change as English sixpences. But the clipping was worse

| * NAME OF COIN. | Sterling money. | | New England and Virginia. | | | New York and North Carolina. | | | New Jersey, Penna., Dela., and Maryland. | | | South Carolina and Georgia. | | |
|---|---|---|---|---|---|---|---|---|---|---|---|---|---|---|
| GOLD. | £ | s. | d. | £ | s. | d. | £ | s. | d. | £ | s. | d. | £ | s. | d. |
| Johannes ..... | 3 | 12 | 0 | 4 | 16 | 0 | 6 | 8 | 0 | 6 | 0 | 0 | 4 | 0 | 0 |
| Half-johannes.. | 1 | 16 | 0 | 2 | 8 | 0 | 3 | 4 | 0 | 3 | 0 | 0 | 2 | 0 | 0 |
| Doubloon.. ... | 3 | 6 | 0 | 4 | 8 | 0 | 5 | 16 | 0 | 5 | 12 | 6 | 3 | 10 | 0 |
| Moidore....... | 1 | 7 | 0 | 1 | 16 | 0 | 2 | 8 | 0 | 2 | 5 | 0 | 1 | 8 | 0 |
| English guinea. | 1 | 1 | 0 | 1 | 8 | 0 | 1 | 17 | 0 | 1 | 15 | 0 | 1 | 1 | 9 |
| French guinea.. | 1 | 1 | 0 | 1 | 7 | 6 | 1 | 16 | 0 | 1 | 14 | 6 | 1 | 1 | 5 |
| Spanish pistole. | 0 | 16 | 6 | 1 | 2 | 0 | 1 | 9 | 0 | 1 | 8 | 0 | 0 | 18 | 0 |
| French pistole.. | 0 | 16 | 0 | 1 | 2 | 0 | 1 | 8 | 0 | 1 | 7 | 6 | 0 | 17 | 6 |
| SILVER. | | | | | | | | | | | | | | | |
| Crown........ | 0 | 5 | 0 | 0 | 6 | 8 | 0 | 8 | 9 | 0 | 8 | 3 | 0 | 5 | 0 |
| Dollar........ | 0 | 4 | 6 | 0 | 6 | 0 | 0 | 8 | 0 | 0 | 7 | 6 | 0 | 4 | 8 |
| Shilling....... | 0 | 1 | 0 | 0 | 1 | 4 | 0 | 1 | 9 | 0 | 1 | 8 | 0 | 1 | 0 |
| Sixpence...... | 0 | 0 | 6 | 0 | 0 | 8 | 0 | 0 | 10½ | 0 | 0 | 10 | 0 | 0 | 6 |
| Pistareen...... | 0 | 0 | 10¾ | 0 | 1 | 2 | 0 | 1 | 7 | 0 | 1 | 6 | 0 | 0 | 11 |

than the counterfeiting, for scarce a coin from a joe to a pistareen could be found which had not at some time been subjected to the shears. For much of the clipping and paring
the people were to be held responsible; but the Government
itself had, in an hour of dire extremity, resorted to the same
practice as a desperate means of increasing its funds. In 1782
a great sum came over from France, as another addition to
the thousands of livres already loaned by Louis, and with it
came a solemn assurance that this loan was indeed the last;
that the royal treasury was empty; that the King could loan
no more. The coins were therefore to be doled out with the
utmost frugality. Many were bright and of full weight, and
full weight in France was far above the weight required in
America. The people, moreover, were then paying and receiving coin in payment by tale. If at such a time the Government were to pay out by tale the overweight guineas, the
Treasury would be the loser by a goodly sum; for it was as
certain as anything could be that the very first man who received a handful of the pieces would at once carry them to
the nearest goldsmith, and, for a penny each, have them reduced to the lowest limit allowed by law. That the Government should be impoverished that creditors might be enriched beyond their just dues, seemed quite unreasonable.
When, therefore, some of the coins were sent to Timothy
Pickering to be used in payment of the debts of the quartermaster's department, there came with them orders that he
himself should clip them, as the Government was too poor to
bear the charge of the goldsmiths. The duty was one from
which naturally he shrank, but the letter is still preserved in
which he begs that the necessary implements—the anvil, the
punch, and the shears—may be sent him, and asks that he be
informed how the goldsmiths put in their plugs.*

* The correspondence that took place between Hodgdon and Pickering is worth
quoting. "The Financier," says Hodgdon in his letter of December 23, 1782,
"will not permit the Continent to be a loser by the gold. The consequence is
obvious. You must select all the French guineas and leave them for exchange in
this city, as well the light as the overweight, as their current value is not equal in
the State of New York; the other pieces must be clipped. The price demanded
is one penny for each piece; but this, it seems, cannot be allowed. It only remains, therefore, for you to say whether you will pay it or cut the pieces to the

The clipping done by the Government differed from the clipping done by the rogues in that it stopped when the last grain the law would allow had been taken. At this point sharpers and counterfeiters began their work, and went so far that it was no longer safe to take any sum of money in discharge of a debt till every coin in the batch had been duly weighed in the balance. The day, indeed, seemed near at hand when, as Washington said, every man would be constrained to travel with a pair of balances in his pocket, or run the risk of receiving gold and silver at one fourth less by weight than by count, and when, as Teague complained, there would be five quarters to every dollar.*

But the evils Teague treated in jest were soon to be treated in earnest. All men who made large purchases, who handled large sums of money, or who travelled from Boston to Charleston, felt that the state of the currency was most lamentable. To be one day paying bills with silver dollars in Boston at six shillings, the next week in New York at eight shillings, four days later at seven shillings and sixpence in Philadelphia, and a month afterward at four shillings and sixpence in Charleston, had become an intolerable nuisance. There seemed to be no reason whatever, now that the war was over, now that the States were united in one Confederation, why something should not be done, and speedily done, to make

standard weight yourself. The last mode has been preferred by Mr. Peirce, and he informs me it is easily and speedily executed with common shears." Mr. Peirce was paymaster-general of the army, and had undoubtedly a large experience in cutting and clipping the coin paid out to the troops. To the note of Hodgdon, Pickering replied on December 24, 1782: "I must trouble you for the necessary apparatus for clipping. 'Tis a shameful business, and an unreasonable hardship on a public officer. I am not certain that I will receive any more bank gold on such odious conditions. A pair of good shears, a couple of punches, and a leaden anvil of two or three pounds' weight. Will you inquire how the goldsmiths put in their plugs?" Life of T. Pickering by O. Pickering, vol. i, p. 388.

* "Without a coinage, or unless some stop can be put to the cutting and clipping of money, our dollars, pistareens, etc., will be converted, as Teague says, into five quarters; and a man must travel with a pair of scales in his pocket, or run the risk of receiving gold at one fourth less by weight than it counts." Washington to Grayson, August 22, 1785. "Teague" was, one hundred years ago, used in much the same way that "Pat" is at present. It was the popular name for an Irishman, and may in that sense be found scattered through the comedies and novels of the time. See Modern Chivalry; also, Independent Gazetteer, Sept. 22, 1792.

a dollar contain the same number of coppers in the rice-swamps of the Carolinas, in the inns and coffee-houses of New York, on the exchange at Boston. This sentiment was as strong in Congress as among the people. Twice since the close of the war the House had brought the state of the currency under discrssion, and had twice listened to schemes for relief. Each of the two schemes proposed the establishment of a new unit of value, the erection of mints and the coinage of a national currency as the most expeditious, the most simple, the most economical way out of the difficulty. The first was the work of Gouverneur Morris. The second was the work of Thomas Jefferson. The idea of a national mint was not, it is true, a new one. Three years before the plan of Morris was read in Congress it was proposed, in an hour of danger and of gloom, to strike copper pennies. The currency was then so debased that forty dollars in paper could not purchase one in silver. Change was so scarce that it was a white day when tradesmen could lay down a few coppers in return for the dirty Continental bills offered in payment of bushels of wheat and slices of bacon. To relieve this pressing want of small coin it was suggested that a great number of copper pennies be struck and thrown into circulation. The suggestion was favorably received, and the designs for the coppers made ready; but it is well for the good name of our country that what was proposed in a day of wrath was never carried out to be bitterly repented in a day of peace. For the coins were to serve not merely as a medium of exchange, but were to teach principles of sound morality and strict economy while they inflamed the passions of the people by keeping awake the recollection of deeds that could not too soon be forgotten. On one side of the pennies were to be stamped representations, prepared by the best French artists, of the barbarities which the English officers were then inflicting on the unhappy captives in the prison-ships and churches of New York. On the other side were to be short sentences drawn from the wisdom of Solomon or the wisdom of the people. Great care was to be exercised in the selection of the passages, that men of every occupation in life might find a precept exactly fitted to themselves. Merchants were to be reminded that "Honesty is the best pol-

icy"; housekeepers, that "A penny saved is a penny got."
For ploughboys and farmers there were to be the lines,
>  " He who by the plough would thrive,
>  Himself must either hold or drive,"
while shopkeepers were to receive the injunction, "Keep thy
shop and thy shop will keep thee." It requires no critical
sagacity to recognize in this the handiwork of Benjamin
Franklin.*

But the coinage of a few pennies was a very different
thing from the coinage of a new currency, nothing short of
which was what Morris proposed. On the seventh of January,
1782, a resolution was passed by Congress calling on the Financier to submit a statement of the values at which foreign coin
should be received and paid out at the Treasury. A week later
the report was read; but all that portion which relates to the
creation of a national currency was, as he afterward frankly
owned, not his work, but the work of his assistant, Gouverneur Morris.

He began with a succinct and clear statement of what he
believed were the three essentials of the new currency.† In
the first place, it was, he said, necessary that the new pieces
should be perfectly intelligible to the multitude, and in order
to be perfectly intelligible to the multitude it was necessary
that they should bear a close relation to the coins then in use.
This was undoubtedly true. It would have been the height
of folly to expect that after having been accustomed all his
life to buy and sell and make change with one kind of
money, the merchant would, on a sudden, throw away the
familiar coins and adopt new ones bearing no relation whatever to those they had displaced. In an instant all business
would have been at a standstill. Tradesmen would have
been at a loss to know what sum of the new currency to
demand for their calamancoes and durants. Buyers would
have been tortured with apprehensions of extortion. Dis-

---

* See a letter of Franklin to Edward Bridgen, October 2, 1779. **Franklin's
Works**, vol. viii, p. 383.

† The plan as laid out by Morris is given in Diplomatic Correspondence of the
American Revolution, vol. xii, p. 91. See also Sparks's Life of G. Morris, vol. i,
pp. 273–276. To him we are indebted for the word *cent*.

trust and suspicion would have been everywhere great, but greatest among the most ignorant and helpless.   Every field-hand, every laborer, every housemaid would have felt sure that the wages received in the new money were far less in amount than the wages received in the old money.   Morris had determined, therefore, that the coins he proposed to bring in should square with the coins he proposed to drive out.

In the second place, he believed it to be necessary, in order to meet the demands of commerce, that the lowest divisible sum of money, or the unit, should be very small.   For it was, he said, only when the unit was small that the price could, in little things, be made to bear some proportion to the value.

In the third place, it was desirable, though not absolutely necessary, that money should increase in decimal ratio. When the ratio of increase was a decimal one, the calculation of interest, of exchange, of insurance, was simply and easily performed.   When the ratio of increase was not a decimal one, such matters required time, labor, and reflection, and were much too puzzling to be performed by the ignorant. Then was it that the great number who did not know were sure to be made the dupes of the small number who did know. As to the unit, it was hard to determine what it should be. The coins which had circulated in America had undergone so many different changes that none among them could be looked upon as a standard, unless, indeed, it was the Spanish dollar; and the Spanish dollar passed at five shillings, at six shillings, at seven shillings and sixpence, at eight shillings, at thirty-two shillings and sixpence.   Taking this dollar, however, as the most available standard, and disregarding the last value, the money unit to agree without a fraction with the remaining values of the dollar would, he said, be the fourteen hundred and fortieth part of a dollar, or, what was the same thing, the sixteen hundredth part of a crown.   It was not, of course, necessary that the unit, equal in value to the quarter of a grain of pure silver, should be exactly represented in coin. All purposes would be served by striking two copper coins, one containing five units and called a Five, and one containing eight units and called an Eight.   Three Fives would make a penny New York and North Carolina money. Four Fives would make a penny lawful or Virginia money. Two Eights would make a penny Proclamation or Pennsylvania money, while three Eights would make a penny Georgia money. By this means the dullest of men could rapidly convert pennies of the present currency into pennies of the proposed currency, and once in the proposed currency, he could with still greater ease proceed to express them in dollars, or quints, or crowns, by simply dividing by the proper number. For purposes of coinage, he proposed that ten quarters, a quarter was to be the name of the unit, should make a penny ; ten pence a bill ; ten bills a dollar ; ten dollars a crown. The crown American money was not to be confounded with the crown English money. The name had been suggested by the device, and the device was an Indian standing with his right foot on a crown, and holding in his left hand a bow, in his right hand thirteen arrows. About him was to be the inscription, " Manus inimica tyrannis."

To this report of the Financier Congress listened with great attention, and with its usual dilatoriness suffered the matter to drop for another year. In 1783 the money question was again taken up, was again expounded in a letter from the Financier, to be once more laid aside for another year, when the whole subject was referred to a committee of which Jefferson was a member. The report of the committee was his work, and differs in but few respects from that of Morris. The principle, he said, of the Financier was sound and ingenious. The suggestion of the Spanish dollar as the unit, and the decimal system of subdivision, were, to his mind, particularly deserving of commendation. The dollar was an excellent unit, because, in the first place, of all coins it was the most familiar to the people, and because, in the second place, it might almost be considered to have been already adopted as a unit. The public debt, the requisitions and their apportionments, were invariably expressed not in pounds, but in dollars. Indeed, the pound was the only unit that could be brought forward in competition with the dollar. But what was the pound? It had one value in the New England States, another value in the Middle States, a third value in North

Carolina, and a fourth in Georgia. Which of these should be adopted? To which State should be given that pre-eminence of which all were so jealous? As to the pound sterling, that was not to be thought of, for if it were hard to accustom the people to a new coin, it was much harder to make them famil· iar with a new coin with an old name. Happily, none of these objections could be lodged against the dollar.

The decimal system was excellent because it was so easy. Every one who would recall his school days must remember how, when learning the money arithmetic, he used to be puzzled with adding the farthings, taking out the fours and carrying them on; adding the pence, taking out the twelves and carrying them on; adding the shillings, taking out the twenties and carrying them on; and how, when he came to the pounds, where he had only tens to carry forward, the work became perfectly simple. The same applied to men. In truth, the bulk of mankind were school-boys through life. Little perplexities were always great to them, and they always felt thankful when an easy was substituted for a difficult process. But the plan of the Financier, good as it was, had one serious defect. His unit was to be the fourteen hundred and fortieth part of a dollar. This was entirely too small. It was much better to keep strictly to the decimal system, and have the dollar contain but an hundred units. This would, moreover, differ but little from the penny of New England, of which one hundred and eight made a dollar; still less from the copper of New York, which was the ninety-sixth part; and but a little more from the penny of the rest of the Middle States, where a dollar contained ninety.

Adopting the dollar, therefore, as the unit, and the decimal scale as the system of subdivision, eight coins should be struck. A gold piece equal in value to ten dollars; the silver dollar, or unit; the silver half-dollar; the silver double-tenth, equal to the pistareen; the tenth, equal to a Spanish bit; the five copper piece, also of silver, and equal to a half-bit; and the hundredth of a dollar, or the copper. The gold piece would then be a fifth more than the half-joe, and a fifteenth more than a double-guinea.

When Morris heard of his plan as modified by Jefferson,

he declared it to be open to grave objections. The proposed penny, or cent, said he, or one hundredth of a dollar, will not apply to any currency in America. It is nothing better than a British half-penny. Nine of them, to be exact, will go for eightpence New York currency; six will make fivepence Pennsylvania money; three will pass as twopence in New England and Virginia; nine will equal fivepence in Georgia, while twenty-seven will be counted as fourteenpence in South Carolina. Nay, more, the dollar itself is a fractional sum when compared with present currencies. This being the case, it was past his comprehension that any one should suppose the people of America would throw away their local moneys to take up a general money that was accurately related to nothing but the pounds, shillings, and pence of Great Britain. The thing was preposterous. The same reasoning should apply to the manufacture of coin that should apply to the manufacture of scythes. Suppose the Government was about undertaking to make these implements of agriculture. Would not every rational man expect them to choose to make such as would be most suitable to the mowers of America, though perhaps longer or shorter than the scythes in use among the Alps? In like manner it would be prudent for the moneymakers to turn out such kind of coin as would please the merchants, though it might not square precisely with the currency of Amsterdam or London. To make a money that involved the assumption or rejection of fractions was to imitate the bed of Procrustes. If the patient is too short for the bed, stretch him; if too long, clip him.*

The arguments of Morris, sound as they were, failed to

---

* Sparks's Life of Gouverneur Morris, vol. i, p. 279. Morris then urged on the committee another plan, in which the unit was equal to twelve shillings and sixpence sterling, which he called a pound, and made equal to one thousand parts. A tenth of this, or one hundred parts, was to be a shilling; a tenth of this a penny, and a tenth of a penny a doit. To this, he claimed, all the currencies of the States were reducible without a remainder. Thus in New England five doits made a penny. Hence £10 19s. 6d. New England money equalled 2,633 pence, equalled 13,165 doits, or £13 1s. 6d. 5 doits in the new money. His table of coin was:

| | | | |
|---|---|---|---|
| 20 doits | = groat. | 600 doits | = half-crown. |
| 100 " | = shilling. | 1,200 " | = crown. |
| 300 " | = dollar. | | |

convince the committee, and the scheme as modified by Jefferson was favorably reported. But the House, despite the urgent need of a national coinage, suffered the matter to drop for another year. At last, on the sixth of July, 1785, a resolution was reached, making the dollar the unit, and the smallest coin a half-penny, of which two hundred were to be contained in a dollar. The plan of Morris, as amended by Jefferson, thus became the basis of our present national coinage. What changes were made in after years are to be ascribed to Hamilton.

A few days after the passage of Jefferson's Land Bill, Congress decided to adjourn till October. Never, perhaps, since legislative assemblies came into use had there appeared quite so remarkable a body of men as the Continental Congress then, for the first time in its existence, about to take a recess. History indeed preserves the memory of but two which can with any justice be compared with it—the Long Parliament that cut off the head of Charles I., and the National Convention that cut off the head of Louis XVI. Both the Long Parliament and the National Convention, like the Continental Congress, seized upon the Government, made themselves for many years the chief power in the State, levied taxes, raised armies, waged wars, concluded treaties, and at last fell from power, overwhelmed with hatred and contempt. But here the resemblance ends. The memory of the Long Parliament and the National Convention is bound up with much that is darkest and saddest in the history of England and of France: with the murder of kings; with the confiscation of estates; with civil war; with bills of attainder and acts of proscription; with all the miseries of the prison-house and all the horrors of the guillotine. The memory of the Continental Congress is bound up with that portion of our national history which we contemplate with feelings of peculiar pride: with the sacrifices and the sufferings, more cruel than the grave, of the eight years of war; with the poverty, the struggles of the six years of peace that preceded the organization of the Federal Government. The republics which the Long Parliament and the National Convention set up have long since disappeared from the face of the earth. The republic which the Continental Congress set up still endures.  The work attempted by the Parliament and the Convention was left half done.  The work undertaken by Congress was most completely done.  From the day when, as a gathering of consulting delegates, Congress met at Philadelphia, it boldly seized the reins of Government, assumed the leadership of the States, declared independence, levied taxes, issued money, raised armies, contracted foreign loans, guided the States successfully through an eight-years' war, and won from the mother country an acknowledgment of the independence so fearlessly asserted.  But there its usefulness ended.  The decline of its authority, which had begun while the war was still going on, became, after the peace, astonishingly rapid.  It had, in the language of the pot-house, more than once been made to eat dirt.  The daily session resembled the play of boys rather than the deliberations of men.  To make requisitions that never were paid, grants that came to nothing, resolutions that never were carried out, constituted, with the bickering, wrangling and disputes, and the reports of all manner of committees, the business of the House from one week's end to another.  Meanwhile, the people, disgusted by the inertness of the members of Congress, and alarmed by the perpetual session and the demands for more extensive powers, became clamorous.  The newspapers abounded with jibes, taunts, and scurrility.  The great Whig party, indeed, was split into two sections—the impost and the non-impost men; the defenders and the detractors of Congress.  In the first section, decidedly the more respectable, were to be found the merchants and importers of the great towns, the holders of loan certificates, the hard-money men, and that little band of stanch patriots from which in after years came the heads of the Federal party, and the first five Presidents.  On the other side was the great body of the middle orders, the farmers, the shopkeepers, the supporters of paper money, all those who clamored for State rights, and all those who found themselves steeped in debts they could not pay.  With them were associated many good, brave, and moderate men, who, while they gave an earnest support to the established Government, looked with painful misgiving on every attempt to enlarge its powers as an attack

on the independence of the States.  Such an one was Samuel
Adams.  But the reasons which Adams advanced against the
appeals of Congress for more extensive powers were such as
became a man of integrity, sober, moral, diligent, and accustomed to reflect.  The reasons which his followers gave for
their conduct were such as should not have imposed on a tavern club after the second bottle had gone round, or been made
use of by a ranting politician in the course of his wildest
stump-speech to a gathering of backwoodsmen on the banks
of the Great Kanawha.  The demands, they said, of Congress
were simply unreasonable.  But that was not all.  For every
demand was accompanied by a threat, or a menace, or an announcement of the most fatal consequences to the Confederacy
if it were not instantly complied with.  Where did these honest gentlemen get so much foresight?  Were they all seventh
sons of seventh sons?  If one could believe their predictions
he would wish he had been a negro, and carried off to St.
John by the Tories.  Now, nothing would do but the congressmen must have the right to levy impost, and fill every
seaport, from the province of Maine to Georgia, with a well-
paid army of excisemen, tide-waiters, and cellar-rats.  Next,
they must have an endowment, or, as they were pleased to call
it, an assured revenue, settled on them.  If they were not allowed to take the affairs of commerce out of the hands of the
States, and regulate them as they saw fit, the Confederation
would go to pieces and American shipping be driven from
the sea.  The Indians would overrun the country unless they
were permitted to pack every frontier settlement and fort with
an armed force in times of peace.  The lands beyond the
mountains must be given up and sold to speculators to pay
the interest on the domestic debt.  But how, in the mean time,
did these gentlemen dispose of the fund which, by stinting
and scrimping and hoarding, the people were enabled to pay
into the Treasury?  Did they guard it with the utmost vigil-
ance?  Did they dole it out with a frugal hand?  No.  They
squandered it with reckless profusion.  Ten thousand dollars
was given to this noble foreigner, five thousand to that, and a
gold sword to the other.  Another great sum was to be given
to the late army.  One hundred thousand was to be set apart

to build a Federal city. No wonder that they wanted an impost. But it was well to be wary. Little by little Congress, with the best intents, perhaps, was seeking to take away the most sacred privileges of the States. It had power enough, and if any change were to be made, the question was whether there should not be a curtailment of what already existed.

The men who talked in this strain were numerous everywhere. But in Rhode Island they abounded. Of the thirteen States, Rhode Island and Providence Plantations had always been the most lukewarm and discontented, and was now entering on that infamous course which makes it impossible to read her history down to the day when she entered the Union under the Federal Constitution without feelings of indignation and contempt. No State paid its quota more grudgingly. None was so often without representation. None, not even New York, was actuated by so selfish and ungenerous a policy. The vague theories, the wild schemes of finance, of government, and of trade, which in other States were stoutly combated by the good sense of the community, seemed, in Rhode Island, to have been adopted by the rabble, and there the voice of the rabble was heard with great respect. No sooner, therefore, was the cry raised against the perpetual sitting of Congress than the Legislature sent instructions to the delegates at Annapolis to move a recess. Partly from courtesy and partly from hope of profit, Congress was invited to resume its session at the city of Newport. A motion to this effect was accordingly brought in on the fourteenth of April.* An exciting debate followed. Few of the members felt it a grievance to be relieved from the heat and dirt of the town and sent back to the cool shade of their plantations and their country-seats for the five hottest months of the year. But where they should again assemble was a question of great sectional interest. The States to the south of the Potomac would gladly have the session held at Annapolis. The Middle States were for Philadelphia or Trenton. The New England States, with much apparent indifference, were for some city well to the north, that the three weeks they were used to spend in journeying to Annapolis might be cut down to at least one.

---

* Journals of Congress.

The moment, therefore, that Jefferson could obtain a hearing, he moved that the word Newport be struck out. The question was put, and when the ayes and nays had been taken, the President announced that the ayes had it. Mr. Montgomery then moved that the word Philadelphia be substituted. But the memory of the insult of the soldiers and the cowardice of the city fathers was still fresh, and the motion was quickly voted down. It was then moved to postpone. But the ayes and nays were again called, and the President declared that the motion had passed in the negative. Jefferson suggested the word Alexandria. But Alexandria was less to the liking of the House than Newport or Philadelphia. Even the most staid and precise of the members were little disposed to banish themselves to a country town where there were no assembly nights, where a company of actors never came, and where the chief divertisement was a card-party or an evening out to tea. The President therefore soon announced that the motion was lost. Trenton was next moved as the place of meeting, and, when the vote was taken, it was found that the ayes had it. Jefferson then moved an amendment by the insertion of the condition that a committee of the States should be appointed. But the previous question was instantly moved by Massachusetts, and the business went over to the twenty-sixth of April. Howell, who, with Ellery, sat for Rhode Island, then moved that the present Congress do adjourn on the third of June to meet on the thirteenth of October at Trenton, and that a committee of the States be appointed to sit in the recess of Congress. To this the House agreed.

And now that the end of the session was close at hand, the business before Congress was hurried up. Several minor bills were disposed of, and, four days later, the House listened to the report of the committee to which had been intrusted letters and papers relative to commerce and navigation. And it was high time. For nothing, the finances alone excepted, was in so ruinous a condition as the commerce of the country. Men began to look back with tender regret to the evil days when trade was hampered by the most unjust laws, when it was a high offence to carry a ship-load of rice to France, and when the skipper who entered the port of Cadiz with a cargo of tobacco stood in imminent danger of being laid by the heels on his return.  The state of commercial affairs, the grumblers said, was now far worse under the liberal rule of Congress than it was fifteen years ago under the iron rule of England.  Then, it was true, the trader was forbidden to carry his rice, his indigo, his tobacco, his pitch, to any ports but those of Great Britain.  Now the ports of England were closed to him, and the markets of all other nations open. Yet those were the flush times.  Trade was brisk, smuggling was most profitable, money circulated freely, and the exports far exceeded the imports.  Now trade was stagnant, the balance of trade was with the foreigners, and the country was being so rapidly drained of specie that the day seemed near at hand when the people would not have one joe to rub against another.

Old traders and importers might well talk in this wise. Twenty-five years before, their ships were to be seen at Surinam, at Hispaniola, at the West Indies, at the Canaries, in the waters of the Mediterranean, and in the waters of the North Sea.  Their captains drove bargains in the Levant, and bartered rice and indigo for rum and molasses in Jamaica.  They sold great stores of corn at Lisbon and Madrid, and every year brought home five thousand pistoles for the liquor and grain purchased by the Dutch.  The New England fleet numbered six hundred sail.  The trade of the mother country with her colonies gave employment to eleven hundred ships and twenty-nine thousand sailors.  Much of this was destroyed by the Navigation Act of 1760, but was soon made up by a most extensive system of smuggling.  The Hudson Bay Company found no mean rival in New York, whence went out annually great bales of furs valued at more than half a million of pounds sterling.  The lumber of Maine was still in demand.  Nowhere could such splendid trees be had for masts and yard-arms, and not a few stately pines, which in colonial days had been marked with the axe of the forest inspector, and set apart for the vessels of the Royal Navy, found their way to foreign shipyards.  The exports from Virginia in the opening year of the war rose to seven hundred and sixty thousand pounds; the exports of the Carolinas to five hundred and eighty thousand pounds sterling. But the shipping was thickest in New England. Scarcely a town along the coast, Boston, Gloucester, Barnstable, Falmouth, New London, Martha's Vineyard, but was deeply concerned in the fisheries. The whaling fleet numbered two hundred and four sail, more than half of which hailed from Nantucket. The prosperity of that little island was indeed a matter of boast to all New England. Then came the war; and when peace returned, trade, commerce, the fisheries, were gone. Many of the fishermen had set off to Halifax; many more would have followed but for the timely letter of Lafayette; a few old hulks rotting in the harbor were all that remained of the great fleet. The fate of Nantucket was but a type of that of the whole country. The merchant marine had been driven from the sea. The ports of European countries had been so long closed to American shipping that little demand existed for American goods. The old markets were shut. Yet the consumption of English goods was as large as ever. The imports from England to America in 1784 summed up to three million seven hundred thousand pounds sterling. The exports from America to England amounted to but seven hundred and fifty thousand pounds. The consequence was a great drain of specie. Dollars, guineas, joes, moidores grew scarcer and scarcer every day. Merchants were unable to meet their payments; embarrassment and distress followed, and a great cry for paper money was raised. Nor were matters at all benefited by the action of the States. Congress had no power to regulate commerce, but each State, left to itself, ordered its own trade in its own way; and the way of one State was always different from the way of another. The commerce which Massachusetts found it to her interest to encourage, Virginia found it to hers to restrict. New York would not protect the trade in indigo and pitch. South Carolina cared nothing for the success of the fur interests. New England derived great revenues from lumber, oil, and potashes; Pennsylvania from corn and grain, and were in nowise concerned as to the prosperity of the trade of their neighbors. Articles which Connecticut and New Jersey excluded from their ports by heavy tonnage duties entered New York with scarcely any other charges than light money.

But the evils produced by the narrow policy at home were slight compared with the evils produced by the narrow policy abroad. The duties laid by the States affected particular localities, and particular branches of industry and trade. The restrictions imposed by England affected every State and every article of commerce, for she had forbidden American goods to enter her ports unless they came in English ships. And now the merchants cried out that ruin stared them in the face. The demand, they said, for goods of English make, tammies, calamancoes, durants, brocades, damasks, and Irish linens, was greatly in excess of the demand for the fabrics of French or Dutch make. Yet from this lucrative traffic they were cut off. They could no longer load their ships with the products of the plantations and the farms, dispatch them to Liverpool, to London, to Queenstown, and bring home in exchange bales of the stuffs which found so ready a market even in the smallest inland towns. And for all this there seemed to be no help. When one State laid some burden on the commerce of another, a cure might be hoped for in retaliation. But with England retaliation was quite out of the question. The very first State patriotic enough to close her ports to English goods unless they came in American ships would speedily find her sister States, far from imitating her example, smothering all feelings of national pride, and holding out every inducement for English merchantmen to come to their ports. Nay, more: should any twelve States band together, settle on some scheme of retaliation, and carry it rigidly into effect, the thirteenth would be the Judas to betray them all for British gold. In such a pass it was clearly the duty of Congress to take the state of commerce into serious consideration, and seek diligently for some cure for the evils that threatened so soon to destroy it.

Such also was the opinion of the House, and early in the spring a grand committee was appointed, to which were intrusted numerous letters, addresses, and memorials on commercial matters, which had, for some time past, been accumulating in the hands of the secretary. On the committee were

Jefferson, Williamson, Gerry of Massachusetts, Read of South Carolina, and Chase of Maryland. They reported on the thirtieth of April. The trust, they said, which the people had reposed in Congress made it the duty of that body to prevent, or at least restrain, everything likely to prove injurious to the United States. The condition of commerce at the present time was most injurious to the United States. Few subjects indeed of greater importance could present themselves to the attention of the people. The fortune of every citizen was bound up in commerce. It was the constant source of wealth; it was the incentive to industry; with it rose or fell the value of produce and the value of land. And now Great Britain had adopted regulations ruinous to the West Indian trade. It had seemed at first but reasonable to expect that measures so unequal and so ill-suited to promote mercantile intercourse would not be persisted in for any great length of time by an enlightened people. But this was a mistake. They were rapidly growing into a system, and unless Congress was given power to lay similar restrictions on the commerce of England, that of the States must decline and inevitably be annihilated. It was therefore urged that the House most strenuously recommend the Legislatures to make over to Congress, for fifteen years, the management of commercial affairs, and give it power to forbid goods, wares, and merchandise to enter their ports unless brought in ships owned or sailed by American citizens, or the subjects of such powers as should from time to time make treaties of commerce with America. In this motion the majority concurred.

May was now at hand, and as the day of adjournment was not far distant, what little business was before the House was hurried on. Notice was read that his gracious Majesty the French King had been pleased to declare Bayonne, Marseilles, L'Orient, and Dunkirk to be free ports. It was explained that by a free port was meant one at which all goods could be brought in and carried out free. A duty was, however, laid upon tobacco at Marseilles, as the tobacco revenue had been farmed and could not therefore be abolished. This news, it was thought, would be joyfully received by the merchants, and as Lafayette was known to have had a principal hand in the business, a vote of thanks was awarded him.

The matter of salaries of the foreign ministers was next taken up. The sum annually paid them was eleven thousand one hundred and eleven dollars. This was pronounced to be excessive. The public expenses must be retrenched some where, and a good place to begin at was the pay of the ministers. They were living in luxury while their countrymen at home were in rags. Nine thousand dollars it was determined was all they should receive in future.

Leave was then granted Franklin to come home, and Thomas Jefferson elected Minister to the Court of Versailles. An officer was dispatched to Canada to find out when the British would give up the posts on the frontier. The Treasury was put in commission, and Oliver Ellsworth, William Denning, and Daniel of St. Thomas Jenifer made commissioners; the Committee of the States chosen, a day appointed in December for the hearing of the delegates of New York and Massachusetts on the boundary dispute, and, on the third of June the House rose.

The thirteen members in whose hands the management of affairs was now left had indeed but little power and small responsibility. They could make no treaties; they could borrow no money; they could put out no bills; could do nothing, in short, that required the affirmative vote of nine States. Yet it was not long before they betrayed even this mild trust, separated with angry words, and betook themselves home. Every one felt that he was an ill-used man. Some complained bitterly at the hard fate that kept them mewed up in a hot town, reading dry papers, and listening to prosy reports, while their fellow-delegates were enjoying themselves at home. Others pronounced it an outrage that they should be compelled to hold sessions day after day at Annapolis. There were many cities in the North where the thermometer never reached such heights, where there was no blinding glare from the bay, where the committee could have been much more comfortable, and business just as well done. The eastern men, moreover, had gone into the measure with but half a heart. Four of them never attended. The sittings from the first were far from harmonious, grew more and more stormy as the weeks wore on, till at last, one day in August, as the chairman was about to put a motion to vote, several of the eastern delegates rose from their seats, rushed from the room, destroyed the quorum, and firmly refused to return. Next day the gentlemen from New Hampshire, Massachusetts, and New Jersey started for their homes.* Two months went by before Congress met at Trenton. The country in the meanwhile was left without a government.

The same post that brought to New England the news of the adjournment of Congress brought also a startling account of the harsh and savage treatment of the Yankee settlers in Wyoming. Wyoming was the name once applied to such part of the hill-country of Pennsylvania as lay to the north of the forty-first degree of latitude. The tract had been extensively settled by men from Connecticut, and had till within a few years been claimed by that State as part and parcel of her domain. But the dispute had been settled in favor of Pennsylvania, and the New Englander who spoke of his friends in Wyoming was understood to refer to one particular valley of the Susquehanna river. In the Delaware tongue Wyoming signifies the broad flats, and in truth that valley is, of all the valleys along the whole course of the river, the flattest as well as the richest and most beautiful. The Susquehanna, issuing from Otsego lake, receives at Tioga Point the waters of the Chemung, and, entering a deep ravine, flows to the southeast. Huge precipices of naked stone rise on either side. Steep hills and mountains shut it in till, as it nears the mouth of the Lackawanna, it suddenly breaks through its lofty barriers into the broad plains of Wyoming. The heaps of sand covered with smoothly rounded pebbles, the rich alluvial soil, the fresh-water shells high above the utmost limits of the river, the rounded hills, the endless succession of bottom-lands and extensive flats, give color to the belief that the valley was once the bed of a great fresh-water lake. But, be this as it may, the spot has from the earliest times been a favorite among men. Along the hill-tops are still discernible the rings of earth, the mounds, the fortresses made by

---

* The committee adjourned August 19, 1784.

that mysterious race whose name is utterly unknown. The Delawares, the Shawanese, and in later times the Six Nations, made it their hunting-ground till the white men drove them out. Nor was there on that terrible day when Brant and his Indians swept through the land a happier, more prosperous settlement in all Pennsylvania. Six years had gone by since the massacre, and the valley had begun to wear its old aspect. Settlers had come in, houses had been put up, farms had been laid out, and great loads of corn and wheat went every autumn to Philadelphia. But this prosperity was of short duration. In 1784 it was again devastated, first by the violence of Nature, and then by the violence of man.

The winter had been one of unusual severity. The weather had been bitterly cold, and the snow lay thick upon the ground till March was far spent. Then, on a sudden, a change came. The wind set in from the south, rain fell in torrents, melted the snow, and turned every stream and creek that fed the Susquehanna into a roaring torrent. In a single night the water of the river rose many feet, broke up the ice on the rapids, and, whirling it down in great masses, lodged it against the frozen surface of the more gentle parts. Three immense ice-dams were thus formed, which caused such an accumulation of water that the river overflowed its banks, and one great inundation hid the flat land from sight. Yet even this afforded no relief to the waters which came pouring in from the hill-country. Every day the dams grew thicker and higher, and with the blocks of ice were soon mingled fragments of barns and houses, rails of fences, ricks of hay, many carcasses of cattle, and innumerable ears of corn. But at last the upper ice-dam, unable longer to sustain the thrust of the water, gave way, and the flood, rushing upon the lower dams, broke through them and swept down the Susquehanna. Then the river fell as rapidly as it had risen, leaving its course marked by ruin. Nowhere over the area covered by the water was a house, or a fence, or a shed to be seen. The farmers could scarcely recognize their own fields. Where a few hours before had been a rich bottom-land was now a bed of gravel. Where had been a promising orchard now stood

a few bent and broken saplings.* Over the flats and along
the margin of the current lay great heaps of ice wedged in
with roofs of houses and trunks of trees.  One such ice-heap
covered the plain where is now the little city of Wilkesbarre,
and so thick was it that the summer had wellnigh gone before
the last block disappeared.  But to all these were added other
evils still more serious.  The corn and the wheat, the potatoes
and the apples, the fruit of the harvest just passed, had been
washed down the river by the flood.  Such indeed was the
scarcity of food that, had it not been for the immense schools
of shad which, on the return of every spring, go up and down
the river, starvation would have ensued.  As it was, the cry
of misery that went up from the valley reached even to the
ears of Dickinson.  He sent an urgent message to the Assembly recommending measures of relief.  But the hatred the
Pennsylvanians felt for the Yankees was not on a sudden to
be turned to pity.  Their sufferings, it was said, were no greater than their deserts.  What business had they in the valley?
Many devout persons declared they saw in the desolation of
Wyoming a manifestation of divine anger, a signal instance
of the way in which God turns into foolishness the councils
of the wise.  No spot had once been more prosperous.  No
spot was now so forlorn.

The prayers of the settlers were therefore disregarded, and
in place of bread the Assembly sent them soldiers.  The duty
of the militia, it was given out, was to restore order in the
valley, to put down the contentions of the Yankees and the
Pennymites, as the Pennsylvania settlers were nicknamed,
and to protect each party in the possession of its rights.  But
the true purpose of the army sent thither was to drive out
the Connecticut claimants in the interest of a company of
land-speculators.  The military were placed in command of Mr.
Justice Patterson, a man whose narrow mind well fitted him
for the work in hand.  So soon as the roads became passable
he led them to Wyoming, and at once began operations.
Fences were torn down from the grain-fields and set up across

---

* See An Account of the Effects of the General Thaw in March, 1784, upon
the River Susquehanna and the Adjacent Country.  Columbian Magazine, November, 1786, pp. 123, 124.

the roads and highways. The farmers were forbidden to hunt in the woods, to fish in the river, to draw water from their wells, or to cut timber to make a shelter for those rendered houseless by the flood.* Meanwhile the soldiers lived at free quarters, wandered over the fields shooting poultry, insulting the women, and prodding the men with their bayonets. Such acts of violence were stoutly resisted. This was precisely what Patterson wished, and quite in accordance with his plans. He raised the cry that the soldiers were being withstood, and, to prepare the way for what was to follow, he wrote to the President of the Council a most carefully worded letter. " I therefore humbly hope," said he, " that if any dangerous or seditious commotion should arise in this county, so remote from the seat of government, that it may not be construed into a want of zeal or love for the Commonwealth if we should, through dire necessity, be obliged to do some things not strictly consonant to the letter of the law."

No sooner had he dispatched this note than the soldiers were turned loose, and, at the point of the bayonet, drove out one hundred and fifty families and set fire to their homes. Desolate and oppressed, they implored permission to go up or down the river in boats ; they urged the helplessness of the women and the children, the long journey which separated them from their friends, and the lack of food. But this request Patterson ungraciously refused, and curtly ordered them to take the Lackawaxen road as the most direct to Connecticut. Again they expostulated. The Lackawaxen road had, they said, fallen into disuse during the war, and was now all but impassable. Bushes had grown up on it ; there were no bridges over the streams it crossed, and for more than sixty miles the road lay through a wilderness where not a house was to be seen. But Patterson was firm in his commands, and more than five hundred men, women, and children were driven hastily toward the Delaware. Not a few fell down by the way and were buried under logs and fallen trees, whence the wolves dug up and ate them. Others died from exposure and fatigue on reaching the settlements.

---

* Boston Gazettes, June 7 and October 25, 1784, contain letters giving accounts of these proceedings.

When the news of Patterson's action reached Philadelphia some show of indignation was made. Patterson and his troops were instantly dismissed. The sheriff of Northumberland was sent down to bring back the settlers, and, under the most solemn assurance from him of protection, many came back. But Patterson had, upon his own authority, re-enlisted the discharged soldiers, fortified a cave on the cliffs of the mountain, which he named Fort Lillope, and bade the sheriff do his worst. The worst the sheriff could do was to carry back the news of his defeat to those who sent him. Meanwhile the valley was a scene of violence and confusion. The men who had returned were bent upon gathering the ripening crops. Patterson and his men were equally bent upon destroying the crops. Armed bands were constantly passing up and down the river, were constantly meeting, and, whenever such meetings took place, shots were sure to be exchanged. One such encounter happened late in July. A party of the Connecticut settlers went down from Kingston to Shawnee to protect the crops, but fell in by the way with a party of Pennsylvanians who instantly opened fire and killed two of their number. Immediately the whole Connecticut element was aflame. Franklin, a New England man well known in Wyoming, collected a number of men, started from Kingston, swept down the west side of the river, dispossessed all the Pennsylvanians, and drove them to Fort Dickinson, where Patterson and his men were cooped up. A summons to surrender was received with jeers. The siege then began in earnest. But the garrison made a sortie and burned the houses occupied by the besiegers. And now four hundred militia appeared in the valley. They were commanded by General Armstrong, a man of some parts and courage, but brutal and utterly destitute of any sense of truth and honor. He had served with distinction in the war, had risen to be a general in the Continental army, and is still remembered as the father of the author of the Newburg Addresses. No sooner had he reached Wyoming than he put forth a proclamation. He came, he said, in the name of the Commonwealth of Pennsylvania, to suppress violence, to administer impartial justice, to insure protection, and to summon the contending parties to lay down their arms. He first began to treat with the Connecticut party. But some natural doubts were aroused touching his good faith, and he was plainly told so. Then he began to curse and to swear, and pledged what he was pleased to call his honor as a gentleman and his faith as a soldier, that Patterson's men should also be disarmed. On this double assurance the New Englanders surrendered. They were ordered to draw up in line; to ground arms, to right-about, to march ten steps, to halt, and again right-about. Armstrong then commanded his men to pick up the muskets. This was promptly done, and the soldier who had pledged his honor and his faith announced to the little crowd of disarmed men that they were his prisoners. Thirty of them were sent in irons to Easton. Forty-six more were marched under a strong guard to the jail at Northumberland, while Armstrong, delighted with his stroke of cunning, hastened back to Philadelphia.

But there was in that city a body of men who looked with no favor on Armstrong and his acts. The Council of Censors had assembled. The Censors met every seventh year. It was their duty to inquire whether the Constitution had been kept inviolate; whether the taxes had been justly levied; whether the public money had been wisely expended; whether the laws had been duly carried out. And they were of the opinion that in the deeds of Patterson and Armstrong the laws had not been duly carried out. The whole affair was therefore soon before them, and a message sent to the Assembly demanding papers and documents. To this an ungracious reply was made, which was, in fact, a refusal. The Censors thereupon gave it as their opinion that the treatment of the settlers in Wyoming was a high-handed outrage. The Assembly retaliated by making Armstrong Adjutant of the State, and authorizing him to raise more troops and complete the expulsion of the settlers. But from this they soon went back.

To oppress the settlers in Wyoming was one thing. To defy the Council of Censors was quite another thing. So long as the Assembly sent its soldiers to drive the hated Yankees from a section of the State far away from the seat of government, nobody cared. The Pennsylvanians were not harassed, their fences were not pulled down, their fields were not laid waste, their wives were not abused, their houses were not burned, nor were they sent across the wilderness to die of hunger by the way. But when the Censors were withstood— the Censors who were the bulwark against the tyranny of officials and the unjust acts of law-makers—the people were greatly alarmed. Then on a sudden much sympathy was felt for the expelled settlers. The action of the Assembly was severely criticised. Armstrong and Patterson were pronounced brutes, and were, under the pressure of popular indignation, speedily recalled. At the same time the Legislature commanded that the Connecticut claimants should be restored to the full possession of their property.*

When this news reached New England, the angry feelings awakened by the ill-treatment of the Wyoming settlers rapidly subsided, and the attention of the multitude was drawn off to the progress of an illustrious visitor. Indeed, the journey which Lafayette was then making through the States resembled a royal progress much more than the tour of a noble foreigner. Everywhere he was heartily welcomed and sumptuously entertained. He landed on the fourth of August, went directly to Mount Vernon, hastened thence to New York, and, on the fifteenth of September, went up the Hudson in a barge to Albany. There he was invited by the Indian commissioners to attend the conference at Fort Schuyler. He accepted, and, to the surprise of many, addressed the assembled chiefs of the Oneidas in a speech that would not have misbecome the commissioners.† From Fort Schuyler he hastened across country to Boston, entered that city on the even-

---

* My authorities for the account of the disorders in Wyoming are: Miner's History of Wyoming, Chapman's History of Wyoming, Peck's History of Wyoming, Stone's Poetry and History of Wyoming, Hollister's History of Lackawanna Valley, and Pearce's Annals of Luzerne County. See, also, Pennsylvania Packet, May 27, 1784, and Boston Gazette for June and October, 1784.

† As Lafayette was not one of the commissioners, many wondered that he should have the impudence to address the Indians on a matter it was not his business to meddle with. But Madison, who accompanied the Marquis on his trip, and heard the speech, gives a long explanation of Lafayette's conduct in a letter to Jefferson. He says, moreover, that the speech was a good one, that he entirely eclipsed the commissioners, and that one of them was greatly annoyed thereby. Madison to Jefferson, October 17, 1784.

ing of the fifteenth of October, and put up at the Bunch of Grapes.*

The presence of the distinguished Frenchman created no little excitement in the city, and the townsmen determined to give him such a reception as he should not soon forget. The seventeenth of October, the seventh anniversary of a great event, was close at hand; but the nineteenth, the third anniversary of a day yet more memorable in the history of our country, was chosen for the reception. On that day three hundred of the most respectable of the citizens assembled in Faneuil Hall, which had for two days past been given over to the carpenters and decorators to be made suitable for so splendid an occasion. Thirteen arches, adorned with flowers and made gay with bunting, had been put up. The arches grew smaller from the centre toward the ends of the room, and in the one immediately over the Marquis's head was a fleur-de-lis. Music was played during the dinner, and, when the cloth had been removed, thirteen toasts were proposed. As each toast was drunk off, thirteen cannon were discharged in the market-place, and three rounds of claps given, a new fashion of applause but lately come in. But no toast brought out such vociferous shouts as the toast of General Washington. No sooner had the name of that well-beloved general been announced than a curtain, which hung behind the Marquis, was rent asunder, and displayed the picture of Washington, crowned with flowers and laurels, and supported by the ensigns of America and France. The Marquis quickly arose from his seat, his face beaming with mingled pleasure and surprise, began to applaud, and was instantly joined by the assembled company.†

From Boston he went to Marblehead. There a great gathering of people came out to meet him. But as the multitude were pressing and cheering round him, he was much struck by the fact that the women far outnumbered the men. He inquired the cause, and was told that the women he saw were

---

* See Letters of Madison to Jefferson, September 7, 1784; September 15, 1784; October 11, 1784.

† New Jersey Gazette, November 8, 1784. See, also, Boston Gazette, Boston Mercury, and other papers.

the widows of men slain in the war, and were come out to welcome him in their husbands' stead. Nor was this by any means a romantic tale. For the official census of the Government revealed the fact that more than one half of the male inhabitants of Marblehead had joined the Continental army and never returned.

From Marblehead Lafayette went on to Salem. But while he was yet far off he was met by the citizens in carriages and on horseback, and escorted to his lodgings. As he entered the town all the church-bells rang out, and the throng in the street set up a joyous shout. At his lodgings he was waited upon by a number of Continental officers, and by a deputation of gentlemen, who presented him with an address. He then went, preceded by the officers, to the Concert Hall, where a sumptuous repast was spread.*

His eastern tour over, the Marquis sailed from Boston in the Nymphe, and went by water to Annapolis. From Annapolis he returned to Mount Vernon, and a second time visited his chief. This concluded, he rode on to Philadelphia, which he reached on the ninth of December. Ten miles beyond the city limits the officers of the late army and the militia were drawn up to receive him and escort him to the City Tavern. The streets, the windows, the house-tops, were crowded with gazers, who saluted him with cheers as he passed along. The bells were rung from the moment of his entrance into the city till ten at night. Through all the evening the streets were ablaze with bonfires. † Two days later he reached Trenton, and was complimented by a committee of Congress. The same day he received the address of New Jersey. On Christmas day he quitted New York for France.

While half the towns in the country were thus vying with each other in doing honor to the illustrious foreigner, it was noticed, in no kindly spirit, that New York suffered him to depart with no other marks of distinction than a few salvos of cannon and an invitation to dine with the Mayor. ‡ The citizens were in no frame of mind to entertain even so distinguished a guest as Lafayette. They had, through the whole

---

* New York Packet.                    † Pennsylvania Packet.
‡ New Jersey Gazette.

year, been engaged in what they believed to be a losing fight with the Tories, and were much exercised over the prospect of the coming spring election. Many petitions, signed by hands well known at the Chamber of Commerce, on 'Change, and at the Bank, urging sharp laws against the Tories, had been suffered by the Legislature to pass unnoticed. Meanwhile, the Tories had been most untiring in their plots, and had obtained a judgment in the Mayor's Court which seemed to strike at the very root of government. The case of Rutgers against Waddington had come up for trial early in the summer, and, to the horror of the Whigs, decision had been rendered for Waddington. The exultation of the Tories was unbounded; the mortification and rage of the Whigs was great. This, it was said, was too much! The Mayor's Court to set aside a law of the Legislature and give a decision in direct opposition to its letter and spirit! This was the end of all liberty. Henceforth, when any law was enacted offensive to the Tories, they had but to trump up some cause of action under it, take it to the Mayor's Court, and have the law set aside. There was, however, one remedy left to a free people which, happily, it was not in the power of the Mayor's Court to take away : the right to meet, consult, and deliberate on the best means of relief from the dangers that threatened them. To this they had recourse. Early in the fall a meeting was called at Van-dewater's-in-the-fields. The attendance was great, for many cases yet remained for trial that were likely to be affected by the late decision of the Mayor. To this meeting the aldermen were summoned. Some few came, were sharply questioned, and gave so ill an account of themselves in the matter that many present were heard to mutter that they believed the aldermen were at heart Tories. The meeting then selected a committee to draw up an address to the tax-payers, and adjourned. This address came forth early in November. It was, the committee said, the happiness of the people of a free land that, on every occasion when they conceived their rights to be in danger, they could meet, and consult and deliberate on the mode of relief. In the exercise of this privilege a number of free citizens had assembled and charged them to address the tax-payers on the late decision of the Mayor's Court on the law commonly called the Trespass Act. That any court should have power to set aside acts of the Legislature was, they believed, absurd. They were addressing an enlightened people, a people awake to everything that might affect their dearly earned freedom, who well knew that the consequences which would flow from the establishment of such a power would be most pernicious, and would render abortive the great privilege of making their own laws by their representatives. They fully believed that the principle of the decision in the case of Rutgers against Waddington was most dangerous to the Government, and that a perseverance in that principle would leave to the Legislature nothing but a name, and make the session nothing but an expense.*

While this address and the indignant feelings that had called it forth were yet fresh, the citizens were not a little pleased to learn that Congress had fixed on their city as a place of permanent residence till a Federal town should be built.

* The address was printed in full in the New York Packet of November 4, 1784.

# CHAPTER III.

### THE LOW STATE OF TRADE AND COMMERCE.

In the Congress which soon assembled in the City Hall at New York one familiar face was wanting. Jefferson had been sent abroad. Early in the previous May, Congress had judged it wise to appoint three commissioners to negotiate treaties of commerce with foreign powers. One of the three was John Adams, who at that time represented the country at the Hague. A second was Franklin, who had for more than six years been minister to the Court of France, and in casting about for a third the lot fell on Jefferson. No sooner had the House adjourned than he set forth, travelled through New Jersey, stopped at New York, went thence to Boston, visited New Hampshire, made himself familiar with the commerce of the various States, and early in July sailed in the packet Ceres to Cowes. He then went on to Paris, which he reached on the sixth of August, and there found himself in the midst of a society the most remarkable the world has ever seen. Our estimate of that society is apt to be a most erroneous one. We are prone to think only of its brilliancy, and to forget that the French King, who stood by us in the dark hour, who recognized our independence, who loaned us money, and sent us ships and troops, ruled over a people much poorer and much more unhappy than our own. The Court and the nobility were indeed still great and splendid. The arts and manufactures had never before been so liberally patronized. Never had the sciences been so assiduously cultivated. Lavoisier had just replaced the obscure language of alchemy with a simple and luminous terminology. Lagrange had made geometry attractive even to the frivolous, and had put forth that fine work on rational mechanics which still holds its place in the schools, and is still looked upon as an authority. No other country could boast of an astronomer so profound as Bailli or Laplace; of a naturalist as acute as Buffon; of a physicist so daring as Pilâtre de Rozier. Jouffroi had steamed down the Saône in his little boat; Lesage had been close upon the discovery of the telegraph. Experimental physics was indeed quite the mode, and all classes were hurried along by the prevailing taste. The Duc d'Orléans forgot his amours and his stud, his fashions and his schemes of reform, to dabble in it. The Marquis d'Arlandes stole a few hours from Court to pursue a series of experiments which cost him his life. The brothers Montgolfier, whose business it was to make paper, had found time in the press of business to devote to physics, had thought much on the ascent of vapors and the formation of clouds, and soon delighted the little town of Annonay with the spectacle of the first balloon. But a party of amateurs in physics at Paris, not to be outdone by Montgolfier, constructed an oil-silk bag, filled it with inflammable air of one tenth the weight of atmospheric air, and, in the midst of a great storm, launched it from the Champ de Mars. It speedily rose above the clouds, and came down four miles beyond the city. The marvellous art, it was said, of making bodies traverse through space was now discovered. Dreams of wings with which men were to fly from Calais to Dover gave way to dreams of balloons in which men were to navigate the globe. The golden age was believed to be close at hand. Indeed, men of sense and judgment forgot themselves, and made predictions which neither they nor those who heard them understood. Physical ills would rapidly disappear. There would be no more war, no more injustice, no more oppression of the weak by the strong. Man, purified and reformed, would go forth, like a beneficent god, in his balloon, to carry to the savages of the South Sea the laws of science and good order.*

* These absurd predictions seemed about this time to be well grounded, as Blanchard had just crossed the Channel in a balloon, and landed on the heights of Calais. The news of this journey was accompanied by a story which was not a little flattering to French vanity. Blanchard was accompanied by an Englishman named Jefferies. Each had, it was said, at the start hung out the flag of his nation. But as the balloon drifted on the aëronauts were compelled to throw

Meanwhile, the Treasury was empty and the people starving. The earth refused her increase, and the farmers, unable longer to live by the products of their lands, had abandoned them. In many hamlets the population had, in the course of a few years, fallen from fifteen hundred to six hundred. Whole provinces were destitute of cattle. Women did the work of oxen, dragged the ploughs, hauled the carts, and brought home the scanty harvests on their backs. Bread was no longer made of wheat, but of roots and pounded herbs. To this miserable poverty was added a gross licentiousness, which pervaded all ranks. Virgin purity and conjugal fidelity became jests. Marriages ceased to be made, and, as one of the bread memorials plainly set forth, half the children born were the offspring of debauchery. In truth, the French society of that day bore no small likeness to the foul and monstrous portress which Milton placed at the gate of hell. Half was divinity; half was snake. All was majestic and beautiful above; all was loathsome and grovelling below.

On this society Jefferson looked with profound disgust. He was, he wrote, just savage enough to prefer the woods, the fields, and the independence of Monticello to the splendors of Paris.* For there the fate of humanity was most deplorable. The truth of Voltaire's saying, that in France every man must be either the hammer or the anvil, was constantly before him. It was a true picture of that strange land to which, we are told, we shall pass in the hereafter, and where we shall see God and his angels in splendor, and crowds of the damned trampled under their feet.†

While thus occupied in observing the condition of the men he had so lately come among, Adams and Franklin joined him

---

over first the ballast and then their clothing, and, as the balloon still continued to descend, the Englishman in despair threw away his flag, but Blanchard retained his, which alone floated over England. The excitement awakened by these experiments was not confined to France. It spread rapidly to England and America. Great numbers of balloons were constructed, and many ascents made. See Pennsylvania Packet, June 29 and July 20, 1784. New York Packet. See, also, a letter from Washington to Duportail, April 14, 1784, and a poem entitled **The Balloon**, in the Columbian Magazine, November, 1786, p. 148.

\* Jefferson to Mr. Bellini, September 30, 1785.
† Jefferson to Mrs. Trist, August 18, 1785.

at Paris. The duty performed by the two ministers with whom he was associated was, to say the least, a thankless and unenviable one. The time of the gentlemen who now represent the Republic at the Courts of Europe is largely taken up with the performance of duties of a social and agreeable nature. They attend levees, they go to state balls, they eat state dinners, and, at regular intervals, send home dispatches to the Secretary of State. Their salary is fair. Their burden is light, for rarely are they called on to perform a more arduous task than to adjust disputes, to look after the interests of their countrymen when in trouble, and dispatch home each week a carefully written account of the state of politics at the Court to which they have been sent. They represent a great, opulent, and prosperous country, holding the first rank among nations. They are at no pains to explain the form of government. They are never under the necessity of setting forth the advantages likely to come from a treaty of commerce. They are never called upon to borrow money, to seek recognition for their country, to explain that the resolutions of a few town-meetings are not the law of the land, that a grumbling letter to a newspaper does not convey the sense of the community, that Americans are white, and do not adorn themselves after the fashion of savages. Yet it was precisely such things as these that American ministers to foreign cou(s were, at the close of the Revolution, compelled to do over and over again. Of the country and the three millions of men Adams and Franklin were proud to represent, far less was then known than is now to be learned from an encyclopædia regarding the Sandwich Isles or the inhabitants of Oceanica. Whether Boston was in Massachusetts or Massachusetts in Boston, whether New Hampshire was a city or a State, whether the Ohio ran into the Mississippi or the Mississippi into the Ohio, were matters concerning which nine tenths of Englishmen and Europeans knew absolutely nothing. Nor were the climate, the products of the soil, or the character of the people any better understood. When Benjamin West went out as a young artist to study in the galleries of Rome he was as much an object of curiosity as a polar bear or a Esquimau. The Italians came in crowds to see what impression would be produced by the marvellous productions of Raphael, of Angelo, and of Titian on the young savage from America, and went away expressing surprise that his face was whiter than their own, and that his clothes were not adorned with bits of glass and pieces of shell.* The American Revolution was almost over before Parmentier succeeded in convincing the starving peasants of France that the American potato was fit for human beings to eat, and astonished the men of Sablon and Grenelle with the sight of great fields of growing maize. Campbell, in that fine poem in which he describes the loveliness of the Valley of Wyoming, makes Gertrude and her lover to wander over broad savannas, and watch the red flamingo reflected like a meteor in the lake.†

Nor is it in the least surprising that this should have been so. In colonial times no one in Europe troubled himself about what took place in a little cluster of towns and hamlets three thousand miles away. Few Americans ever came to the continent. Scarcely any traveller from the continent ever found his way to America. When the war opened, when France recognized the independence of the States, when the war closed and that independence was secured, European interest in America rapidly increased. But the only sources whence information could be obtained were English newspapers or Englishmen, and both the newspapers and the men were fully bent on presenting the United States in the worst possible light. While five hundred ships were engaged in bringing English tammies, durants, Irish linens and brocades to

---

* When Benjamin West was introduced to Cardinal Albani, who was quite blind, the Cardinal asked, "Is he black or white?" On being told that West was very fair, he exclaimed, "What, as fair as I am?" Life and Labors of Benjamin West, Esq., by John Galt, London, 1806, p. 103. For the curiosity of the Italians respecting him, and his behavior before the masterpieces of painting and sculpture, see pp. 104–107.

† This is by no means peculiar to the time. Thackeray, who, had he stopped to think, should have known better, has the Virginians making maple-sugar in the fall of the year. For the English ideas of the use of Indian corn in the United States at the present day, and for some remarkable definitions of "corn-cob," "mush," "samp," "hog and hominy," see Food, by A. H. Church, M. A. Oxon., etc., ed. 1877, p. 78; Foods, by Edward Smith (International Scientific Series), p. 159, and The Complete Works of Charles F. Browne (Artemus Ward), English edition. p. 257, note.

the United States, and taking home cargoes of rice, tobacco, and lumber, Frenchmen and Dutchmen were assured that the commerce of the United States was scarcely worth the wind it took to waft a ship there. The stately pines of Maine, which before the war had furnished masts to half the ships in the Royal Navy, were suddenly found to be quite rotten. Every Gazette that came out had some new evidence of American atrocity. The readers were assured that across the water justice was never administered, that debts could never be collected, that only a few months before a Virginia colonel, a nephew of the Governor, had cheated a stranger out of a hundred thousand livres, and another gentleman had been thrown into prison for merely mentioning the fact.* Other nations might, of course, make commercial treaties with the Americans if they liked, but nothing would come of it. Their commerce amounted to little, and, such as it was, had long ago come back into the old channels and was entirely in English hands. As to the attempt being made by Congress to prohibit the importation of goods in English bottoms, that need excite no alarm, for the States never could be brought to unite on anything. There was a spirit of revolt among the people who in no short time would turn upon their leaders. The stories, indeed, which then passed current in the papers and coffee-houses of London, and were firmly believed on the continent, touching the ill-humor the Americans were in with their great revolutionary leaders, seem too absurd to have been listened to with a sober face, yet they imposed on men of sense and experience. Jefferson tells us how, when Franklin came back, in 1785, a Swiss gentleman expressed his solicitude for the Doctor's safety, as he understood, he said, the people would receive the great philosopher with stones. " Yes," said Jefferson, "your apprehensions are just. The people of America will probably salute Doctor Franklin with the same stones they have thrown at the Marquis Fayette."†

---

* Franklin to R. Price, August 16, 1784. Franklin to Ingenhousz, April 29, 1785. James McHenry to Franklin, August 24, 1784. Adams to Jay, August 6, 1785. Id., July 19, 1785. Id. to Maréchal de Castries, December 9, 1784. Id. to Jay, October 21, 1785. Jefferson to Hogendorp, October 13, 1785. See, also, complaints in the Boston Gazette, December 5, 1784.

† Jefferson to Monroe, August 28, 1785. In the same letter he goes on to say : " The English papers are so incessantly repeating their lies about the tumult,

Meanwhile the ministers resolutely combated such fictions, and labored hard to support the credit and good name of their countrymen, only to be in turn heartily reviled by them. Some wretched specimens of humanity scarcely deserving the name of men had gone abroad, had presented themselves to the ministers, had been courteously received and hospitably entertained, and had then come home with lying stories of the splendor in which the representatives lived. It was stated that they actually rode in carriages, that they had so many dishes on their tables at a meal, and that their clothing and the rich furniture of their houses were sights to behold.* In Connecticut the newspapers were particularly loud in their demands for reform; nor did they cease till Congress yielded to the outcry and cut down the salaries of ministers from twenty-five hundred to two thousand pounds. Had this reduction been made in view of the straitened condition of the Treasury, it would at least have been plausible, though neither just nor wise. For never before had the finances been in quite so desperate a state as in the early months of 1784. Adams, who seems to have been charged with the business of begging money, was at that time in London, whither he had gone to recruit his health. But his rest was soon broken by a dispatch from his Amsterdam bankers conveying tidings of a most alarming nature. Morris had drawn bills to the amount of one million of florins. They had but four hundred thousand florins wherewith to cash the drafts. Bills sufficient to consume half that sum had already been presented. They had, however, succeeded in putting off the holders with excuses for a few days, but if measures were not speedily taken to meet these demands, the paper would all go back protested. †

Adams now felt that American credit was indeed at stake, and, despite his ill-health and the rigors of the season, set off

---

the anarchy, the bankruptcies, and distress of America, that these ideas prevail very generally in Europe." See Jefferson to Madison, September 1, 1785. Also, Boston Gazette, December 5, 1784.

* "Our too liberal entertainment of our countrymen here has been reported at home by our guests to our disadvantage, and has given offence." Franklin to Adams, August 6, 1784.

† See the letter of Willink and others to Adams, December 2, 1783, in the Works of John Adams.

in January for Amsterdam. The trip, which may now be made under the most unfavorable circumstances and in the worst of weather with comfort and with ease, was then beset with as many dangers as would be encountered in a journey through Siberia in the depth of winter. From London he hastened to Harwich. But at Harwich he was obliged to wait several days for fine weather before the packets put out to sea. The weather was bitter cold. The vessel pitched and rolled so terribly that fires could not be kept up in the cabin, and the sea ran so high that three days were consumed in going thirty-three leagues. When at last the windmills of Holland came in sight, the ice lay so thick along the shore that Helvoet could not be reached. The passengers were therefore landed on the island of Goree. Here boors' wagons were obtained to carry the baggage, and the whole party set out on foot through the snow for the town of Goree, six miles distant. There Adams expected to meet ice-boats, but none were to be had, and he was again forced to travel in an open boor's wagon across the island to Midel-Harnis. At Midel-Harnis he was detained several days in the worst of lodgings till the ice-boats came to carry him over the little arm of the sea to Helvoet. The boats at length appeared, and he embarked amid the waste of ice which every day went in and out with the tide. Sometimes the little boat was rowed, sometimes pushed by boat-hooks between great blocks, and at others dragged over vast fields of ice which now and then gave way and let it down. Before the day closed, however, the little craft reached the opposite shore. And it was most fortunate, for the boat which immediately followed became wedged in the ice, was carried out to sea and brought in by the tide, and did not reach land till fifteen hours had been spent in the water. But even when a landing was effected Adams found himself on the dike some two miles from Helvoet. Once more a boor's wagon took him to the Brille, where the night was passed. In the morning another sheet of water filled with floating ice was crossed in the boats, but when the Maese was reached it was so firmly frozen that he crossed it on foot. Thence he went on by wagon to Delft, and from Delft by coach to the Hague. Two days later he entered Amsterdam, to find, as he pathetically expressed it, American credit dead, never to rise again.* Not a single obligation had been sold since the arrival of the news of the mutiny of the troops at Philadelphia, and the reluctance of the States to grant the impost. One hope remained. Would not the regency of Amsterdam do something? The bankers assured him they had already appealed to the regency. But the members of that august body were men of form and precedent. They expressed themselves well disposed toward the young republic, yet they could not in this matter be obliging. To make a loan under the present circumstances would be a departure from the usual rule. It would create a precedent, and the very moment a precedent was created a dozen other powers as distressed for money as America would rush in and demand the same, and how could the regency refuse to mete to them from the same measure? Much the wiser course would be to take back the application, as a decision would surely be made against it.

The advice was taken, and Adams, much disheartened, went back to the Hague. But no sooner was he there than he wrote to the bankers entreating them to again seek aid of the regency.† He would have them reminded that the commerce of Amsterdam was much concerned in the matter. The city had a right to do what it would with its own. No power could cite it as a precedent, because it was no precedent. He came not as demanding a right, but as begging a favor. And surely, if the city saw that it could without injury to itself confer a favor on a friend, nay, at the same time improve its commerce, it had a perfect right to do so, whatever other powers might think. But the regency could be brought to no such mind.

In this extremity recourse was had to the brokers and money-lenders. But they too were alarmed by the reports of the tumults and bankruptcies in America that came out in every issue of the London Gazettes, and were as loath to take up the paper as the regency. They would choose, they said, to see certain means provided for the payment of the interest before they ventured their fortunes any deeper in the Ameri-

---

* Adams to Franklin, January 24, 1784.

† Adams to Willink, January 29, 1784.

can loan. Adams, however, was determined the bills should not go back protested. His bankers were untiring in their efforts, and toward the close of February a loan of one million guilders was secured at what was then thought to be a ruinous interest. This would, he wrote Jay, raise a tremendous clamor in America. But he could not help it. His situation was very disagreeable. Could not Morris be induced to withhold his hand? It was not for him to question the justness of the drafts. He was only a minister. His duty was to borrow money, even if he went to the full extent of his instructions. But it was hard to go to such extremes, well knowing that great numbers would blame him, because they could not be made to believe in the necessity of it. There was in Holland a despotism in the government of loans as absolute as that of the Grand Seignior. All the money was in the hands of five or six men, and they were as avaricious as any Jew in Jews' quarter. This was one of the ways Holland took to revenge itself on the rest of Europe for the insults it received in negotiations and in wars.*

Meanwhile, a question was submitted to him of no small importance to hundreds of young men in America, and which not long after was made the subject of a diplomatic correspondence. There was at that time in London a young man named Mason Weems. He was, he wrote Adams, a native of Maryland, and a student of divinity. He had come over some two years before to complete his studies and take orders, for there was then no Bishop of the English Church in America, and all candidates for holy orders were compelled to travel three thousand miles to be ordained. Weems had taken this course, had gone to London and made application to the great Lowth, Bishop of London. But Lowth had received him most ungraciously, and flatly refused to lay his hands on any man who was going back to America to preach. He then went to Watson, Bishop of Llandaff. Watson received him graciously, sympathized with him on the distressed state of the Church in America, and even went so far as to hold out hope that a letter from the Governor of Maryland would gain for him admission to the vineyard of the Lord. This he procured and

---

* Adams to Jay, February 13, 1784.

carried to Watson, but was then plainly told that nothing could be done without consent of the Archbishop. To the Archbishop he went accordingly, had several interviews, but was informed that the business was not in his Lordship's hands. It was a parliamentary matter, and, till a law was passed authorizing the ordination of Americans without putting them to the pain of swallowing the oaths of supremacy and allegiance, nothing could be done for him in England. In this extremity he applied to Adams to know if the Bishops in Holland, in Sweden, or in Germany could ordain him without administering the oath of allegiance.* The reply of Adams reminded Weems that there were no Bishops in Holland, and suggested that he should write to Franklin and Jay. But a few days later, falling in company with the Danish minister, Adams asked, as a matter of curiosity, if the rite could be performed in Denmark. The envoy did not know, but would take pains to inform himself. This he did; and not long after his secretary waited on the American minister with the reply. His Danish Majesty had submitted the question to the College of Theology, which gave it as an opinion that the test-oath could be omitted, and that, as Americans were not supposed to have any knowledge of the Danish tongue, Latin would be used in the ceremony.†

But in the mean time Weems, with a fellow-student, had written to Franklin and received in return a letter highly characteristic of the man. It began with advice and ended with a story. He had applied to a French clergyman, but was told that the candidate for orders would be expected to swear allegiance to the Archbishop of Paris. He had applied to the Papal Nuncio, but no help could be expected from that quarter unless the gentlemen became Catholics. He for his part did not see the necessity for being connected with the Church of England. Was not the Church of Ireland just as good? Or, if they could obtain ordination neither from the English Church, nor the French Church, nor the Swedish Church, and

---

* Mason Weems to Adams (no date).   See on this subject a letter from Adams to Jay, January 4, 1786.

† Adams to Mason Weems, March 3, 1784.   This kind offer was declined. White to Adams, November 26, 1785.

did not care to become Presbyterians, why not make a Bishop of their own? The Scottish Church had done so when the King of Northumberland refused to lend one of his Bishops. If the British Islands were sunk in the sea, and the world had seen greater changes than that, they would have to take just such a course. And indeed, a hundred years later, when people became more enlightened, it would be a matter of wonder that men in America, fully qualified by their learning and their piety to pray for and instruct their neighbors, should not be permitted to do so till they had made a journey of six thousand miles out and back, to ask leave of a cross old gentleman at Canterbury, who seemed to have as little regard for the souls of the people of Maryland as did King William's attorney-general for the souls of the people of Virginia. And he then went on to relate one of those apt stories for which at no time was he ever at a loss.*

Not long after the letter was dispatched, Jefferson reached Paris, and the three commissioners turned their attention to the more serious business in hand. They were instructed to conclude treaties of commerce with all the independent States of Europe. Treaties had already been concluded with Holland and Sweden, and notes had long been passing and repassing between the Baron de Thulemeier, the Prussian Envoy at the Hague, and Adams, on the subject of a treaty with Prussia.† Early in February Thulemeier had called on the American minister, had thrown out some significant hints, and finally stated in so many words that his master was of the opinion that it would not be difficult to effect some arrangement on the subject of trade between the Court of Prussia and the United States highly beneficial to both. Frederick had observed that Carolina rice, indigo, and Virginia tobacco found a ready market at the ports of Embden and Stettin, and believed that the fine linens of Silesia and the excellent porcelain of Saxony could not fail of an equally ready sale in the ports of America. A year, however, passed away before the treaty was signed, and in the meanwhile great changes had taken place. Jay had returned to the United States and become

---

* Franklin to Weems and Grant, July 18, 1784.
† Adams to the President of Congress, March 9, 1784.

Secretary of Foreign Affairs.  Franklin had received his longed-for permission to come home; Jefferson had been appointed minister in his stead, and Adams had been sent as ambassador to England.  The choice was a most happy one.  Of all the men in the service of the republic, he alone was, by nature and by experience, fitted for the place.  There were indeed many men of more brilliant parts and more engaging manners.  Franklin was such a one.  He was renowned throughout Europe as a philosopher; nor has his just fame been cast in the shade by any investigator our country has since produced.  His manners were courtly.  His sprightly conversation, his shrewd observations, his wit, his repartees, his stories, his good-nature, and the ease with which he accommodated himself to every class of society, made him an agreeable companion at all times and to all men.  For such a man France was at that time precisely the place, and he there rendered services to his country which are simply inestimable.  But the work to be done at the English Court required other qualifications than a fine mind and ability to please; and these qualifications were possessed by Adams in a high degree.  Diligent, cautious, painstaking, he was an excellent man of business and a careful observer of events.  His mind was in no danger of being drawn aside to investigate the ascent of balloons, to examine the pretensions of Mesmer, or to write up pamphlets on emigration to America.  He was constantly intent on matters of state, and was as familiar with public opinion in England touching American affairs as with public opinion in Holland.  He had indeed given it as his belief, long before the appointment was made, that the post of Minister to England would be far from a pleasant one, and that whoever should occupy it would find himself in a thicket of briers from which he could barely expect to escape without tearing his flesh.*

With such feelings he reached London on the twenty-sixth of May, was presented to the King four days later, and wrote home to Jay a full account of his reception.  How the master of ceremonies waited on him and conducted him to the Secretary of State.  How kindly Carmarthen received him and took him off in a fine coach to Court.  How the master of

* Adams to Jay, April 24, 1785.  Adams to Dumas, May 11, 1785.

ceremonies again met him in the antechamber, and stayed with him while the Secretary went in to inform the King. How full the room was of ministers and lords, bishops and courtiers ; how hard they stared at him, and how the Swedish and Dutch ministers came and held him in conversation till Carmarthen returned. How he was led through the levee-room to the closet of the King; how he made his three reverences ; how moved the King was by his speech ; and how gracious was the reply. How, when the audience was over, the master of ceremonies met him at the door and conducted him through the apartments to his carriage, while, as he went along, the servants, the gentlemen porters, and the under-porters, roared in a voice of thunder, " Mr. Adams's servants, Mr. Adams's carriage." * Nor was he the only one who filled his dispatches with accounts of the presentation. All the ministers then assembled at Saint James from all the Courts of Europe had speculated with no small interest as to what manner of reception George III. was likely to give to the envoy of his late rebellious colonies. No sooner, therefore, was the ceremony over than they hastened to inform their masters that the minister of a petty confederation of thirteen discordant States had been received with the same marks of honor it was customary to bestow on the ambassadors of the proudest kings.

Adams himself was much pleased with the treatment accorded him, and went, two weeks later, with a light heart to make his first official visit to the Secretary. His Lordship was good enough to begin the conversation. He could, he said, answer for himself, and he believed he could reasonably do so for the rest of the King's servants, that they were sincerely desirous of cultivating the most cordial friendship with America. Some animosities would, of course, remain among individuals, but it might be in their power to do much toward soothing them. Adams expressed his delight at hearing such amicable expressions from his Lordship, and reminded him that there were six points to be discussed. The most pressing was perhaps the occupation of the posts along the frontier by British troops. It surely was not unknown to his Lordship that the retention of the posts had deprived the merchants of a

---

* Adams to Jay, May 27, 1785.

most profitable trade in fur, which they justly considered as
their right. The skins that would have been obtained from
the Indians, had the posts been given up in accordance with
the treaty, would assuredly have come to England in payment
of the debts. Their money value would have exceeded several
hundred thousand pounds.* And even one hundred thousand
pounds would, as his Lordship well knew, have gone far toward
satisfying the demands of the creditors. The carrying off of
the negroes was another matter yet to be adjusted. The injury done by this act was little felt north of the Potomac, and
it would be very difficult to say just how much it was felt to
the south. The loss indeed was threefold, for it was a loss
not merely of the money-value of the slaves, but also of their
labor, and the profits of the products of their labor. Had the
seventh article of the treaty been kept inviolate every one of
them would at that moment have been at work in the tobacco-
fields or the rice-swamps, and the fruits of their toil would
have gone to pay the debts. But distressing as these things
were to the planters, the restrictions lately put upon American commerce were still more distressing to the merchants.
Believing that trade would speedily return to its old channels,
and be managed in the old way, English merchants had made
large advances, and American merchants had contracted large
debts. Both expected that remittances would be made in the
articles used for such purposes before the war. But this was
not to be. Hindrances were set up in the form of imposts
laid by England on all American exports. Neither rice, tobacco, pitch, tar, turpentine, ships, nor oil, in short, none
of the articles which had in times past been sent out in payment of debts could now be sent out at all. The consequence was that the debtors, in their zeal to make payments,
had drained the country almost of its last penny. The rate
of interest had doubled. The price of bills of exchange had
gone up to ten per cent above par, and every kind of pro-

---

* A list of furs advertised at London for the spring sales of 1787 contained
over three hundred and sixty thousand skins. All came from the United States,
and were valued, at a low computation, at two hundred and twenty-five thousand
pounds sterling. See Consequences of the Retention of the Frontier Posts by the
British. American Museum, April, 1787, p. 280.

duce become so dear that a great quantity lay rotting in the London warehouses because it would not bring in England the price that had been paid for it in America. The construction, again, which had of late been put upon the armistice was another matter of just complaint. It was well known that a number of valuable ships had, after the conclusion of the month stipulated in the treaty, been captured off the coast of America, and were still withheld from their rightful owners. A large balance in favor of the United States, in the account of the charges of prisoners, was likewise kept back.*

Carmarthen expressed his willingness to give every one of these points a due consideration as soon as something was given him in writing to begin on. He was sure that with a little patience and a little time all would be happily adjusted. Many rubs would undoubtedly be met with; passion and private interest would frequently have to be overcome. But if the ministers on both sides took care to keep right, there was much reason to expect success. What he said was indeed quite true, for it then seemed to the most dispassionate observers that much time would be expended, that much patience would be consumed, and not a little mediation gone through with before the debtor and the creditor could be brought to an amicable understanding. Each stoutly maintained that his view was the only just one, and complained loudly of the severity of the demands of the other. What, the debtor asked, were the facts in the case? Before the war there existed between England and America a free commerce founded on common faith. The English merchants had, just before the Lexington fight, sold to the American merchants and planters great quantities of goods. The merchants were to pay for such goods as they received when disposed of. The planters were to make remittances for such goods as they received when their crops of rice, of indigo and tobacco had ripened and been sent to market. But long before the merchants had sold their bales of calamancoes and durants, nay, while many of them still lay in the holds of the ships that carried them over the sea, England sent an armed force and

---

* Adams to Jay, June 17, 1785.

seized them. Nor did this suffice. She carried off also the indigo, the tobacco and the rice the planters had provided in payment of their debts, and the negroes on whose labor they depended for future crops. And now she had the impudence to demand recompense for the things she had herself carried off. It was difficult to see on what principles of justice or of common sense she could refuse to make compensation for the seized property. Suppose a draper who had sold a piece of linen to a neighbor on credit should, the moment he had quitted the shop, run after him, take the linen away by force, and send the bailiff to arrest him for debt. Would any court of law in the land award judgment to the draper without ordering the restitution of the linen? Let England give back the goods she had seized, and it would then be time to talk of a reckoning. But this was not all. Having required payment for property they had seized, the English creditors now went on to insist that interest should be allowed on the debts for the eight years of the war. Some big-wigs had been consulted and had given it as their opinion that interest could be collected, that war never interrupted the interest nor principal of debts, and that there was no difference between the late war and any other war. But the best lawyers in America held that there was a great difference. The war for independence, they said, was a complete dissolution of all laws and all government; and, consequently, of all contracts made under those laws. It was a familiar maxim of the law that a personal right or an obligation once suspended was lost forever; the rights of the creditors were during the struggle in a state of non-existence, and no interest could therefore grow out of them, as they were not revived till the intervention of the treaty. But even this was not all. Every sensible man who had a sum of money owing to him would naturally think it to his interest to aid the debtor to the utmost in the payment, or at least not to strive to hinder him. But the conduct of the English merchants was precisely the reverse of this. While on the one hand they clamored for payment with interest, on the other they were at great pains to make the remittances they so much desired impossible. The only gold-mines America possessed were her lands and the sea. Yet by an odious Navigation Act they forbade American merchants to send them the products of the land and the sea. Remittances of rice, tobacco, ships, whale-oil and fish were no longer received.

The view taken by the creditors was a very different one. The debts, they said, had been contracted in times of peace, in the usual way, and were justly due. It was therefore harsh and unreasonable for many of the States, in direct violation of the treaty, to place legal impediments in the way of a recovery of them. The spirit of migration into the back wilderness of America was most alarming. Every month numbers of debtors were going off into the canebrakes of Kentucky and Tennessee. Yet there was not a sheriff in the land who would or could attach the property or arrest the persons of these men known to be removing to places where they could never be come at.* As to the Navigation Act, that was an eminently good thing. Every nation had an unquestionable right to govern its own commerce, its own imports, its own exports, in its own way. What right, then, had American merchants to think hard of them for wishing to encourage their shipwrights and their whale-fishery? If they were to be so foolish as to listen to the complaints of their friends across the water, the day would soon come when the Americans would be their ship-carpenters,† when merchants would be compelled to man their ships with American seamen from the banks of Newfoundland, and when the Board of Admiralty would have to send to Boston or New York every time they wanted a frigate or a man-of-war for his Majesty's navy. The whale-fishery and the Newfoundland fisheries were the great nurseries of British seamen, and the moment foreigners were allowed to carry oil to England and quintals of fish to the West Indies, that moment English shipping

---

* This complaint was set forth by Colquhoun, the Provost of Glasgow, in his conversation with Adams. Colquhoun had been sent to London by the Glasgow merchants to confer with those of London on the matter of seeking government aid in the recovery of their debts. See Adams to Jay, June 6, 1785.

† Adams to Jay, August 30, 1785. The letters of Adams written at this time contain a most excellent account of the public feeling in England on the Navigation Act, and a commercial treaty with the United States. See letters of June 26, 1785; July 19, 1785; August 6, 1785.

would begin to decline and English seamen to become fewer in number. It was merely a wise endeavor to make the most of their own means and their own nurseries that had prompted the act so bitterly reviled in the States. If the Americans wished to enjoy the liberty and the profit of carrying their salt fish, their tobacco, their lumber, their tar, their pitch, and their turpentine to the West Indian colonies, they should be able to give something in return. And what could be given in return? The privilege of going to New York or Boston with cargoes of tammies and laces? That, as every one knew, was given simply because it could not be withheld. Congress did not possess the power to levy imposts and duties, and the several States could never be induced to give that power. Of what use, then, was it to make a reciprocal treaty with America when they were sure of getting all the commerce with that country it was desirable to have? The experiment had been tried. After the close of the war French and Dutch merchants had entered into competition with them for the American trade. But three fourths had been ruined by the venture. Americans had found that they could not supply themselves elsewhere. Nor was it difficult to make an explanation. During the war business had stagnated. But manufactures had been largely carried on, and the rapid progress the fine arts had of late made in the kingdom gave to the manufacturers great taste and skill. Their wares therefore surpassed those of all other makers in elegance of design, in cheapness and utility. They stood in no danger of being outstripped.*

But while the multitude held such language as this Adams labored hard to convince the ministry of the manifold advantages of a commercial treaty. Late in August he obtained for the first time a conference with Pitt. Pitt was then enjoying a height of power and popularity which he never surpassed in the whole course of an administration which lasted till the nineteenth century had come in. At an age when most young men, even of remarkable abilities, are still pursuing their studies or fitting themselves for professions, he was renowned as an orator, as a statesman, as a great parliamentary leader.

* Adams to Jay, June 26 and July 19, 1785.

He was now in his twenty-sixth year, and was by far the greatest subject that had been seen in England since the days of Oliver Cromwell. He was adored by the nation; he was petted by the Court; he domineered over Parliament; he was absolute in the Cabinet; he had put down the coalition under his feet; he had put up the stocks to sixty-five; he was extolled as a financier greater than Montague. As a parliamentary tactician he was placed above Walpole and Chatham. The influence he held over George III. was believed to be greater than that which Villiers had held over James I. His haughtiness, his pride, his contempt for titles, for garters, and for money, had gained him a greater share of the favor of the multitude than had ever been accorded to Monmouth or to Wilkes. But it was not till after the Houses had risen and the news of the Massachusetts Navigation Act had been made public in the Gazettes, that he found time to turn his attention from the twenty resolutions concerning Ireland to affairs concerning America.

As soon as Adams presented himself Pitt graciously asked what were the points to be discussed between them. He was told that they were the evacuation of the posts, the construction put upon the armistice, a treaty of commerce, and the negroes carried off by Sir Guy Carleton. The carrying off of the negroes was, he said, so clearly against the treaty that measures would be taken to satisfy that demand as soon as it could be proved how many were taken. He then went on to consider the armistice. This was contained in the twenty-second article of the preliminary treaty, and provided that all ships taken by either side in the North Sea or the British Channel after twelve days, reckoning from the ratification of the treaty, should be restored. From the mouth of the Channel to the Canary Islands the term was to be one month. From the Canaries to the equator, and in all other parts of the world, the space was to be five months. The language seemed too clear to admit of misconstruction. It was precisely such as was to be found in all the treaties made during the eighteenth century. But no sooner had a vessel taken off the coast of America by a British cruiser within the second month been brought into the port of New York, than the judge of admiralty condemned it as a lawful prize. The tidings spread to Rhode Island and Connecticut where similar decrees were thereafter rendered against English vessels. All this had already been explained to Carmarthen, and the assurance given that the aggrieved Englishmen had but to carry their cases to the Admiralty Court appointed by Congress and the decisions of the inferior court would instantly be set aside.* When, therefore, Pitt mentioned the armistice, Adams showed the construction put on it to be absurd. It would, he said, place the whole coast of America within the period of five months. The United States was not between the Canaries and the equator. Surely, then, it was not within the period of two months. Neither was it in the Channel nor the North Sea. Hence it was not within the period of twelve days. It must, therefore, be either in the period of one month or five months; but that it should be in the five-months' time was an idea never for a moment entertained by the contracting parties. Pitt said he thought this was clear, and might easily be arranged. But as to the posts, that was a point connected with the debts, and must be settled at the same time. To this Adams made reply in much the same language he had held with Carmarthen; assured him that interest on the debts was out of the question, and that it was highly improbable a jury could be found from Georgia to New Hampshire who would by their verdict give interest to a creditor. Pitt observed that such decisions would surprise the creditors, that war never interrupted interest, and that the late one was no different from any other. He then passed to the treaty of commerce and asked what were the lowest terms the States would accept. Adams said he could not undertake to answer as he did not know. But one thing he did know: that all men of sense and judgment in America had long been weighing in their minds the advantages and the disadvantages of a free commerce on the one hand, and a Navigation Act on the other. The present time was a most critical one. The news lately brought over from all parts of the States, and the Navigation Act recently adopted by Massachusetts, indicated in a manner not to be mistaken which way the balance had begun to incline. Whether

---

* Adams to Carmarthen, July 27, 1785.

the balance went on inclining more and more in that direction would depend entirely on the conduct of England. And just what that conduct should be was for Mr. Pitt to decide. The more Americans thought on the advantages of a Navigation Act such as that in force in England, the more they would be drawn toward it. He had heard that there were five hundred foreign ships entering and clearing every year at the ports of the United States. How easy it would be to have every one of these ships built in America, owned in America, manned by American crews, and commanded by American captains! Once there was in England a law "that none of the King's liege-people should ship any merchandise out of or into the realm but only in ships of the King's liegance, on pain of forfeiture." What hindered America from adopting this very act in all its rigor? No one would deny that every nation had a right to regulate its own commerce as it saw fit. To this Pitt agreed. No one could doubt the ability of the Americans to build ships, nor the abundance of their materials. Pitt assented. Nobody would pretend that rice, ginseng, indigo, tobacco, grown on American soil and transported in American ships, would not find a market in Europe. Nor would anybody pretend that cargoes of European goods could not be had to carry home again. Nay, even England, though she should make ever so strict laws against exports and imports in American ships, would still be glad to obtain, through France or Holland, large quantities of American produce, and to sell through the same channel as much of her manufactures as Americans would pay for. Pitt smiled at this and owned that there were American articles of much importance to England. "But," said he, "Englishmen are much attached to their navigation." "And Americans, too," said Adams, "to theirs." "But," answered the Prime Minister, "the United States having become a foreign power, our Navigation Act would not answer its ends if we should dispense with it toward you." "I beg your pardon," said Adams to this, "for I think your Navigation Act will completely defeat its own end as far as it respects us. The end of the Navigation Act, as expressed in its own preamble, is to confine the commerce of the colonies to the mother country; but now we are become independent States, instead of confining our

trade to Great Britain, it will drive it to other countries." Pitt
did not deny this.  "But," said he, "you will allow we have
a right."  "Certainly I do; and you, sir, will allow we have
a right too."  "Yes, I do; but you cannot blame Englishmen
for being attached to their ships and seamen, which are so
essential to them."  "Indeed, I do not, sir; nor can you blame
Americans for being attached to theirs, which are so much
fewer and so much more essential to them."  "No," said Pitt,
"I do not blame them."    And he then proceeded to ask
whether any advantage could be given to England that would
not immediately become the right of France; what was the
state of the American whale-fishery; what that of the French
whale-fishery Calonne was laboring to introduce; and whether
American whalers had found a market for their oil out of
France.   Adams thought they had found a good market at
Bremen.   Indeed, he did not doubt but that spermaceti-oil
would be salable in any of the great European cities that
were illuminated at night.  The fat of this whale yielded an
oil that was cheaper and better than any vegetable-oil in use.
No substance in nature gave such a clear and beautiful flame.
He for one was surprised that Englishmen preferred darkness, and, consequently, burglaries, murders, and robberies in
their streets, to receiving, as a remittance, spermaceti-oil.  The
lamps around Grosvenor square, he knew, were dim by midnight and out by two.  Those in Downing street, he had no
doubt, were the same.  But had they been fed with whale-oil
they would have burned till the sun was long up.

And now that the Cabinet had obtained from the American
envoy as much information as they were likely to get, they
maintained a contemptuous silence, which was, he wrote home,
both galling and perplexing.  No answer was made to his
notes.  No heed was given to his memorials.  No consideration was accorded to his requests.  He was indeed treated with
great civility.  Audiences were granted to him by the Secretary as often as he demanded them.  But upon such occasions
he was, he complained, made to do all the talking while Carmarthen acted the part of a civil and attentive listener.  The
most that he could at any time wring from him was a short,
testy, unmeaning answer.  Whenever he mentioned the posts

he was invariably told that was a matter connected with the debts. Whenever he pressed for an answer to his notes, Carmarthen, in broken sentences, would express a wish that the ministry would answer everybody. Whenever he offered a gentle remonstrance against the silence with which his most urgent memorials were treated, a hint was dropped that they were in the hands of Pitt. With these few exceptions Adams was, at all the interviews, the sole speaker. He was suffered to introduce such topics as he saw fit, in such order as he saw fit; to discuss them without interruption to the end; and when he would pause, in the hope that Carmarthen would drop a hint, or make some comment, or start a fresh topic, a dead silence would be maintained till such time as, mortified and abashed, he passed on to a new theme.*

From that time forth to the day when, three years later, he returned to America, he continued to fill his letters with reproaches, with entreaties, and with grave advice. How long would the Boston merchants tamely submit to pay thirty, or even fifty per cent, duty in the port of Liverpool, and exact but ten in the port of Boston?† There was but one way to escape from such unjust exactions, and that was by a Navigation Act as severe as that enforced in England. He most earnestly besought the States to lose no time in passing a like act. Were the measures much longer delayed the country would become an endless theme of derision. The more it suffered, the more would it be laughed at. But once in force, the reputation of America would instantly rise all over Europe. The act would, moreover, be of great help in treating with France and Holland, as well as with England. For the very moment these foreign powers saw the States on the right way,

---

* It may not be uninteresting to transcribe a few of the sentences from the letters of Adams in which he sets forth his troubles. "I am sorry," says he, on one occasion, "that, in representing all these conversations, I am obliged to make myself the principal speaker; but I cannot get them to talk." August 25, 1785. Again he says: "I can obtain no answer from the ministry to any one demand, proposal, or inquiry." To Jefferson, October 11, 1785. "In short, sir, I am like to be as insignificant here as you can imagine. I shall be treated, as I have been, with all the civility that is shown to other foreign ministers, but shall do nothing. I shall not even be answered." December 3, 1785.

† Adams to Jay, August 30, 1785.

and united in determined measures, they would esteem more
highly the commerce, the credit, and the good-will of America.
Frenchmen were asking quite as often as Englishmen, What
have you to give in return for this and that privilege, for this
and that article of trade? Maréchal de Castries was perpetually demanding, What have you to give in return for leave
to trade with the French Indies?* When once a Navigation
Act had been made, then it could be said, when questions of
this kind were sneeringly asked, We will repeal our Navigation Act, or take off our impost in return for your taking off
yours. Sometimes his faith in his countrymen seemed to fail
him, and he plainly told them their actions were ruinous to
their dignity abroad. It was now in the hands of the States
to determine whether there was or was not a union in America.
If there were, then might they easily make themselves respected.
But if there were not, they would be little regarded and would
soon be at war with England. It behooved the great seaport
towns to look well to their defence. Let them put the fortifications they had in as good condition as possible, provide
arms and ammunition, and have the militia well drilled. It
was quite impossible for a man who did not live in England to
imagine the bitterness felt toward America. The parliamentary factions led by Shelburne, by Buckingham, by North,
and by Fox, were united as one man against her. The Navigation Act was highly popular, and though it was well known to
give much encouragement to smuggling, the Government did
not dare to meddle with it. Some hot heads went so far as to
say they would distress America till she petitioned to come
again under English government, when they would spurn her.
Others would most willingly embarrass Pitt in every rational
plan of agreement and plunge him into a new war. He knew
that some of his countrymen were thoughtless enough to say
that one way out of the difficulty was to end all commerce.
There was some truth in this. It was true that if all intercourse between Europe and America were to stop forever,
if every ship in her docks were to be burnt and the keel of
another never to be laid, the people would still be the happiest
people on the face of the earth, and in fifty years the most

---

* Adams to Jay, October 21, 1785.

powerful. The luxuries brought over from the Old World destroyed prosperity, enfeebled the race of men, and retarded the increase of population. But to talk of annihilating commerce was idle. The character of the people must be considered. The tortoise and the sea-fowl were not more aquatic. The love of commerce, with its pleasures and its conveniences, was as unalterable as their natures.* Connections with Europe, with Asia, and with Africa must be made, and that speedily. It was, however, a true maxim of diplomacy that he negotiated ill who could not make himself feared,† and there was little in the course now followed by the States to inspire fear. An American army awakened no dread in England, for no thoughts were there entertained of again sending an army to America. On the navy Englishmen looked with profound contempt. They could be made to smart only by restrictions and imposts.

But to the warnings and advice of the minister a large part of his countrymen turned a deaf ear. The opinions which many then held touching the importance of commercial relations and the principles of trade were most lamentable, and not a little singular in a country which had for a century past been so deeply concerned in commercial ventures. When the advocates of the impost and the regulation of trade by Congress bitterly complained that their ships were shut out of British ports, and that while London merchants enjoyed the benefits of a free trade with the States, American oil was taxed eighteen pounds a ton,‡ and tobacco sixteen pence a pound in Liverpool,# they were told the world was all before them where to choose. That if the seaports of the British isles and colonies were shut, those of all other nations were open, and why not send their oil and tobacco-leaves to Lisbon, to Amsterdam, to Bordeaux? Why not carry their rice and timber to the Azores, to the Canaries, to Cuba, and the islands of the West Indian sea? When they answered that these ports were closed to foreigners, and that they could never hope to bring sugar from the Brazils, or Madeira from Lisbon, till they could give something in exchange, and that so long as Dutchmen and Spaniards, Frenchmen and Portuguese, were

---

* Adams to Jay, December 6, 1785.     † Ibid., May 5, 1785.
‡ Ibid., July 19, 1785.     # Adams to Jefferson, July 24, 1785.

free to come and trade at Boston or New York, they had nothing to give in reciprocity, the opponents of the impost were
dumfounded, and gave it as their opinion that if commerce
were carried on in that way the sooner it ceased the better.
No amount of argument, however lucidly and favorably expressed, could make it clear that commercial compacts between
nations bore any resemblance to the commercial compacts that
were made every day between individuals on the Exchange.  It
was easy to understand that, in the dealings of importers with
merchants, or merchants with tradesmen, each party was guided
in his conduct by what seemed to him to be best for his own
personal interest.  But that great and opulent nations should,
in their commercial treaties, be influenced by such sordid motives, was unheard of.  If France would not let Americans
carry fish to her West India islands unless some reciprocal
advantage were given by America, the merchants had but to
wait a bit; the French would soon find out that their colonies
could be supplied with this necessity much cheaper from American fisheries than from any other source, and the restrictions
would speedily be removed.  Trade was a thing that should be
left to take care of itself.

With this much - abused maxim on their lips, the non-
imposters looked on in complacency while the ships of their
neighbors were excluded from the Brazils, from the East Indies,
from the West Indies, from the Dutch colonies, from the English colonies, from the Spanish colonies, and from the Mediterranean, where, behind the Pillars of Hercules, the Barbary cor-
sairs were believed to lie in wait for American merchantmen.
Foreigners had indeed been admitted to trade, under certain
restrictions, with the French colonies.  But the merchants of
Marseilles, of Bordeaux, of Rochelle, Nantes, and Saint-Malo,
cried out that they were ruined, opposed the free ports, opposed the admission of lumber, of hemp, and tar, and besieged
the ministers with petitions which at one time seemed likely
to be granted.  The commerce of the country meanwhile was
entirely at the mercy of these powers.  Congress was, by the
Articles of Confederation, fully empowered to make treaties
of commerce.  But if any power refused to enter into such
a treaty, excluded American shipping from its ports, and laid

heavy duties on every kind of American produce, it was for the individual States, and not Congress, to say whether the vessels of such a power should be suffered to trade free at the ports of the United States. And on such a matter as this, it was often urged, every man of sense and judgment knew the thirteen States never could be made to think alike. It was folly to suppose that if South Carolina shut up her ports to Spanish vessels because her rice and her indigo were excluded from the colonies of Spain, New Hampshire, which produced no rice and indigo but whose forests of stately pines furnished masts and spars to the navy of the Catholic King, would immediately do the same. Or that Virginia should refuse to suffer Portuguese ships to go out from her ports loaded with hogsheads of tobacco because the Lisbon merchants would not take Nantucket oil in payment for pipes of Madeira and hogsheads of olives. If things really came to such a pass as this, and each State undertook to regulate its own commerce, the upshot would be that each would have to send ministers to all the courts and maintain consuls at all the great seaports of Europe. No man in his wits could for a moment entertain the idea of thirteen American plenipotentiaries meeting in the antechamber of every foreign King, each with full powers and distinct instructions from home, without having presented to him such a picture of confusion, of altercation, expense, and endless delay as would show him the utter folly of the thing. There was indeed an alternative. All the States might bestow ministerial power on one and the same person. But this, too, could not be carried out, for there had not been, was not, and never would be, a man to whom each member of the Confederation would intrust its affairs of trade. They were far too jealous of each other. Besides, the heterogeneous mass of papers, full of different objects, conflicting views, and inconsistent commands, he would pull out of his portfolio every time he wanted to know if Rhode Island would join with Massachusetts and Connecticut in taking tea at Cadiz in payment of staves and hemp, or if Pennsylvania would be content to barter ship-loads of grain for jars of olive-oil, must make such a scheme useless. Nor was it likely that any gentleman of spirit could be found to consent to be held accountable for his behavior to thirteen masters.* There was then but one way out of the trouble, and that was to give over the whole matter to the care of Congress.

But this remedy was pronounced by the foes of the measure to be worse than the disease. If, said they, sarcastically, it be so great an evil to the country to be unable to send, year after year, thousands of joes, moidores and carolins abroad in exchange for luxuries that make women of men, nourish a taste for outrageous extravagance, and put an end to home manufactures, is it not a still greater evil to endow Congress with authority that will render its yoke more uneasy than the yoke of the British King? And then they went on to express their alarm for the safety of the States in fables and in figures of speech. One non-content gravely warned the public on no account to pass over to Congress the right to manage trade. That body already held so much power as to be dangerous to the liberties of the people. But, because their liberties were endangered, was it necessary to rush on to destruction? Was it sensible to shut the barn-door when the horse had gone? It was true indeed that members whose conduct was displeasing could be put out and other men put in; but the body was Congress all the same. Pluck out the limbs of a lobster and in a very little while new ones would take the place of those destroyed. Indeed, every one of the new claws would be larger and stronger than the old claw it replaced and would hold whatever was given to it with increased avidity. The difference between the British lobster and the American lobster was just this: the one was all of a color; the other was a streaked, thirteen-tailed wretch, seven times as big and growing bigger and fatter every day. It was really laughable to talk of the imbecility of Congress. Facts were stubborn things. Congressmen rolled in their coaches, built Federal towns, voted salaries, and gave away pensions. Was this imbecility? †

Another malcontent set forth the foreign relations of the country in an effusion which to our ears sounds coarse and vulgar. Yet it richly deserves to be cited in evidence of the manners of the time, and of one of the many ways in which men of sense were then accustomed to discuss grave questions of state. Should one, said the writer who carefully

---

* Adams to Jay, May 8, 1785.    † New York Packet, April 4, 1785.

hid his name, travel through all the cities of Europe, he could not find a coquette so expert as Miss Columbia. In 1775 she lived at the expense of Mylord who kept her indeed not very sumptuously. She therefore soon began to traffic in her charms and was by this means enabled not only to provide for her own livelihood, but to gratify a thousand wants which Mylord fancied to have. First among her lovers was Monsieur. But while Monsieur was exhausting his purse to please her she was eating *petits soupers*, sometimes with the crooked-nosed Don, sometimes with the Swedish Gentleman, but more often with the stanch old Cheese-monger. Monsieur, in consequence, now sustains a loss by Miss Columbia of some eighty thousand pounds sterling, besides another sixty thousand pounds in loans and moneys for which he went security. Considering that all this has been spent during an acquaintance of six years, Monsieur has much reason to be out of sorts. As to the three sullen lovers—the Don, the Cheese-monger, and the Swede—they have seldom been farther off than large promises; and were it not for about fifty-four thousand pounds advances Mynheer has made, the poor girl would not have found in the acquaintance of these gentlemen the expenses of her toilet. She now shows the greatest coolness toward them, not only in her letters, but in the secret connections she still keeps up with Mylord. But Mylord, knowing how to appreciate her, stands fast and laughs at her Ladyship.*

It may well be supposed the papers that came out in the Packet were read, bitter and coarse as they were, with much interest by the members of Congress then assembled at New York. Indeed, the controversy was watched with anxiety everywhere. Rarely did a week go by but the mails carried out bundles of the papers for Washington or Madison. Jay never suffered a packet to sail without a number for Adams and Jefferson. The session had opened early in January, but it was not till the month was well spent that enough members came in to make a quorum. One of the first measures was the election of a Board of Treasury.† Gervais, Livingston, and

---

* New York Packet, August 23, 1784. This style of treating public events was very common.

† January 25, 1785. Journals of Congress.

Osgood made the Board, and these three were to exercise all the functions lately possessed by the Financier. Two days later an ordinance was passed defining the duties of the Secretary of War,* and two months later † Henry Knox was appointed to the place. He was to be charged with regulating the military affairs of seven hundred men. Some minor matters then occu-pied the attention of the House till the eighth of February, when the clerk announced that the election of three commis-sioners to choose a site for a Federal town had been made the order of the day.‡

The plan for such a town had for two years past been many times under discussion. The idea had naturally been suggested when, in the early summer of 1783, Congress was driven from Philadelphia by the mutiny of the Lancaster line. At that time the need of a permanent residence was severely felt, and the claims of several places as the best site were as-serted. But it was not till October that a resolution passed directing that ground be chosen and buildings put up on the banks of the Delaware not far from the falls. # This, how-ever, gave much offence to the southern delegates. In a matter of this kind, they said, with truth, the convenience of one set of States ought not to be sacrificed to that of an-other set; that the site chosen for the Federal town should be central; that the falls of the Delaware was not a central spot, and the selection of it was therefore most unjust to them. Two days later, accordingly, they attempted to have the matter reconsidered, but failed.‖ With this the matter rested for a few days, when a resolution was reached that it was not wise to have a single place of residence, and order-ing that buildings should also be put up on the lower falls of the Potomac not far from Georgetown. This satisfied the southern delegates and nothing more was heard of the Fed-eral town till the end of December, 1784.△ The whole sub-ject was then reviewed, the plan for two capitals rescinded, and, after a stout fight by the Virginia representatives, an ordinance passed ordering commissioners to lay out a Federal town on

---

* Journals, January 27, 1785.                    † Ibid., March 8, 1785.
‡ Ibid., February 8, 1785.    # Ibid., October 6, 1783.    ‖ Ibid., October 8, 1783.
△ Ibid., December 20, 21, and 23, 1784.

the banks of the Delaware near Lamberton. On the motion of Mr. Hardy to strike out "on the banks of the Delaware" and put in "at Georgetown on the Potomac," the vote stood: ayes, one; nays, eight.

The plan, as it appeared on paper, was then thought to be a bold and magnificent one. The commissioners were to select a tract of land not more than three nor less than two miles square on the banks of the Delaware, purchase it, and there lay out a Federal city. The structures, which they were charged to erect in an elegant manner, were a house for Congress and suitable buildings for the executive departments. Residences were also to be provided for the president and secretary of Congress, the secretaries of war, of foreign affairs, of the marine, and for the officers of the Treasury. It was further expected that each State would put up a fine house as a home for its delegates. But to pay for the four square miles of land and for the erection of the necessary buildings, an amount was put aside which was, it has often been asserted, ridiculously small even for that time. The commissioners were empowered to draw upon the Board of Treasury for one hundred thousand dollars, a sum but twice as large as that now paid each year to the President as salary; which would not now suffice to meet the expenses of the Government for one day, and which falls far short of the sums almost every month paid down in the city of New York for single building lots, twenty-five thousand of which would not equal the smallest area of land the commissioners were commanded to buy. But to a government that could not raise three millions of dollars a year the sum was a great one. That such was the opinion of the multitude is shown by the bitterness with which the scheme was assailed in pamphlets, and by the assaults which were made on Congress in the papers. That Congress was serious in the matter is plain from the exhibit of sectional jealousy which the debates on the site for the town never failed to call forth. The truth is, the money appropriated was then believed to be not only a sufficient but a liberal allowance. That it now seems so contemptible is but the natural consequence of the astonishing advance which the nation has, since the time of the Confederation, made in opulence and power. Yet it is hard for one who for the first time climbs to the dome of the noble Capitol, and looks down on the stately buildings which overhang the Potomac, to believe that ninety-nine years ago Congress seriously thought of providing the Government with offices and its members with homes, for a sum that would not at present purchase the tenth part of an ocean steamship, and has often been exceeded by the cost of a half mile of railroad. On the tenth of the month Philip Schuyler, Dickinson, and Morris were appointed commissioners, but Schuyler refusing to serve, his place was filled by Brown.

This troublesome matter disposed of, the course of parliamentary business went smoothly on. Little of much consequence was done till the autumn was well advanced. In March the slave question was again brought forward. Rufus King laid before the House a proposition to exclude slavery from the new States to the northwest of the Ohio, and make it a part of the Federal compact. A warm discussion followed, but the proposition was finally committed by a vote of eight States to four.

At this point in their proceedings the attention of Congress was much occupied by the excitement of the approaching election in the city. Scarce had the month of April opened when several prominent citizens were put in nomination for the Assembly. Such things as organized political parties did not exist, but their places were largely supplied by the two great orders of society, the rich and the poor. It is true that many questions of a national and local nature parted men in their opinions; but when an examination is made it will be found that those who supported the one side were the rich, and those who upheld the other were the poor. The manner of making a nomination was a simple one. As the day of election drew near, a number of gentlemen would meet at one of the coffeehouses, discuss the situation, and select one of their number to represent them in the Assembly. His name, with a few remarks on his high character and a pledge to support him, would then be sent to the Packet and Advertiser for publication. The pledge was commonly signed by a long list of merchants and characters of note. He then became the subject of abuse far more violent and shameless than in our time is poured out

even on a candidate for the Presidency, and many things
combined to make the spring canvass of 1785 more exciting
than ever.  The discussion which had taken place on the impost and the power to regulate trade had caused much bitterness of feeling.  The presence of Congress it was foolishly
thought would be felt, and that every member of the House
would spare no pains to elect men who would firmly support
the wishes of the national Legislature.  But there was also a
question of a local nature that came into the canvass.  Since
the election of 1784 decision had been given in the famous
case of Rutgers against Waddington.  The Mayor's Court had
set aside a law of the Legislature.  That the act had been set
aside because it was an unjust and iniquitous one was impossible
to believe.  Every one knew that it was a just act and a good
one, and that decision had been given directly against its express stipulations because a rascally lawyer had so tricked out
the wrong as to make it appear the right.  The whole profession was as a consequence denounced.  They were growing rich at the expense of poor debtors who had lost all in
the glorious cause.  They were selling themselves to the Tories.  As soon, therefore, as it was known that some attorneys were to run the indignation of the multitude became
great.  The papers were filled with exhortations written in
the style of the hangman, beseeching all true patriots to have
a care how they voted.  Are we not, said one of these, are
we not convinced by this time that we have among us a set
of men so audacious that they venture, even in public, to
wrest, turn, twist, and explain away the purport and meaning
of our laws?  Beware of the lawyers!  These men are the
very rulers of our fate.  Call to mind the wormwood and
the gall Great Britain strove to force down your throats.
Rise!  Be wise, be vigilant, and you may yet escape the chains
and fetters which are being made ready for you by a set of
designing men who wish to lord it over you.  The mechanics
were then assured that aristocracies were the bane of society.
That of all aristocracies that of the lawyers was the worst, and
that they would surely be set against the Mechanics' Incorpora-
tion Bill.  The bill alluded to was one to come before the next
Legislature, by which the mechanics of the city hoped to get

leave to form themselves into a society for many purposes which they held praiseworthy.*

In the midst of the canvass news of an agreeable nature came from Boston. There was probably no State in the Union which at that time suffered so severely from the British orders in council as Massachusetts. The source of her prosperity had always been the fisheries and the carrying trade. Both of these were taken from her. One order had forbidden American fish of any kind to be brought by vessels sailing under any flag, not excepting the English, into the ports of the West Indies. Another had placed a duty of eighteen pounds a ton on whale-oil. A third had, by prohibiting any but English bottoms to fetch American goods to English ports, all but destroyed her once lucrative business of ocean carrier. While to these three a fourth grievance was added, the merchants complained, by the English traders. They had, it was said, supposed that if they could no longer export American goods, they could at least freely import English goods. But they were mistaken. Scarcely had the ink of the treaty dried when the city swarmed with factors and agents of the English merchants. These undersold every importation an American made, and in a little while had all the trade in their hands.

Like complaints came from Charleston. When the evacuation took place, sensible and patriotic men supposed, it was said, they had seen the last of the British. But the troops had hardly gone when the Pumping Club and the Smoking Club were disputing and wrangling about letting the British come back, and while the whole city, torn by these two factions, was hot in the debate, the English settled the matter by sending out a standing army of merchants, factors, clerks, and agents. They came in shoals, outmanœuvred, undersold, bullied, and drove off the French and Dutch merchants, monopolized the whole trade of the State, speculated on the wants of the people, tempted them in every way to buy, plunged them into debt, and, when they could not pay, seized their lands and goods. Not a week went by but some fine estate was put up by the sheriff at public vendue to satisfy the demands of British fac-

---

* See the New York Packets for the month of April, 1785. Boston Gazette, April 18, 1785.

tors. England, unable to conquer America with an army of
soldiers, was now about to conquer her with an army of traders.
So great a number of young clerks had poured in from Great
Britain and had found employment in the stores of the large
towns, that the sons of citizens had no chance to be brought up
to trade except with a few old merchants. Let the policy
continue, and Britain would soon have the South Carolina trade
in her own hands, for the citizens would not know anything
about trade. Was this wise ?*

The answer came from Boston. The matter was there
felt to be too serious to be muttered about and silently endured. Nothing but vigorous measures could remedy such
evils, and these were soon on foot. On the fifteenth of April
the merchants of Boston held a meeting at the long room at
Colonel Marston's. † The trouble was discussed, and a number of remedies, some of an extreme kind, proposed. They
determined, however, that the best plan was to prepare two
petitions, and instructed a committee to draft them. One
was addressed to Congress and set forth the embarrassments
under which trade was laboring. The other was to the home
Legislature imploring it to call the attention of the delegates
in Congress to the importance of speedy action. They next
established what they called a Committee of Correspondence.
The duty imposed on these gentlemen was to write to the merchants of every seaport in the States and induce them, if possible, to take a like action. They ended by pledging themselves
to make no more purchases of goods from the British merchants and factors then in Boston. As these had lately made
heavy importations, this resolution, it was believed, would be
severely felt. On the third of May the mechanics and artisans met in the famous Green Dragon Tavern, came to a like
conclusion, and adopted similar resolutions.‡

When these proceedings became known the supporters of
Congress were much elated. They expressed much pleasure
at seeing Massachusetts come into line. It was pleasant to

---

* See a pamphlet entitled, A Few Salutary Hints pointing out the Policy and
Consequences of admitting British Subjects to engross our Trade and become our
Citizens. Charleston, S. C., 1786, p. 10.

† Grayson to Madison, May 1, 1785.     ‡ Boston Gazette, May 9, 1785.

know that in at least one city of the Union the merchants were fully awake to their own interests, and had the courage to come to such strong resolutions. There was now some prospect of retaliation, if the merchants of the other great towns would but follow the lead and listen to the urgent appeal of their brothers at Boston. The smiter might yet in turn be smitten, in spite of the halting conduct of those faint-hearted ones who, alarmed by the insidious suggestions of the Tories, delayed giving to Congress power to put upon Great Britain the same restrictions she had put upon America. Indeed, when they came to read the comments made by the London papers on the action of the Boston merchants, they flattered themselves that the sting was felt already. How just the belief was is shown by the accounts which Adams, in a casual way, sent home to Jay. He had, he wrote on one occasion, been honored with a call from a noble lord who, in the course of conversation, took pains to reflect in strong terms on the Boston proceedings, and had expressed his fear that they would obstruct the return of friendship, and prove a bar to what every one should wish to see, a good treaty of commerce.* He was told that the resolutions were introduced by the words, "Whereas there is no treaty of commerce," and that there could be no doubt but that, as soon as a good treaty was made, the merchants would give them the go-by. He merely answered that he was sorry they had ever been passed. On another occasion, when Adams had an audience of Carmarthen, his Lordship mentioned that he had seen in the Gazette some account of the Boston resolutions, and went so far as to say he was very sorry to hear of them. But Adams thought they had, with other matters, contributed very much toward enabling Mr. Pitt to find time to listen to his demands.†

However this may have been it is certain that the report of the proceedings had scarce reached London before their effect became apparent in New England. Bowdoin took them into serious consideration and on the last day of May addressed the Massachusetts Legislature on the subject. They must, he said, be aware that the state of foreign trade gave general uneasiness. There was an extravagant use of imported articles.

---

* Adams to Jay, June 17, 1785.        † Ibid., June 26, 1785.

This drew away great sums of money, and, as the old-time remittances were refused, caused heavy balances against the country. England undoubtedly had a perfect right to manage her own trade as she saw fit; and in this management she was to be guided solely by her own interest and her own sense of it. The United States, too, possessed this same right. But, unhappily, the power to exercise it was wanting, for many States still refused to grant the necessary permission. This might possibly be the result of a caution to reserve to the States all powers not necessary to be delegated to Congress. But surely a bitter experience had shown that it was necessary to bestow on Congress control of trade which could on the same principle of caution be limited to a certain time. He then suggested that the States should appoint delegates to meet and settle, once for all, precisely what power it would be safe to make over to Congress for the regulation of commerce.*

The address was duly considered. The suggestion was well received, and, after some debate, the General Court gave it as their opinion that the powers Congress then enjoyed were not adequate to the great purposes they were designed to effect. A resolution then passed, with small opposition, that it would be expedient to have a convention of delegates from every State in the Union meet at some convenient place for the sole purpose of revising the Articles of Confederation. The Governor was also instructed to write to the executives of the twelve States, urging them to recommend the passage of laws likely to hinder the contracted and monopolizing policy of Great Britain, and to send on a copy of the resolutions to Congress.† Gerry, Holten, and Rufus King were the three Massachusetts delegates at New York. They received the letter of Bowdoin and the resolution early in July, and flatly refused to lay any such documents before Congress. But the first of September was come before they assigned any reasons for their

---

* Governor Bowdoin's Message to the Legislature, May 31, 1785.

† July 1, 1785. The act is given in full in Pennsylvania Packet, July 18, 1785. When the news of the Boston meeting reached Philadelphia, a similar meeting was held in that city, and resolutions sent to the Legislature. For the action of the Legislature, see Pennsylvania Packet, September 22, 1785. For New Hampshire resolutions, Pennsylvania Packet, July 20, 1785. Annual Register, vol. xxvii, p. 356.

conduct.  The members of that body were, it seems, entirely unprepared for any such course.  Their policy was a time-serving policy.  They had no wish to see a single Article of the Confederation revised, or a single line of one of them altered, though it were to give, for all time, the very power they were so earnestly begging for a little time.  They were well pleased if they could, after much begging, pleading, and threatening, obtain for a short time such small loans of power from the States as would enable them to tide over present ills, and were much disposed to let the future take care of itself.  They looked, too, with alarm on what was called the growing taste for an aristocracy.  Indeed, it was the fear of this more than anything else that moved the Massachusetts delegates to take the course they did.  They were apprehensive, so they wrote to Bowdoin, and believed it to be a duty to declare it, that such a measure could have but one result. *  The moment the call for the convention went out there would be from one end of the Union to the other a great exertion on the part of the friends of aristocracy to send members who would, by every means in their power, strive to bring about a change of government.  In place of discovering and amending the defects of the Confederation, the whole system would surely be condemned, a new plan reported, and of what the character of that plan was likely to be they could, they thought, form a very correct judgment.  But should the members be all of them ardent republicans, matters would not be bettered.  For such had been the clamors of designing men against the Confederation, against the rotation of members, which was after all the best check to corruption, and against the present way of altering the articles by the unanimous consent of the Legislatures, that there seemed great danger that a report would be brought in bestowing on Congress powers the States had not the most distant intentions of giving up.  These reasons were held to be good, and the Legislature soon after repealed the resolution.  This happened in October, five months after the occurrence of an event which many predicted marked the beginning of a prosperous trade in the far East.

On Washington's birthday, 1784, as some enthusiastic ones were careful to observe, the ship Empress sailed from New

---

* Boston Magazine for 1785, p. 475.

York for Canton, and had, after a voyage of fifteen months, again passed through the Narrows on the eleventh of May, 1785. A few days later Samuel Shaw, the supercargo, drew up a brief report of the voyage and sent it to Robert Morris. Morris forwarded it to Jay, and Jay in turn made haste to lay it before Congress, where it was read with much interest. It is curious to observe how little the two countries, soon to be so intimately connected, were then known to each other. Not one, perhaps, in a million of the polished and enlightened race that dwelt behind the wall of China had ever so much as heard the name of the little horde of barbarians with whose grandchildren their descendants would be proud to form treaties and to hold intercourse, whose civilization was to improve their civilization, and to whose land Chinamen would one day come by tens of thousands. To the most intelligent Americans China was still a fairy-land. The English, the French, the Portuguese and the Dutch had indeed been graciously permitted to send consuls to the few open ports, and ships bearing the flags of these nations were constantly to be seen sailing round the Cape of Good Hope laden with boxes of tea and bales of silk. But as yet none of the merchants had been allowed to go back into the country, or to set foot outside of the prescribed quarters of the free towns. Of the interior of China, therefore, nothing more was known than could be derived from the narratives of the Jesuits, and this knowledge was very scanty and very crude. Men of enlightened understandings fully believed that between the wall and the sea lay a rich and fertile country, teeming with vegetation, looking like a garden, and swarming with many hundreds, nay, as some said, thousands of millions of men. And of these millions nothing more was known than that their skins were tawny, their eyes askew, that they wore paper clothes and wooden shoes, that they beat their wives, that they lived in queer-shaped houses of many colors, drank tea as an American drank water, and carried bundles tied to the ends of long sticks slung over their shoulders. There were probably, with the exception of the little crew of the Empress, not ten men in the United States who had ever in the course of their lives so much as seen a Chinaman.

But to the stock of information already possessed on these points the report of the supercargo contributed nothing. It was of little value to any but merchants and men immediately concerned in trade, and was by them pronounced to be most interesting and important. It appears from the letter of Shaw that from the time the vessel stood out to sea nothing unusual happened till she entered the Straits of Sunda, where she fell in with two French ships of war. Salutes and compliments were exchanged, and, when the Frenchmen came on board, the captain learned to his delight that the frigates were, like his own ship, bound for Canton. The visitors pronounced themselves equally pleased. The admiral hastened to make known his signals to the Americans, furnished them with much useful information on the navigation of the eastern seas in case the vessels should become parted by storms, and set out in company with the Empress. The first stop was at Macao. There the French consul came on board with congratulations and profuse offers of help. He would be delighted, he would be ravished, to be of any aid to the good allies of his illustrious master, and begged for the honor of taking them ashore and introducing them to the Portuguese consul. The captain and the supercargo went, and were treated with marked civility. From Macao they sailed on without hindrance to the mouth of the Canton river. There a mandarin graciously suffered the barbarians to go up the river and drop anchor opposite the city of Canton.

But ere the sails were furled the precaution was taken to salute the shipping with a discharge of thirteen guns. The salute was quickly answered, and soon an officer from each vessel came on board. Not, however, till the twenty-ninth of August did the Chinese dignitaries consent to be rowed out to the Empress. They called the Americans the new people, inspected the ship with great interest, and when a map of the United States was spread out on the cabin-table, expressed surprise at the extent of the country, asked about its products, and seemed much pleased at the prospect of so fine a market for silks and tea.

These amicable relations were for a time interrupted. A party of Chinese merchants visited an English man-of-war lying

in the river.  As they were going home a salute was fired in
their honor.  But one of the gunners directed his piece so care-
lessly as to kill a Chinaman outright and wound another.  The
law in the Celestial Empire was blood for blood.  A demand
was accordingly instantly made on the English commander to
give up the murderer.  This he stoutly refused to do, and sent
an assurance that the unhappy event was just such a one as
often came of the use of gunpowder.  But the Canton authorities could see no difference between a death caused by accident
and a death brought about by wilful means, and in great anger
drove all foreigners out of the city, shut the gates, and confined
them to a small district without the walls.  The Governor began to gather troops.  The English in alarm begged all foreigners to stand by them, and for a while matters wore a serious
look.  Care was taken meanwhile to do nothing that could give
the least offence, and soon an invitation came from the Canton
rulers to the master of each ship, except the English, to send
an officer to a conference.  This was done.  The conference
was held, the trouble talked over, and on the solemn assurance
of the Chinese that the gunner should be fairly tried, and if
found guiltless set free, the allies promised to urge the English
to give him up.  The arbitrators were thereupon thanked for
their services, and dismissed with a gift of two pieces of pongee
silk each.  The supercargo on that day represented the Americans.  The two rolls he received were forwarded to Congress
with the letter, and examined with much interest.

As soon as the letter of Shaw had been read, Congress expressed its high sense of the importance of the voyage, thanked
the supercargo for the public spirit he manifested in so promptly
making known the result of his trip, and sent him back his rolls
of silk.*

Toward the close of May, the western lands being again
under discussion, a resolution was carried urging North Carolina to reconsider her act of the previous November, and once
more cede to Congress her possessions beyond the mountains.†
Had the request been granted, there can be no doubt the

---

* Diplomatic Correspondence of the Revolution.  Journals of Congress, May,
1785.  American Museum, March, 1787.

† Journals, May 23, 1785.

measure would have speedily brought peace and quiet to that distracted region.   But North Carolina was too intent on bringing her rebellious subjects to terms to think for a moment of bestowing them with their lands and goods on Congress.

Indeed, when the news of the request was carried into the district some months later, the malcontents expressed much surprise.   They could not, they said, understand why Congress should apply to North Carolina ; North Carolina had nothing to do with them.   The parent State had, by her act of 1784, given them away.   Congress did not take them under its protection.   They belonged, therefore, to nobody, and while in this condition had called a convention, had framed a constitution, had formed a new State, had chosen for it a name, and elected a Legislature which was actually in session at the time the act of the twenty-third of May was passed.   The request was simply absurd.   Congress was treating them as if they were rebels.   That was a great piece of injustice.   They had never thrown off their allegiance to North Carolina.   North Carolina had thrown it off for them.   They were now a free State, and all Congress had to do was to say whether they should come into the Union or stay out of the Union.   Much of what they stated was strictly true.   The delegates to the second convention had assembled early in 1785.   These had given the State the name of Franklin,* and had drawn up a constitution which they submitted to the people.   It was expected that the men of the district would consider it carefully, and select delegates to a third convention, which should have full power to ratify or reject.   The place fixed upon for the meeting of the convention was Greenville.   But as there was then no printing-press nearer than Charleston or Richmond, and as much time must elapse before the constitution could become known to all, the delegates were not to convene till the fourteenth of November.

Meanwhile the Legislature was to organize.   Elections were

---

* The name of the State has often been asserted to be Frankland, the land of the Franks or Freemen (Albach's Western Annals, pp. 507, 509).   But letters are extant from high officials of the State to Benjamin Franklin declaring that it was named after him.   See letter of William Cocke to Franklin, June 15, 1786. Franklin to Cocke, August 12, 1786.   Sevier to Franklin, April 9, 1787.

held without delay ; members were chosen after the manner in which the settlers had long been accustomed to elect representatives to the Assembly of the parent State, and these, meeting at Jonesboro, conducted their business with so much dispatch that on the last day of March they adjourned. Many acts were passed by them. But one alone excited general comment, and was the cause of unbounded merriment across the mountains. A list of articles at that time scarce to be met with in the State of Franklin would be a long one. But there would be no article in the list less plentiful than money. A few Spanish milled dollars that had come up from Natchez, some bad coppers, some sous which had been gilded over to look like moidores, and dirty fragments of Carolina paper currency, were, it is true, to be found there as everywhere. Yet even this made up so small a sum that the settlers on the Watauga and the Holston had from the earliest times resorted to barter. Some one could always be found who would take a raccoon-skin for a pound of sugar, or would exchange a gallon of good peach-brandy for a yard of flax linen. When, therefore, the Legislature came to determine what should be the legal currency of the State, it most wisely contented itself with fixing the value of such articles as had, from time immemorial, been used as money. One pound of sugar, the law said, should pass for a shilling-piece ; the skin of a raccoon or a fox for a shilling and threepence. A gallon of rye whiskey, it was thought, was worth twice that sum, while a gallon of peach-brandy or a yard of good nine hundred flax linen was each to pass for a three-shilling piece. Some difficulty was met with in selecting articles that could be easily carried from place to place and expressive of large values. It was, however, finally determined that a clean beaver-skin, an otter- or a deer-skin, should each of them be the representative of six shillings. In this kind of money, the law further prescribed, the salary of every officer of the State, from the Governor down to the hangman, was to be paid.*

When this act became known in the East the wits were greatly amused. Franklin, they said, was a happy State, for it had a currency which need not be locked up in secret drawers, which stood in no danger of being sent abroad by the mer-

---

* The acts are given in Ramsey's History of Tennessee.

chant, and which could not be counterfeited.   There was a land where debtors would be unknown, and where lawyers might starve.   For the moment a man was out of money, instead of applying to the Legislature to loan him some on his lands, he had merely to shoulder his gun, throw his traps across his back, go off to the forests, and there, far away from sheriffs and jails, trap beaver and track deer till he had accumulated enough money to pay his way for months to come.   Others expressed a hope that the judges would be paid in skins of the mink. But in the belief that the new money could not be counterfeited they were much mistaken.   Many bundles of what seemed to be otter-skins were soon passing about, which, on being opened, were found to be skins of raccoons with tails of otters sewed to them.   Those who laughed at the currency of Franklin would have done well to remember that old men still crept about among them who could distinctly recall the time when, in North Carolina, they had themselves paid quit-rents and debts in furs, in hides, in tallow, indeed, in every kind of thing that was marketable and easy to carry about.*

The same day on which Congress begged North Carolina to give up her western lands a new slur was cast upon the dignity of that body by Massachusetts.   The three gentlemen who represented her moved to bring in a resolution they had lately received from home.   This resolution set it forth as the sense of the Legislature that the United States Government was well formed.   But whatever marks of wisdom and of skill might appear on the face of the system, it could not be expected that every kind of corruption ambition or avarice might seek to introduce for the ruin of the Confederation had been guarded against.   It became the United States, therefore, in the early years of its life, to form such principles as would tend to hinder designing men in future ages from sapping the roots of the Union.   The world admired the prudence and wisdom which, by providing for a rotation of members in Congress, fixed a barrier against corruption.   But the Legislature of Massachusetts saw with concern that no provision had been

---

* These distressed times occurred in 1722, and again in 1738, when farm produce was made a legal tender.  See, for other instances, Ramsey's History of Tennessee, p. 298.

made to prevent members of Congress appointing themselves to office. No very great share of sagacity was needed to foresee that unless this point was timely guarded the lucrative places in the Federal Government would become filled by men who would not be the most capable of serving the people, or the most remarkable for integrity, and that some men, forsaking the good of the country, would take corrupt means to become members of Congress, that they might appoint themselves to well-paid posts. When the reading of the resolution was ended its commitment was moved and carried without a dissenting voice.

Meanwhile, the friends of government, nursing no such fears, were earnestly striving to create new offices. Everywhere the need of an impost and a vigorous management of trade was the absorbing topic of conversation. Many plans were proposed, many remedies suggested, discussed, and abandoned, till early in March a memorial, addressed to the State Legislature then in session, was actively circulated through the coffee-houses and taverns for signature. Some names of men well known in all occupations and professions were put down, but the merchants, as was to be expected, were far the more numerous. The subscribers set forth that they highly approved of the impost. They advanced, indeed, no new argument in its behalf, but contented themselves with a plain statement of such reasons as might any day have been heard in conversation between merchants on the street. They believed it was now admitted by all men of sense to be a principle in finance, as incontrovertible as any of the axioms of geometry, that a revenue raised in a State by an impost of the nature proposed by Congress was less felt, and therefore more cheerfully paid, than a revenue collected by any other means known to tax-gatherers. The great objections to a duty were that it acted as a check to commerce and as a bounty to smuggling. To neither of these was the impost open. The duty of five per centum was not high enough to stop importation. The gains to be had by avoiding it were not great enough to pay for the risks of smuggling. As for the idea of a misuse of the money that would flow into the Treasury, it was not to be thought of for a moment. The past behavior of Congress forbade it. Nor was it easy to be lieve that men who were chosen from the body of the people, who enjoyed but a temporary power, and who were in a little while to step down from their high places and mingle once more with the people, would attempt any very daring scheme of fraud. The proposal to grant to Congress for fifteen years sole power to regulate commercial matters was also warmly recommended. The Legislature was reminded that the Confederation was composed of thirteen independent republics; that each one of the thirteen was individually more or less commercial; that the whole collectively had, in times gone by, made no bad figure in the trading world, and would most assuredly make a still better figure in times to come. It were well, therefore, if certain general principles of trade were at once laid down and steadily followed out. But how could they be carried out unless the direction of commercial affairs was placed in the hands of a body of men whose laws each one of the States was in duty bound to obey? With what body could such power be so safely lodged as with that which had, ever since the United States began to exist, been in charge of the general welfare of the people? *

But, while the memorial was still passing from coffee-house to coffee-house, and was still being eagerly signed, a reply to it came out in the Packet under the signature of Sidney. In this paper all the points advanced in the memorial were, one after the other, taken up, and, in the opinion of the writer, refuted. The recommendation of Congress, he went on to say, was to levy an impost to fund the national debt. Every one who had read Dr. Price or Monsieur Necker knew what funding meant. Funding had been the ruin of England. What, then, was to prevent the United States, if she followed in the steps of England, from meeting the fate of England? The people were told, as they had been told a thousand times before, that the payment of the debt was just and necessary. Who said that it was not just and necessary? But was it necessary that the people should sacrifice their liberties to pay it? Perhaps there never was an action so fatal to freedom as that lately adopted by Congress to compass the darling object of getting the purse into its hands. Deputations from its own body had been sent

---

* New York Packet, March 7, 1785.

to the Assemblies of Virginia and Rhode Island. Should this be tried on any other Legislature, Sidney sincerely hoped the body so afflicted would remember its dignity, and show that the freedom of debate was not to be overawed by such means. The memorial further set forth that a tax collected by impost was least felt by the people. So much the worse. Its imperceptible operation would only make it the more easy to be continued and made everlasting. That members of Congress were chosen yearly, might be recalled at any time, could not be re-elected more than twice, and so must, at the end of three years, return to the body of the people, was another ballad sung in the people's ears. This sounded well enough. But the effect of the change was to take away all responsibility from the whole. As to recall, who in Congress would be restrained by fear of being called home when the sessions of that body were held with closed doors, and no one could find out who was the mover of a hateful measure? Besides, all who had returned to private life were, almost to a man, noisy advocates of the increase of the powers of Congress. It should therefore be remembered that the Legislature which should give the last fiat to the impost and regulation of trade would sign the death-warrant of American liberty.*

And now the arguments and replies of both parties came out fast. Indeed, it soon became manifest that the great struggle would be in New York. The temper of Massachusetts had been clearly shown in the strong resolutions adopted by the Boston merchants. Pennsylvania had not long after followed in her track, and imposed heavy duties on foreign vessels and foreign goods. In South Carolina murmurs of discontent were heard, and the whole subject of commercial regulations was being warmly debated. But the contest was nowhere carried on with as much acrimony and spirit as in New York. There three great parties were diligently striving for the accomplishment of their aims. On the one side were the non-impostmen, bitterly set against the extension of the power of Congress, and devoted adherents of State rights. On the other side were the impost men, eager for change, and confident that the stability of the Union depended on the power of Congress.

---

* New York Packet, March 17, 1785.

Between these extremes was a third, and by no means contemptible, party of trimmers. They were as much disposed to distrust the one set of extremists as the other. The States, they felt, should not have all the power. Neither should Congress. There was a golden mean, and this golden mean was to be found not far from either extreme. There was undoubtedly much truth in the assertion that trade and navigation matters were in a sad plight. Something must be done, and done soon. But it was by no means clear whether that something could be best done by Congress or by the States, or by both jointly. It was quite certain that the people could not do without many articles from over the sea; and what they deemed so essential they would import either directly or indirectly. At the present moment England would not suffer them to carry any of her manufactures in American bottoms. Suppose that, in retaliation, Congress forbade English vessels to bring English goods to American ports. Would the prohibition stop the goods coming? Assuredly not. They would still flow in, and the fifteen years during which Congress had power to keep on the impost would be fifteen years of smuggling, of remonstrances, and of vain expectation. A general and sweeping prohibition was therefore to be rigidly guarded against. But special navigation acts, acts which should decide what goods should come into one State and be excluded from another, Congress was scarce the body to make. The States could do this much better. It was, of course, quite possible that special acts might in the end fail. Very well. Let it be so. The States would then be quite ready to make over to Congress power to regulate trade. But perhaps the safest way was to let trade alone. A strong prohibition, some held, would go far toward establishing home manufactures. This was true. But was it well to set up manufactures in a country not fully or but sparsely settled, where the villages were a day's journey apart, and the houses out of sight of each other? What the country wanted was men, not manufactures; and an impost could not, unhappily, produce them. What it would bring forth was monopolies. Nor was there, when the matter came to be looked into, much real cause for the cry of ruin going around. What were the facts to support it? Would some one name the State whose staples were rotting for want of a purchaser? Did Virginia find any trouble in disposing of her tobacco? Was South Carolina burdened with unsalable indigo and rice? Where was it that the produce of the fields did not command a higher price than before the revolution? What farmer did not find his grain taken the minute it reached the market? But England had laid a heavy duty on oil. Very well. The world was full of markets for oil. Take it to Ireland. Take it to any of the ports at which, in colonial days, no American ship was ever to be seen. All would come right in time. It was to the interest of England to make a treaty of commerce with the United States.*

But neither the efforts of the trimmers nor the supporters of the impost could bring over the Governor and the Legislature to their way of thinking. The memorial which had been framed early in the spring, and sent in covered with the names of wealthy merchants and distinguished citizens, met with so little success that the Chamber of Commerce determined to again appeal to the Assembly. Several meetings were held. The matter was gravely discussed, and a committee appointed to draw up the memorial.† The paper was speedily made ready, and at the same time two circulars were prepared. One was addressed to the States, and one was addressed to the counties.

The memorial called the attention of the Assembly to the folly of a system which, while it empowered the United States in Congress assembled to make treaties with foreign powers, deprived them of the means of making such treaties with advantage. For no one could be ignorant that all relations between nation and nation were founded on common interest. Nothing was ever yielded by one save as payment for something gained of the other. It was much to be lamented that the power to regulate trade had not been vested in the national Legislature, but had been reserved by the States. The States

---

* This style of reasoning is well exemplified in an article called Cursory Thoughts on the Regulation of Trade, which came out in the New York Packet of October 27, 1785.

† The memorial and the two circulars are printed in full in the New York Packet for November 10, 1785. Another memorial by the same body is printed in the Packet for March 14, 1785.

could not possibly use it for the common good.   They could
not make treaties.   Trade could not, therefore, left to them,
be made the basis of commercial compacts.   Nor was it at all
likely that anything approaching a regular system could be
adopted by thirteen assemblies, bent upon thirteen different
objects, and seeing the same object in thirteen different lights.

The circular to the States was of a somewhat different
tone.   They could not but see, it was there stated, that merchants and landholders had been led to the false belief that
their interests were really quite unlike.   It was not surprising,
therefore, that one State should suppose advantage was to be
gained, or danger shunned, by inflicting injury or oppression
on another.   Reason seemed to be unable to dispel this illusion.
But if reason were not sufficient to show the fallacy of such a
belief, a severe experience in the past, and a much severer experience to be apprehended for the future, would show that in
the union of the States lay the source of their greatness and
their power.   Commerce was the basis of the marine.   It was
only by the marine that the States could ever hope to make
themselves respected as a nation.   And, unless the nation was
respected, the citizens would be despised; unless the nation had
the power to exact, the citizen would, in foreign lands, demand
his rights in vain.

The circular sent to the counties likewise contained some
wholesome truths.   The small farmers and petty landholders,
who detested commerce as the bane of the country, and looked
upon it as the main channel through which the gold and silver
of the land flowed out and all manner of foreign luxuries
flowed in, were given to understand they were mistaken.
The instrument plainly told them that the interests of the land-
holder were so closely bound up with the interests of the merchant that the moment commerce began to languish agriculture
must do the same.   They were assured that if they supposed
the products of their fields and their dairies were entirely consumed at home, they were much in error.   The merchants constantly sent great quantities abroad.   But unless the United
States were speedily vested with such power as would make
it the interest of foreigners to seek a commercial alliance, the
merchant would not be able to persist any longer in the ruin-

ous experiment of exporting grain and timber, tobacco and hemp, at a certain loss. Then a total stop would be put to the purchase of produce. The States would be drained of their last pistareen, and the people made unable to discharge their debts. They were reminded that the meeting of the Legislature was near at hand. It became them, then, to give pointed instructions to the delegates to support every measure tending to bestow on Congress that authority without which the commerce of the country never could be placed on an equal footing with the commerce of England, of Holland, and of France.

While the circulars contained, indeed, no reasons likely to carry conviction to the minds of men who, from ignorance or prejudice, held contrary opinions, they were by no means without effect. Every mail-coach that went out from the city took many packages of them addressed to distant parts of the country. Not a few found their way to the inns of remote hamlets, and were read by some who heard for the first time that there was in New York such a thing as a Chamber of Commerce, and that the English Navigation Act was, after all, a very serious matter. And now the discontent which had arisen in Boston, had spread thence to Philadelphia, and had been taken up with so much spirit in New York, broke out in Virginia. But the agitators for the regulation of trade in Virginia belonged to that class of the community which in the Eastern and the Middle States was most bitterly set against the measure. In Massachusetts and New York the merchants were the supporters and the farmers the opponents. In Virginia the planters were to a man united in the opinion that some steps must be taken to mend commercial affairs, and the merchants quite disposed to let trade alone.*

The reason is obvious. The condition of things to the south of the Potomac was precisely the reverse of the condition of things to the north of the Potomac. Beyond the north bank of the river the farmers throve and the merchants did a losing business. Beyond the south bank the merchants were daily

---

* "The mercantile interest," says Madison, writing of the investment of Congress with power to regulate trade, "which has taken the lead in rousing the public attention of other States, is in this so exclusively occupied in British commerce that what little weight they have will be most likely to fall into the opposite scale." To Monroe, August 7, 1785.

growing more prosperous and the planters more impoverished.*
The trade of Virginia was perhaps more in the hands of England than was that of any of her neighbors. She possessed no
ships or seamen. Her merchants were every one of them connected in business with Great Britain, and with Great Britain
alone. The planters did most of the exporting. The merchants did all the importing, and the value of the imports footed up each year to more than twice the value of the exports.
The price, again, which the imports and exports of Virginia
fetched in the home markets, when compared with the price
the same goods brought in neighboring markets, was greatly in
favor of the merchants over the planters. It was only after
much higgling that a hundred-weight of tobacco could be made
to bring a guinea on the Rappahannock and thirty-two shillings
on the James. But at the same time in Philadelphia forty-four
shillings, Virginia currency, was paid down for tobacco of the
James river inspection, and a proportionate sum for tobacco of
the Rappahannock inspection.† As to imported merchandise,
the price asked in Richmond and Norfolk was almost double
that asked in New York. The merchants, therefore, having
no cause for complaint, kept still. But the planters, finding
that they were selling their staple for less and buying their
goods for more than their neighbors, were highly dissatisfied,
and with much reason. Yet they were slow to action. Indeed,
the fall was far advanced when the House of Delegates raised
the question whether relief for the present commercial distress
could better be accomplished by Congress or the State.

The attention of the House had been called to this by
petitions which came up from the four great towns of Norfolk,
Portsmouth, Suffolk, and Alexandria. The memorials presented a picture of the state of affairs both gloomy and disheartening. They showed how the prohibition laid by Great Britain
on the trade of the West Indies had produced much distress;
how American bottoms had rapidly decreased, how ship-building had totally stopped, how even the carrying trade from town

---

* "Our internal trade is taking an arrangement from which I hope good consequences. Retail stores are spreading all over the country." Madison to Jefferson, August 20, 1785.

† Madison to Monroe, June 21, 1785. Also to R. H. Lee, July 7, 1785.

to town along the coast had gone into foreign hands, and that
the very ships which went up and down the rivers were not
owned by Americans.

Under this pressure the House determined to take speedy
action, referred the petitions to a committee of the whole on
the state of the commonwealth, and on the seventh of November
resolved itself into a committee of the whole, and took the
papers into consideration. A warm and full discussion followed.
Harrison, Braxton, and Meriwether Smith were for
State measures. Nor were there, in the House of Deputies,
three men whose opinions were heard with greater respect.
They were perhaps the oldest members of the House, and
possessed all that traditional influence which in legislative
bodies is always exercised by the old men over the new.
They had, all three of them, been members of the Continental
Congress, had often been employed in the councils of the
State, while Harrison and Braxton added the further renown
of having set their names to the Declaration of Independence.

Benjamin Harrison was a bold, frank, outspoken man. He
had all his life been active in the cause of liberty, and had, in
the early movements of the revolution, borne a part marked
with zeal and decision. A story is told of him which deserves
to be narrated as it finely illustrates the character of the man.
In the Congress of 1775, when the second petition to the King
was under discussion, John Dickinson, who had the chief part
in framing it, said that there was but one word in the paper he
disapproved of, and that word was Congress. Scarcely had he
said so when Harrison jumped to his feet and exclaimed :
" There is but one word in the paper, Mr. President, which I
approve, and that word is Congress." In the war he carried
arms with distinction, rose to be colonel of a regiment of foot,
had lately been Governor of Virginia, and had commenced the
present session of the Legislature with an animated contest for
the Speaker's chair.

Braxton, like Harrison, was early distinguished for the
firmness and zeal with which he defended the rights of the
colonies. No one had been more active in behalf of Henry's
resolutions on the Stamp Act. Yet his popularity was for a
time under a cloud. He had, while a Virginia delegate to

Congress, recommended to the Virginia Convention of 1776 a plan of government under the signature of A Native. The scheme was coldly received. The author was believed to be much biased by his two years' residence in England, and soon after lost his seat in Congress.

But of the three, the political career of Meriwether Smith had been the most singular. He was a merchant, and believed to be quite familiar with public affairs. His pursuits, indeed, as a merchant, gave him great aptitude in the dispatch of business. But they were believed by his friends to have affected his political views as nothing else could. No man, as a delegate to Congress, ever went through so many stages of favor and of disfavor with his constituents. For his conduct on one occasion he was warmly thanked. For his conduct on another he was strongly censured. Several times he was subjected to charges and investigations, which, though ending indeed in a full acquittal, marked him out as an eccentric and impracticable character.*

Joined with these three was Charles Thurston. He had been bred to the ministry, but had, when the war opened, thrown aside his gown, deserted his flock, become a soldier, and was now a most active politician.

When, however, these advocates of a State navigation act were bluntly asked what they had to propose, they were not a little puzzled. Braxton then came to their relief, and answered that he would have all British vessels from the Indies excluded from Virginia ports, and that he would have no merchant allowed to do business in the State till after a residence of a certain number of years. But he was plainly told by those who were for the regulation of trade by Congress that such talk did not in the least aid his side of the question. Much was said about public faith; about the injury each State would continually be doing to her neighbors if suffered to make her own commercial laws, and the want of unity and distrust of Congress such law-making would exhibit to England. But the most masterly reply was the speech of James Madison.†

---

* Journals of the Virginia House of Delegates, October session, 1779, p. 30. May session, 1780, pp. 22, 46. May session, 1781, p. 14. October session, 1781, p. 40.

† Madison to Washington, November 11, 1785. The notes of this speech will be found in Madison's Writings.

Madison assured his hearers, who, because they every year sent a few ship-loads of tobacco across the Atlantic, thought themselves able to speak with authority on matters of commerce and trade, that general regulations were both wise and necessary. In no other way could foreign acts be counteracted, treaties made, ships and seamen encouraged, embargoes laid in time of war, and strife among the States prevented in time of peace. They were reminded how, the moment Massachusetts closed her ports to English shipping, Connecticut made hers free, how bitter the dispute was growing between New York and New Jersey, between Pennsylvania and Delaware, and how all these things showed that, whatever goods Virginia prohibited coming into Norfolk, or Portsmouth, or Alexandria, would be admitted to Maryland or North Carolina, and thence, by fair means or by foul, surely come over her borders. But the measure was not only necessary, it was safe. If it were wise to intrust Congress with power to manage war, it was equally wise to intrust Congress with power to manage trade. Madison then went on to show them how the peculiar situation of the United States increased the repellent power of each State, and how easily this might lead to the utter dissolution of the Confederation. Of such a breaking up there could be but one result. In every State a standing army, taxes made perpetual, and each petty squabble decided by an appeal to arms. When the vote was taken, the Speaker announced that the Ayes had it, and that the sense of the House was that power over trade ought to be vested in Congress with certain restrictions. In accordance with the custom of the House, a committee was then appointed to prepare instructions for the Virginia delegates in Congress. The instructions were speedily drawn up, presented to the Legislature, and discussed in a committee of the whole.*

And now the opposition party of Harrison and Braxton mustered its full strength. The discussion lasted through several days, and was marked by the bitterness and intemperance

---

* Madison, in his account of the debate, says: "Its adversaries were the Speaker, Thurston, and Corbin; they were bitter and illiberal against Congress and the northern States beyond example." Madison to Jefferson, January 22, 1786.

of the attacks on Congress and on the North. The bill was first discussed on the grounds of its general merits, and, in the heat of debate, Thurston, after a savage attack on the eastern States, so far forgot himself as to assert that it was very doubtful "whether it would not be better to encourage the British than the eastern marine." But the remarks raised such a storm of invective that the attack was soon shifted to the ground of perpetual duration. Here the opponents of the resolution were more successful, and, after much talk about tyrants, about liberty, and the power of Congress over the States, succeeded in cutting down the term of the impost first to twenty-five and then to thirteen years. But the limitation to thirteen years made the resolution worse than none. The movers abandoned it with disgust, and suffered it to lie on the table till the last day of the session, when a substitute was moved which led to consequences of which not even the far-sighted judgment of Madison, who prepared it, had any conception whatever. This was the beginning of that movement which went on step by step in a direct and unbroken progression to the establishment of our present Government. From this motion came the National Trade Convention at Annapolis in 1786. From the Annapolis Convention of 1786 came the Philadelphia Convention of May, 1787; and from the Philadelphia Convention of 1787 came the Constitution under which we live. It is therefore well worth our while to narrate, with some fulness of detail, the history of this movement from its insignificant beginnings.

The Potomac river had always been regarded as the boundary line between Maryland and Virginia. The charter of Lord Baltimore had so defined it, but had made the jurisdiction of the colonial governors extend across the river to the southern shore. By the constitution of 1776, Virginia recognized this charter, released to Maryland all the territory claimed by it, and all rights demanded, except the free use and navigation of the Potomac and Pohomoke from their sources to their mouths. The language conveying the grant was broad and general, and might, without much sophistry, be construed into a complete relinquishing by Virginia of all jurisdiction over the rivers. Yet it seems to have escaped notice till the year after the peace when Madison brought it to the attention of the Virginia Legislature. He had, it seems, early in 1784, been travelling along the Potomac and had then been told of many flagrant evasions successfully practiced by foreign vessels loading at Alexandria. On his return to Orange he immediately wrote to Jefferson who at that time sat in Congress as one of the delegates from Virginia.* He quoted the language of the grant, mentioned the evasions which had come under his own observation, urged Jefferson to sound the Maryland delegates on the matter, and threw out the suggestion of a joint commission from the two States to define the power of each on the river. The time, he thought, was at hand, as Maryland, put into a good humor by the cession of the back lands, would be all the more ready to listen to reason. The suggestion for a joint commission was warmly approved by Jefferson. A bill was soon brought into the House of Delegates, and three commissioners appointed. Three more were, in the fall, appointed by Maryland, and in March, 1785, the commissioners met at Alexandria but soon adjourned to Mount Vernon. Everything that bore upon jurisdiction over the river and the bay was carefully gone into, all conflicting claims were amicably adjusted, and the terms of a compact quickly settled.

But, as the discussion went on, the commissioners could not fail to observe that there were many things closely bound up with the welfare of the two States which they had no rightful power to touch. It was doubtless of great moment that each State should have equal and well-defined rights on the waters of the river and the bay. But it was also of much importance that every hundred-weight of tobacco that went over the Potomac to Maryland, and every barrel of corn that came from Maryland to Virginia, should be made subject to a uniform system of duties. Nor was it less desirable that all disputes about the currency, or the meaning of the commercial laws, should be settled in accordance with some uniform principles. The commissioners were well aware that, however needful these things might be, it did not fall within their instructions to meddle with them. Yet they felt sure that, as good men and true, they might with perfect propriety draw up a supple-

---

* Madison to Jefferson, March 16, 1784 ; also, April 25, 1784.

mentary report setting forth how, in the course of their labors, they had been deeply impressed with the want of legislation on the currency, on duties, and on commercial matters in general. This indeed they did. And added the suggestion that each year two commissioners should be appointed to report upon the details of a system for the next year.

The Legislature of Maryland was first to act on the report. And, in doing so, went beyond the suggestion of the commission and proposed that Delaware and Pennsylvania should be invited to join Virginia and Maryland in a common system of commercial policy. This was in November. At that time neither the proceedings of the joint commission nor the action of the Maryland House of Delegates had been laid before the Legislature of Virginia. But Madison, who was a commissioner, was well aware of what had been done and now saw his opportunity. The resolution granting Congress power to regulate trade for thirteen years was, in his opinion, likely to do more harm than good. He determined, therefore, to attempt to baffle the arts of the opposition, and to further the good cause by enlarging the recommendations which he knew would shortly be presented to the House, into a call for a convention of commissioners from all the States. He accordingly drew up such a resolution. But when he had made it ready a new difficulty presented itself. Who should introduce it? He had long been a member of Congress. He had on several occasions, in set speeches, defended the extension of the powers of that body, and particularly in matters of trade. He was therefore often accused of undue bias in favor of Congress, and he knew that any resolution he might bring in would be viewed with more jealousy, and scrutinized with more severity than if brought in by any one else. In this difficulty he had recourse to Mr. Tyler, who agreed with him in politics, who had never sat in Congress, and whose popularity in the House was great. Tyler introduced the resolution. It was moved as a substitute for the original motion, and, as it was not pressed, was laid on the table. But at last, on the fifth of December, the Maryland resolutions were brought before the House of Delegates and referred to the committee on commerce. A week later the report of the joint commission under·

went a like fate. This, however, was reported back a month after, in a series of resolutions similar to those of Maryland, and passed. As for the supplementary report, a copy was ordered to be sent to each State. With the copy was to go the request that each of the eleven would appoint commissioners to meet with those from Maryland and Virginia for the purposes expressed in the instrument. And now the way seemed open. The recommendation of the commission fell, indeed, far short of the resolution of Madison. Yet it was a step in the right direction. The commissioners had contented themselves with urging a uniform system of duties between the States. Madison proposed that the convention should go beyond this, should examine the condition of the trade of the Confederation, and should report such an act as would, when adopted by each State, enable Congress to provide for the trade of the whole country in the most effectual manner. In this form his resolution was taken from the table on the last day of the session and rapidly passed through both branches of the Legislature. Seven commissioners were appointed. Among them was Meriwether Smith, who had from first to last opposed it with bitterness and asperity.

A few weeks after the breaking up of the Houses the seven commissioners held their first sitting at Richmond. The business before them was to determine a time and to select a place of meeting for the proposed convention. The day was soon fixed upon as the second Monday in September, 1786. But the place was not chosen till after much discussion. For the seven were agreed that wherever the convention met it should at least do so at a place far removed from the sittings of Congress and the neighborhood of great commercial towns. Were the delegates to assemble at New York, or indeed at Philadelphia, the cry would surely go up that they had been awed, or browbeaten, by members of Congress to adopt such measures as would gratify what Brutus and Gracchus, Cassius and Junius, called "the lust of power." Were they to deliberate near the large seaports, where the merchants were numerous and powerful, nothing would be able to dissuade the multitude from the belief that every member of the convention had been button-holed by dozens of distressed merchants, or had his ears filled with complaints and his pockets with petitions, till he was made to believe that matters were a hundredfold worse than they were, and could only be remedied by extending the power of Congress. It was thought, however, that all ground for such charges was completely removed by selecting Annapolis as the place of meeting.*

The call for the Trade Convention, however, excited much less discussion than was expected. The attention of the people was wholly taken up with a subject which was to them much more pressing. There were at that time, as there have been and still are, in every State select companies of incorrigible fools who thought that a State could, by merely calling a bundle of old rags a hundred thousand pounds, really add one hundred thousand pounds to the wealth of the community, and that if any man were rash enough to doubt this he should be locked up in jail till he came to his senses. These men had, during the summer and fall, been unusually active and clamorous, and succeeded in bringing over to their way of thinking great numbers of converts. Nor was it a very difficult matter to make converts. For money had become so scarce that many men who at any other time would have scouted the talk of the paper advocates as the babble of fools, were easily made to believe a debased currency which circulated freely was, after all, much better than a good currency of which they rarely saw a coin. Indeed, with the recollection of the dark days of 1779, when forty dollars were paid for a hat, fifty pounds for a hundred of sugar, and as many dollars for a hundred of flour, still fresh in their memories, the multitude was not ashamed to cry out for a new issue of paper money, and for new gag-laws to make it circulate. The consequences were soon apparent. The elections came on, and in the Legislatures of seven States out of the thirteen the paper men counted a majority. No sooner did they find themselves in power than they brought in all manner of bills for the issue of paper, and hurried them through with all possible speed. In most instances the opposition encountered was small in numbers and broken in spirit. But in a few States the struggle was bitter and protracted. Such a one was

---

* Such was the statement made to Madison by Edmund Randolph. Madison to Jefferson, March 18, 1786.

Maryland. More than a year before a paper-money bill had
been framed, had been strongly defended in petitions to the
House and heartily reviled in letters to the Gazette, had been
passed by the House, and, most happily, thrown out by the
Senate. This merely increased the clamor and indignation of
the people, and in November, 1785, a petition praying for the
emission of paper money came in from the town of Baltimore.
Nine hundred and ten men put their hands to the instrument.
The whole subject was at once up for discussion. The troubles,
it was said, which afflicted the State were not to be cured by
building up manufactures, by encouraging commerce, by passing navigation bills. These were the things which made the
troubles. The true panacea was paper money. From the very
day on which the bills began to issue from the Treasury the
burden of taxes would grow lighter, debts be discharged with
ease, arts and commerce flourish, and the faces of all men wear
a contented expression.

To this childish talk were opposed arguments which might
be perused with profit by those mischievous schemers who in
our time, under the name of Greenbackers, advocate a money
policy as vicious and absurd as that which, ninety-eight years
ago, was vainly combated by our ancestors. Those who had
been led away by the large promises of the paper men were
told by the specie men that the main support of paper money
was public opinion. The support of the many was also the
foundation of all power in the Government. A Government
in which the people had no faith was doomed. A currency
in which the people had no faith was likewise doomed; it
had no value whatsoever. But public opinion as applied to
paper money meant something very different from public
opinion as applied to Government. It meant a firm belief
that a dollar in credit-bills was equal to, and would answer all
the purposes of, a Spanish dollar in silver. If such faith existed among men, then the road to an issue of paper money
would be smooth and easy to travel. Such confidence did not
prevail, nor could any fair-minded man deny that it ought to
be firmly set up before they ventured on an expedient which
had so many times before been productive of miserable consequences. It was easy to understand the motives which led

men to favor the plan. Dishonest debtors held the delusive hope that a new tender law would be passed. Merchants who found the gains arising from the fluctuations of paper to be the most profitable part of their business, would, of course, give it a warm approval. The multitude, heavy laden with taxes, would welcome with delight any means of paying them with as much ease as in the days when red money was taken at par. But suppose this new money did come out; was there a farmer or a planter who would take it in payment for barrels of corn or hogsheads of tobacco? Would a moneyed man with his specie out at interest take it? Would the merchants take it for an assortment of goods at the current price? The truth was, the wit of man could devise no method of supporting paper money the moment public opinion failed it. Bills of credit, when unsustained by this prop, stood on exactly the same footing as private bills. Let the richest, the most highly esteemed man in the State issue a bond of one hundred pounds for five years and what would become of it? He could not sell it for half that sum. The same was true with paper money. When the debtor knew he could discharge specie obligations with it; when the merchant knew he could pass it as coin in other States; when the Government took it for taxes, and the money-lenders exchanged it for silver and gold at par, then would paper money be as good as specie, and not before. To talk of ample funds for redemption at a distant day betrayed a lack of information on the subject that was really lamentable.*

In the midst of the discussion the term of the Senate expired, and the whole body was to be chosen anew. Then the excitement rose to fever heat. Never had there been such electioneering, such wire-pulling, such pamphleteering known in the State. Members of each House canvassed openly among the people, and, when the election was over, it was found that, although the House of Deputies was made up almost exclusively of the paper men, and though many old members of the Senate had lost their seats, the hard-money men still presented a formidable majority in the Upper House. The result was

---

* These arguments are set forth in a paper in the Maryland Gazette, December 2, 1784.

inevitable. The House of Deputies almost immediately passed an act for the issue of credit-bills. But the Senate stood firm, threw out the bill, and, at the fall election of 1787, the paper-money scheme was once more made the question of an exciting canvass.*

In other States, however, the struggle was soon over. In Pennsylvania almost the only man of ability and note who held out vigorously against the rag-money party was Pelatiah Webster. Very little information regarding him has come down to us; but his works show him to have been a man of parts, clear-headed, and a student of political economy and finance. Indeed, no one among his contemporaries maintained sounder views on these matters, or labored more diligently to instruct the people. An ardent free-trader and a hard-money man, he spent much leisure time in writing little tracts on his favorite hobbies. Now it was a pamphlet on the danger of too much circulating cash in a State; now a neat essay on the Test Act, on Credit, or a paper embodying severe strictures on the Tender Act. But more commonly his theme was Free Trade and Finance. Six essays on this subject had already come out when, in January, 1785, he published the seventh. Like all its predecessors, though treating of things which to most readers are tiresome and dry, it was pleasingly written, and contained much wholesome advice. The idea that there was a great scarcity of cash was, he said, erroneous. There was a full sufficiency. Everything that had a cash value, labor, and indeed all the great staple commodities produced by it, would and did command not only immediate payment, but high prices. On an average, forty to fifty per cent more was obtained for labor and for country produce in 1784 than in 1774. It was then absurd to talk of the lack of money when labor and the fruit of it had quick sales, good prices, and cash. To say that it was hard to

---

* See a letter from Madison to Jefferson, August 12, 1786. Writing to Monroe four months later, he says: "We hear that Maryland is much agitated on the score of paper money, the House of Delegates having decided in favor of an emission." In 1787, April 15th, Franklin writes: "Maryland, too, is divided on the same subject (paper money), the Assembly being for it, and the Senate against it. Each is now employed in endeavoring to gain the people to its party against the next election, and it is probable the Assembly may prevail." Franklin to De la Rochefoucauld.

borrow money, and that all kinds of public securities were down far below par, was no argument. If capitalists would not put out their money, if loan-office certificates, depreciation certificates, and final settlements were to be had at two shillings sixpence in the pound, or eight for one, that did not prove money to be scarce. What it did prove was a want of public and private faith, and a distrust of all security. He then showed most forcibly that an issue of paper money would not mend matters in the least.* But his arguments fell on deaf ears. The House yielded to the rage for paper money, and ordered bills of credit to be issued by the State Treasurer. Rittenhouse accordingly notified the President, on the tenth of May, 1785, that bills to the amount of seven thousand pounds had been signed, and were ready to issue; that the signers were working industriously, and that he felt sure in future at least ten thousand pounds would come out each week.† The sum emitted was small. The funds for sinking it were good, and it was not made a legal tender. It went into circulation partly by way of loans to the farmers on their lands, and partly by way of payments to the public creditors. It was believed, therefore, to be as good as money of the kind could be made, or, as the supporters said, as good as specie. Yet before the first of August, 1786, was come, the depreciation had reached twelve per cent.‡

North Carolina came next. The amount put out had been quite large, had been made a legal tender, and been issued in that way which, of all ways, was the surest to cause a depreciation at the start. A little was loaned on landed property, and as much as possible passed off on creditors who had bills against the State. But this proved far too sluggish a channel, and, under the pretence of throwing the new money rapidly into circulation, large purchases of tobacco were ordered by the State. The agent charged with this duty received strict commands to make all payments in paper, and to put down for each pound of leaves twice as much as the planters could, in the best market, obtain for it in specie. Every debtor, there-

---

* Essays of Pelatiah Webster.

† Rittenhouse to Dickinson, May 10, 1785. Pennsylvania Archives, 1785.

‡ See a letter from Madison to Jefferson, August 12, 1786.

fore, who could lay hands on a hundred-weight of tobacco, carried it to the agent, received double its specie value in paper, and then hastened off to pay his creditors in paper shillings and dollars, which the law declared to be quite as good as silver ones. But something more than the votes of a Legislature was needed to transmute rags into silver. From the day on which the paper first appeared, depreciation went steadily on till the new bills were paid and received at a discount of thirty per cent.

In South Carolina the advocates of soft money denied that the paper had suffered any decline whatever. The bills had been issued as loans to individuals, and had not been made a legal tender. Yet, in spite of boasts and promises, depreciation showed itself in the rapidity with which the price of every kind of goods went up. Indeed, matters soon came to such a pass that the paper men, in desperation, called a meeting of planters at the State House. Judge Heywood took the chair, and stated that the purpose of the meeting was to induce the planters to do something for the support of the credit of the new medium. A spirited debate followed. In the course of it Mr. Bradsford spoke for the merchants. The merchants, he said, were fully determined to give the bills every degree of support in their power. They had, in fact, entered into a solemn league to do so. It was greatly to be hoped a like disposition would not be found wanting in the planting interest. For at least a month past no difference had been made by the members of this league between paper dollars and silver dollars, which circulated much more freely than they had done for years. He had himself received many payments in specie, and he had exchanged bills to the amount of several hundred dollars with the vendue masters in order to oblige friends who wished to go out of the State. But this equality had been destroyed by some impatient ones. They wished to leave the State. They were in want of specie, and, to get it at once, had given orders to their agents or factors to sell for one half paper, one half specie. This distinction had alarmed the distrustful, and paper was now going down.

Bradsford was followed by De Saussure. He announced himself as a merchant, and told the meeting that in his house the paper of South Carolina was held to be as good as gold. This paper had been put out for the sole purpose of enabling the planters to extricate themselves from debts and embarrassments. As soon as it came forth, the merchants, out of pity for the planters, had given it every support they could. Suppose they had not done so. Suppose they had adopted a different line of conduct, and, instead of taking, had refused the paper. What would then have happened? It would have instantly lost value. But while the merchants were striving to keep up the value of paper, the planters were striving to pull it down. They were asking more for rice if paid for in paper than if paid for in gold. Nor was it in this article alone that the increase in price had taken place. It was common for planters to ask six shillings for indigo in paper, or four shillings sixpence in specie. Those who had corn demanded eight shillings paper, or a dollar in silver. If this went on, the credit of the paper then circulating would surely be ruined. Before the meeting broke up, every one present agreed to take the paper as equal to silver and gold, and solemnly pledged himself to buy no goods of any kind on which an abatement was offered for payment in coin.*

Meanwhile, some hot-heads at Charleston determined to try what threats and a little coercion could do. They accordingly formed themselves into an organization called the Hint Club, held regular meetings, and appointed a secret committee. The precise purpose of the club, and the duty of the committee, is, it must be owned, obscure. But, so far as can now be known, it was the business of the secret committee-men to hunt out among the planters and merchants all such as favored hard money, to watch them closely, and, if their conduct seemed likely to injure the prosperity of the credit-bills, convey to them a forcible hint that it would be well to desist. When the hint failed the club was notified. A meeting was called, a night and a rendezvous chosen, and, when the time came, three rockets let off. Then the members hastened to the appointed place and went thence in a body to hurl down, as it was said, public vengeance on the destroyers of the commonwealth.†

---

* New York Packet, August 28, 1786.
† New York Gazetteer and Country Journal, July 21, 1786.

In Georgia the opposition to the paper money was equally strong, and the means taken to force it into circulation equally unjust. The Legislature had, at its late session, ordered an emission of paper currency, had made it a legal tender, and the bills were almost ready to come out. While the matter was still under discussion, the laborers and mechanics had begun to murmur against it, and some talk of a petition was heard. They had not forgotten what became of the late issue. How it had steadily gone down in value till the bills would scarce bring the sum expended in printing them; and how this caused great distress and misery, which they would not willingly a second time undergo. But no sooner did it become known that the act had passed, and that the paper was really coming out, than they resorted to strong measures, held meetings, drew up resolutions, and lay down their course of conduct. One of the first meetings was held early in September at the Court-House at Savannah, and was composed entirely of· mechanics.* They understood, they said, in the resolutions framed on that occasion, that the paper money shortly to be put out was a legal tender for all debts present and to come. The funds had, however, in their opinion, no better security for redemption than the paper issued in times past, and declared by law to be sunk at one thousand dollars in bills for one dollar in silver. They could not therefore, in justice to their families, take the money of the new issue at par, but only at so much as they could sell it for in coin.

The merchants took a different view of the matter. They had, to a man, worked hard to have the money issued, and, now it was out, were determined to support it. They knew, moreover, where their strength lay, for they were the purchasers and exporters of the rice, the indigo, the pitch, whatever, in short, the plantations around Savannah produced. A little concerted action on their part could therefore, at any moment, prevent a single ship-load of produce quitting the river. This action was taken. A bill was hurried through the Legislature, and the planters informed that if one of them should refuse to take paper in payment for his rice, not a sack of

---

* New York Packet, September, 1786.

it should be suffered to leave the State.* To effect this no produce was to be exported from any part of Georgia unless a sworn
statement was produced, signed by the planter and the merchant, that neither of them had at any time refused to take the
paper money of the State at the value expressed upon its face.†

Against measures such as these Virginia alone, among the
States south of the Potomac, stood firm. The itch, as Madison called it, for paper money had never very seriously afflicted the people. The disorder did indeed break out, and rage
quite fiercely toward the close of 1786; but was limited to
the counties of Brunswick and Campbell. From each of them
petitions came up praying for a paper emission to be a legal
tender for all contracts made since the glorious day when the
ploughmen of Middlesex drove the British out of Lexington and
down the road to Boston. But when a bill came before the
House of Delegates for discussion, almost every member had
something to say against it, and, when the vote was taken, the
Nays had it by a crushing majority of eighty-five to seventeen.‡

In other parts of Virginia the people contented themselves
with forming societies for the encouragement of economy and
home-trade. One such sprang up in the four counties about
Richmond, and numbered among its members all the first
characters of the place. A gentleman whose name was on the
roll declared one aim of the Patriotic Society to be to instruct
the delegates. Another was to teach the people. They showed
a total heedlessness of the public good. This came not so much
from depravity as from a lack of knowledge. The members
of the Patriotic Society purposed, therefore, to meet, talk over
matters of general concern, and make known their thoughts to
the people in the shape of instructions to the delegates. Should
these be approved, they were to be signed and sent to Richmond.

To the political duties were added others of a more praiseworthy kind. A pledge was drawn up which declared the pres-

---

* Boston Gazette, October 23, 1786.

† New York Gazetteer, October 11, 1786.

‡ See Journals of the House of Delegates of Virginia, session of 1786, pp. 15
and 16. The strong and sensible language of one sentence of the resolution
passed on that occasion is worth quoting. "An emission of paper money would
be unjust, impolitic, and destructive of public and private confidence, and of tha
virtue which is the basis of republican government."

ent embarrassments could be honestly and thoroughly remedied in no other way than by a spirited exercise of industry,
by enlarging the productions of the land, and by practicing a
strict frugality.  All who put their hands to this pledge bound
themselves, on their honor, to encourage these things by their
example, to shun dissipation, and to give a warm support to
any plan of trade the fruits of which should go to their countrymen.  Prizes were also offered for the most useful discovery in farming, and for the best method of fencing to save
timber.*

In New York the paper party had, for a year past, been
steadily growing in numbers, had gained many seats at the
late election, and, believing themselves strong enough to carry
their measures, brought in a bill.  This at once led to a violent
opposition, and split the State into two parties.  On the one
side were the importers, the holders of stock, the speculators in
cash, as they were called, the moneyed men, and the great body
of creditors, who, having made their advances on a specie basis,
were determined to take nothing but specie in return.  These
put as good a face on the matter as possible, and went about
assuring their friends that scarcity of cash was a mere fiction.
It had been the cry of idle and extravagant fellows in all ages.
That there really was a circulating medium in the country, no
more convincing proof was wanted than the state of the market.  Any one having a bushel of rye, or a bushel of wheat, or
a bushel of corn, or, in truth, any kind of produce, had merely
to carry it to the Bear Market to receive, in cash, as much for
it as in days before the war.  If some men found themselves
unable to pay their debts, it was because of idleness or profusion.  But taking up money of the State on loan was a delusion.  It afforded, at best, but a temporary relief; put off the
evil day for a year or two, and then left them deeper than ever
in debt.  The injuries suffered so recently by the depreciation
of a paper currency would surely make men loath to take it.
And if it were not freely taken, it would depreciate; and de-

---

* See New York Packet, November 17, 1786; American Museum, August,
1787, p. 166 ; Letters of Bushrod Washington to George Washington, September
27 and October 31, 1786; George Washington to Bushrod Washington, September 30 and November 15, 1786; Washington's Writings, vol. ix.

preciation could only be prevented by making it a tender, and to make it a legal tender would be cruel.\*

With the friends of the emission were the shopkeepers in the great towns, the merchants in the country villages, manufacturers, and debtors.   The arguments which these advanced were that, by the ravages of war, the depreciation of the continental money, and a long train of unavoidable misfortunes, numbers of the most industrious and frugal citizens had become deeply involved in debt.   There might, they said, be money enough at the Bear Market to buy a few bushels of corn or rye, yet this fact was very far from proving the existence of a circulating medium.   Such a thing did not exist. And did any one want a better proof than that lands were sold every day, at sheriff's vendue, for one half their real value? They further insisted that the speculators in cash were taking advantage of the distress of their neighbors to reap great harvests.   That they were lending money at exorbitant rates of interest, and exacting payment the moment it became due. That the bank was a nuisance.   Instead of affording a useful relief to the mercantile interests, it had degenerated to a scandalous scene of usury and extortion.   That, if paper money were emitted, all men would be helped; that the ill effects of usury would be stopped, while all its profits, then going to a combination of usurers, would be enjoyed by the State.

Both parties betook themselves to a newspaper and pamphlet war.   Most of the papers were by anonymous hands. Yet the names of the writers were no secrets.   One dreamer, who called himself Honestus,† filled several columns of the Packet with a plea for paper money, and the abolition of the bank, which was to his mind the cause of all the trouble.   Another, who wrote on the same side and subscribed himself A Spartan, ironically recommended that the best thing to be done was to do away with money and go back to barter.   Copy, said he, the laudable example of Lycurgus.   Banish money, and with it all the evils of which money is the root.   Let barter, the first and simplest mode of dealing, be once more established.   Then truly will men be industrious.   Then will the

---

\* See a paper by A Citizen of Dutchess County, in the New York Packet for March 6, 1786.                     † New York Packet, March 27, 1786.

streets be crowded.  Then will the carters and porters meet
with full employment.  Nay, even people of the better class
will be seen lugging pieces of furniture to exchange for barrels of flour or pairs of shoes.*

But of all the papers the excitement called forth, the two
most widely read were a pamphlet by Thomas Paine and a petition from the Chamber of Commerce to the Legislature.  The
stirring words of "Common Sense" and the "Crisis" were still
so fresh in the minds of men that anything by the same hand
was read with consideration and delight.  Nor would it be easy
to find among the many pamphlets by the author of "Common Sense" one more distinguished for common sense than his
little tract on paper currency.  He began with the observation
that he remembered to have once heard a German farmer say
in a few words about as much as the subject required : "Money
is money, and paper is paper."†  All the inventions of man,
said he, cannot make it otherwise.  If paper can be metamor-
phosed into gold and silver, or made to answer the same purposes with all men, then it is time for the alchemist to cease
his labors, and for the hunter after the philosopher's stone to
go to rest.  Gold and silver are the emissions of nature.  Paper
is the emission of art.  The value of gold and silver is ascertained by the quantity which nature has made in the earth.
The fact that these metals were stamped into coin added much
to their convenience, but nothing to their value.  Their worth
was in the metal; not in the stamp.  Gold, again, had all the
requisites of money.  Paper had none of them.  Paper was too
plentiful, too easily got at.  The only use it should be put to
for money purposes was to write notes and obligations on to pay
in coin.  But when an Assembly undertook to issue paper *as*
money, all safety and certainty were overturned and property
set afloat.  Of the many sorts of base currency, the basest was
paper.  It had least intrinsic value of anything that could be
put in place of specie.  A hob-nail or a piece of wampum from
the Indians far exceeded it.  To suppose, therefore, that the
breath of an Assembly whose authority expired in a year could

---

* New York Packet, February 16, 1786.

† Dissertations on Government; the Affairs of the Bank, and Paper Money.
By the author of Common Sense, p. 43.

give to paper the value and duration of gold, was absurd. Indeed, it was utterly beyond the power of the Legislature to engage that the very next one would not refuse to take their money for taxes. As for a Legal-tender Act, any member who moved such a thing ought to be punished with death.

The petition of the Chamber of Commerce came out late in February. In tone it was not unlike the many similar instruments which that vigilant corporation had from time to time laid before the Assembly. It shared also the usual fate.*

But pamphlets, petitions, remonstrances, were alike in vain. The paper men stood firm. The bill was carried. The Governor set his hand and seal to it, and an emission to the amount of two hundred thousand pounds York money came out. Eight shillings made a dollar. The issue was therefore believed to be equal to five hundred thousand Spanish milled dollars. Something, indeed, was gained by the opposition. For the money was made a legal tender in suits only, and was loaned to none who could not furnish excellent security.

Late in July the notes began to come from the press. The rush for them was not so great as had been expected. Many who had been clamorous for the money a few months before held back that they might see what kind of a reception would be given it. In this extremity a few men of means determined to make a public showing of their implicit faith in the bills. For several days, therefore, after the first issue, they went about among the inns and taverns of the city at the hour when the company was the most numerous, threw down upon the counters handfuls of shillings and Spanish bits, and asked to have them exchanged for the light and portable money of the State. Everywhere they found ready takers, and, ere the week was ended, coin to a considerable amount had in this way been exchanged for paper.†

New Jersey, in the mean time, had put out thirty thousand pounds in paper, had made seven shillings sixpence a dollar, and had declared it to be a legal tender. An additional hundred thousand pounds soon followed. In that State a wholesome dread of popular associations long stifled any open dis-

---

* New York Packet, March 6, 1786.

† New York Gazetteer and Country Journal, July 28, 1786.

crimination between the paper and coin.* But much of the trade of New Jersey was then carried on at Philadelphia and New York. Large sums in the new paper were therefore soon offered at these cities in payment of debts. But, as the merchants were in no fear of the clamor of angry Jerseymen, they refused it as a legal tender, depreciation began at once, and, before the end of the year, had spread to New Jersey.

While State after State was thus printing money to satisfy the cry of the multitude that they had no circulating medium, an event happened in New England which filled the whole country with mortification and rage. Late in the summer the bark Mary Barnard had set sail from Boston, and, after a month's voyage, had reached the port of London. The English papers had mentioned the arrival, and had noticed with delight, as one of many signs of the prosperous trade the home merchants were doing with America without a treaty of commerce, that the ship was fairly loaded down with specie. No such cargo had come over from the States for twelve years past. She brought, it was said, forty-six thousand one hundred and twenty-five dollars; twelve hundred and twenty-nine joes; one hundred and ten half-joes; eight hundred and six crowns; two thousand and eighty-seven guineas; eighty-five pistoles; two hundred and sixty-four dollars in silver; one moidore, and five hundred and fifty-six ounces of gold. But on this side of the water there was thought to be little cause for rejoicing. Men who had not so much as seen a half dozen guineas, or joes, or moidores for a year past, stood aghast at

---

* See a letter from Madison to Jefferson, August 12, 1786. It seems scarce worth while to give a list of the innumerable papers and pamphlets which came out on the subject of paper money during the year 1786. A few of the best of them are: The True Interest of the United States, and particularly of Pennsylvania, Considered; Extracts from an Address to the Representatives of the People of Virginia; Queries and Replies Relative to Paper Money, by Z.; Essay on Paper Money, by An Old Soldier; Thoughts on Paper Money, by Nestor; Paper Money Advocated, by a Branch of the House of Shandy; Essay on Money, as a Medium of Commerce: with Remarks on the Advantages and Disadvantages of Paper admitted into General Circulation, by a Citizen of the United States, 1786; The Primitive Whig; New Jersey Gazette, January, 1786, five numbers; Pelatiah Webster's Free Trade and Finance; Letters from Sylvius to the Freemen Inhabitants of the United States, Containing some Remarks on Scarcity of Money, Paper Currency, etc., 1787.

the news.   What a sum to go out in hard money, said they,
from a place which has for above a year suffered the most inconvenience from being drained of that article!   Can it be
that New England, which had just cause to raise the first cry
against the importation of British goods; that New England,
where men and women formed societies for the promotion of
American manufactures;  that that small part of America
which in reality employs a greater number of manufacturers
than all the rest of the continent put together, has sent out
such a treasure for British gewgaws?   The vulgar cry had
long been, Encourage home manufactures, discourage importation.   Yet here was New England, doing the most manufacturing and having the least cash of any of the thirteen
States, exporting the most money.*   And this anomaly was
quickly seized upon by the grumblers.   Those who had lands
for sale, or looked with distrust on the growing favor of manufactures, asserted that he who expected that mills and factories
would import money looked no further than his nose.   The
only way to bring in money was to cover the earth with corn
and with rye, with acres of wheat and with fields of flax.
Then, when the harvest was over, a triumphant fleet of ships
would sail from every port, and would in a few months come
home heavily laden with gold.   Others contented themselves
with alluring pictures of the happiness of the farmer, contrasting the low of cattle and the bleat of lambs with the din of
mills and factories, the pure air and the green fields with the
stench that rose from the docks, and with the crowds that stood
upon 'Change.

It is a significant fact, however, that while half the country
was indulging in language such as this, New England had
already begun that splendid line of manufactures which, in the
course of two generations, grew rapidly to astonishing proportions, covered her streams and rivers with workshops and factories, built up new towns more populous and opulent than the
old, and, among many substantial benefits, gave to the world
that innumerable host of articles which, under the name of
Yankee notions, are now to be found in the markets of every
people.   The humble beginning of so much prosperity was in

---

* New York Packet, October 16, 1786.

the manufacture of cotton and woollen cloths.  At last patterns
had been obtained, and rude models set up, of the Arkwright
machines.  More than eighteen years before Arkwright had
made known his spinning-jenny.  Since that time it had been
wonderfully improved, and had become, with the machines of
Compton and Cartwright, the marvel and envy of the world.
It was indeed with this at first as with every great invention,
from the alphabet to the printing-press, from the printing-press
to the railroad, from the railroad to the telegraph.  It was
bitterly opposed.  The jennies were long operated in secret.
The life of the inventor was threatened.  On more than one
occasion the machines were broken to pieces by an angry mob.
But, in spite of threats and violence, they began to multi-
ply.  It was soon discovered that the spinning done by hand
was inferior in quality to the spinning done by the jenny;
and Arkwright, whom hundreds of men could remember as a
raw lad wandering over the heaths persuading the peasant-girls
to sell their hair, was raised to the dignity of knighthood.
Then a complete revolution took place.  The same men who a
few years before denounced the jenny as an impious thing,
and the inventor as a man who richly deserved a halter and
might possibly get his deserts, soon clamored that not a machine should, on any account, be suffered to leave the kingdom.  The year after the Boston tea party, Parliament, accordingly, forbade that any drawings, models, or memoranda
of any machine used in the manufacture of textile fabrics
should leave the realm.  Some attempts were made a few months
later to carry models of the jennies to Germany, and also to
France.  But it was not till peace had been restored that any
effort was put forth to bring them to America.  It was at that
time quite fashionable for men of wealth and leisure to form
themselves into societies for the encouragement of whatever
they had most at heart.  Societies for the encouragement of
manufactures, societies for the promotion of agriculture, societies for the furthering of arts and sciences began to spring
up in every great city.  But the most active among them was
at Philadelphia, and the most active of all its members was
Tench Coxe.  No man deserves better than he to be called the
father of the American cotton industries.  At a time when the

plant was rarely seen outside of a flower-garden, when the custom-house officers at Liverpool denied that all America could produce six hundred pounds, he plainly told his countrymen that cotton would one day be the source of their wealth and their power.* He stood up before the Federal Convention and begged southern delegates to go home and urge their people to cultivate it. He bitterly opposed the article of Jay's treaty which forbade the export of cotton for twenty-five years. Nor did he, to the end of a long and eventful life, grow cool in the encouragement of his favorite industry. No sooner was the war ended than he set his heart on obtaining a series of the Arkwright machines. An agent was procured in England to undertake the matter under promise of a large reward, and a full set of models was made in brass. But the work could not long be kept a secret. In 1786, upon the very eve of shipment, the pieces were seized.

Help, however, came from another quarter. Scarcely had the English Government laid hold of the models of Coxe than Hugh Orr, of Bridgewater, sent up a notice to the General Court of Massachusetts. He had, he said, in his employ two Scotchmen by the name of Barr who had some knowledge of cotton-spinning machines. The news was received with delight. A committee was appointed to examine the two Barrs, to find out what they knew, and to report with all speed to the Legislature. The report is still extant, and recommends that two hundred pounds sterling be granted to the men to complete certain machines, and to reward them for their public spirit. So great a sum was not then to be spared from the Treasury. Six tickets in a State Land Lottery which had no blanks were therefore voted to the Barrs, and out of the money they drew the first stock-card and spinning-jenny in the United States were made.

But while these were making, another petition came up to the General Court from William Somers. He was, he said, a member of a Baltimore society for the encouragement of agriculture. He had been brought up to the manufacture of cotton, and knew how to adapt the thread for weaving dimities,

---

* See An Address to an Assembly of the Friends of American Manufactures, by Tench Coxe, Esq., reprinted in American Museum for September, 1787.

plain and checked muslins, calicoes, jeans, and jeannettes. In-deed, he had, at his own risk and expense, gone to England, had studied the machines for carding and spinning wool, and had, after much difficulty, brought back models and descriptions to Baltimore. But at Baltimore he had found nothing to do, had set out for Boston, and had, upon the way, lost much of his property. He now sought help of the Legislature. So prom ising a petition was not to be thrown out, and twenty pounds were accordingly placed in the hands of Orr for the encourage-ment of Somers. In a short time a rude model of an Ark-wright machine was completed and exhibited under the name of the State's Model, with the spinning-jenny made by the Barrs. These were confided to the care of Orr, and, as a reward for his pains, full permission was given him to use them. He was, however, at the same time strictly enjoined to show the ma-chines to all whom interest or curiosity prompted to come and examine. Many gladly availed themselves of the chance, and before long rude imitations of them were set up at Worcester, at Beverly, and at Providence. It was not, however, till Washington had been one year President that Samuel Slater put up in the workshops of Almy & Brown the first series of machines worthy to be called copies of the famous inventions of Arkwright.*

Thus, while the ignorant rabble of Massachusetts were loudly declaiming against the evils of trade and manufacture, a few clear heads were founding that lucrative branch of manu-facture which now in the same State gives employment to more men and women than could a hundred years ago be found in the two great cities of Boston and New York added together, and consumes each year in wages a sum more than sufficient to have paid off the national debt.† But it was not in the line of cotton goods alone that a beginning was made. Other manufactures were not suffered to languish. Indeed, when in the following year Tench Coxe made his address be-

---

\* An entertaining account of the rise of American manufactures is to be found in Bishop's History of American Manufactures, vols. i and ii ; and in White's Memoirs of Samuel Slater.

† The census of 1880 gives the number of hands employed in the cotton-mills of Massachusetts as 62,794. For the six New England States the figures are 129,228,

fore the Pennsylvania Society for the Encouragement of Agriculture, he told his hearers many things on this subject which they were loath to believe. How that Massachusetts made such quantities of linen that the price had gone down from New York to Georgia; how that the importation of English goods had fallen off to one half what it had been twenty years before; how that there were in one factory as many as ten thousand pairs of cotton and woollen cards; in another a hundred tons of nails, and in the town of Lynn a hundred and fifty thousand pairs of stuff and silk shoes; and how, with a population of four thousand five hundred, Ipswich had in a year produced forty-two thousand yards of silk lace and edgings. He then delighted the women of his audience by showing them thirty-six specimens of Ipswich trimmings.

Astonishing as all this was to many who listened to the oration of Coxe, the internal affairs of Massachusetts gave, in the autumn of 1786, little promise of the opulence and prosperity of the future. The State was just then passing through one of those periods of gloom which so often in the lifetime, both of individuals and of nations, follow, and go before, periods of great prosperity. The evil consequences of the war were everywhere making themselves keenly felt. The year in all the States was one of unusual distress. The crops had indeed been good. In many places the yield had been great. Yet the farmers murmured, and not without cause, that their wheat and their corn were of no more use to them than so many bushels of stones. That produce rotted on their hands. That while their barns were overflowing, their pockets were empty. That when they wanted clothes for their families they were compelled to run from village to village to find a cobbler who would take wheat for shoes, and a trader who would give everlasting in exchange for pumpkins. Money became scarcer and scarcer every week. In the great towns the lack of it was severely felt. But in the country-places it was with difficulty that a few pistareens and coppers could be scraped together toward paying the State's quota of the interest on the national debt.

The cause of so much misery, and the cure, are to us as we look back, quite apparent. Yet it is highly interesting to recall to what our ancestors in their day attributed the malady which afflicted the body politic, and with what dangerous remedies they sought to destroy it.    Every man who then frequented the taverns of an evening, or attended the town conventions got up by the malcontents, was accustomed to hear the troubles accounted for by a system of reasoning which was a singular compound of truth and absurdity.

By the best computation that can now be made, the private debts in the State summed up to at least one million three hundred thousand pounds sterling.    There were, besides, two hundred and fifty thousand pounds due to the soldiers of the late army, and one million five hundred thousand more as the State's proportion of the Federal debt.    The law required that one third of this last should be raised by taxes on the ratable polls.    And the ratable polls did not reach ninety thousand in number.    The burden of three millions of pounds sterling would, in the best of times, in a commonwealth not numbering three hundred and seventy-nine thousand souls all told, have been a heavy one.*    But it was to be borne by men destitute of ships and commerce, without manufactures and without agriculture.    Governor Bowdoin had, in a message to the General Court in 1785, urged as a remedy that farmers in the interior towns where there was much wood to be cleared away, should devote themselves to the production of pot- and pearl-ashes.    That the ashes should be deposited with an agent of the State, should be sold by him, and the money used to pay the taxes of the men who brought them.    But the advice was never taken.    Why indeed should the farmers rise up early and lie down late that they might pay taxes unjustly put upon them?    Every man who knew anything knew that trade and the merchants were at the bottom of this ruinous taxation.    The duty of meeting it should therefore be thrown on commerce and not on agriculture.    It was doubtful whether trade could bear the load.    But in any case good only could come of such a measure.    If commerce did support the weight of taxes, the commonwealth would be greatly eased.    If commerce went down under the pressure, the commonwealth would still be the

---

* The population of Massachusetts, by the census of 1790, was ascertained to be 378,787.   This does not include Maine.

gainer, for it would then be rid of a prolific source of evil. The merchants, the malcontents asserted, had grown rich on the great gains of traffic, and now vied with each other in luxury and display. This was foolishly imitated by the less opulent, who, drawn away from those principles of industry and frugality which are the best prop of a republican government, manifested a taste for foreign trumpery. This market the importers had determined to supply. Their credit was sound, and they had, therefore, most rashly bought more goods than could either be used or paid for. Bad as this was, the evil had been greatly aggravated by the decayed condition of commerce, and the little attention which had been given to producing articles of export. In nothing, it was said, was negligence so apparent and the results so disastrous as in the fisheries which might well be called the gold-mines of Massachusetts. The whale-fishery in particular was a constant source of complaint with men who were never weary of contrasting its ruinous condition in 1786 with its prosperous condition in 1776. From contemptible beginnings in 1701, it had, they said, in three quarters of a century, grown to such dimensions that Nantucket alone poured into the State each year one hundred and sixty thousand pounds sterling, employed a fleet of one hundred and fifty sail and twenty-five hundred seamen. But this magnificent navy was no more. Some of the seamen had found service in foreign lands. Others, from sheer hunger, had laid aside the harpoon and were fast becoming cobblers. In this and in like ways the articles once sent out as remittances were no longer to be had, and nothing but specie was left wherewith to satisfy the demands of importation. But America had no gold-mines from which to supply the loss of so much coin; and, as money was constantly going out and none coming in, it was merely a question of time how long it would be before shillings and joes would utterly disappear, and men be compelled to traffic with one another as their ancestors had with the Indians and buy meat with corn and bread with hatchets. To prevent matters coming to such a pass as this, either of two things must be done. Commerce must be destroyed and the outflow of specie stopped, or the place of the coin carried abroad must be filled by an issue of paper.

With the merchants, in the condemnation of the multitude, were joined the lawyers. Indeed, of the two classes, the members of the bar were the more hated and despised. The mere sight of a lawyer as he hurried along the street was enough to call forth an oath or a muttered curse from the louts who hung round the tavern. The reason is plain. During the years of the war the administration of justice had been almost wholly suspended. After the war, debts had increased to a frightful extent. The combination of these two circumstances had multiplied civil actions to a number that seems scarcely credible. The lawyers were overwhelmed with cases. The courts could not try half that came before them. For every man who had an old debt, or a mortgage, or a claim against a Tory or a refugee, hastened to have it adjusted. While, therefore, every one else was idle, the lawyers were busy, and, as they always exacted a retainer, and were sure to obtain their fees, grew rich fast. Every young man became an attorney, and every attorney did well. Such prosperity soon marked them out as fit subjects for the discontented to vent their anger on. They were denounced as banditti, as blood-suckers, as pick-pockets, as wind-bags, as smooth-tongued rogues. Those who, having no cases, had little cause to complain of the lawyers, murmured that it was a gross outrage to tax them to pay for the sittings of courts into which they never had brought and never would bring an action.

Meanwhile the newspapers were filled with inflammatory writings.* The burdens that afflicted the State were attributed to the attorneys. One paper repeatedly insisted that this class of men should be abolished. Another called upon the electors to leave them out of office, and to bid their representatives annihilate them. The advice was largely followed. In almost every country town a knowledge of the law was held to be the best reason in the world why a man should not be made a legislator. But nowhere was this feeling stronger than in the capital. In the representation of Boston was one place which her citizens had for many years past delighted to bestow on men whom eloquence and learning had raised to the first rank

---

* The most celebrated of these were the papers which appeared over the name Honestus. See, also, Boston Gazettes for March 27 and May 1, 1786.

at the bar. That place had been successively filled by Pratt, by Thatcher, by Otis, and by Adams. It was now given to a man of a less hateful calling.

This folly was combated with ridicule. One writer remarked that it was truly laughable to hear his townsmen gravely voting that the lawyers were a grievance. Did not every man of sense know they were a result, not a cause, of public evils? They grew out of laziness, out of dilatoriness in paying debts, out of breaches of contracts, out, in short, of the vices of the people, just as mushrooms sprang out of dung-hills after a shower, or distilleries from a taste for New England rum. The sober and frugal Dutchmen of New York had no use for lawyers. Before the war there was, in the whole of Orange county, but one action for debt tried in eighteen years. The industrious Quakers and Germans of Pennsylvania had no use for lawyers. A tax-collector never called upon them twice. They had no grievances. Neither would the New England man when he learned to save. Scarce a day went by but a farmer might be seen riding into town with a bushel or two of flaxseed. Flaxseed was a cash article, and cash paid taxes. But did this farmer put aside his cash to pay taxes? Not a bit of it. When he turned homeward his saddle-bags would be found full of coffee and his stomach of rum. Another would bring a lamb to market. Lambs commanded cash, and cash paid taxes. But the moment the worthy countryman got his cash he would go, not to the collector, but to the store and lay down five shillings for a feather. If these men, every time they got a shilling, would only put sixpence away, they would soon find their grievances redressed without the trouble, noise, and expense of town-meetings, conventions, and mobs.*

In this state of the popular mind the Houses met. It was evident from the beginning that a stormy session was at hand. For many of the members were new men, and all the new men were zealous in the cause of the people. One of the first things undertaken was a redress of grievances. Many wild schemes were proposed, warmly debated, and at last a bill was

---

* On Redress of Grievances. By an Industrious Man. American Museum, February, 1787.

passed by the House which closely affected the lawyers. It was believed that the best way to silence the clamor on this matter was to throw open the courts to all persons of good character, to fix the fees of attorneys, and to restrain the practice of champerty. But when the bill in form was sent up to the Senate, that body, disliking it and dreading a conflict with the Assembly, stoutly refused to consider it before the recess. So the bill went over.

The next struggle was over the paper-money bill. Seven towns in Bristol county had sent in a petition for the issue of a paper currency on a plan as novel as it was dangerous. The petitioners were well aware that money of the kind they so much desired was almost sure to depreciate, and must, at least, be accompanied with a promise of redemption. To avoid these troublesome peculiarities they had, they thought, hit upon a most happy plan. The money never should be redeemed, but should, in certain given times and at fixed rates, depreciate till the entire issue was extinguished. The petition was, to the great surprise of its authors, bitterly assailed on every side. Indeed, when a trial of strength was made, it was thrown out by a great majority, the Nays mustering ninety-nine and the Ayes but nineteen, in a House of one hundred and eighteen members.

A still more popular bill, making real and personal estate a legal tender, soon after met with a like fate, the Nays being eighty-nine and the Ayes thirty-five, in a House of one hundred and twenty-four. A most unpopular bill granting supplementary funds to Congress was, however, passed. On the eighth of July the Houses rose.

To the friends of good order the session had been most encouraging. But the malcontents had, by the loss of so many measures in a Legislature from which they had expected so much, become more angry and noisy than ever. They had no longer any faith in the Senate, and but little in the House. They determined therefore to betake themselves to the old-fashioned way of stating and correcting their troubles. County and town conventions had come into use before the revolution, and had then and during the war served a good and a high purpose. But, like many other good things when out of time and place, they had now ceased to do good, and had begun to do harm. From being a support to constitutional authority they had commenced to wear a strong appearance of opposition to constitutional authority. Thus, in 1784, a proposition went out from the towns of Medway and Wrentham to the remaining towns of Suffolk county to meet in convention to take measures for the redress of the grievances of commutation and the impost. Not long after, the town of Sutton sent a similar summons through the county of Worcester. Yet both these things of which they complained had received the sanction of the Legislature. In later times the proceedings that went on at the county conventions were even more unjustifiable. They censured and condemned their rulers. They voted the Senate and the courts to be grievances, addressed the people in language dangerous at any time, and finally attempted to set up a body of men that should supplant the Legislature itself.*

No sooner had the Houses adjourned than the malcontents of Hampshire determined to call a convention. They did so, and, on the twenty-second of August, delegates from fifty towns were assembled at Hatfield. What they considered grievances were there carefully gone over, and a paper drawn up which set them forth in twenty-five articles. They began by voting themselves to be a constitutional body, and declaring that they detested mobs and riots. They next went on to condemn the Senate for being what every Senate ought to be. It was, they said, not a representative body, but a re-

---

* A shrewd observer has left us an amusing and doubtless just description of the small politicians and county conventions of New England. "When a measure," says he, speaking of the General Court of Massachusetts, "has been there agitated that has been disagreeable to Individual members—They will *rise* and for lack of argument say, M^r Speaker, this measure will never do—the *People*, Sir, will never bear it. The particular measure is determined against their Opinion, these Small Politicians returned home misrepresent the doings of the Legislature—tell their Constituents such and such measures are taking place altho' I did my utmost to prevent it. The People must take care of themselves or they are undone. Stir up a County Convention, and by Trumpeting lies from Towne to Towne get one collected and consisting of Persons of small Abilities—of little or no property, embarass'd in their Circumstances—and of no great Integrity—and these Geniuses vainly conceiving they are competent to regulate the affairs of State—make some hasty incoherent Resolves, and these end in Sedition, Riot & Rebellion." See a letter from David Sewall, October 16, 1786, in the Thatcher Papers, Hist. Magazine, November, 1869.

straint on the representative body, and ought therefore speedily to be abolished. The Court of Common Pleas was also unnecessary. The fees of the judges were too great. The present practice of the attorneys was bad; they had an undue influence in the State, and were growing rich at the expense of the poor. The use of the impost and the excise for the payment of continental taxes and notes due to the army was then denounced in severe language, the mode of apportioning taxes voted to be iniquitous, and a paper medium called for. After a session of three days they adjourned.

However sincere the delegates may have been in the assertion that they detested mobs and riots, events soon showed that the men who chose them held no such doctrine. On the last Tuesday in August, 1786, the Court of Common Pleas was to sit at Northampton, for the county of Hampshire. But when the judges came they found the court-house in the possession of an armed mob of fifteen hundred men, and adjourned. The news spread rapidly through the counties of Worcester, Middlesex, Bristol, and Berkshire, and set them all aflame. Worcester, indeed, had been the first to act. A month before the Hatfield convention met a paper was carried from town to town through the county, and thousands of names had been put to it.* By this instrument the subscribers bound themselves to prevent, to the utmost of their power, the sitting of the Inferior Court of Common Pleas for the county, or of any other court that should attempt to take property by distress. They also engaged to prevent all public sale of goods seized by distress, even at the risk of their lives and fortunes, till the grievances were legally redressed. And they kept this engagement most faithfully.

On the fifth of September the court was to be holden at Worcester, and early on the morning of that day a hundred men armed with old swords and muskets, and as many more carrying sticks and bludgeons, drew up on court-house hill. After some delay, the judge, accompanied by the sheriff and the crier, came out of the house of a Mr. Allen and started for the court. As he went on the crowd divided to let him pass; nor was any opposition made to him till he reached the

---

* New York Packet, August 11, 1786.

steps of the court-house.  There five men with muskets, and
one with a sword, were drawn up.  The judge, General Arte-
mas Ward, a noted revolutionary soldier, called on the sheriff
to clear the way.  But the guards instantly drew back and
opposed him.  Meanwhile, the crier broke through them and
opened the door.  The judge then advanced, but was quickly
covered by the muskets of the five sentries at the door.  He
turned to Wheeler, who commanded the men, and demanded
to know who their leader was.  But he was not answered.
He said that he would speak of their grievances to the proper
authorities.  But he was told that he must put whatever he had
to say in writing.  This he stoutly refused to do; yet said, if
if they would take away their bayonets, and let him stand on
some eminence where all the people could see him, he would
talk to them.  This was refused; and, forgetting himself, he
began to curse and to swear.  " He did not give a damn," he
said, " for their bayonets.  They might, if they liked, plunge
them into his heart."  Then, becoming still more angry, he
stamped his foot and cried out that he would do his duty, and
held his life of small consequence when opposed.  Wheeler
then ordered his men to put up their muskets and let him
stand upon the steps.  He harangued the crowd for two hours,
though they constantly interrupted him with jeers, and cries
of " Adjourn without day."  When he had finished speaking,
he went on to the United States Arms tavern, and there
opened court.  Next day, however, finding that the militia
were taking sides with the malcontents, the court was adjourned without day.  The mob then demanded this decision
in writing, and he gave it.*

The next week the Court of Sessions was to sit at Concord.
Orders were therefore issued that the militia of Middlesex
and Bristol should turn out and protect it.  In the meanwhile,
the citizens of Concord, thinking that pacific measures might
perhaps have more effect with the insurgents than the appearance of force, named committees to confer with the leaders.
These were found so well disposed to listen to reason that an
understanding was soon reached.  The malcontents were to

* See a letter in the New York Packet, September 18, 1786; also, Massachusetts Spy.

make no demonstration, and the citizens were to promise that the militia should not be called out. The order summoning the Middlesex men to arms was accordingly wholly counter-manded, and that for the Bristol men conditionally so. This was precisely what the insurgents wished; and the day before the court was to sit they appeared, to the horror of the citi-zens, in great force at Concord. They were commanded by Job Shattuck and one named Smith. The whole of Monday was spent in making rude huts out of fence-posts and boards. In these they passed the night. When Tuesday came, for that was the day on which the court was to meet, the entire force marched to the ground opposite the court-house, took posses-sion of it, drew up in line, and kept guards marching up and down before them. The order was good, and the movements of the mob had much of military precision. But the towns-folk noticed with alarm that barrels of rum were constantly on tap. At length, becoming impatient of the long time taken by the judges to deliberate, and being heated with rum, the mob demanded that a detachment should be sent to find out the cause of the delay. Some horse and foot accordingly set out. When they came to the tavern where the judges were, they marched up and down in front of the building several times, halted, and faced about in a threatening manner. The judges, understanding this display of force, sent out word that no court would be held. The insurgents then withdrew. It was now past noon, and about two o'clock a fellow acting as sergeant went off, with two drums and a fife, and soon came back with about ninety men, well armed. They came from Hampshire and Worcester. As the men from Worcester marched by Jones's tavern, where the court was then at din-ner, Smith called on the crowd to fall in. "He would," he said, "give them two hours to think about it. At the end of that time, every man who did not follow his drum and join the Regulators should be driven out of town at the point of the bayonet." Then he became outrageous, cursed and swore, and declared that any man who escaped him would be a monument of God's living mercy.* Shattuck also harangued

---

* One who claims to have been an eye-witness reports the words of Smith to have been: "As Christ laid down his life to save the world, so will I lay down

the by-standers, and told them it was high time to wipe out all old debts and begin anew. "Well said, well said, Job," cried one who overheard him; "for I know you have bought two farms lately which you can never pay for."

And now a few of the malcontents, who had carried back the message of the judges to the main body at the court-house, came again. They brought with them a written message that it was the sense of the people that the court should not sit, and demanded that the answer which they had received in the morning should be put down in writing. The judges referred them to the clerk. The clerk, however, told them he was but a recording officer, that he had no orders from the court to do the thing they required; and, while they were yet wrangling with him, the judges made good their escape.*

While these disturbances were taking place in the lower counties, the rage of the disaffected broke out with equal violence in Berkshire. It had indeed at one time seemed as if, in that county at least, the farmers and ploughboys were of a better mind. Late in August a convention had been held at Lenox. In it many friends of good order and government found seats. Nor did the most rancorous members seem quite ready to go to such an extreme as their neighbors had gone to at Hatfield. The men who were for order even succeeded in passing a few measures of a strong character. The convention declared that it approved of the way the impost and excise revenue was expended, and of the grant of supplementary funds to Congress. That it disapproved of all systems of paper money, and promised a hearty support to the courts. But however great might be the influence of these men over the convention, they had none over the mob. Scarcely were the resolutions passed than eight hundred malcontents entered Great Barrington, prevented the sitting of the Court of Common Pleas, broke open the jail, set the prisoners free, and

my life to suppress the Government from all tyrannical oppression, and you who are willing to join us in this here affair may fall into our ranks. Those who do not shall, after two hours, stand the monuments of God's living mercy." Pennsylvania Packet, September 23, 1786.

* My account of the scene at Concord is taken from letters published in the New York Packet for September 21, 1786; New York Gazetteer, September 20, 1786; and Pennsylvania Packet, September 23, 1786.

compelled three of the judges to sign a paper. By this instrument they bound themselves not to act under their commissions till the grievances of the people were fully redressed. But the fourth judge, who was also a Senator, stoutly refused to sign, nor could they by threats force him to do so.

The complaints and demonstrations had, up to the middle of September, been directed against the Courts of Common Pleas, the Courts of General Sessions of the Peace, and to some hateful features in the manner of holding the Courts of Probate. But now the rioters began to tremble for their safety. The opposition, it was openly said, which had been made to the lower courts, left but one course open to them. They must at all hazards prevent the sitting of the Supreme Judicial Court; for that court had the power, and doubtless would exercise it, of indicting them for past offences. To the friends of Government there seemed little ground for this fear. For the Supreme Court had, since the affair of the fifth of September, held a session at Worcester; yet not a single bill had been brought in against the rioters by the jury. The leaders, however, were determined, and announced that the Supreme Court soon to be held at Springfield should not sit. The Governor, on the other hand, announced that it should. And that this might not prove an empty assertion six hundred militia were ordered under arms and took possession of the court-house. The command was given to General Shepard, an officer who had served with distinction in the late war.

On the morning of court-day the malcontents mustered to the number of five or six hundred, and marched to the court-house under the command of Daniel Shays. Shays had once held a captain's commission in the Continental army, and now strove to maintain something of military order and discipline among his followers. They went, accordingly, in good style to the ground. But the moment they caught sight of the militia their rage broke forth in shouts and curses. When quiet was restored Shays sent an insolent message to the court forbidding it to find any indictment against his people. To this the judges returned a firm answer. They had, they said, sworn to carry out the laws and they intended to do so. But as little business could be done in the midst of confusion they soon after adjourned to the next day. On Wednesday, the panel of jurors not being full, the few who came were dismissed. On Thursday the court rose.

Meanwhile the rioters, mortified and enraged, began to take violent measures. At one time they drew up in line of battle and marched down upon the militia with drums beating and muskets primed. For a moment it seemed that a general action was near. In truth, it was only by the utmost exercise of authority that Shays prevented his men from firing on the troops. At another time they insisted on marching through the streets of Springfield in the very face of Shepard and his army. This was too much; nor was it till Shays had given the most solemn assurance that no demonstration should be made that leave was granted. When word came that the court had adjourned, a demand was instantly made for the ground occupied by the troops. This was acceded to; and while the rioters were hastening to take possession of it with as much joy as if it had been a hard-won field, Shepard marched to the protection of the Federal arsenal.

Great Barrington was the next point of attack. The announcement had been made that the Supreme Court would not sit at that place. But the Regulators, as they called themselves, denounced this as a ruse. They were not, they said, to be deceived in that way. They knew that the court would surely hold a session unless they were on the spot to prevent it. They would therefore take good care to be upon the spot. A large crowd accordingly marched into the town on court-day. But when they discovered that they had merely deluded themselves, their shame and disappointment were great. They first became insolent and then riotous, drove some of the friends of Government out of town, searched several houses, and fired on two of the first characters in the place.

This done, they behaved for a time more peaceably. For the General Court had, on the twenty-seventh of the month assembled at Boston, and great numbers of the rioters were hurrying off to the county conventions. One in Middlesex comprised delegates from eighteen towns. Forty-one towns formed another in Worcester, while all the villages but one in Boston made up a third. In each of these the troubles of the people were carefully gone over, and, after much wrangling, a petition sent up to the Legislature. These three documents were instantly taken into consideration, and such grievances as were common to them picked out for redress. One of these was the sitting of the General Court at Boston. Another was the Court of Common Pleas, the Court of General Sessions of the Peace, and the present manner of holding the Probate Court. Scarcity of money was a third. The use made of the impost and excise tax was a fourth. In one way or another remedies were applied to each. An act was brought in for the payment of back taxes in specific articles. A plan was agreed upon by which civil action could be begun before a justice of the peace. A tender act was framed which was believed to be quite unobjectionable. A promise was also given that, if possible, the General Court should in future hold its sessions out of Boston. On the eighteenth of November the Legislature adjourned.

It might as well have never assembled, for the malcontents were more angry than ever. Indeed, they were too irritated to know whether the great concessions made to them were such as they wished, or whether they wanted any concessions at all. Five days after the adjournment of the General Court the towns of Worcester formed a new convention, went over the late acts of the Legislature, denounced them in unmeasured terms, and finally put out an address. The people were, they said, perfectly right in examining, and, if need be, censuring and condemning the conduct of their rulers. Any one who would take the trouble to go over the roll of the General Court would see that many of the rulers of Massachusetts were born to affluence. They all were perhaps in very easy circumstances. To expect men in such circumstances, men who had never known what it was to want for a shilling, or to be dragged off to jail by a harsh creditor, to feel for the poor was absurd. Undoubtedly they meant well; but they were, after all, but fallible men, and had shown their fallibility most signally in the policy they had lately pursued. It was true that this, bad as it was, did not justify the stopping of the courts of justice by armed bands. That was wrong, and the people were earnestly entreated not to do so again. Such lan-

guage from such an assembly was rated at its true value by all
who read it.	When the Court of General Sessions attempted
to sit at Worcester, the court-room was found to be filled with
armed men.	It seems that early on the morning of Tuesday,
the twenty-first of November, some sixty men, under the lead
of a fellow named Gale, came into the north end of the town.
During that evening and on Wednesday the Hubbardston and
Shrewsbury men came in and swelled the number to one hun-
dred and fifty.	These took possession of the court-house, and
quietly awaited the coming of the judges.	As the court ap-
proached, the crowd gave room, and let them go unmolested to
the steps, where a triple line of bayonets barred the way.	Then
the court, after the ancient fashion, called upon the sheriff to
clear a passage.	The sheriff, Colonel Greenleaf, who made some
pretensions to oratory, thereupon addressed the crowd, warned
them of their peril, and went on to remark in severe terms on
the conduct of those about him.	But the crowd, who knew him
well, were determined to have some sport with him.	So one of
the leaders answered him and said they were come to seek redress for grievances ; that the most intolerable of all grievances
was the sheriff himself and that next to his person were his
fees, which were, for executions in particular, excessive.	" If,"
said the Colonel, who was much nettled, " If you think the fees
for executions excessive, you need no longer seek for redress,
for I will hang you all for nothing with the greatest of pleas-
ure."	This raised a laugh, and, as the crowd pressed close
about him, some hand put an evergreen sprig, the badge of
rebellion, in his hat.	But the Colonel, ignorant of this, led the
court with great dignity back to the United States Arms, amid
shouts of laughter from the crowd.*

While the disaffected were thus associating for evil purposes, the better-minded were equally active in forming so-
cieties for good purposes.	Scarce had the Legislature broken
up when one of the members conceived the project of forming
a league.	Every one who came into it was to pledge him-
self to discourage the use and importation of foreign goods,
and to promise to wear home-made clothes, and by every
means in his power to encourage economy, frugality, and in-

---

* Lincoln's History of Worcester.

dustry. The plan was quickly put into execution, and the Governor, the Lieutenant-Governor, the members of the Council and the Senate, put down their names as members. Some rich merchants, in the hope of taking off the reproach that had been fastened upon them, made haste to join it.* And now the garrets were ransacked for old spinning-wheels. The spinning-bee came again into fashion; spinning-schools were started in almost every town, and for a time damsels were more ambitious to be renowned for their skill at the wheel than for their performances at the harpsichord and spinet. Nor must we fail to make mention of a like association which about this time sprang up in Connecticut. The disturbances in Massachusetts had greatly alarmed the women of Hartford. They were now quite convinced that the cry they had so long heard, that extravagance and importation were ruining the country, really meant something. For they could not fail to see that money was fast going out of the States, and that it was going out in payment for goods of which fully two thirds were consumed by women. They determined to seek a remedy, and after vigorously canvassing the matter, called a meeting for the sixth of November. They ended by drawing up an address for public circulation. This set forth that the women of Hartford had taken into consideration the unhappy state of the country. They had found it most deplorable, and had made up their minds to retrench as far as possible all unnecessary expense, as a duty they owed as well to their country as to their families. A resolution therefore had been adopted that for the space of eight months they would not buy any gauze, any ribbons, any laces, any feathers, any beaver hats, silks, muslins, or chintzes. There were, however, two occasions in life which seemed, even in the most distressing times, to justify a woman in the purchase of these foreign goods. The resolutions accordingly very properly stated that an exception was to be made for weddings and mournings. With this reservation they further resolved to dress their persons in the plainest manner, to encourage industry, frugality, and neatness,

---

* See Association entered into by the late Governor, Lieutenant-Governor, Speaker of the House of Representatives, several members of that body, etc. American Museum, August, 1787.

and that, whenever they received visits or made feasts, they
would study to avoid all unnecessary expense, especially in the
matter of imported goods.*

A month later the disturbances broke out afresh. The
regular term of the Court of Common Pleas was to be held at
Cambridge early in December. Some muttered threats had
been reported to the Governor, and led him to believe that
measures for obstructing the sitting were on foot. So he ordered seven regiments of militia to hold themselves in readiness
to move on a moment's notice. But some well-disposed persons in Middlesex undertook to promise the malcontents that
if they would only keep quiet the militia would not be ordered
to march. The desired pledge was readily given, accepted,
and no military orders issued. In spite of the assurance of
good behavior, however, a large number of insurgents met at
Concord. They had expected to find there bands from Bristol,
Worcester, and Hampshire, and go on with these to Cambridge. As it was, they actually went quite a distance on the
road from Worcester.

And now the patience of Bowdoin gave out. This new
piece of deception was too much. He issued warrants against
the Middlesex leaders, and placed them in the hands of the
sheriff for execution. The sheriff speedily collected a company
of cavalry, and with some gentlemen of Boston under Colonel
Hitchburn, and a party from Groton under Colonel Wood, set
out, by daylight, on the morning of the twenty-ninth of November. They came first to Concord. There a discussion took
place as to who should go forward. Finally it was settled that
the Groton horse should be dispatched. They were, it was
said, best acquainted with the country, and, being known there,
would not excite alarm from an unfamiliar appearance to the
inhabitants. About dusk these returned with two prisoners—
Parker and Page. Shattuck had taken the alarm and fled.
But the sheriff was determined to make one more attempt to
take him, and at the dead of night, in a blinding snow-storm,
the whole party set off for Shattuck's house in Groton. But
the darkness of the night, the severity of the storm and the

---

* New York Packet for November 14, 1786. See, also, Patriotic and Œco-
nomical Society of the Ladies of Hartford. American Museum, August, 1787.

great drifts of snow that lay across the road, so delayed the march of the little band that it was not till late on the morning of the thirtieth that they came in sight of Shattuck's home. Meanwhile, he had taken the alarm and fled to the woods. A diligent search was instantly begun, his tracks were soon discovered in the snow, and himself surrounded. And now, when he saw that his chances of escape were few, his courage revived. He determined to sell his life as dearly as possible, and made a desperate effort to cut his way through; nor was he taken till many wounds were given and received.

While this was going on in Middlesex, the malcontents were gathering in Worcester. At last, early in December, though the cold was more intense than had been known for many years, and the roads made almost impassable by snow, a thousand of them marched into the county town. Shays commanded them. A few he placed as guards about the houses where the judges were, and some were lodged at the Hancock Arms. The rest he billeted on the townsfolk.* It was at Worcester, while living at free quarters, that the news of the captures at Groton reached them. In a few hours all was in a ferment. Some, disheartened by the cold, by repeated defeats, and the resolute front the Government was beginning to show, began to murmur. It was time, they said, to go home. Matters might take a favorable turn before spring. But it was plainly useless to contend against the weather and the troops. Shays himself was of this mind, and, at a time when his voice should have been raised to encourage the faint-hearted, was overheard to say: "For God's sake, have matters settled peaceably; it was against my inclination I undertook this business; importunity was used which I could not withstand; but I heartily wish it was well over." † Others of a more determined mind were for marching straight to Boston and effecting the release of Shattuck and Page. There seemed indeed but little disposition on the part of the insurgents to carry out their threat; yet it was on that account none the less alarming to the Bostonians. Preparations to defend the capital were instantly made. A post was sent to General Brooks, commanding him

---

* Boston Gazette, December 11, 1786, and January 29, 1787.
† Lincoln's History of Worcester, p. 147.

to have the militia of Middlesex up and ready to move on the shortest notice. The duty of defending the city was laid upon General Lincoln. He placed the Boston militia under orders, and notified other companies in Suffolk to come in the moment they heard the discharge of cannon on Fort Hill.*

But when the ninth of December came, Shays and his party, instead of advancing, fell back. The retreat, as was to be expected of a band of rustics, was disorderly and confused. But there were other incidents which made it long remembered in the Worcester villages. While they were still enjoying comfortable quarters, many had heartily cursed the folly that brought them on such an errand at such a season of the year, and had a thousand times wished themselves well out of the business. When, however, the retreat began, the suffering of the whole body became extreme. The thermometer was far below zero; many had a long journey before them, and could with the greatest difficulty obtain a crust of bread or a piece of bacon. In this distressed state numbers of them, weak from cold and hunger, and weary with plodding through banks and drifts of snow, fell down in the fields and died. Of those who escaped death, scarce one reached home without a frozen hand or a frost-bitten foot. Even the zeal of Shays seems to have been greatly cooled. An officer who fell in with him asked, leaving it optional with him to answer, if a pardon were offered, would he take it and leave his people to themselves. Shays, with the spirit of a craven, instantly replied, "Yes, in a moment." His words were soon carried to the authorities, and the officer commissioned to offer a pardon. The two, however, never met again, the commission was returned, and Shays gave his name to the rebellion.†

---

* Boston Gazette, December 4, 1786.

† The retreat of Shays caused much delight, and was celebrated in prose and verse. A single specimen of the poetry and the wit will suffice:

"Says sober Will, well, Shays has fled,
    And peace returns to bless our days.
Indeed! cried Ned, I always said,
    He'd prove at last a *fall-back chaise;*
And those turned over and undone
Call him a worthless *Shays to run.*"

It was later suggested that the names of Shays and his band should be handed down to posterity in some such rhyme as this:

The Governor now determined to raise an army. And it was high time. For the friends of Government had of late manifested a great dislike to appearing in arms against men who were their neighbors and acquaintances, and on whose votes they counted for seats in the Assembly, or for county and town offices. Indeed, in several places the malcontents were greatly enraged at the opposition they met with, and had gone off vowing vengeance. In some towns officers of the militia, and noted characters who had been active on the side of Government, were threatened with violence. In others, scarce a week went by but the sky was reddened by burning barns or blazing hay-stacks. Under these circumstances men were loath to leave their shops and their homes, seize their muskets, and hasten to protect a court, to receive in return for their pains the thanks of the Governor and the destruction of their property by the mob. This difficulty, it was thought, could readily be overcome by sending the men raised in one county to contend against the disaffected in another. They would then no longer find themselves opposed to friends and acquaintances, but to men they did not know, for whom they cared nothing, and who did not know them. Plans, therefore, were soon on foot for collecting an army of four thousand four hundred men. Seven hundred of these were to come from Suffolk and five hundred from Essex. Middlesex was to furnish eight hundred more, while Hampshire and Worcester were each to send up twelve hundred. Suffolk and Middlesex were also called on for two companies of artillery. The men from Suffolk and Essex were to assemble at Boston on the nineteenth of January. Those from Hampshire at Springfield on the eighteenth. The Worcester men were to join the troops from the eastern counties at Worcester. All were enlisted for thirty days, unless sooner discharged, and were to receive the same pay as during the war had been given to the continentals. The command was bestowed on General Lincoln.

And now a new difficulty arose. The Quartermaster-Gen-

---

" R—stands for Rebels who mobs dare to raise.
S—stands for Satan, Smith, Shattuck, and Shays."
New Jersey Journal, January 17, 1787.

eral reported that munitions of war for so large a body of
men were not on hand; nor was there money enough in the
Treasury to purchase them.  The Legislature was not then in
session.  It might be summoned.  But that would not better
matters.  For the money would have to be raised by tax, and
no tax that could be laid would yield the needed sum in season.  In this situation a number of wealthy gentlemen made
an offer of a loan of the necessary funds, which was gladly accepted.

The nineteenth of January, therefore, found the troops
streaming into Roxbury.  There preparations were speedily
completed, and when all had come in the line of march was
taken up for Worcester which was entered on the twenty-
second.  The march through the country between these two
towns was performed with the greatest regard for the feelings
of the inhabitants.  Nothing was omitted which could quiet
the alarm so naturally excited by the passage of twelve hundred armed men.  Every command, every movement, was
executed with the orderly precision of old warriors.  For the
troops which the State had assembled, while they passed under
the name of militia, were very different from the holiday
soldiers which could now, in a like emergency, be gathered
from the same places.  They were an army of veterans.
Scarce an officer among them but had gained his rank by
meritorious services in the late war.  In the ranks marched
many men who had taken up arms in the early days of the
revolution, had joined the continentals, and had served with
the illustrious chief to the close; had participated in the disastrous retreat along the Hudson, and had been present at the
surrender of Yorktown.  Even the greenest had seen something of battles and sieges.  Some had lined the fences on that
memorable day when the British were driven out of Lexington
town.  Some had stood in the trenches with Warren, and had
seen the redcoats twice come up, and twice in confusion go
down the slope of Breed's Hill.  Others had formed part of
that army which had laid siege to Boston, and had looked on
with grim pleasure as the ships bearing the troops of Howe
stood out to sea.

Among the malcontents were likewise many men of great

military experience. But they were in a position where their knowledge was of small use. The party whose cause they had taken up was without funds, without provisions, and without organization; nor was it in the power of the leaders to compel obedience even to the most reasonable commands. It was the chiefs who obeyed, not imposed commands. When, therefore, the multitude demanded to be led to Springfield, Shays readily consented.

In December a great crowd under Day and Grover had come into the town to obstruct the court. But no disturbance had arisen. "The court was," they said, "mellow enough." And they had good reason to say so, for the judges sent out and invited the leaders to dine with them at the tavern. It was not, however, to hinder the sitting of a court that they came in January. On that plot of ground now covered with the gun-shops and sword-factories of one of the most magnificent armories in the world, was a mean-looking building which had long been used as a Federal arsenal. In it were a considerable quantity of military stores, stoves, camp-kettles, saddles, a few hundred kegs of damaged powder, a few thousand muskets, and several field-pieces. To protect these was the object of the State. To get possession of them was the object of the mob. While the troops were mustering at Roxbury, orders were sent to General Shepard to take possession of Springfield. The village at that time was made up of a few hundred houses scattered along the post-road, from the banks of the Connecticut eastward toward Boston. On the heights back of the town was the arsenal, and there Shepard posted his twelve hundred men. The plan of the malcontents was to surround him and cut the army to pieces before Lincoln could come on from Worcester. Eli Parsons, with four hundred Berkshire men, accordingly took possession of the north parish of Springfield. Day, with an equal number, entered West Springfield, while Shays, with eleven hundred, moved toward the Boston road on the east. This placed the Connecticut between Day and Shays, and as the river could be crossed by bridge or by ferry strong guards were placed at each. From travellers he had stopped and examined, Shays learned that Lincoln, with some four thousand men, would soon be upon

him.   He determined to act at once, and, on the twenty-fourth
of January, sent word to Day that on the twenty-fifth Springfield would be attacked on the east, and urged him to cross the
river and attack it on the west.   But Day was ambitious of
military renown.   He would have all the glory of Shepard's
surrender or none.   His answer was that he could not attack
on the twenty-fifth, but would on the twenty-sixth.   The messenger, happily, was taken, the dispatch carried to Shepard, and
Shays, hearing nothing from Day, took it for granted that he
would assist.

About four on the afternoon of the twenty-fifth, Shepard,
as he expected, saw Shays advancing quickly along the Boston road.   His men were in open column, and many of them
wore evergreen boughs in their hats.   When they had come
to within three hundred and fifty yards of the arsenal, an
aid was sent to demand the intention of the mob, and to
warn them of their danger.   The answer came back that
they would have the barracks.   Then they approached nearer
still.   Shepard sent a flag and warned Shays that if he crossed
a certain line he did so at the peril of his life.   At this
Shays became furious; said that was just what he wanted,
called his Maker to witness that he would march on, and did.
The troops were instantly ordered to fire.   But as the purpose was merely to frighten, the muskets were pointed in
the air.   And now Shepard saw his mistake.   For there
were in the ranks of Shays many old soldiers who had
been in too many battles to be alarmed by the rattle of mus-
ketry or the noise of a sham fight.   They continued advancing in good order till the troops were a second time
commanded to fire.   Four men immediately fell.   Some, not
used to such scenes, raised the cry of murder and fled.   In
a moment the ranks were in confusion.   Shays threw himself
into the thickest of the crowd, and, with curses and threats,
sought to stay the fugitives and deploy his column.   But the
terrified ploughmen that rushed by him were deaf to his entreaties and soon the eleven hundred were in full retreat; nor
did they stop till the village of Ludlow, ten miles from Springfield, was entered.   The next day they joined Parsons at
Chicopee.   There a count was taken.   To the dismay of all it

was found that two hundred deserters had gone off to their homes.*

Meanwhile Lincoln had been hastening toward Springfield and came in on the morning of the twenty-seventh. His troops had suffered greatly from their long marches in the cold and the snow. Numbers of them were worn down with fatigue; others badly bitten by frost. Yet they were ordered under arms at half past three on the afternoon of their arrival. Four regiments of foot and four pieces of artillery, with some of the horse, were then led across the river on the ice. Shepard, at the same time, with the Hampshire men and the light horse moved up the river on the ice. The intention of Lincoln was that Shepard's troops should prevent Shays, who was on the east bank, joining Day, who was on the west, while his own troops were to cut off Day's retreat.

When the Hampshire militia were seen coming up the river as fast as the slippery ice would permit, the guard at the ferry-house turned out and made some show of resistance, but soon retreated. A few troops and some horse were sent after them, and another stand was made near the meeting-house. This lasted but a minute or two, and they once more retreated in confusion till they were overtaken at the west end of the village by the horse, when they scattered and took to the woods. That night Shays collected his men, and, in great disorder, fell back through South Hadley to Amherst, plundering as he went.† So great was the confusion that when a party of stragglers were suddenly overtaken by their own rear-guard, they supposed Lincoln's advance was upon them, opened fire, and killed several.‡

The pursuit, however, did not begin till two in the morning of the twenty-eighth, and was then continued till Amherst was reached. Shays, in the meanwhile, had gone on to Pelham and taken post on two high hills known to the townsfolk as east hill and west hill. His position, naturally a strong one, was made yet more sure by the great drifts of snow that lay all along the foot of the hills. Finding no accommodation for

* New York Packet, February 2, 1787. Boston Gazettes, February 5, 1787, and later. The papers are full of letters.

† Boston Gazette, February 12, 1787. ‡ New York Packet, February 2, 1787.

his army at Amherst, Lincoln stayed just long enough to search the houses and to learn that most of the men, with ten sleighs of provisions, had gone on to Pelham. He then led his army to Hadley. But no sooner were the men comfortably quartered than news came that some of Shepard's force had fallen into the hands of the enemy at Southampton and were still there. Immediately the Brookfield volunteers, numbering fifty men, were sent in sleighs, with about one hundred light horse, to effect a recapture. They were soon upon the track of the rebels and about midnight overtook them at Middlefield. From hints thrown out by the villagers it was discovered that fifty of them, under Luddington, had gone quietly to bed at a certain house which was quickly surrounded. Luddington had during the war been an officer in the Continental army, had been aid to General Tupper, and was not a little disconcerted to be roused from his sleep at dead of night to hear the familiar voice of his old commander calling on him from the darkness to lay down his arms. When he had collected his senses a parley was held ; and, while this was going on, the remainder of Luddington's party came up under arms. In a moment each party drew up in line, and were about to fire, when the cry was raised that the troops were coming. Thereupon the rebels surrendered. When it was day, Tupper, with fifty-nine prisoners and nine sleighs of provisions, went back to the army.

And now letters began to pass and repass between Lincoln at Hadley and Shays at Pelham.* The malcontents were reminded of the heinous crime they were committing, of the punishment that justly awaited those who took up arms against the state, and of the pardon which a mild government would even then bestow on all who laid down their arms and went to their homes. Some show of repentance was made on this appeal, and finally a request came that one of the leaders might hold a private conference with one of the officers on the subject of a pardon. This was readily granted, and the third of February set as the day. The whole proceeding was a ruse. For while the conference was going on and the attention of the army drawn to it, Shays collected his men and

---

* New Jersey Journal, February 21, 1787.

marched rapidly to Petersham. About noon on the day of the conference the news that the enemy were in motion was brought in to Lincoln. At first he was disposed to think that, like all reports which pass from mouth to mouth, the account as given to him was much exaggerated, and that Shays was merely moving his men from the east hill to the west hill in Pelham. That he might not, however, be found unprepared for a general retreat of the enemy, the troops were ordered to be in readiness to march, with three days' provisions, at a moment's notice. Scarce were the preparations completed when positive information came that the rebels had left Pelham and were rapidly marching eastward. This word was brought in at six in the evening. At eight the army was under way. Nothing of note happened to delay the advance till about two in the morning when the houses of New Salem came in sight. Then a strong north wind arose which sharpened the cold till it became all but unbearable. Clouds at the same time began to gather, and, before the troops had gone far a blinding snow-storm overtook them. The way on to Petersham lay over a high country thinly settled and with few trees. If they went on they would therefore be exposed to the full force of the wind and the snow. If they stood still, it seemed hardly possible that flesh and blood could long withstand the cold. The nearest shelter for so many was eight miles away. Thus, deprived of covering by want of buildings, and of food by the severity of the cold, which prevented them taking any on the road, Lincoln felt that the life of his men depended on continuing the march to the enemy's quarters. This accordingly was done, and the whole thirty miles was made with scarcely a halt. About nine in the morning the advance guard, under Colonel Haskill, with a company of artillery and two cannon, entered Petersham. It was then discovered that the rear was five miles behind them.

This undoubtedly was the time for action by the malcontents. They were numerous. The advance guard of Lincoln was small and the main army was yet far away. They had been well fed and comfortably lodged in warm houses. The troops were numb and half frozen by the cold, and had just finished a march of thirty miles, through drifts of snow knee-deep. But the rebels were taken completely by surprise. They had not expected a pursuit so soon, and had gone quietly to bed feeling sure that Lincoln was still at Hadley, and that the cold and the snow would keep him there for some days to come. When, therefore, the cry was raised that the militia were come, they rushed from the houses, and without stopping to ask about numbers thronged into a narrow lane that led to Athol, and quitted the town in confusion. They were closely followed, and about two miles out of town a hundred and fifty were taken. Many more fled to their homes. The rest went over the borders, some to New Hampshire, some to Vermont, and some to New York.

The rout at Petersham was most complete. The rebels continued, indeed, for some months, to collect in small bands, come over the line and harass the border towns. But they never at any time thereafter appeared in force.

Lincoln, feeling sure that the rebellion of Shays was now over, dismissed three companies of artillery and ordered two regiments back to Worcester. He then set out for Northfield, where some of the fugitives had collected. But on the way an express met him from General Patterson, who commanded in Berkshire.

It seems that while the militia were hastening from Worcester toward Springfield the malcontents of Berkshire, who had gone over to Shays, thought to distract the Government and render good service to their cause by appearing in arms at several places. But the friends of Government were likewise not inactive. They felt satisfied that Lincoln would speedily disperse the rebels. And in that event it was, they thought, more than likely Shays would fall back to the heights that lay between the counties of Hampshire and Berkshire, fortify the passes and the strong points, draw his supplies from the towns well affected to Government, and seize on the chief characters as hostages. They determined therefore to form an association for common defence, and soon five hundred names were given in. It was well that they did so, for scarce was the league formed when one hundred and fifty of the rebels under Hubbard appeared at West Stockbridge. Hubbard had taken his post at the meeting of three roads, was stopping all travellers, and drawing a considerable number of recruits from the country round about. But while he was thus occupied news was sent through the neighboring towns and a force was speedily upon each of the three roads and hastening toward him. The first to come up was a party of thirty-seven foot and seven horse. On their appearance Hubbard's sentries discharged their muskets and fell back. The whole force was instantly drawn up in line and word given to fire. They hesitated. Seeing this, one of the horsemen who was well known to many of the rebels, rode up and commanded them to lay down their arms. Some readily did so, whereupon the rest broke and fled, firing as they retreated. These were hotly pursued and eighty-four of them, with Hubbard, were made prisoners. It is perhaps interesting to note that the horseman who on that day commanded the rebels to disperse was Theodore Sedgwick, the ancestor of that famous General John Sedgwick who, after many gallant services in the Mexican War, went down, sword in hand, in the battle of the Wilderness, and of that Catharine Sedgwick who wrote "Hope Leslie" and "The Linwoods."

The dispatch which told of the skirmish at West Stockbridge further stated that the rebels had afterward met at Adams; had been scattered by Patterson; had again assembled at Williamstown; had once more been dispersed, and were now marching in such numbers to Washington that the General felt much alarmed for the safety of his troops. This at once changed the plans of Lincoln. He gave up his intention to march to Northfield, and hastened with one division of the army through Amherst, Hadley, Chesterfield, Partridgefield, and Worthington, to Pittsfield. Shepard, with the other division, set out for the same place by a different road. But the malcontents had fled. Parties in sleighs were sent to Dalton and to Williamstown, and these returned soon after with twenty prisoners.

Meanwhile, a letter from Eli Parsons, who was safe over the border, was going from hand to hand through the State. The language was that of a village tavern orator. Will you, said he, tamely submit to have your arms taken from you, your estates confiscated, and yourselves made to swear allegiance to a constitution which common sense tells you is iniquitous? Will

you sit still and look on while the yeomanry of the commonwealth are parched and hewn in pieces by the merciless tools
of tyranny ? He then expressed a pious wish for the tongue of
a ready writer, that he might impress on their minds some
idea of the duties of freemen. What these duties were he
went on to specify. He was collecting troops, he said, at New
Lebanon, in York State, and at Pownal, in Vermont. He was
fully determined to carry his point, if fire, blood, and carnage
could do it. In this laudable purpose it was the duty of every
freeman to assist. He begged, therefore, that all friends of his
cause would, without delay, hasten to meet him in Berkshire,
and there help him to "burgoyne" Lincoln and his army. The
letter was dated February fifteenth and ended with a request to
pass it along.*

Had Parsons been as ready with his sword as he was with
his pen, the threat of burgoyning Lincoln might easily have
been accomplished. Six days after the date of the letter, the
thirty days for which the militia had been called out expired. Their place was to be filled by fifteen hundred troops
lately enlisted for four months. But during the exchange Lincoln had at one time only thirty men. This opportunity, happily, was lost to the malcontents. It was not indeed till the
twenty-sixth of February that a considerable force came over
the line from New York. Captain Hamlin commanded them,
marched them to Stockbridge, plundered it, and went off with
a number of the first characters in the town as prisoners. The
militia of Sheffield and Great Barrington flew to arms and
hastened after them. But the troops were ignorant of the
movements of the enemy, marched now in one direction and
then in another, as the leaders saw fit to command, and at last,
in disgust, started home by way of Springfield, where, to the
surprise of all, the rebels were found in force. On the approach of the militia, Hamlin ordered his prisoners to the front
and gave the word to fire. But the troops came on steadily, in
good order, and firing as rapidly as they could. For six minutes the action was severe and many of Hamlin's men fell.
This alarmed them and they broke and fled in every direction,
leaving two dead and thirty wounded on the ground. The loss

* United States Chronicle, March 1, 1787.

of the troops was two killed and one wounded, while two strip-lings who were with them died from exposure and fatigue.

Once more the fugitives found a secure resting-place over the border. But it was not long before even this was taken from them. Several weeks before the fight at Springfield, letters had been dispatched to the Governors of the neighboring States acquainting them with the fact that they were harboring rebels, and urging them to take measures for bringing the refugees to justice. And now the replies began to come in. All, with the exception of that from Rhode Island, were gracious and full of promises. The Governor of Rhode Island did indeed, on the same day that Parsons put forth his letter, assure Bowdoin that he would do all in his power to assist in keeping good order. But he soon found that he had promised for himself alone. When the motion was made in the Assembly to instruct the Governor to issue a proclamation for the apprehension of the rebels, a violent debate followed, and, when the question was put, it was discovered that the Nays had it by a majority of twenty-two. While the voting was going on, as the Massachu-setts authorities were greatly enraged to learn, one of the rebels was honored with a seat in the chamber.

The Governor of Connecticut sent assurances on the twen-tieth of February that if any rebels came into the State they should instantly be given up. That the farmers along the State line might be stimulated to be vigilant and prompt to act, a large reward was promised to any one who should be so fortu-nate as to catch a leader. In New Hampshire a major-general was instructed to arrest all bodies of armed men coming into the State. Clinton, so soon as he received the letter of Lin-coln acquainting him of the support the malcontents had in New York, and of the incursion of the twenty-sixth of Febru-ary, hastened to lay the matter before the Legislature. There a resolution was passed urging him to go with all speed to the towns where the rebels were. He was also bidden to call out such militia as he might need, and, whenever he saw fit, to leave the State. Three regiments of militia were accordingly commanded to be put under arms. The Governor then set off from New York, met Lincoln, and went with him to New Con-cord.

Measures so vigorous caused much alarm among the refugees, and soon small bands of horsemen were seen moving
quickly along the roads that led to the Vermont border.    For
once over the line they had good reason to think they would
be in a safe place.    Indeed, for a time it seemed likely that
Vermont would follow the example of Rhode Island.    So early
as the thirteenth of February, Lincoln sent Royal Tyler, who
was then acting as one of his aids, to urge the Governor of
Vermont to assist in capturing the rebels.    After some difficulty
he obtained an audience of the Governor and made known his
mission.    The Governor heard him with attention, expressed
regret at the lamentable turn of affairs in Massachusetts, and
said something about doing what he could, and did nothing.
When he was pressed to act he offered first one excuse and
then another for the delay.    At last Tyler, greatly disgusted at
his reception and feeling convinced that no aid was to be had
from Vermont, put his demands in writing and took his leave.
This communication was in time laid before the Legislature,*
was referred to a committee, and a report brought in recommending a proclamation to be issued forbidding the people to
harbor or abet the rebel leaders.    In this the Lower House
concurred, and sent the report up to the Council.    There it
was supported by eight or nine assistants, and would indeed
have passed, but the Governor for the first time spoke out.
It was, he said, plainly the interest of the State of Vermont to
encourage immigration.    If, however, the proclamation came
out, emigration from the neighboring States would surely be
checked, for no one would dare to come over the border lest he
should be stopped and treated as a Massachusetts rebel.    The
sense of the people, too, was against the measure.    There
could be no mistaking the meaning of the armed mob that was
fast gathering in the next town.†    These arguments were
deemed conclusive by the Council.    A proclamation did, however, come forth on the twenty-seventh of the month.‡    But
it was well understood to be a mere matter of form.    No attention was paid to it, and the rebels were free to come and go

---

* In Council, February 17, 1787.    Laid before the Assembly the same day.
† In Council, February 24, 1787.    See Governor and Council of the State of
Vermont, vol. iii, pp. 375–379.        ‡ Vermont Gazette, March 5, 1787.

as they pleased.* On the first of March Pennsylvania set a price on Shays and his fellow-leaders.

The rest of the spring and summer was spent in the trial of the prisoners. A few of the most malignant suffered punishment; but the others were thought to have been sufficiently punished by their long confinement in the jails, and were permitted to go free. A general pardon was also extended to such of the rebels as should, before a fixed time, return to their allegiance and take the oaths. It was not, however, thought prudent to disband the army till the twenty-first of September.

The conduct of Rhode Island in sheltering the Massachusetts rebels surprised no one. The control of that State was in the hands of men who sympathized heartily with the malcontents, and she was now about entering on that long career of infamy which did not terminate till Washington had been some months President. When the war ended and the people once more returned to peaceful pursuits, it became apparent that men were nowhere so discordant, so dissatisfied, so hard to please, as in Rhode Island. Grievances such as elsewhere were borne with a few grumbles were there thought to be quite intolerable. The people were especially disposed to give a trial to every one of the innumerable schemes for reform which then distracted the country. No plan that the brain of man could concoct seemed too absurd. Any one who could suggest a new way of paying debts, cutting down taxes, or increasing trade, was sure of a patient hearing and a large following; but the favorite just then was the establishment of what was called a

---

* It is stated that on February 17th a troop of horse from Massachusetts rode into Marlborough, Vermont, in search of Luke Day, and, on being asked for their authority, said they had license from Governor Chittenden. Vermont Gazette, February 26, 1787. On April 30th about one hundred of the fugitives met at Shaftsbury, but the people, becoming alarmed, called on the judge and the county sheriff to disperse them, and they went on to White Creek, in New York. Vermont Gazette, May 7, 1787. But on June 5th Governor Hancock informed the Legislature of Massachusetts "that those who have been in opposition to Government have, from Vermont and New Hampshire, repeatedly made incursions into this State, with the intent to plunder and carry off the friends of Government." Vermont Gazette, July 16, 1787. See, also, a letter from Ethan Allen to Colonel Benjamin Simmons, in Clinton Papers, No. 5,863. Durham and Baker, two of Shays's party, were afterward taken on the Onion river. Vermont Gazette, July 30, 1787.

bank of paper money. It was not a new scheme. So early as
1784 the supporters of the idea had attained to very formidable numbers. But January, 1785, came before the first trial of
strength was made. A petition bearing scores of names and
praying for the issue of a bank was then sent to the Legislature. But the sentiments of the people were not shared by
their representatives. The long list of signatures had no
weight with men who held estates, who had money out on
mortgage, who saw in the list the scrawls which passed for the
names of debtors owing them large sums, and who looked with
dread on the day when, for the coin they had loaned, they
should receive back bags and pillow-cases full of paper. When,
therefore, the time came for taking action on the petition, a
great muster was made, all the seats were filled, and, the votes
being counted, it appeared that the Nays were greatly in the
majority.

The result enraged but did not dishearten the petitioners.
It was, they said, now quite evident who were and who were
not their friends, and it would go hard with them if the paper
bank did not in the next Legislature find ample support. Nor
was this threat by any means an idle one. A new party was
quickly organized, the State actively canvassed, and, in the
spring of 1786, the paper advocates went to the polls confident
of success. The difficulty of communicating between the capital and the remote parts of the State was such that some time
elapsed before the results of the election were known. Indeed,
they were not accurately known till the Legislature met on the
first Monday in May, when it was found that fully one half of
the assistants and thirty-eight out of seventy deputies had lost
their seats, and in their stead were men devoted to the paper
scheme. The bank men were delighted. Their victory was
complete. The call for the land-tax was instantly remitted.
The excise law was suspended. A paper bank of one hundred
thousand pounds was ordered.* In the course of the debate
which preceded the passage of the bill it was noticed that the
speakers on the affirmative were invariably from the country
districts, and the debaters on the negative as invariably from

---

* Arnold's History of Rhode Island. Rhode Island Colonial Records, vol. x,
May, 1786.

the rich seaboard towns. Newport, Providence, Bristol, Westerly, each sent up men trained in the great school of commerce and trade, familiar with all questions of finance, and who well knew that a Spanish milled dollar was a very different thing from a promise to pay, some time in the future, a Spanish milled dollar, and that no body of deputies under the sun had skill enough in alchemy to transmute paper into coin.

But no argument which they could advance could turn the votes of men who had come up for the express purpose of abolishing taxes, suspending the excise, and emitting a currency which was, in their belief, to flow into their pockets much faster than it could possibly flow out. The bill was passed, the paper came forth, and, as the Newport and Providence men had asserted, the depreciation began with the issue. The law declared that the bills should be loaned according to the apportionment of the late tax, that they should be paid into the Treasury at the end of fourteen years, and that every one of the farmers or merchants who came to borrow a few hundred pounds must pledge real estate for double the sum demanded. Many from all parts of the State made haste to avail themselves of their good fortune, and mortgaged fields strewn thick with stones and covered with cedars and stunted pines for sums such as could not have been obtained for the richest pastures. They had, however, no sooner obtained the money, and sought to make the first payment at the butcher's or the baker's, than they found that a heavy discount was taken from the face value. This, in the opinion of the large holders of the paper, was an outrage. Things were come to a pretty state if the Legislature were not to be allowed to say what was and what was not money. The very right which justified the Government in taking a piece of copper or a piece of silver, stamping it, and calling it a penny or a sixpence, justified the Government in taking a piece of paper, stamping it, and calling it a sixpence or a shilling. If it were lawful for the State to issue hard money, it was surely lawful for the State to issue paper money. The metal of the coin had, it was true, an intrinsic value which the paper had not; but to say that gold and silver were on that account better than paper was to talk nonsense. The hard currency was secured by the intrinsic value of the metal which was an imaginary security, one that could neither be touched nor seen. The security of the paper money was far better; it was real; it was broad acres of land which fire could not consume and which water would not destroy. In fact, the paper money was as good as metal money, and every man who did not take it willingly should be made to take it unwillingly. A call was made for a forcing act, which the Legislature quickly passed. Every one who should, according to this act, refuse to take the bills in payment for gold, or should in any way discourage their circulation was to be fined one hundred pounds and lose the rights of a freeman. The effect of the law was to make worse the matter it was designed to mend. The merchants denounced it as iniquitous, and declared that they would pack up their goods and set off for another State before they would submit to so wicked an act. Indeed, they refused almost to a man to make any sales. The traders followed their example and closed their shops or disposed of their stock by barter. For a time business was at an end, and money almost ceased to circulate except among the supporters of the bank. Rent was paid in grain; nor was it by any means, in some towns, a rare thing to see cobblers exchanging shoes for meat, and shopkeepers taking cords of wood for yards of linen.

Providence and Newport presented a most doleful appearance. Half the shops were closed. Scarce any business was done. On the street-corners stood crowds of idle men, chattering, it was said, like magpies. Some were denouncing the paper party for having made the tender laws; others for not carrying them out.* The disputes often ended in blows, and street fights became of almost daily occurrence.†

The refusal of the merchants to sell provoked the farmers to retaliation. If, they said, the merchants would not dispose of any goods to them, they in turn would not sell anything to the shopkeepers. They would not bring a pound of produce to market till people came to their senses and took the bills for what the Legislature had declared them to be worth. And to this determination they strictly adhered. Travellers along the roads were no longer forced to turn out to make way for long

---

* New York Gazetteer, August 24, 1786.
† New York Gazetteer and Daily Evening Post, July 28, 1786.

trains of wagons creaking under the weight of tons of hay, sacks of corn, kegs of cider, of boxes filled with huge cheeses, and baskets overflowing with vegetables and fruit.  On the farms the butter accumulated on the dairy-shelves.  The cattle feasted on produce that used to be sent to town.  When market-day came round, the farmer slept many hours later than was his wont, while his daughters no longer dispatched him with little commissions and counted the hours till his return.

Some attempts were indeed made to dispose of the produce at Boston, in Connecticut, at New York.  But a notice was put up in all the coffee-houses warning merchants against a combination of the abettors of the iniquitous paper money of Rhode Island.  These farmers, the notice stated, had failed in their credit with the merchants of Rhode Island, and were now endeavoring, by offering quantities of flaxseed, barley, and cheese, deliverable in the fall, to get a credit for West India goods at New York.*

It was, however, only in the great towns that real distress was felt.  There the scanty stock of food grew scarcer and scarcer every day.  Corn rose to fifteen shillings a bushel.  New England rum stood at ten shillings a gallon.  But not a drop was to be had at any price in paper.†  For a time this was submitted to in patience.  It was hoped that the merchants would give way, or the farmers of Massachusetts, tempted by the high prices, would send in provisions from their farms.  But even these hopes failed, and measures of relief became imperative.  At Newport the sufferers grew violent.  The town at that time laid some claim to commercial importance, and contended with Providence and Bristol for the honor of being the first city of the State.  Her shipping brought together many men who followed the sea for a living, or managed to gain a livelihood by rendering such services as were required by ships just come in, or just about to depart.  They cared nothing for principles and much for comfort.  Whether money was made of paper or silver was, they thought, a small matter, for little enough would in either case come to them.  It seemed the

---

* New York Gazetteer and Daily Evening Post, August 24, 1786.  Boston Gazette, September 4, 1786.

† New York Gazetteer, September 13, 1786.

height of folly to go hungry in order that a few rich men might keep up one side of a controversy which, however it ended, would not help them a whit.  Whether the farmers or the merchants had the better cause of complaint they knew not.  But they did know that the merchants held the grain, and they made up their minds to get it.

A number of them accordingly came together, put two men named Wanton and Anthony in command, and began to insist that the stores where corn was lodged should be opened and the grain sold for paper.  Most of the merchants gave the rioters no heed.  But among them was a Quaker, who, alarmed by threats of violence, felt it to be his duty to give his cheek to the smiter, and consented.  This the merchants would not suffer.  In a few hours a great crowd of friends of hard money were assembled about the Quaker's store to defend it.  Words were bandied with the mob, threats exchanged, and the passions of each party so much excited that a conflict seemed at hand.  At this stage the Governor and two of the Council appeared, went about among the crowd, and succeeded in restoring order.*

And now the anger of the people turned against the farmers, and threats of breaking open cribs and robbing rich barns were made openly on all sides.†

At Providence the distress caused by the scarcity of food was felt with equal severity.  But better counsel prevailed than at Newport.  No disturbance broke out, and when July came, and the two parties were still determined to hold out, a town-meeting was called to decide on a plan of relief.  The attendance was large.  The speakers were numerous.  The discussion was animated.  The suggestions were as many as the debaters.  But the sense of the meeting was finally announced to be that it was no more than fair each side should give up something.  It was recommended to the farmers that, if any one among them saw fit to bring his sheep or his grain to market, they should not molest him, but suffer him to do so in peace and quiet.  It was recommended to the shopkeepers that they should open their doors and make sales to every well-disposed farmer, and that the terms of all sales should be such as the buyer and the seller

---

* New York Gazetteer and Country Journal, August 1, 1786.
  † Ibid., August 1, 1786.

should agree upon for themselves. It was resolved that five hundred dollars should be borrowed and sent into some other State to buy corn for the relief of persons destitute of bread.

The meeting then broke up. The delegates went home with the comfortable assurance that they had by a few wise suggestions saved their fellow-townsmen from the horrors of a famine. They were sure that each party would make the concessions asked; that the shopkeepers would take down their shutters, that the great merchants would dispose of their goods, that the farmers would, after some bluster, once more bring in their produce, that trade would revive, and food be plenty. But they were much mistaken. Many to whom the recommendations were addressed received them with open contempt. Indeed, a few weeks had scarce gone by when a call came out for a convention of towns to devise means for enforcing the bank act. Scituate was named as the place, and the tenth of August as the day of meeting. But nothing was done. For the delegates were no sooner met than they adjourned and went off to East Greenwich, where the State Convention was to sit. When the roll was called it appeared that sixteen towns had sent up representatives, most of them picked men, and pledged to support none but vigorous measures. What these vigorous measures were soon became evident. It was moved and carried to stand by the acts of the General Assembly. That body, which happened to be in session at the time, was next urged to enforce the penal laws in behalf of paper money. The farmers were asked to make no sales of produce to the enemies of the bank. But the convention was by no means unanimous even upon these points. Five delegates had come up from Providence fully determined to labor in the cause of the merchants and traders, and as the three motions were brought forward, they combated them with great energy and patience. The five repeatedly rose up one after the other to protest, to counsel moderation, to beg for concessions, to offer plans for a compromise, and succeeded in changing a few votes. But the majority stood firm, and the motions passed. The same day a new forcing act was carried at Newport. Providence, Bristol, North Shoreham, Newport, and Warren protested. But the only notice taken of the protest was to forbid the clerk to make any entry of it on the minutes.

And now the rage for town-meetings and county conventions was at its height. Those of Providence, Scituate, and East Greenwich followed hard upon each other, and before the first of September it was known that a convention for Providence county would be held upon the thirteenth. All the towns and villages sent up delegates. The whole state of the country was gone into. But the state of trade particularly arrested their attention. It was pronounced most deplorable; and in searching for some persons on whom to lay the blame, they fell upon the merchants, flatly accused them of exporting specie, of importing costly goods, and of producing the manifold ills from which society was suffering. A new way of trading was then recommended. The State of Rhode Island and Providence Plantations, it was asserted, possessed many things for which there was great demand abroad. Her fish, her produce, her lumber, were much sought after. But few things came from abroad which her people could not easily dispense with excepting gold alone. The proper course to be pursued was manifestly for the Government to take commerce into its own hands. Let the Legislature name a committee. Let the committee provide ships, and the tax-collector cargoes. For labor, lumber, produce, fish, and oil might be received in payment of taxes as well as money. Let these be carried across the water and sold for specie, or traded for such goods as were really needed. Then would the balance of trade be turned, money would be easy and taxes would be light, for the great gains of traffic would flow into the coffers of the Treasury instead of the pockets of the merchants. If some men persisted in trading on their own account, well and good. Let them do so; but make them in return for this liberty pay heavy duties in hard money, and not, as was their wont, in interest certificates.

But while the convention was wrangling over the best way to regulate trade, and the easiest way to drive paper into circulation, the whole question of the legality of the forcing acts came up in the courts. A Newport butcher named John Weeden had among his customers a strong paper-money man named John Trevett. Trevett, who was a cabinet-maker, presented himself at the market one day, purchased a few pounds of beef, and tendered in payment some of the new money. Weeden refused to take paper shillings at their par value, and Trevett, in a rage, lodged a complaint against him. As this was the test case, the excitement attending it was intense. The hearing began almost immediately. Indeed, it was expressly stated in the forcing act, passed at the summer session of the Assembly, that all offences against the bank law should be tried within three days after the complaint was entered ; that there should be no jury ; that three judges should make a quorum; that their decision should be final; and that, if any man were hardy enough to refuse to obey it, he should be locked up in jail. The framers of this shameful law had hoped by these means to place the goods, the estates, the liberty of every hard-money man in the State at the mercy of the courts. And as the judges were removable at the will of the Assembly, there seemed much reason to believe that the law would be vigorously executed. When the day of trial came, the benches in the court-room were packed, every inch of standing-room was taken, while a great crowd, unable to get in, stood under the windows or jostled each other about the doors. Each side was represented by able counsel, for the contest was in truth not between Trevett and Weeden, but between the farmers and the merchants, between those who, having mortgaged their lands for the paper issue, now struggled hard to keep it at par, and those who, recalling the disastrous times of 1779, struggled hard to prevent a shilling of the paper from ever getting out of the hands of its holders. The first day was taken up in listening to counsel on each side. The excitement of the audience was intense. The debate was warm, and conducted with great animosity. Indeed, two of the judges so far forgot themselves as to speak against the act from the bench. On the second day the court rendered its decision. Howell was appointed to deliver it. When he began to speak a death-like stillness was in the room, but when he was done the shout of exultation that went up from the benches announced to the crowd without that Weeden had won, and that the odious act had been pronounced unconstitutional by the court.* Then the spirit of the victorious party swelled up high and strong. But Trevett and his friends, deeply mortified and enraged, went off muttering threats of vengeance against the court. In this frame of mind were many of the assemblymen, and before their anger had begun to cool they were summoned to Newport to a special session of the Legislature. The first act of this body was to command the five stubborn judges to come before it. Two pleaded sickness and stayed away.† Three came, were sharply questioned as to their behavior, browbeaten, and finally told that their case was laid over till the fall session by which time it was hoped their sick brethren would have quite recovered. The members then went on to do the worst act of their lives.

The paper was still in the hands of its first takers. No one else could be found who would receive it at the face value.‡ Many would have nothing to do with it on any terms, and there seemed much reason to believe that the late decision of the court would make these people more determined than ever. It was felt that a new forcing act must be passed, and that the new one must be stringent. An iron-clad oath, to which the name of the Test Oath was given, was accordingly framed and brought in. Every man who took this swore in a most solemn manner to do his utmost to support the paper bank, and to take the money at par. But as it was wisely believed no one would take the oath of his own accord, a long list of penalties was provided for those who did not. Ship-captains were forbidden to come in or go out of the ports of the State till they had taken the oath. Lawyers were not to practice, men were not to vote, politicians were not to run for office, members

---

* New York Gazetteer, October 6, 1786. See, also, a pamphlet entitled The Case of Trevett against Weeden, on Information and Complaint for Refusing Paper Bills in Payment for Butcher's Meat at Par with Specie, by J. M. Varnum, Providence, 1787. See, also, Boston Gazette, October 2, 1786; United States Chronicle, October 5, 1786; Providence Gazette, October 7, 1786; Newport Mercury, October, 1786.

† Annals of Providence. Colonial Records of Rhode Island, vol. x. Varnum's pamphlet, The Case of Trevett against Weeden.

‡ The rate of exchange when paper was negotiated was four dollars in paper for one in coin. See New York Gazetteer, September 13, 1786.

of the next Legislature were not to take their seats, till they had, upon their solemn oaths, declared that paper was as good as gold.* In this form the law went before the people. Town-meetings were immediately called to discuss it. But the partisans of the bank had by their own violence inflicted a deep injury upon their cause. Many honest and fair-minded men, who were prepared to welcome with delight the appearance of a paper currency, were not prepared to vote for the bill. They believed that the new money would lighten many burdens. To them, taking the oath would be a small matter. But they shrank from the thought of giving their assent to a law that forbade men of a different mind to sail their ships, to cast their votes, to practice their professions, to hold any office of public trust, till they had come before an officer of the law and, stammering and stuttering from shame, called their Maker to witness that they would do a thing they thought to be both foolish and wicked. There was also some fear of a great exodus. It seemed likely that a number of rich merchants and prosperous tradesmen would, before submitting to so degrading an act, pack up their goods, desert their homes, and set off for a neighboring State. Everywhere the oath was denounced in the strongest terms; and when the returns were all in, it was found that but three towns had given an assenting vote. At North Kingston, Scituate, and Forster, those who approved so far outnumbered those who opposed the bill that the delegates were instructed to support it in the Legislature. Their support was of no use. In November the Test Act was thrown out by an overwhelming majority. Four of the judges were at the same time dismissed. The forcing acts declared void by the courts were repealed, and death pronounced against all forgers of the new currency.

Meanwhile, the effects of the issue began to be felt. The paper went down steadily till six dollars in rag money would not buy one dollar in coin. Then landholders who had covered the few acres they called their farms with mortgages made haste to lift them. The Court of Common Pleas at every sitting was thronged with suitors anxious to make de-

* New York Packet, October, 1786. United States Chronicle, October 12, 1786.

posits.  The newspapers were filled with notices by the judges that sums in lawful money-bills had been deposited with the court by men who had in every respect complied with the law respecting paper money.*  In Washington county alone more than twenty bills in equity for the redemption of estates were on file.  On the day put down for the sitting of the court the petitioners came, bringing with them their money.  But as the sums were large and the money bulky they found it impossible to bring it in their pockets.  Some, therefore, carried the bills in handkerchiefs, some in pillow-cases.  One huge bag containing more than fourteen thousand dollars in paper was dragged in, and the court asked to count it and record the tender.  This the judge stoutly refused to do, told the petitioner that it was not for the court to prove a tender, and that he would not touch the money till after judgment had been reached.  He then put off the trial of all cases till the following term.†

The shameful course which the paper party had thus for a year past been following in Massachusetts and Rhode Island was undoubtedly an extreme one.  Yet it was closely imitated in New Hampshire.  The State then contained a population of less than one hundred and forty thousand souls; and if the accounts the people gave of themselves are to be trusted, there was not anywhere another one hundred and forty thousand men so burdened with taxation, so bowed down with debt, so short of money.  Their troubles had first become unbearable about February, 1785.  They then resorted to the usual mode of correction.  Town-meetings were held.  Commerce, the state of trade, the courts, the lawyers, the taxes, and the finances were fully looked into.  The conclusion was that the easiest and speediest way to obtain relief was to put out more paper money.  A petition was drawn up, signed by many hands, and sent in to the Legislature.  But a new difficulty arose.  Some men, who clearly understood what the petitioners did not,

---

* New York Gazetteer, September 27, 1786.  Pennsylvania Packet, September 23, 1786.  The Newport Mercury, and the United States Chronicle, a Providence paper, have each of them whole columns of such notices during the months of September, October, and November, 1786.

† Bull's Memoirs of Rhode Island.

undertook to expostulate with them. What, they were asked, would be gained by a new issue? No paper money unsecured by coin was worth the trouble of printing. The State had no funds, and it was not in the power of the State to establish any funds with which to secure paper from depreciation. Make the bills, it was said, a legal tender, and secure them with land. To this it was answered, with great force, that the State Constitution expressly forbade the Legislature to make a retrospective law. It could not therefore make paper a tender in the future for contracts made on a coin basis in the past. It might enact that paper should be a legal tender for the payment of debts to be contracted in times to come. But this would not mend matters, for the debtors were suffering from past engagements, and these would still exist. As to loaning the bills on land, that would be to put it in the power of the public debtor to buy up the paper at a discount and pay his taxes with it at the Treasury. This would be most disastrous to the State. For while the coffers were overflowing with paper, the Government would suffer all the embarrassment of poverty. There was, they were assured, but one way to cure their ills, and that way was to be diligent and frugal; to build up manufactures and to practice agriculture.

This plain statement of the truth was received with derision. Be diligent! Where was there a set of men who rose earlier, toiled harder, and lay down later than they. Be frugal! How could they be otherwise. Scarce able to keep clothes on their backs and food in their mouths, deeply in debt, with all the money in the State in the hands of the rich, and not a shilling to be borrowed except at a ruinous interest, it would be very hard to be spendthrifts. As to manufactures, they would have none of them. Massachusetts had ventured largely in manufactures, and was poorer than ever.

In this determination they clamored yet more loudly for a new issue of bills. The newspapers, too, lent their aid; called on their readers to assert their rights, and published long tirades the burden of which was that the Governor and the representatives were public servants, and that public servants must be made to do the public will. This advice was speedily taken. A demand was made for a tender law, and a tender law was passed.   It was then the fashion in New Hampshire, as indeed it was everywhere, to lock men up in jail the moment they were so unfortunate as to owe their fellows a sixpence or a shilling.   Had this law been rigorously executed in the autumn of 1785, it is probable that not far from two thirds of the community would have been in the prisons.   At least that number stood in hourly fear of the sheriff.   All such were therefore delighted to hear that when a debtor, so the new law provided, should tender to his creditor, in satisfaction of an execution for debt, either real or personal estate sufficient to cover the debt, his body should be exempt from jail.   But many of the men who made this law were creditors, and, knowing that they would often be forced to take great quantities of worthless property, inserted what they believed was a saving clause.   If the goods tendered were not to the liking of the creditor, he could refuse them, keep his claim alive, take out an alias within a year, and levy on any property of the debtor he could find. But the benefit was all with the debtor.   When an execution was about to be taken out, the farmer made haste to evade it. His good clothes and his good furniture were concealed.   His cattle were driven to a neighbor's pasture.   His rich lands, his house and chattels were made over to a relative, and when the sheriff came he was found to possess meadows which grew nothing but iron-weed, thistles, and mulleins, cattle too weak to stand up, hens too old to lay, a few dilapidated wagons, and a barn just ready to tumble about his ears.   The result was that those to whom debts were due ceased to press for payment, and those who owed were slower than ever to pay.*

Yet the courts and the lawyers grew more detested every day.   They were expensive.   They were unnecessary.   Those who had cases to be tried complained that between attorneys' fees, entrance-fees, and taxes, they were almost ruined before judgment was reached.   Those who had no cases to be tried complained that it was the height of injustice that they should be made to contribute to the support of institutions from which they had not derived and never would derive the least benefit. Such language had long been confined to a few, and had excited no very general comment.   Sometimes an angry farmer

---

* Belknap's History of New Hampshire, vol. ii.

would set forth his views upon the subject in the Gazette. Sometimes a disappointed office-seeker would stand up at town-meeting and declare that the courts and the lawyers were grinding the faces of the poor; that the attorneys grew rich while their neighbors approached beggary; that their fees were too large and their numbers too great. But in June, 1786, the matter was taken up in a serious way. The tender act had then greatly increased the number of cases in the courts. The judges were run down with business. The hands of the sheriff were full of writs. The people became exasperated. The Inferior Court was, they said, nothing better than a sinecure for clerks and judges. The whole process of justice so called, the defaulting, the demurring, the abatements, the fees, and the bills of cost, was a burden that could no longer be endured. But they determined, before proceeding to extreme measures, to go through the form of a convention. Concord was chosen as the place. The time was to be during the June session of the Legislature, for it was thought that a little intimidation might have a wholesome effect on that body. The appointed day came, and found but five of the delegates in town. Some had been detained by the length of their journeys, some by the difficulties. There was, however, at Concord a noted wag, who determined to turn the wisdom of the council into foolishness. He accordingly sought the acquaintance of the five, pretended to be a fellow-delegate, introduced some ten or twelve boon companions as on a like mission, talked much of the value of time, and urged the delegates to send out a call for the convention to meet immediately.* They quickly fell into the trap. The call was posted. The meeting was held, and some sixteen, including the five regular members, were present. Everything that touched on the situation was debated in the most absurd manner. Finally a set of extravagant resolutions passed, which the convention, in solemn procession, carried to the Assembly. It was recommended that three millions of dollars should be put out on landed security, that the Inferior Court should be abolished, and free trade established with the whole world. The number of the lawyers, moreover, was too great. Two were ample for each county. This instrument was received by the

---

* Belknap's History of New Hampshire, vol. ii.

Legislature with a great show of gravity, for the members had been let into the secret, was laid upon the table and ever after suffered to remain there. The convention then dissolved and the five started for home. But scarce were they out of town when the regular delegates began to come in. The joke was soon known to every one, and the real representatives, mortified and enraged, went to their homes.*

July and August passed away in comparative quiet. With September came the first signs of violence. Early on the morning of the twentieth, four hundred men, horse and foot, assembled at the little village of Kingston, some six miles out of Exeter, where the General Court was sitting. There they chose a leader and got hold of a drum. Several militia-men who had borne arms in the revolution, and who happened to be among them undertook to teach the raw ones such military tactics as the time would allow, and showed them how to form in column, to march, to deploy, to form in line of battle, and to fire.† It was then found that near one hundred had muskets; the rest were armed with swords and staves. Toward afternoon all arrangements were completed, and about four o'clock the mob entered Exeter. At first they effected a military parade up and down the main street, but soon drew up in front of the meeting-house where the General Court was in session. An officer they called Moderator was then sent in with a paper, and told to demand an instant reply to an old petition sent in on September fifth. The House in great alarm appointed a committee of three to meet three from the Senate and consider what answer should be made. But the Senate, not to be overawed by a display of arms, unanimously non-concurred in the resolution of the House.‡ A conference was then asked for, was granted, and the two bodies met. The President informed the House of the reasons that had led the Senate to non-concur. They were, he said, surrounded by a crowd of men carrying arms in their hands. To grant the petition under such circumstances would be simply to destroy all freedom of action for the future. To grant the petition under any circumstances would be folly, for it was the petition

* New York Packet, September 11, 1786.    † Ibid., October 2, 1786.
‡ Belknap's New Hampshire, vol. ii.

of but thirty towns out of three hundred. The House acknowledged the force of this reasoning; the conference ended, and the mob were curtly told that the General Court would not consider their paper. When the Moderator announced this, shouts of indignation went up on every side. The drums beat to arms, and, after something like order was restored, the whole line, muttering vengeance, marched off and surrounded the meeting-house. Those who carried muskets were ordered to load with ball. They did so. Sentries were then placed at the doors and strictly enjoined to suffer no one to go in or come out. Meanwhile the business of the House went on with as much deliberation as if the crowd at the doors were spectators and not rioters. It was long after sunset when the President left the chair and attempted to quit the building. The sentinels stopped him. He reasoned very coolly with them, pointed out the foolhardiness of the course they were pursuing, called on them to lay down their arms, and assured them that the forces of the State would support the Government to the last. This they told him flatly was a great lie. He attempted to respond, but was interrupted with cries of "Paper money! Equal distribution of property! Annihilate our debts! Release us from the taxes!" In the midst of the shouting he went back to his seat to wait patiently till relief should come. Nor did he wait long. Shortly after dusk a drum was heard beating in the distance. Then came huzzas for Government, and cries of "Bring up the artillery." The rioters, thinking that a great force was upon them, made a hasty retreat, and their prisoners walked out unmolested.* That night was spent in preparation for the morrow. The militia were collected; the services of a number of gentlemen were accepted, and just after sunrise the next morning the whole body, with the President at its head, sought the insurgents. They were found drawn up in front of a tavern out of town. On the approach of the soldiers they wavered, broke, and fled. Some few came to a stand at King's Fall bridge, and made a show of fighting. The order, indeed, to fire was given by the leader of the mal-

---

* New York Packet, October 2, 1786. New York Gazetteer, October 2, 1786. New Brunswick Gazette, October 5, 1786. An Account by an Eye-witness. See Historical Magazine, January, 1869, pp. 37, 38.

contents. But a rush was made by the Government forces; and, when the confusion was over, the Moderator with forty of his followers were prisoners. This ended the affair. Some time later the Assembly prepared a plan for the issue of paper money, and sent it to the towns for ratification. The returns were not all in till January, 1787. It then appeared that the number of towns that had voted No was very greatly in excess of the number of towns that had voted Yes. Two questions were next put to vote in the Assembly : Could the Legislature pass an act making paper money a legal tender for debts contracted before the passage of the act? Ought paper money to be put out on any plan yet proposed? Each of these questions passed in the negative.

The acts of the paper party in Vermont must be narrated more briefly. Vermont had not at that time been admitted to the Union. Her citizens did indeed exercise all the rights of sovereignty, but it was not till the Constitution became law that they were suffered to send representatives to the Federal Council. Nine years before, in the darkest hour of the war, the men of the southern counties of what was then known as the New Hampshire Grants had risen up, renounced their allegiance, asserted their independence, chosen a Governor and Assembly, formed a State and called it by the name of "New Connecticut, alias Vermont." * The independence of New Connecticut was soon after acknowledged by New Hampshire. But many settlers had come in from New York, had made clearings, laid out farms, built villages and towns, and had paid their taxes to New York. The great State, proud of so prosperous a community, steadfastly refused to give up jurisdiction over it; and in a little while the peace of New Connecticut was disturbed by the contentions of two parties. To one the name of Yorkers was given; the other assumed that of Vermonters. For seven years their treatment of each other would have delighted two Indian tribes on the war-path. Their history during this time is a shameful record of wanton attacks and reprisals, of ambuscades laid in the dead of night, of murder, arson, and bloodshed. At last, after the spring of 1784,

---

* Slade's Vermont State Papers, pp. 68–73. Hall's History of Eastern Vermont, vol. i, p. 253.

New York ceased to press her claims with violence, and thence-forth the Vermonters governed their State in quiet. But no sooner had one set of evils been removed than another presented itself. One half the community was totally bankrupt; the other half was plunged in the depths of poverty. The year which had elapsed since the affair at Yorktown had not brought all the blessings that had been foretold. They were still out of the Union; money had never been so scarce; taxes had never been so large; their debts had never been so many; their creditors were as merciless as the Yorkers. Nobody seemed to thrive but the judges, who drew fat salaries out of the taxes, and the attorneys, who wrung large fees out of the people.

The evils of this state of affairs were indeed great; but the irritable temper in which the people then were, and the labors of men sent, it was believed, by the authorities of New York, magnified them a hundred fold.* For a time their complaints were confined to the tavern and the fireside. But soon a countryman, who had brooded in indignation over his troubles till he could contain himself no longer, prepared an address to the farmers of Bennington county, and published it, over the signature of A Poor Farmer, in the Gazette. His paper was long, but the gist of it may be given in a few words. If any one would be at the pains of examining the tax-list for the year 1784, he must surely see that one half of the sum set down for Bennington county was to pay the court for sitting. What right, reason, or justice was there, he wished to know, in this? Why should he, and a hundred other poor farmers like him, who owed nothing and owned less, who never had a case in court, and who never intended to have a case in court, be made to pay the cost of its sitting? The tax was too severe, and he felt some desire to know how long the men of Bennington would bear it.†

A few weeks after the appearance of this address a number of men from Wells and five or six of the adjoining towns held a meeting, discussed the matter, and drew up resolutions for a

---

* On the presence of agents from New York in Vermont, see some letters in New York Gazetteer and Daily Evening Post, November 6 and December 13, 1786.

† Vermont Gazette, January 31, 1786.

redress of grievances. They were not printed and are now lost. Yet it is possible to form some idea of them from a doggerel poem, in Hudibrastic metre, that came out in the Gazette and was largely copied by the other newspapers. The strain of this poem was that attorneys ought to be expelled from the courts, debts cancelled, and that if the legislators would not pass these laudable acts, it would be an easy matter to make them. But the interval between discontent and open rebellion is always a long one, and more than two years and a half went by before the threats were carried out.*

Matters, in the mean time, in place of mending, became more and more disheartening, till in the summer of 1786 they reached such a pass that they were made the subject of an address by the Governor. Chittenden then filled the chair of state, and the address he put forth was quite characteristic of the man and the times. The coarseness of the style, the flippancy of some of his remarks and the intemperance of others, was such as might be expected in a political pamphlet gotten up for campaign purposes, but would now be thought singularly out of place in a grave state paper. The causes, he said, of the trouble were not hard to find. As Joshua of old had commanded the sun to stand still, so, during the war, men had

---

* As poems of this kind were by no means uncommon in the newspapers of that time, it may be worth while to give a few lines as a specimen:

> Whereas the Assembly of the State
> Have dar'd audaciously of late,
> With purpose vile, the Constitution
> To break or make a wicked use on,
> By making laws and raising taxes,
> And viler still (so truth of fact is)
> By keeping up that smooth-tong'd clan,
> For ages curs'd by God and man,
> Attorneys, whose eternal gabble
> Confounds the unexperienced rabble.
>
> .    .    .    .    .    .
>
> These lawyers from the courts expel,
> Cancel our debts and all is well—
> But should they finally neglect
> To take the measures we direct,
> Still fond of their own power and wisdom,
> We'll find effectual means to twist 'em.

Vermont Gazette, February 28 and March 6, 1786. Vermont Journal, March 24th.

commanded their creditors to be patient. The consequence was that debts had greatly accumulated, that payment for them all, now the war was over, was demanded at the same time, and suits followed. Law-cases had become so numerous that there was not money enough in the State to pay for entering them, to say nothing of the fees of the officers and attorneys. Yet but few of them were disputable. Most of the time of the court was taken up in hearing what the lawyers call shunage, an attempt to put off execution. As a remedy for this, one cried, "A tender act"; another, "A bank of money"; a third, "Kill the lawyers." These were but temporary cures, and could not remove the cause of the disease. He then told them that if they would attend to their own business, be frugal, be diligent, practice agriculture, stop importing English linens, and set their wives to spinning, their troubles would soon end. Vermont was an inland State; transportation was very expensive. Everybody ought therefore to raise whatever he could, and if he did so he would find that nineteen twentieths of his wants were supplied. The other twentieth might come from abroad and should be well taxed. The present system of taxation was all wrong. Revenues ought not to be raised on the commodities, but on the luxuries of life; and among the luxuries were importations and lawsuits. None but idle and litigious men went to court, and they should be made to pay for it. If, however, a bank of money was insisted upon, a very small one should be struck, the funds loaned to such as would pay a reasonable interest, and made a legal tender for all debts on which a prosecution had been commenced. Then four fifths of the lawsuits would instantly stop, and half the sheriffs, a great part of the constables, and all the pettifoggers might go to work.*

The address came out in the Gazette of the twenty-eighth of August. The very next number contained news of the first outbreak.† On the fifteenth of the month the Supreme Court held a sitting at Rutland. Two hundred gentlemen, who, as the writer expressed it, "were not directly touched or infringed upon by that banditti of pick-pockets, the attorneys," rode into Rutland as representatives of ten neighboring towns. No vio-

---

* Vermont Gazette, August 28, 1786. Vermont Journal, September 4, 1786.
† Vermont Gazette, August 31, 1786.

lence took place, but a great show of strength was made, and a spirited resentment manifested that so many good subjects of the State should be harassed, confused, and put to extreme cost by those unhappy members of society. A postscript to this piece of news called upon all lawyers who read it to have a care how they imposed upon men who had passed through the wilderness, and had endured fire, famine, and the sword in defence of their rights.

Windsor was next visited. It had been announced that the Court of Common Pleas for the county would sit at that town on the last day of October. Some threats had been muttered at the tavern that whether the court sat or not would depend on the wishes of the people. But as the mutterers were deep in their cups, the threats excited no attention till, on the day the court was to open, some thirty men from the villages round about came into town in a body. Stebbins, a broken-down farmer, and Morrison, a blustering fellow who shod the horses and mended the carts of the farmers for several miles around Windsor, commanded the mob. As soon as their business was known, the sheriff, with the State's attorney, hastened to the malcontents, expostulated with them, read the riot act, and called upon the crowd to disperse. Some of the more turbulent became excited, stoutly refused to move, and flung stones at the sheriff. An attempt was made to arrest them, but they were dragged off by their better-disposed comrades and lost in the multitude.*

At the very time the malcontents were annoying the court at Windsor the General Assembly was voting on a resolution framed for their relief. It seems that during the fall months men who were not yet ready to take up arms had been busy all over Vermont holding town-meetings and preparing petitions to the Assembly. Nine had been sent up, and were read by the clerk on the eighteenth of October. They were all of a piece: the taxes were unjustly levied; the lawyers were a nuisance; the costs of the courts were excessive. The bad spelling, the lack of punctuation, and the misuse of words told precisely from what class of men the papers came. Yet it seemed not unlikely that the wildest requests of the petitioners would

---

* Pennsylvania Packet, December 27, 1786.

be granted, for in the House then assembled all the passions, prejudices, and turbulence of the people were fully represented. One of the first acts of a stormy session was a Specific Tender Act. By this the creditor was made to take on execution, after the time of agreement, such articles of personal property as the debtor had agreed to give. But this gave small relief, for most of the debtors were as destitute of personal property as they were of money. Some clamored for a general tender forcing the creditor to take anything the debtor offered. Others as strenuously insisted on a bank of paper money. And there seemed much reason to think that both parties would be gratified. At this stage of the affair Nathaniel Chipman came up to Rutland. Chipman was a judge of the Court of Common Pleas, a man of considerable parts, and thoroughly familiar with the temper of the House. He became alarmed, sounded several members, and, finding them much of his mind, urged them to come to his room and talk over matters. They did so. The grievances of the people, both real and imaginary, their inflamed passions, the turbulent spirit of the greater part of them, the violence of the Assembly, and the ruinous measure it was about to pass, were quietly discussed. It was agreed that to attempt to stem such a current would be foolish. The wisest course, they thought, would be to yield, and, while they went with the tide, seek to guide and check it.* To accomplish this end a preamble and set of resolutions were made ready and presented the next day. The instrument was framed with much care. In the preamble were mentioned some of the measures the Assembly had already taken, and some of the measures the multitude were very anxious it should take. The resolutions instructed the first constable in each town to summon the freemen of the place to meet on the first Tuesday in January, 1787, and to count their Yeas and Nays on the two great questions before them : Should a paper bank be issued? Should the Tender Act be continued? † When the resolutions came up for debate in the House they were vigorously attacked; for a few were sharp enough to see that such a document, coming from the opposition party, meant not concession but delay. The framers, how-

---

* Thompson's Civil History of Vermont, p. 79.

† Vermont Gazette, November 13, 1786. Journal, November 20, 1786.

ever, were ready with a popular argument. The sufferings of the people, it was said, were severe. Relief of some kind had become absolutely necessary. The great question of the hour was, What is the best way of giving relief? Of this the people, no one surely would deny, were the best judges. It ought therefore to be submitted to their decision.* This reason prevailed, and the resolutions were passed. It was afterward remarked by superstitious housewives that no good would ever come of the bill. Every noted day in its history had been one of disturbance. The day it was carried through the House the Court of Common Pleas was attacked at Windsor. The day it was made public in the Gazette the Superior Court was broken up at Windsor. The day it was printed in the Journal the County Court was set upon at Rutland.

When the four judges had taken their seats, word was brought in that the court-house was surrounded by a great multitude, armed with bludgeons, with rusty muskets, and with old swords. Many in the crowd were mere lads; others were tavern-haunters, demagogues, and men of the lowest order. There were, however, scattered here and there among them a few of the first characters of the place.† So soon as the judges were told of the gathering, the sheriff was commanded to adjourn the court till afternoon. The order had hardly been obeyed when a committee came in from the malcontents, bearing a petition that the court should adjourn without day. They were heard with civility, and dismissed with the answer that when the docket had been called, and the business of the day dispatched, their request would be thought over.‡ This reply was carried back to the mob. Instantly they flew into a rage. But as nothing could be done, they waited with great impatience till the court met in the afternoon. Then a hundred of the malcontents rushed into the room in a most insolent and riotous manner. A certain Thomas Lee was at the head of them. Lee passed among his fellows as a man of

---

* See the account given by Daniel Chipman in Records of Governor and Council, Vermont, vol. iii, pp. 364, 365.

† Caverly's History of Pittsford, p. 252.

‡ The written answer of the court may be seen in the Vermont Gazette, December 11, 1786.

some education; had served in the late war, had risen to the rank of colonel, had become beggared, had been locked up in the jail for debt, had liberated himself by being admitted to the poor man's oath, and was ready for the most desperate enterprise. The moment he was in the room he began to harangue and threaten the court for not having complied with the petition of the morning. His language indeed became so insolent and offensive that he was cut short in the midst of his speech by a command to the sheriff to adjourn the court. This was quickly done. But when the mob saw the judges had risen, they positively refused to let them through the door-way, called for arms stored at a neighboring house, posted sentinels, and kept judges, sheriff, and lawyers close prisoners for two hours. Finding the spirit of the court was not to be broken by a show of force, the mob, toward supper-time, began to fall away, and in a little while none were left. The judges hastened to their lodgings, where the committee of the rioters a second time waited on them. The sheriff meanwhile sent off to alarm the county and raise the militia. Though it was between eight and nine in the evening before his orders went out of Rutland, so speedily were they executed that before nine the next morning troops under Colonel Pearle came streaming into town from Pawlet. Soon after, Colonel Clark and Lieutenant-Colonel Spafford came in with more, and the Regulators, as they called themselves, fell back from the court-house and broke up into small knots.* The business of the court was no longer hindered, and just at dusk the sheriff ventured to arrest seven of the leaders and lock them up in the jail. A party of forty, who, under an excitable militia-captain named Cooley, had taken refuge in a house a mile out of town, were next surrounded by a detachment of horse and foot; but not till several shots had been exchanged, and some blood shed, did they give themselves up and come back to Rutland prisoners.

To all appearances the rebellion was crushed; but as the troops had brought three days' rations with them, it was believed to be on the side of prudence to keep them till the last moment. Late on Saturday afternoon, however, the militia

---

* A Letter to the Printers. Vermont Gazette, November 27, 1786.

were drawn up, reviewed by Colonel Clark, thanked, and discharged. But it was then so near dark that they spent the night in Rutland, and early on Sunday morning set out for home. They were hardly out of sight behind the hills which encompassed the town when word was brought in that two hundred of the Regulators had assembled to the west of Otter creek. Horsemen were instantly dispatched by the court to recall the troops. Clark was overtaken at Pine Hill, hastened back to Centre Rutland, and placed a strong guard at the bridge over Otter creek. Pcarle took up his position at Blanchard's Corners. The malcontents lay between them. And now some earnest friends of law and order spent the rest of Sunday in persuading the Regulators to go back to their farms. They had, they were told, been misinformed. Artful and designing men had imposed on them with absurd stories about the fraudulent dealings of the court and the harsh treatment of its prisoners. Nothing of the kind had taken place. But if they persisted in the course they were pursuing, they surely would bring up in bloodshed and in ruin. Great numbers were convinced of their error, abandoned the enterprise, and took service under Government. When Monday came, all was again peaceful, and the militia once more turned homeward.*

---

* For accounts of the troubles at Rutland, see Caverly's History of Pittsford, pp. 252–258; Hollister's History of Pawlet; Hall's Eastern Vermont; and the Vermont Gazettes of November 27 and December 11, 1786.

# CHAPTER IV.

### THE BREAKING UP OF THE CONFEDERATION.

BAD as was the condition of the finances of the States, that of the national Government was much worse. The very men who announced themselves ready to go to any extreme in hopes of finding a means of paying their own debts, could not be induced to take the first step toward providing the means of paying the national debt. The state of the Treasury had become desperate and alarming. At the opening of the year 1786 the entire debt of the country summed up to forty-two million three hundred and twenty-five dollars. A little over thirty-four millions was due at home. Of the remaining eight millions, a part was due in France, some in Holland, and some in Spain.* To a generation which has expended three thousand millions of dollars on a civil war, which is accustomed to see Congress each year appropriate several hundreds of millions to the service of the state, and pays down annually for postage-stamps and postal-cards a sum but little less than the whole debt of the United States in 1786,† the burden under which our ancestors bowed down seems light. But it was then thought a heavy one. So great was the poverty of the people that the tax-gatherers found it impossible to wring from them the two and a half millions necessary to pay the annual interest. Every year the requisitions were sent out, and every year the interest fell more and more in arrear. During the fifty months which elapsed from the first day of November, 1781, to the

---

* The precise sum of money due to creditors at home was $34,115,290. The foreign debt was $7,885,035. The interest amounted to $2,415,956.

† The amount collected by the post-offices of the country during the fiscal year 1882 was $41,368,062

first day of January, 1786, requisitions to the amount of ten
millions of dollars had been made on the States, and less than
two and a half millions had come into the Treasury.  For the
last fourteen months of this time the receipts were much less
than four hundred thousand a year, while for the same time
the interest on the foreign debt alone was much more than five
hundred thousand.  To make matters still worse, the first instal-
ment of the principal became due in 1787, and thenceforth
one million fell in each year till all was paid.

With this the multitude were as familiar as with any fact
in daily life; as with the price of wheat or the cost of living.
For three years the impost system had been before them for
consideration.  The imperative need of an assured revenue
had been made known to them repeatedly.  Yet the Treasury
was as empty as ever.  Some few States, after much deliberation, had yielded a reluctant consent.  But even these had so
bound their concessions with absurd restrictions that they might
much better have withheld them.  New York and Rhode Isl-
and, Maryland and Georgia, would not listen to so dangerous a
thing as a revenue system of any kind.  It was not the intention of these States to see the fine ports of New York and
Providence, Baltimore and Savannah, crowded with gaugers
and tide-waiters busy collecting great sums of money, not a
penny of which reached the State Treasuries.  Delaware had
no objection to the impost or the supplementary fund; she
thought indeed that they were good things, but nothing could
induce her to consent to their establishment unless every other
State did the same.  North Carolina had assented to everything
Congress asked.  Massachusetts had granted the general impost,
but withheld the supplementary fund, and with Massachusetts
were joined New Hampshire and Connecticut, New Jersey,
Virginia, and South Carolina.  Pennsylvania sent word that
she too granted the impost and the permanent fund, but would
collect them in such way as the Legislature from time to time
saw fit to prescribe.

The seriousness of this condition of affairs was keenly felt
in Congress.  It was on the authority of that body that the
loans and the debts had been contracted, and the House had, in
the name of the whole country, pledged its faith for their pay-

ment. The year, therefore, was scarcely come in when a grand committee was appointed to examine into the state of the finances, and report the best way of discharging the debt. Early in February the report was read to the House.*

The document began with a recital of the sums due, and then went on to the consideration of the means of payment. The Articles of Confederation, it was said, provided three ways: requisitions, loans, bills of credit. As to the success of requisitions in the future, it was easy to form a judgment from the success of requisitions in the past. In October, 1781, eight millions; in October, 1782, two millions; in April, 1784, two millions six hundred and seventy thousand; in September, 1785, three millions of dollars had been called for. But the sums sent in under these requisitions were not sufficient to pay the interest on the foreign loans. Happily a part of one of the loans had not been expended, and had been used to discharge a part of the debt; but all the loans were now exhausted.

As to contracting new loans, that was something not to be thought of. Unless the Treasury could promptly meet the interest due on the money already borrowed, it was foolish to seek to be trusted for more. Besides, the country being at peace, enjoying the blessings of a free and extensive commerce, and having but the expenses of Government to attend to, Americans should blush to admit that they could not discharge their engagements without the help of foreign nations.

The emission of bills of credit was likewise objectionable. They would not serve to pay off even the domestic debt, for, bearing no interest, they would place the credit in a worse condition than before. The States, it was indeed true, were in possession of another fund arising from the sale of vacant and unimproved lands, but as public securities were taken in payment for these lands, little specie would come into the Treasury from that source. They were to be looked on rather as a means of extinguishing the domestic debt; and as not an acre of them could be sold till they were surveyed, and as some time must elapse before the geographer could survey them, no immediate aid was to be expected. All this the committee said they had considered, and could, after mature deliberation, see

* Journals of Congress, February 15, 1786.

no way out of the trouble but to recommend the impost. This
they did. And as all the States, save New York and Georgia,
had in some wise assented, it was advised that these States be
most earnestly urged to take into immediate consideration the
resolution of the eighteenth of April, 1783. When the report
had been read, Houston, of Georgia, rose and moved to postpone; but the motion was lost by a vote of nineteen to two.
The matter was then referred to a new committee of five.

On the fifteenth of the month the House was informed that
the committee was prepared to submit the result of its deliberations. Rufus King read the paper, for he had, with the hearty
consent of the other four, been chosen as the best qualified
to set forth their views. Though in years the youngest man
who at that time sat in the House, he was in experience among
the oldest. He had just turned thirty, but had come early
into public life, and was already known as a jurist, a statesman, and an orator. His first public service happened the
year after quitting Harvard. The British were at that time
overrunning Rhode Island, men were greatly wanted, and
King went out as a volunteer under Sullivan. This duty discharged, he settled at Newburyport and began the practice of
law. There the remarkable talents which in after years raised
him to the highest dignities and gained for him the conduct of
great affairs, began to show themselves, and it was not long before he went up to Boston and took his seat in the General
Court as the representative of his fellow-townsmen. In the
Assembly he distinguished himself as a man of business, a
ready debater, and a pleasing orator. Whenever he stood up
to speak he was always sure of a patient hearing from the
House, and the House was always sure of getting from him
much light on the matter under debate. One speech in particular, in support of the five-per-cent impost, was greatly admired,
and aided not a little to secure for him an election to Congress.
The report on the finances which he now submitted was a most
carefully prepared and exhaustive production. He called the
attention of the House to many things which depended on a
sure supply of money. Without funds, he said, the interest on
the debt could not be paid; the merchants could not be protected against the Barbary powers; the frontiersmen could not

be defended from the savages; magazines, so indispensable to public safety, could not be formed; public servants could no longer be maintained abroad; the Federal Government could no longer be run at home. All these things depended on the prompt payment of the yearly requisitions, and all these things, it seemed not too much to say, were likely to be involved in a common failure and ruin. The committee had felt it to be no more than their duty candidly to look into the principles of the impost and find out, if they could, what reasons had stood in the way of its adoption. This they had done. They had in the most impartial way examined all the laws passed by the States on the matter of the impost, and they were unable to find that a single member of the Confederation had stated one objection against it. The result of this inquiry was that they were clearly and decidedly of the opinion that of all systems of collecting revenue the wisdom of Congress could devise, the impost was the freest from well-grounded objections, and the most likely to meet with the approbation of the States. A further reliance on the old way would be madness. For eight years past the requisitions had been most irregular in their working. Their collection had been most uncertain. Their unproductiveness was evident. To look to them, therefore, as a source whence to draw moneys to meet engagements, definite in amount and fixed in time, would be folly. It would be dishonorable to the understanding of any man who entertained such confidence. It would be dangerous to the safety, honor, and welfare of the Union. Seriously impressed with these facts, they believed it to be the plain duty of Congress to represent to the States how utterly impossible it was to maintain the faith of the Federal Government by requisitions made from time to time, and to once more urge a speedy and full concession of all to the impost system of April, 1783.[*]

It had been long since language so strong and decided had been listened to by Congress. The report met with a hearty approval, was adopted, and a set of resolutions expressive of the sense of it drawn up and quickly passed.

The attention of the House was then turned to the regulation of trade. Another grand committee was appointed. All

---

[*] Journals of Congress, February 15, 1786.

the acts of the States granting Congress power over trade were examined, and another report listened to on the third of March. As had been expected, the acts were found to be most conflicting and incongruous. One State granted everything that had been asked, but clogged the grant with the condition that when the twelve others had done likewise the regulation of trade by Congress should become an article of the Confederation.* Three had determined the date when the act was to take effect.† Another had settled upon the time the act was to run.‡ Four had suspended their acts till all had complied.# Three had not given the request any consideration whatever.‖ One prescribed how the trade of the State should be regulated.ᴬ Nothing was to be done under such circumstances, it seemed to the committee, but to send back the acts with a civil request that the States would reconsider and make them agree one with another. This the House accordingly did.

The appeal was well timed. The regulation of trade by Congress was highly popular with a very large and very influential class of the community, and great activity had been manifested in its behalf. In North Carolina, one of the three that still withheld consent, a grand jury returned in their list of grievances the fact that Congress did not possess enough power to regulate trade.◊ The grand jury of Wilkes county, in Georgia, did the same, complained bitterly that the State had refused to allow Congress to lay an impost of five per cent on foreign goods, and earnestly besought the Legislature to make haste to do so.‡ Merchants in the great cities continued to fill the Gazettes and Packets with most distressing accounts of the depredations of Algerine cruisers. The Barbary powers, it was said, were plainly at war with the States. One merchant had heard from his agent in the Barbadoes that two Algerine war-ships, one of twenty-two guns and one of fourteen guns,

---

* North Carolina.  † Connecticut, Pennsylvania, and Maryland.
‡ Rhode Island extended the time to twenty-five years.
# Massachusetts, New York, New Jersey, and Virginia.
‖ Delaware, South Carolina, and Georgia.
ᴬ New Hampshire granted power to regulate trade by restrictions on duties.
◊ Pennsylvania Gazette, January 25, 1786. The statement is copied from the Charleston papers.
‡ Pennsylvania Gazette, January 25, 1786.

and a xebec of twelve guns, were cruising about the islands, that they had overhauled an Englishman by mistake, had questioned him closely, had declared he was an American, and compelled him to show his papers.* Another had received notice that four Moorish cruisers had put in at Madeira, had made many inquiries about American ships, and had gone off asserting that they were at peace; but their manner gave the lie to their words.† Indeed, an American ship, which happened to be going out just as the pirates were coming in, had only managed to escape them by showing no colors and running close to shore.‡ A third furnished an account of the capture and treatment of a ship's crew.#

Of these facts a most skilful use was made. Between British restrictions and Barbary piracies there would, it was said, soon be an end to American commerce. If the ships of the States were not to be driven from the seas, these things must stop instantly. And they never would stop till Congress had full power to retaliate upon Great Britain and make war upon the Moors. The force of these arguments was much strengthened by news of an alarming nature which came from New Jersey. The Legislature of that State had long been out of humor. It began by quarrelling with New York about the duties, and went on to quarrel with Congress about the requisitions. Late in September, 1785, a call had been made for three millions of dollars.‖ This according to the common usage had been apportioned among the States, and one hundred and sixty-six thousand seven hundred and sixteen dollars of it fell to New Jersey. But the State, imitating the conduct of Rhode Island, stoutly refused to pay one shilling. One hundred and sixty-six thousand dollars, it was said, to be taken out of the pockets of an overtaxed people, and for what? To support the Confederation? And why should New Jersey contribute funds for the continuance of so weak and unjust a Government? She had, in an hour of public danger, waived her objections, humbled her pride, and gone into the Confed-

---

* Charleston Evening Gazette, April 3, 1786.
† Pennsylvania Gazette, February 15, 1786.
‡ Ibid., February 1, 1786.          # Ibid., May 3, 1786.
‖ Journals of Congress, September 27, 1785.

eration on terms most disastrous, simply because the necessities of the hour were great and because she entertained a firm belief that all things in which she was aggrieved would be remedied.  Her quotas had been unjust.  She had been made to bear more than her share of the expenses.  She had been for years ill used by a neighboring State.  All this Congress was aware of, and had refused to right her.  She had been very patient; but there was a point beyond which patience ceased to be worthy of men and became the badge of cowards.  She would no longer submit to be fettered with a compact so unjust, so unequal; she would assert her independence and refuse to pay one penny of the new quota till every grievance had been righted.  A resolution expressing these sentiments was accordingly brought in, and passed the Legislature by a great majority on the twentieth of February.  A few days later one of the members who sat for New Jersey announced the fact to Congress.

The blow was a heavy one.  One hundred and sixty-six thousand dollars seems in our time a trifling sum; but it bore a greater proportion to the revenue of the country in 1786 than twenty millions bore to the revenue of the country in 1882.*  The loss of so large a part of the income of the Government would, in the best of times, have been severely felt; but that in times of such distress it must be attended by disastrous consequences was obvious.  Even if every one of the others paid up her quota in full, there would still remain a large deficit; and while this deficit existed, the interests of the whole country must suffer and its good name be disgraced.  Peace could not be purchased of the Barbary powers, and every merchant-ship that entered the Pillars of Hercules would soon be moored to the docks, or stranded on the beach of Tunis or Tripoli.  Magazines could not be put up, troops could not be employed, and in a little while every promising hamlet of frontiersmen along the banks of the Ohio and the Holston would be a smouldering ruin, strewn with mangled corpses.  Part of the interest on the debt would remain unpaid, or perhaps the salaries of the ministers abroad fall in arrear.  All this was bad enough to make the most stubborn opponent of the

---

* The net revenue of the Government for the fiscal year 1882 was $403,525,250.

impost give way; but it was not the worst. Want of money was a great calamity; but want of unity between the States was a greater calamity still. If New Jersey, it was felt, persisted in her determination, the Confederation would in the eyes of every foreign power stand forth as the most impotent Government on the face of the earth. What king would make treaties, would exchange ministers, would engage in commerce with a confederation forced to beg compliance with its lawful acts from a member by no means the most powerful, whose territory lay not two miles away from the seat of Government, and who was fully aware of every circumstance that ought to have made it ashamed to disobey. Every friend of America would hang down his head from very shame; every enemy would be filled with exultant joy. But nowhere would the delight be so extravagant as in England. There, ever since the peace, the speedy downfall of the Union had become the common talk of the coffee-house and the street. The Gazettes and the refugees, who were still looked upon as a safe authority for American affairs, were confidently predicting a dissolution. "Leave them to themselves," it was said; "they will soon fall out, and gladly seek to come back, one by one, under the old Government, and then—" Sometimes the speaker would end his sentence with a gesture or a look which left his meaning quite plain. Sometimes he would openly declare that when the day of repentance did come he hoped his Majesty's ministers would have spirit enough to spurn the petitioners, or at least treat them with such severity as would make them repent heartily of their late rebellion.* The American States were not, and could not be, united. Nothing could induce the landed interest to join with the commercial. The States to the south of the Potomac were bitterly set against the States to the north of the Potomac.† What effect the behavior of New Jersey would have in England was therefore not doubtful. The King would continue to hold the posts on the frontier, and firmly refuse to enter into any commercial relations.

In this pass Congress determined to try what a little per-

---

* See a letter from Adams to Jay, October 21, 1785.

† Adams to Jay, August 6, 1785. See, also, Adams to Jay, July 19, 1785.

suasion would do. A committee was appointed, instructed to expostulate with the angry Legislature of New Jersey, present to it the distressed state of the country, beg it not to increase the embarrassments of the hour, and were dispatched with all speed to Trenton. There they were courteously received by the Assembly, and the tenth of March set down as the day for their hearing. Gorham and Grayson were of the committee. But Pinckney, who represented South Carolina in Congress, made the address. The States had, he said, come together, formed a government, and put the administration of its concerns in the hands of one controlling power. The act was a purely voluntary one. Each State was therefore in honor and in duty bound to bear such a share of the expenses of the Government as its abilities would allow. New Jersey complained that her portion was too large. It was difficult to see the fitness of this complaint. The first system made use of by the Confederation for raising a revenue had indeed been found impracticable and unjust. It had been changed. A new system had been introduced; and to this New Jersey not only assented, but sent in the very returns on which the assessment she now thought a grievance had been made. How, under such circumstances, could she with justice assert that she bore an undue proportion of the debts? How could she, with any show of consistency, refuse the requisition sent her? If overrated, let her give proofs of it to Congress. If oppressed, let her state to Congress the oppression of which she complained. She had indeed a controversy with New York. Had her resentment in common with that of Connecticut been directed against New York alone; had she by every proper means in her power, by levying duties, by opening a free port just opposite the great city, sought to force that State to do her justice, she would have received the countenance and support of every other government in the Union. But another and a most unhappy course had been pursued. She had refused the lawful requisition of Congress till New York did her justice. Such conduct would defeat, not further, the ends in view. It would turn the animosity of the States from New York, and direct it to her. For with what consistency could force be used against one State for not assenting to a measure on which it was confessed she had a perfect right to deliberate, while another was suffered with silence and with impunity to refuse the requisitions she was constitutionally bound to obey ? It was not too much to say that by a persistence in her refusal New Jersey would inevitably dissolve every tie that bound the States together. Others would soon follow her example, refuse their requisitions, and withhold their supplies from the common Treasury till she in turn had yielded. Then the existence of the Federal Government would be endangered ; it would perhaps cease. He ended by reminding his hearers of the critical plight of commerce, then languishing under the most ruinous restrictions, of the hostile behavior of the Indians on the frontier, and the insulting conduct of England in holding the posts.*

When he had made an end of speaking, the Legislature rescinded its resolution. It had not, it declared, the most remote intention of doing anything to embarrass Congress, or to injure the general welfare of the nation. Not a word, however, was said about raising funds to meet the requisition. Indeed, five months slipped by before any such provision was voted. In the meanwhile the impost was granted by New York.

So soon as the last appeal of Congress for the tax was known, many warm friends of the measure, not choosing to be discouraged by repeated failures, determined to make one more effort in its behalf. Among them was Hamilton. Ever since Congress began to exist, Hamilton had with justice been numbered among its most unflinching friends. No one had written or said more in its behalf. No one had been more active in combating that extreme jealousy of power which seems to be inseparably bound up with republican government, or had given a more hearty support to even its most unpopular measures. Five years before, while the war was still waging, he had, in a series of papers which he called the Continentalist, expressed the heterodox belief that the many fatal mistakes which so seriously endangered the good cause were to be ascribed to nothing but the weakness of Congress. At a later period, when Tory scribblers and pot-house politicians were re-

---

* New York Packet, March 23, 1786.

viling that body as impotent and useless, he had, in his Vindication, again blamed the people for withholding the authority which could alone make it respectable, and had, in the famous letters of Phocion, laid down unanswerable reasons why the States ought cheerfully to comply with every recommendation Congress made. He was now for the impost, and was in precisely that place where his vote and his voice could be of most use. He was a member of the Legislature of New York. With the temper of the Assembly he was thoroughly familiar, and it seemed to him, as to many of his friends, that the chances of the impost passing the House were small. It was determined, however, to make the attempt. A new petition was decided upon. Hamilton drew it up, and notices were sent out that copies could be signed at Bradford's Coffee-House, at Vandewater's in the Fields, at Abraham Marlin's, or at the Bear Market on the North river.* Great numbers made haste to read it, and of those who read almost all affixed their names.

The instrument was a clear, forcible, and concise statement of the reasons why the impost should be passed, and closed with an observation as pointed as it was just. Whenever any one held forth on the merits of the system, it had been usual to silence him with the observation that the good points about it were undoubtedly many; but that it would be ruinous to all liberty to put into the hands of Congress so much money, patronage, and power. The petitioners now plainly told the Legislature that they felt their interest and liberties would be quite as safe in the hands of men sent to represent them in Congress for one year as in the hands of men sent to represent them in the Legislature for four years; that all government implied trust, and that every government must be trusted just so far as was necessary to enable it to perform the high functions for which it had been created.†

While the petition was being signed, both parties kept up a bitter conflict through the press. One writer, who signed himself Gustavus, addressed the Senate.‡ The present was, he

---

* New York Packet, March 27, 1786. † Hamilton's Works, vol. ii, pp. 333, 334.

‡ The paper came out in the New York Packet, April 6, 1786, and was addressed to the Senate of the State of New York.

said, the last session of the Assembly before the first interest, for which the impost was to provide funds, fell due. It surely was not necessary to remind the members that, should the first interest on the Dutch loan not be satisfied, the principal could be demanded. Congress had a claim to the gratitude of every American for having made the loans. It had pledged itself and the country for the payment of the sums lent, and had a right to do so. Should Congress be authorized to make national contracts and not fulfil them? As to the dangers of granting a revenue to Congress, until the political dotards and dreamers who first suggested them could advance some solid reasons, it was not worth while to confute them. The members of the Senate were too well informed to be alarmed by the awful figures of the sword and purse, which, like halberds in a militia train-band, were interspersed and brandished throughout the dull harangues of the demagogues. The argument which some used of the advantage New York would derive from a separate impost was a base one, and would soon be disproved. Her provoked neighbors, spurning her selfishness and avarice, would no longer pay a tax to the citizens of New York for which their public account was not credited.

In the same number of the Packet appeared some arguments by a member of the non-impost party. The paper was by an unknown hand, was addressed to the Congress of the Thirteen States, and was written in that coarse and bombastic style common to the political writings of the age.* Do you expect, said the writer, by threats of coercion, to terrify us into the embrace of despotism? Shall the independent State of New York be made a dupe to your body? Central in situation, extensive in domain, strong in numbers, important in commerce, fruitful in agriculture, invincible in war, and inexhaustible in resources, we dare all the terrors of your resentment. Behold the resistless flood of the Mohawk, view the rolling waves of the Hudson, and see a picture of our importance and our strength. He then went on to ask why, if they must have an impost, one granted till the next session of the Legislature would not answer their purpose. A committee of revision, said he with gross insolence, could then be appointed,

---

* New York Packet, April 6, 1786.

your accounts looked into, and, if no suspicion of collusion existed, an extension easily obtained.

To this tirade Congress gave no heed, for the members had long become accustomed to insult and abuse, and they well knew that the reasons advanced for refusing an impost were precisely the ones which had from first to last guided the political conduct of Clinton. It is impossible to mention the name of George Clinton without calling up the recollection of a man to whose memory a grateful posterity has been more than kind. To believe that he was a really great man, to extol him in terms too exalted to be applied to the founders of the republic, is in our day a common thing. His reputation, indeed, is immense. But when an even-handed justice is meted out, it must be owned that he has been much over-rated. That he was a man of force and no mean ability is quite true; but that he was in any sense a statesman is not true. He was, in fact, the most shrewd, the most crafty, the most pushing and successful politician of his time. Quick-sighted rather than foresighted, he raised himself, despite his humble birth and scanty means, partly by time-serving, partly by the skilful use he made of every chance opportunity, to the high post of Governor of the State of New York and held it for many years. From the day on which he thus became the most powerful man in the State he toiled persistently to make the State the most powerful member of the Union. He would see her waste lands along the Mohawk turned into gardens. He would see her noble harbor filled with ships. He would have her Treasury run over with gold. But his cramped and narrow mind knew no way by which his State could attain to so much prosperity save that by which he himself had climbed to greatness, by selfishness, by cold-heartedness, by pulling down the rivals that struggled at her side. The course, therefore, pursued by New York, from the November morning when the enemy left her soil to the day when she finally adopted the Constitution, forms the most shameful portion of her annals. There is nothing like it save in the history of Rhode Island. And this course, there can be no doubt, was prescribed by Clinton. While others were striving to give strength and dignity to the Union, he was steadily laboring to break it down. To weaken the power and thwart the wishes of Congress had with him long been a guiding principle, and he now found in the impost a means of doing both.

After innumerable petitions had been presented, and many sharp debates and addresses listened to, the Legislature passed the act. But they inserted in the bill a clause which, as they well knew, made the grant of the impost useless. They would not, it was understood, part with one jot of the power of the State. They would have no men swarming upon their docks, prying into every ship that came from abroad, setting valuations and collecting revenue, unless they were creatures of their own making. It was therefore made a condition of levying the impost that the collectors of the duty should be appointed by the State of New York. When Congress took up the matter, toward the middle of August, their committee announced this fact.* Instantly a resolution was passed recommending New York to amend the act, and, as the Legislature had then broken up, a letter was ordered to be written to Governor Clinton urging him to call a special session.† The letter was sent, and on the sixteenth of the month the answer was read to the House. He had, he protested, the highest deference and respect for Congress. He wished it was always in his power to comply with the recommendations of Congress. But, unhappily, he had no power to convene the Legislature except for extraordinary purposes. The present business had often been before the Assembly during the late session. He could not, therefore, consider it as anything extraordinary. ‡ In a word, he plainly told Congress that he did not think it of much importance whether the impost succeeded or failed, whether the national Treasury was full or empty, whether the interest on the loans was paid or unpaid; and he undoubtedly told the truth. His reply was deemed evasive, and before the month had gone out it was again moved that he be urged to assemble the Legislature.# There the matter rested for the present. Some minor

---

\* The act was passed by New York on May 4, 1786. Congress was notified on May 12th, and referred it to a committee, which reported July 27, 1786.

† Journals of Congress, August 11, 1786.    ‡ Ibid., August 16, 1786.

# See the Report of the Committee on the Governor's Letter, August 22 and 23, 1786.

business then took up the attention of the House; but a week later, after a warm debate, a vote was reached which threw the country into a ferment, and for a time still further impaired what little harmony existed between the States.

On the twenty-ninth of May the Secretary of State for Foreign Affairs wrote to the President of Congress. He had, he said, in the course of his dealings with Gardoqui, met with great difficulties. The negotiation indeed was at a stand-still till these hindrances were removed ; but, in his opinion, it was expedient that they should be so managed that their very existence should for the present remain a secret. He begged, therefore, that a committee might be appointed to instruct him.* His request was granted. King, Pettit of Pennsylvania, and Monroe were named. The secret soon came out, and in a few months the right to navigate the Mississippi was hotly debated by the whole country.

The difficulties of which Jay hinted arose from a secret article of the English treaty. The second article of that instrument described the southern boundary of the country given up by England as the thirty-first parallel of latitude from the Mississippi to the Appalachicola, down the middle of the Appalachicola to the Flint, from the Flint to the head of St. Mary's river, and down that river to the sea. These were the southern limits of British possessions in America ; for that splendid region which lay yet nearer to the Gulf, and passed under the name of the Floridas, was Spanish ground. The mildness of the climate, the richness of the soil, the luxuriance of its vegetation, were well known. Travellers pronounced it to be one of the most highly favored regions on the globe. There, they said, the rigor of the northern winter and the intense heat of the tropical summer were alike unknown. There men grew old without ever having seen snow, or ever having felt the heat of a day when the thermometer rose to one hundred and ten. The fertility of the soil was described as simply inexhaustible. The oranges, the figs, the bananas, the pomegranates that grew in the gardens or sprang up in the woods, were thought to be as fine as any that came from the Indies. On this region England had long looked with wistful eyes. In-

---

* Secret Journals of Congress, May 31, 1786.

deed, when the treaty was framed it seemed not unlikely that as soon as peace was made with Spain, England would come into possession of at least a part of it. A secret article was therefore agreed on which stipulated that, should Great Britain gain West Florida, the southern boundary of the United States should be a line running due east from that point where the river Yassous mingles its waters with the Mississippi to the Appalachicola.* The eighth article stipulated that the Mississippi should always be open to Englishmen and Americans alike.

But before the treaty was signed the secret article was well known at Madrid. The indignation of the King was great. In truth, it seems strange that men should have supposed for a moment that the stipulations could long be kept a secret, and that, when they were known, Spain would look on with complacency while land still her own was parcelled out between her neighbors. Spain had indeed become the most impotent and torpid of nations. But, torpid as she was, there still remained one point on which she was exquisitely sensitive. Whoever touched her there, touched her to the quick. Her Treasury might be empty, her finances might be in frightful disorder, her army a rabble, her ships lie rotting at the docks. A horde of pirates might exact from her a yearly tribute, competition might drive her merchants from the sea, and she might in European politics exert far less influence than the single city of Amsterdam, or the little State of Denmark. All this could be borne. But the slightest encroachment on her American domains had more than once proved sufficient to rouse her from her lethargy and to strengthen her feeble nerves. It was so on this occasion. The news of the ratification was scarce six months old when a letter from his Catholic Majesty to Congress was on the sea. Congress was informed that until such time as Spain should admit that the boundary between the United States, Louisiana, and the Floridas had been truly described in the English treaty, she would assert her claim to the exclusive control of the Mississippi. Nor would she under any circumstances suffer boats from the States to sail up or down its waters while under her control.†

---

* Secret Journals of Congress, iii, 338.

† June 25, 1784. Communicated to Congress November 19, 1784.

The letter occasioned much uneasiness and alarm. Some hot-headed men, and there were many such in the settlements along the Ohio and the Holston, were for hurling foul scorn at Spain, sending pirogues down the river, and, if the worst came to the worst, taking possession of Louisiana by force of arms. Others, who lived in the great sea towns, who knew nothing of the country beyond the Alleghanies but that it abounded in savage beasts and savage men, and who cared much for their own prosperity, took a very different view. The navigation of the Mississippi might, they said, become very important to the country in course of time. But that time was not the present. Before that day would come, many thousands of settlers must go over the mountains, many thousands of acres of forest-land be cleared, many towns must spring up on the river, many battles with the Cherokees be fought, and the whole valley turned from a wilderness to a garden. All this was very remote. So remote that it was not worth while to give up the good-will of Spain to secure it. There would be time enough in the future for that. The friendly offices of Spain were at present much more needed than the navigation of a river a thousand miles away. Was the need of a commercial treaty immediate and pressing? Spain was willing to enter into such a treaty. Was gold and silver demanded? There was scarce a product of the States, lumber, tar, pitch, wheat, indigo, whale-oil, that could not be rapidly exchanged for specie in the ports of Spain. Were foreign markets desirable? Here again the friendship of Spain would be most useful. France would turn a deaf ear to the clamor of the merchants of Bordeaux and L'Orient the moment Spain began to plead in our behalf. Portugal would open her ports in response to the friendly intercession of her neighbor. Backed by Spain, American ships and merchants would be graciously received in the Canaries, in the Levant; nay, every power along the whole shore of the Mediterranean would hasten to make treaties and exchange consuls. Even the Barbary powers, whose ships lay in wait for the first American packet hardy enough to enter the strait, would listen to terms of amity and peace. Was it worth while to give up all this, plunge into a war, and expend great sums of money to secure the navigation of the Mississippi? Was any man so weak-minded as to suppose that the richest cargoes that would go down the river would yield any returns comparable to the returns that must come from the cargoes that would go over to and come back from Spain?

Between these two extreme parties was a third, less hot-headed than the first, more far-sighted than the second. They were not, they said, prepared to rush into a war. Yet they were not prepared to give up their claims to the Mississippi. The present advantages of a trade with Spain were undoubtedly many and great. Yet, whoever had beheld that fine western country, whoever had seen the majestic rivers rolling through broad valleys to the sea, the great prairies, level as the floor, vieing in fertility with the most favored spots on earth, and capable of feeding millions of cattle or growing hundreds of millions of bushels of grain, would be slow to throw away so splendid an opportunity for the petty gains of trade. There, too, was a population, bold, hardy, full of energy and grit; such an one as any nation might be proud to own. Adopt the policy of exclusion, and in a few years the Atlantic States would be to the people of the Kentucky district no more than England or Spain. They would throw off their allegiance. They would raise a government of their own. They would perhaps, to secure the great blessing nature had provided for them, put themselves under the protection of Spain. Then, with a chain of British posts along the northwest, and a prosperous Spanish colony along the southwest, the States would find all too late how dearly they had paid for the privilege of sending fish to the Canaries and pitch to Madrid. This calamity might, it was quite likely, be prevented by negotiation. It might be possible, by a little firmness and a little diplomacy, to hold on to the one without giving up the other; to make an amicable treaty with Spain, yet obtain the free use of the Mississippi.

Such was, in the main, the opinion of Congress. The House indeed, after some bickering as to the propriety of dispatching so important an officer as the Secretary of State for Foreign Affairs, determined to send Jay to Spain. But long before he was ready to set out, Don Diego Gardoqui arrived.

Gardoqui came with the modest title of encargado de negocios. But he was in truth Minister from Spain. He presented his credentials on the second of July, 1785, was received, and declared that he was charged to conclude a treaty of amity and commerce. The affability, the easy good manners of the Spaniard, the interest which he shrewdly manifested in American affairs, but, above all, the gracious letter of his master, did much to remove the fears of a rupture with Spain. Congress became so bold that in its first instructions to Jay he was commanded to be very firm in his demands for the free use of the Mississippi. But the minister was equally firm in his refusal. A long negotiation followed. Notes, visits, papers were exchanged. A whole year slipped away, and matters seemed no nearer to a close. His master, Gardoqui said, was ready and willing to enter into a treaty; he would concede many things to the merchants of the States, but not the use of the Mississippi. That point the King would not yield. It was simply a waste of time to talk of it. It had always been, and was, an inflexible maxim of Spanish policy to shut out all mankind from the American dominions. Jay expostulated, persuaded, argued; and at last thought he saw an easy way out of the difficulty. He had but to get rid of the restriction laid upon him by the resolution of the twenty-fifth of August, 1785, and all would go on well. He accordingly wrote to Congress that his way was beset with difficulties, and begged that a committee might be appointed to instruct him in secret.

That the difficulty to which he alluded was the resolution of the previous August, and that the purpose of the committee was to have that resolution revoked, was well known and openly asserted. The members of the committee had indeed been carefully selected, were men touching whose opinions no doubt existed, and were chosen as the representatives of the three great sections of the country: the East, the middle States, and the South. King, who sat for Massachusetts, had, on the very day the Secretary's letter was read in Congress, stood up in his place, and in a long speech denounced the insidious conduct of France, declared that no reliance was to be placed on her in future, and pronounced what was thought to be a high eulogium on Spain. Pettit came from a State where public opinion on the proposed treaty was almost equally divided. But he was himself known to be a steady supporter of Spain. Of the three, Monroe alone represented the interests of the South and West. He was a Virginian, and every Virginian was deep- ly concerned in the prosperity of what he called the back country.

But while Jay was composing his letter the right to navigate the Mississippi was being tested. A Kentucky flat-boat, laden with hardware, was, despite the claims of Spain, slowly descending the river. The goods were the property of Thomas Amis. Amis was a North Carolinian, bold, enterprising, and reckless. As to whether the States were or were not entitled by the law of nations to use the river he neither knew nor cared. He was sure that a lucrative trade might be carried on with the Spanish towns scattered along the banks, and felt confident that if a well-selected cargo came down the river the Spanish authorities would wink at its sale. He made a purchase accordingly of some Dutch ovens, pots, skillets, ploughs, and fifty barrels of flour, carried them to the Ohio, procured a boat, and began his journey. Everything went well with him till the morning of the sixth of June, when he came in sight of the high bluffs at the foot of which stood the filthy and squalid huts of Natchez.

Natchez was, with the exception of New Orleans, the most important Spanish town on the river. There were a fort, some soldiers, a church, a few hundred huts, and a population made up of Spanish, French, negroes, half-breeds, and Indians. At Natchez, Amis was stopped. His pots, his ovens, and his boat were brought on shore and confiscated. The commandant indeed went through the form of giving him a receipt, and, as a mark of particular favor, suffered him to return to the States.

No boat at that day ever undertook to stem the current of the Mississippi. Amis was therefore forced to go home by land. The journey was long. The way lay through a wilderness. He was in constant danger of falling into the hands of the Indians. It was not till the summer was far spent that he found himself once more on the banks of the Ohio. Yet he had, in the course of his journey, found some compensation for the ills he endured. Wherever he went he told the story of his wrongs, and wherever he told it he was sure to find sympathetic and indignant listeners.    In a little while his narrative, greatly exaggerated, spread over the whole State of Franklin and the district of Kentucky.    And everywhere the news of the seizure at Natchez was met by news more exasperating still.    Congress, it was said, had made a treaty with Spain, and had agreed to close up the Mississippi for twenty-five years. The story, though false, contained a large grain of truth.    No such treaty had been made; but the day when it would be made seemed near at hand.

After working for two months with the committee, Jay, on the third of August, laid before Congress a statement of the difficulties he had so long kept secret, and suggested a way out of them.    A treaty with Spain was, he represented, greatly to be desired.    But of making such a treaty there was no hope whatever while the claim of the United States to the waters of the Mississippi was insisted on.    The Spanish minister on this point was inflexible.    The best that could be done under the circumstances was to put aside the Mississippi question, consent to the terms offered, and make a treaty, but distinctly state that the instrument should be binding for twenty-five years and no longer. . He then went on to urge the fitness of this course with arguments that might have become the mouth of a New England merchant, but which did small credit to the head and the heart of the first minister of state.

John Jay was descended from an old Huguenot family, had been bred to the law, and had held many public offices of dignity and trust.    When the war seemed upon the eve of breaking out he had been made a member of the Committee of Correspondence.    He was afterward raised to the high place of Chief Justice of New York, was sent to Congress, had been made President of that body, went thence to Spain, had been one of the Peace Commissioners, had put his name, with Franklin and Adams, to the treaty with England, and had come home to be made Secretary of Congress for Foreign Affairs.    He brought to the office a good knowledge of continental politics, was painstaking and diligent.    Yet the policy which he followed during the whole of his administration was one of procrastination.    He was much more disposed to put off a difficulty than to grapple with it, and felt quite satisfied if he could, by some happy expedient, arrange matters for the time being.

The proposition he now made to Congress was heard by some members with unconcealed delight; by others with mingled feelings of indignation and alarm. For three weeks it was fiercely debated. But the discussion had not gone far before it became manifest that in the House, as among the multitude, there were but two great parties, and that the lines separating them were precisely those separating the great sections of the country. On the one side were the New England States clamoring for the conclusion of the treaty. On the other side were the southern States insisting, with equal firmness, that the resolution of the twenty-fifth of August, 1785, should be rescinded, and Jay forbidden to treat further with the minister from Spain. Between them, hesitating which way to turn, were the middle States. New Jersey and Pennsylvania indeed leaned strongly to New England. Precisely what course would be taken by New York no one could tell. But every one was aware that Clinton ruled New York, and every one who knew Clinton knew that the course he would urge would be the most selfish possible.

Was it reasonable, such was the language of some noted southerners, to demand so great a sacrifice from one section of the country for the benefit of another? Massachusetts seemed to think it very hard that the South would not fall in with Spain; would not sell the affections of her western colonies; throw away her richest possessions; distrust an ally able and willing to befriend her; and court, by the most precious sacrifices, an alliance with a power whose impotency was notorious. But what would Massachusetts say to a proposition to give up to Great Britain her right of fishery as the price of some stipulation in favor of tobacco?

Blind as the eastern States seemed to be to the fact, it was really a matter of very serious concern to them to gain possession of the trade with the West. Without such a trade the ties of blood, which were every day growing weaker and weaker, would soon be no ties at all. Then there would be no bonds to bind the East with the West. The ease, as Washington said, with which men glide down stream would give a new bias to the way of thinking and acting of the western settlers, and what went on across the mountains would be to them of no concern whatever.  The navigation of the Mississippi was not, it was true, needed by the settlers at present.  But the day would come when it would be needed, and when that day came no earthly power could deprive them of it.  Why, then, stir up the restless and impetuous spirits of Kentucky to acts of extravagance and desperation ?   Why urge a matter it was clearly to the interest of the country to let sleep ? *

To this it was answered that nine tenths of the ills which so sorely afflicted the country grew out of a decayed and languishing commerce.  A treaty with Spain would revive trade, bring in gold, and relieve the present embarrassments.  And what was the price of this ?  The shutting up of a useless river for a few years.  To a country so sparsely settled that it was near a week's journey from one little hamlet to another, and where one might ride all day and never see the smoke of a hut or hear the sound of an axe, what was now done with the Mississippi could not be of the least importance.  To the East what was done with the Mississippi was of the utmost importance.  There could be no prosperity without commerce. There could be no commerce without a treaty.  There could be no treaty without giving up the use of the river.

This was the foundation for the story that went down the Ohio valley as Amis came up.  The people were soon aroused. Clark, a man of no mean parts, who passed among his fellows under the title of General and had acquired a widespread notoriety along the Ohio, took the lead.  He called a board of field officers of the late Wabash expedition.  The board met at Fort Vincennes, indulged in harangues against Spain, Congress, and Mr. Jay, and at length decided that the alarming state of the West required a strong garrison at Vincennes.  A body of men was soon enlisted for one year, and Clark put in command.  But he had not been many weeks in charge before he began to commit acts which he looked upon as just re-

---

* See a letter from Washington to Henry Lee, June 18, 1786 ; again, July 26 and October 31, 1786.  Lee supported the Spanish side till, at the fall election, he lost his seat in Congress.  Referring to the causes of Lee's defeat, Madison writes : " One of them is said to have been his supposed heterodoxy touching the Mississippi."  Madison to Jefferson, December 4, 1786.

prisals, but which the State in whose name he perpetrated them regarded as thefts. Vincennes was at that time a collection of squalid huts, where some enterprising Spaniards carried on a lucrative trade with the settlers. One of them lived in the town, and kept in a cabin of unhewn logs smeared with mud what was known as a store. There the trappers bartered skins for sugar and coffee, and laid in supplies of Jamaica rum. There the better class of farmers found such articles of finery or use as were the delight of their sweethearts or their wives, sun-bonnets, gayly colored ribbons, tin spoons, and iron pots. On this store Clark had long had his eye. The owner was a Spaniard. A Spanish officer had seized the goods of Amis, a native of the States, and he saw no reason why he, an American officer, should not seize the goods of a native of Spain. He accordingly, one dark night, dispatched a fellow named Dalton with a guard of soldiers to take the store. It was late when Dalton reached the place. The Spaniard was asleep, but was roused by the noise at his door, and, in that mixture of bad Spanish and bad English which did duty as a language at Vincennes, demanded what was wanted. Dalton made him understand that his cellar was to be searched. He struck a light, opened the door, and led the way to the cellar. Dalton made a hasty survey of the barrels and boxes that littered the floor, came out, set a guard about the cabin, and went back to his quarters. Early the next morning he returned with a force of men, plundered the cellar, and went off with great quantities of taffy, sugar, coffee, wine, kegs of brandy, bundles of peltry, and bales of goods. Whatever could be used to clothe the troops Clark retained. The rest he put up at public auction and sold, while the despoiled and ruined merchant fled down the river, vowing vengeance on his spoilers. An officer of the recruits named Bussaroon was then dispatched to the settlers on the Illinois. He was charged to urge them to conciliate the Indians; to notify them of the capture at Natchez, of the reprisal at Vincennes, and to advise them to lay hold of any Spanish property they could.*

---

* My account of the seizure at Fort Vincennes is taken from the deposition made to the Committee of Investigation by Daniel Neeves, one of Dalton's guards. See Diplomatic Correspondence of the Revolution, vol. vi, p. 211.

Meanwhile, the Kentuckians were appointing committees of correspondence, and preparing two papers which indicated most clearly the spirit they were in. One was a petition to the Virginia Assembly, and was the work of the delegates who sat in that body from the district of Kentucky. The other was a pretended letter from a gentleman residing at the falls of the Ohio to his friend in New England, and was the work of an unknown hand. The petition was a vigorous protest against the hated proposition of Jay, and a bold assertion of the right of the United States to use the Mississippi.* The language, indeed, was so strong that many who declared themselves in favor of it expressed a fear that it would give great offence to Gardoqui, and were for softening some expressions and leaving out others. But among those who thought differently was Madison. He fully sympathized with the indignation of the western men, and he thought he now saw an excellent chance to assist them, while at the same time he helped forward a favorite project of his own. Nothing lay nearer to his heart than to have Virginia adopt the report of the Annapolis Convention. But the great change which had in the course of the autumn come over the feelings of leading Virginians, made him despair of success. He was, he said, on his return to Richmond, shocked to find that the behavior of Congress in the Mississippi affair had produced such ruinous results. Some men, who had always been conspicuous as stanch supporters of the Federal authority, had become greatly soured. The ardor of others had been cooled.† He determined, however, to do what he could; he went to the Kentucky delegates, assured them of his support, presented the importance of sending representatives to Philadelphia, won them over, and struck a bargain. He agreed to speak for the petition. They agreed to vote for a delegation; scarcely had this been arranged when the question came up in the House. On the third of November it was decided that a law in conformity with the report of the Annapolis Convention ought to pass, and a committee was named to prepare one. On the seventh of the month the bill was

---

* Journal of the House of Delegates of Virginia, 1786, p. 46.
† Madison to Washington, December 7, 1786.

reported ; two days later it was passed. The vote was unanimous.*

Three weeks now went by before the Kentucky petition was reached. At last, on the twenty-ninth of November, the House went into a committee of the whole to consider it. The discussion was long and full, but the opinions of the members were all one way. Indeed, before the day closed, a set of resolutions, couched in language less violent than that of the petition, was voted without one dissentient voice.†

The pretended letter from the gentleman at the falls of the Ohio bore date five days later. It did not upon its face differ greatly from the hundreds of epistles which at that time swelled the mail-bags and were read by the post-riders. The complaints with which it was filled were in sentiment, if not in language, much like those in which, under the excitement of the times, the most austere patriots and trained statesmen were accustomed to indulge, such as Washington expressed to Lee, and such as may be found scattered through the letters of Jefferson, of Madison, and Monroe. Yet the paper was so artfully constructed as to be well calculated to arouse the very sentiments it affected to describe. The late commercial treaty, said the writer, has given the west country a universal shock. To sell us, and make us vassals to the Spaniards, is a grievance not to be borne. The acts which brought about our revolt from Great Britain were not half so barefaced and impudent. To give us liberty to carry our corn, our beef, our pork down the river, only to find that at the end of the journey it becomes subject to Spanish laws, is an insult to our understanding. We know by a woful experience what becomes of such goods. We know that it is in the power of the Spaniards to take our produce at what price they will. We know that large quantities of flour, meal, and tobacco have been confiscated. This the West will not endure. The country has been settled but six years, and that in the face of a savage foe ; yet, in spite of this, and of the great market emigration has made, the produce that is on hand each year is simply enormous. Flour and pork are

---

* Journal of the House of Delegates of Virginia, 1786. Madison to Jefferson, December 4, 1786.

† Journal of the House of Virginia Delegates, session 1786, pp. 66, 67.

selling at twelve shillings a hundred; beef is in proportion. Any quantity of Indian corn can be had for ninepence the bushel. Shall all this be done for the good of the Spaniards? Shall we be bondsmen of the Spaniards, as the children of Israel were bondsmen of the Egyptians? Shall one part of the Americans be slaves and another freemen? Our state is so bad that any exertion to better it will be just. We are indeed preparing to make that exertion. Spanish goods at Vincennes and Illinois have already been taken, for we are determined, if we cannot trade down the Mississippi, they shall not trade up. Twenty thousand troops can easily be raised west of the Alleghanies and the Appalachians to drive the Spaniards from their settlements at the mouth of the river. If this is not countenanced in the East, we will throw off our allegiance and seek elsewhere for help. Nor will we seek in vain, for even now Great Britain stands with open arms to receive us.*

Many copies of this letter were made and sent over the river to Franklin, were there widely circulated, and read at the musters, the town-meetings, and the court-openings with great effect. In truth, the people of Franklin were in so irritable a frame of mind that no story that could come to them respecting the intentions of Congress was too wild to be believed. They were sure they were about to be, if they had not already been, made over to Spain as the price of some commercial concessions to the East. Their condition was, in fact, most lamentable. Two governments contended for their obedience. Both levied taxes. Both enacted laws. Each government had its courts, its justices, its sheriffs, its militia captains, and its dignitaries of state. Whatever act was done by one side was sure to be imitated and surpassed by the other. The contest resembled somewhat the fencing scene in Hamlet, but was less bloody. Laertes wounds Hamlet; then, in scuffling, they change rapiers, and Hamlet wounds Laertes. Sevier's followers attempted to hold court at Jonesboro. But while the law-

---

* Secret Journals of Congress. The letter is given in full in the Independent Gazette or Chronicle of Freedom for July 7, 1787. In the same paper are two other letters of like strain. One of them, "Copy of a Circular Letter Directed to the Different Courts in the Western Country," contains a call for a meeting to frame "a spirited but decent remonstrance to Congress."

yer for the prosecution in a case was in the midst of an impressive harangue to the court, Tipton entered with a body of men, seized upon the papers, and turned the judge and the lawyers out of doors. A few days later a party of Franklinites came upon a log hut where a justice was sitting under the authority of North Carolina. Recalling the scene at Jonesboro, they went in, took the papers from the clerk, broke up the court, and drove the company into the road. Tipton then went to the house of Sevier, where the papers were deposited, and carried them off by force. Sevier in turn repaired to Tipton's house, regained possession of the documents, and hid them in a cave.*

But while the Governor was busily engaged chasing judges and hiding briefs, his attention was suddenly drawn to a matter which required for its management the exercise of all his authority, courage, and skill. The Indians rose on the frontier. Lulled by the willingness with which Old Tassel and Hanging Maw had signed the late treaty, settlers had pushed along the north side of the Holston as far as Beaver creek. There a large clearing had been made, and several houses, built of tree-trunks laid one upon another, roofed with strips of bark, and provided with openings wherein greased paper did duty as glass, had been put up. But the sight of so flourishing a settlement, so remote from the source of defence, and exposed on three sides to attack, was too tempting for the Indians. They sacked it, killed two men, and drove the rest back to the towns. And now the frontier swarmed with Indians. War parties went out from the Cherokees, the Chippewas, the Twightwees, the Tawas, the Pottawattamies, and Shawanese. It was feared that before many weeks had passed a thousand braves in war-paint would be on the march for the settlements, burning and killing as they went. Such a prospect might well make the heart of the stoutest frontiersman quake. For of all wars, an Indian war was the most terrible. The miseries of a rupture with Spain would be as nothing to it. The fighting would then be done in the full light of day, in an open field, and would be mollified by all the usages of civilized men. Every

---

* See Haywood's History of Tennessee. Ramsey's Annals of Tennessee, pp. 339, 340. Marshall's History of Kentucky.

one would know that, if he were so unfortunate as to fall into
the hands of the enemy, he would be treated with a reasonable
amount of kindness and consideration.  His wounds would be
dressed, he would be well housed and fed, and he would, at the
first opportunity, be exchanged.  Not so with the Indian captive.  With his hands bound behind him, he would be driven,
hungry, thirsty, and smeared with blood, to some distant village,
and might count himself most happy if the friends who came
to deliver him and his companions were not forced to pick his
bones out of a heap of ashes, or carry home his corpse scalped,
scorched, lacerated, and maimed.

So soon, therefore, as the news came, Sevier was all activity.
A call was made for volunteers, and in a few days one hundred and sixty horsemen were on the march for the heart of
the Indian country.  They came first to Houston station on the
Little river, then crossed the Tennessee at Island Town, passed
by the Tellier plains, and went over the Unaka mountains to
the Hiwassee.  There were three Cherokee towns known among
the trappers as the valley towns.  Sevier at once attacked them
with great energy, took them, killed fifteen Indians, and set fire
to the lodges.  Thence scouts were dispatched, but they had
not been long gone when they returned with word that a trail
had been discovered a few leagues away, that it was fresh, that
it was large, and that all signs indicated a considerable force of
Indians near at hand.  A pursuit was ordered.  Horses were
saddled, guns loaded and primed, and the trail soon reached.
But when those of the party who had grown old fighting Indians saw it, they declared that upward of a thousand braves
must be in the band.  To go on would, they said, be madness.
The trail undoubtedly led to some narrow defile in the hills, or
to some carefully planned ambuscade, where the pursuers
would on a sudden find themselves surrounded and over-
powered by tremendous odds, and be cut off to a man.  The
punishment, too, already inflicted on the Indians was severe.
There was therefore no good reason for taking the risks of a
further advance.  This counsel prevailed, and Sevier ordered
his men to go back to the settlements.

A very different fate meanwhile awaited a much larger
expedition that went out from Kentucky.  The result was in

truth a shameful failure, and the men came home without having fired a single shot or seen a single foe. General Clark was in command, and to this fact is to be ascribed no small part of the ills encountered. Clark was, like Sevier, a demagogue and an agitator; but he was not, like Sevier, a man of dauntless courage and iron will, quick to think, quick to act, and a natural-born ruler of men. The raid into the Cherokee country was well planned, rapidly executed, and successful. The Wabash expedition was from the start badly arranged, badly led, mutinous, and disastrous. Early in the summer about a thousand men had answered to the call for volunteers, and assembled at the falls of the Ohio. There a short delay occurred, while food and ammunition were collected; but, as soon as the quartermaster reported that enough had come in, the army took up its march for Vincennes. The rations and the powder were sent by water in nine boats. The troops went by land, driving a herd of cattle before them, and came first to the fort. There they had hoped to find the boats, but three days, five days, a week dragged by, and none came. At last, on the morning of the ninth day, the little fleet of keel-boats and barges was descried coming slowly up the river. Shoals and low water in the Wabash had detained it. The news that the boats were in sight was welcomed by the men with every manifestation of delight; but their joy was speedily followed by bitter murmurings and complaints. Half the provisions had rotted on the voyage, while of the stock of food brought by land, nothing save a few bullocks remained. To obtain more supplies was out of the question, and the troops were instantly put on short rations. From that time forth all was disorder and discontent. As the march progressed the mutterings grew louder and louder, orders were obeyed with less and less alacrity, and when the deserted Indian towns on the Vermilion were reached the troops mutinied. Clark, in an evil hour, had sent out runners to offer the Indians war or peace. That so old a soldier should have been guilty of so gross a bit of folly is indeed strange. If his mission were one of peace, he ought never to have quitted the falls of the Ohio. If his purpose was to make war, and it undoubtedly was, he ought not to have thrown away the many advantages

of a surprise, especially when contending with so crafty and
so cunning a foe. In this opinion his officers and his men
shared. A march through the wilderness and over the plains
was, they said, bad enough even when food was plenty and no
enemy near; but to make such a journey with hungry stom-
achs, in order to fight Indians, and then to find, after all done
and suffered, that their own leader had betrayed them, was
too much. Three hundred of them one morning refused to
go a mile farther, saddled their horses, and turned their faces
homeward. Clark, overwhelmed with shame, remonstrated,
argued, threatened, and at last begged them, with tears running down his face, not to desert him. No heed was given to
his entreaties, and the mutineers set off for Vincennes.

Scarce were they out of sight when the few that remained
held a council, discussed the perils of their situation, and
speedily resolved to go after their friends. In a moment all
was confusion in the camp; blankets were hastily collected,
rations distributed, and, before many hours had gone by, the
whole band was in full retreat. They came up with the deserters toward evening, and camped with them that night.
Next morning the troops, scorning order and discipline, went
by the nearest route to their homes.*

The sudden return of the expedition without having struck
a blow caused general alarm. Great preparations had been
made for it, and great things expected in return. When the
call for troops was issued, men had hastened from all quarters
to put down their names in the list of volunteers. So many
of the first characters of the district joined the army that the
meeting of the convention to decide the question of the independence of Kentucky had to be postponed. Yet what, it
was asked, had come of all this? The provisions had been
wasted. Time had been squandered, and the men had gone
muttering, grumbling, and half fed to within two days' march
of the Indians, had sent word to the chiefs that they must
make peace or fight, and had then, in a moment, turned about
and fled. What was to prevent the Shawanese coming out of

---

* The account of Clark's Wabash expedition has been mainly taken from
Marshall's History of Kentucky, vol. i, pp. 248, 249; Dillon's History of Indiana,
pp. 201, 202; and Albach's Western Annals.

their ambuscade among the defiles of Pine creek and marching straight upon the settlements? There was, however, much to prevent such a calamity. For, while the alarmists were complaining, Colonel Logan, a brave and skilful officer, crossed the Ohio, where Maysville now stands, with five hundred mounted riflemen, penetrated the Indian country to the head of Mad river, burned eight towns, laid waste many hundreds of cornfields, killed twenty braves, and, with eighty prisoners, hastened back to Kentucky.

There he found the settlers greatly excited over the affair at Vincennes, and anxiously awaiting the result of their memorial to the Virginia House of Deputies. Every emigrant that came down the river was stopped and closely questioned as to the state of feeling beyond the mountains, and the latest information concerning the treaty. One of the malcontents, named Thomas Green, was particularly active in this work. He seems to have been one of those restless, aspiring characters that are never happy unless stirring up strife or fomenting discord. He had allied himself closely with Clark, had written the famous letter to the gentleman in New England, had agreed with Clark to bear half the expense of a letter to the Governor of Georgia, and now addressed himself to Jay. His language was strong, but it expressed no more than the ill-humor of the settlers warranted. The commercial treaty with Spain was, he said, cruel, oppressive, and unjust. The whole West was astonished at the proposition to close the Mississippi. It was truly surprising to every man of sense that the Legislature of the United States, which had been so applauded for the assertion and defence of the rights of man, should in so short a time seek to subject the greater part of its dominion to a slavery worse than had ever been imposed by Great Britain. Ireland was a free country to what the West would be when navigation was shut, and all the benefits of toil given to the Spaniards.*

But his letter to the authorities of Georgia proved most disastrous. He had intrusted the instrument for safe delivery to a messenger named Wells. Ignorant, talkative, and proud of his charge, Wells boasted wherever he went of the

---

* Green to Jay. Diplomatic Correspondence of the Revolution, vol. vi.

mission he was on, of the great sum he was to get for performing it, and showed the letter freely. Among those who saw it as he passed through Danville were some stanch friends of government. By them a careful copy was taken, sent at once to the Governor of Virginia, and in a few weeks the whole matter was laid before the council. Clark solemnly protested on his honor that he never so much as saw the letter, that he did not know the contents, and that he was an ill-used man. But it was thought a little singular that one so old in public affairs should, with childlike simplicity, contribute to the expense of a letter firmly binding him, on the slightest encouragement, to raise an army, go over the border and take possession of the disputed land, yet never read the writing. His word was therefore doubted. His conduct was denounced, the powers assumed by him disavowed, the prosecution of all concerned in the seizure of the Vincennes goods ordered, and a formal notice dispatched to Congress.

Much of the excitement, however, had by this time spent itself, and much had been allayed by the vigorous language in which the Virginia Assembly had protested. The free navigation of the Mississippi, such was the language of the memorial, was a bountiful gift of nature to the United States. It had, too, been secured to them by the late revolution. The Confederation was constructed on the broad principle of equal rights. A sacrifice of the rights of any one part to the real or supposed interests of another would therefore be a flagrant violation of justice, and an alarming innovation in the system of the Union.* This passed the Houses by a unanimous vote on the twenty-ninth of November. Next day Madison announced that he would, on the fourth of December, move the election of delegates to the Federal Convention to be held at Philadelphia in the spring.

The convention of which he spoke was that body of men to whom we owe the Constitution. The commissioners who met at Annapolis in the previous September had recommended Congress to call it. At Annapolis the attendance had been slim. No delegates came from Georgia, from South Carolina,

---

* Journal of the House of Delegates of Virginia, session 1786, pp. 66, 67.

or from any State to the east of the Hudson. Three times they had been chosen in Massachusetts. Twice they refused to serve. The third time they accepted and set out, but, like the delegates from Rhode Island, were met on the way by news that the convention had broken up. The session indeed was a short one, for the few who came had such limited powers that the delegates contented themselves with lamenting the wretched state of national affairs, and urging a new convention of delegates, with enlarged powers, to meet at Philadelphia in May. Hamilton furnished the draft of the report, the convention spent two days in debating and amending, and then adopted it and adjourned. From Annapolis it was carried to New York, where Rufus King, with that narrowmindedness which he so often displayed, prevented Congress recommending it to the States.

But the men of Virginia were happily of a better kind. There the Assembly took up the report of the commissioners in the second week of the session, and appointed a select committee of seven to prepare and bring in a bill.* The seven reported four days later.† Madison drew the preamble, which set forth in earnest and dignified eloquence the reasons which prompted the act. No opposition was encountered. The three readings were without debate, and on the ninth of November the bill passed. But it was not till December that the commissioners were chosen on a joint ballot.‡ They were seven in number, were men who had long been in public life, and were thought to be, in Virginia, among the foremost statesmen of the time. Washington was the first elected. Then came Patrick Henry, then Edmund Randolph, then John Blair, Madison, Mason, and Wythe. Two names were wanting in the list, which many declared should have been there. But it was afterward asserted that Edmund Pendleton was then suffering from a dangerous malady which threatened his life,# and that Richard Henry Lee was no longer the favorite he once had been. He was known to be much in favor of shutting up the Mississippi.

---

* Journals Virginia House of Delegates, November 3, 1786.
† Journals, November 7, 1786.      ‡ Ibid., December 4, 1786.
# See a letter from Madison to Jefferson, December 4, 1786.

He was suspected of being in no sympathy with the purposes of the convention.*

And now the example set by Virginia was speedily followed by others. Indeed, before Congress had given its sanction to the Federal Convention, six States appointed delegates.† Massachusetts made a seventh. But the act by which she bound herself to send representatives to Philadelphia was not agreed to till the very day on which Congress, after much deliberation, approved of the call of the convention.‡

By those firm friends of government who waited with feverish anxiety for the action of the States, the hearty concurrence of Massachusetts was hailed with delight. For nowhere had the antifederal feeling been so bitter and so strong as in New England, and of all New England it was strongest and bitterest in Massachusetts. There the sovereignty of the State had always been a favorite principle of legislation.# One of her delegates, long before the definitive treaty was signed, had been bold enough, in a fit of ill-humor, to stand up in the halls of Congress and throw out threats of a separate confederacy beyond the Hudson.‖ Another had, upon a public occasion, ventured to call the Continental Government a foreign one.^ Nay, more, in the summer and autumn of 1786 a project was actually matured to go out of the Union and form a new confederation of New England States. But the rebellion of Shays broke out. In an instant public opinion changed completely. Stern patriots, who, while all went well, talked of the dangers of baleful aristocracies, soon learned to talk of the dangers of baleful democracies. They beheld the Legislature in-

---

* Letter from Madison to Washington, November 8, 1786.

† The six were Virginia, New Jersey, Pennsylvania, Delaware, North Carolina, and Georgia. ‡ February 21, 1787.

# It cannot be doubted that John Adams was a stanch Federalist. Yet Adams, in his Defence of the Constitutions of Government of the United States of America, which he published in 1786, made the remark: "Congress is not a legislative, but a diplomatic assembly." First edition, p. 362. When Jefferson called his attention to it "as not entirely accurate and not likely to do good" (Jefferson to Adams, February 23, 1787), Adams explained that he spoke of Congress as it then was constituted, and not as Congress should be in the future. See letter of Adams to Jefferson, March 1, 1787.

‖ Madison's Debates, vol. i, p. 357. Also, pp. 428–430.

^ See Austin's Life of Gerry, vol. i, pp. 407–415.

sulted, the courts mobbed, justice defeated, the strong arm of the State openly defied. Like men of sense and candor, they at once saw their errors, renounced them, and frankly confessed that, in place of detracting from, it was the duty of every good citizen to add to and strengthen the powers of Congress.* But the most marked of all the conversions was that of Rufus King. King had from the first been among the determined opponents of Federal authority. No arguments could be found weighty enough to convince him that any good could come from a powerful and efficient national Government. He had drawn the letter in which the Massachusetts delegates gave their reasons for withholding the resolutions of 1785, and had, in the October previous, appeared before the General Court to speak against the plan of a convention of the States.† But he now went from one extreme to the other with a rapidity that will surprise no one who has watched the course of men in revolutionary times. He admitted his mistake, and wrote to his old colleague, Gerry, exhorting him to lend his aid to effect a call of the convention. " Events," he wrote, " are hurrying us to a crisis ; prudent and sagacious men should be ready to seize the most favorable circumstances to establish a more perfect and vigorous Government." ‡ From that time forth he was a Federalist.

What action would be taken by New Hampshire nobody knew. What would be done by Rhode Island no one cared. The unhappy condition into which that once prosperous State had fallen was indeed most deplorable. She was scarce looked upon as any longer a member of the Union. Her name had become a byword and a reproach, and was never mentioned without a wagging of the head and a shooting out of the tongue. She was nicknamed Rogue's Island ; # her people were spoken of as Know Ye men, and her acts as Know Ye measures.‖

---

* See a statement of General Knox, referred to in a letter of Washington. Sparks's Washington, vol. ix, pp. 226, 227.

† See an Address made to the Legislature of Massachusetts, by Rufus King, October, 1786. Also, Boston Magazine for 1786, p. 406.

‡ See a letter of Rufus King to Elbridge Gerry, February 11, 1787. Austin's Life of Gerry, vol. ii, pp. 7, 8.

# See A Dream, Boston Gazette, October 2, 1786. See, also, a paper on Connecticut Currency in New Haven Historical Society Papers, vol. i.

‖ New York Packet, June 15, 1787.

It was said, with great truth, that it was impolitic for a Rhode Islander in his travels to own his country unless he was so fortunate as to be able to prove a uniform and decided hatred of Know Ye men and measures. When a merchant violated his engagements, when an agent betrayed his trust, when a tradesman defrauded his customers, the term of reproach applied to him was Rhode Island's faith. When language failed of odious epithets to portray the finished villain, he was declared to be as contemptible as a Know Ye Judge.* When a criminal broke jail, or a debtor fled from his creditors, it was sneeringly said that he would surely be found in Rhode Island. The most sanguine Federalist never for a moment supposed that a State ruled by men so given over to dark and crooked ways would join the convention. No one, therefore, felt any disappointment that she never did. Yet the effect of her shameful conduct, combined with the turbulent scenes in Massachusetts, was, in the eastern States, immense. In three months' time public opinion underwent a complete change. Faith in the stability of the Union went down. A strong distrust of republican institutions sprang up. No money, it was said, is paid into the Treasury. No respect is paid to the Federal authority. Not a single State complies with the requisitions. Some pass them over in silence; some absolutely reject them. It is quite impossible that a Government so weakened and despised can much longer hold together.† The malady has come to a critical stage. None but the strongest remedies will serve. The patient must be killed or cured.

But among those who looked with favor on a dissolution of the Union, many opinions prevailed as to what should take its place. At one extreme of the Antifederal party was a body of men, numerous, respectable, and not without influence, who leaned toward monarchy and were for setting up a King.‡

---

* New Jersey Journal, July 11, 1787.

† See a letter from Madison to Pendleton, February 24, 1787.

‡ "The late turbulent scenes in Massachusetts, and infamous ones in Rhode Island, have done inexpressible injury to the republican character in that part of the United States; and a propensity toward monarchy is said to have been produced by it in some leading minds." Madison to Pendleton. See, also, a letter from Madison to Washington, February 21, 1787. Washington to Madison. Sparks's Washington, vol. ix, p. 223.

They could, they protested, see no way out of the ills that lay so thick on either hand but by abandoning the attempt at republican government, and taking refuge in that very system they had with so much difficulty just thrown off.

At the other extreme were to be found many men of note; almost all the first characters in the country, and a large proportion of the community. They abhorred, they said, the idea of a monarchy; they would never give up the idea of a republic. But they were convinced that no one republican government could rule harmoniously over so vast a country, and over such conflicting interests. They were therefore for three separate confederations, marked off by such boundaries as difference of climate, diversity of occupations, and the natural products of the soil required. Everybody knew that the eastern men were fishers and shippers and merchants, while the southern men were planters and farmers. The late discussion over the Mississippi had shown how impossible it was to reconcile the interests of men so variously employed. It was better, therefore, that they should part; and that, as Massachusetts built her ships and Virginia raised her tobacco and her slaves under different climates, they should do so under different flags. They hoped there would be three republics: a republic of the East, a republic of the middle States, and a republic of the South.*

Between these two parties lay the great body of the people. They too were anxious for a change, and talked much of a vigorous government. But whether it was obtained by a dissolution or a partition of the Confederation was all one to them.†

The Assembly of Connecticut did not resolve to send delegates till Saturday, the twelfth of May, two days before the convention was to open. While the question was under debate, Mr. Huntington, a man of some local fame and a militia general in the late continental army, rose and addressed the Speaker. The measure under discussion had, he said, been recommended by Congress and acceded to by most of the States. This was to him a good reason why Connecticut

---

* Rives's Life of Madison, vol. ii, p. 187, where some extracts from his Diary are given.

† Madison states that this feeling was particularly strong in Connecticut. Rives's Life and Times of Madison, vol. ii, p. 188.

should do likewise. He would gladly stop and say no more. But he felt constrained to go on, as he had much cause to think that some gentlemen who heard him were of the belief that the Confederation was sufficient unto itself, and that others held the country would be better without any. The Confederation had been framed while America was smarting under the hand of wilful power. It seemed to have been the leading object of the framers to set up an authority without bestowing upon it any power whatever. No penalty was fastened to a breach of the contract between the States. No means of forcing obedience existed. The observance of the articles hung solely on the good-will and pleasure of each State. He was no prophet, but his calculations must indeed be wrong if diversity of sentiment and manners, if local circumstances, if the unjust distribution of the debt, and the jealousies that sprang from trade, did not bring forth heart-burnings and strife of the most serious kind. God only knew where and when they would end. Was it wise to trust the event to chance and leave government to arise out of the distractions of the mob? Surely it was far better, in a cool and dispassionate hour, to consult with the sister States on the fitness of making needed changes in the Confederation. A man removed from scenes of danger, blessed with plenty, and compassed by kind neighbors, was apt to hug himself in his ease, and think the independent State of Connecticut a host unto herself. Was this so? Far from it. She was open to the insults and depredations of a single ship-of-war. On all sides were treacherous neighbors. He remembered to have heard a gentleman say, in the debate upon another question, that Poland was cut up out of pity for her people. Who knew how long it would be ere Massachusetts, Rhode Island, and New York would join, and in the excess of their love part out Connecticut among them? What security had she against the turbulent spirit of the one, the selfishness of the other, and the righteousness of the third. How long would it be before the rights of these States began to clash? In twenty years, nay, in ten, Massachusetts would awake to the fact that she had the sole right to the fisheries on her coast. Connecticut fishermen would be driven from Nantucket shoals. Complaints would come in to the Assembly, would be sent on to Congress, and a recommendation made by that body to Massachusetts to give indemnity for the outrage and the loss. Did any one for a moment suppose she would do it? Alas, poor fool! Massachusetts would write a long letter of justification to Congress, and close it with a reminder of the old continental money and the renowned expedition to Penobscot bay. Some might say these fears were visionary, and that his sentiments on government came from a military way of thinking, or the baneful influence of the Cincinnati. Yet he would always speak the dictates of duty and of truth, and declare himself for the convention, the impost, and an efficient General Government.

When he had sat down Mr. Granger got up and spoke against the measure. He feared it would displease his constituents. He thought it would endanger the liberties of the people. Congress had power enough, and if the convention was held, it would likely bring about a kingly government.

On the same side was Mr. Perkins. The State, he was sure, would send to Philadelphia men who had been tenderly bred, were in easy circumstances, and who could not therefore feel for the people in their day of distress. "If," said he, "we send, we shall be under the double obligation to adopt what the convention shall recommend; for if we say A, we must say B also."

Mr. Humphrey approved of the conduct of Rhode Island in refusing to choose delegates, and called upon Connecticut to follow her. Colonel Seymour denounced the behavior of Rhode Island, and said that by her iniquity she had become the reproach and scorn of her neighbors. Colonel Wadsworth hoped the House would never copy Rhode Island in any of her acts of legislation. She had forfeited all claims to the confidence of the country and the whole world. Her acts were a disgrace to the human race. Things were come to a fine pass when men went about declaring that there was no power in the Federal Government, and that it would be better to go back to Great Britain. He saw in the Assembly at least one man who wished America had been conquered at any period of the war. He was told that men would be sent who were delicately bred, and knew nothing of the sufferings of the mass.  Was the Assembly a pack of fools?  Was it so stupid as to send men ignorant of the state of things?  Had this been the custom of the past?  If so, let the House emerge from its stupidity and select men who lived in the country, had been hardly bred, and knew what the people wanted.  No State had stronger reasons to call for a change in the Articles of Confederation than Connecticut.  She imported heavily. The taxes on her importations footed up to one hundred thousand dollars a year.  Every shilling of this went to her neighbors.  Let this go on and the State would be ruined.  Captain Granger had said they should all become asses.  He would liken Connecticut to a strong ass crouching down, not under two, but under twenty burdens that would finally crush the life out of her.

At this point Mr. Fitch found fault with the members for abusing Rhode Island.  To this Colonel Wadsworth stoutly replied that so long as laws were passed founded on injustice, he should claim and take the liberty to say just what he pleased about them.

Colonel Seymour supported the measure.  He was for having delegates.  He was happy that a motion for a general convention had come from so respectable a quarter as Virginia. Affairs had reached an alarming crisis.  Vermont was balancing between Canada and the United States.  The settlements on the Ohio were draining the eastern States.  New York was joined to her selfish interests and become unfederal. Massachusetts was in disorder.  Rhode Island was a reproach. It was indeed a sad picture.  But he flattered himself that the convention would find a balm for all the wounds, and give strength to the Federal Government.

Several other gentlemen spoke.  The question of sending delegates to Philadelphia was then put, and carried in the affirmative.*

In the middle States a better temper prevailed.  New Jersey and Pennsylvania had already given a warm support to the action of the Annapolis Convention.  Delaware was

---

* See Proceedings of the General Assembly of Connecticut.  American Museum, October, 1787, pp. 395–399.  For some arguments in support of the convention, see Goodrich's Connecticut Election Sermon, preached in May, 1787.

soon to follow. New York alone held back. The session of her Legislature had opened with the year, and it soon took up the impost. Clinton brought forward the urgent appeal of Congress, now addressed to them alone, with the curt remark that it was a subject that had been repeatedly before them, and must be well understood. An angry and protracted discussion followed. Hamilton led the defence, and toiled hard to secure a few yeas; but when a vote was reached, the impost was again thrown out by a majority of fifteen.* It was now the fifteenth of February, and the Federal Convention was to meet, if indeed it met at all, in three months' time. Yet Congress had done nothing but listen to the reports of committees and grand committees declaring that the proposed convention was a good thing. Some of the States had made use of this trifling conduct to excuse their own delay. They affected to have grave scruples about the propriety of acting on the report till Congress had formally approved it. To appoint delegates, it was argued, before Congress had time to consider the paper, was, to say the least, to exhibit indecent haste. To name commissioners, and then have Congress refuse to make the recommendations suggested by the gentlemen at Annapolis, would be to add another insult to the already long list, and to strike another blow at the life of the Union. The present was no time for the States to hold a controversy with the National Legislature.

There were not wanting many clear-headed ones to assert that such reasoning was specious, and merely a cloak for deep-laid schemes to break up the Confederation. Among them was Hamilton. He had drawn up the report, was greatly interested in its success, and determined that nothing should be left undone in its behalf. Accordingly, two days after the impost had been voted down, he moved in the Assembly that the New York delegates in Congress should be instructed to bring in a resolution recommending the States to send commissioners to Philadelphia. The motion passed the Lower House, and after a short struggle was carried in the Senate by one vote.† It

---

* Journals New York Assembly, February 15, 1787. The vote was thirty-six Ayes to twenty-one Nays.

† Journals, February 17, 1787.

was not a moment too soon, for Congress had set apart the twenty-first of the month as the day on which to take up the report of their grand committee on the communication from Annapolis. When, therefore, the time came, and the clerk announced the order for the day, one of the New York delegation rose in his place and moved the House to postpone in order to substitute the resolution of his State.* The substance of this was that a convention ought to be held, the Articles of Confederation carefully revised, and the needed amendments reported to Congress and the States. A lively debate followed. So sudden and unexpected a display of Federal spirit † by a State which had but six days before rejected the impost, and perhaps destroyed the Union, excited general alarm. A few saw in the language of the instructions not a wish to accede to the convention proposed, but an attempt to secure a new one under the sanction of Congress. Others suspected New York of seeking to divide the plans of the States, and so frustrating them all. The motion to postpone, therefore, passed in the negative. Eleven States were present. Eight voted against it.

No sooner was this disposed of than Dane, of Massachusetts, came forward with a very similar motion. But he was well known to be, of all men there present, the most bitter and acrimonious Antifederalist. He utterly disapproved of the convention, and had been at much pains to dissuade his State from coming into it. His proposition was thought to be open to the same objections as that from New York, and voted down. It was then agreed by all, except Connecticut, that the resolution should pass as it stood upon the journals. This sanctioned the proceedings and appointments already made by a few States, and advised the others to do the same.

The removal of what so many had been pleased to consider the only hindrance to the Philadelphia meeting produced a general sense of relief. All who possessed estates, who were engaged in traffic, or held any of the final settlements and depreciation certificates, felt safe. Another chance was offered

---

* Journals of Congress, February 21, 1787.

† See some extracts from Madison's Diary of Proceedings in Congress, given in Rives's Life and Times of Madison, vol. ii, pp. 182–184.

them to mend the evils they had so long complained of. It was perhaps the last chance. But this added not a little to their hopes, for they were sure that, knowing this, their delegates would never suffer the opportunity to be thrown away. The multitude, however, were indifferent. That great mass of the community whose lot it was to eat bread in the sweat of the face thought it a matter of no importance whether there was one republic or three, whether they were ruled by a monarch or governed by a Senate. So long as the crops were good, wages high, and food cheap, the sum of their happiness was likely to be much the same under the one form of government as under the other. Whether the Dutch got the interest on their loan, whether the treaty was made with Spain, their sleep would be none the heavier and their burdens not more light. Their wages had indeed never been so high. But while they had no cause to grumble over the returns of their toil, they had much reason to complain of the trash in which those returns were made.

For years past counterfeiters and clippers had been busy with the coin, till a good half-penny or a full-weight pistareen could seldom be found in the States. Scarce a month went by but the Gazettes and Journals all over the country warned their readers to be on their guard against French sous that looked like moidores,* and to take no French guineas till they had carefully examined the hair on the King's head.† There were bad dollars that bore date 1782, and could only be distinguished from the good by the ugly nostril and the long face; ‡ and false English guineas of 1764, that could be told from the true by the downcast eye and the raised brow.# But the copper coinage was in a worse state still, for it had become a lucrative trade to manufacture abroad great quantities of base metal in imitation of pence and half-pence, bring them to America, change them into joes and guineas, and send the gold to England. So many had been thrown into circulation in Rhode Island that the Legislature had found it necessary to

---

* Pennsylvania Packet, May 13, 1784.   New York Packet, May 10, 1784.

† New York Packet, April 21, 1785.

‡ See Pennsylvania Packet, April 27th, May 13th, and June 1, 1784.

# New York Packet, April 21, 1785.

impose a fine of six shillings for every piece taken.* Yet they continued to pass from hand to hand, and numbers of them were to be seen in the taverns and coffee-houses at New York. There they were freely taken, for almost every copper in the city was bad. Shopkeepers and marketmen complained bitterly. The "rap half-pence" current were, it was said, a reflection on the police. There was not a handful of genuine pennies in the town, and every British ship that came into the port added to the quantity of bad ones.† Such a state of things must end in serious loss. Indeed, matters became so bad that the Assembly appointed a committee to examine and report on the copper coins passing in the city. The report was listened to on the third of March, 1787, and is the most valuable and interesting document of the session.‡

The committee had, it should seem, been ordered to bring in a bill to regulate the copper coin of the State. But they were at a loss to know the extent of the intended regulation; whether it was to apply to the coin then in use, or to a new issue in the near future. They had therefore, among other things, ascertained the value of such as were then in the hands of the people. There were, first, a few genuine British half-pence of George II.'s time, and some of an earlier date; but they were greatly worn, and the impression scarce distinguishable. Some Irish half-pence were also in circulation. They had a bust on one side and a harp on the other. With these exceptions, almost all the pieces that were passing about were imitations either of the British half-pence or, what was worse, of the Jersey coppers. The counterfeits of the English ha'pennies were much lighter than the true, were made of low-grade copper, were badly executed, and were commonly called Birmingham coppers ; for it was pretty well known they were manufactured at that city and imported in casks under the name of hardware.# As for the other false coins, a great

---

* Pennsylvania Packet, July 14, 1785.

† New Jersey Gazette, January 9, 1786.

‡ Journal of the Assembly of New York for 1787, p. 78.

# In the New York Daily Advertiser of May 26, 1786, is some information on this point taken from an English paper. "The piece spoken of, bearing the inscription ' Libertas et Justicia,' etc., was not made in America, nor by direction of Congress. It was coined in Birmingham, by order of a merchant in New York.

many of them had lately come into use, but were so far below the weight of the Jersey coppers that they seemed designed to be a catchpenny for the New York market.

The committee then went on to estimate the loss the State suffered from spurious coins. The very best red copper in sheets could, they said, be purchased at any factory in England for elevenpence sterling a pound. To bring it over the water would cost from twenty to twenty-five per cent more, so that the price would, on arrival in America, be about two shillings of New York currency. But old copper kettles and pans could be melted down into ingots, and made into blanks, as the pieces were called before milling and stamping, for at least twenty per cent less. Of the genuine British half-pence, forty-eight made a pound avoirdupois. But of the Birmingham coppers then passing current, sixty went to the pound. The true Jersey coppers weighed each six pennyweights six grains, which gave forty-six and two fifths to the pound. All of these passed by common consent at fourteen to the shilling, which gave a very handsome profit to the coiners. By a careful calculation the committee found the profit to be fifty-seven per cent for the British half-pence, ninety-six per cent for the Birmingham pieces, and fifty-four per cent for the Jersey coppers.

This condition of the small change was indeed most alarming. Yet it was the same everywhere. In New Jersey, an act of January, 1786, provided that fifteen coppers should make a shilling; but, long before the first of August was come, twenty, and even thirty, were demanded and paid to the shilling.[*] In Virginia, pence and half-pence had entirely disappeared. Meanwhile, the New England States were being flooded with great sums of base money [†] from England, and there seemed good reason to think more was yet to come. Upon one occasion Adams wrote that for some time past there had been in circulation in London several hundreds of thousands of pounds of bad coppers; that upon a sudden every one had refused to

Many tons were struck from this die, and many from another; they are now in circulation in America as counterfeit half-pence are in England." From the same town came Birmingham dollars. For a description of some at Beverly, see Boston Gazette, April 29, 1793.

[*] Pennsylvania Gazette, August 8, 1786.

[†] See Plymouth Journal, January 10, 1786.

take them, and that he feared this was but part of a deeply laid plan to buy them up for a trifle and ship them to America, where they would pass as genuine.* Twelve days later he again sent word that he had broken up a nest of counterfeiters who were busy imitating the paper money of the southern States.†

Toward correcting these abuses Congress had made several efforts. In the summer of 1785 two copper coins were ordered to be struck, one called a half-penny, of which two hundred were to make a dollar, and one to be called a penny.‡ But they had never come out. A year later an ordinance was passed providing for an entire national currency.# The decimal system of multiplication was adopted. The mill was to be the lowest money of account, and eight coins were to be put out in three metals. Cents and half-cents were to be of copper; dimes, double dimes, half-dollars, and dollars, of silver; half-eagles and eagles of gold. Three hundred and seventy-five grains of pure silver were to be contained in a dollar. A little over two hundred and forty-six and a quarter grains of gold were to be in every eagle. Matters, however, did not improve, and when, two months later, the bill for the establishment of a mint was passed, a last attempt was made to destroy the evil. The quantity of base coin, it was stated in the bill, daily imported and manufactured in the States was so great, and the injury done to trade and commerce so severe, that the time had come for the immediate interposition of the power vested in Congress by the Articles of Confederation. It was therefore ordered that, after the first day of September, 1787, all foreign coppers should cease to pass current in the United States.‖ Yet this came to naught. A contract with one Jarvis △ for copper coins was, it is true, drawn up, signed, and a few of the pennies struck.◊ But, long after the

---

* Diplomatic Correspondence of the Revolution. Adams to Jay, April 10, 1787.
† Ibid.   Adams to Jay, April 22, 1787.   ‡ Journals of Congress, July 6, 1785.
# Ibid., August 6, 1786.               ‖ Ibid., October 16, 1786.

△ In a newspaper of the time the fact is noted that Mr. Jarvis, who had contracted to supply the United States with copper coin, had sailed for Amsterdam. New York Daily Advertiser, November 12, 1787. See, also, Columbian Magazine for April, 1788, p. 200.

◊ The copper of 1787, commonly called the Franklin penny, had upon the face of it a sun rising above a dial; around this the word "Fugio" and the date 1787.

first of September had come and gone, English pence and half-pence were to be found in the till of every tavern, and were taken at the counter of every store. Nor did the first cent issued by the Government of the United States appear till 1792 was far advanced.*

But the citizens of New York, ere the summer was over, had other things to lament besides the state of the coin. The Legislature, in an evil hour, passed an act aimed full against the commerce of Connecticut and New Jersey. To supply the great city with firewood, vegetables, and fowls had long been a source of income to her neighbors, and a brisk trade had grown up. Early on the morning of every market-day the broad sheet of water that separated Paulus Hook from the city was dotted with shallops loaded to the water's edge with butter and cheese, turnips and carrots, with, in fine, all those varieties of vegetables and fruit for which the Dutch farms of New Jersey were even then famous. Every week there drew up at the docks vessels from Connecticut bringing hundreds of cords of the best firewood the market could supply. To such proportions had the business grown that it was commonly believed that several thousand pounds sterling were in this way drawn out of the city by the Jerseymen and Yankees. This trade the Assembly determined to crush, and framed and passed an act the consequences of which were not foreseen.

Underneath was the curt advice, "Mind Your Business." On the reverse was an endless chain of thirteen circular links; in the centre, "We Are One," and around this, "United States."

* The act creating the United States Mint passed April 2, 1792, and the same year three pieces were struck, the Disme, the Half-Disme, and a trial Cent with a silver centre. But the first regular issue of money was the copper cent of 1793. Of this there are, in the cabinets of collectors, eleven varieties. Yet none seem to have given satisfaction. "The American cent," says one of the grumblers, "does not answer our expectation. The chain on the reverse is but a bad omen for liberty, and Liberty herself appears to be in a fright. May she not cry out, in the words of the Apostle: 'Alexander the coppersmith has done me much harm; the Lord reward him according to his works.'" Boston Argus, March 26, 1793. The Alexander referred to was Hamilton, first Secretary of the Treasury. Since 1793 the cent has, with the exception of 1815, been issued each year, and is the only one of our coins that furnishes so unbroken a succession. A very exact and interesting description of United States coppers from 1793 to 1857, when the nickels began to be coined, may be seen in the Boston Transcript of March 1, 1859. See, also, for the same, the Historical Magazine, May, 1859, p. 338.

Every wood-boat, every shallop, every small sloop from New Jersey of more than twelve tons burden, it was decreed, should henceforth be entered and cleared at the Custom-House in the same manner as packets that came from London or any other foreign port. The moment the law went into operation the boatmen plying between New York and the northern shore of New Jersey cried out that they were ruined men; that almost the whole of their small profit was taken from them and put into the hard, griping hands of the officers of the customs at New York. To retaliate by raising the price demanded for their produce was impossible, for the increase would be so great that half the consumers would cease to buy.

The Legislature at Trenton heard their cry, and resolved to be signally revenged. The corporation of the hated city was the owner of four acres of land on Sandy Hook, in the State of New Jersey. The plot had been purchased from the original proprietor for the purpose of maintaining upon it a light-house, a public inn, and a kitchen-garden. The light-house was already built, and on this was now laid a tax of thirty pounds a month.*

The restrictions placed on boats from Connecticut were much the same as on those from across the Hudson. The rate of dockage was raised, small sloops forced to pay an entrance-fee, and the carting of firewood across the city heavily taxed. No notice was taken by the Connecticut Assembly. But the business men at New London, whence most of the boats went out, were greatly incensed. It seemed, they declared, as if the time was at hand when, between the British Navigation Act, the lack of commercial treaties with continental powers, the Barbary xebecs, and the selfish policy of New York, there would not be a port on the face of the earth where an American vessel could trade. But they would see what could be done. They would strike back with all the power at their command, and flattered themselves they could make the blow felt. A league was formed, and a paper passed about, which bound all who signed it, under penalty of fifty pounds to be collected by a civil process in any court of law, not to send into the State of New York any article whatever, nor to fur-

* See a letter from Brunswick, in American Museum, December, 1787, p. 601.

nish any craft bound for that State with any kind of lading for one year from the twentieth of July, 1787.* The agreement was faithfully kept. Yet little came of it. The supplies withheld by the New London merchants were obtained elsewhere, and, before the year specified in the agreement had passed, ten States had ratified the Constitution, and the power of New York to tax her neighbors was taken away for ever.

The Barbary States were, however, in a much kindlier mood than was represented. A treaty with them had been under discussion for two years. But nothing could be done without money, and as no money was to be had, the subject had not been formally broached. At last, after much pinching and screwing, enough was scraped together to justify the commissioners in making an attempt, and two gentlemen, named Thomas Barclay and John Lamb, were selected, provided with presents, and dispatched to Africa.

The two set off early in February, 1786. But scarce were they out of England when a Tripoline ambassador appeared in London. He refused to speak with the ministers of the Crown, and insisted on an audience of the King. Adams was much alarmed. His Majesty declared that nothing of moment took place, and that what the fellow really wanted was a present and his expenses paid to Vienna and Denmark. Yet the American minister felt that the coming of the ambassador had some bearing on the affairs of the United States, and that there were not wanting in London many men who would gladly stir up the African to persuade his countrymen to wage war on American ships. He had therefore thought it best to shun him. But when he learned that all other foreign ministers had made their respects, and that a longer delay would be taken as an affront, he changed his mind, made his call, and was much surprised to find his Excellency at home; for he had purposely selected a late hour of the evening. He was, however, admitted, when a most ludicrous conference followed. Each indeed conducted himself like a man of sense and temper. But the Christian knew not a word of Arabic, and the Mussulman knew but a few of English. They spoke, therefore, in a strange jumble of Italian, of Lingua Franca, of bad French and worse English.

---

* Pennsylvania Gazette, June 27, 1787.

The ceremonies were such, Mr. Adams wrote, that a description of them might fittingly be sent to Harlequin for the amusement of the gay at the New York theatre, but not to so grave and dignified a body as Congress. Many questions were asked concerning America. How hot the summers were, and how cold the winters. Whether the soil was rich or poor; whether the climate was wet or dry. This over, his Excellency observed that it was a very great country, but Tripoli was at war with it. How, Adams asked, could there be war between the two nations? There had been no hostility, no injury, no insult, no provocation of any kind on either side. This he owned was true, but answered that Turkey, Tripoli, Tunis, Algiers, and Morocco were the rulers of the Mediterranean; that no people could send ships to traffic in that sea till they had made peace with the rulers; that the Americans must make treaties, and that the order to be observed in making them was Tripoli, Turkey, Algiers, and Morocco. With this they parted, agreeing that a further conference should be held at an early day.

Before a week had gone the Tripolitan came with great ceremony to return the call of Mr. Adams. With him was an English Jew named Benamor, a decent man, and very ready in the English, the Arabic, and Italian tongues. He would, his Excellency said, have nothing to do with the court interpreter. He could not trust him, for he had, since his arrival, found much ill-will toward the United States, and a general desire to prevent him from seeing the American minister. He had therefore brought his own interpreter. He then went on, with the help of Benamor, to say that it was the delight of his soul, it was the whole pleasure of his life, to do good. He was zealous to embrace every chance to do good, and he now saw an opportunity to do a great deal. The time was critical. Peace could not be made too soon. Were a treaty to be put off another year, it would be very hard to bring it about at all. By that time the Algerines would have taken many prizes, would be very greedy for more and very difficult to move. Then he spoke of the horrors of a Barbary war. A war between Christians and Christians was mild. No inhuman actions were indulged in, no cruelty was practised; prisoners were kindly treated and readily exchanged. But a war between Turks and

Christians was terrible. Prisoners were sold into slavery. He was himself a Mussulman. Yet he must say he thought it a hard law. As he could not alter it, he wished to soften it. He was never happier than when doing good. Of all the Barbary States, Algiers was the most troublesome to treat with. They were always eager for prizes, and now had more ships, and larger, than ever before. Were an overture for peace made to Algiers, she would instantly reject it. Were a treaty first made with Tripoli, the Algerines would instantly give way. Tripoli, and Tripoli alone, could effect this. Threats and menaces were powerless. No people had a greater armament than Spain. Yet when Spain came with offers of peace, Algiers spurned them, and was upon the point of waging a fierce war when Tripoli interfered, and a firm peace was concluded. Adams here broke in and told him that friendly assurances had come from Morocco, and that agents had been dispatched to treat with her. He was delighted, he was overjoyed to hear it. He was sure success would come of it. As for Algiers, he could promise nothing. But he would undertake to answer for Tripoli and Tunis. He would write, he would send his secretary, nay, go himself, and that was saying more than he had ever said to any minister in Europe. Then he took a great oath, that oath which to a Moslem is the most awful and solemn of all oaths, called upon the name of Allah, and swore by his beard that his only motive in striving for a peace was the love of doing good. When the African went away he left Adams sorely puzzled. " He is," said the minister, " either a consummate politician in art and address, or he is a benevolent and wise man." *

Other interviews followed. The price of peace was discussed, and the cost for the four Barbary powers put down as not far from two hundred thousand pounds sterling.† The sum was indeed great, but if anything was to be accomplished, fear and avarice were, Adams declared, the only agents that could do it. The States must either buy the Barbary powers or fight them. There was something grand in the thought of fighting them. The craven policy of Christendom had made

---

* Letter of Adams to Jay, February 20, 1786.

† Adams to Jay, February 22, 1786.

cowards of the sailors of Europe before the standard of Mahomet. It would indeed be heroical and glorious for the people of the New World to break up that nest of pirates, drive their cruisers from the sea, and restore courage to the mariners of the Old. But it would be hard to bring the States to think so. * The cost of war, too, would far exceed the cost of peace; and when it was happily over, many and costly presents would still have to be given. Did De Massoc carry his point without gifts? Had not France made presents ever since? Did any power ever at any time conclude peace with these rovers without doing the same thing? † But the cost of doing nothing was incalculable. Before that sum was known, six per cent insurance on all imports and exports, the ransom of many captives, and long columns of figures expressing the loss of trade in the Levant, and half the trade with Portugal and Spain, would have to be footed up. Something must be done at any cost. It was intolerable to be so indifferent. His indignation was roused beyond all patience to see his countrymen in a torpor while every robber, pirate, cheat in Europe preyed upon them. Even at that very moment Jews and Judaizing Christians were plotting to buy up the continental paper at two shillings on the pound, and make the States redeem it at twenty. Let this be done, and the Jews would gather a richer plunder than would ever fall to the Algerines or the coffee-house of Lloyd's.‡

While Adams was higgling with Tripoli and lamenting over the conduct of Algiers, affairs in Morocco began to wear a more hopeful aspect. Thomas Barclay, who was charged with the mission to that State, set off early in February, went first to Spain, and thence in a swift-sailing vessel to Africa. John Lamb, who was to treat with Algiers, went with him.#

---

* Adams to Jefferson, July 3, 1786.          † Ibid., July 31, 1786.

‡ See a letter from Adams to Jefferson, June 6, 1786. In the account of the interviews with the Tripoline envoy I have in many places made use of the words of Mr. Adams.

# Lamb sailed from Barcelona. But his vessel was scarce out of sight when the British consul at Barcelona informed M. Logie, consul at Algiers, that the Spanish papers were irregular, that Lamb had with him eighty thousand dollars, and that the vessel could be seized by the Dey as an American bottom. This Logie instantly communicated to the Dey. But word came back that the American

The simple and unpretentious manner in which he performed his journey aroused some apprehensions for his success. For it was then the custom of European powers when treating with the Barbary States to send with their ministers a great fleet of ships of the line, to enter the harbor with decks cleared for action, and, while they offered peace, make threats of war. Some therefore expressed a fear that the Emperor and the Dey would be affronted and refuse to treat with an agent who came in a merchant ship, landed like a common traveller, and had no armed force to support his demands. They were, however, mistaken. Barclay was well received, and, while the negotiation dragged slowly on, spent much of his time in studying the habits, customs, religious practices, and daily occupations of the Moors.

In truth, the letters in which he communicated his observations to those who sent him form by no means the least valuable and interesting part of the state papers of the day. They may still be perused with profit and amusement; and were at that time, when scarce anything was known of the country, most eagerly read. The Emperor he declared to be a man possessed of many amiable qualities, and in learning greatly above the average of his subjects. But his private life was, to one bred up in the decorous notions of the West, disgusting and loathsome. In his palace were four queens and forty women, who, though never married, were treated with the same respect and honored with the same attentions as if they were his lawful wives. In his seraglios were two hundred and forty-three concubines, attended by eight hundred and forty-six women and an army of eunuchs. As for his subjects, they were fierce, lazy, delighting in cruelty, and avaricious to the last degree. Fear of man had indeed forced the idle Moors to bestir themselves and defend their town with heavy fortifications. Fear of God had made them put up some costly and beautiful mosques. But they had done nothing more. Their streets were despicable. Their houses were a sight to behold. Nor had they, though an eminently

---

officers had been allowed to land, had gone away, had taken the money with them, and that the consul would do well in future to mind his own affairs. See a letter of William Carmichael to Jefferson, July 15, 1786. Diplomatic Correspondence.

maritime people, any dock-yards worthy of the name. There was, in fact, small need of such. For, with great shrewdness, they obtained from one half of Christendom ships which they forced the other half to keep in good repair. Anchors, rigging, barrels of tar, coils of rope, and bales of canvas were con. stantly coming over from England, Holland, and Sweden. The greater part of their cruisers had been built out of prizes. Much of this work was done at Gibraltar, without any cost to the Emperor. One ship, that had just come off the stocks at that place, had been overhauled by the British Government at a cost of seven thousand pounds. But there were in the navy other vessels which had been obtained ready built as the price of peace. Indeed, his Majesty was at that moment impatiently awaiting the result of a demand on Frederick the Great for three fully armed frigates.

The first audience of the Emperor took place in the garden of the palace. His Majesty was on horseback. About him were a thousand attendants. The Americans were presented by the Pacha. They were asked what kind of a journey they had, whether they came in a frigate, how America lay as to Great Britain, and why it separated; how many troops were kept up, between what latitudes it lay, and if there grew in its forests timber fit for ships. When these questions had all been answered to his satisfaction, he exclaimed, " Send your ships and trade with us. I will do everything you can desire." Then he looked round upon his people, and they all cried out in a loud voice, " Allah preserve the life of our Master!"

The second audience was likewise in the garden. As Barclay came toward him, bowing and bending low, the Emperor cried " Bona, bona," and began to complain of the English. But his complaints were silenced as soon as the gifts were spread before him. Among them were an atlas and a watch. The watch he examined with much care, for it was an alarm-watch, and the first he had ever seen. With the atlas he seemed familiar ; called for a map of the United States, took a pen and wrote down off the coast the highest latitudes to which his cruisers sailed. It was a rare event when the flag of Morocco was seen to the north of the coast of Portugal, or much to the

west of the Canaries and the Western Isles.* The result of
Mr. Barclay's visit was that, late in January, 1787, Sidi Hadge
Ben Abdelleck Fennish informed the American minister at
London that his master had, on the first day of the blessed
month Ramadan, 1200, concluded a lasting treaty with the
United States. But when the instrument came to the hands of
the Secretary for Foreign Affairs he was again greatly occupied
with the Spanish treaty.

Early in March some of the Virginia delegation, among
whom was Madison, held an interview with Gardoqui. In the
course of conversation the Mississippi trouble was broached
and fully discussed. The shrewd envoy, well knowing that
he was addressing men most firmly set against the treaty,
sought to move them first by fair words and then by menaces.
Spain, such was his argument, would not for a moment listen
to the idea of opening the Mississippi. To be debarred the
use of the lower part of the river was undoubtedly a great
hardship to the United States. But it was a hardship which
Spain herself endured. His most Christian Majesty was asking no more than he was ready to give, nay, than he actually
did give. If the free use of the Mississippi was of importance
to the back country, so was the navigation of the Tagus to
Spain.† But the Tagus also flowed through Portugal. His

---

* See the letters of Thomas Barclay, written during September, October, and
November, 1786, in Diplomatic Correspondence.

† To other men Gardoqui held other language. " Mr. Gardoqui has told me
confidentially that he regards that navigation as a matter of great indifference to
his Court; and that, whatever may be the pretensions of the inhabitants of Kentucky, they never could gain great advantages from their expeditions upon the
Mississippi. . . . To carry on a profitable trade there is need of means to make
return voyages. Every one knows that it requires several months to ascend the
Mississippi as far as the Ohio, that a season and a special time is necessary in
order not to run aground, and that the profits of this navigation can never compensate for its dangers. . . . It is not therefore the Mississippi which causes us
the greatest embarrassment, but it is the incontestable principle of reciprocity."
Otto to Vergennes, New York, December 20, 1785. See Bancroft's History of the
Constitution, vol. i, p. 472. Two years later a writer, discussing the navigation of
the same river, says : " And it is worthy of observation that in all probability steamboats will be found to do infinite service in all our extensive river navigation."
Cutler's pamphlet, called An Explanation of the Map which delineates that part
of the Federal Lands comprised between Pennsylvania West Line, the River Ohio,
Scioto, and Lake Erie. Salem, 1787, p. 10. At that time neither Rumsey nor

Majesty had therefore never thought of claiming the right to send his ships down that river to the sea. The possession of both banks at the mouth of a river settled the question of ownership. He was told that, in estimating the rights of nations in such cases, regard must be paid to the proportion of territory owned by each. Suppose Spain had but five acres on each bank of the Mississippi; would he maintain that two such garden-plots gave her an exclusive right to the waters that ran between? But that, Gardoqui said, was not the case; Spain controlled a great proportion of the territory. "How much?" said Madison. After a moment's thought Gardoqui answered, with some hesitancy and confusion, that she claimed to the Ohio. The Virginians smiled. He was then asked, if her dominion went so far to the north, how far it extended to the east. But he turned the question off by insinuating that he had already discussed that matter with Jay, lost his temper, lamented that he had been in the country so long and accomplished nothing, and declared that he foresaw very disagreeable consequences. One of the delegates asked what they were; but he again parried the question, and muttered something about Spain making her own terms with Great Britain. He was sorry, very sorry about the Virginia instructions. They would prove very disastrous. He had written to his master to soften the matter as much as possible; but he was sure troops and provisions would instantly be sent to New Orleans. He wished he might not be a true prophet, but America would see she had mistaken her interest; Spain would make her feel the vulnerable side of her commerce. Then he recovered his good-nature, and said, jestingly, that the people of Kentucky would make fine Spanish subjects. With this the interview ended.*

A week later the action of Virginia denouncing Clark's seizure of Spanish property at Vincennes was brought him. At the same time he was reminded of the bad spirit that was becoming manifest in the West, how that the settlers blamed the Government, how that they looked with no friendly eye

---

Fitch had made a success of their boats. The expression of such an opinion therefore does great credit to Cutler's foresight.

* Madison's Debates, vol. ii, p. 594.

on Spain, how they threatened to go over to Great Britain, and how impossible it would be for Congress to shut the Mississippi. To this Gardoqui replied that the end of the negotiation would be no treaty at all; that the Spanish trade was most valuable to the country, and would surely be lost. He had, he protested, long seen and lamented the weakness of the Union. No one wished more earnestly than he did to see it preserved and strengthened, and that was more than France or any other power did. The kindly offices of Spain to America had been many and great. This was not denied. But he was plainly told that his country had an interest in the independence of the colonies, for they were now lost to a power that had brought down the pride of certain princes, had given law to the House of Bourbon, and had in times past made his Catholic Majesty renounce all claim to the sole use of the Mississippi. The taunt was a bitter yet a just one, for the language of the envoy had been high and menacing. With this the second interview closed; and no more was heard of the matter till, a few weeks later, it came up in Congress.

On the eleventh of April the secretary made his report on the state of the negotiation with Spain. The day following, the twelfth of the month, he submitted his report on the papers from Virginia and North Carolina. Each was unsatisfactory. The Articles of Confederation set forth that the assent of nine States was necessary to the conclusion of a treaty. This could not possibly be misunderstood. It was stated as plainly, as concisely, as emphatically as the English tongue would permit. Yet the Secretary for Foreign Affairs had the effrontery to stand up before Congress and assert that he thought himself warranted by the assent of seven States to go on with the negotiation with Gardoqui, that he had done so, and that he had, after many conferences and many debates, drawn up an article for the non-usage of the Mississippi. But he had taken good care not to commit Congress to its acceptance.* About the Virginia papers he had little to say. The troubles in the West had greatly embarrassed him. He feared the time was not remote when the United States would be forced to fight Spain, or to make peace on the best terms it

---

* Secret Journals of Congress, April 11, 1787.

could. Between war and peace there was, in his opinion, no reputable middle way. " It will therefore," said he, " be expedient to prepare, without delay, for the one or the other, for circumstances which call for decision seem daily to accumulate." *

Both reports were listened to by Congress on the thirteenth. When the reading was finished, Mr. Madison rose and moved to send them to a committee. The friends of the Spanish interest strongly opposed it; said much about the terrible state of trade and the goodness of Spain. But when the division was taken it was found that five States had voted for and three against the motion.† Yet it was lost, for it was necessary, in order to carry any question whatever, that a majority of the States in the Union should vote yea. It was observed, however, that three States had changed sides. New Jersey had sent up positive instruction to her delegates to vote against the treaty. Pennsylvania, by a late change in her representation, had made it strong in behalf of the West. Rhode Island, too, had abandoned the eastern alliance, for her congressmen were assured that the true motive the eastern States had for closing the Mississippi was to check emigration to the rich lands of the Ohio, and so increase the demand for their own.

The vote gave renewed hope to the supporters of the southern view. On the eighteenth of the month Madison again came forward with a motion to send Mr. Jefferson as Minister Plenipotentiary to Madrid. In the discussion which followed, Rufus King, who invariably expressed the sense of the East, declared he saw no objection to this, as something must be done, but thought the secretary should be given an opportunity to speak. This was done. The following day the memorial of Virginia against shutting the river was brought in, and a motion made to lay it also before Mr. Jay. King opposed this. The instructions had, he said, been printed in the newspapers, and were not new to the secretary. His argument was clearly an attempt to relieve Jay of the responsibility of disregarding them. For the secretary, if accused of

---

* Secret Journals of Congress, April 13, 1787.
† Ibid. But eight States were present.

neglecting them, could well say that he was not bound to consider as official, information that came to him through the press. King therefore was told that no objection should be raised, because the document had come out in the Packet, and that if Congress referred any measure to Mr. Jay, it ought also to supply him at least with every fact bearing on the matter in the most authentic way. When the motion was put to vote, the President declared that the nays had it. On April twenty-third the secretary's report was taken up. The debate was warm and acrimonious, and in the course of it Gorham, who sat in the Massachusetts delegation, avowed that it would be a good thing for the Atlantic States to shut up the Mississippi, and he hoped it would be done. At this Madison grew angry, spoke with great severity about the illiberal sectional policy of the East, and contrasted Mr. Gorham's words "with the principles of the revolution and the language of American patriots." * In fact, so much incensed was he that he determined at once to attack the action of Jay on the ground of illegality. He came forward, therefore, with a final motion.† He would have the Secretary for Foreign Affairs informed that, in the opinion of Congress, the vote of seven States ought not to be regarded as authorizing the suspension of the use of the Mississippi. The discussion was an angry one. King held, and justly, that the motion was barred. There were, he claimed, twelve States present when the instruction passed. But eight were present now. A rule of the House declared that no question should be revived which had been once set aside by the previous question, unless the same or an equal number of States were present as at the time of the previous question. On the other hand, it was argued that the negotiation was illegal; that seven States were usurping the power expressly given to nine. This was not denied, but in the midst of the debate a motion to adjourn was carried. No more was heard of the treaty for eighteen months.

The attention of the members was indeed almost immediately drawn off to the Federal Convention, for many among them were delegates, and the day of meeting was near at hand.

---

* Madison's Debates, vol. ii, p. 609.

† Secret Journals of Congress, April 25, 1787.

The second Monday in May, which fell upon the fourteenth of the month, had been chosen, but members began to assemble at Philadelphia early in the week before. Madison set out from New York on the second of the month, and was the first to reach the city. A few days later his colleagues, Blair and Wythe, left Virginia. Owing "to the badness of their cavalry," a State boat conveyed them to Yorktown, whence they took packet to Philadelphia. For a long time it seemed doubtful whether Washington would come. He could not, he wrote, in decency do so. He had already declined a re-election to the presidency of the Cincinnati, to meet at Philadelphia, and had alleged private business as the cause.* He could not after this think of accepting a later call and going to the convention. His scruples were happily overcome by the rebellion of Shays and the arguments of Randolph and Madison.† He left Mount Vernon on the ninth of May. Everywhere along his route public honors attended him. At Chester he was met by the Speaker of the Assembly, and by many of the first characters of the place, and escorted to Gray's Ferry. There the city light-horse met his carriage and accompanied him into town. It was the evening of Sunday, the thirteenth, yet the most straitlaced forgot their devotions, poured out of their houses, and, as the little cavalcade moved down the streets of the city, every church-bell sent forth a joyous din, and every voice sent up a shout of welcome to the American Fabius. ‡ His first act was a graceful tribute to genius and worth, for he went with all haste to pay his respects to Franklin who then filled the chair of President of the Commonwealth of Pennsylvania. This over, Robert Morris carried him home to his house.

For several days the delegates from Virginia and Pennsylvania were the only ones on the ground. Of those still to arrive, some were tardy in setting out, while some who started in good time were detained on their way by tempestuous weather. It was not till the twenty-fifth of the month that a quorum of seven States was present. Early on the morning of that day

---

* Washington's Writings, vol. ix, p. 212.   † Ibid., vol. ix, pp. 219, 243, note.

‡ Sparks's Life of Washington, p. 435. See a letter of Madison to Jefferson, May 15, 1787.

the members of the convention met in the State-House, and
by a unanimous vote called Washington to the chair. Major
Jackson was made secretary. His rival for that honor was
Temple Franklin, a young man and a grandson of the illustrious philosopher. But Temple's father was a Tory; he was
himself a mere lad, and, when the ballots were counted, he was
found to have too few for a choice.* The credentials of the
delegates were then examined, a committee appointed to prepare rules, and an adjournment till the twenty-eighth taken.
Meanwhile, delegates from Massachusetts and Connecticut came
in. New Hampshire had named hers. But her Treasury was
empty, no funds could be raised, and her representatives did
not come for some weeks.† When Monday, the twenty-eighth,
came, nine States were present; the doors were closed, a pledge
of secrecy laid on each member, and from that day forth what
took place in the convention was never fully known till Madison had been many months in his grave.‡

The convention which thus continued to deliberate in
secret for four months was undoubtedly a most remarkable
body of men. Every State had sent up in her delegation
some one renowned as a statesman or a soldier, and of whose
services in the cause of freedom she was justly proud. Some
had been members of the Stamp Act Congress of 1765, and
had, eleven years later, put their names with a firm hand to
the Declaration of Independence. A few, when the revolution broke out, had raised regiments, hastened off to the army
of Washington, had fought through the war, and come home
distinguished as brave and skilful officers. Some had been
governors of States, some were renowned as jurists and scholars, while others had, year after year, been sent to represent

---

* Yates's Secret Debates.

† See a letter of Madison to Jefferson, June 6, 1787.

‡ Madison's Debates form the only complete record of the discussions in the
convention that has come down to us. Judge Yates did indeed take notes, which
were published after his death. But Yates, with Lansing, lost his temper, quit
the convention in a huff early in July, and never returned. His notes therefore cover but a third of the time the convention sat, and are, moreover, hasty
and crude. Yates was a rank partisan, represented the Clinton party, and
when he found he could not carry his point, withdrew. His notes are of doubtful fairness. Madison's Debates were carefully prepared, and after his death
published by Congress.

their States in Congress. On the floor of the House sat Washington, afterwards the first, and Madison, afterwards the fourth President of the United States; Gerry, who became the fifth Vice-President; Hamilton, soon to be the first Secretary of the Treasury; and Rutledge and Oliver Ellsworth, who rose in time to be chief justices under the Constitution they were about to form. There too was William Johnson, eminent for his scholastic and legal attainments. He was indeed one of the few Americans whose learning had obtained recognition abroad; for Oxford had made him a Doctor of Civil Laws, and the Royal Society had thought him not undeserving of membership. At home he had sat upon the bench of his native State, and had twice been sent a delegate to the Congress of the Confederation. He came from Connecticut, and with him were associated Ellsworth and Roger Sherman, now remembered as one of the framers and one of the signers of the Declaration.

Massachusetts sent four delegates of great distinction. Elbridge Gerry, a signer, and for many years a distinguished member of Congress; Nathaniel Gorham, Rufus King, and Caleb Strong. From New Hampshire came John Langdon, often a delegate, and once the President of his State, and to whom, a few months later, as temporary President of the first Senate under the Constitution, fell the pleasing duty of notifying Washington of his election to the chief magistracy of the republic. His colleague was Nicholas Gilman, a youth of twenty-five, and the youngest member of the convention. The most noted member of the New York delegation was Alexander Hamilton. The two men who came with him, Lansing and that Judge Yates whose chief service to posterity is his little volume of the Secret Debates of the Convention, were both Clinton men and strong Antifederalists. Four men of renown came from New Jersey: William Livingston, eleven times Governor of the State; William Patterson, ten times made attorney-general; David Brearly, the chief justice; and William Houston, the delegate in Congress.

Gunning Bedford, Jr., Richard Bassett, George Read, a signer, Jacob Broome, and John Dickinson sat for Delaware. Dickinson had been bred to the bar, had early become noted for eloquence and learning, had been sent to the Continental Congress, and there disgraced himself by stoutly refusing to sign the Declaration. But his undoubted patriotism, his courage, and the ability with which he defended the cause of the States, soon regained all the popularity he had lost. He once more sat in Congress, was three times President of Pennsylvania, became a citizen of Delaware, and was by her sent to the convention. Maryland chose as her representatives James McHenry, Daniel of St. Thomas Jenifer, and Daniel Carroll of Carrollton, all of them members of Congress; John Mercer, a gallant soldier of Virginia; and Luther Martin, a noted lawyer and Antifederalist. From Virginia came Washington and Madison, Randolph the Governor, George Mason, George Wythe, and John Blair. Patrick Henry had been chosen, but he refused to serve, and James McClurg took his place. North Carolina sent up Alexander Martin, a battered soldier of the revolution and once a governor, Hugh Williamson, William Davie, William Blount, and Richard Spaight, an Irishman, a congressman, and a firm supporter of Government. Another Irishman, Pierce Butler, was in the South Carolina delegation. Butler was a man of ability, and had attained to some eminence in his State; but no distinction was to him so much a matter of pride as his blood, for he boasted that he could trace unbroken descent to the great family of Ormond.* He came with the two Pinckneys and John Rutledge. Georgia, the youngest member of the Confederation, had four delegates: Colonel Few, Abraham Baldwin, a Connecticut man, William Houstoun, and William Pierce, a Virginian, and once aide-de-camp to Greene. All of them had at some time been congressmen.

But no delegation contained so many and such able men as that of Pennsylvania. Among its members the two men of least note were Thomas Fitzsimmons, a great merchant of Philadelphia, and Jared Ingersoll, who led the Pennsylvania

---

* Butler was often twitted in the lampoons of later years with noble descent. As one of the ten Democrats who voted against Jay's treaty, he is described as
"Pierce Butler next, a man of sterling *worth*,
Because he justly claims a noble birth."
The Democratiad: A Poem in Retaliation for the Philadelphia Jockey Club. Philadelphia, 1795.

bar.  With these were associated George Clymer, one of the signers, Robert and Gouverneur Morris, and General Mifflin, who, after fighting with Washington in the field and bitterly denouncing him in Congress, had received his resignation as Commander-in-Chief, and been forced to publicly thank him for the great things he had done in the war.  There, too, was James Wilson.  Wilson was a Scotchman, had been an inmate of the Universities of Edinburgh, of Glasgow, and of St. Andrew's, and had come over to America while still a lad.  Of the fifty-five delegates he was undoubtedly the best prepared, by deep and systematic study of the history and science of government, for the work that lay before him.  The Marquis de Chastellux, himself a no mean student, had been struck with the wide range of his erudition, and had spoken in high terms of his library.  There, said he, are "all our best authors on law and jurisprudence.  The works of President Montesquieu and of the Chancellor D'Aguesseau hold the first rank among them, and he makes them his daily study." * This learning Wilson had in times past turned to excellent use, and he now became one of the most active members of the convention.  None, with the exception of Gouverneur Morris, was so often on his feet during the debates, or spoke more to the purpose.†

But the fame of no man who sat that day in the State-House was so splendid or went back to so early a time as that of Benjamin Franklin.  His name was known to every learned society of Europe at a time when half the delegates to the convention were in the nursery, and before the oldest among them had come to note.  He was great and famous before Rufus King, before Gouverneur Morris, before Hamilton, before Madison, before Randolph, were born, before Wilson came over from Scotland, while Pinckney was still a lad, and had risen to a high office under the colonial Government while Washington was a humble captain in the army of Braddock.

---

* Travels of Marquis de Chastellux in North America, p. 109.

† Some humble statistician has been at the pains to count the number of speeches made during the convention.  Of these there are put down to Gouverneur Morris 173; to Wilson, 168; to Madison, 161; to Sherman, 138; to Mason, 136; to Elbridge Gerry, 119.  Historical Magazine, January, 1861.

Franklin was in truth the greatest American then living; nor would it be safe to say that our country has since his day seen his like. Others have been more successful as philanthropists, or more renowned as inventors. A few have speculated more deeply in natural philosophy, or have made a more astonishing use of their knowledge of physics. But there has not been one who, to all these diverse qualities of mind, has added that homely wisdom which has so well been named hard common sense. His mind was one of the finest of an age not barren of great minds, and was trained by such a discipline as rarely falls to the lot of any of the children of men. He passed through every vicissitude of fortune, and saw every phase of human nature. He knew poverty, he knew opulence, he knew men, he knew life as few have known it. The son of an English tallow-chandler, his early years were spent among the children of laborers and mechanics. While still a stripling he stole away from his father's house, and, with a few pence in his pocket, went forth to seek his fortune, slept in cock-lofts and garrets, and bore manfully all the misery of poverty and want. Before he was fifty, the low-born, friendless, self-taught Yankee lad by frugality and thrift overcame every obstacle that lay in his path, and raised himself to great reputation and to place. In his old age he came to stand before Kings and Parliaments, was honored by all manner of learned societies, and made the friend of powerful statesmen and men renowned in every walk of science and art. From this school, which would have ruined an ordinary being, he came forth a rounded and perfected man. Suffering such as has sufficed to warp and sour minds second only to his, prosperity such as has turned the strongest heads, served but to make him the most kind-hearted, the most genial, the most unassuming of mortals. Men of all sorts found in Franklin a delightful companion and a common friend. Hume and Robertson never wearied of his talk. Burke and Chatham never spoke of him but in terms of praise. He was the correspondent of Kames, of Shipley, Bishop of St. Asaph, of Buffon, of Mably, of Condorcet, of Vergennes, of La Rochefoucauld. Voltaire delighted to do him honor. Turgot affixed to his name the line, " Eripuit cælo fulmen, sceptrumque tyrannis." His popularity in France was immense.

It was not surpassed by that of Voltaire.  It was not equalled
by that of Napoleon.  When he walked the streets of Paris,
the people followed him in crowds.  Rude copies of his face
hung in the window of every print-shop and over the fire-place
of every man of fashion.  Men of science did him honor;
women of the world wrote him sonnets.  No nobleman's garden was complete till a liberty-tree had been planted therein
by the hand of the great philosopher.  Snuff-boxes and walk-
ing-sticks, hats and ties were all "*à la Franklin.*"  The newspapers delighted to print his maxims and good sayings, and
one of them, uttered when all seemed lost to his country, was
treasured up by the people of France, and became, long after
he was dead, a popular revolutionary cry.*

The task to which these men now applied themselves was
not an easy one.  They were expected to find a sovereign
remedy for all the evils that afflicted the body-politic.  But to
say what were and what were not ills was a puzzling question.
A few summed up their troubles in a general way, and declared the times were hard.  Others protested that the times
were well enough, but the people were grown extravagant and
luxurious.  For this, it was said, the merchants were to blame.
There were too many merchants.  There were too many attorneys.  Money was scarce.  Money was plenty.  Trade was
languishing.  Agriculture was fallen into decay.  Manufactures should be encouraged.  Paper should be put out.  No
mind seemed capacious enough to take in all at a glance, and
go at once through a mass of deceptive appearances to the real
cause of distress.

One shrewd observer complained that his countrymen had
fallen away sadly from those simple tastes which were the life-
blood of republics.  It was distressing to see a thrifty farmer
shaking his head and muttering that taxes were ruining him
at the very moment his three daughters, who would have been
much better employed at the spinning-wheel, were being

---

* For Franklin's popularity, see Franklin's Works, viii, p. 303 ; ix, p. 22.
Adams's Works, iii, pp. 134, 135, 220, 221.  Campan, Mémoires sur Marie Antoi-
nette, t. ii, p. 233.  Capefigue, Louis XVI., t. ii, p. 11, note.  Mémoires de Mme.
Vigée Lebrun, t. i, p. 251.  Mémoires et Corres. de Mme. d'Epinay, t. iii, p. 419.
Also, Rosenthal's America and France, pp. 57–59, 70–74.  The saying alluded to
was "Ça ira."

taught to caper by a French dancing-master. It was pitiable to see a great lazy, lounging, lubberly fellow sitting days and nights in a tippling-house, working perhaps two days in a week, receiving double the wages he really earned, spending the rest of his time in riot and debauch, and, when the tax-collector came round, complaining of the hardness of the times and the want of a circulating medium. Go into any coffee-house of an evening and you were sure to overhear some fellow exclaiming, "Such times! no money to be had! taxes high! no business doing! we shall all be broken men!" Language such as this one might expect to come from some poor wretch in ragged clothes and destitute circumstances. But the speaker was invariably a spruce young fellow in an elegant silk waistcoat, satin breeches, shoe-buckles *à la mode à Londres*, with a hat cocked with ineffable grace, and a fine bamboo cane. Ask the waiter who he was, and you would learn he was shopkeeper to a merchant. The country was full of like men. Mechanics were held in such low esteem that every farmer's son must needs be a merchant. His father might not have a single hogshead of tobacco with which to set him up. But it mattered not. He would get a clerk's place, dress, powder, wait upon the ladies, make friends as fast as he could, procure letters of credit, send to England, and after a while open a store with a cargo of goods for which he had never paid a shilling, become bankrupt, and immediately raise a cry about hard times, high taxes, and lack of money. Of course there was a great lack of money. Virginia afforded innumerable proofs of this. There horse-racing was become so much a science as to be thought a necessary part of the education of every Virginian. Yet at ten turfs within the State there was only two thousand six hundred and ten pounds paid annually to the owners of winning horses. During the two past winters the American Company of Comedians had condescended to spend much time in the State. But such was the prodigious scarcity of money that even in the city of Richmond, and in the large and opulent borough of Petersburg, not more than two hundred people could be got together of a night, though the tickets were at the moderate price of a dollar. Again, an industrious man had, with much labor, expense, and assiduity, brought a dog of uncommon sagacity to dance on his hind legs, and in point of gesture and address equal any puppy whatever.  Yet he had the cruel mortification to receive no more than one hundred dollars a night. Three hundred and fifty pounds were paid in prizes for cock-fights in a single spring.  At one of these no more than three fellows lost ten dollars each on a single battle, and paid it before the face of a sheriff, who had for six weeks been trying to get five dollars out of them for their specie-tax.  In a word, so extreme was the scarcity of money that the sum expended by rich Virginians in concerts, balls, barbecues, puppet-shows, legerdemain tricks, and dancing dogs, did not much exceed twenty-seven thousand dollars a year.

If further proofs were wanted of the unparalleled scarcity of money, New England would furnish them.  There persons could get no more than double the value in cash of their axe-helves and hoe-handles, their wooden trays, their cider, their carrots, their parsnips, their cabbages.  Nothing, in fact, cost more than half as much again as it did ten years ago.  This, it was answered, might all be so, but it could not alter the fact that the times were hard and the country on the brink of ruin. In Massachusetts the leaders of the late rebellion were making laws to exempt themselves from punishment.   In Rhode Island the bonds of society were dissolved by paper money and tender laws.  Why did the people of New Jersey nail up the doors of their court-houses?*  Why did the debtors of Virginia set fire to theirs in order to stop the course of justice? †  The newspapers were full of bankrupt notices.  The farmers' taxes amounted to near the rent of their farms.  Mechanics wandered up and down the streets of every city destitute of work.  Ships, shut out from every port of Europe, lay rotting in the harbors.  The American name was insulted at every court.  Would any person of sense declare, after beholding such a picture as this, that times were not hard, that the country was not upon the brink of ruin, that a new and vigorous Federal Government was not needed?  What was to become of the people?  Trade was gone.  Manufactures were dead.

---

* Pennsylvania Gazette, April 26, 1786.

† See the account in Independent Gazetteer, September 21, 1787.

Everything was coming in from abroad, and the money fast going out. There was nothing left but to become a farmer or a merchant, and a merchant was thought the more honorable of the two. It was better to weigh out coffee than to plant corn; to draw molasses than to drive a plough. The whole nation was like to turn into merchants.

There was, however, one man clear-headed and temperate enough to look calmly on what went on about him, and take a correct view of the state of affairs. He had himself endured many hardships and undergone much suffering, but had never in the darkest hour looked upon the gloomy and hopeless side of things. He now put forth a neat little essay which he called "Consolation for America." In his usual way, for Franklin was the author, he began with an apt anecdote, and then went on to take a dispassionate view of the real condition of the country. He saw, he said, in the newspapers complaints of hard times, deadness of trade, scarcity of money, and the like. He could not say that these complaints were without foundation. There were in all countries people so circumstanced as to find it hard to gain a livelihood; people with whom money was scarce simply because they had nothing to give in exchange for it; and it was always in the power of a small number to make a great clamor. But, on a cool examination, the prospect would appear less gloomy than was imagined.

The chief business of the continent was agriculture. For one artisan or one merchant there were perhaps a hundred farmers. Each cultivated his own land, drew from it not only food, but clothing, and, after taking out for himself, had some to spare for commerce. For the part thus disposed of he never was better paid than at that moment, as the prices current sufficiently showed. In truth, when one who had travelled through Europe and seen how small is the proportion of persons in affluence to those in poverty, the few rich and haughty landlords, the multitude of abject, rack-rented, tithe-paying tenants, and half-paid, half-starved laborers, beheld the happy mediocrity that so generally prevailed in the States, he would be convinced that no country enjoyed a greater share of human felicity than America.

In the cities, the owners of houses and lands had their

interests vastly augmented in value.  Rents had risen to an astonishing height.  This made a demand for new buildings. New buildings gave employment to many workmen, who asked and were paid higher wages than any other part of the world would afford them.  If merchants found trade languishing, it was because they had imported more goods than the people could buy.  If shopkeepers found trade dead and money scarce, it was not from the fewness of buyers, but from the excessive number of sellers, that the mischief arose.  There were too many artisans and farmers turned shopkeepers.  Let them return to their tools and their ploughs, leave the shops to women and widows, and money would soon be plenty enough. Some were apprehensive for the future.  The increase of luxury alarmed them.  The States, they were sure, were on the high-road to ruin.  This could hardly be.  It rarely happened that the amount of idleness and prodigality of a people, which tended to dissipate, surpassed the amount of industry and frugality, which tended to accumulate property.  The luxury of a few seaports was not likely to ruin a country so full of industrious and well-to-do farmers as the United States.  Farming and the fisheries were the sources of wealth.  Every man that put a seed into the ground was recompensed forty fold.  Every man that drew a fish out of the waters drew up a piece of silver.*

Both the grumblers and the hopeful were, however, of the same mind on one matter.  They were sure the convention then in secret session would construct such a form of government as would cure these manifold ills of the country, and bring peace and quiet to the distracted States.  Meanwhile, the people of Philadelphia were much diverted by two other attempts at reform.  Neither was highly thought of at the time,

---

* Consolation for America, or remarks on her real situation, interests, and policy.  By his Excellency Benjamin Franklin, Esq., etc.  American Museum, January, 1787.  My authorities for the statements in the text are chiefly American Manufactures.  Three Letters by A Plain but Real Friend to America.  The Devil is in You, by Tom Thoughtful.  A Word of Consolation for America, by An Honest and Cheerful Citizen.  Present Situation of Affairs, American Museum, 1787. Cause of and Cure for Hard Times.  Causes of A Country's growing Rich.  Thoughts on the Present Situation of Affairs.  A View of the Federal Government.  Three Letters by a Bostonian.  Hard Times, Columbian Magazine, 1786, p. 31.  The Primitive Whig, New Jersey Gazette, January 9, 1786.

yet each was the forerunner of great things to come. One was the result of the labors of Noah Webster to improve the English tongue. The other was the work of John Fitch, and marks the beginning of that splendid series of American inventions that is without a parallel in history.

Noah Webster was a man of some learning, narrow-minded it is true, yet able, of unflagging industry, and of great self-reliance. But he was unhappily afflicted with the most offensive of all faults, gross self-conceit. Though a young man, he had risen to some notoriety in New England as a zealous Whig, a firm friend of Government, and as the author of some political essays which may still be perused with interest, and an excellent spelling-book for schools. Webster was himself a school-master, and had conceived a strong disgust for the ancient Dilworth and Jonson, which were at that time the only spelling-books in use. He set about correcting them, and as he worked upon his book the idea of a still greater reform seems to have started in his mind. He would improve the English tongue. He would simplify English spelling and grammar. He would destroy those dialectical differences that made the New England man a laughing-stock of the Virginian, and establish an American language that would in time go over the ocean and replace the ancient speech of England. The scheme was a bold one. But Webster was young, ardent, and began his task with a spirit worthy of so high a purpose. Like most reformers, he commenced by laying down a theory of perfection, which he carried out unswervingly to its logical extreme. Some words were to be proscribed; the spelling of others was to be materially altered; all silent vowels were to be cut out. But the most daring innovation was in the alphabet. The new language was to have every sound represented by a letter, and no letter was to be suffered to remain that did not stand for a distinct sound. Many new characters were therefore to be introduced, and many old ones cast aside. Such was his enthusiasm and conceit that he felt quite sure that letters familiar to hundreds of generations of men, and older than any other institution, human or divine, then existing, letters that had seen the rise of every language of Western Europe, that were old when the first Saxon set foot in

Britain, when Christ came on earth, when Cæsar invaded Gaul, when Rome was still a petty hamlet on the banks of the Tiber, would at his suggestion be ruthlessly swept away. Nor was he the only one who thought so. Franklin was made acquainted with the plan, and wrote to Webster that he had himself often thought of such a change; that he believed it not merely practicable but necessary, and that for his part he was ready to give it all the encouragement and all the support in his power.

To bring his plan to the attention of the public, Webster wrote a series of lectures which he read during the winter of 1785 and the spring of 1786 at Annapolis, at Baltimore, at Philadelphia, and New York. Everywhere he met with much applause. One who heard him at Annapolis declared that he had gone with indifference and come away with regret. After all that had been written on the subject, he looked for nothing new, especially from an American. But he was agreeably disappointed. The lecturer was bold enough to call in question opinions of eminent English writers which had till then passed for truth, and if he received the attention he deserved, England would be indebted to America for the last improvement in her tongue.*

At New York, Ramsey and many of the congressmen who heard him were much pleased, approved his plan, and urged him to go on. But in Philadelphia were many who looked coldly on so radical a change.† This Webster well knew, and, before lecturing in that city, cast about him for some public character whose good services he might secure. He selected his countryman Timothy Pickering, and to Pickering he now

---

* Pennsylvania Gazette, January 16, 1786.

† Webster was never popular at Philadelphia. Peter Porcupine (William Cobbett), in his attack on Dr. Rush's quack medicine, written thirteen years later, narrates an anecdote of Webster which, true or false, illustrates the conceit of the man. When he came to take charge of the Episcopal Academy he is said to have met Dr. Rush in the street, when the following dialogue took place:

"*Scene, a Street.* Enter Rush and Webster.

"*Rush.* How do you do, my dear friend? I congratulate you on your arrival in Philadelphia.

"*Webster.* You may, if you please, sir, congratulate Philadelphia on the occasion!!! (*They embrace.*)" See The Rush-Light, February 28, 1800, p. 51.

wrote.  He had, so the letter ran, begun a reform in the language.  His plan was still in embryo, yet he proposed to make it the subject of a set of lectures to be read in Philadelphia some time during the winter.  As he was the first American to undertake so bold a plan, a Yankee, and a youth, he felt the need of the countenance of gentlemen of the established character of Mr. Pickering.  He wished, therefore, that a notice of his coming might be inserted in a Philadelphia newspaper, in order to prepare the minds of the people for such an event.*  In a word, he wanted what in the language of our time would be called a puff.

When the lectures came off, Pickering made one of the audience, and has left us, undoubtedly, a just estimate of the performance.  With a competent share of good sense, the lecturer had, he declared, a *quantum sufficit* of vanity, and greatly over-estimated his own talents.  Such, in truth, was his egotism that his hearers were prevented from receiving that satisfaction which they must otherwise have drawn from his ingenious observations.  As to the encouragement he met with, it was nothing to boast of.  But then the Philadelphians had ever seemed to have an overweening opinion of their own literary acquirements as well as other excellencies.†  This, before a year had gone by, Webster found to be quite true.  It was long before the recollection of his offensive egotism, and the strictures he laid on the improper pronunciation of many words, were forgotten by the Philadelphians.

Late in April, 1787, the Independent Gazetteer, a scurrilous sheet even for those times, and strongly tinged with Antifederalism, published a communication in which, among other things, Webster was accused of being a Tory and an enemy of the public debt.‡  Webster had no liking for the Philadelphians, who had indeed given a poor reception to his book.  In truth, he had complained to Pickering that while the " Institute " found a ready sale at Charleston, at New York, and in

---

* See a letter from Noah Webster to Timothy Pickering, October 28, 1785.

† Pickering to John Gardiner, July 4, 1786.  Life of Pickering, by O. Pickering, vol. i, p. 537.

‡ Independent Gazetteer, May 9, 10, 15, and 23, June 4, 6, 7, 11, 26, and 30, 1787.

the East, there was scarce a call for it at Philadelphia.* This new offence was therefore hard to bear. He quite lost his temper, and had the bad taste to reply. But this only made matters worse, for the reply was, to say the least, full of bitterness and conceit. Had he not, he said, a thousand testimonials of his patriotism, love of government, and justice; had he not written the substance of volumes in support of the revolution and the Federal measures; had he not crushed, almost with his single pen, a State combination against these measures, there might be some appearance of truth in the charge. He then went on, in a long letter, to show that he really was an ill-used man.†

This was precisely what the Gazetteer wanted; and from that time forth for two months scarce a number came out but it contained some fling at Webster.‡ A host of pretended school-masters attacked him, half in sport, half in earnest, sometimes as Mr. Webster, sometimes as Mr. Grammatical Institute, and again as the Institutical Genius. Did Mr. Webster, said one of them, suppose for a moment that any man in Pennsylvania would submit to be instructed by a man from New England, where, so far from being acquainted with their own language, they stupidly spoke a mixture of all? Mr. Webster had much fault to find with some words often in the mouths of Pennsylvanians. But were they much better off in New England? Where under the sun did they get kaow for cow? Nan, a word much in use among the Quakers, was far better, and could not possibly be thrown aside. In truth, if he were to pick out all the awkward, old-fashioned words that continued to be as current among them as the Jersey six-pound bills, he would have to peruse the dictionary from A to Z.#

On another occasion he was derided for placing after his name the word 'Squire, and this in the eyes of many was the greatest fault of all. For the old reverence for titles and marks of rank had not yet become extinct, and it was thought

---

* Webster to Pickering, October 28, 1785. Life of Pickering. Nathaniel Patten, in his attack on Webster's Speller, asserts that the sale was twenty thousand copies annually. Connecticut Courant, May 24, 1790. American Mercury, May, 1790.　　　　　　　　　† Independent Gazetteer, May 10, 1787.

‡ See the Independent Gazetteers for April 25, May 26, May 29, May 30, May 31, June 1, 1787.　　　　# Independent Gazetteer, May 26, 1787.

a piece of impudence for an upstart Yankee school-master to assume so dignified a title.*

But in general the jests and sarcasms were directed against his book. In a mock address to the Federal Convention, that body was asked to see to it that the English tongue was properly established. One Webster, a New England man, had put out a book which he called an "Institute," and which contained some new things. On the title-page was the word systematic. This strong propensity to clip off the *al* from systematical and like words was noticed with concern. It was an innovation. It was to be looked to, for was not the *al* essential to the language and the main pillar of the Feder*al* Government? On another page he used need for needs, which every schoolboy knew was false. Could the States exist when a verb did not agree with its nominative case. The same Institutical Genius declared that all adjectives could be compared by more and most. What child did not know that one thing could not be more square or more cubical than another? Adjectives such as broad and long followed, he said, the nouns they qualified. It would therefore be proper to say hereafter that Chestnut was a street long and Market a street broad. Could a New England man be right? His attempt to introduce his "Institute" into the schools and displace Dilworth and Jonson was a Whig scheme.

But a still greater revolution was at the same time well under way. Steam navigation had begun. The first boat in the United States, and almost the first in the world, had been moved by steam. The glory of this invention is most commonly ascribed to Fulton. But an equal share must in justice be meted out to Rumsey and to Fitch. Both were men of wonderful mechanical bent; both were familiar with the power of steam, and both, almost at the same time, conceived the idea of using it to drive boats through the water.

John Fitch was a native of Connecticut, had been bred a mechanic, and had, at his trade, shown much ingenuity and skill. He was, in truth, a born inventor, and to wonderful originality of mind joined two traits of character, for lack of which many minds as fertile as his have gone to waste.

---

* Independent Gazetteer, June 1, 1787.

Calamities and humiliations, such as have bowed down and broken the spirits of hundreds of inventors, failed utterly to check his ardor or to cool his zeal.   It was not till late in life, however, that his remarkable powers began to display themselves.   He had passed his fortieth year before he ceased his wanderings, settled down on the banks of the Delaware, and built his first boat.   In April, 1785, while at Neshaminy, an obscure village of Bucks county, Pennsylvania, the idea of moving a carriage by steam seems to have come to him.   He was, he afterward declared, quite ignorant at that time of the inventions of Watt, and felt much disappointment when one Irwin, a minister at Neshaminy, showed him a picture of a steam-engine in " Martin's Philosophy."   After turning the matter over in his mind for a few days he abandoned it, and took up a plan for propelling boats by steam.   His first model, with paddle-wheels at the side, was quickly built and tried on the waters of a small stream that flowed by the town of Davisville.   It was crude in the extreme; but Ewing, who was president of the University of Pennsylvania, saw it, was pleased with it, and urged Fitch to seek aid of the General Government.   He gave him, indeed, a letter to Houston, who had for some years been a member of Congress.   Houston sent him to Lambert Cadwalader, a New Jersey delegate, and with his help an application was made, in due form, to Congress.   But the members of that weak and despised body were too busy with the impost and the regulation of trade to give any heed to the prayer of a hare-brained mechanic.   His plan was coldly put aside, and, half in anger, half in disgust, Fitch turned to Gardoqui.   But he was once more disappointed. The Spaniard would have all or none, and refused to subscribe a dollar unless all the profits and a monopoly of the invention went to his master the King of Spain.   This Fitch had the spirit to decline.   " If," he said, " there be any glory and profit in the invention, my countrymen shall have the whole of it."

And now the future began to look bright to him.   New Jersey gave him a patent-right to navigate the streams and rivers of the State for fourteen years.   Some gentlemen at Philadelphia became interested, formed a company, and raised a purse of three hundred dollars to help him on with his work.

He was at the same time joined by one to whose aid he soon owed great things. There was in the city a Dutch watchmaker named Voight.* Voight was a skilled mechanic, was of an ingenious turn of mind, heard of the new company, went to Fitch, made an offer of his services, and the two were soon at work on a small boiler and engine. The first trial was made on the Delaware early in the summer of 1786. But the condenser was found to be imperfect. The valves were not tight. The piston leaked. Water ran in streams from the cylinder-heads, which were of wood. These defects were remedied, and a second trial made. The engine, by a clumsy arrangement of levers, was first made to move a single paddle at the stern; then an endless chain, with many paddles fastened to it, was placed on each side of the boat; then paddle-wheels at the sides; and finally a system of six upright oars on each side. This gave the best results, and the boat moved off at the astonishing rate of seven miles an hour. Fitch was elated. If so small a craft, driven by so small an engine, could reach so high a rate of speed, there was, he declared, no reason why a large boat, with a larger engine, should not go at a more rapid pace. A vessel forty-five feet long was accordingly built, an engine of twelve-inch cylinder put in, and, late in August, 1787, the steamer was, in the presence of a great crowd of spectators, run up and down the Delaware river. Many members of the Federal Convention looked on, for the delegates had on that day adjourned in order that a committee might deliberate on a clause of the proposed constitution relating to the passage of navigation acts by Congress. All were delighted. Some drew up and gave to Fitch special certificates setting forth the merits of the strange experiment they had seen. Among them were Randolph, Governor of Virginia; Doctor Johnson, of Connecticut; Andrew Ellicot, and that David Rittenhouse whose name is, unhappily for himself, associated with the most absurd of all mechanical contrivances, an orrery.†

---

* Voight afterward became an officer in the United States Mint, and gained some notoriety for an improvement in the manufacture of steel. See Pennsylvania Journal, May 27, 1793; also, Pennsylvania Gazette, May 29, 1793.

† For an account of John Fitch, see his Life by Westcott. For an account of his boat, see Description of a new invented Steamboat. Columbian Magazine, De-

But while Fitch was experimenting at Philadelphia, James Rumsey was hard at work upon another steamboat at Shepherdstown, a small Virginia village on the Potomac.* The method of propulsion he employed was to suck water in at the bow and eject it at the stern, a system that has ever since his time tormented inventors, has been repeatedly tested, and as often thrown aside. No precise account of his machine has come down to us. But the boast has been preserved that it would not cost more than twenty guineas for a ten-ton boat, nor consume more than four bushels of coal, or the equivalent in wood, in twelve hours. The trial-trip was made on the eleventh of December, 1787. The vessel carried half her loading and a crowd of guests. Gates was among them, and has borne testimony to the fact that a run of four miles was made in one hour against the current of the Potomac river. The vessel's speed would, it was thought, have been at least eight miles in the same space of time; but, unfortunately, some water had been suffered to stand in the pipes, had frozen,

---

cember, 1786, and January, 1787. The description is by Fitch, and an engraving of the boat is given. See, also, The Growth of the Steam-Engine, by R. H. Thurston; and an interesting sketch of early steam navigation in America, in the Historical Magazine, April, 1859, p. 125, and vol. iii, pp. 3, 4. One of the earliest of Fitch's experiments was made on the Schuylkill, at Gray's Ferry, in the spring of 1785. Rembrandt Peale saw it, and has left an account of it in a Letter on the First Experiments of Fitch and Fulton in Steam Navigation. Collections of the Historical Society of Pennsylvania, vol. i, May, 1851, p. 34.

* So early as March, 1785, Washington appears to have been much interested in the experiments of Rumsey. See a letter of G. Washington to Hugh Williamson, March 15, 1785. Rumsey was well known as an ingenious man, and had from time to time invented a number of useful things. Some of these are favorably mentioned in the Virginia Gazette for December 16, 1787. The boat and saw-mill are mentioned in the Pennsylvania Gazette, September 10, 1788. Fitch, a year later, when his boats were running from Philadelphia to Bordentown and Trenton, became involved in a pamphlet-war with Rumsey as to priority of invention. See The Original Steamboat Supported; or, a Reply to Mr. James Rumsey's Pamphlet, showing the True Priority of John Fitch and the False Datings of James Rumsey, Philadelphia, 1788. See Rumsey's Short Treatise on the Application of Steam, 1788. Also, A Plan wherein the Power of Steam is Fully Shown by a new constructed Machine for Propelling Boats or Vessels, of any Burthen, against the most Rapid Streams or Rivers with great Velocity. By James Rumsey. His notice of patents from New York and Pennsylvania may be seen in the Freeman's Journal, October 28, 1789.

had fractured them, and the broken pieces were rudely held together by bits of rags.*

Far less notice was taken of these experiments of Fitch than their importance and success deserved. The attention of men of all sorts was turned to one object, and to one alone, the Federal Convention. From the day in May when that body began to sit with closed doors, the anxiety of the multitude had been steadily increasing, and had, long before August came, risen to fever heat. Boasts, idle conjectures, prophesies, and anxious letters filled the newspapers, and poured in upon the delegates from all parts. The conduct of the thirteen States was likened to that of the Prodigal Son. Each had, it was said, taken of the portion of independence that should have lodged in Congress, and wasted it in riotous living in a far land. They were now coming back, burdened with diseases and with debt, to their father's house, which was a Federal Government. Yet a little while, and the Federal robe and ring would be put upon them, the fatted calf would be killed, and every city, village, farm-house, and cabin in the land would resound with joy, since the States that were dead were alive again in a strong, efficient national Government.†
The United States was like unto an old man with thirteen sons among whom he had divided his substance. Twelve abode with him, watched over their goods, and proved themselves in many ways good and faithful sons. But the thirteenth had gone out from his father's house, had spent his portion, and hanged himself by his garter to a tree.‡ The convention, it was asserted, had resolved that Rhode Island should be considered as out of the Union; and that for the share of the national debt yet due from her she should be held responsible. Gentle means would first be used to collect it; but if these failed, the sum should be exacted of her by force.# Many plans of government, it was believed, had been talked of. One seemed to keep the form, but effectually destroyed the spirit, of democracy. Another, regarding only

---

* Virginia Gazette, published at Winchester, December 16, 1787. Copied into the Middlesex Gazette or Federal Advertiser, February 25, 1788.

† Pennsylvania Gazette, August 15, 1787.      ‡ Ibid., August 22, 1787.

# New York Packet, June 15, 1787. New Jersey Journal, June 13, 1787.

the necessity of a strong executive power, openly rejected even the semblance of a popular constitution.* There were plans to cut the States into three republics,† and plans to set up a King. All the details of a monarchy closely resembling that of England had been arranged. A constitution had been drawn up, titles, orders, and social distinctions provided for, and a commission was soon to be dispatched to lay the crown at the feet of George's second son.

This wild talk, which ought not to have imposed upon a village clown, was fervently believed. The post-bags came filled with letters to the delegates, reproaching them for their wickedness, or begging to know if it were true. To these one answer was invariably given. "While we cannot affirmatively tell you what we are doing, we can negatively tell you what we are not doing; we never once thought of a King." ‡ Emboldened by this credulity, some Tories and malcontents of Connecticut drew up and passed round for signature a paper recommending, half in jest, half in earnest, a kingly government for the States. The people, it set forth, had found by a bitter experience that they lacked wit enough to govern themselves; that all their declamation and parade about liberty, republicanism and property were mere stuff and nonsense, and that it was high time to tread backward in the path they had walked in for twelve years.# The monarch of their choice was the young Bishop of Osnaburgh, second son of the King of England, and who, as Duke of York, came not many years later to bear a great part in a famous scandal.‖ Others ventured to express the hope that, whatever the convention should do, the name Congress would at least be laid aside. The word was, they protested, associated in their

---

* New Jersey Journal, June 20, 1787.   New York Packet, June 15, 1787.

† Pennsylvania Gazette, June 27, 1787.        ‡ Ibid., August 22, 1787.

# Pennsylvania Gazette, August 15, 1787.   Pennsylvania Journal, August 22, 1787. Writing from New Haven, the day before the convention broke up at Philadelphia, Colonel Humphreys says: "It seems, by a conversation I have had here, that the ultimate practicability of introducing the Bishop of Osnaburgh is not a novel idea among those who were formerly termed Loyalists. Ever since the peace it has been occasionally talked of and wished for. Yesterday where I dined, half jest, half earnest, he was given as the first toast." Colonel Humphreys to Hamilton, New Haven, September 16, 1787.

‖ See Life of George IV., by Percy Fitzgerald.

minds with weakness, instability, and scanty power. It was quite impossible to mention it without calling up the recollection of continental money, of the forty-for-one measure, of tender laws, and of a huge pendulum vibrating for two years between Annapolis and New York.*

But the guesses of the multitude went, as usual, wide of the mark. Rhode Island was not ruled out of the Union. The States were not divided. The name of Congress was not abolished. No attempt was made to set up a King. A wise and just Constitution was, however, patiently and laboriously worked out. To those who looked forward so eagerly to the breaking up of the convention the result of its deliberations alone was given. The steps that led to it were most wisely hidden from them. Indeed, a new generation sprang up, and the secret process of fabrication was still unknown to the world. But the journals of the convention have now become public property. The notes of the debates taken down by Madison and Yates have been published, and we are perhaps in possession of all the information concerning the secret session of that body that will ever be collected. This information is far from complete; yet it is quite enough to enable us to form a tolerably correct idea of the labors of a most remarkable assemblage of men, to whom, under God, we owe our liberty, our prosperity, our high place among the nations.

The serious work of the convention began on the morning of Tuesday, the twenty-ninth of May. When the roll had been called, and the delegates of eight States had answered to their names, Governor Randolph rose in his place and addressed the House in a long and vigorous speech. He pointed out, precisely and clearly, the manifold faults of the Confederation, declared it to be quite unequal to preserving the safety, honor, and welfare of the country, and besought all who heard him to aid in setting up a strong and energetic Government. He then unrolled a manuscript which he held

---

* Pennsylvania Gazette, August 22, 1787. For some of the arguments then in use among the supporters of the convention, see To the Freemen of the United States in Support of a Federal Government. On the Means of Promoting a Federal Sentiment in the United States.

in his hand, and read a series of resolutions. These, he said, he offered as leading principles for a good system of government. He did not intend them for a Federal Government. He meant them for a strong, consolidated Union, in which the idea of States should be almost done away with.

His resolutions, which became known in the course of the debates as the Virginia plan, were fifteen in number, and were not his own work. The seven delegates from Virginia had indeed framed them with great care and labor, and had chosen Randolph to lay them before the House; for he was, of the seven, the highest in political rank, and renowned as a man skilled in the art of public speaking. The substance of the plan was that the right of suffrage each State had in Congress should be proportional to the sum of money it paid into the Treasury as quota, or to the number of free inhabitants of its soil; that Congress should consist of two branches; that the people should elect the members of the one; that the State Legislatures should choose the members of the other; that there should be a national executive elected by the national Legislature; a national judiciary, to hold office during good behavior; and that a republican government and a right to the soil should be guaranteed to each State.

When he had read the resolutions he moved that the House go into a committee of the whole on the state of the Union, and sat down. Some debate followed, but the motion was carried, and the next day set as the time.

And now Pinckney rose and presented a second plan for a Federal Government, which he had himself made ready. Of this, unhappily, no record has come down to us. It was indeed referred to the committee of the whole; but from that time forth no entry of any kind concerning it is to be found on the minutes. When, therefore, thirty-two years later, the Secretary of State was preparing the journals of the convention for publication, he wrote to Pinckney for a copy of his plan, and received in reply a document that was inserted in the printed journals and has been copied by biographers and historians as the South Carolina plan. But the instrument sent Mr. Adams is not in any sense a copy of the instrument laid before the convention.

Early on the morning of the thirtieth the clerk read the order of the day, and the House went into a committee of the whole on the state of the Union. Randolph moved his first resolution. Some discussion followed, in the course of which the younger Morris pointed out that it was unnecessary, as the next resolution would not agree with it. Randolph then withdrew it, and moved in its place : that the union of the States merely federal would not fulfil the purposes of the Articles of Confederation ; that no treaty between the States would accomplish it ; and that a national government ought to be set up consisting of supreme judicial, legislative, and executive powers. To this member after member rose to offer an amendment. But as soon as Pinckney could get a hearing he said that, if the motion were agreed to, it seemed to him all work was done. The instructions of the delegates in general were to revise the existing Articles of Confederation, and to alter or amend them, as the case might be. To flatly declare that they were insufficient, and could not be amended or improved, was, he thought, to put the matter out of the reach of the powers of the House. The argument had its weight. The first and second resolutions were dropped and the third taken up. The word "supreme" required explanation. Was it, some one asked, intended to destroy the State governments? The answer was, Yes, to a limited extent. When the powers of the national Government clashed with those of the States, the States must give way. The question was called, and six States voted in the affirmative. Connecticut voted in the negative. New York was divided. For there were few questions on which Hamilton could agree with Lansing and with Yates.

The resolution next in order was that the system of representation was unjust, and ought to be based on quota or population. Mr. Read moved that it be postponed. The State of Delaware had, he said, expressly forbidden her delegates to consent to any change in the system. He would therefore, if the question passed, feel it his duty to withdraw. Madison spoke on the other side ; but it was finally agreed to postpone.

On the following day, which was Thursday, the last of May, the New Jersey delegation came in. When the credentials had been examined and the members taken their seats, it was moved that the national Legislature ought to consist of two branches. This was passed. The fourth resolution of the Virginia plan, that the members of the first branch should be chosen by the people, was then taken up, and a spirited discussion provoked. Gerry, who could not forget the late scenes of rebellion in Massachusetts, told the House that the ills of the country came from an excess of democracy. "The people," said he, "do not want virtue, but are the dupes of pretended patriots. In Massachusetts it has been fully established by a long experience that they are daily led into the most baneful measures, and made to hold the most dangerous opinions, by the false reports of designing men, and which no one on the spot can deny." Sherman, of Connecticut, was of the same mind. The people, he thought, should have as little to do directly with the Government as possible. They wanted knowledge, and were constantly liable to be misled. Mason spoke against this. He would allow there was too much democracy. But he would hold to the belief that the first branch of the national Legislature ought to be the popular branch. It ought to be the American House of Commons, if he might use the words. It ought to come directly from the mass. When, after a long debate, the vote was taken, the Ayes had it by six to two. Connecticut and Delaware were divided.

The fifth of Randolph's resolutions, and the sixth, that there ought to be a national executive to hold office for seven years, were soon disposed of. But when the number of the executive came up for discussion, the wildest opinions were expressed. For three days no other business was touched on, and, before the debate was over, almost every delegate had spoken. Randolph was for dividing the country into three sections, and having an executive from each. Sherman urged a single executive and a council of revision. Rutledge and Wilson, a single executive without the council. This, the Governor of Virginia protested with much warmth, would never do. It would be a monarchy, and the temper of the people would never brook a King. The requirements of a good executive were vigor, dispatch, and responsibility, and he for one did not see why they could not be found in three men as well as in one. Every one, Wilson said, knew that a single executive was not a King. One fact had been over-looked. Yet it had great weight with him. The thirteen States agreed in few things; but they had all agreed in placing a single executive at the head of Government. Not a State could be named that had ever for a moment thought of three heads. In such a triumvirate he saw nothing but fierce and undying animosity. They would be sure to fall out; public business would be sure to be stopped; the poison would spread to the people, and everywhere there would be jealousy, suspicion, and contention. When the ballot was counted, seven were for a single executive and three against.

It was now Monday, the fourth of June. The rest of the week was taken up with discussing the eighth resolution, and amendments to the fifth and fourth. On Saturday the great debate of the session began. The cause was a motion by Patterson to reconsider that clause of the second resolution which bore on the question of representation. Judge Brearly spoke first. The matter was an important one. On the principle that each State was sovereign, the Articles of Confederation had given to each one vote in Congress. If the States were to remain sovereign, a right of suffrage on any other plan was unjust. Were population the basis, there would be ninety votes: one for Georgia and sixteen for Virginia. Was this just? Not in the least. Such a system must defeat itself or end in despotism. If there must be a national Government, there was but one thing to do. Lay the map of the Confederation on the table, wipe out the State-lines, mark down new ones, such that each State should have the same representation, and then a government on the proposed plan would be a just one, and not before. It is strange so shrewd a lawyer should, even in the heat of debate, have been misled by so foolish a piece of reasoning. Had he stopped for a moment to think, he must have seen that it would be quite as impossible to keep up an equal distribution of population as to maintain an equal distribution of wealth.

Patterson spoke next on the same side. "Let us," said he, "consider with what powers we are clothed." He then moved to have the credentials of the Massachusetts delegates read. This was done. "By these," continued he, "and by others, it is plain that our business here is to go over the Articles of Confederation and to alter or amend them in such wise as we judge best. Can we on this ground form a national Legislature? I fancy not. We are met in this room as the representatives of thirteen independent States for Federal purposes. Can we then form one government and destroy the sovereignty of the very States that have sent us here to make that sovereignty yet more secure? I fancy not. What, pray, is a property representation? Is a man with four thousand pounds to have forty times as many votes as a man with a hundred pounds? And what, pray, is a representation founded on numbers? If State sovereignty is to be kept up, shall I submit the welfare of New Jersey with five votes in a council where Virginia has sixteen? Suppose, as was in agitation before the late war, America had been represented in the British Parliament, and had sent over the sea two hundred delegates. What would they have availed against six hundred? I tell you we should have been as much enslaved as when without representation. Nay, more enslaved, for we should then have been without even the hope of redress. Some one has said this national Government is to act on individuals and not on States. Cannot a Federal Government be framed to act in the same way? I say it can. I will never consent to the proposed plan. I shall make all the interest against it I can. Neither my State nor myself will ever submit to despotism or to tyranny."

The angry tones and menace of the speaker had their effect, and the moment he was done Wilson rose. He reminded the gentleman from New Jersey that a majority, nay, a minority, of the States had a right to confederate with each other, and the rest might do as they pleased. Numbers were the true basis of representation. It was absurd to say that New Jersey with her population should have the same weight and the same influence in the national councils as Pennsylvania. " I say," said he, " it is unjust. I never will confederate on such a plan. The gentleman from New Jersey is candid. He declares his opinions boldly. I commend him for it. I will be equally candid. I say, again, I never will confederate on his principles."

The discussion was then postponed, and the remaining resolutions of the Virginia plan taken up, till, on the morning of the thirteenth of June, it was found that all had been disposed of. It was then moved that the committee of the whole report to the House. This was done, and the House, after hearing the report, put off the consideration of it to the next day. But at this stage of the debate Patterson asked leave to bring in a new and totally different plan. The leave was given, and on Friday, the fifteenth of June, he read to the convention the New Jersey plan.

A few members were found hardy enough to support it. But the men whose legal learning made them the leaders of the debate spoke strongly against it. Randolph denied that the delegates had not power to form a government on the Virginia plan. Wilson drew a close comparison between the two. "The only difference between the plan from Virginia and the plan from New Jersey is," said he, "in a word, this: Virginia proposes two branches to the Legislature, Jersey one. Virginia would have the legislative power derived from the people, Jersey from the States. Virginia would have a single executive, Jersey more than one. By the Virginia plan the national Legislature can act on all national concerns. By the New Jersey plan, only to a limited extent. By the one, the Legislature can negative all State laws. By the other, the executive can compel obedience by force." Much had been said about the New Jersey plan agreeing with the powers of the convention. The argument had no force with him. For himself, he believed his powers extended to everything or to nothing. He had a right, and was free to support either plan, or to reject both. The people cried out for relief from their ills, and looked up with fond hopes to the National Convention. They expected a national Government, and such the Virginia plan would give them.

To this stage in the debates Hamilton had hardly said a word except aye and nay. His position was in truth a trying one. He was almost the youngest man on the floor of the House, and had been forced on almost every question to vote against his colleagues, Lansing and Yates. But the time had now come, he thought, to speak out boldly and plainly. On

the morning of the eighteenth of June, therefore, in a long
and able speech, he went over the good and bad points of the
plans before the convention.  He liked neither of them much,
and he liked the Jersey plan the least.  It was the old Articles
of Confederation with a few new patches.  It was pork still
with a change of sauce.  He then read to the House eleven
articles, which were not to be considered as a plan, but which
he would, some time in the future, move as amendments to
the Virginia plan.

The best debate on the Jersey plan, however, was made by
Madison.  Patterson, in presenting his resolutions, had dwelt
much on the Articles of Confederation, and the duty of every
State to obey them.  Not much notice was taken of the argument at the time.  But when, on the nineteenth of June, the
first resolution of the Jersey plan was taken up for discussion,
Madison refuted him in a few words.  It was quite true that
all the States had agreed to the Articles of Confederation.  Yet
those very articles declared that the infraction of one of them
by a single State broke up the compact.  Had not such an infraction been made?  Did not New Jersey, said he, with sour
pleasantry, flatly refuse to obey a lawful requisition of Congress?  The States were forbidden to make wars and treaties.
Yet had not Georgia made wars and concluded treaties with
the Creeks?  Had not Maryland and Virginia entered into a
partial compact?  Had not Pennsylvania and New Jersey set
bounds to Delaware?  Had not Massachusetts at that very moment a great body of troops in pay?  Many of the States had
infringed the rights of individuals, had issued paper money,
and established ways of paying debts differing from the forms
of contract.  Were not these infractions of the articles and acts
of tyranny?  And what check did the Jersey plan put on
these?  None.  It was indeed provided that when a State dis-
obeyed it should be made to obey.  But how would military
coercion work?  The small States could easily be brought to
obedience or crushed.  But what if the great States proved refractory?  Was the gentleman so sure that he could by force
effect submission?  Suppose, again, as he had threatened, no
plan could be agreed to, what then would become of the little
States?  Would Delaware and New Jersey be safe against

Pennsylvania? Would Rhode Island be secure from Massachusetts?

As soon as he was seated, King moved that the committee rise, report the New Jersey plan to be inadmissible, and recommend that of Virginia. It was carried by a vote of seven to three, one State being divided. The plan was now formally before the convention, and the next week was spent in an amicable discussion. Should the national Legislature consist of one branch or two? Should there be one executive or three? Should the members of the first branch be twenty-five years old, or thirty? Should they be paid by the States or the nation? Should they serve for four years, for six years, or for seven? Such were the questions that took up the attention of the House. Not till the twenty-seventh of the month was that resolution reached which, from the opening to the close of the convention, was never once mentioned without exciting a violent display of sectional feeling, and a long and fierce debate. The language of the first clause was that the right of suffrage in the national Legislature ought not to be according to the rule established in the Articles of Confederation, but according to some other. The great speech was from Martin.

Martin was a fluent speaker, a ready debater, and had raised himself, by what his friends called his eloquence, to the high place of Attorney-General of Maryland. He had acquired, from nature or by art, the habit of saying much, yet meaning little. No lawyer who contended with him in the courts could, from such meagre evidence, produce so long an argument. No one knew better how, under the appearance of clearness, to be most obscure; and on this occasion he made full use of his powers. For three hours he addressed the House. Indeed, when the time for adjournment came he was still speaking, and was forced to finish his oration on the following day.

When at last he was done, Lansing moved to strike out the word "not." "I oppose the motion," cried Madison. "How can any of the States be endangered by an adequate representation? There has been much talk of a combination of the great States against the little. What likelihood is there of such a thing? What inducements? Where that similarity of customs, manners, religion so necessary? If there can possibly be a diversity of interest, it is in the case of the three large States. They are far apart. Their trade is different. Their religions are unlike. Massachusetts is deeply engaged in the fisheries and the carrying trade. The staple of Pennsylvania is wheat and flour. Virginia cultivates tobacco. Can such States ever form a combination? Does not the history of every country on the face of the earth disprove it? Is it not the strong States that fall out, and the weak ones that combine?" He then went on, after his fashion, to illustrate his remarks by passages drawn from the history of Sparta, of Athens, of the House of Bourbon, the House of Austria, and with examples taken from the conflicts of Carthage and of Rome.

But the force of his argument was lost on Gorham. He could, he said, for one, see no difficulty in supposing a union of interests among the States. In Massachusetts there were once three provinces. They had united, and no man could now find the faintest trace of the old distinctions. Thus was it that the little States would unite in a General Government. New Jersey in particular, lying between Pennsylvania and New York, could never become a commercial State. It would be to her interests to be divided, and some day part would go to Pennsylvania and part to New York. Nor could Massachusetts long remain a great State. The Province of Maine would soon become independent of her. So too with Pennsylvania. Her western possessions must in time be made into a new State. Gorham sat for Connecticut.

On the motion to agree to Lansing's amendment the Nays had it by a vote of six to four, one State, as usual, being divided. The question to agree to the original motion was then put by the chair and carried in the affirmative, the Ayes counting six, the Nays four. This disposed of for the time being, it was moved that in the second branch each State should have an equal vote. But again the State-rights men flew into a passion, another rancorous debate occupied all Friday and Saturday, nor was it till Monday that a vote of five to five was reached. Indeed, at no time during the sitting of the convention were the members so angry and the debate as personal and bitter as on the afternoon of Saturday, the thirtieth of June. At one time Wilson, who had quite lost his temper and his patience, was heard to exclaim: "If the minority withhold their consent to the new plan, if they will have their own way or go out from the Union, then let them go. The opposition to the plan is as twenty-two to ninety in the general scale; not a fourth part of the Union. Shall three fourths be ruled by one fourth? Shall three fourths give up their right for the support of an artificial being called State-interest? For whom do we make a constitution? Is it for men? Or is it for imaginary beings called States?" "The last speaker," said Ellsworth, "asserts that a General Government must depend on the equal suffrages of the people. Where is or where was there a confederacy ever formed where equality of voices was not a fundamental principle?" "Lycia," said Madison, "was such a one." He then went on to attack the arguments of the Connecticut delegate one by one. The last speaker, said he, has appealed to our good faith to observe the Articles of Confederation. "I have already impeached many States of an infraction of them. I have not spared my own State, nor can I justly spare his. Did not Connecticut refuse her compliance to a Federal requisition? Has she paid a shilling into the Treasury for two years past? Does this look like the observance of a solemn compact?" This was too much, and in a moment Ellsworth was on his feet clamoring to be heard. "My State," said he, "has all along been strictly Federal, and I appeal to your Excellency," turning to Washington, "for the truth of it during the war. The muster-rolls will show that she had more troops in the field than even the State of Virginia. We strained every nerve to raise them. We feel the effect of it to this day. But we defy any gentleman to show that we ever refused a Federal requisition. If she has proved delinquent, it has been through inability only, and that is no more than others have been without the same excuse."

At this point Gunning Bedford, one of the five who sat for Delaware, broke in. The great States, it seemed to him, went on as if the eyes of the smaller ones were utterly blind. Impartiality with them was out of the question. The Virginia plan was their political creed, and they were bound to support it, right or wrong. Even the petty State of Georgia, with an eye to her future wealth and greatness; South Carolina, puffed up with the possession of money and negroes, and North Carolina too, were all three on the side of the great States. It was said they never could coalesce. Their interests were different. Yet even then they were firmly united in a scheme of interest and ambition. Did they think to crush the smaller States? Sooner than be ruined, there were foreign powers who would take them by the hand. "Take a foreign power by the hand!" cried King. "I am sorry he mentioned it. I hope he will be able to excuse it to himself on the score of passion."

It was now quite plain that nothing could be done in the convention. So much had been said, and so many members had been upon their feet in the course of the long debates, that the sentiments of each State were well known. On the one side were the powerful and opulent commonwealths of Massachusetts, Pennsylvania and Virginia, the two Carolinas and Georgia, insisting that representation in both branches of the national Legislature should be according to population or to wealth. On the other side were the four small States of Connecticut, New Jersey, Delaware, and Maryland insisting with equal vehemence that the right of suffrage in each branch should be equal. New York was divided. New Hampshire and Rhode Island were not represented.

In this pass, Pinckney came to the relief. He moved a select committee to take into consideration both branches of the Legislature. But scarcely had it been put by the chair when Martin flew into a passion. "It is again attempted," said he, "to compromise. You must give each State an equal suffrage, or our business is at an end." "It seems to me," answered Sherman, "we have got to a point where we cannot move one way or the other. Such a committee is necessary to set us right." Nor did he express more than the opinion of the House. For when the question to agree was put, but two dissenting votes were cast. After eleven members had been balloted for, the House adjourned for three days.

But the meetings of the committee were no more harmonious than the meetings of the convention. Again the proposition to compromise was brought up, and again resisted. You propose, such was the language used by the opposition, to yield to an equal representation in the second branch, provided we will consent to an unequal representation in the first. We will not. There is no merit in it. It is merely offering, after a long and bitter struggle to put both feet on our neck, to take one off if we will peacefully suffer one to remain. But we well know that you cannot keep even that foot on unless we are willing, and that, having one firmly planted, you will be able to put on the other when you please. You will grow rich. You will grow populous. And with this increase of men and money will come more power. What security can you give that you will not then force from us that equality in the second branch which you now deny to be our right, and submit to from necessity? Will you tell us that we ought to trust you because you now enter into a solemn compact with us? You have made such a compact before, and now treat it with the utmost contempt. Will you now make an appeal to the Supreme Being, and call on him to guarantee your observance of this compact? This also you have done before for the observance of the very Articles you now so wantonly violate.

Before the committee rose, however, a better spirit prevailed, and a report was drawn up. This recommended that each State should be given one representative in the first branch of the Legislature for every forty thousand inhabitants free or bound to servitude for a number of years, and a three-fifths representation for all others except Indians; that all money-bills should originate in the first branch, and not be amended in the second; that no money should be drawn from the Treasury except by bills originating in the first branch; and that in the second branch each State should have an equal vote.

On the fifth of July the House listened to the report of their committee. Some ill-natured remarks were made, and some apologies offered for hasty speeches on the previous days. But with those exceptions the debate was orderly and the report well received. The clause fixing the representation at one for each forty thousand free inhabitants was, however, recommitted. The next day the committee reported that in their judgment the first House of Representatives should consist of fifty-six members. This was again recommitted. It was then observed that two delegates were not in their seats. Yates and Lansing had, in a fit of ill-temper, quitted the convention and gone home to New York.

On the ninth of the month the number of representatives for the first House was fixed at sixty-five. The debating then went smoothly on till the seventeenth, when the manner of choosing the executive came up. The younger Morris, who was firmly attached to popular government, declared that the executive ought not to be elected by the national Legislature. If it were in the power of that body both to choose him and impeach him, he would assuredly be its creature. His election would be the work of intrigue, of faction, of cabal. The people ought to make the choice. Then some man, distinguished for great public services or fine character, a man, if he might so express himself, of continental reputation, would be raised to the office. Sherman replied. It was beyond the scope of his narrow mind to suppose that the time would ever come when the means of communication with which he was familiar would be supplanted by new and better ones, of which the world had then no idea. He spoke, therefore, for election by the national Legislature. The people, said he, can never know enough about the character of a man, and besides, they will never give a majority of votes to any one man. They will vote for some one of their own State or their own town. On the same side was Mason. To his mind, to leave the choice of a chief magistrate to the people was as unnatural as to leave a choice of colors to a blind man.

When the question of a popular election was put, but one State voted yes. When the question of a choice by the national Legislature was put, all voted yes. But the matter was not suffered to rest. Again and again it came up, till at last, a week later, it was moved and carried that the executive be chosen by the national Legislature, that he serve for seven years, and be ineligible to re-election. Two days after, the articles agreed to were referred to a committee of detail. The House then adjourned till the sixth of August.

On that day, as the members took their seats, they received

each a copy of the draft of the Constitution printed in large type on a broadside. For another month the debating went on, a few changes and additions were made, and on the eighth of September the House, convinced that the Constitution could not be improved, referred it to a committee to revise the wording and arrange the articles.

When Monday, the seventeenth of September, came, the convention assembled for the last time, and the Constitution, as we now have it, was laid upon the table for signature. For some minutes nothing was said. Then Franklin, about to close the last national service of his life, got up, with a paper in his hand, as if to speak. But his voice and his body were far too weak, and he handed the paper to Wilson, who read it. The document was highly characteristic of the man. He had, he said, lived a long time, and had often been obliged to change his opinion on matters on which he was once sure he was right. The older he grew, therefore, the more apt was he to doubt his own judgment, and to pay more respect to the judgments of others. Steele, in one of his dedications, told the Pope that the only difference between the Church of England and the Church of Rome in their opinions on the certainty of their doctrine was this: The Church of Rome was infallible. The Church of England was never in the wrong. He then went on, in his habitual way, to narrate an apt story. A certain French lady, in a quarrel with her sister, said: "I do not know how it is, sister, but I meet with nobody but myself that is always in the right; ' *il n'y a que moi qui a toujours raison.*' " In this sentiment he agreed to the Constitution, with all its faults, if it had any. He had expected no better, and he was not sure it was not the best. He hoped that each member who still had objections would doubt a little of his own infallibility and put his name to the instrument. He then proposed as a form, "Done in convention by the unanimous consent of the States." Governeur Morris drew up this ambiguous form, in hopes of gaining the dissenting members, and put it into Franklin's hands, that it might have the better chance of success. But sixteen refused, and began, one after another, to excuse themselves. Gerry feared a civil war. Randolph knew that nine States would never ratify. Washington was the first to sign. It was long popularly believed that, as he stood beside the table with his hand upon the Constitution, he held up the pen and said : " Should the States reject this excellent Constitution, the probability is that opportunity will never again offer to cancel another in peace; the next will be drawn in blood." * When he had signed, the other members went up, one by one, in the geographical order of the States, beginning at the East. As the last members were affixing their names, Franklin, looking toward the President's chair, back of which a rising sun happened to be painted, said to a few who sat near him, that painters had found it difficult in their art to distinguish a rising from a setting sun. "I have," said he, often and often, in the course of the session, and the vicissitude of my hopes and fears as to its issue, looked at that behind the President without being able to tell whether it was rising or setting. But now, at length, I have the happiness to know that it is a rising and not a setting sun."

Before the convention rose, it was ordered that the journal should be left in the keeping of the President until such time as the new Government should see fit to intrust it to other hands. If it were published, an evil use, it was feared, would be made of it. If it were destroyed, no evidence would then exist with which to refute the false charges of political enemies. The President was also bidden to draw up a letter of transmittal and send it, with the Constitution, to Congress. This he accordingly did.†

---

* Pennsylvania Journal, November 14, 1787. New York Packet, November 20, 1787.

† My authorities for the proceedings of the convention are : Madison's Debates, Yates's Secret Debates, and the Journal of the Convention. Many other valuable papers were wantonly burned by Secretary Jackson, as he himself states in his letter to Washington.

# CHAPTER V.

### THE CONSTITUTION BEFORE THE PEOPLE.

THE ship Constitution, as the friends of that instrument delighted to call it, was thus fairly launched. From that moment dates the existence of the two great national parties which, under many different names and on many different platforms, have ever since continued to struggle for supremacy in the State. In all parts of the land, it is true, men were, after the return of peace, divided by their political opinions into at least two classes. Everywhere there were Imposters and Non-imposters; Hard-money men and Soft-money men; patriots who favored the strengthening, and State-righters who urged the weakening of the power of Congress. But these classes were in no sense national parties. They had no organization, they had no leaders, no platforms, no watchwords, no names. They were purely local, and the followers of the one as of the other would have denied with vehemence that they were anything else than stanch and honest Whigs. When, however, the people were bidden to choose between the old Articles of Confederation and the new Constitution, between a sham union of the States and a strong national Government, a change came about. An issue was raised. Something was at stake; and the Whig party was quickly rent in twain. Leaders appeared; standards were set up. The name of Whig fell for a time into disuse, and, under the appellation of Federalist and Antifederalist, the two sections of a once harmonious party drew farther and farther apart and began a contest on a national scale.

The conflict opened in Pennsylvania. Such, indeed, was the zeal which animated the little band of Federalists in that

State that, twenty hours after Congress had formally submitted the Constitution to the people, a call for a convention
was hurried through the Assembly.* The matter had, it is
true, been under debate the day before, and had been marked
by the first show of party violence.   Late in the morning session of Friday, September twenty-eighth, 1787, Clymer, who
sat for Philadelphia, and had been one of the delegates to the
Federal Convention, rose in his place and, without previous
notice, moved a State Convention to consider the Constitution.  The Antifederalists were astounded.  The session of the
Assembly was all but over.  A new election was at hand, and
they had therefore never for a moment supposed that the
instrument would be taken up by the House so soon to adjourn.  Their plan was to make it a question in the ensuing
canvass, and to secure, if possible, such a majority of men of
their own mind in the next Legislature as would prevent the
hated document being submitted to the people.  Clymer's
motion accordingly found them off their guard, and forced to
combat it with such plausible arguments as came to them at
the instant.  This haste, they said, was both unseemly and un-
parliamentary.  The Convention had sent the Constitution to
Congress.  Congress had not yet sent it to the States, and till
this was formally done it was simply indecent to know anything about it.  It was, too, a constant practice with the members, when any business of great moment was to come up, to
give notice and have it made the order of the day some time
beforehand.  Besides, no bill was ever passed without at least
three readings.  This was not a loose but a strict rule of the
House; so strict, indeed, that not even the building of a
bridge or the laying out of a road could be determined till
the formality had been gone through with.  Yet here were
members clamoring for the passage of a most important bill,
sprung upon the House without the usual notice and without
the usual readings.  It was all wrong.  The House would on
the following day break up, and the whole matter should be
left to the next Assembly.  But their arguments were of no
use.  Their voices were drowned amid cries of " question,"
and when the Speaker put it, of the sixty-two members pres-

---

* New York Packet, October 9, 1787.

ent, forty-three voted for and nineteen against it. The House then adjourned till four in the afternoon.

The rage of the nineteen flamed high. It was impossible for them to find words wherewith to express their indignation. They met hastily, declared that if they could not defeat the attempt to call a convention by their votes they could by their absence, gave a solemn pledge not to return to the House, and kept it.

When four o'clock came, but forty-five, two more than those who had voted for the convention, were in their seats. This number was two less than a quorum, and till a quorum was assembled no business could be done. After waiting some time, and no more members coming in, the Speaker commanded the sergeant-at-arms to go out and summon the absent ones. He went, was gone a long while, and when he came back was questioned at the bar. He had, he said, gone to the house of one Boyd, had there found Whitehill, Smilie, Antis, and some other noted Antifederalists, had summoned them in the name of the House, and received in reply a firm assurance that they would on no account obey.* Nothing was left the Speaker but to adjourn the Assembly till Saturday.

Meanwhile, news of what had happened in the State-House, and the names of the nineteen seceding members, spread fast through the town. All that evening and till late in the night crowds filled the taverns and coffee-houses, or stood on the street-corners, angrily discussing the situation and forming plans for the morrow. The Antifederalists were triumphant and defiant. The Federalists were much disheartened. Some were for concession. But a few, more zealous than the rest, determined that a quorum should be formed, come what might. If two of the dissenters could not be persuaded to go, they should be made to go. The two chosen for this treatment were James McCalmont, who sat for Franklin, and Jacob Miley, who represented Dauphin. Early on the morning of Saturday a great crowd gathered, accordingly, about their lodgings, broke open the doors, laid hold upon them and dragged them, cursing and struggling, through the streets to the State-House. There they were forced into their

---

* Pennsylvania Gazette, October 3, 1787.

places and held down in their seats with clothes disordered and torn, and faces white from rage.*

When the roll was called, forty-seven members answered to their names. This made a quorum, and the House so formed went on with the business of the day.

Much time was spent in reviling the behavior of the nineteen, in lauding the merits of the Constitution, and discussing the fitness of naming an early day to consider it. Some were for having the election of delegates to the State Convention held at the same time as the annual elections, then nine days distant. But the first Tuesday in November was moved as election-day, and the thirtieth of the same month for the meeting of the convention. When the question was put, the Ayes had it by a vote of forty-five to two. Scarce was the result announced when the crowd that filled the halls and lobby and stood about the doors, testified its approval by three hearty cheers, and set off to spread the news. The shops were shut, business ceased, and the bells in all the churches were rung through the rest of the day. Before the debate was over on Saturday an express came spurring into town with word that Congress had submitted the Constitution to the States. He had been sent on by Bingham, one of the delegates at New York.†

The first of October was now come, and the day on which the delegates were to be chosen was but six weeks away. The whole State was in commotion. The inhabitants of every town and hamlet from the Susquehanna to the Ohio were arrayed against each other as Federalists or Antifederalists, supporters or detractors of the Constitution. The canvass would, under any circumstances, have been conducted with much acrimony and zeal. The State was one of the largest and most populous in the Union. Within her borders lay the greatest and richest city of the western world, and that city had for many years been the seat of the national Government. Each party knew, therefore, that the eyes of the whole

---

* See the statement of their treatment as published under their signatures in Pennsylvania Gazette, October 10, 1787. New York Packet, October 12, 1787.

† New York Packet, October 9, 1787.

country were on it, and that failure or success would be the undoing or the making of its friends in the neighboring States. But a peculiar bitterness was given to the electioneering by the fact that the principles of government as laid down in the Federal Constitution were almost precisely the opposite of the principles of government laid down in the State Constitution. Pennsylvania was at that time one of the few commonwealths of America where men had been bold enough and weak enough to make trial of the wild theory of government Turgot had propagated and Condorcet had praised. The State Constitution provided for but one legislative body. The Federal Constitution provided for two. The President of Pennsylvania was chosen by the Assembly. The President of the United States was to be chosen by electors. The State Government was a centralized democracy. The national Government was to be a Republic of Republics. Every voter, therefore, who helped to send a Federalist to the convention, declared the Government under which he lived to be bad in form, and so it was.

It may well be supposed that, while so much was at stake, the two parties strove with unwonted fury. The newspapers were not large enough to contain half the addresses, thoughts, letters, observations, that poured in from Cato and Brutus, Cincinnatus and Biscayanus. One of the earliest of these was an address from sixteen of the assemblymen who had, when the call for the State Convention was under debate, left their seats and refused to return. It bore date the twenty-ninth of September, and was the first formal protest against the Constitution. They had, the signers said, stood out against the instrument because the House had not received any official information from Congress touching it, because the delegates sent to the Federal Convention were all of them Philadelphians, were none of them fit to represent the landed interest of Pennsylvania, and were almost to a man strongly opposed to the Constitution of the State.*

---

* Address of the subscribers, members of the late House of Representatives of the Commonwealth of Pennsylvania, to their constituents. Independent Gazetteer, October 3, 1787.

A dozen replies came forth instantly.* Every one of them branded the statements of the address as wicked and malicious falsehoods. One of the writers declared that he was at a loss what most to be surprised at, the impudence of the lie, or the boldness of the insult to the understanding of the people. An official submittal of the Constitution to the State, addressed by the hand of the Secretary of Congress to the Speaker of the Assembly, had most assuredly arrived and been made known to the House, not indeed at the time of the first debate, but before the adjournment on Saturday evening. They knew such official information had come. They knew it was in the possession of the Speaker. They were careful, therefore, to keep away. Where were they likely to get officially such information as they pretended to want? In the public streets? In Major Boyd's house, from the Major's hand? or in the State-House, and from the Speaker? †

It was astonishing, another writer said, what short memories some of the rebels had. No name at the foot of the address was in bolder hand than that of William Findley. Did Mr. Findley forget that he was actually offered a seat in the convention, that he was put in nomination, that he told the House it would not suit him, as no wages were to be joined to it, and that withal he received two votes? If it were such a shocking thing to send rich Philadelphians to the convention, why did not the sixteen vote for Mr. Findley, who was from the country? How did it happen that Robert Morris and George Clymer and Thomas Mifflin, all citizens of Philadelphia, received the unanimous vote of the Assembly? What were the sixteen about? Why did Mr. Whitehill, whose name was also among the signatures of the rebels, rise in his seat and say that the choice ought to be confined to the great city because it would be too costly for country members to attend? ‡ This pertinent reply was signed by six members of the Assembly, and was held by the Federalists to be final.

---

* See Remarks on the Address, October 6, 1787. To the Freemen of Pennsylvania, by Federal Constitution, October 10, 1787. To the Freemen of Pennsylvania, by One of the People.

† To the Freemen of Pennsylvania, October 10, 1787.

‡ Remarks on the Address, October 6, 1787. Independent Gazetteer. See, also, American Museum for October, 1787.

Indeed, the reasons given by the deserters were soon met with such overwhelming evidence of untruth that they ceased to be seriously considered, and began to be made sport of. Whitehill, Findley, Judge Bryan, and their friends, were nicknamed the Antifederal Junto. The place where the sergeant-at-arms had found them was called Boyd's Cellar, and to their address a mock protest came out.* One squib told of a farmer near Philadelphia who had sixteen sheep, but sold one when he read the address, remarking that he did not want anything about his farm to remind him of the sixteen addressing assemblymen.† Another suggested the names Washingtonians for the Federalists and Shayites for the Antifederalists.

In the midst of this newspaper war the annual elections came on. It was some time before the returns from the back counties were known ; but when the last had been heard from, it appeared that the Federalists had been eminently successful. They had lost nothing and had gained much. Whitehill, who had signed the address as one of the sixteen, and had been put up for a seat in the council, was rejected by the voters of Cumberland county. Samuel Dale, whose name was also at the end of the address, and Antis, who made one of the Junto at Major Boyd's, shared a like fate in Northumberland. All three were replaced by avowed supporters of the Constitution. ‡

But the election to which the two parties looked forward with mingled feelings of hope and fear was still remote. Four weeks were to come and go, and during these weeks the Constitution was scrutinized with extreme jealousy. The objections of the Antifederalists were many and weak. The new plan was, in the first place, they complained, not merely, as it ought to be, a confederation of States, but a government of individuals. The sovereignty of the States was destroyed in its most precious parts. The form, indeed, of a republican

---

* Pennsylvania Gazette, October 10, 1787.

† Pennsylvania Gazette, October 10, 1787. See, also, a coarse poem, in Hudibrastic metre, called "On the running away of the Nineteen Members of Assembly from the House." Pittsburg Gazette, November 3, 1787.

‡ Pennsylvania Gazette, October 17, 1787. Just before the election, posters were put up in all the public places of the county denouncing Antis and Dale, and likening them to Satan on the Mount.

government was guaranteed to each by express words; but any one who would read the instrument carefully, and not suffer his understanding to be clouded with a multitude of fine phrases, could see that it was the form, and not the substance, that was promised. The most baleful results were certain to come. Either the Union, cemented with so much blood and treasure, would go down in a bitter struggle, or the sovereignty of the States would be gathered by silent encroachments into one huge aristocracy. For was it not clear that if two powers were given equal command over the purse of the people, they would fight for the spoils? Was it not clear that the weaker would in the end be forced to yield to the stronger? This power the new Congress was to have. Not only could it overawe the States, but it could reach down and lay hold on the life, the liberty, the property of the meanest citizen in the land. Yet there was no safeguard, no bill or declaration of rights. Trial by jury, too, that sacred bulwark of liberty, was done away with in civil cases, while the liberty of the press was not secured. In a word, every check to the ambition of wicked and intriguing men had been studiously removed. There were to be no more annual elections, there was to be no more rotation in office.* There was to be a standing army kept up in time of peace; a Prussian militia; general search-warrants; excise laws; customhouse officers; tide-waiters and cellar-rats; a free importation of negroes for one-and-twenty years; poll-taxes for the heads of the people if they chose to wear them, and death if they dared to complain.†

To these strictures some temperate and well-considered answers were put forth by the Federalists. It is idle, said one pamphleteer, to discuss the need of a central government. We have tried separate governments quite long enough to see and to feel that they are at best puny and weak. It is likewise idle

---

* These popular arguments against the Constitution are clearly stated under twenty-three heads in a paper called "Objections to the Proposed Plan of Federal Government. By an officer of the late continental army." See, also, George Mason's Objections to the Federal Constitution. New York Packet, November 30, 1787. And R. H. Lee's Objections in New York Journal, December 24, 1787. They were answered in detail by "Plain Truth."

† See Independent Gazetteer, October 6, 1787.

to discuss the right of the convention to frame the document called the New Plan. The gentlemen who sat at Philadelphia have not gone an inch beyond their authority. The States did not say to them, Do this, and do not do that; amend this article and strike out that. They were simply told to amend the Articles of Confederation. And amendment in parliamentary language means, if it means anything, add, diminish, or strike out the whole. The Constitution is before us. We have crossed the Rubicon; and the question now to be decided is, Shall we reject the New Plan and break up into twenty petty hordes and classes, each with a chief as despotic as he dares to be, or shall we adopt the Plan, unite, and form one strong and vigorous Government? Adopt by all means. No argument lodged against the Constitution is sound. Some have said a Bill of Rights ought to be added. It can, they hold, do no harm, and may do much toward quieting the minds of the people. Not so. It is not at all sure that such a bill will be quieting. To do so, it must contain everything the citizens of the United States claim as a national or a civil right. The omission of a single one will produce more heart-burning and dissent than is either felt or made on the present occasion. But suppose the convention had put out a Bill of Rights. Would not designing men have clamored as loudly against its presence as they now do against its absence? What! they would have exclaimed, do these exalted spirits imagine that the natural rights of man, the rights for which we have fought and bled, depend on their gracious concession? If a man owns six hundred acres of land and sells a half, must he take a release from the buyer for the other half? No! Then why is it necessary for a people to have a grant of natural rights from a government which derives every power it has from the grant of the people.

But nothing can please these grumblers. They mutter that one representative for thirty thousand men is too small, and call the House of Representatives a shred, a rag of representation. Suppose their complaints listened to, and the ratio raised to one for five, ten, twenty thousand, as they may choose. What then will happen? They will instantly cry out about the expense of a mobbish Legislature. What is it that makes men think there is safety in numbers? Who can defend large popular assemblies when he thinks how they are chosen? By our system we are as likely to put in fools as wise men, and knaves much rather than honest men. Is it not true that when such assemblies get together they flatter and cajole the people? To sit and hear the speeches made in such bodies one would think the good of the people was the only thing in pursuit. The word "people" is sounded from all parts of the House. "The people wish this." "The people wish that." "The people, Mr. Speaker, will never hear of the other." Yet these same demagogues who think so much of the people and cry for equal rights are quite willing, nay, insist, that the one hundred and eighty thousand freemen of Maryland shall have no more to say in the affairs of Government than the thirty thousand of Delaware, and that the great State of Virginia shall have no more votes than the little State of Rhode Island.*

While the idle reasons thus answered were passing from mouth to mouth among the Antifederalists, a great meeting of the Federalists was held at the State-House. Wilson addressed to them a speech remarkable among the speeches of that troubled time for coolness of reasoning and dignity of language. It had been urged of late, he said, that the Constitution was of pernicious tendency, because it tolerated a standing army in time of peace. A standing army had always been a popular topic of declamation. Yet he knew of no nation in the world which had not found it necessary and useful to keep up, even in seasons of the most profound tranquillity, the show of armed strength. To this America herself had been no exception. Was she not at that very moment maintaining cantonments along the banks of the Ohio? It had been said again that trial by jury was in civil cases abolished. This was a mistake. The business of the convention that framed the Constitution was not local, but general. It was not limited to the views and usages of a single State, but to the views and usages of thirteen States. When, therefore, the subject was up

---

* See a pamphlet entitled, Remarks on the Proposed Plan of a Federal Government, addressed to the Citizens of the United States of America, and particularly to the People of Maryland. By Aristides, 1788. Also, Thoughts on the Political Situation of the United States of America, in which that of Massachusetts is more particularly considered. By a Native of Boston, 1788.

for discussion, the members had found themselves beset with difficulties on all sides, and without a precedent to shape their course. Cases open to a jury in one State were not open to a jury in another. In none were admiralty cases, and such as were agitated in courts of equity, sent to a panel of twelve jurors. This lack of uniformity made it impossible to lay down a general rule. The convention had accordingly most wisely refused to discriminate, avowed the task too hard, and left it as it stood in the fullest confidence that no danger could ensue. He then went on to take up the other objections in their order.

The speech was widely read and called forth innumerable letters in reply. The Federalists held it to be a masterly performance, quoted it upon all occasions, and went so far as to say that Mr. Wilson would undoubtedly fill some high place under the new Government. The Antifederalists ridiculed it as "a train of pitiful sophistries, unworthy of the man who uttered them"; * and as they could not refute the sophistries, attacked the man. One lampooner abused him as Jimmy. Another vilified him under the name of James de Caledonia.† A third summed up a long list of objections with a sketch of his character, which was a strange mingling of truth with falsehood. Mr. Wilson, he allowed, was a man of varied learning. But, unhappily for him, he was never to be found on the popular side of any question. During the late war he had narrowly escaped hanging by the people. The whole tenor of his political behavior had always been strongly tinged with the spirit of aristocracy. His talents had ever been devoted to the patrician interest. It was easy to see in his lofty strut the lofty mind that animated him; a mind able indeed to plan and to do great things, but which unfortunately could descry nothing great beyond the pale of power or out of the glow of worldly grandeur. On what he was pleased to call the lower ranks of the people, on popular liberty and popular assemblies, he looked down with contempt. Men of a sublime mind were, he thought, born of a different race from the other sons

---

* Objections to the Proposed Plan of Federal Government. By an officer of the late continental army.

† Independent Gazetteer, March 4, 15, 18, 1783.

of men. To them, and to them alone, had high heaven given the reins of government. The fact that the new plan received the warm support of such a haughty aristocrat was the best reason in the world why it should be rejected by the people.*

To this it was answered that Mr. Wilson was not the only signer of the Constitution. His was but one in a long list of great names. Was it not signed by a Washington, a Franklin, a Hamilton? It was absurd to suppose for a moment that men whose patriotism had been tried by the hardest of all tests and never found wanting would on a sudden turn traitors. The name of the American Fabius was of itself enough to carry conviction to the mind of every honest Whig who hated tyranny, and whose blood boiled at the thought of a kingly government. Behold him in 1775 taking leave of his family and his home, and hastening to the relief of a distant and then unknown part of America. See him transforming and cementing a band of rustics into an army. Follow him to the field of battle, and see him first in danger and last out of it. Go with him into Valley Forge, and see him sharing the hunger, the cold, the fatigue of every soldier in the camp. Was there ever such fortitude in adversity? Was there ever such moderation in the hour of victory? Such tenderness at all times for the civil power of the land? But, above all, behold that glorious scene at Annapolis in 1783, when he gave up his commission, laid his sword at the feet of Congress, and took up the toils of a farmer on the banks of the Potomac. Was there ever such a man? Where was the villain black-hearted enough to say that Washington was recommending a Constitution ruinous to the liberties he had done so much to secure? Was the name, too, of Franklin to go for nothing? Think of him, in the seventieth year of his age, cooped up for weeks in the cabin of a small packet, tossed by the waves, exposed to danger on a sea crowded with British cruisers. See him winning from France that aid which in the end enabled America to close the war with glory and success. See him signing the treaty. See him coming home bent with age,

---

* Objections to the Proposed Plan of Federal Government. By an officer of the late continental army.

loaded with honors, and followed by the applause of all Europe. Was he the man to disgrace a long life spent in the service of his country by urging on his countrymen a bad form of government? The thing was absurd. To mention it was to refute it.*

But the Antifederalists were not, they maintained, to be misled by the glamour of great names. They had seen names as great as any at the foot of the Constitution subscribed to the present reprobated Articles of Confederation. Nay, some of the very men who had put their hands to the one had also put their hands to the other. Had not Roger Sherman and Robert Morris recommended the Confederation? If these patriots had erred once, was there any reason to suppose that they, or a succeeding set, could not err a second time? Had a few years added to their age made them infallible? Was it not true that the Federalists, who so warmly supported the new plan and would force it down the throats of their fellows because Franklin had signed it, affected to despise the Constitution of Pennsylvania which was the work of no one so much as of that same venerable patriot? † What, then, was the value of these boasted great names? Many of the signers, it was quite true, had done noble deeds. No one could forget the debt of gratitude the continent owed to the illustrious Washington. But it was well known that he was more used to command as a soldier than to reason as a politician. Franklin was too old. As for Hamilton and the rest of them, they were mere boys.‡ These unkind remarks called forth the highest indignation from the Federalists. But party spirit ran high, and it was not long before one of their antagonists went so far as to assert, that to talk of the wisdom of the Great Commander and the

---

* Address to the Freemen of Pennsylvania. By Federal Constitution. October 10, 1787.

† See Objections to the Proposed Plan of Federal Government. By an officer of the late continental army. Philadelphia, November 3, 1787. American Museum for November, 1787, p. 432.

‡ See a paper entitled, To the People of Connecticut. New Haven Gazette, December, 1787. Pennsylvania Gazette, December 26, 1787. Address to all Federalists, by Curtius. New York, September 27, 1787. Remarks on the late Insinuations against General Washington. American Museum for October, 1787, p. 385.

Great Philosopher was to talk nonsense; for Washington was a fool from nature, and Franklin was a fool from age.*

It must not, however, be supposed that all criticisms on the new plan of government were in a serious or ill-natured strain. No weapons of political fence were then such favorites with the multitude as ridicule and satirical allegory. Men who had neither the patience nor the wit to wade through the scholarly arguments of the Federalist, and who could see nothing but dry facts and barren statements in the pleasing letters of Tench Coxe,† would read and re-read with increasing delight a piece of foolery by Francis Hopkinson, or a neatly turned allegory by John Mifflin. Hundreds of carpenters and journeymen tailors who knew nothing about the needs of a Declaration of Rights, or the fitness of a national judiciary, were sure to have their minds strongly biassed by an address which, under the title of the New Roof, or the New Breeches, set forth the good points or the bad points of the Constitution in the language of their workshop or their trade. An unsparing use was therefore made of these means of instruction. One squib asserted that the ministers were against the Constitution to a man because there was nothing in it about the iniquity of going to plays and the duty of keeping holy the Sabbath day. Another did not see how any Protestant could support it, as it gave both Jews and Catholics an equal chance to become President.‡ A third represented that while it was bad enough to be without a Bill of Rights, it was much worse to be without a bill guaranteeing the right to eat and drink. A Turk remarked that he had read the Constitution without his spectacles, and was much taken with the likeness it bore to the Sublime Porte. The President would closely resemble in his powers the mighty Abdul Ahmed. The Senate would be his Divan; the standing army his Janizaries; the judges, unchecked by

---

* See a paper signed Centinel. Independent Gazetteer, October 5, 1787. For an attack on Few, Telfair, and Baldwin, of Georgia, see Independent Gazetteer, February 11, 1788.

† Letters on the Federal Government. By Tench Coxe, Esq.

‡ Pennsylvania Gazette, November 14, 1787. In the Massachusetts Convention, a Worcester farmer declared, on January 19, 1788: "There is no provision that men in power should have any religion; a Papist or an infidel is as eligible as Christians."

jurors, his Cadis; while the new-made Bishop Seabury would do very well for his Mufti.* Peter Prejudice complained of the ill-treatment he had met with at the hands of his tailor. He had sent an old pair of breeches to be patched, and, as they were full of holes both behind and before, had provided cloth enough for the mending. The wretched tailor had kept them four months, and, in place of repairing them, had declared they were worthless and made a new pair of small clothes out of the stuff sent for the mending. This was a vile conspiracy on the part of the tailor, the journeymen, and the apprentices, against the liberty of his thighs and knees.†

It is easy enough, said another, to get an endorsement to the Constitution. You have but to draw up a set of stirring resolutions, enclose them with a five-dollar note in a letter to a partisan in the country, and observe these directions: Select a small town, the more out of the way the better, and bid your friend get all the people into the tavern he can, and after expending the five dollars in grog, beer, and gin, and all have grown cheerful, put a hero in the chair and read the resolutions. Then ask all who disapprove to hold up their hands. Not one will have the impudence to do so. Thereupon have the resolutions signed as the unanimous resolve of a number of highly respectable inhabitants of the county. But see to it that no stir be made. Get the men together quietly, ten or twelve will do, and let them separate as soon as possible. Above all, avoid cheering and firing of cannon, lest the farmers get wind of what is going on and spoil the game.‡

Another offered a receipt for an Antifederal essay. Take, said he, well-born nineteen times, aristocracy eighteen times, liberty of the press thirteen times, negro slavery once, trial by jury seven times, great names six times, Mr. Wilson forty times, and, lastly, George Mason's hand in a cutting-box nineteen times.# Put these all together and dish them up at

---

* A Turk.  Independent Gazetteer, October 10, 1787.
† American Museum.        ‡ Independent Gazetteer, January 10, 1788.
    # "Redoubted Mason! challenger of steel!
    With *cutting-box*, in letters large, thy *Hand*
    Long time spread terror thro' th' astonished land."
                    Aristocracy, an Epic Poem, 1795, bk. ii, p. 13.

pleasure. These words will bear boiling, roasting, or frying, and, what is most remarkable of them, will bear being served a dozen times to the same table and palate.*

Another gave the political creed of every Federalist. The creed was a bold imitation of that of the Apostles, and, like that of Athanasius, ended with a fearful curse.† But in most of the squibs and pasquinades that filled the papers the Federalists were reviled under the name of "the well-born."

The term "well-born" was a contemptuous nickname given to the Federalists. It had just come into use, and was borrowed from an unfortunate expression in a late work of John Adams. That minister had for a year or more past spent much of his leisure time in the preparation of a defence of the constitutions of America. The book was meant to be a reply to a letter Turgot had written to Doctor Price, one of the few Englishmen of note who sincerely sympathized with America, and was at best but an ill performance. The most just criticism pronounced upon it was perhaps that of Madison. Men of learning, he said, would find nothing new in it. Indeed, the volumes were scarcely out at Philadelphia and New York before they were assailed as a vigorous defence not of the constitutions of America, but of the constitution of England. One sentence in the preface gave particular offence. In writing of the advantages of a triple form of government, a house of representatives, a senate, and a supreme executive, Mr. Adams took occasion to urge the imperative need of a senate. "The rich, the well-born, and the able will," he declared, "acquire an influence among the people that will soon be too much for simple honesty and plain sense in a house of representatives." The chief among them ought therefore, for prudence sake, to be separated from the mass and placed in a senate by themselves. He then went on to show, by the example of Chatham, that they could do less harm to the State in such

---

* Pennsylvania Gazette, November 14, 1787.

† New York Journal, December 12, 1787. For other squibs and satires, see Duetto sung by W—h—ll and F—dl—y, accompanied by G—e B—n with a Violoncello. Tune, "Darby, or the Poor Soldier." Independent Gazetteer, October 15, 1787. Also, "Cobbler, Stick to your Last," in American Museum for June, 1788.

a select body than in a more miscellaneous one.* The statement undoubtedly contained much truth. But many who admired the book as a whole felt great indignation at this remark, and the worst construction was put upon it. Mr. Adams was represented as recommending an aristocratic and therefore kingly form of government. That some men in the republic were richer than others, that some were more gifted than others, no one undertook to gainsay. But that some men were well-born and some ill-born was asserted to be utterly at variance with the principles laid down in the Declaration of Independence and the Articles of Confederation. It was hard, such was the language used by many, to tell which of the two sights was the more diverting: the British Government paying a British general † for writing such farces as " The Maid of the Oaks" during the siege of Boston, or the thirteen United States of America keeping an ambassador in England at the enormous cost of eight or ten guineas a day for no other purpose than to write eulogiums on the British Government under the pretext of vindicating the Governments of America.‡ He had been at great pains to exhibit the British constitution as the model of perfection. But America would scarcely canonize him for his sermon. The fact was, he had figured awhile at the brilliant Court of St. James, had become dazed at the splendor and comfort he saw about him, had put it down as the work of the English Constitution, and now imagined that the three-headed Legislature he recommended would be a fine thing for America. But he was mistaken. He should look beyond the Court. He should peer into the ditches which served as graves for multitudes of the dead, and under the hedges which served as habitations for multitudes of the living; he should go into the cottages of the poor and miserable, and see with how much parsimony the mechanics and laborers of England lived that they might maintain in ease a set of pampered lords; and when he had seen this he would not perhaps be quite so ready to persuade America to take the same

---

* See the Preface to A Defence of the Constitutions of Government of the United States of America. By John Adams. Ed. 1797, p. xi, or London ed., 1787, p. xiii. † The reference was to General Burgoyne.

‡ Independent Gazetteer, October 4, 1787.

road to greatness.* Throughout the book he was constantly harping on the balances, the balances, like the graces, the graces, of Lord Chesterfield. Yet could any man say that he had given a rational account of the balancing powers of a single State? † But it was peculiarly amusing to read his observations on the need of one of his three balancing powers being composed of the well-born. In what part of the United States, pray, were the well-born to be found? Was it Massachusetts? Or was it New England generally? ‡

While these questions were still unanswered, the election of delegates to the Pennsylvania State Convention took place. The Antifederalists were in high spirits, and confidently predicted success. The Junto, indeed, had been unwearied in its exertions. Whitehill, Findley, Smilie, and John Bryan, one of the justices of the Supreme Court, had repaired to their districts, and gone from place to place for the purpose of inflaming the country against the Constitution. The Quakers, in spots far removed from Philadelphia, were assured that the Society of Friends in the great city were bitterly opposed to the new plan, and angry that so noted a member of their body as Robert Morris had signed it. The small farmers were told that if they were tired of serving on juries, and wished to see tax-collectors helped by bands of soldiers taking their savings from them to support a standing army, a pack of national judges, and a three-headed Federal Government, they would do well to send a Federalist to the convention.

In some places this kind of reasoning had much effect. Smilie, Whitehill, Findley, and a score of other avowed enemies of the Constitution, were elected. But in Philadelphia the Antifederalists suffered a crushing defeat. Five delegates were to be chosen, and when the polls were closed at the State-House, it appeared that the name standing highest on the Federal ticket had received twelve hundred and fifteen votes, and the name that stood lowest eleven hundred and fifty-seven votes.

---

* New York Packet, October 6, 1787.

† Independent Gazetteer, October 4, 1787.

‡ See a paper by Biscayanus. Independent Gazetteer, June 28, 1787. For other similar criticisms, see Virginia Gazette, July, 1787, and Maryland Gazette, August 17, 1787.

Pettit, who was at the top of the Antifederal poll, got but one hundred and fifty, while Irvine, who was at the bottom, got but one hundred and thirty-two.  One name, indeed, ran far ahead of Pettit; but that was the name of a man well known to have but little sympathy with the party on whose ticket it appeared.  Franklin had not been put up by the Federalists as a delegate, partly, as was explained, because of his great age and feebleness, but chiefly because he then filled the high place of President of the Commonwealth, and it was not thought fitting that any officer of the State should occupy a seat in the convention.  He was therefore used by the Antifederalists as a decoy.  But the ruse was detected, and though some votes were drawn to the ticket, they were not sufficient to elect him.  He received two hundred and thirty-five.*

On the morning of the twentieth of November the convention met in the State-House.  The session was long and stormy.  Indeed, on more than one occasion it seemed likely that the members would stop disputing and betake themselves to blows, for the men of both parties had come up to town in an angry and determined mood.  The Federalists, united to a man, looked up to Wilson as their chief, assigned to him the burden of debate, and followed with alacrity and vigor his lines of attack.  Among the Antifederalists, Whitehill, Findley, and Smilie contended for the lead.  They were deeply hurt by what they were pleased to think the shameful behavior of the Assembly, and had made up their minds to leave no means untried to defeat the plans of James de Caledonia.  Every method of obstruction known to the time was therefore made use of.  Whole days were spent in discussing the meaning of words with which every member on the floor was as familiar as with his own name, and which were almost every day in his own mouth.  Whole hours were consumed in hurling abuse backward and forward from one side of the house to the other.  One writer in the Gazette complained that the convention had not got through six words of the Constitution after expending two thousand pounds, and that if this thing went on there would not, when the session was over, be a shilling left to pay the public debt and the wages of the

---

* Pennsylvania Gazette, November 14, 1787.

public officers.* Another † said with truth that five days had been taken up in disputing about the meaning of the two words "annihilation" and "consolidation"; that during this debate Findley had spoken for nine hours, Whitehill for seven, and Smilie for five, and that the gabble of these three men had cost the State a thousand pounds.

At last, on the twelfth of December, 1787, after a sitting of three weeks, the Constitution was ratified by a vote of forty-six to twenty-three. The Federalists were wild with joy. The next day, which was Thursday, the supreme council, the convention, and the faculty of the University of Pennsylvania went in procession to the Court-House, where the ratification was formally read to the crowd. When the reading was over, the bells of Christ Church rang out a merry peal, and a company of artillery fired a Federal salute. At three in the afternoon the members of the late convention sat down, in Epple's Tavern, to as fine a dinner as the host of that renowned inn could provide. In the evening some sailors and ship-carpenters put a boat, manned and rigged, upon a wagon, and drew it up and down the chief streets of the city. For a time the towns-people were at a loss to know what this meant. But the meaning soon became clear. A sailor who stood in the bow threw out a sounding-line and cried, sometimes, "Three-and-twenty fathoms, foul bottom," and sometimes, "Six-and-forty fathoms, sound bottom, safe anchorage." ‡ It was then noticed that the number of fathoms were meant to denote the strength of the two parties in the convention.

And now the minority published an address. It was not, they said, till the termination of the late glorious contest that any defects were discovered in the Confederation. Then of a sudden it was found to be in such a shocking condition that a convention was called by Congress to revise it. To this convention came a few men of the first character, some men more noted for ambition and cunning than for patriotism, and some who had always been enemies to the independence of the States. The session lasted four months, and what took place during that time no one could tell. The doors were closed.

---

* Pennsylvania Gazette, December 5, 1787.     † Ibid., December 19, 1787.
‡ Ibid., December 19, 1787.

The members were put under the most solemn engagements
of secrecy. The journals of the conclave were still hidden.
Yet it was well known that the meeting was far from peaceful. Some delegates had quitted the hall before the work
was finished; some had refused to lend their names to it when
it was done. But the plan came out in spite of this, and was
scarce an hour old when petitions, approving of the system
and praying the Legislature to call a convention, were to be
found in every coffee-house and tavern in the city. No means
were spared to frighten the people against opposing it. The
newspapers teemed with abuse; threats of tar and feathers
were liberally made. The petitions came in, the convention
was called by a Legislature made up in part of members who
had been dragged to their seats to make a quorum, and so
early a day set for the election of delegates that many people
did not know of it till the time had passed. The lists of
voters showed that seventy thousand freemen were entitled to
vote in Pennsylvania, yet the convention had been elected
by but thirteen thousand. Forty-six members had ratified the
new plan, yet these represented but six thousand eight hundred voters. Some freemen had kept away from the polls
because of ignorance of the plan, some because they did not
think the convention had been legally called, and some because they feared violence and insult. The ratification was in
their opinion worthless. Twenty-one of the twenty-three put
their names to the address.*

In the mean time, while the convention was listening to the
harangues of Smilie and Findley on the freedom of the press
and the right of trial by jury in the Federal courts, the Constitution was unanimously ratified by Delaware. This was done
on the sixth of December.† On the eighteenth of the month
the delegates to the New Jersey Convention came to the same
decision without a dissenting voice, and on the next day the
news was received with every manifestation of public joy, with
cheers, with discharge of cannon, and with military display.

One third the necessary number of States had now ratified,

---

* See a broadside entitled, The Address and Reasons of Dissent of the Minority of the Convention of the State of Pennsylvania to their Constituents.

† New York Journal, December 14, 1787.

and as the news spread westward, the Federalists of Carlisle determined to have a celebration. The last Wednesday of December was chosen as the day, and late in the afternoon bells were rung and guns fired, to bid the friends of the new plan assemble on the public square. Thither had already been brought a cannon and some wood for a bonfire. But scarcely had they begun to assemble when a body of men in military order were seen marching across the square. Many were armed with clubs or bludgeons, and when they came up to where Major Wilson was loading the cannon, they ordered him to stop, and made threats against any one who should attempt to light the fire. But Wilson, who had won his title of Major in the revolution, replied stoutly that if they did not like the proceedings they might go home. Thereupon several of the rioters snatched up barrel-staves that lay on the pile of wood, and hurled them at him. One struck him on the breast. In an instant Wilson seized a stick, rushed at the man who threw the stave, and struck him. The mob now attacked Wilson, threw him down, and would have beaten him to death had not a fellow-soldier lain upon his prostrate body and received some of the blows. This over, the cannon was spiked, wood heaped about it, and, with its carriage, committed to the flames. An almanac for 1788, which contained the Constitution, was then sent for and burned, after which the mob went off, cheering the minority, and shouting damnation to the majority of the convention.

Next day the Federalists, fully armed with guns and bayonets, returned to the square and celebrated for two hours. When they were done, the Antifederalists assembled, went to a vacant lot, brought out two effigies, labelled, "Thomas McKean, Chief Justice," and "James Wilson, the Caledonian," marched to the square, and burned them with every manifestation of delight.* Then they separated. But their anger had not begun to cool when it was yet more excited by news from Georgia.

Of all the States Georgia was, with the exception of Rhode Island and Delaware, the most insignificant. Her soil was

---

* An account of the riot is given in the Independent Gazetteer, January 9, 1788, and in the Boston Gazette, January 28, 1788.

rich.  Her area was indeed great.  But it was half a wilderness.  So sparsely was the land settled that the number of the
inhabitants fell short of the number of those who struggled
for a living on the barren hills of Vermont, and was not much
more than two and a half times as large as the population of
Philadelphia.  But the feeling of the Georgians was intensely
southern, and when it was known that the State Convention
had, on the second day of January, 1788, ratified the Constitution without an amendment or one dissenting voice, the hearts
of many firm Antifederalists failed them.  It seemed as if no
help was to be expected from the South, and they began with
great anxiety to wait for news from the East.

But so slowly was the news carried northward that the
delegates to the conventions of Connecticut and Massachusetts
had done their work and gone home before it was known in
Boston that one State beyond the Potomac had warmly approved the Constitution.  The State Convention of Connecticut broke up on the fourth of January, 1788, after a stormy
session of five days.  The vote stood one hundred and twenty-
eight Ayes to forty Nays, and was hailed by the Federalists with
delight.  Indeed, they had much reason to be pleased with
their success, for the Antifederalists were nowhere so strong as
in New England.  Rhode Island was completely given over to
them.  In Massachusetts and New Hampshire they had lately
been in open rebellion.  In Connecticut they had been upon
the point of taking up arms, had passed round a petition begging for a King, and had seriously meditated withdrawing from
the Confederation.  That the Federalists were able to command
so large a majority in so large a convention, chosen by men so
minded, seemed a great victory, and led the friends of government to look forward with renewed hope to the meeting of the
Massachusetts delegates.

The prospect in that State was not a pleasing one.  John
Hancock, the Governor, gave the Constitution at best but a
lukewarm support.  Samuel Adams was strongly opposed to
it.  Dane, one of the congressmen, had denounced it in the
halls of Congress, and Gerry, one of the delegates at Philadelphia, had stoutly refused to sign it.  With these men were
the small farmers, the petty traders, and the inhabitants of the

back-country villages and towns. For some time it was believed that the tradesmen of Boston were Antifederal. But they held a mass-meeting early in January, denied the charge, and declared that they had at the late election taken pains to choose men who should give a warm support to the plan.*

The character of the men who were thus expected to defend the Constitution is a sure index to the character of the great classes of the community among which the new system of government found favor. Of the one hundred and eighty-seven Federalists who sat in the convention, twenty-four were ministers whose piety and eloquence had made them renowned throughout the State, fifteen were members of the Senate, twelve were among the first lawyers of the bar, three were judges of the Supreme Court, one had been Governor of the State. There too were judges of probate, high sheriffs of the counties, and generals of the army; for Lincoln, Brooks, and Heath had been rewarded for their services in Shays's rebellion with seats in the convention.† Such an array of men, noted in every walk of life, might well have made the hearts of the boldest Antifederalists sink low within them. Yet it served but to render them more savage and determined than ever. Their objections, as was truly said by one who knew them well,‡ were not lodged against any part of the Constitution, but against the men who made it and the men who praised it. They were sure some injury was plotted against them. They knew the system was the work of the ambitious and the rich. "These lawyers," exclaimed Mr. Singletary on one occasion, "and men of learning and moneyed men that talk so finely and gloss over matters so smoothly to make us poor, illiterate people swallow down the pill, expect to get into Congress themselves. They mean to be the managers of the Constitution. They mean to get all the money into their hands, and then they will swallow up us little folk like the great Leviathan, Mr. President; yes, just as the whale swallowed up Jonah." "It is an old saying," observed Mr. Randall on another day, "that a good thing don't need praising; but, sir,

---

* Boston Gazette, January 14, 1788.  American Museum, January, 1788.

† Boston Gazette, January 14, 1788.  See a letter of Gorham to Madison.

‡ See a letter of King to Madison, January 27, 1788.

it takes the best men in the State to gloss the Constitution, which they say is the best that human wisdom can invent. In praise of it we hear the reverend clergy, the judges of the Supreme Court, and the ablest lawyers exerting their utmost abilities. Now, suppose all this artillery turned the other way, and these great men would speak half as much against it, we might complete our business and go home in forty-eight hours." *

Language such as this was heard every day from all parts of the House. Indeed, not a member from the country districts who got up to speak sat down without indulging in harsh words about lawyers and judges, rich men and rulers. One cautioned the House to be very jealous of rulers. Another reminded it how all the godly men of Scripture had failed, and declared that for himself he "would not trust a flock of Moseses." At last, as the session drew to a close, a weather-beaten face and a pair of sunburnt hands came to be looked upon as the outward signs of an Antifederalist, and so many were they that no one could say whether the number of the friends or of the enemies of the Constitution was the greater.

In this state of uncertainty both parties displayed unusual energy. All manner of means were used to secure votes. Meetings were held, petitions were signed, resolutions were drawn up, members were button-holed in the coffee-houses and on the street, and, when entreaty failed, there is some reason to believe, were offered money. Such a charge was actually made by the Boston Gazette.† A most diabolical plan, the writer said, was on foot to corrupt the members of the convention who opposed the Constitution. Great sums had been subscribed for the purpose in a neighboring State, and if the matter were looked into it might be found that collections were making nearer home. The matter was looked into, and the printers summoned to appear before the House. But they stayed away, pleaded sickness, and sent a letter full of lame excuses and apologies. The vote of one great man was, however, changed by fair means. Samuel Adams had come to the convention a firm Antifederalist, and had, by the influ-

---

* Elliot's Debates.    † Boston Gazette and Country Journal, January 21, 1788.

ence which his spotless character and illustrious public services
gave him, done more than the harangues of a hundred delegates to bring over the waverers to the side he believed to be
the right one.  But a number of shipwrights and mechanics, to
whom Adams was well known, determined to make an effort
to win him over to their side.  A great meeting accordingly
was held at the Green Dragon Tavern, resolutions passed in
support of the Constitution, and a committee named to carry
them to Adams.  Few on the committee were known to
him.  But at the head of it, with the resolutions in his
hand, stood that Paul Revere who, in the dead of an April
night thirteen years before, rode through the Middlesex villages
and towns, woke the sleeping patriots, and sent them with
their old Queen's arms to the fights of Concord and Lexington.  Adams took the paper, read it, and turning to Revere,
said : " How many mechanics were at the Green Dragon when
these resolutions passed ? "  " More, sir, than the Green Dragon
could hold," said Revere.  " And where were the rest, Mr.
Revere ? "  " In the street, sir."  " And how many were in
the street ? "  " More, sir, than there are stars in the sky." *

The mission was successful.  Adams gave way and changed
his vote, for he had to the end of his life a strong faith in
the hard sense and patriotism of the people.

The question of ratification was put to the convention on
the sixth of February.  One hundred and eighty-seven delegates
voted yes, one hundred and sixty-seven voted no.  When the
vote was announced in the street a yell of exultation went up
from the expectant crowd.†  The bells were rung.  The cannon were fired.  The whole night long bonfires blazed in the
streets.  The noise and the fires were indeed soon forgotten,
yet one testimonial of the joy of the people has come down to
our time, for on that day the Long Lane that ran by the meeting-house where the convention sat lost its name, and has ever
since been called Federal street.

---

\* Works of Daniel Webster, vol. i, p. 302.  See, also, Wells's Life of Samuel
Adams, vol. iii, p. 260.

† " The Boston people have lost their senses with joy."  Knox to Livingston,
February 13, 1788.  When the news came to New York, the pine-tree flag was
run up and a salute fired.

The Antifederalists were amazed, began to cast about them for the cause of their defeat, and soon found it in the post-office. Information, it was said, which surely would have changed many votes in Massachusetts and Connecticut, was purposely kept back. The productions of many able writers were detained till their point was lost. No one, for instance, at Boston knew that there had been a minority in the Pennsylvania Convention. Since the beginning of the year the printers in the eastern States had received scarce a single paper printed beyond the Hudson. For weeks past not a copy of the New York Packet or the Journal had been seen in Boston. Some were foolish enough to lay all the blame on the carriers. But it had at last become palpable to all that the well-born were at the root of the trouble, and were busy stopping the transmission of news from State to State by tricks in the post-office. The post-office was in their hands, and these sons of power had such control that not a paper printed in New York could find its way to Philadelphia or Boston, nor could the papers of the South get out of the offices in which they were dropped unless they contained fulsome praises of Franky's New Roof, which was to cover them and the office-hunters of the continent.*

For a time the Federalists contented themselves with flatly denying that they were guilty of such mean practices, asserting that Rufus King had carried the news of the dissent to the Massachusetts Convention,† and declaring that the Constitution was too good to be hurt by the slurs and sarcasms of Tory scribblers. But the matter was made so much of at Philadelphia and New York that steps were taken to disprove it. The Postmaster put forth a circular in which he said that the post-office, officially, had nothing whatever to do with the newspapers; that they had never been taken as mail matter, and had not till within a few years been admitted to the same portmanteaus with the letters. The post-riders and the postmasters were alone in the business. The riders carried the papers,

---

* These complaints and charges are set forth in the New York Journal, December 17, 1787; Independent Gazetteer, January 16, 1788; New York Journal, January 23, 1788; Independent Gazetteer, January 31, February 5, and February 8, 1788; Pennsylvania Gazette, March 5 and 26, 1788.

† Pennsylvania Gazette, April 9, 1788. See, also, some remarks on aristocratic influence in the Boston Gazette, November 26, 1787.

bargained with the printers about the postage, and put the
money in their own pockets as perquisites. The local postmasters, to oblige the public, undertook, not officially, to dis-
tribute the papers, and got, as the price of their labor, the
compliment of a paper from each printer. If, therefore, the
papers went astray, the printers must look to the post-riders,
not to him, for redress.*

Meanwhile, a paper was passed about for signature among
the printers at Philadelphia, stating that while the convention
was sitting the newspapers had come as usual. Many put their
names to it. But the printer of the Freeman's Journal, a violent Antifederal sheet, stoutly refused. The reason was demanded, and he named seven consecutive numbers of Green-
leaf's New York Journal which he said had not come during
the session of the convention. These he thought were particularly valuable, as in them were the effusions of Brutus, of Cato,
and of Cincinnatus. That containing the fifth number of the
address of Cincinnatus to James Wilson was put out at New
York on the twenty-ninth of November, but not a copy reached
Philadelphia till the fifteenth of December, two days after the
convention broke up. The reason was plain. Cincinnatus
gave some information about the way Robert the Cofferer had
conducted the finances of the Union, and struck at some arguments in favor of the New Roof. The paper, therefore, had
carefully been kept back. To this it might well have been said
that the absurd charges against the Constitution trumped up by
Cincinnatus were more than refuted in the able papers which,
in each issue of the Packet and the Gazette, came out over
the name of Publius.†

Nine years before, Hamilton brought the name of Publius
into notice at the foot of a series of letters on the misconduct
of a congressman. He now made it famous by subscribing it
to the numbers of the Federalist. The plan of these papers
was all his own, and seems to have started in his mind as soon
as he got back from the Convention at Philadelphia and be-

---

* Independent Gazetteer, March 24 and 26, 1788.
† The Federalist, Nos. I to IV, appeared in the Pennsylvania Gazette, October
24, 1787. The Federalist No. I appeared in the New York Packet, October 30,
1787.

held the evil fruits of the behavior of the deserters Yates and
Lansing.  The city for so many years strong on the side of
Government, the city that had sent petition after petition to
the Legislature recommending the impost, urging the regulation of trade by Congress, and denouncing the paper-money
schemes as iniquitous, now seemed given over to the Antifederalists.   The coffee-houses were crowded with men who
worked each other into fury by talking against the Constitution.   They denounced it as the "triple-headed monster."
They nicknamed it the "Gilded Trap," and declared it was
"as deep and wicked a conspiracy as ever was invented in the
darkest ages against the liberties of a free people." *   Politics, it was said facetiously, were so much the rage that two
friends could not meet on the street but one was sure to cry
out, "Hello, damme, Jack, what are you, boy? Federal or
Antifederal?" †   Not a Journal or Packet came out but it
contained a savage attack on the well-born, or the new plan.‡
On these monstrous slanders Hamilton looked down with a
just contempt, for he well knew that it was an unsafe thing to
answer a fool according to his folly.   Yet it seemed to him
much good might be accomplished and many votes secured if
the meaning of the Constitution were set forth in a series of
scholarly and dispassionate essays.   The idea pleased him, and
with all haste he laid it before three men in whose readiness to
help him he had great faith.

The names of two of the three were soon whispered about
among a little band of trusty friends.   But the secret was well
kept, and it was not till Hamilton had been long in his grave
that a public disclosure was made, and it became generally
known that some of the most admired numbers of the Feder-

---

* New York Journal, November 30, 1787.

† Ibid., December 27, 1787.

‡ Ibid., December 12, 1787; December 24, 1787.  Ibid., November 8, 1787.
In a play called The Politician Outwitted, the state of popular feeling in the city
is humorously shown in the dialogues between Loveyet, his servant Thomas, the
school-master Trueman, and the French barber.  That the absurd language in
which Trueman extols the Constitution is not overdrawn may be seen by com-
paring it with some passages in An Examination into the Leading Principles of
the Federal Constitution Proposed by the Late Convention.  By A Citizen of
America, 1787.

alist were by the hands of Madison and Jay. With them for a time was associated William Duer. Duer had come to the city a poor boy, had amassed a great fortune, had married a daughter of that Lord Stirling whose exploits in the revolutionary army are well known, and had come into some note as a politician. He sat in the first Provincial Congress, had been sent to the Assembly, and was one of the committee to frame a constitution for New York. He was twice ruined financially, and finally died, as the phrase went, on the limits of the jail. To the last, however, he was a firm friend to Hamilton, and when Hamilton rose to be Secretary of the Treasury, often acted as his agent. It was doubtless to this friendship rather than to political sagacity and knowledge of the subject that he owed his connection with the Federalist, for Hamilton must surely have foreseen that the Constitution could not at so early a day be interpreted by one who had taken no part in its formation, and who knew no more concerning it than was to be obtained from the perusal of its articles in the Gazettes. Duer, however, engaged to write.*

The first number, written by Hamilton as he came down the Hudson in the cabin of a sloop, appeared in the Independent Gazetteer of October twenty-seventh, 1787. From that day on till the fourth of April not a week went by but three or four Federalists came out. In April they ceased. By that time the labor of preparing them for the press had fallen entirely on Hamilton and Madison. Duer, after three brief pieces, wrote no more; and it was well he did not, for, though sprightly, they were judged ill performances. Jay, after the fifth number, fell sick, and contributed none till the sixty-fourth was reached. In the dullest months of winter the weekly tale of four numbers was a hard one. Indeed, it often happened that while the printer was setting up the opening lines of a copy the closing sentences were still under the pen. But when the spring opened, when the courts began to sit and the elections came on, Hamilton put aside the Federalist for other things. Nothing, therefore, was heard of Publius till the State Convention met at Poughkeepsie. Thereafter his writ-

---

* The papers contributed by Duer are published in the edition of the Federalist edited by J. C. Hamilton.

ing appeared regularly till the middle of August, and then stopped.

It is not easy for us to form a notion of the effect these papers had on the men who for the first time saw them in the Packets and Gazettes. We read in the most ancient of books how a stone rejected by the builders became the chief stone of the corner. Much the same has been the fate of the Federalist. To our ancestors it was little more than a huge Federal pamphlet.* To us it is the interpreter of the Constitution. There is no reason whatever to suppose that the followers of Clinton gave any more heed to the writings of Publius than did the followers of Hamilton to the foolery of Brutus and the nonsense of Centinel. Indeed, six administrations passed away and a new generation sprang up before it was discovered that the modest volume of essays about which editors and biographers were wrangling was after all the best commentary on the Constitution that could be written. That the work is a true statement of what the framers of that instrument meant it to be cannot be doubted. Two of the authors had sat in the convention, had taken part in the debates, had listened to the objections lodged against every article, and had come away with note-books and memories full of that precise information the task required. Nothing was left to conjecture; everything was known. They wrote, therefore, as having authority.

The same day the fifty-sixth and fifty-seventh numbers of the Federalist appeared the New Hampshire Convention met at Exeter. Great things were expected of it, for every mail that came from the East brought most comforting news. Many, by no means given to dreaming, went so far as to predict a ratification without one dissenting voice. But such a host of country members came up bidden to vote against the New Roof that, after struggling for a week, the Federalists were glad to consent to an adjournment till the third Wednesday in June.

This was the first check the Constitution met with, and as the account of it travelled slowly southward the friends of gov-

---

* The common opinion of the Federalist was well expressed by a senator who sat in the first Senate. Under date of June 12, 1789, he says: "Get if I can the Federalist without buying it. It is not worth it." Sketches of Debates in the First Senate, 1789-1791. By William Maclay.

ernment were much depressed.  The disaster could not, they said, fail to do harm in Maryland, where a convention was soon to meet.  The great men of Maryland were all against the Constitution.  Luther Martin,* whose influence was strong at the bar and in the Legislature, was hostile to it, and Samuel Chase, whom the people still loved for the bold way in which he had, when the State was a British colony, stood up and pleaded for the Declaration of Independence.  These men, they were sure, would use the action of New Hampshire to defeat the Constitution, or at least procure an adjournment of the convention; and if this were done, the chances of success were few indeed. But, most happily, their fears were groundless.  The eloquence of Martin and the boundless influence of Chase were vain. Nothing could persuade the electors that the New Roof was a bad covering, and more than sixty delegates pledged to ratification were chosen.

They assembled at Baltimore on the twenty-first of April. It was clear from the first morning of the session that the few Antifederalists who had secured seats could do nothing by their speeches and their votes.  But they determined to put on a bold front, talk much about the danger of being too hasty, about the wisdom of waiting till Virginia or New York, or some State more deeply concerned in the new plan, had been heard from, and watch for a seasonable opportunity to carry an adjournment.  So soon, therefore, as the discussion opened they began, by every means known to parliamentary law, to place obstructions and to cause delay, and when the patience of the members seemed utterly exhausted, brought in a motion to adjourn.  But the Federalists were on their guard.  Two thirds of them were indeed chafing at the harangues that kept them from their spring planting and ploughing.  But they had fully made up their minds not to separate till the Constitution had been ratified or rejected, and so the motion to adjourn was voted down.  A few days later, after sitting one week, the convention ratified the Constitution by a vote of sixty-three to eleven.

This immense majority of almost six to one more than re-

---

* Luther Martin's Genuine Information Furnished the Legislature of the State of Maryland is worth reading.

paired the damage done by New Hampshire. The hopes of
the Federalists rose higher than ever. It was now, they said,
easy to see where opposition to the Constitution would come
from. It would come from the Hudson and the East. That
section was a hot-bed of Toryism, of Shayism, of Antifederalism. Not a State to the south of the Hudson had considered
the new system of government but had adopted it unanimously
or by a glorious majority. But, happily, it was of small moment what men might think of the Constitution among the
hills of New Hampshire or in the stupid Dutch towns of New
York. Seven States had ratified it. The assent of but two
more was needed to make it the law of the land, and one of
these States would be South Carolina and one would be Virginia. Some one who knew the power which strange coinci-
dences and auspicious days have over the mass of men, went
further and declared that the outlook for the future was bright ;
that all was now well. For, by a wonderful stroke of fortune,
four of the five conventions next to meet were to do so on
days memorable in American history for signal displays of
patriotism and courage. The twelfth of May, 1780, was still
remembered in the South. On that day three thousand patriots, after a siege of three months, surrendered the city of
Charleston to nine thousand British. Now, after the lapse of
eight years, many of the same men were to meet in the same
city, on the same day of the same month, to deliberate whether
they would again give up the country to Tories, or assist in
founding a strong and safe government. This time there
would be no surrender. But the brightest of all days in the
American calendar were the seventeenth of June and the
fourth of July. On the former the conventions of New
Hampshire and New York were to meet. On the latter the
convention of North Carolina.*

The twelfth of May was looked forward to with interest.
South Carolina was, with the exception of Virginia, the most
populous, the most wealthy, the most commercial of the southern States. Indeed, on the list of exporting States her name
was third. The sums obtained for the pitch, the tar, the indigo,
and rice that each year came down the Ashley and the Cooper,

---

* New York Packet, June 10, 1788.

and went out in a hundred ships to Amsterdam and Boston, would, it was firmly believed, have sufficed to pay her share of the debt the nation bore with so much murmuring. Every one therefore felt anxious to know how the powers to regulate commerce which the Constitution gave to Congress would be received in so commercial a State. Early in January this matter had been severely examined by the Legislature, and in the course of some rambling talk on that occasion, Rawlins Lowndes, an alarmist, and a man of small attainments, had cautioned the House to have a care what it did. If the Constitution became the law, the East would, he said, get all the carrying trade into its hands, and lay the South under payment of whatever freightage it chose. The reply of Pinckney to this is curious. He did not attempt to deny that the eastern States would get the carrying trade, but declared that they would not abuse it. There was, he said, no danger of rivalry. There was every prospect of firm union. What one had the other wanted. The East had all the ships. The South had all the goods to put in them.* Some concessions must no doubt be made by the South to the East, for it was the nursery of seamen, and could in time of war furnish a navy to protect commerce. But the East, too, would have to give something to the South, for any blow struck at commerce must be felt by those whose business it was to carry the articles of commerce. The true course was to leave the whole matter to the General Government. †

The arguments of Pinckney had their weight, and so great a number of Federalists were sent to the convention that on the twenty-third of May the Constitution was ratified. The ayes were one hundred and forty, the nays seventy-three.

Eight States had now declared for the new plan. New Hampshire made the ninth. The convention that adjourned in February reassembled on the seventeenth of June, sat four days, and adopted the Constitution by a vote of fifty-seven to forty-six. But so hard was it to get word from that remote

---

* South Carolina during the years 1786–'87 gave employment to 947 ships, of a total burden of 62,118 tons. American Museum, June, 1789. During 1788 the ships cleared amounted to 56,977 tons. Massachusetts for the same time, 85,000. Virginia for nine months, 56,000. New York Packet, April 25, 1789.

† American Museum.

part of the Union that the express-riders who carried the news were met at Alexandria by the shouting, the bell-ringing, and the bonfires which announced that Virginia had given her assent and, as the phrase went, come under the New Roof.

The convention had assembled at Richmond on the second day of June, and for six weeks before the people had been in a state of unusual excitement. Such canvassing, such electioneering, such open bribing and threatening had never been known. The Federalists, who were strongest in the upper and lower country and about the northern neck, bestirred themselves but little, and trusted much in the goodness of their cause. But the Antifederalists, or the Antis, as they were nicknamed, who held the counties that lay in the middle country and along the south bank of the James, distinguished themselves by their violent and unscrupulous behavior. The turning-point, they openly boasted, was now come. Everything hung on Virginia. What she did, that also would New Hampshire and New York do, and it would go hard with them if they did not have a handsome majority at Richmond. Indeed, many of the most hopeful Federalists thought for a while that these vauntings would come true, for the canvass was carried on with alarming impudence and bitterness. Merchants and planters were solemnly assured, by men of no less note than Colonel Mason and Richard Lee, that the eastern States were eager to get control of the carrying trade, and that, as they would have a majority of votes in the new Congress, they would surely get control. Letters were sent to the Kentucky district positively declaring that the East was ready to close the Mississippi in return for Spanish help in securing foreign treaties. Even church matters were brought in, and numbers of well-disposed tax-payers were shocked and alarmed to hear that a religious establishment was to be set up under the new Government.

Had such reckless statements been confined to the mouths of county politicians and pot-house orators, they might have sufficed to alarm some weak and timid men, change a few votes, and send a few Antifederal delegates to the convention. But no one made so free a use of them as Patrick Henry, and Henry was a man not to be despised. He was of Scotch blood, and connected through his father, an Aberdeen man, with that

David Henry who followed Cave in the management of the Gentleman's Magazine, and with the famous William Robertson who wrote the first readable history of America. But it was from his mother, a Virginia woman, that he inherited the fluent and sonorous eloquence which made him great and powerful. The most obsequious of his biographers has been unable to find that he was in his youth precocious, or gave any sign of the possession of this wonderful gift. He was indeed the most idle, the most shiftless, the most slovenly and awkward lad in Hanover county. He was thirty before he gained a reputation for knowing anything more useful than where the largest fish were to be caught, or a fox unearthed with the least pains. At fifteen he was behind the counter of a country store measuring off yards of calamancoes and weighing out pounds of snuff. At sixteen he was attempting to keep a store of his own, but was really learning to fiddle and to play on the flute. At eighteen he was married and on a farm. At twenty-one he was back once more at store-keeping, and at twenty-four he was a ruined man. Then it was that the idea of becoming a lawyer first occurred to him. In six weeks he read Coke upon Littleton and the Virginia Laws, went up to Williamsburg, appeared before the examiners, and, with many promises on his part and many misgivings on theirs, got his license. With his license he went back to Hanover Court-House, where his father-in-law kept an inn, and for three years tended travellers and drew corks.

The clergy of the established church had in the meanwhile fallen out with the Legislature on the question of their stipends of tobacco, and John Camm's vigorous pamphlets, "The Two-Penny Act" and "The Colonels Dismounted," were in every hand. The clergy were clearly in the right, and when one of the rectors in Hanover county brought suit against the tax-collector and filed a demurrer, the court sustained it. In this pass the counsel for the collector deserted him, and in his distress he turned to Patrick Henry. Henry took the case, argued it for near an hour, and affected the jury so powerfully that, clearly in defiance of the law, they brought in a verdict for the defendant. From that day forth Henry was a marked man. His practice increased, money flowed in, and in no long time he was made a

member of the House of Burgesses.  From the House of Burgesses he went as a delegate to the first Provincial Congress,
was chosen the first republican Governor of Virginia, and was
offered a seat in the convention that framed the Constitution he
now so fiercely attacked.

But, most happily, the contest in which he was engaged was
one for which the great powers of his mind quite unfitted him.
No one spoke so well or reasoned so badly as Henry.  He was
to the end of his days an orator and an actor, and nothing more.
Had he, indeed, gone upon the stage, he would have rivalled
Garrick.  The attitudes which he struck, the way in which he
walked, his gestures, his sonorous voice, and the wonderful play
of his features must, if we may trust the descriptions of those
who heard him, have been most remarkable.  He would have
been fine as Othello, and have done well as Sir Andrew Ague-
cheek.  But a statesman he certainly was not.  Whatever could
be done by eloquence he could do.  He could deliver a fourth-
of-July oration, move a jury, conduct a canvass, or entertain
the Legislature with tirades on liberty and the rights of man
in a way that would have excited the envy of Pitt and Burke.
When, however, the end sought was to be gained not by good
speaking, but by good reasoning, he was unable to cope with
men whose limited vocabulary, whose mouthing and stammering and monotonous tones it was painful to hear.

In the convention, therefore, though he came up as the
leader of the Antifederalists, he was much less formidable than
during the canvass.  Rants on the iniquity of shutting up the
Mississippi, on the dangers of allowing the Indiana claim, on
established churches and monarchies, might impose on the men
of the Ohio valley, but they were lost on men long accustomed
to weigh evidence carefully, who had sat in Congress, who were
familiar with the secret history of the Spanish negotiations,
and had taken a part in framing the Constitution.  No arguments that Henry could bring forward could refute the close
reasoning of Madison and the careful statements of Randolph
and Marshall.  His speeches, in truth, were a singular mingling
of appeals to God and the American spirit, with such reasons
for hating the Constitution as were every night hiccoughed out
in the taverns, or printed every week in the Chronicle.  Would

Virginia give to Congress a right to collect taxes, duties, impost, and excise? Were Virginians about to abandon their country to the depredations of excisemen? Did they intend that any Assembly but the General Assembly should tax them, or any tribunal but the courts of Virginia adjust their disputes?* This was precisely the style of Henry.

The moment the Speaker recognized him he fell to abusing the new plan. It was a pernicious, an impolitic, a dangerous system. It was a great consolidated Government. Under it neither the rights of conscience, nor the liberty of the press, nor trial by jury could be secure. An aristocracy of the rich and the well-born would spring up and trample on the masses. A standing army would do the will of tyrants. The Mississippi would be closed, and the Ohio valley given up to red men and buffalo. The Indiana claim would be revived, and twenty thousand families in northwestern Virginia be turned out of their cabins in a single day. These and a hundred other arguments just as shallow and absurd he continued for ten days to set forth with all the eloquence and ingenuity of which he was master. They won him, indeed, no converts; but they were alarming enough to keep the men from the Kentucky district from deserting him and going over to the Federal side.

At last, on the fourteenth of June, the House determined that what Henry had called the discussion at large should stop, and ordered the text of the Constitution to be taken up clause by clause. The debating under this rule took up the time till the twenty-fourth. On the morning of that day Wythe, who was chairman of the committee of the whole, left his seat, came down into the body of the House, and moved to ratify, with such amendments as it should seem best to make. The instant his seconder sat down Henry rose and moved as a substitute that, before ratifying, a Bill of Rights and some twenty amendments he had made ready should be referred to the other States for consideration. Two more days were then spent in useless wrangling, and when the vote was counted the chairman declared that the nays had it by eight

---

* See a piece by Cato Uticensis in the Virginia Independent Chronicle, October, 1787.

majority. On the question to ratify, which was then called for, two members came over to the Federalists, and the majority rose to ten. One hundred and sixty-eight delegates were present. The convention next day broke up.

The same night the post-riders brought word of the ratification to Alexandria. In that little town almost every man was a Federalist, and by common consent the next day was set apart for festivity. The near prospect of a strong and lively Government would of itself have been enough to call forth every manifestation of public joy; but the delight of the townsmen was given a keener zest by the recollection that they were the first to rejoice over the adoption of the new plan; that the day was the anniversary of the battles of Monmouth and Sullivan's Island; and by the arrival, two hours before dawn, of a post bringing word of the assent of New Hampshire.*

Philadelphia was the first large city to receive the news, and there the popular rejoicings put on a more impressive form.† It was known so early as the twenty-sixth of June that New Hampshire had assented; but every one felt that the Constitution could never be firmly set up while so great and populous a State as Virginia held out. When, therefore, the post that came in on the evening of the second of July brought letters telling that Virginia was Federal, the doubts and fears that had tormented men for seven months were put at rest. It was instantly determined that the coming fourth of July should be made the occasion for a great display of Federal spirit; that there should be speeches and toasts and a procession, and that the procession, it was said, should be such a one as the continent had never seen.

---

* See a letter from Washington to Charles Cotesworth Pinckney.

† While the Philadelphians were rejoicing over the good news, an event took place which at another time would have aroused little interest, but, in the excited state of public feeling, was thought most significant. Oswald, a rank Antifederalist and editor of the Independent Gazetteer, had been sued by one Brown for libel. His arrest took place on the day the news of the ninth ratification came, and was instantly denounced by the Antifederalists as a vile Federal scheme. When, a few days later, the court convicted him of contempt for refusing to answer some question, the cry was raised that this was another type of the tyranny that might be expected under the new plan. See Independent Gazetteers for July 1, 1788, and later.

Not a moment was wasted, and by the night of the third all was ready. The pavements had been swept, the trees had been lopped. Ten ships had been procured, dressed in bunting and anchored in the Delaware, one at the foot of every street from North Liberties to South street. They were typical of the ten ratifying States. As the first rays of the morning sun came over the eastern bank of the Delaware, the ship Rising Sun, which lay at the foot of Market street, fired a national salute, the bells of Christ Church rang out, and each of the ten vessels on the river ran up to her mast-head a broad white flag which, spread by a stiff breeze from the south, displayed the name of the commonwealth for which she stood. Meanwhile, the procession was fast forming in the city, but the sun had been four hours up before it began to move. Every trade, every business, every occupation of life was represented. There were saddlers and gunsmiths, stone-cutters, tanners, brewers, merchants, doctors, shipwrights, and stocking-makers. The cordwainers sent a miniature shop. The rope-makers marched each with a bunch of hemp and a piece of rope in his hand. The Manufacturers' Society delighted the crowd with the spectacle of a huge wagon drawn by ten horses and neatly covered with cotton cloth of their own make. On the wagon were a lace loom, a printing mill, a carding and a spinning jenny of eighty spindles. Compared with the cunningly and exquisitely wrought machines now to be found in the mills and factories of New England, they would seem rude and ill-formed. But they were among the newest inventions of the age, and were looked on by our ancestors as marvels of mechanical ingenuity. There, too, were represented in succession Independence, the French Alliance, the Definitive Treaty, the Convention of the States, and the Federal Roof, a huge dome supported by thirteen Corinthian columns. But the cheering was never so loud as when the Federal ship Union came in sight. She had, it was whispered among the crowd, been built in four days. Her bottom was the barge of the ship Alliance, and was the same that had once belonged to the Serapis and had been taken in the memorable fight by Paul Jones. She mounted twenty guns, and had upon her deck four small boys, who performed all the duties of a crew, set sail, took a pilot on board, trimmed the sheets to suit the breeze, threw out the lead, cast anchor at Union Green, and sent off dispatches to the President of the United States. When the end of the procession had passed Union Green, Wilson gave the address. Hopkinson wrote the ode which, printed in English and in German, was scattered among the people and sent off on the wings of carrier pigeons to the ten ratifying States. That night the streets of the city were bright with bonfires and noisy with the shouts of revellers who had taken too many bumpers to the French King, to the American Fabius, and the builders of the Federal Roof.* But the rejoicings did not end with the day. For months afterward the newspapers gave unmistakable evidence of the pleasure with which the great mass of the people contemplated the new plan. The word Federal became more popular than ever. It was given by town committees and select-men as names to streets in numberless towns, and was used as a catchword by tradesmen and shopkeepers. One advertisement informed the public where the Federal minuet was to be obtained.† In another a dancing-master announced that he would give instruction in the Federal minuet. A third invited gentlemen who visited the city to put up their horses at the Federal stables. A number of designs were suggested for a lady's Federal hat.‡ Federal punch became the drink of the day. In the shipping news, in the list of packets that had arrived and brigs that had sailed, appeared notices that the sloop Anarchy, when last heard from, was ashore on Union Rocks; that the scow Old Confederation, Imbecility master, had gone to sea; and that on the same day the stanch ship Federal Constitution, with Public Credit, Commercial Prosperity, and National Energy on board, had reached her haven in safety.#

Elsewhere the day was less peaceably kept. At Providence a riot seemed imminent. On the twenty-fourth of June, when

---

* An account of the procession is given in the Pennsylvania Gazette of July 9, 1788. See, also, Pennsylvania Gazette Supplement No. 3,032.

† Federal Gazette, October 15, 1788.

‡ United States Chronicle, June 19, 1788. Federal Gazette, October, 1788.

# United States Chronicle, July 17, 1788. Massachusetts Centinel, August, 1788. Connecticut Courant, September, 1788. Gazette of the United States, May 13, 1789.

the news of New Hampshire's ratification came, all business was stopped, the church-bells rung, and a great rejoicing held on Beacon Hill.* It was there determined to have a still finer celebration on the fourth of July. A large plain in the cove just without the town was chosen as the place, a great tent put up, an invitation inserted in the Chronicle bidding the farmers to come, and the largest ox the butchers could find, roasted whole. But the farmers were strongly Antifederal, and while the citizens of Providence were preparing the feast, the countrymen were making ready to spoil it. Toward evening, therefore, on the night of the third, they began to gather, with arms in their hands, near where the ox was roasting. Early on the fourth, when about a thousand were assembled, the townsmen sent out a committee to confer with the leaders and find out what was wanting. To their surprise, they saw at the head of the mob three members of the Assembly, and a judge of Know Ye fame. The judge declared the purpose of his followers to be to break up the festivities. The committee reminded him that the day was a public one, that the land where they stood was private property, and that it was a great stretch of power to surround and disturb with guns and bayonets people who were eating and drinking and making merry on their own land and at their own expense. The judge was then civilly requested to state his grievances. His friends would, he said, be satisfied if thirteen cannon were fired and thirteen toasts drunk, and none of them in honor of the nine ratifying States. He was told that thirteen cannon had been fired at sunrise, and thirteen toasts were to be drunk. These were then shown him. He insisted that the words of one of them should be changed from "the nine States" to "the day," which was done. He then went off. And now the mob were at a loss what to do. They had no food with them, for their leaders assured them they should carry off the ox. Some, therefore, hid their guns in the brush, came over to the cove, and joined in the Federal rejoicings. Some bought food at the tavern, and some went home tired, hungry, and ashamed. On the fifth came the news of Virginia's ratification, when a new procession

---

* United States Chronicle, June 26, 1788.

was formed, and more cannonading and bell-ringing indulged in.*

At Albany some blood was shed. When the news from Virginia came, the friends of government determined to have a parade. But being warned that such a performance would greatly offend the Antifederalists, they gave it up and contented themselves, on the morning of the fourth, with ringing the bells and firing ten guns at the fort. They had, however, scarcely separated when the Antifederalists, led by Peter Yates and Abraham Lansing, came in a body to the same spot, discharged thirteen guns, and burned the Constitution. They then went to dinner at Hilton's Tavern. The Federalists dined at Lewis's, and when the cloth was removed, the whole party being pretty full, it was agreed to raise the Constitution where Yates and his band had burned it. While some hastened to get a copy of the document, others went to the pine-brush, cut down a tree, took it to the fort, nailed the Constitution to the top of it, and raised it on the very spot where the ashes of the morning's fire were yet smouldering. Ten guns were then fired, a procession formed, and the Constitution, made fast to a tall pole, was carried before the pine-tree through the streets of the town. Meanwhile, the diners at Hilton's had filled their pockets with stones and set off in search of their opponents. They met them in a narrow lane, and in a moment the air was thick with stones, bricks, and pieces of iron. For a while the fight was hot; but the Antifederalists soon broke and ran.†

While Peter Yates and his friend Abraham Lansing were burning the Constitution and stoning the Federalists at Albany, another Yates and another Lansing, animated by the same spirit, were urging on the faction at Poughkeepsie. There the State Convention was assembled. For two weeks the session had been dragging along, yet the business of the meeting seemed as far from a speedy ending as on the day when Clinton was

---

* See a letter from a gentleman in Providence to his friend in Boston. New York Packet, July 18, 1788. Also, Staples's Annals of Providence, pp. 329–335. United States Chronicle, July 10 and 17, 1788. United States Chronicle, July 31, 1788.

† Extract of a letter from a gentleman in Albany, dated the 7th inst., to his friend in this city. New York Packet, July 11 and 18, 1788. The battle was afterwards ridiculed in The Albaniad, an Epic Poem. By Pilgarlic, 1791.

put in the chair.  The debates had been savage.  The delegates had not been sparing of abuse ; much bad feeling had
been stirred up, but no work done.  The Antifederalists could
indeed, had they been so disposed, have settled matters and
gone home in a week, for they came up to the convention
in such numbers that at least two thirds of that body were of
their party.  They were much more inclined to delay than to
hasten a vote.  Clinton kept them from ratifying the Constitution.  Fear kept them from rejecting it.  They were well
aware that if the instrument before them were thrown out, yet
adopted by nine States, New York would be left out of the
Union, and that to be left out of the Union meant endless
misery and expense.  It meant treaties, it meant a navy, it
meant a string of forts along a frontier still to be wrested from
the British, it meant ministers at every foreign court, consuls
at every great seaport abroad, and an army of tide-waiters and
gaugers at every dock at home.  Bitterly as they hated the
Constitution, they were not ready to pay such a price for the
privilege of rejecting it.  They did not dare to go back to
those who sent them and say that the Confederation was broken
up, that New York was a free and independent State, and that
to support this new dignity the taxes, already unbearable,
would have to be increased twenty-fold.  They determined,
therefore, to await the action of the other States.  Nor did
they wait long.

On the twenty-fourth of June word was brought that New
Hampshire had ratified.  The news was discouraging, but it
did not break the resolute spirit of Clinton and his band.  New
Hampshire was a very little State, and a poor one.  Her population was small and scattered, she had no ships, she grew
nothing fit for commerce.  The whole number of human beings
that struggled for a living on her hundreds of thousands of acres
was scarcely four times as great as that crowded together on
the four square miles that made the city of New York.  And
of these many thousands had never in their lives heard the
roar or smelled the salt air of the sea, or looked on a sheet of
water larger than Lake Winnipiseogee.  To track bears, to
hunt elk and deer, to cut down trees, make potashes, and raise
a little Indian corn, was in the opinion of New Yorkers the

chief occupation of New Hampshire farmers. Whether such a State came into the Union or stayed out of the Union was to them of small moment while two such States as Virginia and North Carolina were firmly Antifederal. And then they began to have dreams of a league. Perhaps it might be possible to form with the South a new confederation on much the same principles as the old. And what, they said proudly, what a confederation that would be! In it would be many of the largest cities, the finest seaports, the greatest, the most prosperous, the most commercial States on the continent. Its power would be irresistible. In a little while it would have the commerce of America under complete control. New York, possessed of the Hudson and the Mohawk, held the key to the Canadas and the great lakes. Virginia and North Carolina owned the rich districts that lay along the Ohio and the Mississippi, and would manage the trade of that splendid region. To make a treaty with Spain would be a matter of a few months. To make treaties abroad would be a matter of a few years; and then would go out each twelvemonth from New York, from Alexandria, from Norfolk, from Wilmington, from some seaport yet to be built on the shores of Pamlico Sound, hundreds of ships freighted with furs, with tobacco, with grain, with indigo, pitch, tar, and rice. But unhappily, in the midst of their magnificent day-dream, came word that Virginia had ratified. Strong hopes were now entertained that the Antifederalists would give way. But they seemed as determined as ever not to surrender, and when a resolution was offered to adopt the Constitution after the manner of Virginia, threw it out by a great vote. The next three weeks were spent in bickering, in higgling, and in endeavoring to frame some form of ratification in which much should be said yet nothing meant. At last, when the patience of each party was all but worn out, the Clinton men announced that they would consent to a compromise. They had, they said, some amendments to offer, and were ready to do either of two things. They would adopt the Constitution with the express condition that the amendments should be made part of it, or they would adopt the Constitution with the reservation of a right to quit the Union if at the end of a certain time the amendments were not accepted.

More they would not do.   This offer, which was declared to
be a most generous one, was far from inviting.   But such was
the zeal of the Federalists to bring the State into the Union at
once that they were for accepting it.   Indeed, so much encouragement was held out that a plan for a conditional ratification
was laid before the House, and, to the surprise of many, was
stoutly withstood by Hamilton and thrown out.   Hamilton had
in the meanwhile been consulting with Madison.*   Everything
was now to be done over again.   The Antifederalists, knowing
their strength, and angry at the slight put upon their proposition, assumed a haughty manner, talked much of flatly rejecting the Constitution, and for a time could not be brought to
listen to reason.   Indeed, several days were wasted in talking
and factious squabbling before both parties agreed upon a plan
which of all the plans devised was the worst.   A resolution
was first presented to the House calling for a new convention
of the States to amend the Constitution ; and when the President put the question, every member present voted Aye.   An
act of ratification, which was little more than a jingle of
words, was then brought in, a long declaration of rights
prefixed, thirty-two amendments tacked on, and in this form
passed.

In New York city the Federalists, who heard the news
about nine on the evening of the twenty-sixth, pretended to
be thoroughly pleased, fired cannon, formed a procession, and
went shouting and cheering through the streets to the houses
of the Federal members of the convention.   But before they
dispersed, some among them disgraced the good cause by a
wanton attack on the office of the New York Journal.   The
issue of the twenty-fourth of July contained some remarks
ridiculing the Federal procession on the day before.†   The
paragraph was no more galling than a hundred others that
had been written on the Federalists, nor worse than their own
party editors were constantly printing about their opponents.
But the potters were particularly incensed at the sport made
of their display in the Federal procession, and some of them
being in the crowd, raised the cry of revenge.   A number ac-

---

* See a letter of Madison to Hamilton, in Works of Hamilton, vol. i, p. 465.
† New York Journal, July 24, 1788.

cordingly surrounded the office, beat in the door, and carried off a quantity of type.*

Beyond the limits of the city the shameful concession at Poughkeepsie was heard with regret.

It was felt everywhere that the victory was with the Antifederalists. The friends of the Constitution openly declared there was no need of compromise. Their brethren of New York should, they said, have stood firm. The Constitution was safe. Ten States had in the most handsome manner adopted it, and steps were, at the very moment the final vote was counted at Poughkeepsie, being taken to put it into operation at New York. The more dignified, the more honorable course would under such circumstances have been to turn a deaf ear to the offers and suggestions of the enemy, firmly refuse to give one inch of ground, and let them, if they dared, go out of the Union. That moment a reaction would have begun. Hundreds, nay, thousands, of simple-hearted, well-meaning Antifederalists, who, while it was still doubtful if nine States could be found to accept the Constitution, were its bitter foes, would, the instant they saw the New Roof up and completed and New York not under it, have become its warm friends. New fears, new dreads would have tormented them; a great cry for another convention would have gone up, and before a year was out the Constitution would have been ratified by a splendid majority, despite the machination of Clinton and his band. But all this was impossible.

The circular letter of Clinton urging the States to call a new convention to amend the Constitution was made ready with all speed, came forth, and was received with delight in North Carolina and Pennsylvania.† The convention of North Carolina assembled on the fourth of July, and before it had been many hours in session a motion was made by an Antifederalist to put the question of ratification. It was certain, he said, that every member who heard him had made up his mind.

---

* American Museum, vol. iv, pp. 100, 102. Life of General John Lamb, by Leake, pp. 333, 334.

† In answer to this call a convention met at Harrisburg in Pennsylvania, and proposed twelve amendments to the Constitution. Among the delegates from Western Pennsylvania was Albert Gallatin.

It was therefore a matter of votes and not of arguments which way the question went, and much time and expense would, he thought, be saved by having the votes counted at once. The general opinion seemed to be decidedly in favor of voting at once.  But one of the Federalists, in a vigorous harangue, pointed out with such force the impropriety of haste in so weighty a business that the motion was withdrawn.

The House then went into a committee of the whole, took up the Constitution clause by clause, and was deep in the debates when reports of the ratifications by Virginia, by New Hampshire, by New York, and the letter of Clinton, came in hard upon each other.  For a moment the delegates were dumfounded.  What to do they did not know.  They had not the impudence to reject the Constitution which eleven States had accepted.  They had not the courage to ratify it, for they had been expressly told by their constituents not to do so.  From this dilemma some brain, fertile in expedients, suggested the way out.  A bill of rights and a long list of amendments were drawn up after the manner of Virginia and referred to the convention proposed by New York.  In a House of two hundred and sixty-six members the majority for the bill was one hundred and two.  On the second of August the convention, after ordering a copy of the amendments to be sent to Congress, adjourned.*

---

* The dates of ratification of the Constitution by the Thirteen States are:

Delaware, December 6, 1787.  Unanimously.

Pennsylvania, December 12, 1787.  46 to 23.

New Jersey, December 18, 1787.  Unanimously.

Georgia, January 2, 1788.  Unanimously.

Connecticut, January 9, 1788.  128 to 40.

Massachusetts, February 6, 1788.  187 to 168.  Proposed nine amendments.

Maryland, April 26, 1788.  63 to 11.  Minority proposed twenty-eight amendments.

South Carolina, May 23, 1788.  149 to 73.  Proposed four amendments.

New Hampshire, June 21, 1788.  57 to 46.  Proposed twelve amendments.

Virginia, June 25, 1788.  89 to 79.  Proposed a Bill of Rights and twenty amendments.

New York, July 26, 1788.  30 to 27.  Proposed thirty-two amendments.

North Carolina, November 21, 1789.  Declaration of Rights and twenty-six amendments.

Rhode Island, May 29, 1790.

But, by the time this paper reached New York, every-thing had been done by the Congress about to end to put the new Government into operation. The first Wednesday in January, 1789, had been named as the day for choosing the presidential electors, the first Wednesday in February for the meeting of the electors, and the first Wednesday in March for the assembling of the Senate and House of Representa-tives.* This latter day happened in the year 1789 to fall on the fourth of the month, and hence was it that three years later Congress decreed that each presidential term should be-gin on the fourth of March next following the day on which the votes of the electors were cast. In obedience to this law, our Presidents have ever since, with seven exceptions, been sworn into office at noon on the fourth of March. Four times the Vice-President has succeeded to the office on the death of the President. Three times the day named by Congress for holding the inauguration has fallen on a Sunday, and the oath was therefore taken on the fifth. The first of these occasions was in 1821. The other two have followed at intervals of twenty-eight years.

To fix upon a date whereon the Constitution should be-come the law of the land was easy. But a place for the meet-ing of the officers of the Federal Government was not chosen without a struggle. It was agreed by the people everywhere that the spot should be central, and that central should be understood to mean the middle States; but in the middle States were many great and opulent cities, and which had the best claim to be called central was hard to say. What did the term mean? Should it be interpreted in a geographical sense? Or should it be construed with reference to popula-tion? Some declared that distance was the thing to be con-sidered, and urged Trenton. Trenton had, they said, been the scene of a most glorious victory, had already been the seat of Congress, was well inland, and therefore out of reach of ships of foreign powers, and was about as far from the southern border of Georgia as from the eastern limits of the province of Maine. Some maintained that as more men dwelt south of the Potomac than north of it, the city selected should be on

---

* Pennsylvania Gazette, September 17, 1788.   Journals of Congress.

the shores of Chesapeake bay, and strongly recommended Baltimore.  A few held for Philadelphia.  Others would have it at
Lancaster or Princeton.*  When New York was mentioned
a shout went up.  Meet at New York!  The thing was absurd!
Vast importance and many great advantages would go to that
city where the national Government was seated and the national treasures kept.  And was any one weak enough to
bestow this honor on the chief city of the State that had killed
the impost, refused the power to regulate trade, laid heavy
duties on the exports of her neighbors, and adopted the Constitution in a way that was worse than rejection?  Were the
Federalists mad?  The city, too, was open to the sea, was
without forts, and far removed from the centre of population.
Any one who would take the pains to look into the matter
would soon find that in the new Congress forty-two representatives and sixteen senators were to come from the country
south of New York, against seventeen representatives and
eight senators from the region east of New York.  Nor was
this all.  The main source of revenue would be the impost,
and the impost would nowhere be so productive as in the importing States of the South.†  To an impartial mind, therefore, the shore of the Hudson was clearly not the place.
When the question came up in the Old Congress, a great display of sectional feeling was made.  Philadelphia and New
York were urged and rejected.  Lancaster was then suggested, but Baltimore was thought a better town; so Baltimore
was chosen.  Two days later Congress once more changed its
mind, threw out Baltimore, and selected New York.  But
when, the week following, the question to agree came up, the
Rhode Island delegates, who had steadily voted for New
York, had withdrawn, the motion was lost and the matter
again in confusion.  The leaves had begun to turn before the
House finally ordered that the new Congress should meet at
New York.

This disposed of, Congress listened to a report on the army.
That little body of men, on which the politicians affected to
look with dread, was scarce more than half the size of some of

---

* Pennsylvania Gazette, September 10, 1788.
† Pennsylvania Gazette, January 7, 1789.

the militia regiments which in our time parade the streets of
our great cities on the fourth of every July and the thirtieth of
every May.   Five hundred and ninety-five men and two companies of artillery numbering seventy-one non-commissioned
officers and privates were all the rolls the War Office could
show to be in active service.   A few, with a sergeant, were
guarding gunpowder and rusty muskets at West Point.   The
rest were garrisoning forts and block-houses among the Shawanese and Iroquois.   One of these posts was called Fort Franklin, and stood on the banks of French creek, hard by the ruins
of the old French Fort Venango.   Another was named McIntosh.   It was a regularly stockaded work, with four bastions,
and mounted, in troubled times, six pieces of cannon.   But the
country had long since become so thickly settled that the fort
was about to be demolished and a block-house built.   A third
was on the site of Jeffersonville, Indiana, and called after the
German Baron von Steuben; there were two companies, a
major, and one gun.   Two companies, a major, and four guns
were at Fort Vincennes, lately put up on the Wabash to overawe the Wabash Indians.   The headquarters of the army were
at Fort Harmar, a heavily bastioned stockade that rose on the
banks of the Muskingum close to the Ohio, and gave protection to the cluster of cabins that made the thriving town of
Marietta.

Six huge pieces of iron cannon, such as would now be
thought unfit to be used for political purposes on a village
green, frowned from the bastions, and gave a feeling of safety
to the hundreds of emigrants that went by on the river.   To
keep a strict count of these travellers was as much the duty of
the commandant as to protect them, and his list had never been
so long as in the autumn of 1788.   From the day ice broke up
on the Ohio scarce a week went by but a score of flat-boats,
loaded with cattle and household goods, floated slowly past the
fort, or made fast to the bank, while the men came up to seek
for water or to ask concerning the behavior of Chickasaws and
Cherokees.   They were in general bound for the settlements
down the valley, and seldom made a long stay.   But early one
bright morning in April a boat was seen to quit the Ohio, turn
into the Muskingum, come up the river, and land its inmates on

the bank opposite the fort.  The commandant was at a loss what to make of so unusual a proceeding.  Nor was his surprise removed when he learned that the strangers had come to settle; that they were from New England, and that they had been sent out by a great land company which owed its existence to the enterprise and push of two Massachusetts Yankees.

These two men were Rufus Putnam and Benjamin Tupper.  Both were men of high integrity, had seen some service in the French and Indian war, and had fought through the revolution with such distinction that, by the time Cornwallis surrendered, each had risen to the rank of General in the continental army.  So highly, indeed, were the services of Putnam esteemed that when in 1785 the office of United States Geographer was created, he was offered a surveyorship under Hutchins.  He declined the place, but urged the claims of his old friend and companion in arms, Tupper.  Tupper readily accepted the office, set out in the early summer of 1785, and went, it seems, as far as Pittsburg, and there stopped.  The Indians were becoming troublesome.  Numberless parties of Miamis, Shawanese, and Twightwees had taken the war-path and were burning, scalping, and murdering not far from the very region it was his business to survey.  He deemed it no more than prudent, therefore, to delay his journey, and when winter set in went back to the East.  Tupper had long been eager to see the West, and had often been heard to declare his intention of some day selling his farm, packing up his goods, and going out there with his family to settle.  But he had been turned from his purpose by the dangers and hardships of the trip, and by the solicitations of family and friends.  No sooner, however, did he behold the magnificent country of which he had heard so much than the longing to emigrate returned with increased vigor, and he instantly made up his mind to go out and possess the land.  But he would not go alone.  He would gather a number of the most hardy and robust young men of New England, take them to the Ohio, make a clearing, form a settlement, and, it might be, lay the foundation of a city that in time to come would rival in wealth and power the most prosperous cities of the East.

With his head full of his plan, he went one night after his

return to visit Putnam. As the two sat talking of other days Tupper made known his scheme of colonization, gave a glowing description of the richness of the soil, of the mildness of the climate, of the abundance of game, and it is not unlikely urged the shrewd old general to join the company about to be collected. However this may be, it is certain that the result of the evening's talk was a notice which, under the head of Information, came out late in January, 1786, in a few of the newspapers of Massachusetts.

The notice informed the public that the subscribers, who were none other than Putnam and Tupper, took this way of addressing the officers and soldiers of the late army and such others as might be, under ordinance of Congress, entitled to lands in the Ohio country. They had personally inspected the region, had gathered much information of a most reliable kind, and were sure that the lands in that delightful valley were richer and more inexhaustible than any known to the people of New England. The climate, the seasons, the fruits of the earth surpassed even the most flattering accounts that had been published. They were determined, therefore, to form a company, become purchasers, go out to this marvellous country and start a settlement, and warmly invited all of a like mind to join them. The name of the association was to be the Ohio Company. The members were all to be residents in the commonwealth of Massachusetts. That no time might be lost, it was proposed that all who took a lively interest in furthering the undertaking should meet in their counties on the morning of Wednesday, the fifteenth of February, 1786, and choose delegates to consider and perfect the scheme. The men so selected, it was provided, should meet in the Bunch-of-Grapes Tavern at Boston on the first of March.

The plan, though as yet disclosed only by glimpses, was highly applauded, and on the day named delegates from eight counties came up. For two hours they listened to the glowing accounts of Tupper and Putnam, were greatly delighted, and instantly appointed a committee to draft a plan in writing. Two days later the report was read. The sole purpose of the Ohio Company was then declared to be to raise a fund in continental certificates and apply it to the purchase and settlement of lands in the western territory. The fund was not to exceed one million dollars, a great sum in those days, and was to be cut up into one thousand shares of one thousand dollars each. The owners, it was provided, of every twenty shares were to form a division, each division was to choose an agent, and the agents were to elect directors and a treasurer.*

The books were then opened for subscription, and before a year had gone by so great a number of what was thought to be a ruined, bankrupt, and broken community put down their names for a share each that a meeting of the agents took place in Brackett's Tavern on the eighth of March, 1787. Putnam, Samuel Parsons, and Manasseh Cutler were made directors. Cutler was a man of varied and extensive learning. He had been bred first to the bar and then to the ministry; but his true calling was politics. He was clear of head, sound of judgment, of great push and energy, and in the pursuit of his aims not over careful of the means used. He was chosen, therefore, to go before Congress and purchase the land, and the choice could not have fallen on a better man.

When he reached New York the memorial of the Ohio Company, drawn up by Parsons, had already been before Congress several months.† Indeed, Parsons himself had presented it on the ninth of May. The time was most fortunate, for, by order of the House, the next day had been named for the third reading of the Ordinance for the Government of the Territory northwest of the Ohio.

The petition of the Ohio Company, it may well be supposed, was heard with delight. Here was a body of men, veterans of the war, and veterans of that line of the army which had distinguished itself by courage, by perseverance, by the firmness with which it suffered hunger, nakedness, and cold, asking leave to buy acres of that land Congress was most desirous to sell, and standing ready to go out and make clearings and put up cabins in that wilderness Congress was most

---

* Articles of an Association by the Name of the Ohio Company. Worcester, 1786. The idea was not a new one. Early in 1783 Rufus Putnam and a number of officers of the New England line formed a plan and drew up a scheme for a settlement northwest of the Ohio. On that occasion Timothy Pickering urged the exclusion of slavery from the new States. Life of Pickering by O. Pickering, vol. i, p. 546.        † Papers of Old Congress, vol. xli.

anxious to see well settled. They were the very men wanted, and their memorial gave a new aspect to western affairs. Unhappily, two days later Congress lost a quorum, and from that time till the fourth of July no session was held. On the fifth a quorum was again wanting, and that night Cutler, with a portmanteau full of letters to congressmen and citizens of note, rode into New York.

Carrington received him kindly, introduced him to congressmen, took a lively interest in his plan, and on the tenth of July reported it favorably to the House. Meanwhile, the ordinance had been referred to a new committee. The weather was warm and little conducive to mental toil. But such was the industry of the committeemen that two days later the ordinance was read for the first time. It parted out the region into three States; it provided that when any of them acquired a population of sixty thousand souls it should be admitted to the Union; it guaranteed freedom of worship, but said not a word about slaves. Grayson noticed this, and to him, perhaps more than to any one else, is to be ascribed the honor of introducing that clause which at the second reading of the bill became the Sixth Article. Involuntary servitude was forbidden forever; but fugitive slaves from other States were to be given up. On the thirteenth of July the question was put, Shall this bill pass? Eighteen members were in their seats, and as their names were called seventeen answered Aye.* One alone stood out. He came from New York, and was a member of a family whose men never missed a chance to display their narrowmindedness, their want of feeling, and their lack of common sense. He was connected with that Judge Robert Yates who eight days before quitted the Federal Convention in disgust, and with that Peter Yates who a few months later led the street attack upon the Federalists at Albany.

While these things were going on in Congress, Cutler spent his time in making friends and furthering his plans. St. Clair, who was President of Congress, and whom he soon won over by asserting that there was no other man he so longed to see governor of the company's purchase, introduced him to the

---

* The States that voted for the antislavery article were Massachusetts, New York, New Jersey, Delaware, Virginia, North Carolina, South Carolina, Georgia.

foreign ministers. He was delighted to find that Van Berckel, the Dutch Chargé, took a lively interest in the proposed settlements. He dined with Hillegas, the Treasurer. He supped with Grayson and some congressmen from the South. He passed an evening with Osgood, head of the Board of Treasury, and was astonished at the variety of his knowledge and the largeness of his views. He was much in the company of Dane, of Winthrop Sargent, of that William Duer who the next year contributed a few numbers to the Federalist, and of that David Rittenhouse whose services in mathematics are still remembered, and whose Dutch clocks are still held in high repute.

By Rittenhouse he was introduced to Hutchins. Hutchins had been Geographer to the King, was then Geographer to Congress, and knew the West better than half the frontiersmen who hunted buffalo and tracked bears from the Monongahela to the Illinois. From Hutchins he drew the only just description of the Ohio valley he had ever heard, was surprised to learn that the Muskingum watered the richest and most salubrious part of the whole western country, and determined that its banks should be included in the purchase.*

This important question decided, Cutler turned next for help to Duer. From some hints dropped by friendly congressmen, he was led to believe his scheme was violently opposed by a few members of the House. To find out who they were, that they might be worked upon, was, he thought, most desirable; and as he could do nothing by himself, he cast about in search of aid. Duer seemed to be the man. He was a politician of local reputation, was rich, kept a fine house, was intimate with almost every member of Congress, and could, therefore, easily ascertain who were for and who were against the plan. No sooner did Cutler make known his wish than Duer undertook the business, and succeeded so

---

* "Was introduced by Dr. Ewings and Rittenhouse to Mr. Hutchins, Geographer of the United States. Consulted with him where to make our location." Cutler's Journal, July 7, 1787. In the entry of Monday, July 9th, is the following: "Waited this morning very early on Mr. Hutchins. He gave me the fullest information of the western country from Pennsylvania to the Illinois, and advised me by all means to make our location on the Muskingum, which was decidedly, in his opinion, the best part of the whole western country."

well that the opponents were speedily known to be Clarke,
Bingham, Yates, Kearney, and Few. These men he declared
must be attacked at their lodgings.* But before this determination could be carried out an ordinance passed Congress
that was little to Cutler's liking.

The moment he read it the shrewd Yankee chose his
course. He affected to be quite disheartened. He announced
his intention to spend no more time and money on the matter,
gave out that he was going home, and said that he knew
more liberal treatment would be given him by some of the
States owning western lands, or even by the Indians.† This
had the desired effect. Numbers of congressmen called at his
lodgings to dissuade him from quitting the city. The business was, they said, one of very grave importance. The contract, when entered into, would be the largest private contract
ever made in the country. He must expect opposition, and
would do wonders if he closed the matter in two or three
months.‡ Indeed, they were at a loss to know by what address he had induced Congress to act so promptly, and to lend
so favorable an ear to his proposals. But Cutler stood firm,
pretended to be very indifferent, talked much of the advantages of a contract with Massachusetts or Connecticut, and repeated his determination to go back to Boston.# This he

---

* " As there are a number in Congress decidedly opposed to terms of negotiation, and some to any contract, I wish now to ascertain the number for and
against, and who they are. . . . This I have mentioned to Colonel Duer, who
has promised to assist me. . . . Clarke, Bingham, Yates, Kearney, and Few are
troublesome fellows. They must be attacked by my friends at their lodgings."
Journal, July 19th.

† "Informed the Committee of Congress that I should not contract on the conditions proposed ; should prefer purchasing lands with some of the States, who
would give incomparably better terms ; and therefore proposed to leave the city."
Cutler's Journal, July 20, 1787.

‡ " They assured me I had many friends in Congress who would make every
exertion in my favor; that it was an object of great magnitude, and must not expect to accomplish it in less than two or three months." Journal, July 20, 1787.

# " Several members of Congress called on me early this morning. . . . I was
very indifferent, and talked much of the advantages of a contract with one of
the States. This I found had the desired effect." Journal, July 21, 1787. " I
was convinced it was best for me to hold up the idea of giving up a contract
with Congress and making a contract with one of the States, which I did in the
strongest terms." Journal, July 20, 1787.

surely would have done, for the sake of keeping up appearances, had not Duer come to him at this moment with an offer that completely changed his mind.

It seems that some of the principal characters, both in Congress and in the city, had been much taken with the plan. The terms given by the Government to individual buyers were liberal. But the terms demanded by the Ohio Company were, they thought, more than generous, and they felt loath that so good a chance to speculate in western lands should be suffered to slip by. A meeting was accordingly held, the subject talked over, a plan concerted, and Duer sent to urge Cutler to extend his contract and take in the new company. The whole matter was to be kept a profound secret.* Cutler, after some pretended hesitation, struck a bargain with Duer, and informed Congress that if it would grant the terms he asked he was ready to increase his purchase to near five millions of acres. He reminded the House at the same time that the money paid down for the land would be enough to discharge four millions of the public debt, that the price of Federal lands would go up, and that, in the disordered state of affairs in Kentucky, it would be a good thing to have in the valley settlements of robust and industrious men warmly attached to Government.† There was much force in what he said, and Congress determined to consider the matter once more.

And now the work of lobbying began in earnest.‡ The support of the southern members was secured by promising St. Clair the governorship.# Sargent was won over by the

---

* "Colonel Duer came to me with proposals from a number of the principal characters in the city to extend our contract and take in another company, but that it should be kept a profound secret. . . . I spent the evening (closeted) with Colonel Duer, and agreed to purchase more land, if terms could be obtained for another company, which will probably forward the negotiation." Cutler's Journal, July 20, 1787.

† Cutler's Journal, July 21, 1787.

‡ "I immediately went to Sargent and Duer, and we now entered into the true spirit of negotiation with great bodies. Every machine in the city that it was possible to set at work we now put in motion." Cutler's Journal, July 26, 1787.

# "Having found it impossible to support General Parsons as a candidate for Governor, after the interest that General A. St. Clair had secured, I embraced this opportunity to declare that if General Parsons could have the appointment of first judge and Sargent secretary we should be satisfied; and that I heartily wished

offer of the secretaryship; and it was arranged, if the worst came to the worst, that he should go to Maryland, interest the delegates of that State in the company, and bring them on, for they were not then in Congress, while Cutler went on a like mission to Connecticut and Rhode Island.* Meanwhile, to Duer and Sargent was assigned the duty of lobbying the opponents of the scheme in Congress. It was no easy task. In some cases, where the men were not well known, two, three, and even four persons were engaged before they could be reached. A great difficulty was encountered by those who undertook to influence Bingham, Yates, Kearney, and Few. But the friends of Cutler stopped at nothing, and the refractory congressmen found themselves beset on all sides. They were remonstrated with on the street. They were argued with at their lodgings. They could find no peace even on the floor of Congress or behind the tables of the coffee-house. Under such pressure Yates and Bingham soon gave way. Few held out some time longer; but Kearney stood firm to the last, and was denounced by Cutler, in a fit of anger, as a stubborn mule.

It was now the twenty-seventh of July. Cutler, weary of business, had selected that day for his return to the East, rose early, and after packing his portmanteaus went out on a round of visits to members of Congress to wish them good-by.† Eleven o'clock struck before the last call was made, and as he passed the City Hall the congressmen were hurrying in. Carrington, who sat for Virginia, saw him as he went by, pulled him aside, and whispered that Few was secured, and that one more trial was to be made in Congress that morning. He had but a few minutes before been assured that Lee was ready with an hour's speech and confident of success. Cutler determined,

---

his Excellency General St. Clair might be the Governor; and that I would solicit the eastern members in his favor. This I found rather pleasing to southern members." Cutler's Journal, July 23, 1787. "I am fully convinced that it was good policy to give up Parsons and openly appear solicitous that St. Clair might be appointed Governor." Journal, July 26, 1787.

* "Duer, Sargent, and myself have also agreed, if we fail, that Sargent shall go on to Maryland, which is not at present represented, and prevail on the members to come on, and to interest them in our plan. I am to go to Connecticut and Rhode Island to solicit the members from those States to go on to New York and lay an anchor to the windward with them." Journal, July 26, 1787.

† Cutler's Journal, July 27, 1787.

therefore, to wait till the close of the day's session. But he had not long to wait, for about three in the afternoon word reached him that an ordinance had passed granting all he asked. Immediately he set off for the Treasury in company with Sargent, made some verbal arrangement with the board, and, leaving everything in the care of Sargent, started for Boston.*

The contract was signed late in October. By it the Government disposed of near five millions of acres of land at two thirds of a dollar per acre.† Of this great area one million and a half was bought by the Ohio Company for one million dollars. The remaining three and a half millions of acres were for a private speculation, in which some of the ablest men in Congress were deeply engaged.‡

Immediate possession was given to the company. Putnam was made superintendent. Carpenters and surveyors, boat-builders and blacksmiths, farmers and laborers, were enlisted, and by the end of November the colonists, forty-seven in number, were ready to set forth. The boat-builders were sent for-

---

* Cutler's Journal, July 27, 1787.

† One third of a dollar was allowed for "bad land," cost of surveying, etc. The nominal price was therefore 66⅔ cents. But as this was to be paid in United States certificates of debt, and as such certificates were worth but 12 cents on a dollar, the real price of the land was not far from 8 or 9 cents per acre. See, The Contract of the Ohio Company with the Honorable Board of Treasury of the United States of America, made by the Rev. Mr. Manasseh Cutler and Major Winthrop Sargent, as Agents for the Directors of the said Company at New York.

‡ "By this ordinance we obtained the grant of near five millions of acres of land, amounting to three millions and a half of dollars; one million and a half of acres for the Ohio Company, and the remainder for a private speculation, in which many of the principal characters of America are concerned. Without connecting this speculation, similar terms and advantages could not have been obtained for the Ohio Company." Cutler's Journal, July 27, 1787. The "private speculation" of which Cutler writes was undoubtedly the famous Scioto Company, the first great "land job" of the republic. Of the history of that company only a few obscure facts remain. But it is safe to say that most of the public men of that day were deeply concerned in it, and that chief among them were Hamilton, Duer, Lee, and St. Clair. Congress indeed, some years later, went through the form of an investigation of the affairs of the Scioto Company. But the only member they would have dared to punish was Duer; and Duer was then, most happily, dead. The investigation, therefore, was quietly dropped. Regarding these land sales, see a letter from Madison to Jefferson, October 24, 1787.

ward at once.* But the rest of the party met at Hartford on New-Year's-day, 1788, and went with all speed to Lumrill's Ferry, then a cluster of eight or ten log huts on the bank of the Youghiogheny river, thirty miles above Pittsburg. There they spent the winter, and while they waited for the river to open, built their first boat. The craft was forty-five feet long and fifty tons burden. Her bows were raking and heavily timbered. Her sides were made bullet-proof, and she was named the May-Flower.†

April came before the ice broke up in the Youghiogheny.‡ On the second of the month, all being ready, the May-Flower was pushed into the river and the journey begun. The boat glided slowly on to the Monongahela, down the Monongahela to Pittsburg, stopped there a few hours, went thence to the confluence of the Muskingum and the Ohio, where, after a voyage of five days, it was pulled ashore.#

The landing was made in the wilderness opposite Fort Harmar. At that time the country was thickly covered with noble forests of oak and sycamore, and under their branches some huts of rough boards torn from the flat-boats were hastily put up to serve as shelter till a clearing could be made and the city laid out. Meanwhile, the directors were not idle. A pamphlet, written by Cutler in praise of the western territory, was widely distributed. Absurd reports were circulated describing the country as a new land of promise, as the garden of the world, as the seat of wealth, as the centre of a great empire. Emigrants were offered farms at a few shillings an acre and transportation free, and so many made haste to avail themselves

---

* See proceedings of meetings held at Brackett's Tavern, November 21 and 23, 1787, in a pamphlet called Contract of the Ohio Company with the Honorable Board of Treasury, etc. Also, New York Journal, December 14, 1787.

† Western Monthly Magazine, May, 1833, vol. i, p. 395. Albach's Western Annals.

‡ Youghiogheny, or Youghioghany, is the English spelling of one of the many names the Indians gave the Ohio. Indeed, Ohio was derived by the French from yOugHIOghany. Bancroft's History of the Formation of the Constitution, vol. i, p. 169, note.

# My account of the New England Ohio Company is taken chiefly from Letters on the First Settlement of the Northwest Territory, by Jacob Burnet. A Fragment of the Early History of Ohio, by Arius Nye. Indian Wars of the West, by Flint. Harris's Tour in the West. Walker's Annual Discourse, and the extracts from Cutler's Journal published in the North American Review, October, 1841.

of the company's offer that by the middle of April a second party set out under Cutler. They went by land, driving their wagons and stock before them, to Wheeling. There they took flat-boats down the Ohio, and on the morning of the first of July came in sight of the log huts of their companions. Next day a meeting of all the settlers was held at the water's edge to name the place. Many terms were discussed. But it was finally decided to call the city after Marie Antoinette of France, and to bestow upon it the name of Marietta. The great square where the block-house stood was to be known as Campus Martius, another was called Quodranaou, a third Cecilia, a fourth Capitolium. The broad road chopped through the woods to Quodranaou was dignified with the appellation of Via Sacra. Thus was founded the first settlement in what is now the State of Ohio. But two months had not gone by before a rival city sprang up a few miles farther down the river.*

A month after the sale to the Ohio Company an offer was made to Congress by John Cleve Symmes to buy two millions of acres between the Little and the Great Miamis. Symmes was a Jerseyman of wealth, had visited the Shawanese country, had been greatly pleased with its fertility, and had come away declaring that every acre in the wildest part was worth a silver dollar. It was too, he thought, only a question of time, and a

---

* An Account of the Campus Martius at the City of Marietta, Territory of the United States Northwest of the River Ohio. Illustrated by an Elegant Engraving. Columbian Magazine, November, 1788. A letter from Rufus Putnam in Vermont Gazette, January 12, 1789. A description of Marietta in the New York Packet, August 27, 1789. See, also, a pamphlet called Oration at Marietta, Ohio, July 4, 1788, etc., with the Proceedings of the Inhabitants of the City of Marietta. Newport, R. I., 1788. The orator was J. M. Varnum, the lawyer for the butchers in the famous case of Trevett against Weeden. Cutler went out with the party in the summer of 1788. Some extracts from the diary of his journey from Hamilton to Marietta are given in the New England Historical and Genealogical Register for April, July, and October, 1860. The entry under date of Friday, August 15, 1788, is worth quoting. "This morning we went pretty early to the boats. General Tupper had mentioned to me a mode for constructing a machine to work in the head or stern of a boat instead of oars. It appeared to me highly probable that it might succeed. I therefore proposed that we should make the experiment. Assisted by a number of the people, we went to work and constructed a machine in the form of a screw, with short blades, and placed it in the stern of the boat, which we turned with a crank. It succeeded to admiration, and I think it a very useful discovery."

very short time, when this value would be doubled and tripled. Thousands of immigrants were pouring into the valley each year, hundreds of thousands of acres were being taken up, and the day would soon come when the rich land along the Miamis and the Ohio would be in great demand. There was therefore a mighty fortune in store for the lucky speculator who should buy land from Congress for five shillings an acre and sell it to immigrants for twenty. But Symmes, while he had the foresight, wanted the energy, the shrewdness, the keen knowledge of men and of the world that so eminently distinguished Cutler. His business lagged, and though his offer to purchase was made in August, 1787, it was the fifteenth of May, 1788, before the contract was closed. In the mean time he put out a pamphlet and made known his terms of sale. A copy soon fell into the hands of Matthias Denman. He became interested in the scheme and purchased that section on which now stands the city of Cincinnati. One third he kept, one third he sold to Robert Patterson, and the remainder to John Filson.

The conditions of the purchase•from Symmes gave them two years in which to begin making clearings and building huts. But the three determined to lose no time, and at once made ready to lay out a city directly opposite that spot where the waters of the Licking mingle themselves with the Ohio. Denman and Patterson were no scholars. But Filson had once been a school-master, knew a little of Latin and something of history, and to him was assigned the duty of choosing a name for the town. He performed the task in a way that must have excited the admiration of the humble race of pedagogues to which he belonged. The melodious Indian names were too barbarous for his scholarly taste. And as he could recall none among cities ancient or modern quite to his liking, he determined to make one, and produced a word that was a most absurd mixture of Latin, Greek, and French. He called the place Losantiville, which, being interpreted, means the city opposite the mouth of the Licking. A few weeks later the Indians scalped him.

Though the spot was selected and named in August, Christmas came before Patterson left Maysville with a company of fourteen backwoodsmen to mark out the streets and put up the first huts of Losantiville.* As they picked their way between the cakes of ice that obstructed the river, they came in sight of the Little Miami, and there, on a broad flat, beheld the block-house and the half-finished cabins of Columbia.

Emigration to the West now became the rage of the time. Every small farmer whose barren acres were covered with mortgages, whose debts pressed heavily upon him, or whose roving spirit gave him no peace, was eager to sell his homestead for what it would bring, save what he could from the general wreck, and begin life anew on the banks of the Muskingum or the Ohio. And so many did so that at the return of every spring hundreds of boats went down the Ohio heavy with cattle and household goods. One observer at Fort Pitt wrote home that between the first of March and the middle of April, 1787, he saw fifty flat-boats set off for the settlements.† Another at Fort Finney saw thirty-four boats pass in thirty-nine days.‡ The adjutant at Fort Harmar had taken the pains to count the boats that floated by the garrison from October, 1786, to May, 1787, and declared that they numbered one hundred and seventy-seven, and carried upward of twenty-seven hundred souls.# Another safe authority estimated that no less than ten thousand emigrants went by Marietta in 1788.‖ Indeed, forty-five hundred were reported as having passed Fort Harmar between February and June.△ In New England the success of the Ohio Company in procuring emigrants was immense. They advertised, they put out pamphlets assuring the

---

* The first huts were, like those of Marietta, made from the settlers' boats. The custom of building houses with boards that had once made the rude "arks" that floated down the river continued long after saw-mills had become numerous. A writer who saw Cincinnati in 1797 remarks: "There was not one brick house in the city. The houses, and there were very few of them, were principally of boat-planks taken from the flat-boats in which emigrants had descended the river." Reminiscences of Judge McLean. Historical Magazine, June, 1860, p. 177. See, also, Historical Magazine, vol. iv, p. 316. A description of the houses of the early settlers in the West is given in Drake's Pioneer Life in Kentucky. For some facts regarding the early settlement of Cincinnati, see the testimony of Denman, Patterson, Ludlow, and others in the Chancery Suit of the City of Cincinnati against Joel Williams in 1807.

† Pennsylvania Gazette, June 20, 1787.        ‡ Ibid., March 29, 1786.
# Independent Gazetteer, July 10, 1787; also, American Museum.
‖ Columbian Magazine for October, 1788, p. 390.
△ Albach's Annals of the West, p. 478.

people that a man of push and courage could nowhere be so prosperous and so happy as in the West. The climate was delightful. Rain was abundant. The soil rich and watered by broad rivers, along whose banks were great bottoms and natural meadows from twenty to fifty miles in circuit. There the forests of oak and black-walnut, sycamore and maple were free from underbrush, and the noble trees thrust out their branches so far on every side that a man in a single day could clear an acre of land fit for planting Indian corn. Indeed, the trees were so far apart he need not chop them down. He had but to girdle them, while each maple he spared would yield him ten pounds of sugar every year.* In no long time, therefore, the company's lumbering wagon, with its black canvas cover and flaming inscription, "To Marietta on the Ohio," became a familiar sight.† At first the departure of so many men from the States was little heeded, for they were believed to be broken-down farmers and Shayites going to retrieve their fortunes and their honor in the West. But when it was noticed that behind the wagon rode numbers of most robust and promising youths, the alarm of the people broke forth in bitter complaints. The scheme was denounced in the coffee-houses as a wicked plot to drain the East of its best blood. The opponents of the company put out a number of pamphlets against it,‡ and wrote much bad verse on Cutler. The poor fools, it was said, were being enticed from comfortable homes under the promise that they were going to a land of more than tropi-

* See An Explanation of the Map which delineates that part of the Federal Lands comprised between Pennsylvania West Line, the River Ohio, Scioto, and Lake Erie. Salem, 1787, p. 10.

† Flint declares that he "distinctly remembers the wagon that carried out a number of adventurers from the counties of Essex and Middlesex, in Massachusetts, on the second emigration to the woods of Ohio. He remembers the black canvas covering of the wagon, the white and large lettering in capitals, 'To Marietta on the Ohio.'" Flint's Indian Wars of the West, p. 143.

‡ A number of these curious pamphlets are still to be found in old family garrets. Some of them were illustrated with rude cuts. Says Walker: "I have a distinct recollection of a picture which I saw in boyhood prefixed to a penny anti-moving-to-Ohio pamphlet, in which a stout, ruddy, well-dressed man on a sleek, fat horse, with a label, 'I am going to Ohio,' meets a pale and ghastly skeleton of a man, scarcely half dressed, on the wreck of what was once a horse . . . with a label, 'I have been to Ohio.'" Annual Discourse in Transactions of the Historical and Philosophical Society of Ohio. Part ii, pp. 194,

cal richness; to a land where they should reap without having sown, and gather without having ploughed. But in truth the climate was cold, the land sterile and sickly, and the woods full of Indians, panthers, and hoop-snakes.*

The East, however, stood in much less danger of losing her young men and her young blood than the Confederation of losing the whole region between the Alleghany Mountains and the Mississippi. In truth, that the settlements along the Holston and the Tennessee did not revolt in 1788 and go over to Spain, was not the fault of one of the boldest, most unprincipled of men. Nowhere in the United States at that time were the people so discontented and unhappy. The evils of which they complained were near and pressing. Yet everything they had done for the alleviation of their condition served but to increase their miseries. The men of one district had broken away from North Carolina, had formed the State of Franklin, and made Sevier their Governor. But the State of Franklin no longer existed. North Carolina had restored her authority, and Sevier, outlawed and attainted, was hunting buffalo and fighting Cherokees far beyond the borders of civilization. The men of another district had begged Virginia to let them go, and had petitioned Congress to make of their district a State. The request was refused. Angry and excited at the treatment accorded them by friends, they now began to think of seeking aid of ancient foes, and in a short time were broken into five factions.

The most reckless were for taking up arms, quitting the Confederation, forming a new republic, and allying themselves closely with Spain. A second party, composed of men who hated Spaniards even more than Indians, were for fighting Spain and seizing Louisiana. These were opposed by a set who declared they were eager to leave the Union, but wished to see the country under the crown of Spain. Some, remembering the great things which France had done in the late war, were for soliciting Louis to obtain a retrocession of Louisiana, and to spread his authority over Kentucky and Tennessee. Others expressed a firm conviction that by a proper show of force they could extort the free use of the Mississippi from Spain without throwing off the authority of Congress.

---

* Flint's Indian Wars of the West, p. 144.

Chief among these was James Wilkinson. Wilkinson was a great favorite with the settlers. Indeed, since the failure of the Wabash expedition and the disgrace of Clark, no man in the valley stood higher. But in such a state of society he who would lead must be quick to foresee and quick to perform the wish of the people, and must ever be doing deeds that will make him the talk of the country far and near. This Wilkinson well knew, and determined to add to his popularity, if possible, by opening the navigation of the Mississippi. His first step was to try the temper of the Spaniards. For this purpose he procured a flat-boat, loaded it with flour, tobacco, bacon, and hams, and sent it down the Mississippi, bound for New Orleans. A few days later he set out himself. Everything went well with the boat till Natchez was reached. There it was hailed, stopped, and examined. The commandants along the river had orders to seize and sell all American vessels that came in their way. But when the Spanish officer at Natchez learned whose property the craft was, he hesitated, and finally set it free, for he was not disposed to meddle with the goods of a general officer, and of so distinguished a general officer as Wilkinson. At New Orleans, however, the authorities knew nothing of Wilkinson, nothing of Kentucky, and were not inclined to show any forbearance toward the General's flat-boat. Indeed, the intendant was about to confiscate the cargo, when a merchant of some influence in the city, and who knew Wilkinson well by reputation, waited on the Governor. He told Miro, who was as ignorant of Kentucky as of Maine, that the measures taken by the intendant would in all probability give rise to unpleasant consequences. The Kentuckians were, he said, already exasperated beyond endurance at the behavior of the Spaniards. They were a bold and fearless race, were determined to have the use of the river, and if the system of seizing their vessels went on, it was quite likely that they would, in spite of Congress, undertake to open the Mississippi by force, and they were well able to do it. The merchant hinted, also, that Wilkinson was very popular, that he had great influence over the Kentuckians, and that his boat-load of flour and pork was sent down in the hope of finding some excuse to pick a quarrel. If his property were captured, he would raise a great outcry, rouse the whole country, and come over the border with several thousands of the best shots in the valley.

Miro was much alarmed, thanked the merchant for his information, and intimated to the intendant that it would be well to withdraw the guard from the boat. This was done, and the goods were allowed to be sold free of duty. When Wilkinson came, and heard under what obligations he lay to his unknown friend, he went to him, expressed his gratitude, and the two soon formed a plan for future work. He next went to the Governor. That he might not seem to stoop from the high character given of him by seeming to be concerned in so small a matter as a boat-load of flour and hams, he framed and told to Miro a great lie. The barrels and flitches, he said, were not his. They belonged to some Kentuckians who wished to make a trial of the temper of the Spanish Government. It was expected that the vessel would be captured. He was merely to look on, and when he went back to the States, report to Congress what he had seen. He was deeply sensible of all the kindness that had been shown to him. But on no account should the Governor expose himself to the anger of the Spanish Court by refusing to seize the cargo. It was a mere trifle, and the commands of his Catholic Majesty were perhaps imperative.* This confirmed the worst fears of Miro. He was sure that an invasion was meditated. He believed that Wilkinson was a man of much power, and well able to delay, if not to hinder, the attack, which at every rise of the river he expected would be made. He determined, therefore, to win over Wilkinson. No bait was then so tempting as the right of free trade with New Orleans. This the wily Spaniard held out, Wilkinson took it, and the two struck a bargain. The General was to do all that lay in his power to bring the people of Kentucky to the side of Spain. In return for his services he was promised a ready market at New Orleans for all the flour and tobacco he might send. The reward was a rich one, for a hundred-weight of tobacco which cost in Kentucky two Spanish dollars, sold, at New Orleans, for nine Spanish dollars and a half.

---

* See the statement of Daniel Clark, nephew of Wilkinson's agent, in Annals of the West, Albach, p. 489.

Wilkinson hastened home. But he had not been many weeks in the valley when news came to him that Colonel Connolly, of the British army, was at Louisville. Connolly had come through the woods from Detroit to the Big Miami, had there taken a canoe and an Indian guide and paddled down the river to the Ohio and on to Louisville. He declared that his business was to look after some lands he once owned at the falls. But Wilkinson, who was a practised liar, mistrusted him, and resolved to find out the real purpose of his visit. He accordingly asked Connolly to come and spend some time with him, and Connolly did so. Wilkinson treated him with marked kindness, won his confidence, sounded him on the navigation of the Mississippi, and soon found out the secret. Indeed, Connolly confided to him in private that Great Britain was eager to strip Spain of Louisiana, and opened to him the whole plan of operations. Troops could not be spared from Canada and the forts the British still held on American ground. But Sir Guy Carleton, who had become Lord Dorchester, stood ready to help the Kentuckians in a war with Spain. He would send money, clothes, and muskets for ten thousand men the moment such an army was collected. He would raise two regiments in Kentucky, and as it was necessary to have the troops commanded by skilful officers, every veteran of the late war who would enlist was to have the same rank in the British army that he once held in the continental army. As for Wilkinson, he had but to name his terms.

To all this the arch plotter listened with gravity, and the moment he had, to use his own words, "pumped out of Connolly all that he wished to know," began to look coldly on the scheme. It was, he said, not yet five years since peace had been declared. The bitter feelings engendered by the war were still fresh. The Americans hated the British with an implacable hatred, and never could be brought to join with them in any undertaking. This was true all over the continent. But it was especially true in Kentucky. In that district the people had seen their settlements attacked, their houses burned, their friends and kinsfolk shot, scalped, maimed, and tortured by the Indians. And these atrocities they firmly believed had been instigated by the British. Connolly protested that this was a mistake.  Wilkinson assured his guest that it was not, and believing him to be a blusterer and a coward, determined to play upon him.  He sent accordingly for an old trapper and hunter in whom he could rely, made known his wishes, and hired him to make a feigned attack on Connolly's life.  The thing was done.  The trapper was seized, brought before Wilkinson, who was a civil justice, sharply questioned, and declared that the Indians had killed his son, that he believed they had been set on by the British, and that he meant in revenge to have the life of every Englishman that came in his way.  He was remanded to the custody of the sheriff and locked up for a few hours.  The prisoner was scarcely out of the room when Wilkinson assured Connolly that the law was unable to protect him, that he was in great danger, and would be a lucky man if he got off with his life.  The ruse succeeded.  Connolly was terribly frightened, said he would go at once, and begged hard for an escort to conduct him out of Kentucky.  This was readily given, and on the twentieth of November he recrossed, the Ohio on his way back to Detroit.*

When Wilkinson found himself rid of Dorchester's agent he began at once to make ready for a second expedition to New Orleans.  Boats were secured, arms and ammunition laid in, and in a few weeks great stores of flour, bacon, tobacco, butter, and hams were on their way to Louisville.  By the last of December all preparations were finished, and early in January of the new year the expedition set out amid the shouts and blessings of the whole town.  It was a white day for Wilkinson.  Never had he been so popular.  He was looked on as a great deliverer.  He had opened the Mississippi.  He had made a market, and emptied countless rude warehouses and barns where for three years the kindly fruits of the earth had been stored up, and where, but for him, they might have stayed till they were eaten by rats and worms, or become foul from decay.  The little fleet which was to carry this produce to New Orleans numbered twenty-five flat-boats of the largest size.  Each bore the Kentucky colors, and was armed with a swivel gun.  Some few had three-pounders.  The fighting

---

* These facts are related in a letter written by Wilkinson to Miro, February 12, 1789.  See Gayarré's Spanish Domination of Louisiana.

force was one hundred and fifty men, well drilled and officered, for it was thought not unlikely that some severe fighting would be done before the boats made fast to the levee at New Orleans.*

The example of Wilkinson was soon followed by others, and dozens of flat-boats were hastily put together, filled with produce, and dispatched to New Orleans. So much wheat, pork, and corn went down the Mississippi in the winter months that, when spring came, in the rich counties of Westmoreland and Washington the cost of food had risen sixty per cent.†

---

* Extracts of a letter from a Gentleman at Louisville (falls of the Ohio) to the editor of the New York Journal, January 16, 1789. See New York Journal, March 5, 1789.

† See a letter dated Marietta, March 10, 1790. Freeman's Journal, May 12, 1790.

# CHAPTER VI.

## THE FEDERAL GOVERNMENT.

THE same issue of the Journal that informed its readers of the departure of Wilkinson's fleet also made known to them the ceremonies with which the citizens of New York bade farewell to the Confederation, and gave a welcome to the Constitution.

While the Kentuckians were busy making ready for their voyage to New Orleans, their friends in the East were not less occupied choosing electors and members of the new Congress. In obedience to the provisions of the law, elections were held on the first Wednesday in January, 1789, for presidential electors. Everywhere the day passed off quietly, and before night electors were chosen in all the ratifying States save New York. In that commonwealth the voting was to be done by the Legislature, and there, at the very start, the absurd law produced a quarrel. The Assembly was full of the creatures of Clinton, and strongly Antifederal. The Senate was strongly Federal. The Lower House demanded a joint ballot, which would have sent two Antifederalists to the Senate and ten to the Electoral College. The Upper House demanded a concurrent vote, which would undoubtedly have given it one senator and five electors. But the Assembly refused, the Senate stood firm, and the Legislature adjourned. New York, therefore, cast no vote for the first President, nor did she, during much of the first session of the first Congress, have any representative on the floor of the Upper House.*

A less serious quarrel took place in New Hampshire. The

---

* A report of the debates in the Legislature during this dispute is given in the New York Daily Advertiser, January 10, 12, 1789.

Senate claimed the right to negative the choice of the House. The Assembly indignantly denied it, but toward midnight yielded, entered a solemn protest, and chose electors, every one of whom was an undoubted Federalist.* The most exciting election was perhaps in Maryland. There the choice of electors was with the people, and the State being much given to Anti-federalism and paper money, two tickets were soon before the voters. Meetings were held, addresses published, each party accused of fraud, and the country districts actively canvassed. But the Federalists assured the people that Washington was their candidate, and won a handsome victory.† In Virginia, also, the choice was left to the direct vote of the people. In Massachusetts much the same thing was done. Two electors were chosen at large. Eight more were selected by the Legislature from twenty-four names sent up by the eight congressional districts. Elsewhere the election was by the Legislatures; in some by a joint ballot, in others by a concurrent vote of both branches.

A whole month passed before the electors met. Meanwhile, there was no electioneering. No great questions were as yet at stake. There were no rival candidates, there was no hand-billing, no pamphleteering, no lampooning, no abuse. The selection of a President lay with the electors, and as none of them were pledged to any name, it was impossible to do more than speculate on the result of the balloting. But the man must indeed have been ill-informed who did not know that every one of the sixty-nine gentlemen would cast his vote for the American Fabius. But it would have been hard to say on whom the choice for the second place would fall. The name of John Adams was much in the papers. But Adams had many enemies. He came of New England stock, and that was held by many to be a good reason why the southern electors should vote for some one else. He had been long abroad, and some thought he had acquired strong monarchical notions during his residence at the Hague and the Court of St. James. He had

---

* Freeman's Journal, February 4, 1789.

† The accounts of the meetings, addresses, and election returns are given in the Maryland Journal, January 2 and 6, 1789, and later. See, also, Pennsylvania Mercury, January 6, 1789.

written a book which he called a " Defence of the Constitutions of Government of the United States of America." But many who read it declared it was not a defence, but an insidious attack. Yet Adams withal was strong. So strong, indeed, that some of his enemies, who sought to ruin his chances, stooped to means which, to say the least, were not respectable. Among them, to his shame, was Hamilton.

The stronghold of the opponents of Adams was New York. That city had long been foremost in a show of Antifederal spirit, and there, in the autumn of 1787, not long after the Constitution had been submitted to the people, the Clinton men organized themselves for opposition under the name of Federal Republicans.* The great body of the party was made up of State-righters and paper-money men, those who had resented the return of the Loyalists, had defeated the impost, had stood out against the Federal Convention, and had loudly praised Lansing and Yates for what they were pleased to call a display of patriotism when those two gentlemen left Philadelphia in a huff. The chiefs of the party were the men who, in the troubled time before the war, had risen to note as the leading spirits of the Sons of Liberty. But the most active, the most partisan, the most bitter among them were Marinus Willet, Smith, Tillinghast, and his father-in-law, General John Lamb. Lamb, indeed, was chairman, and presided at the weekly meetings at Fraunces's Tavern, when the conduct of the party at Poughkeepsie was discussed, when the explanation was drawn up, and the urgent circular to the States calling for a new convention was sent out. †

Meanwhile, the day for the choice of electors drew near, and the Federal Republicans were all activity. Against Washington they had not a word to say. But the man for the vice-presidency was to their minds George Clinton. They canvassed, they disputed, they corresponded, and finally sent out a circular letter in his behalf. It was necessary, such was the substance of their appeal to the voters, to have in the new Government some man eager to further the constitutional

---

* Life of General John Lamb, by J. Q. Leake, p. 306.

† The Circular to the States and Counties is among the Tillinghast Papers in the New York Historical Society.

amendments so many States had made the condition of ratification. Such a man was Governor Clinton. There was every reason to believe that the ten votes of New York would be cast in his favor. Some gentlemen from Virginia had been consulted, and had declared that the people of that State also had it in view to support him. It was hoped, therefore, that the voters of every State would favor the scheme of making Clinton Vice-President, and instruct their electors accordingly.*

Such was the opposition of open and avowed enemies. Very different, however, was the opposition of Hamilton. He was great as a party manager. No one in his day, not even Clinton, nor Burr, surpassed him. But the political world of Hamilton's time was ruled chiefly by caucuses. It was through the agency of caucuses that the revolution was begun, that the first Congress was assembled, that independence was declared, that the Confederation was formed, that war was carried on, that the way was made ready for the framing of the Constitution. And it was by the caucus that Hamilton sought to defeat Adams.† He affected alarm at the poor prospects of Washington and the fine prospects of Adams. He has been accused, by one who surely knew, of exciting equal alarm among the Cincinnati.‡ He sent word to Virginia that New England was not unanimous for Washington. He assured his friends in New England that Virginia was in the same condition. It is certain that he drew away five votes from Adams in New Jersey, and even caused him to lose two in Connecticut.

On the first Tuesday in February, the day before the electors were to meet, a post galloped into Hartford. He had been sent, he told the Connecticut electors, for it was to them he came, by Colonel Hamilton. He reminded them, it is probable, that the earnest wish of every Federalist the land over was that the first presidency of the republic should be bestowed

---

* Leake's Life of Lamb, p. 326. Clinton got but three votes, and these three were given him by Virginia.

† "Alexander Hamilton," says Mr. Adams, "was the greatest organist that ever played upon this instrument" (the caucus). Review of the Propositions for Amending the Constitution, etc. John Adams's Works, vol. vi.

‡ "He made all that he could of these bodies of Cincinnati and others to prevent Mr. Adams being chosen Vice-President." Review, etc. Adams's Works.

on Washington.  Unhappily, there was much reason to fear
that the balloting, even for that illustrious character, would not
be unanimous.  There was doubt about the southern electors.
Even those of Virginia were divided, and it was not unlikely,
if the New England electors did not cast some scattering votes,
that Adams would be chosen President.  This clearly was not
the wish of the people.  The Colonel, therefore, had made a
close and careful calculation, and found that if New Jersey
threw away three votes, and Connecticut two, all would go
well for Washington and Adams.  Trumbull protested against
this, declared it must be all a deception, and said he could
not see how giving two votes to some one else would help
Adams.*  But he was silenced, and bidden to remember that
Hamilton had made a calculation, and been at the pains to send
a post to acquaint them with the result.  Connecticut therefore gave two of her votes to Samuel Huntington.  New
Jersey gave five of her six to John Jay, for there, too, Hamilton had been busy.

That part of the behavior of Hamilton which was so obscure to Trumbull admits of but one explanation.  His anxiety
for the success of Washington was assumed.†  His calculation
was a sham.  He needed no calculation.  If every other source
of information had been closed to him, he would still have
been in the possession of one, which ought to have calmed his
most reasonable fears and carried conviction to his mind in

---

* "Many of your friends were duped on this occasion.  I will inform you
how it was managed in Connecticut.  On the day before the election Colonel
Webb came on express to Hartford, sent, as he said, by Colonel Hamilton, etc.,
who, he assured us, had made an exact calculation on the subject, and found that
New Jersey was to throw away three votes, I think, and Connecticut two, and all
would be well.  I exclaimed against the measure, and insisted that it was all a
deception; but what could my single opinion avail against an express armed with
intelligence and calculations?  So our electors threw away two votes where they
were sure they would do no harm."  Trumbull to Adams.  See Works of John
Adams, vol. viii, pp. 484, 485.

† "If he believed one word," says Adams, "of the apprehensions he propagated, it is very unaccountable; for there was a very great certainty in the public
opinion that Washington would have a unanimous vote."  Review, etc.  John
Adams's Works.  A careful perusal of all the newspapers, both Federal and Antifederal, of the time, published in all parts of the country, shows most conclusively
that the public sentiment was overwhelmingly strong in support of Washington
for the presidency, and that the statement of Mr. Adams is quite just.

its most wavering moments. He had been present in the Federal Convention from the morning when Randolph brought forward the Virginia plan to the morning when Yates and Lansing withdrew, and he had attended on many days after they left. He had listened to the debates, and he well knew with what jealousy, with what animosity, the South even then beheld the growing importance of the East. That he should therefore, with the recollections of these scenes fresh in his memory, have really believed the South would choose Adams and reject Washington, is a supposition not to be entertained. The truth seems to be, he was bent on defeating Adams, and to do this made use of tricks and statements that have left a dark stain upon his character.

As the time drew near for the meeting of Congress, elections for representatives began to take place all over the country. Everywhere the excitement was great, and it seemed when the reports came in as if half the first session of the House would be taken up settling contested seats. In some places the polls were kept open for many weeks. In others the two parties were so nearly balanced that no choice was made till after repeated trials. This was to be ascribed in part to defective laws, and in part to absurd methods of electing. In New Jersey the law was silent as to the time of closing the polls. In the eastern towns of that State, where party spirit flamed high, the polls were therefore kept open for three weeks, nor would they have been shut then had not the Governor named a day after which no returns were to be received.* In Connecticut it was the custom to hold two elections. At the first, three candidates were chosen for each office. Their names were then published, and after some weeks a new election was held and one of the three chosen. But a majority of the votes cast was necessary to a choice. The result was natural. The moment parties became nearly equal in numbers, neither could secure the needed majority; protracted elections followed, party ani-

---

* "In New Jersey, the law having fixed no time for closing the polls, they were kept open three or four weeks in some of the counties by the rival jealousy between the eastern and western divisions of the State." Madison to Washington, March 19, 1789.

mosity grew stronger and stronger, and in the mean time the office was vacant.

The evil of the system was well shown in Massachusetts. There Shayism still throve, and every follower of Shays was a firm Antifederalist. The stronghold of the party was the western counties, and there a most determined effort was made to elect its candidates. But so closely were the two sides matched that election after election took place without any result. At last the Shayites of Worcester county made a desperate effort, brought in voters from the most distant places, and sent Grout, an Antifederalist, to the top of the poll. In the extreme western counties a like contest took place, but after several ballotings the Federalists returned Theodore Sedgwick, a lawyer, a trusty Federalist, and a descendant of the Massachusetts general of that name.*

In Middlesex, Gerry was chosen over Gorham. But not till two trials had been made and he had put out an address to the electors declaring that, now the Constitution had been adopted, he opposed it no longer, and that he believed all citizens to be in duty bound to support it.† In Suffolk, Fisher Ames, a young man of thirty, was elected over Samuel Adams. Adams was voted for by the Antifederalists, and warmly defended by many Federal friends. One writer in the Chronicle expressed the hope that while the people were careful to introduce into the Federal Legislature the American Fabius, they would not be unmindful of the American Cato. Another reminded his readers that Adams was the poor man's friend. A third ventured to declare that it was the vote of Adams that carried the ratification of the Constitution in Massachusetts. But the Federalists asserted with great truth that he was old, that he had passed all his life in destroying, and that the turn of his mind was much better adapted to pulling down than to building up. He was therefore not a safe man to put into a legislature whose chief duty was to

---

* See Vermont Gazette, January 19, 1789.

† He was afterwards twitted with this change:
  "Gerry, whose alter'd mind in one short year,
  Led him its firm supporter to appear."
  Aristocracy, an Epic Poem, book ii, p. 18.

build up. A few, forgetting his great services, denounced him as old and as "an amendment-monger," a name often applied to the Antifederalists.*

The majority of the first House of Representatives was thus formed of new men, not a few of whom had been busy with their books and their sports when Paul Revere made his famous midnight ride. Yet some noted names appear on the roll. Connecticut sent Jonathan Trumbull and Roger Sherman, who, without education and without friends, had raised himself from the shoemaker's bench by dint of hard sense and patient toil. From South Carolina came Ædanus Burke at the head of a strong Antifederal delegation. In his train were Sumter, renowned for many gallant enterprises in the late war, and William Smith, a young man, but soon to become distinguished for debate. Madison was one of the ten from Virginia.

While these men were busy electioneering, great preparations were being made to receive them at New York. The Congress of the Confederation had occupied rooms in the City Hall, which stood on the ground now covered by the Treasury Building. But the building was old and out of repair, and the rooms were thought too mean and shabby to be occupied by the new Congress. The city was appealed to, but could do nothing, for its treasury was out of funds. Congress could do nothing, for the national coffers were empty. Some wealthy merchants therefore took up the matter, and soon the magnificent sum of thirty-two thousand five hundred dollars was collected by subscription. The hall was immediately given over to Major L'Enfant, who made some pretensions to a knowledge of architecture and the fine arts, and had gained some note as the designer of the badges of the Cincinnati. An army of carpenters, masons, and plasterers was turned in, the structure completely remodelled, and renamed Federal Hall.†

So extensive were the changes that when the fourth of March was come Federal Hall was still in the hands of the carpenters. It mattered little, however, for on the morning of that day but eight senators and thirteen representatives were in the city.

---

* Wells's Life of Samuel Adams.

† Description of the Federal Edifice at New York. Illustrated with a Plate representing a View of that Building. Columbian Magazine, August, 1789.

The day had been ushered in with a few pleasing and solemn ceremonies. On the afternoon of the third, as the sun went down behind the low ridges of the Jersey coast, the guns at the Battery fired a farewell salute to the old Confederation. At the coffee-house some jolly gentlemen sat late, and long after midnight continued to drink bumpers to the new era. When the first streaks of gray appeared on the morning of the fourth, at twelve noon, and at six in the evening, salutes were again fired, and the bells of all the churches in the city rang out a welcome to that Constitution under which we have in a hundred years become the freest, the richest, the most prosperous of nations.*

Had it not been for the bell-ringing and the firing there would have been little to indicate that a great change of government had taken place. Some new faces indeed were seen at the coffee-house, and some familiar ones were missed, for many members of the old Congress who had failed to secure seats in the new had already packed their portmanteaus and hastened home. But a sense of duty kept a few in their seats, and these continued to hold daily sessions, and to transact some unimportant business in the name of the United States. Meanwhile the new Government from which so much was expected could not go into operation. The day on which it was to have begun slipped by. Yet its members did not come. This was highly diverting to the Antifederalists, and the source of endless annoyance to the Federalists. They contented themselves, however, with cursing the sloth of their friends in private and apologizing for them in public. The roads, it was said, were in a terrible state. The distances were long. The elections had been so close that in many places a choice had not been made till the last moment. Some had pressing business to arrange, and could not leave home till it was settled. But they would soon come. A week passed, and a few stragglers appeared. Then even the Federalists lost all patience. A meeting was held of such senators and representatives as were in town, and a vigorous appeal sent out to the absent members to hurry. Another week was impatiently spent. Half a dozen new men came

---

* New York Journal, March 5, 1789.

in, and the matter began to look serious. The old Congress was slowly dying. The new Congress showed no signs of life, and it seemed not unlikely that the country would in a short time be left without a government of any kind. Every day the people grew more and more excited. Indeed, in the great cities business almost ceased to be done.* Alarmed and angry, the senators called a second meeting and published a second appeal, more urgent than the first. But no heed was given to it, and March was all but ended when the thirtieth representative crossed the Hudson.

The number of the first House had been fixed by the Constitution at sixty-five. But Rhode Island and North Carolina had not joined the Union, so the number fell to fifty-nine. Thirty made a quorum, and a quorum being present in the city, the House, on the morning of the thirtieth of March, took possession of its rooms in Federal Hall and organized.

The first duty was to choose a speaker. Virginia, it was well known, had secured the presidency. The vice-presidency had been bestowed on Massachusetts. New York, which ranked but fourth among the States in wealth and population, had been most richly rewarded with the seat of Congress. It was thought no more than just, therefore, that the speakership should be given to Pennsylvania, and Muhlenberg, a rich Philadelphia merchant, was placed in the chair.

And now a new delay arose. Nothing could be done till the Senate had a quorum, and another week was passed in grumbling and chafing, in watching every stage-wagon, and asking the name of every traveller that came into the city. At last, on the morning of the sixth of April, a messenger knocked at the door of the House and informed the Speaker that the Senate was ready to count the electoral vote. The members hastened to the Senate-chamber, the ballots were opened, and as Langdon read them off, were taken down by a teller appointed by the House and by a teller appointed by the Senate. The Houses then separated.

When the representatives were once more in their seats the Speaker announced the result. George Washington had received sixty-nine, John Adams thirty-four. A few other

---

* New York Packet, March 31, 1789.

men less renowned for public services received votes.* But they were merely complimentary, and intended to cut down the number for Adams, that he might not come too close to his illustrious chief.†

While the messengers were hastening to inform Washington and Adams of their election, the Houses were supplied by the people with advice. The ills, it was said, that beset the country came from the languishing state of agriculture, from the struggling condition of manufactures, from the importation of British goods. This last was a crying evil and should be put down. The English, ever since the close of the war, had been heaping up indignities on the Americans. Yet their connection was as fondly sought as ever. The stores and shops were full of the tawdry badges of this infamous servility ; and with sorrow should it be remarked that the paltry fashions of England, so eagerly followed by all ranks in America, were disgraceful specimens of pusillanimity, and unless speedily checked, would sully the honor of a free people. Slaves might put on the fantastic gewgaws of their masters. But how shameful for a people styling itself free and independent to be servilely copying the fopperies of those who are forever insulting it!

The first, the very first act, therefore, of the Federal Government should be to restrain commerce with Great Britain, unless on terms of reciprocity. Till this was done tradesmen and husbandmen might look forward to the halcyon days of peace and plenty ; merchants might please themselves with the prospect of a flourishing commerce ; politicians might indulge a thousand agreeable ideas of the growing riches of the country ; but depend upon it, they would never be anything but dreams. Many of Great Britain's manufactures were similar to those of the States, and ought not to be imported. If the country was to prosper, it must spend less on foreign goods than its own would sell for. Suppose, said one grumbler, and his argu-

---

* Samuel Huntington, of Conn., 2 ; John Jay, of N. Y., 9 ; John Hancock, of Mass., 4 ; R. H. Harrison, of Md., 6 ; George Clinton, of N. Y., 3 ; John Rutledge, of S. C., 6 ; John Milton, of Ga., 2 ; James Armstrong, of Ga., 1 ; Edward Telfair, of Ga., 1 ; Benjamin Lincoln, of Mass., 1.

† See a letter from Gerry to John Adams, March 4, 1789. Adams's Works.

ment may be taken as a sample of hundreds of others, the case of a Staten Island farmer. He raises beef, corn, butter, and cheese, and carries them to New York. But he is a prudent man, and bringing home no silks, no teas, no rum, lays by five hundred pounds a year. He dies, and his son succeeds to his land and fortune. But the son is a fashionable young man, and must have wines from France and Spain. The linen made of his own flax is homespun. Therefore he cannot endure it, but must supply himself from Holland and Ireland. He cannot sleep in a bed of his own linen and stuff furniture. He must have chintz, as more genteel. Nothing but a China damask is fit for a morning-gown for him to wear. When he goes to the city he takes in a thousand pounds of produce, and brings home fifteen hundred pounds of rum, spices, sugars, silks, and gauze. In a little while he falls into debt, is arrested, his farm sold, and his body lodged in the jail.

The difference between men and States is no more than less and greater; and it is pitiful to see men ploughing the ocean from the torrid to the frigid zone rather than their own fields; carrying flaxseed to Ireland and owing that country for linen, when they have under their feet the richest soil in the world. It is plainly the duty of Congress to spare no pains to restrain importation and to encourage home manufacture.*

The advice was thought sound, and had already been acted on by the people. In every great city, from Boston to Baltimore, societies for the encouragement of manufactures had sprung up since the war, and were flourishing. That at Boston put forth an address urging the manufacturers of the great seaports to join with it in checking importation.† The members of the society in Delaware took a solemn pledge to appear on the first day of January in each year clothed in goods of American make, to foster the growth of flax and

---

* See a pamphlet called Commercial Conduct of the United States of America considered, and the True Interest thereof attempted to be shown. By a Citizen of New York. Also, An Address to the Independent Electors of the Federal Government. By a Republican.

† See a Circular Letter from the tradesmen and manufacturers of the town of Boston to their brethren in the several seaports in the Union. Boston, August 20, 1788. American Museum, October, 1788.

wool, and to discourage the purchase of cloth abroad.* The society at Philadelphia had, at great cost and labor, secured the models of a cotton-carder and a cotton-spinner, built a factory, and begun the manufacture of cotton goods.†

The result was a speedy return to old habits of simplicity and frugality. Young women wore plainer clothes, and made haste to surpass their mothers in skill at the spinning-wheel.‡ Young men drank American porter and beer, and were not ashamed to be seen in homespun stockings and home-made jeans. Politicians found the surest way to win the hearts of their constituents was to appear dressed in American broad-cloth.# The town of Hartford could think of no gift so appropriate for John Adams, on his way to be inaugurated Vice-President, as a roll of cloth from its own looms.‖ All true patriots heard with joy that on the auspicious day when the American Fabius stood forth to take the oath of office he was clad from head to foot in garments whose material was the product of American soil.△

---

* See the constitution of the society as given in the American Museum, February, 1789.

† Address to the Friends of American Manufactures. By An American Citizen (Tench Coxe). American Museum, October, 1788. Federal Gazette, May 11, 1790.

‡ The interest which the young women of the time began to take in the spinning-wheel is worthy of notice, and is often alluded to in the papers. "The spinning-wheel, long neglected," says one paper, "begins to be held in general reputation by the Fair," and then goes on to give an account of some recent exploits of the Fair. United States Chronicle, June 26, 1788. "On hearing of the adoption of the new Constitution," says the same sheet a few weeks later, "fifty-five young ladies met at the house of the minister and spent the day in spinning." United States Chronicle, July 31, 1788. The town where this took place was Woodstock, Rhode Island. An account of a similar meeting "at the house of the Presbyterian minister at Newbury Port" is given in the Pennsylvania Packet of April 26, 1787. Says another paper: "A company of forty-three ladies, devoted to the encouragement of manufactures in the State of Rhode Island, met, on April 22d, in the State-House of the patriotic and federal town of East Greenwich, and spent the day in spinning. They were of no party and no creed. They spun 173·5 knotted skeins of good linen yarn, and as each spun her own flax and for her own use, the yarn spun from five to ten skeins per pound. Ten of them spun 32 skeins, one-half knot; twenty-nine spun 115 skeins, 4·5 knots; five spun 25 skeins, 10 knots. Sundry gentlemen waited on them with wine, cakes, etc." New York Packet, May 12, 1789.          # American Museum, February, 1789.

‖ Letters of John Adams to his wife, April 19, 1789.

△ Pennsylvania Gazette, May 7 and 13, 1789.

His inauguration fell on the last day of April. Washington quitted Mount Vernon on the sixteenth of the month, in company with Colonel Humphreys and Mr. Thomson, and came by the most direct road through Baltimore and Philadelphia to New York. The journey, even at that time of year, might easily have been made in five days, but he was much delayed by the hearty receptions given him along the entire route. From every village and hamlet through which the road lay the people poured forth to welcome him, and to testify, by shouts and blessings, their love and gratitude for the great things he had done. He was feasted at Alexandria. He was entertained at Georgetown. He was warmly received at Philadelphia. The people of that city had selected Gray's Ferry, on the lower Schuylkill, as the place to meet him, and had taxed their ingenuity to the utmost to devise decorations worthy of the occasion. The bridge, a mean and rude structure, was hidden under cedars and laurel, flags and liberty-caps. Two triumphal arches were put up, and signals arranged to give warning of his coming.

At last, about noon on the twentieth, the flag in the ferry-garden was dropped, and soon after the President was seen riding slowly down the hill and under the first arch, where a laurel crown was let fall upon his head. From the bridge he went on in company with Governor Mifflin and the troops to Philadelphia, where he lay that night.* The moment he entered the city limits the bells of all the churches were rung, and, in the language of that time, a *feu de joie* was fired. The President was much affected, and, says an eye-witness, as he moved down Market street to the city tavern every face seemed to say, Long, long, long live George Washington.† Early the next morning the Philadelphia Horse rode with him to Trenton, where a yet more pleasing reception awaited him. On the Assumpink bridge, over which, twelve years

---

* Account of the Preparations at Gray's Ferry, on the River Schuylkill, and of the Reception of General Washington there, April 20, 1789, on his way to the Seat of Federal Government, to take upon him the High Office of President of the United States. Embellished with an east view of the ferry, the bridge, the decoration, etc. Columbian Magazine, May, 1789.

† Pennsylvania Gazette, April 22, 1789. Pennsylvania Mercury, April 21, 1789. Freeman's Journal, April 22, 1789. New York Packet, May 1, 1789.

before, he led his little army on the night before the battle of Princeton, the women of Trenton had put up a triumphal arch. Thirteen columns supported it, and were surmounted by a great dome adorned with a sunflower, and the inscription, "To thee alone." Beyond the bridge was gathered a bevy of women and girls, who, as the President passed under the dome, came forward to greet him, singing and strewing the way with flowers. Washington was greatly touched, and thanked them in a few neatly turned sentences.[*]

From Trenton the Huntington Horse accompanied him to Rocky Hill, where the Somerset Horse met him and escorted him to Brunswick. Thence the Middlesex Horse took him to Woodbridge, and the Essex Horse to the barge at Elizabethtown point.[†] Once on board, the little craft was rowed by thirteen pilots through the Kill von Kull and out into the broad bosom of the most beautiful of harbors. Around him on every side crowded an innumerable navy of trackscouts and shallops, barges and row-boats, gay with flags and black with shouting men. Before him, just visible in the distance, lay the low hills and the white houses of the great city, and as the barge sped swiftly toward them, the Spanish warship Galveston saluted with thirteen guns. The ship North Carolina replied. A third salute was fired by the artillery as Washington climbed the stairs at Murray's wharf and was welcomed by Clinton, the senators and representatives, and escorted through dense lines of cheering citizens to the house made ready for his use. At night the sky was red with bonfires, and the streets and coffee-houses full of revellers.[‡]

It was the twenty-third of the month. But as a few finishing touches were yet to be given to Federal Hall, the ceremonies of inauguration were put off till the thirtieth. On the morning of that day the people went in crowds to the churches to offer up prayers for the welfare of the new Gov-

---

[*] New York Packet, May 1, 1789. See, also, the Account of the Manner of receiving, at Trenton, his Excellency George Washington, President of the United States, on his Route to the Seat of Federal Government. Communicated in a Letter to the Editor. Embellished with a view of Trenton and the triumphal arch. Columbian Magazine, May, 1789. Freeman's Journal, April 29, 1789.

[†] New York Journal, April, 1789. Gazette of the United States, April 29, 1789.     [‡] Ibid., April 30, 1789. New York Packet, May 1, 1789.

ernment and the safety of the President.  Precisely at noon the procession, which had been forming almost since sunrise, moved from Washington's house on Cherry street, through Queen street,* Great Dock † and Broad streets, to Federal Hall.  As the head of the line reached the building the troops divided, and Washington was led through the midst of them to the Senate-chamber, where both Houses were formally introduced to him.  When the members were again seated and the noise had subsided, Adams, who had already been inaugurated, informed the President that the time had come for the administration of the oath of office.  Washington rose, and followed by the members of the two Houses, went out on the balcony of Federal Hall, from which he could be seen far up and far down Wall street, and by the multitude that filled Broad street.  The Chancellor of New York tendered the oath, and when the ceremony was over, turning toward the people, cried out, "Long live George Washington, President of the United States!"  The crowd took up the cry, and amid the joyous shouts of the citizens and the roar of the cannon on the Battery, Washington went back to the Senate-chamber and delivered his inaugural.  That night there were bonfires in all the streets, and moving transparencies in the windows of the Spanish Minister's house.

It now became proper, in accordance with the ancient usage of the British Parliament, to frame an answer to the President's speech.  But here a new difficulty arose.  By what title should he be addressed?  A decent respect, it was said, for the opinions and usages of civilized nations required that some title of respectability should be given to the Chief Magistrate.  But what?  Should he be mentioned in State papers, and complimented in resolutions, under the title of His Highness, or His Excellency?  Was it consistent with the simplicity of a republic to style him High Mightiness?  Or should he content himself with the more humble appellation of the President?  The question was as delicate as it was puzzling, and had been under debate in both Houses since the day he landed at Murray's wharf.  Committees had been appointed, conferences

* Now Pearl street east of Hanover square.
† Now Pearl street from Hanover square to Whitehall street.

had been held, reports had been made, and a complete disagreement had resulted. The representatives adopted the report of their committee, that it would be unwise to use any other title than that given in the Constitution, and on the eighth of May addressed the executive as the President. But the senators were of a different mind. They were strongly in favor of a high-sounding title, and at the very moment the House was thanking the President for his gracious words in a neighboring chamber, rejected the report, declared the words "His Excellency" were not dignified enough, and appointed three of their members to confer with a House committee and devise better. The resolution was sent down to the House the following day, which was Saturday, and on Monday came up for debate.

A dozen members spoke. But the speech that came nearest the sentiments of the people, and was most applauded out of doors, was made by Tucker, of South Carolina. He was, he said, opposed to such a committee. The matter was one the House had no right to take into consideration. Then, turning to the Speaker, he exclaimed: "What, sir, is the intention of this business? Will it not alarm our fellow-citizens? Will it not give them just cause for alarm? Will they not say that they have been deceived by the convention that framed the Constitution? One of its warmest advocates, nay, one of its framers, has recommended it by calling it a pure democracy. Does giving titles look like a pure democracy? Surely not. Some one has said that to give dignity to our Government we must give a lofty title to our Chief Magistrate. Does the dignity of a nation then consist in the distance between the first magistrate and the citizens? Is it true that it consists in the exaltation of one man and the humiliation of all the rest? If so, then to make our dignity complete we must give first a high title, then an embroidered robe, then a princely equipage, and finally a crown and hereditary succession. This spirit of imitation, sir, this spirit of mimicry and apery, will be the ruin of our country. Instead of giving us dignity in the eyes of foreigners, it will expose us to be laughed at as apes. Let us set up tranquillity and good order at home, then wealth, strength, and national dignity will be the infallible result."

Jackson, one of the three from Georgia, wondered what title the Senate knew of that could add lustre to the man who filled the presidential chair. For his part he could think of none. Would it add to the fame of Washington to call him after the petty and insignificant princes of Europe? Would styling him Your Serene Highness, or Your Grace, or Your Mightiness, add one tittle to the solid properties he possessed? Certainly not. To talk of such a thing was to trifle with the dignity of the Government.

Madison spoke in the same strain. He saw no danger in a title. He did not believe that a President, clothed with all the powers of the Constitution and loaded down with all the titles of Europe and Asia, would be a dangerous person to American liberty. He objected to the principle. If, said he, we give titles, we must either borrow or invent them. If we invent and deck out an airy being of our creation, it is a great chance but its fantastic properties render the empty phantom ridiculous and absurd. If we borrow, our servile imitation will be odious. We must copy from the pompous monarchs of the East, or we must follow the inferior monarchs of Europe. In either case the splendid tinsel and the gorgeous robe will disgrace the manly shoulders of our chief.

When a few more members had been heard, Lee, to get rid of the matter, moved the previous question. It was agreed, however, to appoint a committee of five. A few days later the problem that had puzzled Jackson was solved. The title the Senate had in view was: His Highness, the President of the United States of America, and Protector of their Liberties. Nothing ever came of the conference, and the matter was suffered to drop.*

But the praise the House got for its display of patriotism on this occasion was, a few weeks later, more than outweighed by the abuse it received for passing the Salaries Bill. Some of the members, who confessed that they were well-nigh reduced to borrowing from their friends, brought it up in the midst of

---

* Some expressions of public opinion are given in New York Daily Advertiser, August 1, 1789. Gazette of the United States, June 20, July 8, and September 2, 1789. New York Journal, August 27, 1789. See, also, the reports of the Congressional Debates in New York Journal, May 14, 1789.

a debate on the western lands. There was little discussion over what the pay of the President should be. He had, indeed, plainly said in his inaugural that he would take none. But, as a debater justly remarked, the Constitution declared that he should have a salary, and it was the duty of the House to provide one. Some were for making it seventy thousand dollars a year. Others thought fifteen or twenty thousand quite enough. Twenty-five thousand was at length agreed on, and at that sum it remained till Grant had been some years in the White House.

The sum the Vice-President should receive provoked a long dispute. The duties and the position of that officer were but ill-defined. The Constitution, it was said, was silent as to both. It did indeed declare that he should sit in the chair of the Senate. But no penalty could fall on him if he shirked this duty and followed pursuits more to his liking than keeping order, putting questions, and announcing the results of ballotings. He might, as a member pointed out, follow any business he chose, stay at home, raise corn or tobacco, draw his pay, and never show his face in the Senate-chamber. Under such circumstances it was doubtful whether he should be paid by the year or by the day for the time he actually sat in the chair. The arguments, however, in behalf of an annual stipend prevailed, and five thousand dollars was agreed to. It was then declared that the members of the Senate and House should receive each six dollars a day, and the Speaker twelve, for every day of the session.

Six dollars a day to the members and twelve to the Speaker! exclaimed the news-writers. The wages are twice what they should be. Where in Europe or America can a precedent for such pay to legislators be found? The British Commons get six shillings a day. The colonial assemblymen, in times before the war, had but eight or ten. The wages of the late Congress ought not to be cited, for it was properly not a Congress, but a council of the States. But perhaps no precedent is wanted. To give the Speaker such extravagant pay is yet more absurd. He has the very easiest berth in the House. He is never on a committee. He never draws up a bill. He never frames a message. Twelve dollars a day is seventeen hundred and fifty-two pounds a year, and seventeen hundred and fifty-two pounds a year may be thought by the gentlemen who get it as a very pretty annuity.* But the mechanics and laborers who are to pay it will see it in a different light. Such wages will enable congressmen to live away from home, to support a theatre, to drink fine wines, and will keep other States from coming into the Union. The expenses of the Government at that rate will be near nine hundred thousand pounds a year.†

To this one of the members of the House replied in a letter to a friend, which soon found its way into print. Six dollars a day was, he remarked, no more than for years was given by Pennsylvania to her delegates. Nay, it was less than was paid under the old Confederacy by all the other States except New Jersey. Massachusetts gave a guinea and board. Virginia and South Carolina a half-joe. This, too, was for every day in the three hundred and sixty-five. Now congressmen were paid for only four or five months out of the twelve.‡ Taking seventy days as the average, and allowing, said another defender of the bill, one hundred and forty dollars for mileage, the sum put into the wallet of each member would be two hundred and ten pounds.# Out of this, if a man were frugal and economical, kept away from the theatre, and never tasted fine wines, he might perchance save one hundred and ten pounds. And this was to compensate him, if a professional man, for the loss of patients or clients; or, if a merchant, for a great chasm in his business. As for the Speaker, he was expected to keep open table.‖

To defray what the Antifederalists called this shameful cost of Government, Congress had already made provisions. A few

---

* It should seem, at first sight, as if this computation were wrong. But it must be remembered that the money of 1789 was not the money of 1883; that the place was New York, and at New York eight local shillings made a dollar.

† See Pennsylvania Gazette, July 15, 1789. Letter from a gentleman in New Jersey to his friend in New York. New York Packet, August 1, 1789.

‡ Letter from a member of the House of Representatives. New York Packet, August 26, 1789.

# Pennsylvania money. Seven shillings and a half to the dollar.

‖ New York Packet, August 25, 1789. See, also, Boston Gazette, September 7, 1789.

days after the session began, when the Speaker had been chosen, when the door-keepers had been elected, when the form of oath for new members had been framed, the House went into a committee of the whole on the state of the Union. Page was put in the chair, and when the floor was declared open, Madison rose and addressed them. He recalled to his hearers the imbecility of the late Congress, congratulated them on the establishment of a vigorous Government, and reminded them that one of the first duties before them was to pay the just debts of the country. This required a full Treasury. A full Treasury could only be kept up by a steady revenue, and a revenue to be steady must bear lightly on the people. Happily for the country, such a system of taxation was possible. He then read the impost system of 1783, added a clause or two on tonnage, and urged the committee to adopt it, or at least make it the basis of a temporary impost. Revenue must be had. Spring was at hand, and spring was the season of importation. In a few weeks the great seaports would be full of ships laden with rum from Jamaica and wine from Madeira, with sugar and spice from the Indies, and the fair products of French and English looms. If, therefore, the committee loitered in their work, the Treasury would lose a great sum which could by a light impost be brought into its strong box.

The speech was well received, and with much show of alacrity the matter was instantly taken up. It was provided in the bill that the mass of goods, wares, and merchandise coming in from foreign parts should be subject to a tax of five per cent on their value. But a long list of articles was given on which special duties were to be laid. At the head of the list stood Jamaica rum, which on motion was changed to distilled spirits of Jamaica proof. Two duties were suggested, one of fifteen cents and one of twelve cents the gallon, which speedily divided the committee. Some thought such rates too high. Some declared they were much too low. And before the discussion had gone far it turned into a debate on the good and ill effects of high duties and low duties. One low - tariff member remarked that the first thing to be considered in laying a tax was the likelihood of gathering it, and that as taxes increased this likelihood decreased. " I trust," said he, " it does not need illustration to convince every member of the committee that a high duty is a very strong temptation to smuggling. Just in the proportion which a tax bears to the value of an article is the risk men will run in their attempts to bring in that article in an illegal way. This impairs the revenue, and in time so much comes in through the hands of smugglers that no revenue is yielded at all." Boudinot said "he for one would be glad to see Jamaica rum doing just that very thing. There were three good results that would come of a high rum tariff. The Treasury wanted money, and surely there was no article on the list of taxable goods so likely to furnish a revenue as rum. The importation would be discouraged, and that was beneficial to the morals of the people. The West Indian distillers would have no inducement to turn their molasses into rum, and as they had no markets for molasses save those of the United States, the home stills would be set actively to work."

His remarks on the moral effects of the tax were violently attacked by two members from the eastward. Fisher Ames quite forgot himself, and reminded the committee, with great vehemence of gesture and speech, that they were not in church or at school, to sit listening to harangues of speculative piety. "We are," exclaimed he, "to talk of the political interests committed to our care. When we take up the subject of morality, then let our system look toward morality, and not confound itself with revenue and the protection of manufactures. If any man supposes that a mere law can turn the taste of a people from ardent spirits to malt liquors, he has a most romantic notion of legislative power."

Lawrence, one of the members from New York, took up the attack. He was for low tariff. If, said he, the committee is to reason and act as moralists, the arguments of the member from New Jersey are sound. For it must be the wish of every man of sense to discourage the use of articles so ruinous to health and morals as rum. But we are to act as politicians, not as moralists. Rum, not morality, is to be taxed. Money, not sobriety, is the object of the tax; and if we can from the vices of men draw some of that revenue which one way or another the people must contribute, we are right in doing so. But suppose we yield to the reasoning of my opponent and lay a high duty, and check the importation of rum. What will happen? We shall defeat our purpose. The country will be just as immoral, and much poorer than at present. Not a hogshead of the liquor will be seen on our wharfs, not a shilling of revenue will be collected from it by our custom-house officers. Yet at all the inns and taverns in the land rum will be as plentiful and as cheap as ever. Does any man suppose for a moment that the thousands of artisans, and the mechanics, the tradesmen, and the fishermen, to whom liquor is as much a necessity of life as meat and bread, will upon a sudden cease to drink it because it is taxed with a great tax? Will they not rather set on foot ten thousand schemes to evade the duty? and is there any ingenuity so marvellous as the ingenuity of men who seek to circumvent an unwise law? Lay such a tax, and in a few months every creek, every secluded bay, every swamp along the whole coast from Maine to Georgia, will be a nest of smugglers. There, in the dark of each moon and in the blackness of each stormy night, hogsheads of the forbidden liquor will be run ashore and buried in the marsh, or hidden in the cellar of some fisherman's hut, to be reshipped to the great seaports of the country. Then will spring up a mode of tax gathering odious to all. On the land an army of custom-house officers, tide-waiters, and gaugers. On the sea a navy of ships, hailing every schooner, boarding every packet, giving chase to every shallop that comes in sight. And when the money collected with so much pains has been counted, the cost of ships and officers paid, and the books balanced, it will indeed be astonishing if a single shilling remains over in the Treasury.

The justness of this reasoning was lost on the committee, and spirits of Jamaica proof were taxed at fifteen cents a gallon.

Molasses stood next on the list. What should be done with it was hard to say. Whole sections of country were mentioned where it was shown to be a most common article of diet. Every gallon of it came from abroad, and it was at the same time the substance from which rum was distilled. If, therefore, too high a duty was imposed, a cry would go up which it would be impossible not to hear. If too low a duty were laid, thousands of hogsheads would come into the country, be turned into rum, and the revenue expected from that source be seriously impaired. Eight cents per gallon, it was thought, would not be a burden on the consumers of molasses in the crude state, yet would be sufficient to discourage its importation by distillers. A duty of eight cents was therefore proposed. Immediately every member from Massachusetts rose and protested. It was too much. The people would never bear it. Rum, which was not worth more than forty-five cents a gallon, was taxed at fifteen cents, or one third its value. Then why should molasses, which would scarcely fetch fifteen cents a gallon, be taxed at eight? This, too, fell on particular States and particular classes. Everybody knew that every quart of molasses which the countrymen spread on their bread or put in their tea came from the French West Indies in exchange for codfish and herrings. For nine months of every year a fleet of New England fishermen braved the storms and fogs of the fishing-banks, trolling and drawing the seine. Their smacks numbered four hundred and eighty. The burden exceeded twenty-seven thousand tons. The catch of a single year often went over four hundred thousand quintals. Yet these honest fishermen had but one market for their products, and in that market could purchase but two articles, rum and molasses. The French would suffer nothing else to go out of the ports in exchange for the fish.

The importation was therefore very great. The ships of Massachusetts alone brought into her ports each twelvemonth forty thousand hogsheads of molasses. Part was consumed raw; part was made into rum. The capital engaged in the business of distilling summed up to half a million of dollars. Yet it was now proposed to destroy these two great industries, which contributed so much to the prosperity and welfare of the nation. Rum was to be taxed till it ceased to be imported, and molasses was to be loaded down with such a duty as would make it too costly to eat and too expensive to distil. Then, when it was too late to mend them, the evils of the odious tax would come out fast. Rum and molasses, no longer salable at home, would cease to be purchased abroad. Fish, having no longer a market in foreign parts, would cease to be caught, the smacks would rot in the harbors, and the fishermen turn ploughmen and mechanics. What, then, would become of the country? Were not the fishing-banks the school of seamen? And when these were deserted, whence would come sailors to man the ships in time of war, and to navigate the merchantmen in time of peace? It was idle to talk of such a duty. The poor of New England would never endure a tax on their favorite beverage of spruce, molasses, and water. To cite the example of England was thought to be unpatriotic. Yet it would be well to remember what had been the experience of that great nation in this same matter. She, too, had in colonial days laid her hand upon molasses and taxed it threepence the gallon. But such heart-burnings and contentions sprang up that she was glad to cut down the duty to a penny.

With this picture of distress before them, the committee readily consented to lower the duty to six cents. The work of finishing the list then went on. Some articles were thrown out; some were taxed without discussion. But a few gave rise to sharp debates. The greater part of two days were spent in wrangling over salt. Cordage and hemp consumed as much more. When steel was reached, a proposition was made to admit it free. It was declared to be of great use in the manufacture of agricultural tools. And as enough for that purpose could never be produced in the Union, there seemed to be some reason for making it an article of bounty rather than an article of tax. Clymer, who came from Philadelphia, resented this. There was, he said, in Philadelphia a single furnace which had, with a little aid from the State, manufactured three hundred tons of steel in two years. It was even then making at the rate of two hundred and thirty tons a year, and would, if protected and encouraged, produce enough for the country.

When the whole list had been gone over, the committee rose and reported. The House considered the report, and ordered a bill providing for duties on certain goods, wares, and merchandises to be brought in. Three weeks later it passed the third reading and became a law. The debates on the bill before the House were little more than a repetition of what had already been said in the committee. Member after member from the southern States rose and protested against the duties. The scale was too high. The late Congress, such was the substance of their reasoning, had drawn up for impost a

list of eight articles. It was fair to suppose that the matter
had been carefully studied, and that the estimated annual revenue of nine hundred and fifteen thousand six hundred and
fifty-six dollars which the eight selected articles were expected
to yield was a safe one. An examination of the lists would
show that these same goods were now taxed at a rate four or
even five times as great as that proposed in 1783. They should
therefore produce at least three million six hundred thousand
dollars yearly. But the new list was four times as long as the
old. It was safe to infer, therefore, that between thirteen and
fourteen millions of dollars would come into the Treasury.
This was out of all reason. The public service did not require
it; and if it did, there was not specie enough in the country to
pay it. It was unjust to lay such a burden on imported goods
when equally sure and productive sources of revenue were at
hand. There was tonnage, there was the post-office, and many
other contrivances which the ingenuity of Government could
devise. To order that because a certain thing could be made
cheaply in one part of this country, foreign goods of the same
kind should be heavily taxed to keep them out, was partial
and unjust. It was true that nails and paper, spinning-irons
and shoes, could be bought at Boston and Philadelphia for a
less sum than they could be imported. But could they be
carried and sold at Charleston or Savannah for that price?
Surely not. Even if they could, the makers had no business
connections in the South such as foreigners had. The moment
a lot of brooms or a cargo of linens came into Charleston, they
were carried by agents all over the State and disposed of
without inconvenience to the buyer. But suppose a cargo of
shoe-nails from Massachusetts came into the Ashley. How
could the people purchase it? Were the shoemakers from
every remote village in the State to come down to the dock
and supply themselves? Did gentlemen fancy it was merely
necessary to fill a ship with merchandise and send it to the
dock at Charleston, to have the planters come down and take
them away? The planters could supply themselves at less
cost and less pains under the present arrangement. Now they
could purchase on long credit, and pay when the crops were
gathered. The market for their rice, their indigo, their pitch,

their tobacco, was in Europe, not in America. When, however, duty was laid, and foreign goods ceased to come in, all would be changed. The planters would then be forced to send their crops abroad, sell for what they could get, and bring home the money before they could buy hats or coats, or linen for shirts. This was an imposition on the South. It was wrong to compel her to buy in the home market unless she could do so as reasonably as in a European market.

The New England members used much the same arguments against the molasses duty. But they joined with the middle States in support of a high tonnage. The House was assured that the distress of the East for want of a tonnage duty was truly alarming. Her shipwrights, who a few years before were the busiest of men on the best of pay, were now glad to work for two shillings and sixpence a day, which was simply starvation wages. Her sail-makers were idle. Her lumber lay rotting in the forests where it had been felled, for want of encouragement to frame it into ships. Philadelphia, where before the war five thousand tons of shipping were built annually, had in the last year launched but thirteen hundred. A protective tariff would, however, soon correct this evil. It would give life to ship-building. The sound of the calking-hammer would be heard in every ship-yard, and American merchantmen be seen in every sea and harbor open to them in Europe.

The southern members drew a different picture. The duty, they asserted, which was to do all these fine things for the East would ruin them. The moment foreign ships were shut out of their ports they were broken men. Of the twenty thousand tons employed in carrying the rice and lumber of Georgia across the sea, fourteen thousand tons were foreign. Burke startled the House by asserting deliberately that not one ship was owned in the State of South Carolina. Where were they to find carriers for their produce when the duty was laid? From the East? Certainly not, for the East had not ships enough for herself. Did not Massachusetts give employment to eight thousand tons of foreign shipping besides thirty thousand of her own? The tax would simply make matters worse. The carrying trade would stay where it was, in the hands of the French and English, freightage would go up, and the rice and tobacco of the planters would rot on their hands. Already the rates were so high, and the market value of rice and indigo so low, that it was a white day with a merchant when the goods he sent abroad paid for the goods he brought home. Tonnage duty was a blow to the prosperity of the South. It was unjust to sacrifice the permanent welfare of one part of the country to the temporary interests of another.

The complaints were not heeded, and the duty was laid.* Indeed, the House, it should seem, had reached the wise conclusion that the members from South Carolina and Georgia could be pleased with nothing. No sooner was a tax proposed than Tucker, or Jackson, or Burke was sure to rise and declare that the burden would fall on the South, that it was aimed full at his State, would quote Scripture about the widow's mite and the rich man's coffers, or remind the House that the new Government was not much liked in Carolina, and that it would not be wise to increase the aversion by an unpopular and oppressive tax. The impost on tallow-candles and raw steel, table-salt and Jamaica rum, nails and foreign ships, was talked of as if every penny of it would be collected in the States south of the Potomac. When such a duty really was proposed, so great a clamor arose that the motion was hastily withdrawn.

Parker, of Virginia, was the mover. Though himself a slave-holder and the representative of a slave State, he had the boldness to stand up and suggest that a duty of ten dollars should be laid on every slave brought in from abroad. He was, he told the House, sorry that the Constitution did not forbid the practice altogether. It was a great defect in the instrument to suffer such a business to go on. It was contrary to revolutionary principles. The southern members listened to him in consternation. But they kept their temper, and when he was done Jackson rose to reply.

"When," he said, "he recollected the source whence the motion came, he ceased to be surprised. Virginia was an old settled State. She had been long in the slave-trade, and had all

---

* On vessels built and owned in the United States, six cents a ton; on vessels built but not owned in the United States, thirty cents; on vessels of powers having treaties with the United States, thirty cents; all others, fifty cents.

the slaves she wanted.  Their natural increase was enough for her uses.  But before she laid such a burden on their importation she should let her less fortunate neighbors get supplied. He was well aware that the business was looked on as odious to the eastward.  There the people did their own work.  It had become the fashion of the day to talk of emancipation. He would not go into a discussion of the subject.  But he would venture to express the belief that it could be shown that the blacks were best off in slavery.  Suppose they were set free.  What would they do?  Work for a living?  Maryland had freed her slaves, and did they betake themselves to work for a living?  Far from it.  They turned common pick-pockets and petit-larceny villains.  If Virginia thought slavery an evil, let her begin by setting her slaves free.  Would she do it?  When that time came, the sound of liberty would lose the charms that now made it grateful to the ravished ear."

Burke, who five years before had thundered against the Cincinnati as dangerous to liberty, now proceeded to defend slavery.  He put on an air of indifference, and declared that the House was contending for nothing.  A good, healthy slave was worth about eighty pounds, and five per cent duty on that sum would be ten dollars.  He was at a loss, therefore, to see what difference it made whether slaves were specially taxed at ten dollars, or were left to be taxed at five per cent with the mass of importation.  He was stoutly told in reply that if the House was wrangling about nothing, he was not contending for much.  It made a great deal of difference whether slaves fresh from Africa were subjected to a specified tax or were left to the *ad valorem* duty, and for two reasons.  In the first place, the bill provided for a duty on goods, wares, and merchandise. The customs officers were not used to look upon human beings as either goods, or wares, or merchandise.  The slaves would therefore be supposed to come in free of duty.  But there was, in the second place, something to be gained more important to the country than a few thousand dollars of revenue.  A great principle was at stake.  It was time this nefarious traffic in human creatures was broken up.  It was time the country yielded to the dictates of humanity and taxed slavery out of existence.

On this point the members from the eastward were strongly divided. All agreed in denouncing the practice. They abhorred slavery from their very souls. They wished the Constitution had abolished it. Some, however, declared that they could not bring themselves to lay a tax on flesh and blood. It was degrading to human nature to be treated as bales of chintz and casks of rum. Besides, to tax slaves might look like countenancing the detested business. All this was admitted. It certainly was lowering to humanity to be rated as merchandise. But was it not better to submit to a little degradation than to suffer the shameful traffic to go on a moment longer? It laid the country open to the just charge of inconsistency. It gave the lie to the Declaration of Independence. While the lips of the slave-holder pronounced all men to be born free and equal, he was busy with his hands tearing unhappy negroes from their homes, bringing them in chains across the sea, and selling them into the house of bondage for a price. To say that it was no rare thing in Africa for parents to sell their children, that prisoners of war were always made slaves, that to be dragged loaded with shackles to the rice-swamp and the tobacco-field was merely to exchange one slavery for another, and that of all slaveries that among a Christian people was the least galling, was to talk nonsense. It was about as sensible as it would have been to say that because it was the custom of the Indians to maim and torture their prisoners to death, every Cherokee or Chickasaw brave that fell into the hands of the Kentuckians should instantly be drowned. For that would be merely exchanging one form of death for another, and no one could doubt that drowning was a much more agreeable death than roasting at the stake. If it were barbarous for savages to roast their captives, it would be heinous for civilized men to drown theirs. If it were cruel for pagan blacks on the coast of Guinea, who made no pretensions to equality among men, to enslave the prisoners of their club and bow, what could be said of civilized Christians who, having fought for and gained their own liberty under the pretence that liberty was a natural right of man, proceeded to take away this natural right from others?

Unhappily the debate went no further. Parker yielded to

the advice of his friends, withdrew his motion, and a few days later asked leave to bring in a bill providing for a duty on certain imported persons till the year 1808.

And now for a while business went smoothly on. The import and tonnage bills were disposed of, bills establishing the Department of State, the Treasury Department, the War Department, and the Land Office were ordered to be brought in, and some amendments to the Constitution were discussed. As they passed from the House they were seventeen in number, and were based upon such amendments as had been insisted on by the conventions of Virginia, New Hampshire, and New York. The Senate, by compressing some and striking out others, cut down the number to twelve ; the House agreed, and in this form they were sent to the States. Of the twelve, ten were ratified by three fourths of the States, and became thenceforth part of the Constitution. Two, that which regulated the number, and that which fixed the pay of the members of the House of Representatives, were most wisely thrown out by the States.

It was now the third of September, and the House, agreeable to a previous notice, listened to a motion for selecting a place of permanent residence for the General Government.

The debate began at once, and was one of the longest and the most acrimonious the members had yet been engaged in. It began on a Thursday morning, and was not over when the members adjourned for dinner on the following Monday. Every one of the fifty-nine had something to say, and the reports of the speeches that have come down to us, though broken and meagre, are full of interest. They show most clearly what was the common opinion among men of that time concerning the prosperity and greatness of the country in our own.

The eastern members, it should seem, were ill-disposed to consider the matter at all. The close of the session was near at hand. Much unfinished business was still before the House. The choice of a spot for the national city was not pressing, and might therefore be left over till Congress met again. But when they saw that the House was determined to go on, they organized a caucus, called in a few of the representatives from

the middle States, talked the matter over, decided that the
new city ought to be as near the centre of population, wealth,
and territory as an easy connection with the Atlantic and the
Ohio would allow, and that the desired place could undoubtedly be found on the east bank of the Susquehanna. A motion to this effect was accordingly made and carried. The next
moment the southern members were on their legs calling to
the Speaker for a hearing.

What, such was the substance of their arguments, what
was the use of laying down for guidance principles so vague
and absurd? What was to be understood by the centre of
population, wealth, and territory? There was one centre for
wealth, and another for population, and a third for territory.
Did the House propose to find the centre of these three centres? The thing could not be done. The numbers of the
people were rapidly increasing in some States and rapidly de-
creasing in others. Thousands of foreigners were settling in
the South. Thousands of farmers from the eastward were
pouring down the Ohio valley to the rich lands beyond the
mountains. What was the centre of population when the site
for the Federal city was chosen would therefore cease to be
the centre before half the Government buildings were put up.
And how was the centre of territory to be found out? Was
the uninhabited wilderness to be considered? Should they
take the Lake of the Woods on one side and the Missouri on
the other, and seek the geographical centre? If so, it would
surely fall on a spot far away from the limits of civilization,
and abounding in beasts and savage men. But they were
assured the populated part of the country ought not to be
thought of, and that if the river St. Croix were made the eastern and the river St. Mary's the southern limit, the centre of
territory would be found hard by the banks of the Susquehanna.
Lee hoped that some member well posted in geography would
show how these banks conformed with the guiding principles
laid down in the motion; how they communicated with the
Atlantic, and how they were connected with the territory of
the West.

Hartley took him at his word and answered him. Wright's
Ferry was such a town. It stood upon the east bank some

thirty-five miles from sea-water. As for the Susquehanna, so great was the volume of its waters that ships could at any time of year sail up it to the waters of Otsego lake. Three fine rivers ran into it, from the north, the west, and the south. The Tioga was navigable for a great distance, and was connected by an easy portage with the Genesee, which emptied into Lake Ontario. The Juniata nearly connected with the Kiskimientas, and that with the Ohio. A short land-carriage joined the head of the west branch with the Alleghany, which gave easy connection with the frontier towns of Kentucky. As to the town, it was no mean place. But ten miles separated Wright's Ferry from the great city of Lancaster. The climate was salubrious. The soil and the river yielded plentifully. If the honorable gentleman was disposed to give attention to a dish of fish, he could find none finer than could be drawn from the waters of the Susquehanna. "Then why not," said Lee, "go at once to Yorktown? Why fix on the banks of a swift river when it is possible to occupy the shores of Codorus creek?"

He was assured by Goodhue that the Susquehanna was much to be preferred. There was the centre of territory. The centre of population, it was true, lay to the northward. But the eastern members were ready, from a spirit of conciliation, to let that pass. They well knew that the centre of population would not change for ages, and that when it did, the movement would be to the eastward, not to the south; to the manufacturing, not to the agricultural States.

This remark was too much for the patience of one of the representatives from Georgia. He flew into a passion and demanded to know what the people would say when they learned that the members from New England and New York had fixed on the seat of Government for the United States. This was not proper language to go out to freemen. Jealousies were already abroad, and this would blow the coals of sedition into a consuming flame. Were the other members of the Union not to be consulted? Were the eastern men to dictate to the country, and fix the Federal city where it pleased them? Why not also fix the principles of government while their hands were in? Why not come forward and say to the

South, " Give us up your principles and we will govern you ? "
This looked like aristocracy. It was not true that the geographical centre was to be found on the Susquehanna. From
Wright's Ferry to the nearest point of the province of Maine
was four hundred miles, and to the nearest point in the upper
district of Georgia it was nine hundred miles.

This in turn was denied. From the Ferry to the extreme
of Maine, a member said, was seven hundred and sixty miles.
To Savannah the distance was precisely the same. To Kentucky it was seven hundred and thirty or forty miles. But
aside from all this, there was surely no occasion for such a
display of warmth. It had been merely stated that a consulta-
tion of the eastern members had taken place. Was there anything wrong in this ? So far from being a mark of an aristocratic spirit, it was merely a proof that men, attentive to their
own business, had chosen this way of discussing it. The proposed city ought to be placed somewhere between the Potomac and the Delaware. The Potomac was objectionable. It
was believed in the East to be unhealthy. Vast numbers of
New England adventurers had gone to the southern States,
and all had found graves there. The Delaware was to be preferred. The strength and riches of the country lay in the
North. There, too, was the centre of population. For surely
no man of candor would for a moment pretend that southern
slaves, men with no rights whatever, should be taken thought
of in determining where the seat of Government should be.
As well might they count the black cattle of New England.

At this stage of the debate Vining obtained a hearing. He
was the only representative Delaware had in the House, was a
man of small parts, and never rose to speak but he entertained
the members with a style of oratory for which florid is a mild
term. After some remarks about the rays of Government, the
unpolished sons of earth, and the pains he had taken to chastise
the prejudices of his mind, he declared he had taken no part in
making the bargain. He was at a loss to know whether Congress was to tickle the trout in the stream Codorus, to build
their sumptuous palaces on the banks of the Potomac, or ad-
mire Commerce with her expanded wings on the waters of the
Delaware. For himself he leaned toward the Potomac.

And now a number of places were suggested. One member moved Peach Bottom, a second was for Harrisburg, a third for the Hudson. But the debate was narrowed down to a comparison of the claims of the Susquehanna and the Potomac. The advantages of the latter were well set forth by Stone, of Maryland.

In fixing the seat of Government it was proper, he thought, to have clearly in view not only the present importance of the States, but their weight at a day in the near future. He did not mean a visionary importance or a chimerical expectation, but such a one as could be proved with as much certainty as that effects follow causes. Now, it did not need demonstration to show that the increase of population to the eastward was merely conditional. There was nothing to invite men to settle there. The climate was severe. The winters were long. The summers were short. The soil was cold and barren. Even if a few hardy adventurers did come into New England, they would soon be driven, by the very law which determined the increase of men, to seek the States beyond the Potomac. Men multiplied in proportion to the ease with which they secured food. But food was more plentiful in a warm than in a cold climate. It was clear, therefore, that at no very distant day the population of the continent would be massed in the warm and fertile States of the South. Indeed, this had already begun. Look at that part of the West called Kentucky. Compare its increase in population since the war with that of any State to the eastward. It had surpassed them all. Nothing like it had ever before been known in America. But this vast crowd of adventurers that was daily spreading over the valley of the Ohio should be closely watched. Everybody knew that immigrants were in general bold and hardy spirits, caring little for laws, hating strict government, and ready for any enterprise, however desperate. But those of Kentucky were particularly so. They were near a great rival nation, eager to make them its subjects. They were independent in their condition. Their soil was rich, their crops were abundant; they wanted scarcely anything the East could give them, and what they wanted from abroad the Spaniards would gladly give them in exchange for bacon and flour, butter and hams. Everything tempted them to break the few ties that bound them to the East, form a new government, or go over in a body to the Crown of Spain. To hinder this the Government must go near them; near enough to be felt by them and to be within easy reach of them. The banks of the Potomac were therefore the place for the Federal city. The Susquehanna came down from the north. The Potomac came from the west, and, of all the rivers in the Union that mingled their waters with the Atlantic, was the only one that afforded a practical, short, and safe communication with Kentucky and the West.

The day closed with some savage remarks from the Virginia delegates. Lee had been upon his legs urging the claims of the Potomac, and before he sat down reminded the House of some of the predictions of the Antifederalists. The Constitution, it was well known, was adopted with great difficulty by Virginia. The States east of Pennsylvania, the Antifederalists had said, would form confederacies and destroy the South. To this the Federalists had answered, No! A magnanimous policy would spring from common interests and common dangers, jealousies would cease, the States would unite and henceforth think only of the good of all. The argument had been successful, and Virginia, with many fears, but strong hopes, came into the Union. But how would the Antifederalists rejoice when they learned that their worst predictions had come to pass; nay, that the northern States had not even waited till the Government was organized, before they sacrificed the South to their own selfish ends!

Lawrence replied to him. If he wished to convince the House he must make use of arguments, not terrors. The Federal Government was in no danger. The South was quite safe. His fears, happily, were not shared in even by his colleagues. The House could recall a day not very long since when the tonnage bill was under debate, and how a member from Virginia had stood up, congratulated the House on its moderation and even-handed justice, and declared that, could the proceedings of that day have been foreseen in the Virginia Convention, many objections brought against the Constitution would never have been made. Madison owned having uttered such a remark. " But," said he, warmly, " give me leave now to say that had a prophet arisen up in that body and brought the declarations and proceedings of this day into view, I as firmly believe Virginia would not at this moment have been part of the Union." " Is it to be contended," exclaimed Sedgwick, " that the majority shall not rule? And shall the minority, because they cannot carry their point, accuse us of a lack of candor? Are we to be told to our faces that a great State would not have joined the Union could she have foreseen the proceedings of the House? Certain members brought this business forward themselves. They drove the House into it. We prayed, we supplicated for time. They stood firm. But now on a sudden, when matters are not to their liking, they in turn are clamoring for time, and blaming the House for doing the very thing they began by demanding. Six weeks' deliberation will not change a single opinion." Wadsworth was yet more emphatic for an immediate vote. He was set against bargaining. It would do no credit to the House. He would not excuse himself. He was willing the whole matter of bargaining should be shown up. He did not dare to vote for the Potomac. If the seat of Government went there, he knew the whole of New England would think the Union destroyed. Since members had been forced, nay, dragged by the throat, he might say, to this business, he hoped it would be finished at once.

But the committee rose, reported progress, and spent three more days in ill-natured debate. At last, after all manner of motions and counter-motions, a final vote was reached on the question that a commission be appointed to select a spot on the banks of the Susquehanna, buy land, and put up buildings. When the question was put by the Speaker, twenty-eight stood up on the affirmative; twenty-one remained seated on the negative. So a bill was brought in and sent to the Senate.

The Senate struck out the Susquehanna, put in a site one mile from Philadelphia, passed it, and sent the bill back to the House. The House was very indignant. All kinds of rumors were afloat. It was declared the Senate were keeping the appropriation bill as a hostage, and that the House ought to show a proper spirit. But the members were weary of the matter, concurred in the amendment, and the next day the House adjourned.

It is both curious and interesting to observe how the wisdom of the best statesmen of that day has been turned into foolishness by a long series of events which, had they been foretold, would have been thought the dreams of a madman. The vast stretch of territory then the richest possession of the Crown of Spain, and of which no thought was taken, has since been added to the States, and is now thickly settled by fifteen millions of souls. Nay, Ohio and Illinois, which, when St. Clair governed them, contained but a few block-houses and a half-dozen straggling hamlets, now boast, each of them, of a population but a few thousand less than that of the eleven States represented in the first Congress under the Constitution. The centre of population near which the Federal city was to stand was the next year found to be twenty-three miles east of Baltimore, where Goodhue had declared it would remain fixed for ages, and that when it did move, would travel to the eastward. But when the century closed, the centre of population was eighteen miles to the west of Baltimore, and from that day forth it has gone steadily westward along the thirty-ninth parallel of north latitude. Never has it at any time been more than sixteen miles to the north, nor more than three miles to the south, of that line. At the close of the first decade of the present century the centre of population was forty miles northwest of Washington. In 1820 it was sixteen miles north of Woodstock, in Virginia. When Jackson was President it was nineteen miles west-southwest of Moorefield, a little town hard by the boundary of Maryland. When Harrison died the centre had advanced to sixteen miles south of Clarksburg, in West Virginia. When the middle of the century was reached it stood twenty-three miles southeast of Parkersburg, in the same State. When Lincoln was elected it had entered Ohio, and was twenty miles south of Chillicothe. In ten years it had travelled eighty-one miles. Then came the civil war, the rate of advance fell to forty-two miles, and in 1870 it was forty-eight miles east by north of Cincinnati. The rate then increased, and when the tenth census was taken the centre of population had passed eight miles west of Cincinnati. In ninety years this centre, once thought so fixed that the permanent seat of Government was to be placed near to it, had moved almost due westward four hundred and fifty-seven miles, and gone beyond the eighth city in the Union, which, in the same year the first census was taken, stood in the midst of a vast solitude, and was called by St. Clair, Cincinnati.

While the House was busy debating by what name the President should be called, Washington was troubled to know in what manner he should behave. He was the first of our long line of Presidents. He had therefore no precedents to guide him in private and public treatment of men. The place was one of great dignity. But just how much dignity was consistent with that republican simplicity which was the boast of the time he did not know. The city was gay. The people affected fashion, and many among them who had enjoyed opulence in the colonial days looked back with some regret on the fine clothes, the hosts of servants, the equipage, and the ceremonial of the royal governors. They would gladly have seen the modest, sad-looking gentleman in black, whom they had raised to the chief place in the land, have a guard at his door, ride out followed by a train of menials, and would have gone, on reception-days, with some pride, through lines of liveried servants to bow at the foot of a very low throne. But the extreme Antifederalists, the men who every election-day denounced aristocracy and the well-born, begrudged him even the fine house and the fine furniture already given him by Congress, and cursed the vandals who were levelling the ramparts of the old fort to make way for a new mansion, yet more costly and spacious than the old. Neither party was to be offended. He did not wish by a too great simplicity to lay himself open to the jibes and sarcasms of that influential class whose after-dinner talk was, as Jefferson complained, monarchical to a shocking degree.* He did not wish, by a too great exclusiveness, to call forth the reproaches of those who bitterly bemoaned what they termed the decline of republican spirit. In 1775 they were accustomed, they said, to hear the phrase,

---

* "But I cannot describe the wonder and mortification with which the table conversations filled me. Politics was the chief topic, and a preference of kingly over republican government was evidently the favorite sentiment." Jefferson's Anas. He is referring to the series of dinners given him on his return from France.

"*vox populi, vox dei.*" Now they were daily told that democracies were a volcano. Then it was, "the natural equality of mankind"; now it was, "the well-born." Then it was, "sons of liberty"; now it was, "State demagogues." Then it was, "our excellent State constitutions"; now it was, "the monster with thirteen heads." Fifteen years before, the expression was, "the free and United States of America"; now it was, "the national Government." *

Washington therefore drew up a set of questions as to his official conduct, and submitted them to Hamilton and Adams. Should he, he asked, associate with all, or see none? Should he keep open house after the manner of the Presidents of Congress; or would it be enough to give a feast on such great days as the fourth of July, the thirtieth of November, and the fourth of March? Would one day in the week be sufficient to receive visits of compliment? What would be said if he were sometimes to be seen at quiet tea-parties? When Congress adjourned, should he make a tour?

The answers that came back removed his doubts, and it was soon announced in the newspapers that the President would receive calls on Tuesdays and Fridays.† Thursdays were set apart for congressional dinners. On Saturdays the President might sometimes be seen riding through the outskirts of the city mounted on a fine Virginia horse, or seated in his box at the theatre. The only one in the city at that time was on John street. It was mean and badly furnished, had been put up for the American Company of comedians before the war, and used by the British officers during their occupancy of the city. There, in a box adorned with fitting emblems, the President was to be seen much oftener than many of the citizens approved.‡ On such occasions the President's March was always played. It had been composed by Pfyles, the leader of the few violins and drums that passed for the orchestra, and played for the first time on Trenton Bridge as Wash-

---

* Boston Independent Chronicle. Also, New York Journal, September 10, 1790.

† New York Journal, May 7, 1789.

‡ It was at this time that opera-glasses began to be used in the theatre. The pit treated this as a great piece of affectation, and the fashion of using "spyglasses" was much ridiculed. See New York Packet, July 28, 1789.

ington rode over on his way to be inaugurated.  The air had a martial ring that caught the ear of the multitude, soon became popular as Washington's March, and when Adams was President, in a moment of great party excitement Judge Hopkinson wrote and adapted to it the famous lines beginning "Hail, Columbia."  Thenceforth it ceased to be known as the President's March, and under the name of "Hail, Columbia" has become one of the most stirring of our national airs.*

Shortly after the Houses rose, the President set forth to show himself to the people of the eastern States.  He went through the chief towns of Connecticut, carefully avoided Rhode Island, passed a few days at Boston, rode thence to New Hampshire, and came back by another route from that by which he went.  Everywhere he was received with a great show of Federal spirit.  Bonfires were lit, triumphal arches put up, feasts were made ready, and odes written in his honor. The farmers deserted their orchards and flocked in thousands to the villages to gaze once more on that passionless face and firmly set mouth.†  He was much gratified with the warmth of his reception in States so ill-disposed to the new Government; and, had it not been for one episode, would have brought back none but the liveliest recollections of unalloyed pleasure.  A great affront was, however, offered him at Boston.  John Hancock was then Governor of Massachusetts.  And of all the long line of men who have filled that high place, he was the most narrow, the most pompous, the most vain.  The Governors of other States hastened to the borders, bade the President welcome, and escorted him with troops to the capital city. But Hancock kept his house, suffered Washington to enter the State, ride to Boston, and pass a night there before he could bring himself to make the first call.  Hancock was a strong Antifederalist.  It seemed necessary, therefore, to his warped and narrow mind that he should hold high the extreme doctrine of independent States.  Washington was, he claimed, but

---

* See a note on this in Custis's Recollections and Private Memoirs of Washington.  Also, Historical Magazine, January, 1859, where Baltimore Clipper, 1841, is cited.  The name of the composer is spelled Fyles, Feyles, and Pfyles.

† For account of the President's tour, see Connecticut Courant, Columbian Centinel, United States Chronicle, New Hampshire Gazette, Boston Gazette, and the Mercury.

the chief of a Confederation of States. He was the chief of an independent State. It was clearly the duty of the President to make the first visit. Hancock accordingly pleaded the gout, gave a dinner to some boon companions and officers of a French man-of-war in the harbor, and not till the whole city was crying shame did he send to excuse his folly and beg to know when the President would be at home. The affront was indeed a gross one, and long remembered.* With this single exception the tour was one unending ovation, and the President returned to New York late in the fall most favorably impressed with the state of feeling in New England.†

Once more at home, his time was taken up with the urgent demands of office-seekers, and in consultations with the lately appointed heads of departments. What is now known as the Cabinet did not then exist. But Congress had at the last session authorized the formation of the three departments, of State, of War, and the Treasury, and at the head of each had been placed some man of ability and integrity. Jefferson was hastening home from France to become Secretary of Foreign Affairs. To Knox, the favorite general of Washington, was intrusted the Department of War. Hamilton had been called to the Treasury. Randolph was Attorney-General. The post-office, then an unimportant branch of Government, was given to Samuel Osgood, of Massachusetts.

In point of importance, indeed, the Treasury was first. The army numbered but a few hundred men. The foreign relations of the country consisted in little more than the occasional exchange of formal notes with the ministers of three

---

* The Boston papers, the Mercury and the Gazette, give no account of, and make no comments on, the rudeness of the Governor. The story, however, is fully told by W. H. Sumner in Some Recollections of Washington's Visit to Boston, in New England Historical and Genealogical Register for April, 1860; in Breck's Recollections, pp. 128, 129; and by a writer under the signature of Centinel.

† In illustration of the manners of the times, the following is worthy of notice. The city is Boston. "The ladies, in honor of the President, have agreed to wear the following device in a sash: A broad white ribbon with G. W. in gold letters (or spangles) encircled with a laurel wreath in front; on one end of the sash to be painted an American eagle, and the other a fleur-de-lis." Pennsylvania Journal, November 11, 1789. See, also, Fisher Ames to Dwight, October 21 and 30, 1789; and Sumner's Some Recollections of Washington's Visit, etc. New England Historical and Genealogical Register, April, 1860, p. 161.

or four continental powers. But the patronage of the Treasury was large, and so long as the debts remained unpaid the management of its affairs was likely to be of far more concern to the country than the number of rations distributed to the army, or what went on at Madrid or the Hague. To this responsible post had been called a young man but just turned thirty-two. But such were the powers of his mind that Hamilton at thirty-two was as well fitted for the place as any man of his time at fifty-two. As a politician he was believed by his contemporaries to have been not over-scrupulous, and to have sometimes followed dark and crooked ways. But as a public servant his zeal, his industry, his ability, were never attacked even by Jefferson, who hated him with an animosity more implacable than the animosity of Burr.

The new Secretary had not been many days in office before he was hard at work on a report on the state of the national debt and the best way to pay it. But while his work was still unfinished the Houses met and began a session singularly eventful, a session from which dates that financial policy which has been so fruitful of wonders, a session in which some questions, long afterward set at rest by an appeal to the sword, were for the first time long and fiercely debated.

In neither of the two Houses which met on the fourth of January, 1790, can a party-line be distinguished. There was indeed among the people the great line which separated the Federal party from the Antifederal party, the upholders from the detractors of the Constitution. But the few Antifederalists who found seats in the Senate and the House were too weak in numbers to form an opposition or to keep back the current of public affairs. Indeed, their antifederalism soon wore off, for the heat of party feud was cold and dull compared with the intense fervor of sectional hate ; the hate that sprang up between the East as the East, and the South as the South. No man in the South was a firmer or more bigoted Antifederalist than Burke. But through all that long and rancorous session Burke put away his party feeling and never for a moment forgot that he came from a State where the negro was a slave and where the rice-plant grew to perfection. Grout had been sent by the Shayites of Massachusetts. But little as he liked the new plan, he too forgot, when he voted, that he was an Antifederalist, and remembered only that he was from the greatest, the most prosperous of New England States.

The Houses met, however, in good spirit, and the speech made by the President at the opening of the session was cordially received. He congratulated them on the concord, peace, and plenty which blessed the land. He spoke with much pleasure of the increasing good-will toward the Government, and of the ratification of the Constitution by North Carolina. But he reminded them at the same time that some matters of great weight demanded speedy and earnest attention. The frontier was to be defended; intercourse with foreign nations was to be facilitated; commerce and manufactures wisely encouraged; post-offices and post-roads multiplied and extended. He had seen, he said, with peculiar pleasure, the resolution of the Houses to provide for the support of public credit; it was of the highest importance to the national honor, and he had bidden the proper officers to lay before them such papers and estimates as would give exact information on the state of the Union.

The next day the Secretary of the Treasury asked leave to bring in his plan for the payment of the debt. Leave was granted, and Thursday of the following week was set down as the day whereon the House would hear it, and he was told to put what he had to say in writing.

When the time came, the members listened in profound silence. The debts, they were told, were of three kinds: the foreign debt, amounting to eleven million seven hundred and ten thousand three hundred and seventy-eight dollars, the domestic debt of forty-two million four hundred and fourteen thousand and eighty-five dollars, and the State debts.* Precisely how much was owed by the States could not, the Secretary said, be ascertained to a dollar, but it would not be far from twenty-one millions, and this he proposed should be assumed. The money had been spent in the common cause. It was part of the price of freedom. No more dollars would be required to pay it if assumed by the Government than if

---

* American State Papers.   Finance, vol. i, p. 22.

left with the States, and it could be much more easily collected and much more easily disbursed at one national Treasury than at twelve different State treasuries. Assumption was therefore clearly the policy of the Government. If this were done, the total indebtedness would not fall far short of seventy-five millions of dollars, and the annual interest would in round numbers be four and a half millions. A tax of a dollar and two bits a head on every man, woman, and child in the country was a burden, the Secretary thought, too great to be borne; so he proposed a plan for raising the interest which seemed to his mind far less odious than a direct and crushing tax.

Every dollar of the forty-three millions which made up the domestic debt would draw six cents from the Treasury as interest. But the debt was redeemable at pleasure. When, accordingly, the Government found itself able to borrow money at five per cent or four per cent, principles of sound economy would force it to do so, and with the funds so raised pay off the debt drawing six per cent. It was more than likely that at the end of five years the price of money would be down to five per cent, and that it would go on falling till, at the end of fifteen years, it would be down to four per cent. The public creditor would therefore in five years, and again in fifteen years, be forced either to submit to a lowering of the rate of interest, or take back all his money invested in the certificates. With this certainty hanging over him, the public creditor might, the Secretary thought, be easily induced to accept an assurance of six per cent for a certain number of years as an equivalent for a reduction of the principal, or for a postponement of the interest on a part of it. Thus cut down, the interest might easily be paid from moneys collected from duties on wine, spirits, teas, coffees, and an excise.

To carry out the plan it would be merely necessary to open a new loan, take the old certificates and evidences of indebtedness in payment of the subscriptions, and fix upon some plan for the distribution of the stock. Hamilton suggested three. One was to give in exchange for each one hundred dollars of the debt brought to the Treasury sixty-six and two thirds dollars of the new funds, bearing six per cent interest, and thirty-three and one third dollars in western lands at twenty cents an acre.

If, however, the creditor would not take land, he was to be allowed to convert the third of his claim into stock, receiving twenty-six dollars and eighty-eight cents in the funds for every one hundred of the claim. This was to bear no interest till 1800 ; and after that time six per cent.

But some men were hard to please, and as they might be disposed to grumble at even so liberal an offer, they were to be at liberty to choose from three other plans. They might subscribe to a four per cent stock, and receive as compensation for the low rate of interest fifteen dollars and eighty cents in land for each one hundred dollars paid in. Or they might take out annuities for life, bearing four per cent interest, and contingent on fixing a given age not less distant than ten years. Or they might purchase annuities for life, contingent on the survivorship of the younger of two lives.

In this form the report was read to the House early in February. The day had been especially set apart for its consideration, the news had gone abroad, and when the time came the seats in the gallery of the House were filled with strangers. Little was said. But when the reading was ended, and it was known to the merchants and shopkeepers who crowded the gallery that the paper they had long looked on as worthless, and which they would at any time for three years past have gladly disposed of at three shillings in the pound, was in all probability soon to be funded dollar for dollar, they became eager to possess more of it. Indeed, before noon the following day the market price of certificates went up fifty per cent. Prudent men, who could see nothing in the action of Congress to warrant a hope of assumption, were at a loss to account for so sudden a rise in value. But it soon appeared that the speculators were at work, that their agents were hastening through every back-country village and town buying certificates and final settlements from the farmers for a song, and that some had gone on a swift-sailing vessel, under a press of canvas, to Charleston, to purchase certificates from the planters before the news of the proposed funding reached the South.*

---

* "The people in this city are informed of all the motions of Government ; they have sent out their money, in swift-sailing vessels, to purchase up the property of uninformed citizens in the remote parts of the Union." Speech of Jack-

One of the partners in this last venture, Smith, of South Carolina, brought the plan of the Secretary formally before the House. It was on Monday, the eighth of February, when the House had gone into a committee of the whole, that he rose and moved four resolutions. The first declared that Congress should not adjourn till ample provision had been made for the payment of the public debt. Another asserted that no discrimination was to be made between the original holders of certificates and their assignees. A third set forth that the State debts should be assumed; the fourth that the arrearage of interest on State as well as continental debts ought to be funded. The first resolution passed without debate. But the others were made the subject of a fierce dispute, which was prolonged till the summer was far spent, grew more and more rancorous day by day, broke up the course of business in the House, spread thence to the people, provoked an amount of sectional animosity that finally laid the foundations of two parties, and made the words "funding" and "assumption" hateful to the ears of the whole nation.

The enemies of funding and assumption, and they were to be found in greatest numbers south of the Pennsylvania line, argued in this way : Funding, wherever found, is ruinous to the welfare of states. The first funding system of which history makes any mention sprang up at Florence in 1634. That magnificent republic, into whose coffers had once poured untold treasures from the East, owed the paltry sum of sixty thousand pounds. She was unable to pay it, and in an evil hour turned it into a funded debt. From that instant her prosperity went down. Her trade fell off. Her credit vanished, and the splendid argosies that once crowded her quays and canals were scattered to the four quarters of the globe. Genoa and Venice came next. They took up a like policy, and where is now their ancient splendor? Spain, in a day of trouble, learned

son, of Georgia, in Congress, February 9, 1790.    Benton's Abridgment of the Debates of Congress, vol. i, p. 198, ed. 1857.    Jefferson, in his Anas, says concerning this : " Couriers and relay-horses by land, and swift-sailing pilot-boats by sea, were flying in all directions.    Active partners and agents were associated and employed in every State, town, and county, and the paper bought up at five shillings, and even as low as two shillings in the pound, before the holder knew that Congress had already provided for its redemption at par."

the practice, but heeded not the warning of the Italian republics. She, too, anticipated her revenues, funded her debt, and sank in consequence far below the level of states that were once her colonies. Then the contagion spread to France, and she now languishes under a terrible load of debt. But the most striking example of the ills of a funding system is England. When William of Orange was on the throne she laid the foundation of her national debt. The sum, five millions of pounds sterling, put into the funds, was indeed small. But it was the germ of a frightful malady, and the patient has ever since been going from bad to worse. In 1711 the debt had grown to nine millions of pounds. When Burgoyne surrendered, it was one hundred and thirty-six millions. It is now above two hundred and thirty millions. The most sanguine man can surely never expect to see this burden lifted. Should she become involved yet more, the consequences will be fearful to contemplate. She will either become bankrupt, or cease to be an independent nation. God forbid that, with so long a line of signal warnings before us, we should ever fund our debt. For a moment it will indeed increase our scanty circulation and raise up our fallen credit. But it will be for a moment, and a moment only. The evil practice will surely be followed, and in a century the debt which is now but a few millions will be expressed by figures it makes our blood run cold to think of.*

It is well to consider how much of truth and how much of error this prophecy contained.

The funded debt of the United States amounted, on the first of January, 1791, to seventy-five million four hundred and sixty-three thousand four hundred and seventy-six dollars. From that day it steadily grew in size till the first of January, 1804, when it summed up eighty-six million four hundred and twenty-seven thousand one hundred and twenty dollars. Then a decline began. In 1812 it had fallen to forty-five millions. In 1835 it was paid off. The next year the Government was in possession of a surplus revenue of forty millions of dollars,

---

* These arguments are to be found in a speech delivered in the House, February 9, 1790, by James Jackson, of Georgia. See Benton's Abridgment of the Debates of Congress, vol. i, pp. 191, 192, ed. 1857.

which produced far more evil than the greatest debt the country has ever borne. It was divided among the States. Instantly the wildest extravagance began. Turnpikes and canals, banks and public improvements, sprang up in every
State. The creation of the Banks of Issue is without a parallel in history. They were to be found in every town,
in every village, in every hamlet throughout the length
and breadth of the land. A story is extant of a messenger
with notes to collect, who traced a bank far beyond the limits of civilization to a spot on the prairies where a smithy
and a single cabin were alone to be seen. The blacksmith
was the cashier, the smithy was the bank, and the safe a
barrel in a corner of the shed. The messenger relates that
when the notes were offered, the blacksmith went to the
barrel, took out first a layer of apples, then a layer of vegetables, and finally the bags of gold, from which he told out
the coin and redeemed the bills, saying as he took them that
the messenger was the first man who had found out the bank.
States that had loaned their credit to such banks soon became insolvent. The extravagance caused by the few millions loaned by the Government brought enormous debts.
Some repudiated; some suspended; some cried out for a new
assumption bill. The appeal was most wisely withstood. But
a new debt had in the meanwhile been growing. When the
Mexican war ended, this was sixty-three millions of dollars.
The Texan Indemnity of 1850 added five millions more. In
1851 it was sixty-eight million three hundred and four thousand seven hundred and ninety-six dollars. Then a decrease
began and went steadily on till 1857, when the bonded debt
of the Government was twenty-eight million six hundred and
ninety-nine thousand eight hundred and thirty-one dollars.
When Sumter was fired on it was ninety million five hundred
and eighty thousand eight hundred and seventy-three dollars.
The civil war raised this to two billion eight hundred and
forty-four million six hundred and forty-nine thousand six
hundred and twenty-six dollars, the largest sum our country
has ever owed.* Thus, in the space of seventy-five years, the
debt which the Antifederalists declared would ruin the coun-

---

* These figures were reached on August 1, 1865.

try if funded, was paid off, and a new one, thirty-seven times
as great, created and borne with perfect case.

But, the enemies of funding went on to argue, even if
funding were a good thing, the system proposed by the Secretary is a bad one. It makes no distinction between the debt
due abroad and the debt due at home. The one is not like a
debt. The other has all the true qualities of a debt. The
one was loaned the United States in real coin, at low interest,
by generous men living beyond the sea, and deriving no benefit from the blessed results of the war. This is a true debt.
The other has been rapidly growing at six per cent on money
loaned on depreciated paper, or paid for services rendered at
exorbitant rates, or for provisions supplied at three times their
real value, by men who are now enjoying all the blessings
brought by the war. Every member in this House knows
that much of our domestic loan-office debt arose in this way.
Every member knows that loan-office certificates were issued
as a kind of circulating medium when, in a day of trial, Congress was put to such straits for cash that it could raise the
money in no other way. Every member knows that every
farmer who hauled wood, or sold provisions, or disposed of his
horses or his beeves for this kind of money, raised his prices
from six to ten shillings at least. Is this debt to be placed on
the same footing as the foreign debt, for which we had a hard
dollar for every dollar we agreed to pay? Let the continental
and the State debts be assumed and paid shilling for shilling,
and the home creditor becomes at once the most favored of
men. He will have kept his property safe and sound through
the chaos of seven years of war. For every hundred dollars
loaned he is now to get back a hundred and sixty dollars, and
this, put into the funds at four per cent, will yield him a profit
compared to which the gains of farming or of trade are paltry. Where is the land, improved or unimproved, that will
yield such returns? What merchant can say, with absolute
certainty, at the opening of a year, that his gains will, at the
close of the year, be four per cent of the money invested in
his trade? Men who held real estate before the revolution
have, between taxes and losses, sunk half of it. But the patriots who, when the nation was hard pressed, went in crowds to

the loan offices and put in their worthless paper, or sold their
tons of hay and bushels of potatoes at three times the market
price, are now to have it all back again safe and much increased, and be given, moreover, a fine investment for the future.   This property intrusted to the Government has, it is
true, slept, some for ten and some for twelve years.   But it
has now waked up to some purpose.   Before funding the certificates and final settlements it would be wise, therefore, to determine their true value.   To say the face value of such securities is the true value and the one to be paid is to talk
nonsense.   Look back on the time the contracts were made.
At the close of the war, at the beginning of the issue of final
settlements, there was a claim against the Government for services really rendered.   The soldiers were the claimants.   They
came forward and made their demands.   But Congress had no
money.   What, then, did it do?   It offered them certificates of
a certain nominal value; nay, more, of a certain known value.
Twenty shillings was the nominal value.   Two shillings and
sixpence was the real value.   Did the soldier accept the offer?
He did.   On what motive did he accept it?   Patriotism.   He
knew as well as he knew anything that he was putting the
capstone on the building he had erected by his labor and cemented with his blood.   " I have," said he, " done great things
for you.   You owe me twenty shillings.   But you are poor.
You cannot pay me.   I will take your two-and-sixpence,
therefore, and give you a discharge."   No man of candor can
for a moment maintain that the soldier who took, or the officer
who paid out the settlement ever believed it to be worth one
penny more than two-and-sixpence in the pound.   The whole
transaction was compounding a debt, and the sum Congress
ought to pay on the final settlements is two-and-six.

Gentlemen cry out at this.   They will have it that the certificate is a private contract; that to declare it to have a value
other than the one carried on its face is to alter a private contract, an act Congress has no right to do.   These amiable gentlemen are mistaken.   The House is not a contractor, but a
judge, an arbitrator.   The case is simply this.   One part of
the community has a demand on another part.   This House
is applied to by the creditor part to recover it.   The debtor

part makes answer that the demand is excessive. Congress is simply to decide what is justly due. And what is justly due? The face value? No. Congress, it is indeed true, acknowledged the face value of the bills to be the real one; but this was done out of necessity, out of policy, lest the settlements should depreciate till they were as worthless as the old red money. Money loaned under such circumstances could not surely be said to be lent in a patriotic spirit. It was a speculation in public funds. Some sanguine men had hoped, by putting paper money worth scarce anything into the loan office, to get back hard money by and by. Where is the hardship, the injustice of giving them back just what they loaned, with interest? Is Congress bound to pay them what they expected to get? They took advantage of the necessities of the nation, and if they never receive a farthing, they are still well paid. Have they not liberty for tyranny?

It must be remembered, too, that much of the debt is owned by these speculators. Many of the original holders of the settlements and certificates have parted with them. Here, then, is an additional reason for discrimination. The present holders, supposing the debt is funded, are not to be placed on the same footing as the original holders. They had no claim. They were under no necessity to take a single settlement. They went of their own will to the soldiers and farmers and bought the certificates. Why were the purchases made? To relieve the pressing wants of disabled heroes? No. To help a poverty-stricken country pay her debts? No. To put money into the pockets of men who had never smelled the smoke of battle, or rendered the first service to the land.

These arguments were at length put into the form of a motion, which Madison, with a long speech, introduced to the House. He moved to discriminate between the original creditors and the present holders of settlements and certificates. The former he proposed to pay in full; but where a claim had been assigned, the assignee should receive the highest market value, and the original holder whatever remained over.

To this it was answered that the plan was wicked and impolitic. It consists, said the Federalists, of two parts. First, to take away the property of one man by a mere act of power, and then reinvest it in another man who has lawfully disposed of it for a price. The buyer of a certificate has, by fair purchase, acquired a right to the full amount expressed in the certificate, which this House cannot stop him of. There is not a tribunal on the face of the earth that can do it. If A gives a bond to B, and B parts with the paper to C, there is no longer any obligation on the part of A to pay B; but he must pay C. He has nothing to do with the private negotiations of B, nor to inquire what sum of money was given for the bond. He cannot say to the holder, You gave but fifty dollars for a hundred-dollar security, therefore I will pay you but fifty dollars. The law will compel him to pay the hundred. The plan is so wicked and unjust that the very soldiers, in whose behalf it is devised, will refuse with scorn to profit by it. Suppose I buy a settlement and go to the Treasury to fund it. The Treasurer would say to me, You are to receive but fifty dollars; the other fifty is to go to the man you bought this of. Now, if I go and tell the officer or the private I bought of, that, notwithstanding my purchase of his whole right, I am to get but half of it, what will he say? He will say, " Sir, I will never touch a farthing of the money; it is yours." This is no ideal sketch. Have not the Society of the Cincinnati of the State of New York, by a resolution, disavowed the principle? Was not a member expelled from the society in Rhode Island for using the tender law to pay a just debt in depreciated paper?*

To this it was said sneeringly that it was hard to understand why the same gentlemen who were afraid to give the soldier a part of his original claim, lest they should offend his nobleness of soul, made no scruples of offering the speculator ten times the sum he was entitled to. Were they sure his honor would not receive a wound? The answer was that the question was not a question of feeling, but of right and wrong. The Government owed a debt. There were two ways of settling it: to pay it outright in hard money, or to fund it. To discharge it in coin would require upward of eighty millions of dollars ready money. This could not be had. To fund it, therefore,

---

* Joseph Arnold, of Warwick, expelled at the meeting July 4, 1789. See account in Freeman's Journal, July 22, 1789.

followed as naturally as shadow follows substance. But how fund it? The Secretary has pointed out several ways. The gentlemen of the opposite side of the House have struck on a way of their own. They wish the interest cut down and the certificates funded by paying part to the holder and part to the original possessor. This is an interference in contracts. No matter what the Government may have received for the settlements, two shillings or three shillings, ten shillings or twenty shillings in the pound, they are contracts by which the Government is bound to pay any lawful holder the face value. As a party, Congress cannot alter the contract in the least. If the original holder has, by disposing of his claim, made a bad bargain, that is his business, and not ours.*

These arguments had so much effect that, when a vote was taken on the motion, but thirteen rose on the affirmative in a House of forty-nine. With this vote all thought of funding and assumption was for a while laid aside. The House had found a new subject. The Quakers, at their yearly meeting at Philadelphia, had drawn up a civil memorial to Congress, praying for the abolition of slavery. It was presented on the eleventh of February, read and committed the next day, and on March seventeenth taken up for debate. The discussion had not gone far before it surpassed in bitterness and vulgarity anything the House had yet listened to. Smith, of South Carolina, and Jackson, of Georgia, could not contain their wrath, and when arguments failed them, fell to abusing the Quakers, their religion, their morals, and their memorial. The Quakers were denounced as enemies of freedom, as spies during the late war, and the guides and conductors of the British armies; the names of the signers of the memorial were called over, their characters blackened, and anecdotes relating to them told upon the floor of the House. Even Franklin, who, then upon his death-bed, had put his name to the foot of one of the petitions,

---

* On the subject of funding, see a pamphlet called Fallacy Detected by the Evidence of Facts; or, Considerations on the Impolicy and Injustice of a Compulsory Reduction of the Interest on the Public Debt, in a letter to a member of Congress, 1790; also, Considerations on the Nature of a Funded Debt. New York, 1791.

did not escape.* A member who listened with disgust to the six days' contest has well described the violence, the personality, the low wit, the rambling from the point which marked that strange debate. " The Quakers," writes he to his friend at Boston, " have been abused, the eastern States inveighed against, the chairman rudely charged with partiality. Language low, indecent, and profane has been used; wit equally stale and wretched has been attempted; in short, we have sunk below the General Court in the disorderly moment of a brawling nomination of a committee, or even of a country town-meeting." † The answer to the memorial was in seven paragraphs; but the gist of it was contained in one short sentence. " Congress," said the report of the House committee, " have no authority to interfere in the emancipation of slaves, or in the treatment of them within any of the States." The vote was twenty-nine to twenty-five.

From this wrangle the House came back in no good temper to the funding and assumption bills. The funding bill, though not much liked, commanded a majority; but assumption was held to be a matter as purely sectional as the seat of Government or the emancipation of the slaves. New England and the middle States, except Pennsylvania, were for the measure. The southern States were against the measure.

The Federalists were able, however, after a three-weeks' discussion, to muster votes enough to force the committee, by a majority of five, to report to the House, among other resolutions, one in favor of assumption. This was on the thirteenth of March. On the twenty-ninth the resolution was taken up. Meanwhile, several representatives from North Carolina, every one of them bitterly opposed to assumption, came in. The moment, therefore, the resolution was read, a motion to recommit was made, and carried by a vote of twenty-nine to twenty-seven. The Assumptionists, in great anger, retaliated by recommitting the funding resolution. More dis-

---

* The mildest part of these debates may be found in Benton's Abridgment. But the original journal must be read to form a just conception of the depths to which the House descended.

† Fisher Ames to G. R. Minot, March 23, 1790. Works of Fisher Ames, ed. 1854, p. 75.

cussion followed, till at last, on the twelfth of April, the resolution to assume was thrown out in committee by a strict party
vote. Twenty-nine stood up on the affirmative, thirty-one on
the negative.

The Antiassumptionists were triumphant. The Federalists
were more determined than ever, and began to talk in a way
that gave much alarm to the more cool-headed members from
the South. They openly declared their intention to bring in
a bill to assume, said they would surely oppose every measure
looking toward funding till the assumption bill was passed,
and that if it did not pass, the consequences to the Union
would be serious indeed.* Some who heard them thought
this was merely the language of angry men. But when, two
days later, a motion was made to go into a committee of the
whole for the purpose of providing for the domestic debt, it
was warmly resisted, and when, on the second of June, a bill
passed providing for the debts, Gerry, true to the words of the
Federalists, moved a bill to assume.

And now each party began to labor with redoubled energy.
The Antiassumptionists hoped to win through a bargain they
had just completed with one of the middle States. The Assumptionists hoped to win by defeating the supply bill. But it
was clear that everything depended on the conduct of the
representatives from Pennsylvania. Of the twelve delegations,
that alone was divided. Five of the members were Assumptionists, three were not. And the two parties being almost
equal in numbers, this gave the balance of power to the Pennsylvanians. Each party accordingly spared no pains to secure
their votes for a future day. The North offered sound arguments, and made appeals to their good sense. But the South
held out a bait the greedy members from Philadelphia could
not withstand. Nothing was so near their hearts as that congressmen and lobbyists should once more be seen lounging
about the streets and sitting in the inns of their great city.
The interest on the national debt might go unprovided for, the
State debts might remain unpaid, the credit of the nation might
fall, but come what might, the patronage of Congress must be
drawn from New York and distributed among the grog-shops

---

* See a letter from Madison to Monroe, April 17, 1790.

and taverns of Philadelphia. Lilliput and the Wigwam, Epple's and the Fish-House, must flourish. The moment, therefore, the Southern members approached them on this matter, they yielded and struck a bargain. It was agreed on one side that Congress should remove to Philadelphia for fifteen years, and then to the banks of the Potomac forever. It was agreed on the other that the assumption bill should be voted down.*

When the news of the bargain leaked out, the Federalists were greatly enraged, but they waited their time and it soon came. The bill to remove to Philadelphia had, in an unsuspecting moment, been passed by the House, had been rejected by the Senate, and on the tenth of June the motion was renewed in the House. But the plan of the Pennsylvanians was then well known. Long speeches and motions were made to delay the vote, and finally, on the following morning, Philadelphia was stricken out and Baltimore put in by a majority of two. The triumph was complete, for, by the rules of the House, Philadelphia could not be again inserted.† The Pennsylvanians and their friends in the Senate, smarting under their defeat, retaliated by throwing out the alternatives from the funding bill, offering the creditors simply four per cent, and daring the Assumptionists to reject.‡ The taunt was a bold one, for the eastern men had for eight weeks past been openly and solemnly declaring that they would oppose all provisions for the public debt which did not include assumption. They were now as good as their word. The supply bill was lost by a vote of thirty-five to twenty-three.

The eastern men now assumed a lofty tone, demanded assumption as a right, and plainly told the southern members that if to the insult of removing the seat of Government to the Potomac they added the injury of rejecting assumption, the consequences would be most serious. Such language, and the firm front presented by those who used it, gave great alarm to some who had steadily voted with the South. These feuds, said they, must be composed. It is hazardous to break up in such a temper. Let the matter rest till the next session,

---

* Fisher Ames to G. R. Minot, June 23, 1790.
† Fisher Ames to Thomas Dwight, New York, June 11, 1790.
‡ Fisher Ames to G. R. Minot, June 23, 1790.

and then we shall doubtless assume.* But the New England men would hear nothing of a compromise, and threatened secession. At this stage in the conflict Hamilton came to their help.

It happened one day, when hard by the President's house, that he fell in with Jefferson who then held the place of Secretary of State. Hamilton made known to him, as they walked backward and forward before the President's door, the temper into which both House and Senate had been wrought, the disgust of the eastern States, and the near danger of secession. The matter was, he admitted, not connected with the Department of State; but in a momentous crisis the members of the administration ought to join and support measures approved by their great chief. On the present occasion Jefferson could do much. Assumption had been lost by a small majority, and he might, by an appeal to the good sense and cool judgment of his southern friends, possibly change a couple of votes, remove all trouble, and enable the public business to go on with smoothness and dispatch. Jefferson pleaded ignorance. He had been abroad. The matter was new to him. He did not know its merits. Yet he would be pleased to have Colonel Hamilton dine with him the next day, meet a few Virginians, and discuss the difficulty calmly over Madeira and punch. Hamilton accepted. The meeting was arranged, and before they quitted the table a bargain was concluded. White and Lee bound themselves to vote for assumption. Hamilton and Morris undertook to carry through a bill fixing the seat of Congress at Philadelphia for ten years, and after that time permanently on the Potomac.† On the ninth of July the agreement of Hamilton was punctually performed. The bill to remove passed by a majority of three. Two weeks now went by before the debate on assumption was resumed. Meanwhile, the

---

* "We hear no more of the injustice of assumption; at least it is tacitly allowed that it will promote justice; and it is asked, Let it rest till next session, and then we shall doubtless assume. This looks like coming over. Besides, consequences are feared. The New England States demand it as a debt of justice, with a tone so loud and threatening that they fear the convulsions which would probably ensue." Fisher Ames to Dwight, June 27, 1790.

† Jefferson's Anas.

first letters-patent were issued.   The petitioner was one Samuel Hopkins, and his claim an improvement in the art of making pot and pearl ashes, an art then largely practiced in many of the less populous States.   That the improvement was a very ingenious or a very important one, may well be doubted. Yet the parchment by which Hopkins secured the exclusive right to his invention, after lying ninety years in old trunks and bureau-drawers, has become historical.   It is the first of the two hundred and sixty-nine thousand letters-patent since granted by the Government *; it bears the signatures of Washington, of Jefferson, and of Randolph, and for these reasons Congress was urgently recommended, three years since, to buy the document for the sum of five hundred dollars.† The date of the patent is July thirteenth, 1790.   A week later assumption came up in the form of a Senate amendment to the funding bill, and was carried by thirty-two votes to twenty-nine.‡

While the fate of the bills was yet uncertain, the Packets and Journals nearest the seat of Government had attacked or defended the measure with their usual virulence.   Poems,# serious and sportive, jibes, taunts, and abusive squibs came out in numbers.‖   But when the assumption bill and the residence bill passed, and the bargaining of the representatives became apparent, the Antifederal scribblers indulged in all the scurrility and coarseness so characteristic of the political writings of the age.   The favorite method of attack was under the figure of Miss Assumption and her bastard children

---

* To December 5, 1882, the number of patents issued was 268,773.

† The recommendation was made by the Secretary of the Interior, January 8, 1880.

‡ " Yesterday we renewed the battle for the assumption ; rather, we began it on Friday.   Mr. Jackson then made a speech, which I will not say was loud enough for you to hear.   It disturbed the Senate, however ; and to keep out the din, they put down their windows.   Mr. Smith followed him an hour.   Yesterday Mr. Gerry delivered himself.   Jackson rebellowed, the motion by Jackson being that the House do disagree to the amendment of the Senate.   Voted in the negative ; thirty-two (not including the Speaker, who is on our side) against twenty-nine."   Fisher Ames to Thomas Dwight, July 25, 1790.

# Gazette of the United States, April 14, 1790 ; August 24, 1790, and February 17, 1790.   New York Journal, August 31, 1790.

‖ Gazette of the United States, April 21, 1790 ; July 28, 1790.

Philadelphia and Potowmachus, and for several months this theme was written on with peculiar delight.* Now it was a notice of Miss Assumption's death, with a little account of her parentage, her fondness for cod's-head and molasses, and of the funeral oration delivered over the remains by Mr. Sedgwick.† Now it was a sketch of the life and death of Potowmachus, with a suitable inscription for a memorial-window in a church in some town in the Old Dominion.‡

The stormy session was now fast coming to a close. It was full time that it did. For from one end of the country to the other the mass of the people were indignant at the bargaining, the wrangling, the delays. After the manner of angry men, the contempt of the people found expression in sarcasms and in jibes. It was a matter of surprise to many, wrote an offended New Englander, that the session of Congress had been protracted and nothing done. The reason was plain. The members were paid by the day, and the more days the more six dollars. Should Congress meet on the fourth of December, 1790, and prolong the sitting till the fourth of March, 1791, the representatives would receive three thousand five hundred and twenty dollars each for two years' services, and have been at home seven months of the twenty-four. Did any one suppose the House would cut short the session when money was to be acquired so easily? Seventeen or eighteen hundred dollars a year was not to be despised. What congressman could earn half that sum at home? In future let Congress be hired by the job. For instance, for hearing, granting, and enacting Nathaniel Twining's # memorial, the country undoubtedly would gladly pay them two thousand dollars. For fixing the place of residence of Congress, five thousand dollars. But for a trifling act, such as funding the national debt, five hun-

---

* New York Journal, August 31, 1790. Independent Gazetteer, September 11, 1790. Gazette of the United States, June 2, 1790.

† Gazette of the United States, June 2, 1790.

‡ Independent Gazetteer, September 11, 1790. New York Journal, August 31, 1790.

# Nathaniel Twining was charged with the transmission of mails from Charleston to Savannah. This he failed to do from September, 1787, to January, 1788, and incurred a fine of $567.41. The fine was remitted July 1, 1790. New York Journal, September 21, 1790.

dred dollars was a great plenty.  The country acted with Congress like a man building a house by day labor.  The workmen were lazy, took holidays on Saturdays, and spent half their time debating where they should board, and whether the tenders who brought bricks and mortar should or should not make a low bow every time they entered the presence of a mason.*

Whether the Houses sat at New York or Philadelphia was in truth about as interesting as whether there were rainbows before the flood, or whether Alexander the coppersmith ever compensated Paul the Apostle for the injury he did him. Any fair-minded man could see at a glance that Philadelphia was the place to hold the sessions.  In the first place, the word meant Brotherly Love.  In the next place, it was a finer city than New York, and every one knew that the elegance and splendor of the town where Congress sat was more to be considered than prompt dispatch of business.  In the third place, the theatre was always open in Philadelphia, and there, too, lived Bobby the Treasurer.  Finally, Philadelphia was nearer than New York to the ancient domain of Virginia.  Much weight should be given to this, for the next stride was to place Congress on the banks of the American Nile at Canogochegue,† a spot apparently as much designated by nature for the capital of the country as Kamtchatka or Orahieta.  Had Congress been made up of such stupid politicians as was that of 1774, it might have been content to stay at New York till the trifling question of funding was disposed of, and have felt under some obligation to remain among a people who had laid out fifty thousand pounds to make it comfortable.  All this had indeed been discussed.  It was agitated for eleven days during the last session, and for eight days during the one about to close.  The Ayes and Nays had been taken fifty times. The cost of debating had been upward of twenty thousand

---

* Connecticut Journal.  Boston Gazette.  New York Journal, September 3 and 7, 1790.

† Canogochegue, or Conococheague, is the name of a small stream that flows into the Potomac from western Pennsylvania.  The word came into common use, and was long used in derision by the Federalists as the name of the proposed capital on the Potomac.  See, also, a letter of Fisher Ames to Thomas Dwight, January 24, 1791, and note.  Life of Ames, by his son, ed. 1854, p. 93.

dollars. The cost of removal would be forty thousand more. But what of it? Were not the finances flourishing? Were not all the creditors satisfied? Let Congress sport with forty or fifty thousand dollars.* It was natural for it to wander. In many respects it was not unlike those predatory nations with moving houses, and the creditors of the country would surely not fall out with the name Political Tartars. A moving State-House should be contrived, and the residentiary fever of the Pennsylvanians cooled by giving them the moving of the Federal edifice and the sole contract for furnishing Conastogue horses.† Or better yet. Let the Secretary of the Treasury confer with some eastern shipwrights, and send in plans for four track-scouts : one for the President, one for the Vice-President and Senate, one for the House, and one for the officers of Government. In these they could coast from New Hampshire to Georgia, and their maritime circuits would lay the foundation of harmony and union. An occasional squall might now and then sink the trackscouts. But so much the better, for an entire change of men would follow. There was, however, one objection. The trackscout business would soon become a local scheme between the eastern States and the State of North Carolina. New England would supply carpenters and timber, North Carolina would find the pitch and tar. ‡ On another occasion an advertisement in large letters announced that good calkers would be paid six dollars a day to calk and repair the ship Congress, R. M. master.⁂ The timbers of her bottom had never been properly squared ; the planks were of green stuff, and it was proposed to give her a thorough overhauling before the great and important voyage to Philadelphia. ‖

---

* New York Journal, July 27, 1790.          † Ibid., July 6, 1790.

‡ New York Journal, June 15, 1790. See, also, New York Journal, August 31, 1790.

⁂ The opponents of the removal treated no one so harshly as Robert Morris. Indeed, he is rarely mentioned in the pamphlets of that day except as " Bobby the Cofferer," or "Bobby the Treasurer." In one caricature which hung in the shop-windows at New York for many months, he is represented as carrying off Federal Hall on his back, the members of Congress cursing or encouraging him from the windows, while the Devil, from the roof of Paulus Hook ferry-house, cries out, " This way, Bobby."

‖ New York Journal, July 1, 1790. Connecticut Courant, July 5, 1790. For further comment on the removal of Congress, see Gazette of the United States,

Before rising, the Houses made an attempt to calm the angry feelings of the people, for an election was near at hand.* A million dollars, derived mostly from the sale of public lands, were ordered to be spent in buying up the public debt. This it was hoped would raise the national credit, put up the price of paper, make foreigners pay dear for American securities, restore good humor to the creditors, and send a great sum into circulation.† The money was much needed. So scarce had cash become that it was not possible for legislatures or select-men, by any means now used for the collection of a revenue, to wring out of the people a few hundred dollars to pay the cost of local government, or to carry on works of public improvement.‡ Taxes the people would not bear. To issue bonds would have been useless, for the authorities could not have insured the interest on them for a week. Help, therefore, was sought in a means now universally condemned, and

---

August 29, 1789. Connecticut Courant, July 12, 1790. Federal Gazette, June 30 and July 12, 1790. New York Daily Advertiser. Also, a pamphlet called An Essay on the Seat of Federal Government and the Exclusive Jurisdiction of Congress over a ten miles District, with Observations on the Economy and delicate Morals to be observed in infant States. Humbly offered to the Public. By a Citizen of Philadelphia. 1789. Even Washington did not escape censure. "A correspondent requests, that the worthy M—r of New York would consider the expenditures of his fellow-citizens to accommodate *Congress*, and the *generous returns they have made them*, and then, *if he can*, let him raise a portrait more lasting than brass, to perpetuate the virtues of the P——t. It is asked, which are the virtues that render him so respectable? Why are they not singled out? Is it for that *inflexible justice*, that *distinguished gratitude* to the city of New York in giving his sanction to the *unconstitutional residence bill?*" New York Journal, July 23, 1790.

* It was believed, in districts far away from the seat of Government, that as the members of Congress came out of Federal Hall for the last time, the angry citizens of New York attacked them, killed some and severely wounded many more. New York Journal, August 24, 1790.

† Fisher Ames to Dwight, August 8, 1790.

‡ Such was the scarcity of money in Vermont that the tickets of the Windsor County Grammar School Lottery were sold for two bushels of wheat each. "The scarcity of cash has induced the managers to adopt the plan of receiving wheat notes for the tickets, and paying the prizes in those notes." Vermont Journal, December 2, 1788. "Where are now," exclaims a pamphleteer, "the quantities of coin which have been brought into the American States, and clipt and defaced during the last seven or eight years? They certainly are greatly diminished, to the degree of stagnating even common gaming." On Monies, Coins, Weights, and Measures proposed for the United States of America, p. 11. Philadelphia, 1789

abandoned to church fairs and gamblers. Lotteries sprang up, and in a short time there was a wheel in every city and in every town large enough to boast of a court-house or a jail. Whenever a clumsy bridge was to be thrown across a little stream, a public building enlarged, a school-house built, a street paved, a road repaired, a manufacturing company to be aided, a church assisted, or a college treasury replenished, a lottery bill was passed by the Legislature, a wheel procured, a notice put in the papers, and often in a few weeks the needed money was raised. It was with the money collected from the sale of lottery-tickets that Massachusetts encouraged cotton-spinning and paid the salaries of many of her officers; that the City Hall was enlarged at New York,* that the Court-House was rebuilt at Elizabeth,† that the library was increased at Harvard,‡ that many of the most pretentious buildings were put up at the Federal city.# The custom, indeed, continued for several years, and The State of the Wheel became as regular an item in the papers as the ship news or prices current.‖

---

* Gazette of the United States, April, 1790.

† New Jersey Journal, January 18, 1792.

‡ Federal Orrery, October, 1794.

# Gazette of the United States, 1794, and later.

‖ "The lottery mania," says a correspondent, "appears to rage with uncommon violence. It is said there are nearly twenty lotteries on foot in the different States. The sale of tickets has been uncommonly rapid. Lotteries have been formed, published, and the tickets sold and drawn in the course of ten or fifteen days." Pennsylvania Mercury, August 24, 1790. "Every part of the United States abounds in lotteries," says another writer. Columbian Centinel, January 22, 1791. The following short list of lotteries and their purposes, collected at random from a few of the newspapers for the year 1789-'90, will show the truth of the Centinel's statement:

West River Bridge Lottery, Brattleborough; Vermont Journal, September 2, 1789. Furnace Lottery, Fair Haven Iron Works; Vermont Journal, January–September, 1789. Windsor County Grammar School Lottery; Vermont Journal, December 2, 1788. Massachusetts Semi-Annual State Lottery, Massachusetts Monthly State Lottery; Massachusetts Spy, September, 1790. Leicester Academy Lottery; Massachusetts Spy, September, 1790. Charlestown Lottery; Boston Gazette, December, 1790. Marblehead Lottery; Columbian Centinel, November, 1790. East Hartford Glass Works Lottery; Connecticut Courant, December 7, 1789. Hartford Bank Lottery, to build a bank along the Connecticut river at Hartford; Connecticut Courant, November, 1789. River Bank Lottery, "to build a bank on the river adjacent to the public road through the Longmeadow in Middletown"; Connecticut Courant, April, 1790. Providence Great Bridge Lottery;

But there was, unhappily, one class in the community sorely in need of money that could get small benefit from the proposed issue. Much of the daily purchase of the poor was made with coppers, and coppers had ceased to circulate.

Until the summer of 1789 such pennies as were considered good money, and were not of foreign coinage, bore the impress of either of seven mints.* One of these was at Rupert, a little town in Vermont. Another was for some months at New Haven; but, after consuming twenty-eight thousand pounds of copper, the supply of metal gave out and the coinage ceased. It was at this mint that the few cents made under the Jarvis contract, and now so highly prized by collectors, were struck. A third was at Boston, a fourth at Dedham, a fifth at Solitude, not far from Morristown, in New Jersey, a sixth at Elizabeth. The seventh had been authorized by the Commonwealth of Pennsylvania.

Though the nominal values of the pieces put out at each

---

Columbian Centinel, December, 1790. Bell Lottery, to procure bells for the German Reformed Church; Maryland Journal, January 2, 1789. Petersburg Church Lottery; Virginia Gazette, September 27, 1792. Alexandria Presbyterian Church Lottery; Virginia Gazette and Alexandria Advertiser, January, 1791. Alexandria Lottery, to pave certain streets; Virginia Gazette and Alexandria Advertiser, April 22, 1790. Fredericksburg Academy Lottery; Virginia Gazette and Alexandria Advertiser, June, 1791. Pine Lottery, for the sale of Real Estate and Paintings; Pennsylvania Gazette, November, 1789. Lottery to enable the Hebrews to remove the debt on their synagogue; Pennsylvania Journal, October 8, 1790. Lottery to build a City Hall at Philadelphia; Pennsylvania Packet, December, 1789. New York City Lottery to enlarge the City Hall for the use of Congress; New York Journal, March 18, 1790. New Haven Glass Works Lottery; Connecticut Journal, December, 1790. Lottery for extending and improving the Woollen Manufactory at Hartford; Connecticut Journal, April, 1791. New Haven Long Wharf Lottery, granted in December, 1790; Connecticut Journal, April, 1791. This work was afterwards described as follows:

> "No decent pier receives the freighted bark—
> A cluttered mud-bank (dangerous in the dark,
> Of length enormous, at whose timbered side
> A pigmy fleet of oyster-boats may ride
> Safe moor'd in mud) is all that bears the name,
> Or to a pier or wharf can kindred claim."

New Haven. A Poem, Satirical and Sentimental, with Critical, Humorous, Descriptive, Historical, Biographical and Explanatory Notes. By Selim (S. Woodsworth). 1809, pp. 7, 8.

* See a paper on Connecticut Currency, in Papers of the New Haven Historical Society, vol. i, pp. 175–180.

were the same, their market values changed at almost every town into which they came. Travellers journeying from New York to Philadelphia found the contents of their wallets shrink and swell as they passed through the villages on the road in a way that seemed out of all reason. Coppers, which at New York went at twenty-one, were taken at New Brunswick by the tavern-keepers at twenty to the shilling. If the travellers stopped over night at Princeton to view the college buildings, the coppers they received in change for the milled dollars with which they paid for their lodgings and Madeira were given at the rate of twenty-four to the shilling. But at Trenton, ten miles away, the shopkeepers would not take the same pieces at less than thirty to the shilling.* Once across the Delaware, however, their value again increased. Pennsylvania, by an act of 1786, had given two men the right to strike ten thousand pounds sterling in coppers, to pass at fifteen to the shilling, and by a law of the year following decreed that every man who passed a copper not of the State issue should, as a penalty, forfeit ten. † The law, as was natural, was evaded. Hucksters and innkeepers, who dealt largely with the poor, and whose tills were as a consequence full of the condemned money, gave no heed to a law which on forty-six days' notice deprived them and their customers of many dollars, and put them to great straits for change. Pennies from the mints at New Haven and Boston continued, therefore, to pass, and such quantities came from New York that the days of Wood's famous brass money seemed to have returned. This went on till Washington was inaugurated and the new Government established. Then on a sudden, in all the large towns and cities, men began to refuse to take the State coins, which would, they thought, soon be declared bad. A rapid depreciation began. In New York pennies fell to twenty-five, to thirty, to forty, to fifty, to sixty-four to the shilling.‡ There, for a while, the decline stopped. But ere the summer of 1789 was passed they ceased to circulate. Distress and confusion followed, for large sums in copper

---

* Independent Gazetteer, June 28, 1787.
† Pennsylvania Gazette, July 18, 1787.
‡ Freeman's Journal, August 5, 1789.

were still in the hands of merchants and shopkeepers.* But
the suffering was confined almost entirely to the poor. Their
plight was truly deplorable. Numbers of shops were forced
to close. The cries of the hawkers were no longer heard in
the streets, and it was with difficulty that the laborers could
find means to buy bread at the bakers', or vegetables at the
markets.† So great was the suffering that the Common Council of the City of New York took up the matter, and urged
the citizens, as an act of mercy, to receive the coppers at forty-
eight to the shilling.‡ This was done. Yet no good came of
it. Small change continued to grow scarcer and scarcer, and
the losses of the poor became so great that, early in the spring
of 1790, the Common Council once more interfered. They
ordered a number of tickets to be printed having a face value,
some of one, some of two, and some of three pence. These
the city treasurer gave out to such as wished them, in exchange
for joes and shillings, and assured the public that the tickets
could at any time be exchanged in sums of more than five shillings for silver, or the currency of the State.# Such quantities
were taken that a few months later the Manufacturing Society
followed the example and put out tickets of a face value of

---

* "Many of the merchants and shopkeepers, it is said, have large quantities
of this coin by them, by which they will be great sufferers." Pennsylvania Gazette, July 27, 1789.

† Pennsylvania Gazette, July 29, 1789.

‡ The resolution of the Common Council declares that "this board, conceiving
it their duty to interpose their advice on this interesting occasion, do recommend
it to the inhabitants of the city to receive and pay the said coin at the rate of
forty-eight coppers for one shilling." Passed July 21, 1789. New York Daily
Advertiser, July 23, 1789.

In a letter written a few days after the action of the Common Council, the
embarrassment of the money market is attributed to the payment of one and a
half per cent premium on French coin, and to the importation of copper coin
in immense quantities to make change. "This arrived at last to such an abuse
of the public confidence that their circulation has on a sudden almost ceased."
Some, however, advertised that they would take coppers at sixty to the shilling.
Independent Gazetteer, July 31, 1789. "On the whole," says another authority,
who signs his pamphlet B., "of what I can collect concerning copper coins, it
seems they do not pass so much by virtue of their small intrinsic worth as by
common consent, induced by a degree of necessity. . . ." On Monies, Coins,
Weights, and Measures proposed for the United States of America, p. 15. Philadelphia, 1789.

# See the notice to the public in New York Journal, March 18, 1790.

one, two, three, four, five and six pence, "in order" it was declared, "to accommodate the operations of their Factory." *

In Connecticut a few sharpers from the coast towns made great profits by purchasing quantities of the coins at New Haven, where they were still taken, when necessary to make change, at six to the penny lawful money, and passing them off on the farmers at twenty-seven to the shilling.†

But withal the popular feeling throughout the New England States during the summer and autumn of 1790 was one of contentment. There was, as Fisher Ames wrote a few months later, a scarcity of grievances.‡ The ill-nature provoked by the contest over the new plan had gone down. Men who had been clamorous over the deficiencies of the Constitution had been silenced by the twelve amendments submitted by Congress, and the prompt ratification of ten of them by the States. Even in Rhode Island the tide had turned, the Federalists had prevailed, and the State had, late in May, been brought into the Union.# Much satisfaction had been given by the vigorous financial policy of the Government. Every farmer, every merchant, every man who had a shilling of taxable property, felt that his taxes had been lightened and his comfort increased by the assumption bill. He beheld with pleasure the prices of public securities going up, and the figures of the national debt going down. He saw final settlements which sold at seven shillings and sixpence, and indents that went at five shillings to the pound in January, held at fifteen shillings before the year went out. He heard with unconcealed delight that in Holland the foreign loan had gone above par, and that two hundred and seventy-eight thousand dollars of the domestic debt had been purchased and cancelled at a cost of one hundred and fifty thousand. Trade was reviving. Old manufactures were increasing; new ones were being set on foot. The

---

* See the notice in New York Journal, August 13, 1790. For some ill-natured remarks on these corporation tickets, see Journal, August 10 and 13, 1790.

† Freeman's Journal, August 5, 1789. See allusions to the state of the copper coinage in Gazette of the United States, September 5, 1789.

‡ Fisher Ames to Dwight, April 26, 1791. "People here (Boston) seem to care as little about politics as I think you do at this moment. There is a scarcity of grievances. Their mouths are stopped with white bread and roast meat."

# May 29, 1790. Gazette of the United States, June 2, 1790.

innumerable lotteries which sprang up all over the East were a sure sign of a widely diffused spirit of public improvement, a desire for larger docks, better bridges, finer roads, more commodious court-houses, more numerous schools.  And deeply engaged in works of this kind, the East gave little heed to the political contentions that distracted the South.

Beyond the Potomac everything done by the new Government since its establishment was thought to be wrong.  The salaries bill, the residence bill, the revenue bill, the funding bill, were so many pieces of jobbery in the interest of the East.  But the vilest of all was the assumption bill.  Indeed, for several years no writer for the Antifederal press could use the word without a hearty curse or a string of coarse adjectives. In Virginia the measure was particularly detested.  That State had long boasted of the efforts she had made to pay off her share of the war debt, and had pointed with just pride to the figures which gave evidence of her success.  And now, when her citizens beheld the delinquent States, the States that had refused quotas, that had given so grudgingly, that had always been far in arrears, shift the debts they had never tried to pay upon the whole country, a cry went up that assumption was a wicked and an unjust thing.  Virginia, it was said, "fairly reeked and teemed with Antifederalism."  It was not long, therefore, before a memorial condemning assumption in strong language was passed by the Assembly and on its way to Congress.  In Maryland a motion declaring assumption to be dangerous to the individual existence of the State was lost by the casting vote of the Speaker.  In North Carolina, the excise, assumption, and the quarrel that had sprung up between the State Court and the Federal Court, had produced great indignation.  The Legislature, in a series of resolutions, scolded their representatives, used harsh language toward the administration, and when a motion was made to take the oath of allegiance to the Constitution, threw it out by a large majority.  Georgia was in a ferment over the treaty with the Creeks.

The Indian affairs were, in truth, in a most alarming state. All through the summer stories and rumors of midnight massacres, and cold-blooded murders of emigrants along the Ohio, had been crowding the columns of the Gazettes and Journals.

At first they were supposed to be merely accounts of such barbarities as the Indians had always perpetrated on the settlers of
a new country from the days of John Smith and Miles Stan-
dish down. But ere Christmas came it was well known that
the settlers in the western territory were involved in a general
Indian war.

To form a just conception of the cause of the long series of
Indian wars which now began to disturb the peace and pros-
perity of the West, we must recall briefly the claims of the
Indians and of the Government to the land in dispute.

That part of our country which lies between the Mississippi
and the Blue Ridge, the great lakes and the Gulf, had, in the
century preceding the revolution, been explored and settled by
missionaries and adventurers from France. Far back in the
sixteenth century Cartier explored the St. Lawrence, and led
out a colony to settle on its banks. But the attempt failed,
the colonists perished, and for sixty years the Indians seldom
saw a white man among them. At last, in 1608, Samuel Champlain repeated the attempt, led a band of hardy adventurers,
eager for the souls of men and the skins of beasts, to the Isle
of Orleans, and hard by, on the high bluffs which look down
on the river and the island, marked out the city of Quebec.
The colonists found themselves far from home, in a cheerless
climate, in a vast wilderness, and in the midst of tribes of red
men who beheld the little hamlet with no friendly eye. So
much depended on the good-will of the Indians that Champlain
left nothing undone to gain it. He made them presents,
joined them in an alliance, and went with them on the war-
path to the shores of that beautiful sheet of water which still
bears his name. There a great battle was fought. The arms
and the courage of the French prevailed, and a victory full of
consequences to the white men was won. For three generations after the battle every Algonkin was the steady friend,
and every Iroquois the implacable enemy, of the French;
and to this more than to anything else is to be ascribed the exploration and settlement of the Northwest. The Iroquois
were powerful through all New York. The Algonkins ruled
along the St. Lawrence and the chain of lakes. When, therefore, the French missionaries began their search for proselytes

and furs, they shunned the Iroquois and travelled westward among the tribes of the Algonkin nation.

Le Caron, a Franciscan, went first, and for ten years toiled among the Indians on the Niagara and the shores of Lake Huron. Brebeuf and Daniel went next, reached Sault Ste. Marie, and founded at St. Ignatius, St. Louis, and St. Joseph, villages of Christian Huron. But the Iroquois overwhelmed them, destroyed the villages, and burned the missionaries at the stake. Mesnard went yet farther to the west, saw the waters of Lake Superior, paddled in a canoe around its southern shores, built a church at St. Theresa bay, and disappeared forever at the portage of Keweenaw. Long afterward his breviary and his cassock were found among the Sioux. Allouez followed him, explored both shores of the lake, and on the western end met the Sioux and heard for the first time of the great river the Indians called the Messipi. But all the glory of its exploration belongs to Marquette.

He set out, in May, 1673, from Mackinaw, with six companions, in two birch canoes, paddled down the lake to Green bay, entered Fox river, and dragging the boats through its boiling rapids, came to a village where lived the Miamis and the Kickapoos. There Allouez had preached and taught. But beyond it no white man had ever gone. The Indians would have dissuaded them, told them of warriors that would cut off their heads, of monsters that would swallow their canoes, and of a demon who shut the way and drowned in the waters that seethed about him all who came within his reach. But the zeal of Marquette burned fiercely, and on the tenth of June, 1673, he led his little band, with two Indian guides, over the swamps and marshes that separated the village from a river which the guides assured him flowed into the Messipi. This westward-flowing river he called the Ouisconsin, and there the guides left him, as he says, " alone, amid that unknown country, in the hands of God."

With prayers to the mother of Jesus, the little band shoved their canoes boldly out upon the river, and for seven days floated slowly downward toward the Mississippi. The stillness of the Ouisconsin river, now crowded with villages and towns, seemed oppressive. Never before had they seen such

buffalo, such deer, such stags. The sand-bars that stopped their
way, the innumerable islands covered with vines and groves,
and bordered with pleasant slopes, the paroquets that screamed
in the trees, the "wingless swans" that strutted on the banks,
the great fish that they feared would dash their canoes to
pieces, filled them with indescribable awe. At last, on the seventeenth of June, they floated out on the bosom of the Mississippi, and turned their canoes to the south. Four days they
followed the bends and twists of the river, and on the twenty-
first of the month saw in the mud of the western bank foot-
prints, and a path that disappeared in a meadow. Leaving the
canoes with their companions on the river, Marquette and Joliet
took the path through the meadows to a cluster of Indian villages, on the shore of what is now believed to be the river
Des Moines. There they feasted, spent the night, and went
back next morning to their followers, and, while the savages
crowded the banks of the Mississippi, resumed their journey.
They floated down the stream, past the rocks whereon were
painted the monsters of which they had heard so much, past
the mouth of the Missouri, past the Ohio, and stopped not far
from the mouth of the Arkansas. There the voyage ended,
and the party went slowly back to the lakes.

The discovery of Marquette was the greatest of his age.
Thenceforth every earnest Jesuit of New France longed to
lead an expedition into the unknown country. Neither heat
nor cold, neither ice nor snow, neither hunger nor thirst, the
attacks of savage foes, nor the treachery of faint-hearted followers, could deter them. Physical suffering and physical obstacles such as have more than once brought ruin to bands of
adventurers as hardy as they, served but to increase the ardor
of the zealots. They penetrated forests into which the savages
had never dared to go. They explored rivers down whose
waters no Indian had ever paddled. They founded missiona-
ry-stations, they built churches, they laid out towns, they put
up forts. Such was the zeal they brought to their work that,
when Washington marched under Braddock to the fatal field
of Monongahela, the Mississippi had been explored from the
Falls of St. Anthony to the Gulf, and the famous chain of forts
wellnigh completed. Yet little territory had been acquired

The custom of the French had never been to purchase of the Indians great stretches of land. They were content to secure small grants around their forts and settlements, and it was these detached parcels that they made over to England by the treaty of Paris in 1763. Five years later came Pontiac's war and defeat, the treaty of Fort Stanwix, and the cession by the Iroquois of all land south of the Ohio to England. When, therefore, the independence of the States was acknowledged, Great Britain surrendered what she had received from France and what she had taken from the Iroquois. But in the region to the north of the Ohio, save the title to a few acres about the forts she continued to hold, she transferred nothing; and there lived the Miamis, the Delawares, the Shawanese, the Ottawas, the Wyandots.

In theory, Congress affected to hold that the claim of these Indians to the land had been forfeited by the part they took in the war. In practice, Congress treated them as sovereign nations, made treaties, and sent out commissioners to smoke the calumet and present the wampum and the beads. Indeed, between 1783 and 1790, no less than five treaties were made. The first, in 1784, at Fort Stanwix, secured from the Iroquois all claim to the lands which now make up the States of Ohio, Indiana, and Illinois. The second, at Fort McIntosh, was with the Wyandots, the Delawares, and the Chippewas. The third was with the Shawanese, at Fort Finney, in 1786. The fourth and fifth, at Fort Harmar, in 1789, confirmed the others. But with the Kickapoos, the Pottawattamies, the Miamis, the Weas, and the Eel river tribes, no treaties were made. Indeed, they declared they would make none. The Ohio should be the southern boundary between the Long Knives and the red men, and over that river no settler should ever come and live.

The task which St. Clair found before him when, in 1790, he sailed down the river to Losantiville, was, therefore, no light one. Every trader and hunter who came in from the Indian country brought news of an alarming kind. One had crouched in the bushes while a band of warriors, hideous in paint and feathers, had marched by within gunshot. Another had stood by the British commandant of one of the frontier forts when the Indians offered him coats riddled with bullets and smeared with blood. A third told of a family massacred at the dead of night, or of a boat-load of emigrants waylaid and butchered on the river. To quiet these disorders, St. Clair dispatched an officer named Hamtramck to the Indians on the Wabash. Hamtramck hastened to Fort Knox, and there in turn employed Gamelin, a Frenchman and a trader of Vincennes, to go among the Indians, to find out their purposes, and, if possible, appease their angry mood. Gamelin was gone a month, and then came back with such an alarming report of the temper of the savages that St. Clair went with all speed to Cincinnati to prepare for the defence of the frontier. The militia was called out. The regulars were put in motion, and early in October the army, numbering fourteen hundred and fifty-three men, took up the line of march.

Never before had such a collection of men been dignified with the name of army. The crowd of discarded, unjust serving men and revolted tapsters that followed Falstaff to the field of Shrewsbury would have put it to shame. In place of trappers and hunters, woodsmen accustomed to bearing arms, to enduring fatigue, and skilled in all the arts of Indian fighting, came old men who ought never to have quitted the chimney-corner, and striplings who had never raised a beard. Some had guns without locks. Some had locks and barrels without stocks. Some had no weapons at all. Nor were those who had much better off, for the officers complained bitterly that half of them were too ignorant to take off a lock to oil it, or put in a flint so as to be of use. What discipline was they did not know. When the Kentucky troops arrived, two officers named Hardin and Trotter contended for the command. Colonel Hardin demanded it as the senior officer. But Colonel Trotter was the more popular. A dispute accordingly arose between them, which was settled by the men declaring they would obey none but Trotter, and would go home instantly if he were not placed in command.

At length, when the broken arms had been mended and all disputes adjusted, the march began. The Maumee villages were selected for the first attack, and when about thirty miles away, Colonel Hardin, with some militia and regulars, was sent forward to surprise the enemy and hold them in their wigwams till the main body of the army could come up. And now the blundering began. Hardin spent a day and a half going thirty-five miles. The main army, with artillery, spent three. When the towns were reached, the enemy had left; and the troops consumed four days more in the work of destruction. Harmar had intended to push on to the Wabash and punish the Wea Indians. But so many pack-horses and cavalry-horses had been stolen by the Indians while the troops slept that all thought of the expedition was given up. Trotter, with three hundred men, was thereupon ordered to scour the woods in search of the enemy. When he had gone about a mile, a mounted Indian was seen, chased by the cavalry, and killed. As the pursuers were returning to the column they came upon a second Indian. Instantly the four field officers deserted their command without a word, gave chase to the Indian, and did not return for half an hour. Meanwhile, the troops, left without a commander, wandered about as they pleased. At nightfall they came back to camp.

This manner of fighting was so little to the liking of General Harmar that a party was dispatched the following morning under Colonel Hardin. Hardin was a man of courage, but as poor an officer as the army could produce. When he had gone about five miles from camp he came upon a spot where the smouldering fires and fragments of food scattered about showed the Indians had slept and feasted there the night before. Hardin ordered a halt, placed the companies at some distance from each other, and, after a rest of half an hour, resumed the march. But so negligent was he that no orders were sent to one of the companies. It remained, therefore, upon the ground; nor was it missed till the army had gone on three miles in advance. Presently the smoke of fires was seen curling up in the distance. An officer pointed it out to Hardin, but he gave it no heed. The Indians, he said, sneeringly, would not fight, and rode on. Scarcely had he spoken when the Indians opened fire upon him. Instantly all was confusion. Hardin fled. The militia threw down their loaded arms and ran for the nearest thicket. Armstrong, who commanded the Federal troops, alone stood his ground, fought bravely till the last man fell at his side, when he threw himself into the thick brush and escaped.*

That night, overcome with shame, Hardin led back his militia to camp. Harmar in the meanwhile had been busy destroying villages and burning corn. This work done, he gave the command to return to the settlements. On the twenty-first of October the march began. Toward sunset Hardin, chafing under his shameful defeat, commenced to beg hard for a detachment to go back and renew the fight. The Indians, he was sure, would return to the villages just burned. He could take them unawares. The surprise would be complete. The victory was assured. For a time Harmar remained firm in his refusal, but at length gave way, and sent Hardin back with three hundred and forty men. It was dusk when they set out, but so slowly did the militia march that the sun was well up when the scouts reported the Indians in force just ahead of them. The spot was on one of the bends of the Maumee river, not far from the site of the present city of Fort Wayne. There the troops were drawn up in three divisions. Two were to attack in front. The third was to march round the bend, cross the river, and strike the Indians in the rear as soon as the firing began in front. The manœuvre was well executed. The crossing was made, the ground was secured, and victory seemed certain, when, unhappily, an Indian starting from the brush, the troops, in flagrant disobedience of orders, opened fire. This gave the alarm. The savages fled. The militia pursued them till, seeing one of their leaders fall, they in turn broke and fled.

When Hardin reached the army he again urged Harmar to send back another force to the battle-ground. But the General would hear nothing of it. He could not, he said, divide his force; he had no food for the horses, he must return to the settlements; and, besides, the Indians had already received a very good scourging. The troops accordingly took up the line of march for Fort Washington. All went well till they came to Chillicothe, on the Little Miami, where a number of the militia, contrary to orders, discharged their guns. This

---

* See Captain Armstrong's account of the fight in New York Journal, February 7, 1791.

was too much even for Hardin.  His temper since his two
defeats had been none of the best.  He now lost all control of
it, and for the first time established something like discipline.
Seizing one of the soldiers, he ordered a file of men to drag
him to the six-pound gun, tie him there, and bade the drummer give him six lashes.  "By what authority," demanded
Colonel Trotter, at the head of a crowd of militia, "do you
order that man whipped?"  "In support of general orders,"
said Hardin, stoutly.  A warm dispute followed; but Harmar
coming up he severely reprimanded Trotter, ordered the Federal troops to parade, commanded the drummer to do his duty,
and swore a great oath that he would risk his life in support of
his orders.  The lashes were well laid on.

St. Clair and Harmar affected to consider the expedition
as a great success.  Five Indian towns, it was said proudly,
twenty thousand bushels of corn, and a score of savages had
been destroyed.  Had Clarke done more in 1782?  Had he
done as much in 1786?  And would any one say he failed?
The two commanders therefore talked much of the happy results that must come of their short campaign, and boasted of
the fine scourging they had given the Miamis.  The scourge,
unhappily, stung without harming.  The burning of a few
dozen wretched wigwams of filthy skins that passed under the
name of villages, the loss of one harvesting of corn, the death
of an old squaw and a few braves, served but to rouse the
tribes on the Wabash to a state of fury.  The cowardice of
the militia made them think they were more than a match for
the largest army the settlers could bring against them, and in
truth they were.

In that remote region of the West where lay the possessions of the Ohio Company, two hundred and eighty-seven
men were all that could in any emergency be collected and
made to bear arms.*  Even this little force was scattered far
and wide over the company's purchase, and lived in many

---

* The census of 1790 gives the population of the territory northwest of the
river Ohio as 4,280.  At Vincennes were 1,000 souls, on Symmes's Purchase 1,300,
on the Ohio Company's purchase 1,000.  The rest were at the Kaskaskias, Cay-
hokia, Clarksville at the rapids of the Ohio, and the French settlements opposite
the Kanawha.  New York Journal, November 26, 1791.

small hamlets, each one of which was a tempting bait to the implacable savage. Most of the settlers were at Marietta, already become a busy town of eighty houses. Some held lands at Belle Prairie, where the river Kanawha discharges its waters into the Ohio; others had put up mills and were grinding corn at Duck creek, at Wolf creek, and along the banks of the Muskingum.* A few, indeed, more daring than the rest, had gone forty miles up the river, made a clearing, and formed a little settlement at Big Bottom. Of all the hamlets in the northwestern territory, Big Bottom was the most exposed. Twenty miles of wilderness separated it from any like collection of houses. A dozen families made up the inhabitants. It lay close to the Indian country. It was, in fact, a solitary outpost of ·civilization in a land of savages. There the Indians began their work. The evening of the second of January, 1791, was chosen for the attack, and not long after the sun had gone down a shrill whoop from the neighboring thicket announced to the settlers that their hour had come. They fought with that peculiar courage, the courage of despair, which never fails to be displayed when all hope is gone, and which on many like occasions has animated even weak women and stripling boys with the coolness and intrepidity of veterans. But all they could do was to sell their lives dearly, and when morning broke, Big Bottom settlement had disappeared from the face of the earth.†

As the news of the massacre spread through the valley there was terror and agitation in a hundred homes. There was uneasiness at Marietta when it was remembered that but twenty regulars held the fort, while two hundred miles separated them from the nearest militia. But the alarm was greatest in the little clearings far removed from the river and the fort, and where in general three or four families clustered round a mill. It was believed that a general rising had taken place, that every tribe on the Miami and the Wabash had taken the hatchet, that the settlements were doomed, and that Joseph Brant, at the head of a great host of warriors, flushed with victory and eager for scalps, was sweeping through the valley. Some, in their alarm, were for quitting their lands

---

* New York Journal, February 21, 1791.        † Ibid., January 31, 1791.

and hastening back to the towns beyond the mountains. Many, leaving the goods in their huts and the grain in their barns, fled with their cattle and their families to the fort. Thence Rufus Putnam dispatched a letter to Washington begging for instant help.   He told of the massacre at Big Bottom, described the exposed situation of the settlements, and the sufferings of the families that had left their homes.   But the true misery and danger of their lot was well summed up in one pathetic sentence.   " Unless," says the writer, " unless Government speedily sends a body of troops for our protection, we are a ruined people."

When the letter reached Washington he had already done what he could for the protection of the frontier.   He had called out the militia, he had authorized the expedition of Harmar, he had laid the state of affairs in the West before Congress.   The Houses met on the sixth of December, and listened to his address on the eighth.   He congratulated them on the flourishing condition of American credit, on the rise of stock at home and abroad, on the ease with which a new loan of three millions of florins had been obtained in Holland, referred to the application of Kentucky district for admission into the Union as a State, spoke strongly of the depredations of the Wabash tribes, and ended with some remarks on the judiciary, the militia, the mint, the post-office, and the post-roads.   The Houses separated.   The representatives returned to their own chamber; the Speaker laid the address before them, and they proceeded to consider what answer should be returned.   All went smoothly till the paragraph touching the Indian affairs was reached.   Jackson then arose.   He sat for one of the districts of Georgia, was a man of some ability, a ready debater, and in one sense an effective speaker.   His speaking has indeed been well described by Ames as a bellow. But his views on all measures were so narrow, his feelings so strongly sectional, and his temper so little under control, that he never could speak ten minutes at a time without uttering something that put the House into an ill-humor.   When he rose to speak on the Indian affairs, he began by saying that he was as fully impressed with the importance of an Indian war, and the protection of the frontier, as any man.   But it was his

duty as a Georgian to express astonishment that the President
had taken no notice in his speech of the treaty with the Creek
nation.  "That treaty," said he, "has spread alarm among the
people of Georgia.  It has ceded away, without any compensation whatever, three millions of acres of land guaranteed to
Georgia by the Constitution.  Three commissioners, not one
of them a citizen of Georgia, were sent by the President to
look into the justness of her claims to the land in dispute.
They reported in her favor, and what has been the result?
Has the Government recognized the rights of Georgia?  No.
It has given away her land, invited a savage of the Creek
nation to the seat of Government, caressed him in a most extraordinary manner, and sent him home loaded with favors.*
But it is said there are secret articles in the treaty!  Good
God! are there to be secret articles between the United States
and any nation under heaven?  Treaties by the Constitution
are the supreme law of the land.  And will Congress suffer
the laws of the United States, like those of Caligula, to be
placed where no man can read them, and then punish the
people for disobeying them?  The people, sir, will never submit to be bound by secret articles."

At this stage of his harangue the chairman called him to
order and asked if his remarks were introductory to a motion
on the paragraph before the committee.  Jackson replied they
were not, but that on some day in the near future he meant to
bring in a motion calling for the Creek treaty, and its secret
articles too.  He sat down.  The House heard no more of it,
finished their answer,† and spent the few days that remained
of the year in an amicable discussion of the sale of western
lands.

---

* "The Indian Chief McGillivray is here.  He is decent, and not very black."
Fisher Ames to Dwight, July 25, 1790.

† "We have had the speech from the throne, have answered it, and to-morrow
we are to present our answer.  Both contain some divine molasses.  Mr. Jackson,
of Georgia, yesterday let off a balloon about the treaty with the Creeks  . ."
Fisher Ames to Thomas Dwight, December 12, 1790.

# INDEX TO VOL. I.

(33)

END OF VOLUME ONE.